Computers
for People

—

Concepts and Applications

Computers for People

Concepts and Applications

JACK B. ROCHESTER
Babson College

JON ROCHESTER
Digital Equipment Corporation

IRWIN
Homewood, IL 60430
Boston, MA 02116

A B O U T   T H E   C O V E R

The illustration is called *Interior* and was created by Katherine Hanley, a computer graphics artist at the AT & T Graphics Software Labs in Indianapolis, Indiana. Kathy holds a degree from the John Herron Art Institute, and combined her interest in classical architecture and Renaissance painting to produce *Interior*. She used a three-dimensional modeling and animation software program called TOPAS to create and build the architectural model, including the columns, walls, and floors. She used a scanner to copy the paintings from an art book into her AT & T 386/25 personal computer. A special feature in TOPAS called texture mapping allowed her to paste the various works of art on the walls. Since she likes to add the human element to her art, Kathy scanned in a photograph of the programmers she works with. She used a TOPAS feature called reflection mapping to make their images appear as a reflection in the floating globes. It was also used to create the reflection in the sunken floor. Finally, Kathy used the computer's mouse and a paint program to add the stars and cosmic clouds that surround the building. *Interior* was a fine arts project designed to demonstrate TOPAS, one of several graphics software programs AT & T markets. In her daily work, Kathy splits her time between creating artwork for brochures and advertising pieces and training customers in how to use graphics software.

Senior sponsoring editor: Lawrence E. Alexander
Developmental editor: Rebecca Johnson
Project editor: Susan Trentacosti
Production manager: Irene H. Sotiroff
Designer: Tara L. Bazata
Artist: Rolin Graphics
Compositor: Progressive Typographers, Inc.
Typeface: 10/12 Galliard
Printer: Von Hoffmann Press, Inc.

Library of Congress Cataloging-in-Publication Data

Rochester, Jack B.
    Computers for people : concepts and applications / Jack B.
Rochester, Jon Rochester.
        p.   cm.
    Includes index.
    ISBN 0-256-06680-9
    1. Computers.   2. Computer literacy.   I. Rochester, Jon.
II. Title.
BT160.R58   1990
231′.8—dc20   90–38206

Printed in the United States of America

1 2 3 4 5 6 7 8 9 0 VH 7 6 5 4 3 2 1 0

FOREWORD

By William F. Glavin
President
Babson College, Wellesley, Massachusetts

We live in a world filled with rapid change. In just the past few years we have seen many political restructurings that reflect new perspectives on our global economy. People look at the decade and, indeed, the millennium ahead as a time of tremendous new opportunities. I am sure no one needs to convince you that computer technology plays a significant role in all this change.

I have had the opportunity to enjoy two careers: one in business, the other in education. In my positions with IBM and Xerox, I have seen firsthand how powerful a force the computer is in changing our lives, not only in the United States but in the world. At Babson College, I have come to understand the importance of information systems in the business curriculum.

Clearly, no college student today should enter the world without a thorough understanding of computers and modern information systems. You may not care about the computer's internal workings, but it is essential that you understand the applications it performs and the many ways it influences our society. Information is embedded in everything people do, in every walk of life including the professions, business, and government service. Each of us needs information in both our personal and professional endeavors. We need information to perform our jobs to the best of our ability. Increasingly, that information is being collected, stored, and disseminated by computers and information systems.

Courtesy of Babson College

Understanding how to use this powerful resource has become a prerequisite for entry into the modern world. It is called computer literacy, and it spans occupations ranging from office worker to senior manager. Courses based on textbooks such as the one you are using provide the tools and the skills you need to become computer literate. Here at Babson, this is a required course. Further, we believe every student, regardless of their chosen major, should understand the relationship between information systems and the core subject matter such as finance, marketing, or management. Thus, it has become a component in every course where it is applicable, just as it is in the working world.

I encourage you to pursue your study of computers seriously. Strive to make computer literacy a valuable tool in your college studies, your personal life, and your work. You won't be sorry.

P R E F A C E

OUR PRIMARY GOAL: TO EDUCATE

We feel education proceeds best when all human faculties are involved: reason, curiosity, creativity, and personal involvement. *Computers for People: Concepts and Applications* was written to educate people unfamiliar with computer concepts or how to use computers. As long-term students and users of computers and high tech-

Jon and Jack B. Rochester

Ric Murray Photography

nology, we have developed a text that reflects our own learning process, beginning with fundamentals, incorporating hands-on experience, and infused with the human touch.

THE HUMAN PERSPECTIVE

As the title suggests, we place great emphasis on people in this text. We feel traditional introductory computer textbooks have treated the subject as a *machine science,* rather than as a *human enterprise.* Every word and illustration in this text has been tailored to convey to students that using computers can be an enjoyable and gratifying personal experience. We emphasize the human perspective in several ways. Each chapter opens with a human interest story, to relate an interesting aspect of computer technology or profile the achievements of a leader in the field of computers. History, from a human perspective, is not confined to a single chapter but is incorporated throughout the text to bring emphasis and clarity to the topic under discussion. The essential human qualities of humor, emotion, inspiration, and achievement are highlighted through real-life examples and application stories.

Each chapter includes three DISKbytes, which feature an interesting and sometimes humorous story that enhances the chapter content. Some provide tips on using specific application software packages, troubleshooting hardware, or buying a personal computer. Students can derive additional familiarity with the actual use of computers in short cases. Each chapter ends with a CAREERbyte, a true story of a person working in the area under study, designed to interest the student in a career with computers.

ETHICS

In keeping with the human perspective, the ethical issues associated with computers are a key element in this text. Discussion of ethical issues is integrated throughout the text, and a relevant ethics topic is presented near the end of every chapter. To enhance class discussions, each chapter concludes with several Issues. Our intent is not to preach but to make students aware of ethical concerns in computing, and to encourage exploration and discussion of these concerns.

AN EMPHASIS ON COMPUTER LITERACY

Computer literacy was once defined as knowledge alone. We feel knowledge without experience is incomplete. Therefore, the text is focused on involving the student with computers—specifically personal computers and their applications. Five chapters include hands-on tutorial work sessions to familiarize students with the way people use computer hardware and software.

APPEARANCE AND CONTENT

Computers for People: Concepts and Applications seeks to achieve a balance in its presentation. The figures and illustrations are not intended solely for visual relief. Rather, each piece is tied directly to the text to bring conceptual information into clear focus. We have carefully selected photographs that are interesting, relevant, and enhance the text without overwhelming the eye. We have adopted a conversational tone in our writing so students will find concepts easier to understand. This does not mean that the content is less rigorous. The text's rigor, level, and accuracy have been carefully evaluated through intensive manuscript development, including a focus group and three reviewer panels.

ORGANIZATION

We have developed a modular approach that allows students to progress from simple to more complex concepts, while bringing them in contact with the personal computer as soon as possible. The book is organized into the following modules:

- Module 1, Computer Fundamentals, introduces students to computers and computer system fundamentals, and includes a hands-on work session with the personal computer's operating system.
- In Module 2, Personal Productivity Applications, students are introduced to word processing, spreadsheet, and database management systems concepts with accompanying hands-on work sessions.
- With a sound understanding of *how* software applications work, students can move on to Module 3, Computer Software, which covers system and applications software concepts and software development.
- Module 4, Computer Hardware, explains processing and peripheral hardware concepts and describes the diversity of tasks computers are used for.
- Module 5, Systems Applications, develops a broad perspective of how computer systems are used, literally around the world: through networking (including a hands-on communications work session), in management information systems, and in office automation.

Although the modules are designed to unfold progressively, each can stand alone and be taught in various sequences according to course requirements. For example, Module 4 (hardware) can easily follow Module 1, or software concepts (Module 3) can be taught prior to the hands-on applications chapters in Module 2.

FEATURES

To enhance educational value and a focus on the human perspective, we conducted original research and interviews to create the following distinctive features exclusively for this book:

- Human interest chapter openings.
- Real-life case studies integrated throughout the text.
- DISKbytes that emphasize chapter content.
- CAREERbytes at the end of each chapter that describe the many different career opportunities available to students.
- A section on computer trends at the end of each chapter.
- An examination of ethics relevant to each chapter content.

PEDAGOGY

To help students assimilate concepts presented in the text, we developed these pedagogical features:

- A systematic, integrated set of behavioral *Objectives,* based on key chapter concepts, numbered for referencing in the chapter summary.
- *Memory Checks.* These are mini self-quizzes that follow each major topic in a chapter. Answering the memory checks ensures that students understand the most important concepts they have just finished studying.
- *Key Terms.* Key terms appear boldfaced in the text on first definition and also appear in a page-referenced list at the end of each chapter. These same terms are also defined in a complete glossary at the back of the book.
- *Summary.* Each numbered behavioral objective is repeated, then concisely explained, in the summary.
- *Review and Discussion Questions.* These questions appear at the end of every chapter and test students' comprehension of key concepts and terminology, as well as serving as a source for class discussions.
- *Issues.* This section appears at the end of each chapter and includes two to four issues or ethics-related questions. The issues are an excellent source for in-class discussions.

SUPPLEMENTS

We hope you find *Computers for People: Concepts and Applications* an effective teaching tool and an enjoyable exploration of the computing world. To assist you, we have developed an extensive instructional package for you and your students.

Instructor's Manual

This supplement is a complete guide to teaching the introductory course for both the new and experienced teacher. It includes information on course organization, including alternate ways to teach from the text, instructions on how to use supplements, a sample course syllabus, a student profile questionnaire, lecture notes, answers to all memory checks and review and discussion questions, a pop quiz, references, and additional classroom instruction materials. It is also available on disk.

Transparency Masters

This package includes approximately 100 transparency masters of key figures that illustrate text concepts.

Overhead Transparencies

This package includes approximately 75 full-color transparencies of key figures that illustrate text concepts.

Test Bank

The test bank includes approximately 100 multiple-choice and true/false questions, all graded in difficulty, for each chapter and appendix. There is a short quiz for every chapter, as well as a sample midterm and final exam.

CompuTest 3

This computerized test bank is available to qualified adopters of *Computers for People: Concepts and Applications.*

TeleTest

A complete, high-quality testing service, TeleTest is a system that allows you to obtain laser-printed tests with answer keys by telephoning the publisher and specifying the questions to be drawn from the test bank.

Study Guide

For each chapter and appendix, the study guide includes a chapter outline, a chapter overview, self-test questions, and answers to the self-test questions.

PC Applications Lab Manual

Prepared by Lee Cornell of Mankato State University, this manual provides hands-on work sessions in DOS, WordPerfect 5.1, VP Planner Plus, Lotus 1-2-3 version 2.2, dBASE III PLUS, and dBASE IV.

Application Software Master Diskettes

These diskettes contain the educational versions of WordPerfect 4.2, VP Planner Plus, and dBASE III Plus. The master diskettes are free to adopters of *Computers for People: Concepts and Applications.*

Macintosh Applications Lab Manual

Prepared by Jack Hodgson of Apple Computer, this manual provides hands-on work sessions for Word, Excel, Filemaker, and MacDraw.

Classroom Presentation Software

Available for both the IBM and Macintosh, Classroom Presentation Software can be used for in-class lecture presentations or in the lab for interactive self-study for the student. Classroom Presentation Software combines text, graphics, and animation with interaction to dynamically illustrate all the major concepts in the text. System requirements for the IBM are: 640 K RAM and EGA, VGA, or Super VGA graphics.

ACKNOWLEDGMENTS

Computers for People is the product of a shared vision, and we would like to give special thanks to the people who helped build it. Our editor, Larry Alexander, truly understood the book's objectives; we are grateful for his steadfast sponsorship. Rebecca Johnson, our developmental editor, worked much harder than anyone could imagine to develop and nurture this project. Our project editor, Susan Trentacosti, guided the manuscript and artwork through the complex book-building process with great skill and care. Tara Bazata designed the book; her clear sight and imagination turned our vision into reality. Special thanks go to Laurel Anderson of Photosynthesis for her excellent taste in the photographs that complement the text.

We were fortunate to have a superb team of educators to work with in preparing the ancillary materials for this book. Lee Cornell of Mankato State University has been involved with the book from its inception, and given the high quality of his comments on the personal computer work sessions, it was only natural that he write the PC applications manual. Jack Hodgson of Apple Computer, Inc., has devoted much of his career to the Macintosh; his Macintosh applications manual is a unique contribution to the book's usefulness. Tim Sylvester of the College of DuPage has demonstrated such depth and breadth in his teaching skills that we had to enlist his participation; our thanks go to him for the

excellent test bank. Margaret Zinky of Phoenix College is much admired for her rapport with students in the classroom. We thank her for the outstanding study guide. Our sincerest appreciation to all of our reviewers; even the most critical comments helped make this a better book. And special thanks to the members of the focus group, who volunteered a weekend to help us define the vision, making this a book that students can learn from and that educators can teach from. The reviewers and focus group participants were:

JoDane Autry
Collin County Community College
Lee D. Cornell
Mankato State University
Ralph Duffy
North Seattle Community College
Terry Duke
University of Texas, El Paso
J. Patrick Fenton
West Valley College
Anthony Fini
Camden County College
Connie Fox
West Virginia Institute of Technology
Karla Gentry
Johnson County Community College
Carol Grimm
Palm Beach Community College
Constanza Hagmann
Kansas State University
Lester Hays
Pima Community College
Peter L. Irwin
Richland College
James G. Kriz
Cuyahoga Community College
Joan Krone
Ohio State University
Cornelius Kucius
Merced College
Shelly Langman
Bellevue Community College
Charles E. Lienert
Metropolitan State College
Engming Lin
Eastern Kentucky University

Donna McClelland
Montana State University

King Perry
Delaware Community College

John Rezac
Johnson County Community College

Sandra M. Stalker
North Shore Community College

Timothy W. Sylvester
College of DuPage

Jane Varner
Montgomery College

Misty E. Vermaat
Purdue University at Calumet

Neely B. Wills
Santa Fe Community College

Margaret Zinky
Phoenix College

To our many friends and colleagues who over the past three years have asked us countless times, "How's the book?" We can now reply, "It's great!" Now they can see for themselves. Jack Rochester would like to thank his wife, Mary, for her constant inspiration, sound judgment, editorial guidance, and unflagging support. Jon Rochester would like to thank Marilyn Febles, Joanne Howell, and Patricia Marie McNish for their enthusiastic support and creative contributions. And finally, we both thank our parents, Jacqueline and Lowell, for teaching us to think creatively and showing us the virtues of hard work and self-determination.

COMPUTER SYSTEMS USED IN THE PREPARATION OF THIS TEXT

We spent over three years writing and preparing this book for you. During that time, we went through several computer technology metamorphoses, changing both the hardware and software we used. We used the fastest and most powerful personal computers, equipped with large-capacity hard disk drives and color video monitors. We used state-of-the-art word processing software with desktop publishing capabilities to produce a high-quality manuscript, printed on a laser printer. We used electronic mail extensively, to exchange messages and send chapters to one another. We also used all the personal productivity software applications we describe throughout the chapters. Once the writing was complete, the manuscript was submitted to Irwin on floppy disks, which were used to typeset and electronically publish the book.

Even though we have worked with computers for over 20 years, this has been a learning experience for us. Keeping up with computer technology is a demanding task; making a textbook useful and relevant is even more demanding. We have tried to do both to the best of our ability.

A wonderful parable from Oriental literature says, "Give me a fish and I eat for a day, but show me how to fish, and I eat for a lifetime." In *Computers for People: Concepts and Applications,* we have attempted not simply to *tell* you about computers, but rather to *show* you how to use them. We would like to hear if we have succeeded. Please write to us in care of our publisher, Richard D. Irwin, Inc., 1818 Ridge Road, Homewood, IL 60430.

Jack B. Rochester
Jon Rochester

CONTENTS IN BRIEF

MODULE I

Computer Fundamentals

1 A Computer-Orchestrated World 4
2 The Computer System: People, Software, and Hardware 28
3 Hands On: Using a Personal Computer 60

MODULE II

Personal Productivity Applications

4 Word Processing 94
5 The Spreadsheet 124
6 Database Management Systems 158

MODULE III

Computer Software

7 Software: From Operating Systems to Applications 192
8 Software Development 232

MODULE IV

Computer Hardware

9 Processing Hardware: Computer Power to the People 278
10 Peripheral Hardware: Input, Output, and Storage Devices 314

MODULE V

Computer Systems Applications

11 Networking: Connecting Your Computer to the World 348
12 Management Information Systems: The Strategic Advantage in Business 380
13 Office Automation: Putting It All Together 408

EPILOGUE   The Future of Computing 432
APPENDIX A Number Systems 444
APPENDIX B The Computer Generations 454
GLOSSARY 472
INDEX 483

CONTENTS

MODULE I

Computer Fundamentals

1 A Computer-Orchestrated
World   4

Computers Go Hollywood   5
Do Computers Matter?   6
  What Is Computer Literacy?   6
  DISKbyte: Understanding the
  Information Age   10
What Is a Computer?   11
  The Modern Computer   11
  How Computers Do Their Work   11
  DISKbyte: Early Counting and
  Calculating Machines   12
Types of Modern Computers   14
  The Supercomputer   15
  The Mainframe   15
  The Minicomputer   16
  The Personal Computer   16
  DISKbyte: How Computers Have
  Changed the Auto Industry   18
What Computers Can't Do   20
  Productivity   20
  DISKbyte: Luddites   20
  Reasoning   21

Errors   21
Ethics in the Information Age   22
  DISKbyte: A Computer
  Crime Sampler   23
Computers for People: Concepts
and Applications   23
  CAREERbyte: Ed Milkow and the
  Computer Helping Profession   25
Summary   25
Key Terms   26
Review and Discussion Questions   26
Issues   27

2 The Computer System: People,
Software, and Hardware   28

The Father of the Modern Computer   29
What Is a Computer System?   30
  People: The Creative Component   30
  Software: The Instruction
  Component   33
  Hardware: The Processing
  Component   36
  The CPU: Heart of the Computer   36
  Peripheral Devices   38
  Computer Memory   38
  The Personal Computer
  Hardware System   40
  DISKbyte: Computers Are
  Like Stereos   44

The Computer System in Action:
Data Processing   45
    Data and Instructions   45
    The Four Data
    Processing Operations   45
    DISKbyte: John von Neumann   46
    A Data Processing Example   46
    Two Methods of Data Processing   50
The Computer Advantage   50
    Accuracy and Speed   50
    Chips   51
    Bits and Bytes   52
    DISKbyte: GIGO   53
    Information: The End Result   53
Ethics   54
    CAREERbyte: Joanne Howell:
    Combining an Interest in Writing
    with Computers   56
Summary   57
Key Terms   57
Review and Discussion Questions   58
Issues   59

3   Hands On: Using a Personal
    Computer   60

Tim Paterson: The Man Behind DOS   61
Mastering Your Personal Computer   62
Getting Acquainted with Personal
Computer Hardware   62
    The Flight Check   63
    The IBM PC   63
    The Apple Macintosh   63
    Personal Computer Configurations   64
    DISKbyte: Tips for a Clean and
    Healthy Personal Computer   66
The Many Faces of the Human-
Computer Interface   69
    The Command Line Interface   69
    The Menu-Driven Interface   69
    The Graphic Interface   69
DOS, The Disk Operating System   71
    DOS Files   72
    DOS Filenames   73
    The DOS Directory   73

    Loading DOS   73
    The Prompt   74
    The Command Line   75
    The Cursor   75
A DOS Work Session   76
    Booting DOS from a Floppy Disk   77
    Booting DOS from a Hard Disk   78
    Issuing Commands   78
    Commonly Used DOS Commands   78
    DISKbyte: Issuing Commands on
    Other Types of Personal Computers   84
    Using Application Programs   84
    Ending a Work Session   85
    DISKbyte: Tips for Keeping Your
    Programs and Data Safe   86
Ethics   87
    CAREERbyte: Michael Dell:
    Starting a Computer Business in a
    College Dorm Room   88
Summary   89
Key Terms   89
Review and Discussion Questions   90
Issues   90

MODULE II

Personal Productivity Applications

4   Word Processing   94

Writing in the Modern World   95
The Back Pages of Written
Communication   96
What Is Word Processing?   96
    The Word Processing Advantage   96
Basic Word Processing Features   99
    Using Files   99
    The Word Processing Screen   99
    Editing Modes   101
    Help   101
    DISKbyte: Word Processing
    and Writing   103
A Word Processing Work Session   103

Getting Started   104
Entering Text   104
Commands   105
Revising Text   108
DISKbyte: Word Processing Tips   111
Using Advanced Word
Processing Features   112
Spelling Checker   112
*DISKbyte: Spelling Checkers Can
Be Deadly*   113
Thesaurus   113
Outliner   114
Table of Contents Generator   115
Index Generator   115
Word Processing Applications   115
Mail/Merge   116
Manuscript Preparation   117
The Ever-Evolving Word Processing
Program   117
Ethics   118
*CAREERbyte: How to Get Rich in
the Software Industry*   120
Summary   120
Key Terms   122
Review and Discussion Questions   122
Issues   123

5   The Spreadsheet   124

The VisiCalc Evangelist   125
Working with Numbers   126
What Is an Electronic Spreadsheet?   127
Birth of the Spreadsheet   127
The Spreadsheet Advantage   128
*DISKbyte: Mitchell Kapor and the
Road from Transcendental
Meditation to Computer Software*   129
Basic Spreadsheet Features   130
The Spreadsheet Screen   130
The Menu Line and Command Line   132
The Scrolling Window   133
*DISKbyte: Paul Funk and the
Add-On Market for Spreadsheets*   134
A Spreadsheet Work Session   134
Creating the Spreadsheet   134
Commands   135
Using Advanced Spreadsheet Features   141

Functions   142
Recalculation   143
Templates   144
Macros   144
Spreadsheet Graphics   144
Spreadsheet Applications   145
Balance Sheet, Income Statement,
and Financial Analysis Ratios   146
Payroll Information   147
Classroom Information   149
Wedding or Shower Planner   151
Sports Information   151
Scientific Information   151
DISKbyte: Spreadsheet Tips   153
The Ever-Evolving Spreadsheet   153
Ethics   154
*CAREERbyte: The Spreadsheet
Wizard*   155
Summary   156
Key Terms   156
Review and Discussion Questions   157
Issues   157

6   Database Management Systems   158

Computer Wins Indy 500   159
What Is a Database?   160
The Database Management System   160
The DBMS Advantage   160
Basic Features of the DBMS   162
Types of Database
Management Systems   162
Data Elements   165
*DISKbyte: Wayne Ratliff: Father of
the Personal Computer DBMS*   168
The DBMS Screen   168
A DBMS Work Session   169
Database Design   169
Creating a Database   170
Saving the Database   173
Manipulating Data   176
Printing Reports   180
Advanced Database Management   181
Personal Information Managers   181
Managing a Corporate Database   182

DISKbyte: The DBMS as a
Productivity Tool   184
The Ever-Evolving DBMS   184
DISKbyte: DBMS Tips   185
Ethics   186
CAREERbyte: Building a
Geoprocessing Database   187
Summary   188
Key Terms   188
Review and Discussion Questions   189
Issues   189

MODULE III

Computer Software

7 Software: From Operating
Systems to Applications   192

Helping Make Software Easier to Use   193
The Versatility of Software   194
Understanding Files   194
DISKbyte: The Abstract Industry   195
System Software   195
The Many Faces of an
Operating System   196
The Servant: Providing Command
Languages and Utilities   196
The Traffic Officer: Controlling
Input and Output   198
The Appointment Secretary:
Scheduling   198
The Hotel Manager:
Storage Assignment   199
The Librarian: Data Management   200
Personal Computer
Operating Systems   200
Minicomputer Operating Systems   203
Mainframe Operating Systems   204
Trends in Operating Systems   205
Application Software   206
Integrated Software   208
Computer Graphics   212
Electronic Publishing   217

Utility Software   221
DISKbyte: Multimedia: The Next
Great Application for Computers?   225
What Lies Ahead?   226
DISKbyte: Tips for Buying Personal
Computer Software   226
Ethics   227
CAREERbyte: Jackie Willig Silver:
A Desktop Publishing Pioneer   229
Summary   230
Key Terms   230
Review and Discussion Questions   231
Issues   231

8 Software Development   232

The First Programmer   233
The System Development Process   234
Analyzing Problems and
Designing Solutions   235
Analyzing the Problem   236
Designing the Program   236
Structured Techniques   237
Coding and Debugging the Program   244
Writing Source Code   244
Translating Source Code   246
DISKbyte: Programming Errors
Can Be Expensive!   247
Debugging the Program   248
Testing and Acceptance   248
Maintenance   249
Writing the Documentation   250
Software Documentation   251
User Documentation   252
Reference Documentation   252
Quick-Reference Guides   253
The Evolution of
Programming Languages   254
Machine Language   254
Assembly Language   254
DISKbyte: How to
Motivate Programmers   255
High-Level Programming Languages   255
Statements and Syntax   256
Compiling High-Level Languages   256
Portability   256

FORTRAN: A Scientific Language 257
COBOL: A Business Language 257
DISKbyte: Grace Murray Hopper: A Computer Science Pioneer 259
BASIC: A Personal Computer Language 259
C: A High-Level Language 262
A World of Programming Languages 262
Advanced Programming Languages, Tools, and Techniques 264
Fourth-Generation Languages 264
Object-Oriented Programming 267
CASE: Computer-Aided Software Engineering 267
Ethics 271
CAREERbyte: Clark Gee, Systems Analyst 272
Summary 273
Key Terms 273
Review and Discussion Questions 274
Issues 275

MODULE IV

Computer Hardware

---

9 Processing Hardware: Computer Power to the People 278
Better, Faster, Cheaper Computers 279
Processing Hardware 280
Computer Systems 281
General-Purpose and Special-Purpose Computers 282
Types of Computers 282
The Personal Computer 284
The Personal Computer System 284
Types of Personal Computers 285
The Desktop Personal Computer 285
IBM PCs and PC-Compatibles 286
Types of IBM PCs 286
Types of PC-Compatibles 287
Using PCs and PC-Compatibles 287
The IBM Personal System/2 288

Types of PS/2s 288
Using PS/2s 289
The Apple Macintosh 289
Types of Macintoshes 289
Using the Macintosh 290
The Laptop Personal Computer 291
Portables and Laptops 291
DISKbyte: The Incredible Shrinking Computer 292
Types of Laptops 292
Using Laptops 294
The Workstation 295
Workstation Characteristics 295
Types of Workstations 297
Using Workstations 298
DISKbyte: Reduced-Instruction-Set Computing 299
The Minicomputer 300
Types of Minicomputers 300
Using Minis 301
The Mainframe Computer 302
Types of Mainframes 303
Using Mainframes 303
The Supercomputer 305
Types of Supercomputers 305
DISKbyte: A Chilly Supercomputer 306
Using Supercomputers 306
Parallel Processing 307
The Ever-Evolving Computer 308
Ethics 308
CAREERbyte: Computer Architects 310
Summary 311
Key Terms 311
Review and Discussion Questions 312
Issues 313

10 Peripheral Hardware: Input, Output, and Storage Devices 314
Herman Hollerith and the First I/O Device 315
Peripheral Devices 316
The Interface 316
Input 318
Input Devices 318

DISKbyte: Great Moments in I/O History   321
Input Devices for the Disabled   325
Output   326
   Types of Computer Output   326
   Output Devices   326
   The Video Monitor   326
   Printers   328
   Computer-to-Machine Output   331
   DISKbyte: Cyberspace: The Ultimate I/O?   332
   Voice Output   332
Storage   333
   Direct Access Storage Devices   333
   Sequential Access Storage Devices   339
   DISKbyte: CD–ROM: The New Papyrus   340
What Lies Ahead?   341
Ethics   341
   CAREERbyte: Robert Solomon: A Talent for Innovative Peripherals   343
Summary   344
Key Terms   344
Review and Discussion Questions   345
Issues   345

MODULE V

Computer Systems Applications

11 Networking: Connecting Your Computer to the World   348
Dennis Hayes and the Personal Computer Modem   349
What Is Computer Networking?   350
Network Components   350
   Telecommunications Hardware   351
   Telecommunications Software   354
   Telecommunications Management Software   355
An On-line Work Session   356
Telecommunications Networks   358
   Public Networks   358

Private Networks   360
   DISKbyte: Networking Tips   364
   The Next Wave in Networks   364
Using Networks   365
   Information Services   365
   Interactive Services   367
   DISKbyte: Telecommuting: Working from Home   368
   Business and Governmental Networks   368
Network Security   370
   Protecting Networks   370
   DISKbyte: Radio Modems Fight Credit Card Fraud   371
The Ever-Expanding Network   374
Ethics   375
   CAREERbyte: The Networking Professional   377
Summary   378
Key Terms   378
Review and Discussion Questions   379
Issues   379

12 Management Information Systems: The Strategic Advantage in Business   380
Richard Nolan: Creating a Vision of MIS   381
Living in a Systems World   382
   MIS: A Definition   383
   Why Use a Management Information System?   384
   Who Uses MIS?   384
   A Business Perspective   386
   A Government Perspective   388
   The MIS Concept   390
MIS: Three Components   391
The People Component   391
   The MIS Organization   391
   DISKbyte: Three Top MIS Executives   393
   End-User Computing   394
The Software Component   395
   Distributed Computing   395
   MIS as a Corporate Resource   396

DISKbyte: IBM's Top 10 Customers   397
The Hardware Component   398
  Systems Integration   398
  DISKbyte: Facilities Management:
Don't-Do-It-Yourself MIS   399
  New Computer Architectures   400
What Lies Ahead?   401
  Information Providers   401
  The Changing Role of
the MIS Executive   402
Ethics   403
  CAREERbyte: The PC Manager   404
Summary   405
Key Terms   405
Review and Discussion Questions   406
Issues   407

13 Office Automation: Putting It
All Together   **408**

The Evolution of the Office   409
The Office Automation Challenge   410
  Office Automation: A Definition   410
  People: The Most
Important Element   411
  Office Systems: Software
and Hardware   412
Office Automation Systems   413
  Text Management Systems   413

*DISKbyte: The Evolution
of the Typewriter*   414
Business Analysis Systems   416
Document Management Systems   417
*DISKbyte: Backing Up the
Vatican Library*   419
Network and Communication
Management Systems   420
Office Automation Technologies
at Work   422
  The Integrated Desktop   422
  Large System Integration   424
  *DISKbyte: Two Views of the Office
of the Future*   426
What Lies Ahead?   426
Ethics   428
  *CAREERbyte: Amy Wohl, Office
Automation Consultant*   429
Summary   429
Key Terms   430
Review and Discussion Questions   430
Issues   431

Epilogue   The Future of Computing   432
Appendix A   Number Systems   444
Appendix B   The Computer Generations   454
Glossary   472
Index   483

Computers
for People

—

Concepts and Applications

MODULE I

Computer Fundamentals

It's truly mind-boggling to realize how quickly computers have transformed our world. Consider that when your grandparents were teenagers, hardly anyone had even heard of a computer. Now, consider the fact that by the year 2000, three out of five jobs will require computer expertise.

Is it any wonder we all need to become computer literate?

Understanding how computers work and how to use them is an entry-level skill for citizens of the new millennium. But don't worry. We're here to help you. That's what this book is all about.

In Chapter 1, we'll explore the world around us and the computers that populate it. We'll learn about the different kinds of computers and how they are used. We'll come to understand the important role the computer plays in many different areas: science, government, business, education, and our personal lives.

Chapter 2 gets down to fundamentals. You'll see how people, software, and hardware form the computer system and how essential each is. You'll learn what goes on inside a computer. You'll also learn about that marvelous chunk of beach sand called the silicon chip and about the different tasks it performs.

Chapter 3 is your first hands-on chapter. Here, you'll learn the basics of using the personal computer: how to turn it on and what happens when you do. You'll learn how to use DOS, the disk operating system, which makes it possible for the computer hardware and software to perform their many useful tasks. You'll also learn about the three different kinds of human-computer interfaces, which determine how we interact with the computer.

It may be a pleasant surprise to learn that computers aren't really difficult to understand. What's more, it's interesting to see the many tasks they perform for us. Let's begin.

CHAPTER

I

A Computer-Orchestrated World

CHAPTER OUTLINE

Computers Go Hollywood
Do Computers Matter?
   What Is Computer Literacy?
   DISKbyte: Understanding the Information Age
What Is a Computer?
   The Modern Computer
   How Computers Do Their Work
   *DISKbyte: Early Counting and Calculating
      Machines*
Types of Modern Computers
   The Supercomputer
   The Mainframe
   The Minicomputer
   The Personal Computer
   *DISKbyte: How Computers Have Changed the
      Auto Industry*
What Computers Can't Do
   Productivity
   DISKbyte: Luddites
   Reasoning
   Errors
Ethics in the Information Age
   DISKbyte: A Computer Crime Sampler
Computers for People: Concepts and Applications
   *CAREERbyte: Ed Milkow and the Computer
      Helping Profession*
Summary
Key Terms
Review and Discussion Questions
Issues

OBJECTIVES

After reading and studying this chapter, you should be able to:

1. Understand the role computers play in modern society.
2. Explain why it is important to be computer literate.
3. Name and identify different types of computers.
4. Understand what computers cannot do.
5. Explain the ethical use of computers.

COMPUTERS GO HOLLYWOOD

Harold Buchman doesn't like to get up in the morning, which suits his employer, Rhythm & Hues, just fine — Harold can work until midnight or even later if he likes. You see, Harold is a computer animator. He works at a computer screen, designing animated (or moving) product logos, television program openers and messages, architectural landscapes, and even spaceships. Harold created the Paramount Films logo (with the stars circling up and around the mountain peak) that you see at the opening of each Paramount film.

Courtesy Harold Buchman

"What first caught my attention were some videotapes of Japanese animation a friend showed me in high school," Harold says. "That and *Star Wars.*" Harold attended the University of California at Los Angeles where he majored in art and design. He studied under two pioneers in computer animation and that, coupled with a few computer courses, quickly helped him decide on pursuing computer animation as a career.

Harold uses programs that create the animation. He works on a design or on a series of movements, then plays the resulting pictures on a special color monitor to see how it all looks. He finds it interesting, challenging work: "I get to use state-of-the-art computer tools, and I really like the people I work with." Rhythm & Hues is a small firm, one of only three or four in Hollywood. There is another computer animation clan in New York. "Everybody in L.A. knows one another," says Harold, "and there's cross-fertilization with New York, too." Like many computer companies, Rhythm & Hues takes good care of its programmers. There's a complete kitchen, with food and soft drinks provided by the company. "The kitchen is the social center, day and night," Harold says. "I have to watch the snacking all the time!"

Computer animation is a rapidly broadening field. Harold worked on an "architectural visualization" for the 1986 World Expo in Vancouver, British Columbia. The entire fairgrounds were simulated by the computer, and a camera "flew" over the grounds to point out where things were located.

In another instance, an office building used computer animation as part of a promotional videotape shown to potential tenants. Amusement parks such as Universal Studios in Florida use computer animation for the Flintstones and Jetsons ride. More and more television commercials and feature films use computer animation to either create or enhance scenes. Harold created a chrome spaceship that could alter its shape in *Flight of the Navigator.* Computer animation can add a glowing aura, sparkling, shadows, and other special effects to real-life scenes and images.

Today, the computer systems used for animation are quite expensive, far beyond the reach of the amateur. However, Harold thinks it won't be long before we have computer animation programs for ordinary use. A friend of his has already produced a short film with his Amiga personal computer. "But you have to be a good artist, first and foremost," says Harold. Even so, people from all walks of life are finding they can improve their work or experiment with interests never before possible — thanks to computers.

DO COMPUTERS MATTER?

Picture a world without computers. Grocery store clerks would punch prices into mechanical cash registers at a snail's pace while customers wait in long, slow lines. Your paycheck or student loan check would take weeks instead of days to clear the bank. Most long-distance telephone calls would require operator assistance and would be full of delays and mistakes.

Without the accumulated weather statistics computers have collected over the years, farmers would not have the long-range weather forecasts that help them plant their crops. Without computers to help locate new oil fields, we might have gasoline rationing and be paying more than $10 per gallon. Commercial aircraft would lack computerized automatic pilot equipment that helps fly and land planes safely. Factories without computer-controlled robots would have no better productivity than they did 50 years ago. Without computer process control, many more industrial accidents would occur, resulting in loss of life and in environmental damage.

A world without computers would also be a world without many of the appliances and tools we've come to depend on. There would be no calculators or digital watches, no cellular phones, no compact disc players and digital recordings, no "smart" thermostats in our houses, no programmable ovens, no home security systems that automatically phone the police.

The computer has made an immeasurable impact on our increasingly complex and fast-moving world. Bill Gates, head of Microsoft, one of the biggest computer software companies in the world, says, "I can't think of any equivalent phenomenon in history." The computer has helped us keep pace with modern life but it has increased our own pace, too, for it seems that the faster we find we can do things, the faster we want them done. But the fact remains, we literally could not function without computers in modern society. For this reason, it is important to understand the computer and what it does. Our goal is to achieve computer literacy.

What Is Computer Literacy?

To be literate means to be knowledgeable or educated about something. **Computer literacy** is being knowledgeable about the computer and how it works in our daily lives. It also means being able to operate and use a computer, at least to perform basic tasks. We feel computer literacy is second in importance only to basic literacy in our society.

We chose the title for our book — *Computers for People: Concepts and Applications* — with great care. We wanted to convey precisely how we view computers in modern life, and specifically what we feel is most important for you to know about computers. We believe people should use computers, because there are many ways that computers can enhance our lives.

Computers for People   About 400 years ago, an English philosopher named Francis Bacon said, "Knowledge is power." He was right; the people who controlled the libraries were the ones who ran society. But technology, from the printing press to the computer, has brought knowledge, information — and power — to more people. For many reasons, we see the computer (especially those that an *individual* can use) as a tool for democracy because it takes the control of information resources from the hands of the few and gives it to all. (See Figure 1–1.)

FIGURE 1 – 1   People are the driving force behind computer systems.

H. Mark Weidman   F. Bodin/Offshoot

Concepts and Applications   We live in a busy and complex world. There is little time for the average person to become a jack of all trades — and certainly not a computer scientist. Therefore, our goal is to teach you the basic computer concepts such as how a computer works, what devices help us use it effectively, and what it is capable of doing. We do this without going into electronic circuitry, computer engineering, and other technical details.

As educators, writers, and human beings, we have found that most people learn best when facts can be explained with a story. Therefore, we describe many applications, which show how computer concepts are applied and how computers are used. An **application** is a computer software program that enables people to use the computer in performing specific work tasks or other activities. You can get an idea of the diversity of computer applications by looking at the photo essay in Figure 1 – 2. We've tried to present a wide variety of application stories; some are straightforward, others are curious or offbeat. After all, there is no reason why learning about computers can't be fun.

We feel the best approach is to make good use of the tools available to us. Computer literacy allows us to better understand the world we live in and to reach goals we may not be able to otherwise. Computers make us more effective when we write, manage our finances, and keep track of our schedules and possessions. Computers can also be our chief asset in learning, in running a business, and in exploring our personal interests and pastimes. You can use a computer to speak with a computerized psychoanalyst, develop a fitness regimen, learn a foreign language, study astrology, or converse with Racter, a computerized poet. You can draw, paint, and store video images. You can hold computer conversations with an international community of people. You can get up-to-the-minute news, stock market reports, back issues of newspapers, information from the government, and more — much more.

While our goal is to help you become computer literate, we also hope that you might develop a deeper interest in computers — one that might lead you to a career in the industry. Each chapter features a CAREERbyte that shows you the many interesting jobs people have working with computers.

FIGURE 1-2 Computers: A photo essay.

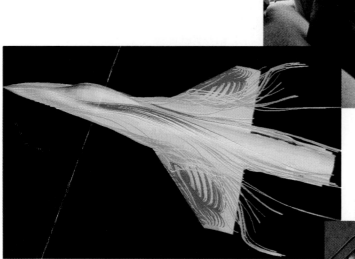

J. Pickerell/Click-TSW

Courtesy NASA

D. McCoy/Rainbow

H. Morgan/Rainbow

F. Bodin/Offshoot

R. Schleipman/Offshoot

J. Moss/Click-TSW

B. Barnes/Click-TSW

H. Mark Weidman

H. Mark Weidman

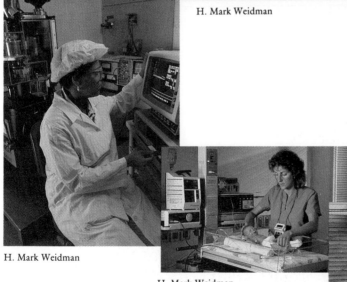

H. Mark Weidman

T. Horowitz/Stock Market

B. O'Shaugnessy/Stock Market

DISKbyte

Understanding the Information Age

The idea of a postindustrial society was introduced by Daniel Bell, a Harvard University sociologist, in 1956. He said the Industrial Age was past and that America would become an information-based, white-collar, service-oriented economy. Bell believed that information used for decision making and forecasting (or predicting long-term effects) was growing increasingly important.

What made it possible to use information in these new ways? It was the computer. By 1956, the United States Census Bureau, a number of large insurance companies, and dozens of businesses were using computers. Computers made it possible to obtain more information than before, and to use it in ways that hadn't been possible. What's more, information could now be used over and over again. Without the computer, there would be no **Information Age.**

Today, information plays a significant role in everyday life. There is a magazine for every taste and interest; thousands of books are published every year; we are assaulted with junk mail that sells everything imaginable. Indeed, computers are

filled with extraordinary amounts of information, much of it available to the average citizen. In addition, vast quantities of information move via telephone, television, radio, and other communications media. We consider being well informed of great value, whether it's knowing current events or having a college education. Therefore, information has value and bestows power and prestige on those who possess it in large quantities. This, in part, is what it means to live in the Information Age.

Yoneji Masuda, who heads the Institute for the Information Society in Tokyo, Japan, wrote a book called *The Information Society* in 1980.[1] In it, he explained how society has progressed, from hunting to agriculture to industry. "Man is now standing at the threshold of a period of innovation in a new societal technology based on the combination of computer and communications technology," he wrote. "This is a completely new type of societal technology, quite unlike any in the past. Its substance is information, which is invisible." The Japanese civilization takes the Information Age very seriously and

is evolving rapidly into an information society.

But the Information Age has its drawbacks. There is little doubt that society is moving at a much faster rate, perhaps accelerated by computers and their high-speed operation. Few of us have the time to assimilate all the information we'd like, even if it's just reading a newspaper or magazine thoroughly. Television mirrors this acceleration by giving us news in "sound bites" or short segments. As a result, because it's harder to retain all the information we encounter, much of it is quickly forgotten.

With today's glut of information, a very real danger is that any information — regardless of form, content, or media — will automatically be considered valuable. We must remember to analyze and evaluate all information before we accept it as correct. The Information Age has brought us useful, versatile tools for science, business, and the creative arts. We must always use them conscientiously.

---

[1] The Information Society as Post-Industrial Society, © 1980 Institute for the Information Society, Tokyo.

MEMORY CHECK

1. Describe some ways the computer has changed the world.
2. What is the meaning of the term *Information Age?*
3. What does being computer literate mean?
4. What is meant by basic computer concepts?
5. What is a computer application?

WHAT IS A COMPUTER?

A **computer** is a device that accepts data, then performs mathematical or logical operations that manipulate or change the data, and finally produces new results from that data. That's quite a concept to take in all at once, so let's take a closer look. Given that definition, you might think there are many machines or devices that qualify as a computer — and you'd be right. Computers come in many shapes and sizes. In the DISKbyte called Early Counting and Calculating Machines, you'll recognize "computers" that date back hundreds of years.

The Modern Computer

In this book, we confine our discussion of computers to those machines that are both electronic and digital. By **electronic** we mean a machine that uses components such as vacuum tubes, transistors, or silicon chips. All these electronic devices require electricity. By **digital** we mean a computer that uses the **binary arithmetic system** as the basis for its operation. Binary arithmetic uses only two digits: the 0 and the 1. We consider the electronic, digital computer the modern computer, which dates from the early 1940s.

Analog Computers   By contrast, there is also an analog computer. **Analog** means the computer does not count in two digits but rather continuously measures and compares changing values. One example is a computerized thermostat, which regulates the heat or air conditioning in a building. An analog radio tuner has a needle or arm that moves from station to station when you turn the knob; a digital radio tuner displays the precise frequency when you touch a button.

How Computers Do Their Work

In our definition, we said the computer accepts data. **Data** consists of facts and numbers suitable for communication or interpretation. When people or a computer act on that data, we call it processing. **Data processing** is the computer system using specific procedures that turn data into useful information for people. Data is the raw material of information. *People* turn the *data* computers produce into useful *information* by understanding and applying it to our world.

Computer Operations   Next, the computer performs mathematical or logical operations on that data. **Mathematical operations** are simply adding, subtracting, multiplying, and dividing. **Logical operations** compare values to perform logical tests and make decisions. For example, is the number 2 greater than (expressed with the > sign) or less than (expressed with the < sign) the number 6? As you can see, the fundamental way computers operate is very simple.

DISKbyte

Early Counting and Calculating Machines

500 B.C. The abacus was used in Egypt; however the abacus as we know it today dates back to China, around 200 B.C. There, it was known as the *saun-pan;* in Japan, it was called the *soroban.*

1620 John Napier, an Englishman, created multiplication tables carved into strips of bone and wood, known as Napier's bones. The bones led to inscribing logarithms on strips of wood and ivory, which evolved into the slide rule.

1653 Frenchman Blaise Pascal, a child prodigy in mathematics, perfected a calculating machine known as the Pascaline. He invented the Pascaline so that his father wouldn't have to work hour upon hour totaling long columns of numbers by hand, a task that made Pascal so sad for his father that he wept whenever he watched him do it.

1673 Gottfried Wilhelm von Leibniz of Germany said, "It is unworthy of excellent men to lose hours like slaves in the labor of calculation which could safely be relegated to anyone else if machines were used." He invented a calculator superior to the Pascaline that became the first general-purpose machine for bookkeepers and mathematicians. Leibniz was also the first to recognize the value of using binary mathematics.

1801 Joseph Marie Jacquard developed the first weaving loom able to repeat a design automatically. The Frenchman used cards with holes punched in them, allowing needles to pass through in some places but not others. The punched card was destined to reappear as a mainstay of computing.

1823 Charles Babbage, a cranky English mathematician, finished the design for the Analytical Engine, a mechanical calculating machine. Like the Difference Engine Babbage toyed with in college,

it was destined never to work, but the basic concepts lived on to form the basis for the famous Mark I computer, built at Harvard in 1944.

1890 Herman Hollerith revived the punched card to count the 1890 United States census. It took human labor seven years to count the 1880 census; it took Hollerith's machine only two and a half years to finish the next one.

1930s American Telephone and Telegraph estimated that if telephone use continues to increase, Ma Bell would need more operators than the entire population of the United States. George Stibitz at Bell Laboratories (the research division of AT&T) built a working model of the Complex Numerical Calculator. It used electricity to activate telephone switching circuits, replacing slower mechanical relays.

Pascaline.

Courtesy IBM Corporation/Neuhart-Donges-Neuhart Design

Difference engine.

Courtesy of IBM Corporation/Neuhart-Donges-Neuhart Design

Punched-card tabulating machine.

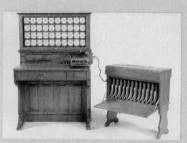

Courtesy of IBM Corporation/Neuhart-Donges-Neuhart Design

Programming Computers   People can make the computer do many sophisticated and complicated tasks by issuing instructions to it. We give the computer instructions, usually in the form of programs, so it will perform the data processing. An **instruction** is typically a group of characters the computer understands. A single instruction might be to total 2 + 2. A **program** is a series, or set, of instructions that gives us a more complex result, such as producing a report listing all the company's customers living in ZIP code 95123.

We commonly turn to computers to help us solve a problem or perform a task that would take too long or is too difficult for people to do themselves. The problem or task must be presented in a very specific and precise manner. If it is not, the computer won't be able to help.

The **programmer** is a person who understands the problem or task the computer is supposed to work on and can translate it into the language the computer understands. And, as you might guess, this process is called **programming.** We commonly refer to these programs and instructions as **software.**

Software   Computer software takes two forms. One is system software, which controls the computer's primary operations. The system software we most commonly come in contact with is called the operating system which, among other jobs, controls the programs we use to accomplish our tasks. You'll learn more about this form of software in Chapters 3 and 7.

The other form computer software takes is application software, the programs we use to produce useful work. This might be a bicycle parts inventory managment application program or a zoological classification application program. There are applications for many thousands of interests and needs. The three most commonly used for personal productivity, schoolwork, and business are:

- **Word processing,** which lets you create and revise your writing.
- The **spreadsheet,** which lets you perform a variety of accounting and mathematical calculations.
- The **database management system,** which lets you organize and obtain data stored in one or more databases.

Module II discusses each of these application programs in great detail. Others are discussed in later chapters as well.

---

1. What is a computer?
2. Describe the two types of operations a computer performs.
3. What are the two most important characteristics of a modern computer?
4. What do we call the facts and numbers we feed into computers?
5. What do we call the process of giving the computer instructions?

MEMORY CHECK

TYPES OF MODERN COMPUTERS

No one had even conceived of the modern computer when your grandparents were born. In 1937, the League of Nations commissioned the world's best minds to forecast future technologies. When these experts submitted their report, there was no mention of the computer. Eleven years later, in 1948, with several computers successfully in operation, IBM declined getting into the computer business—not enough demand, it said. And five years after that, in 1953, Thomas J. Watson, Sr., founder of IBM, declared that the world would only need five computers.

Did these people fail to recognize the computer's potential? Not really. At the time, people thought of computers much as we think of water or power utilities—large, centralized plants designed to serve the needs of whole regions. Watson had no way of knowing there would be computers in our wristwatches, cash registers, cars, and kitchen appliances. When most people thought about computers back then, their mental image was of big metal boxes that hummed and whirred but were otherwise a mystery.

These first computers were developed in the 1940s at universities. **ENIAC, the Electronic Numerical Integrator and Calculator,** shown in Figure 1–3, was the world's first electronic digital computer. Completed in 1946 at a cost of $3 million, it stood two stories high, weighed 30 tons, and covered an area the size of two football fields. It was not much more complicated than a modern hand-held calculator and was able to perform a mathematical computation about as fast.

Computer technology has advanced at a relentless pace since then. Engineers have continually sought ways to make better, faster, smaller, and less

FIGURE 1–3   ENIAC, the world's first digital, electronic computer system.

The University of Pennsylvania Archives

expensive computers. A computer industry commentator once noted that if automobile technology had advanced at the rate of computer technology, you could buy a Rolls-Royce for $2.50 and it would get 2 million miles per gallon.

The first computers were just plain huge. Today, we have computers of all sizes. When we discuss physical computer components and equipment, we call it **hardware.** Let's explore the various types of modern computer hardware.

The Supercomputer

Supercomputers are the most powerful computers on earth. They are most often used in experimental governmental and scientific research facilities such as the Lawrence Livermore Labs in California and Los Alamos National Laboratory in New Mexico. They are also used in military weapons research, atmospheric and earth science research, and natural resource exploration. Figure 1–4 shows one of the most popular supercomputers, the Cray.

The Mainframe

The computer most commonly used in business is the **mainframe computer.** It is made up of many cabinets filled with electronic gear and connected to the main computer cabinet, which led to its being called a mainframe. One is shown in Figure 1–5.

In 1964, after spending four years and $5 billion on research and development, International Business Machines (IBM) introduced the System/360 mainframe computer. Bob Evans, the project manager, called it the "you-bet-your-company computer." Thomas J. Watson, Jr., IBM's chief executive, introduced it himself on April 7, 1964; he called it the most important product in the company's history. It became the most popular mainframe in computer history and set an early standard for the industry.

FIGURE 1–4   The CRAY Y-MP series of computer systems.

Courtesy of Paul Shambroom/Cray Research, Inc.

FIGURE 1–5   A mainframe system.

D. McCoy/Rainbow

The Minicomputer

The **minicomputer** was introduced as a smaller, less expensive alternative to the mainframe. Early minis were used for a variety of special-purpose tasks. They provided guidance systems for aircraft, measured seismographic fluctuations in dangerous mines, and controlled manufacturing processes such as keeping the temperature of cooking vats of beer, soup, and chocolate constant.

This smaller, more mobile computer was designed by Kenneth W. Olsen, an MIT graduate who went on to found Digital Equipment Corporation, the world's second largest computer company. Today, there are minis of all sorts; some are as large or as powerful as mainframes, while others fit on a desktop. Figure 1–6 shows a minicomputer at work in office automation.

The Personal Computer

For many people, the path to computer literacy begins with the personal computer, so that is our primary focus in this book. The **personal computer** is one designed for use by a single individual and is usually small enough to fit on a desktop. The personal computer is sometimes called a **microcomputer,** reflecting the fact that it was smaller than a mainframe or a minicomputer. Today, we commonly use the term *personal computer* generically to refer to many different kinds of microcomputers. Personal computers come in many sizes. The most powerful models are called **workstations** and often have the power and capabilities of a minicomputer. Others range in size from desktop to laptop to briefcase, even to one that fits in the palm of your hand!

The first personal computers were like the old Volkswagen beetle: all they came with was the bare essentials. Their owners had to know a lot more about computers than today's personal computer users. Apple and Radio Shack were

FIGURE 1−6   A minicomputer system.

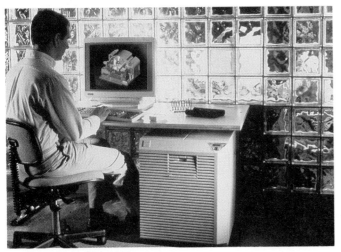

Courtesy of Hewlett-Packard Company

FIGURE 1−7   A personal computer system.

Courtesy of Compaq Computer

the first companies to introduce personal computers to the mass consumer market. Radio Shack's management wasn't sure there would be much interest in personal computers when the TRS-80 Model I came off the assembly line, so they only made enough so each retail store would have one. If the darned thing didn't sell, the store could use it for inventory or something, they reasoned.

Figure 1−7 shows a state-of-the-art personal computer. It shows the **system unit,** where the computer electronics are stored. The **keyboard** is used to enter data and instructions. The **monitor** or video display screen is where you see your work. A separate **printer** (not shown) provides a finished copy of the results. In essence, these are the hardware components of all computers, large and small. Large computers require many cabinets to make up a system unit, and have many keyboards, monitors, and printers, so more than one person can use them at once.

DISKbyte

How Computers Have Changed the Auto Industry

The automobile is a product of the Industrial Age, but the computer has had a dramatic impact on the way cars are designed, manufactured, and even the way they operate. Computers provide tools, supply data, and perform tasks that contribute to building more reliable, less expensive cars.

As you can see in Figure 1–8, computers help design cars, from the curve of a fender to the intricate working of the engine, suspension, and instrumentation. Before computers, engineers and designers built models with wood or clay. By simulating the components in three-dimensional detail, computers greatly shorten the time required to design and test a prototype. This is called **computer-aided design**, or **CAD** for short.

Next, computers play key roles in identifying, refining, and producing the raw materials that go into the car's construction. They assist in locating the richest deposits of iron ore, the source of the car's metals, and do the same in isolating oil deposits, the source of the car's plastic materials.

As you can see in Figure 1–9, computers control the machines that form the metals and plastic, and computer-controlled robots assemble, weld, and paint cars as they roll off production lines. The entire process of manufacturing is monitored and controlled by computers. This is called **computer-aided manufacturing, or CAM.**

Computers are also used for sending orders and invoices between an auto manufacturer and its suppliers, the companies who provide such things as shock absorbers, tires, radios, nuts, bolts, and hundreds of other parts. This is called **electronic data interchange, or EDI.** After the order is filled, the manufacturer pays the suppliers' invoices via computer, using **electronic funds transfer, or EFT.**

Computers greatly enhance the engineers' abilities to test finished cars by supplying hundreds of times more information than unassisted human senses can provide. Cars are tested in many ways: for their aerodynamic qualities in computer-controlled wind tunnels, for the engine's performance, and to determine the overall life expectancy. Once data is collected, computers can compile and report the information in a fraction of the time it would take people to do the job. This is called **quality control or QC.**

In the marketing department, computers dissect and analyze auto-buying trends. The dealers learn what kinds of cars different types of people in different geographic areas want to buy. In the advertising department, computers help graphic designers and advertising copywriters prepare everything from magazine ads to computer-generated television commercials. At the car dealership, computers are used to qualify customers for financing and to send credit data to the bank. Computers are also used to send special orders directly to the manufacturing plant and to analyze parts and service data to determine where problems might arise.

Without computers, manufacturing cars would take longer, cost more, and produce many more inferior products. General Motors has estimated that using EDI in automobile manufacturing saves the consumer between $200 and $500 on the sticker price. And, as you can see in Figure 1–10, computers not only help manufacture cars but now they help us operate them more safely and conveniently, too! Computers are used in the fuel and emissions system, the braking system, and to monitor such things as locked doors, oil pressure, air conditioning, and so forth. Many cars now come equipped with a diagnostic computer that connects to the dealer's service department computer, providing an instantaneous analysis of the car's condition.

FIGURE 1–8   A computer-aided design (CAD) computer system.

A. Sacks/Click-TSW

FIGURE 1–9   Computer-aided manufacturing (CAM) controls processes as well as robot arms.

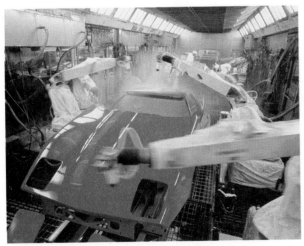

A. Sacks/Click-TSW

FIGURE 1–10   Computers not only help manufacture autos but also guide and control their passenger systems.

G. Haling/Photo Researchers

1. What is the most powerful type of computer called?
2. What type of computer is most often used in business?
3. What computer was designed for special-purpose tasks?
4. What is the more popular term for the microcomputer?
5. What are the four basic components in a personal computer system?

**MEMORY
CHECK**

WHAT COMPUTERS CAN'T DO

There is no doubt that computers are fulfilling their promise to perform certain tasks *better, faster,* and *cheaper.* In terms of the analogy with the auto industry, the 1992 equivalent is that the Rolls-Royce should now cost about 15 cents and get around 132 million miles per gallon. But is it enough to be good, fast, and cheap?

Along with fears about computers, from early on there have been great expectations about how computers would revolutionize our world. But some of the benefits people expected from computers way back in the 1950s just haven't happened.

Productivity

Computers haven't yet met all our expectations as a productivity tool. Sometimes it takes longer to do things with a computer than it would to do it manually. Sometimes it takes too much time to learn how to use an application that's supposed to increase productivity. Consider the following facts:

- In businesses, manual processes such as preparing routine paperwork and forms have been automated but the process itself remains

---

DISKbyte

Luddites

Keeping pace with modern times and technology seems like a good idea, but it *is* optional. Let's take a brief look back at some who chose not to take that option.

A Luddite is someone who irrationally hates technology. The name came from Edward Ludd, who rampaged from about 1800 to 1815 in England, destroying weaving looms in factories. Computers and their predecessors have had their share of Luddites as well, ranging from quiet protesters to wild-eyed bombers.

For example, a Spaniard named Magnus, who lived around the year A.D. 1000, made a counting machine of brass that resembled a human head with figures instead of teeth. We'll never know how it

worked—priests thought it so diabolical they destroyed it. Six hundred years later, French workers rioted in the streets of Paris to protest the use of the Pascaline, fearing it would create unemployment.

In the 1960s, a group of San Francisco anticomputer protesters picketed a computer trade show. They wore cardboard computer terminals on their heads and carried signs reading "IBM: Intensely Boring Machines," and "Office Automation is for Office Automatons."

We concede that people sometimes have a right to be mad about their experiences with computers. George Wittmeier of Kirkland, Washington, mistakenly underpaid his federal income tax by one penny. The Internal Revenue

Service computer counted up interest and fines totaling $159.58 and demanded payment. An IRS spokesman explained the incident by saying, "Obviously, the computer has gone berserk."

Despite such occurrences, it is incorrect to characterize the computer as a bad machine. There is nothing either good or bad about the computer, any more than there is anything good or bad about an automobile. Cars don't cause accidents; people do. Similarly, computers don't make errors in bills or invade your privacy; it's the people using them who do these things. That's why we stress the ethical, responsible use of computers in this book.

essentially unchanged. For example, Smith Sporting Goods types an order to Argus Rod Company for 100 fly rods into its computer and prints it out. The order is mailed to Argus, where a clerk sits down at the Argus computer and retypes the order into its system, then prints it out and takes it to the fulfillment department. This is not a productivity gain.

- Installing a new computer system is just as complicated and full of mistakes as ever. A few years ago, the U.S. Internal Revenue Service installed a new computer system, which then did not work properly. People's income tax returns were delayed for months, and it took nearly two years for the new system to become fully operational.

- Errors in programming occur with astounding frequency. The Space Shuttle Ground Processing System was found, after 2,177 hours of simulation testing, to contain 3 critical errors, 76 major errors, and 20 minor errors in programming.

Reasoning

In 1949, a book entitled *Cybernetics* by Norbert Weiner stated that the computer shared similarities with the brain and human nervous system.[2] Thus, it seems fair to say that in the same way we have built machines to replace human labor, we have also sought to build a machine that does certain kinds of thinking for us. While computers have come a long way, they still lack many of the mental capabilities possessed by five-year-old children. Simply put, computers can't think. They can't discriminate or assimilate widely divergent kinds of data, and they have absolutely no capacity for ethical evaluation. These are still powers possessed only by people—and it may be wise to keep things that way.

Errors

Computers don't make errors, people do; either in the way they program computers or in the way they use them. However, computers are extremely finicky machines and often frustratingly literal. This is because they use the principles of logic; for example, 1 must always equal 1. If you type "one," the computer won't understand it. Every instruction must be precisely entered. Say you are using your personal computer, and you type the instruction "COPY" but your finger accidentally presses the Y twice—COPYY. The computer will flash an error message, "Bad command or file name." It's easy to see why this literalness drives computer people to build smarter computers.

Likewise, computer accidents occur just because the computer can't tell the difference between doing something sensible versus something ridiculous. Erasing all its stored data is no different to a computer than changing a traffic light from green to red. Computers may operate logically, but they are incapable of acting prudently and rationally.

---

[2] Norbert Weiner, *Cybernetics* (Cambridge, Mass.: MIT Press, 1949).

ETHICS IN THE INFORMATION AGE

If you accept that information will improve the quality of life, then you must accept the fact that computers will be full of data about you. The government wants statistical data about your occupation, your race, your age, your income tax status, and so forth. Business wants data on your buying habits, how you like its products, and your address for its mailing lists. The bank wants data on your credit and the insurance company wants data on your health.

It's conceivable that these computers know more about you, in terms of the amount of data amassed, than you realize. How do you feel about that? Back in the 1960s and 1970s, some people thought of computers as intrusive; they were tools of Big Brother, who was always Watching You. Over the years, many of these attitudes have diminished; with the exception of instances involving criminals and political dissidents, there are few cases of personal data being misused by the government.

But what does our government know about us, and who gets to see that information? Within the government computers, there are levels of security which restrict access to computer data, to respect your privacy and prevent misuse of information. In the United States, there is the Freedom of Information Act that allows us to see the files the government maintains on us. In fact, you can request credit records, medical records, and more. If any of the information is incorrect, you have the right to correct it.

In recent years, some federal agencies have balked at releasing information to citizens, claiming the Freedom of Information Act ruling does not apply to computerized records, or that it takes costly programming time to retrieve them. Congress and the American Civil Liberties Union have been working to revise the Act and to ensure that our rights will be maintained.

Ultimately, each of us shares the responsibility for the ethical use of computers. Just as one courteous driver can instill courteous behavior in other drivers, so each of us can set an example for ethical computer behavior. Ethical computer use means many things:

- Respect for someone else's machine and private files.
- Honoring the copyright laws by not making unauthorized copies of programs.
- Using the computer in responsible ways, such as not connecting to another computer without permission to do so.
- Protecting the computer you are responsible for by keeping your secret password (the personal code that lets you use the computer) private; not leaving your computer on for others to use in your absence; and reporting security breaches when you see them.

MEMORY CHECK

1. What three things did computers promise to do?
2. Describe a way computers have not been an effective productivity tool.
3. Why have computers failed at reasoning?
4. When we say a computer has made an error, what has really happened?
5. Describe several characteristics of ethical computer use.

—
D I S K b y t e
—

A Computer Crime Sampler

There are many kinds of computer crime, some minor, some not. Here are a few examples:

- Three clerk-typists were arrested at Ford Motor Company for running an office football pool on the word processing computer. The football pool was pulling in about $5,000 a week; but even more serious, it was part of a larger gambling operation running on company computers and totaling $25,000 a week.
- A student at San Jose State University was arrested for having made over $7,000 in unpaid phone charges while playing the adventure game Dungeons and Dragons.
- Saxon Industries used its computers to maintain two sets of books on its inventory. The falsified records were used to inflate the company's revenues for over 13 years. If the company had been profitable, no one might ever have known its management was milking the company for $5 to $7 million a year in profits.
- A computer criminal called the Cuckoo was tracked down—electronically—after illegally gaining access to computers at Lawrence Berkeley Labs in California. Cuckoo was looking for military secrets to sell to the Soviets. Clifford Stoll, an astronomer, noticed 75 cents of computer time usage that couldn't be accounted for and began searching for the unauthorized user. He eventually traced the Cuckoo to Germany, where he and four other members of the Chaos Club were arrested, tried, and convicted of espionage.

COMPUTERS FOR PEOPLE: CONCEPTS AND APPLICATIONS

We hope this chapter has shown you that the world of computing is a lively world of people, ideas, and activity. We hope to show you more of its many facets as we explain the basic computer concepts and show you the diversity of applications. There are two more chapters in Module I covering computer fundamentals. In Chapter 2, we'll present the fundamental concepts of computers, explaining how people, software (the program instructions), and hardware (the physical components) work together to form a complete system. Chapter 3 is the first of four "hands-on" chapters. It shows you the fundamentals of using a personal computer. You'll learn how to set up and begin operating a personal computer. You'll also learn how to work with DOS, a standard operating system. After studying Chapter 3 you'll be ready to learn some practical uses or applications for your computer.

Module II covers personal productivity applications. Chapters 4, 5, and 6 provide hands-on experience with the three most widely used personal computer applications: word processing, the spreadsheet, and the database management system. Each of these application chapters includes concepts, terminology, and tutorial sessions to help you fully understand how to use these popular applications.

Module III explains the fundamentals of computer software, building on the basics discussed in Chapter 2. Chapter 7 covers the fundamentals of system software and application software, explaining the concepts underlying the operating system you studied in Chapter 3 and extending the applications in Module II. Chapter 8 shows how software is designed and created, explaining software development and programming, discussing the tools and programming languages used to create software.

Module IV explores computer hardware. Chapter 9 covers processing hardware, including personal computers, laptops, workstations, minicomputers, mainframes, and supercomputers, explaining the ways in which different types of computers are used. Chapter 10 surveys peripheral hardware we attach to processing hardware. We will see input devices from simple keyboards to sophisticated scanners; output devices such as video monitors and laser printers; and storage devices such as hard disk drives and CD-ROMs.

After reading Chapters 2 through 10, you will have completed a detailed study of computer concepts and personal computer applications. The remaining three chapters show how computers are used in many different ways to provide information for people. This is Module V, which covers systems applications or ways to make multiple computer systems work together.

Chapter 11 explains the most exciting application of the 1990s. **Networking,** often called telecommunications or data communications, links computers of all types all around the world, via telephone lines, to share resources and data. This chapter discusses the full range of networking, including local area networks, and on-line services such as Dow Jones News/ Retrieval.

Chapter 12 explains how computers are used in corporate and institutional environments to provide Management Information Systems (MIS). Today's business world simply could not function without computers, and this chapter shows the many diverse ways large and small computer systems provide companies with vital data.

Chapter 13 takes everything you have learned in the previous chapters — the diversity of computer processing and peripheral hardware, the wide range of applications, the potency of networking, the resources of MIS, and the versatility of personal computers — and brings it together in the modern office. Office Automation (OA) is people using computers to plan, manage, organize, and strategically control today's business. OA demonstrates how computers and other office machines can be networked; how computer systems produce data used to create important information systems and even new applications; and how computer technology is changing the fundamental way people work. OA is an evolving but highly developed integration of people, software, and hardware.

As you read this book, you'll see many examples of the computer industry's restless need to seek out better, faster, more affordable computer systems. In our final chapter, Epilogue: The Future of Computing, we speculate about where people are taking computers — and where computers are taking people. Appendixes offer additional material on number systems and the five generations of computing. Finally, all the boldfaced terms and their definitions are collected in the Glossary.

We hope this book gives you both knowledge and enjoyment. We hope you come away with both an appreciation of computers and practical abilities to use and understand them. Welcome to the world of the computer.

C A R E E R b y t e

Ed Milkow and the Computer Helping Profession

While other kids were collecting trophies for athletic activities, Edward Allen Milkow was collecting computers. His collection looks like a Who's Who in Computers: the Commodore Pet, the Apple II, a Toshiba laptop, desktop personal computers and more. Ed's always been avid about personal computers; he even started his own software company, Stardust Software, as a teenager.

"I've gone through all the phases," he says, explaining that his early interest in computer games was followed by a desire to explore the computer's electronic innards, taking it apart and installing new devices. He has collected vast quantities of information about another of his passions, collector's editions of comic books. He's also written a novel and several screenplays on his personal computer.

But a few years ago, Ed realized one thing he enjoyed perhaps more than anything else was helping others learn how to use computers. He started his own business, helping people and small businesses set up new computer systems, and later took a full-time job at a small

Photo by Andrew K. Howard

programming company doing the same work.

Then one day he learned of an opening for a customer support specialist at Ergo Computing, Inc., one of the hottest new personal computer startups of the 1990s. Ergo offers the "Brick," a modular personal computer that can be moved from one place to another and connected to existing keyboards and monitors. Thus it is

both a traveling computer and one for the desktop. Customers call Ed when they need answers to questions: What would work best with this system? How do I install this device? What programs should I use?

Ed handles about 25 calls on a normal day, spending about 15 minutes on average with a customer. He has a Brick at his desk that has stored in it all the problems that the customer support specialists have encountered in the past. "It helps us share the problems and solutions with each other, so we aren't constantly reinventing the wheel," Ed says.

What does he like most about the work? "The people. I work with great people. But mostly it's the satisfaction that comes from helping a customer solve a problem. A lot of times it's just a simple problem, like making sure the connections are tight. Sometimes it's a real brainbuster, and it's a tremendous feeling when we finally figure it out. People really appreciate it when you get their computer working for them. I like that."

SUMMARY

1. *Understand the role computers play in modern society.* Picture a world without computers — if you can. Computers have become so much a part of life that it is difficult to imagine how we'd get along without them.

2. *Explain why it is important to be computer literate.* Computer literacy, for everyone in our society, is very important. We need to understand how computers affect our lives and realize that we will be using them and interacting with them on a daily

basis. This means understanding basic computer concepts as well as applications—the ways computers are applied and used. A computer is a device that accepts data and performs mathematical or logical operations on that data to produce new results. We must give the computer instructions, in the form of programs, so it can accomplish its tasks. This book discusses the modern electronic, digital computer, which was developed in the 1940s. Another kind of computer is the analog computer, which continuously measures and compares changing values.

3. *Name and identify different types of computers.*   There are four types of modern computers: the supercomputer, the mainframe computer, the minicomputer, and the personal computer or microcomputer.

4. *Understand what computers cannot do.* Computers perform a great many complicated tasks today. Yet there are ways in which they have not lived up to some of our expectations for greater business productivity. Computers make errors because they have been improperly programmed or used, or because they are so literal in completing their tasks.

5. *Explain the ethical use of computers.*   The Information Age has brought with it a whole new set of concerns. People work harder and longer than ever before, seemingly trying to keep pace with computers. We often face "information overload" because there is so much information to assimilate. Computers also test our ethics and our values, both on the personal and governmental level. Computers make it all the more important for each of us to act ethically and responsibly.

KEY TERMS

analog, p. 11
application, p. 7
binary arithmetic system, p. 11
computer, p. 11
computer-aided design (CAD), p. 18
computer-aided manufacturing (CAM), p. 18
computer literacy, p. 6
data, p. 11
database management system, p. 13
data processing, p. 11
digital, p. 11
electronic, p. 11

electronic data interchange (EDI), p. 18
electronic funds transfer (EFT), p. 18
ENIAC (Electronic Numerical Integrator and Calculator), p. 14
hardware, p. 15
Information Age, p. 10
instruction, p. 13
keyboard, p. 17
logical operations, p. 11
mainframe computer, p. 15
mathematical operations, p. 11
microcomputer, p. 16
minicomputer, p. 16

monitor, p. 17
networking, p. 24
personal computer, p. 16
printer, p. 17
program, p. 13
programmer, p. 13
programming, p. 13
quality control, p. 18
software, p. 13
spreadsheet, p. 13
supercomputer, p. 15
system unit, p. 17
word processing, p. 13
workstation, p. 16

REVIEW AND DISCUSSION QUESTIONS

1. Explain the importance of computer literacy.
2. Why is the computer so important in the Information Age?
3. What are the two types of operations a computer performs?

4. What do we mean by an electronic, digital computer?
5. Explain the difference between a digital and an analog computer.
6. Why do we call data "the raw material of information"?

7. What is a computer program?

8. What is a programmer trying to accomplish in writing software?

9. What do we call the equipment that we use software with?

10. Describe the uses for the four different types of computers.

11. Describe some of the advantages computers bring to manufacturing automobiles.

12. What are the three goals computers strive for in performing their tasks?

13. Can you think of ways that computers might be used to improve productivity?

14. Why might it not be a good idea to have computers that reason?

15. What do you see as the major reasons for computer errors?

16. Do you feel computers, especially government computers, are invading your privacy?

17. Does the Freedom of Information Act address the issue of invasion of privacy adequately?

18. Describe how you might use a computer ethically and unethically.

19. Do you think computer crime is a serious problem?

20. Are computers and the Information Age making the world a better place for us to live?

ISSUES

1. The great scientist Albert Einstein once said, "Since I do not foresee that atomic energy is to be a great boon for a long time, I have to say that for the present it is a menace." Could it also be said that there is a dark side to computer technology? If so, what do you think it is? What are some potential harms and risks that computers present today or might present in the future?

2. Each of us must grapple with ethical and moral issues every day of our lives. What, if anything, makes computer ethics different? Do you think we need a separate set of ethical guidelines to follow when working with a computer? What makes it any different than the ethics we use on the job or in our lives? Do you think computer ethics—or any other kind of ethics—can be taught?

3. What does the term *Information Age* mean to you? Do you feel you are living in the Information Age? How has it affected you? Do you enjoy working with information, or has it caused more stress in your life? What do you think the Information Age will be like in the year 2000?

CHAPTER 2

The Computer System
People, Software, and Hardware

CHAPTER OUTLINE

The Father of the Modern Computer
What Is a Computer System?
   People: The Creative Component
   Software: The Instruction Component
   Hardware: The Processing Component
   The CPU: Heart of the Computer
   Peripheral Devices
   Computer Memory
   The Personal Computer Hardware System
   DISKbyte: Computers Are Like Stereos
The Computer System in Action: Data Processing
   Data and Instructions
   The Four Data Processing Operations
   DISKbyte: John von Neumann
   A Data Processing Example
   Two Methods of Data Processing
The Computer Advantage
   Accuracy and Speed
   Chips
   Bits and Bytes
   DISKbyte: GIGO
   Information: The End Result
Ethics
   CAREERbyte: Joanne Howell: Combining an
     Interest in Writing with Computers
Summary
Key Terms
Review and Discussion Questions
Issues

OBJECTIVES

After reading and studying this chapter, you should be able to:

1. Identify the functions of people, software, and hardware in a computer system.
2. Identify the two types of people who work with computers.
3. Define two kinds of software.
4. Describe the two categories of hardware components.
5. Name the three components that comprise the CPU.
6. Describe the types of computer memory and their uses.
7. Identify the four operations of data processing.
8. Describe the two methods of data processing.
9. Define the terms *bit* and *byte*.
10. Describe the difference between data and information.

THE FATHER OF THE MODERN COMPUTER

John V. Atanasoff had a problem. The year was 1937 and Atanasoff, a professor of mathematics and physics at Iowa State University, needed to find a better way to help his college students solve long, complex math problems called simultaneous differential equations. "We needed practical solutions for practical purposes," he recalls. For Atanasoff and his students, that meant getting more accurate answers and getting them more quickly.

Wrestling with the problem kept him working in his lab, many times until three or four in the morning. "Tormented," is the way he described himself.

Driving helped him work out problems. One night he drove 200 miles before stopping at a roadhouse to rest. "I realized that I was no longer so nervous and my thoughts turned again to computing

Courtesy of Alice Atanasoff

machines. Now I don't know why my mind worked then when it had not worked previously, but things seemed to be good and cool and quiet. During this evening . . . I generated within my mind the possibility of regenerative memory . . . and I gained an initial concept of what is called today the 'logic circuits.'" The concept for the computer was emerging.

Working with a modest grant of $650 from the college, Atanasoff began designing his computer. With help from his graduate assistant, Clifford Berry, the first prototype of the Atanasoff-Berry Computer, or ABC, was completed in 1939.

Atanasoff was quick to realize that vacuum tubes, although subject to failure, were more reliable than mechanical relays. He also developed some of the essential concepts that would be incorporated into future computers, including using binary mathematics over the decimal system. The combination of vacuum tubes and binary mathematics made the ABC an electronic, digital computer.

Atanasoff never permitted a commercial version of the ABC to be built, mainly because the two companies to whom he showed it — IBM and Remington Rand (which went on to develop the UNIVAC) — asked him to sign away all his inventor's rights. In a letter to Remington Rand, Atanasoff wrote, "this procedure would furnish your company with all of my information without any corresponding obligation on your part . . .."

In 1942, Dr. Atanasoff was requested to accept employment with the Naval Ordinance Laboratory in Washington, D.C. He left the details of the patenting process in the hands of Iowa State officials and a patent lawyer. To his chagrin, and despite periodic inquiries, the patent applications were never filed. Even so, the ABC became the prototype of the first large-scale programmable electronic computer, ENIAC.

Patents granted to ENIAC, constructed at the University of Pennsylvania under a U.S. Army contract between 1943 and 1946, were invalidated by an unchallenged U.S. District Court decision in 1973. The court found that basic electronic digital computer concepts in ENIAC were "derived from one Dr. John Vincent Atanasoff." Today John Atanasoff is recognized as the father of the modern computer.

WHAT IS A COMPUTER SYSTEM?

There are systems all around us: the earth's ecological system, the solar system, the international economic system. People are made up of systems, too: we have digestive, nervous, and circulatory systems, for example. In every system, many parts work together to solve a problem.

Computers are systems, too. We define a **computer system** as consisting of *people,* working together with *software* and *hardware* components. When all three are working together, we call it data processing. *Data processing* is the process of utilizing specific *procedures* that turn *data* into useful information.

For example, a researcher might instruct a scientific supercomputer to calculate a mathematical equation. The director of finance at a corporation uses a cluster of minicomputers to prepare the year's balance sheet. The air traffic controller at a metropolitan airport requests that the mainframe computer list all available take-off runways. A college student uses a personal computer with word processing software to create a term paper. These are just a few examples of how people obtain useful information from computer systems.

In this chapter we'll study computer systems, including the human, software, and hardware components. We'll see the vital role people play. We'll learn how software works. And we'll explore hardware, including the heart of the computer: the central processing unit. What you learn in this chapter applies to all computers, large or small, and to all computer systems, regardless of their special characteristics.

People: The Creative Component

People are the most important component of the computer system. As Figure 2–1 shows, the process of computing is circular; thoughtful people put hardware and software to work so that the machine provides benefits to people. The people who work with computers fall into two groups: computer professionals and computer users. A **computer professional** is a person who designs, operates, or maintains a computer system. A **computer user** is a person

FIGURE 2–1   Using computers always involves people.

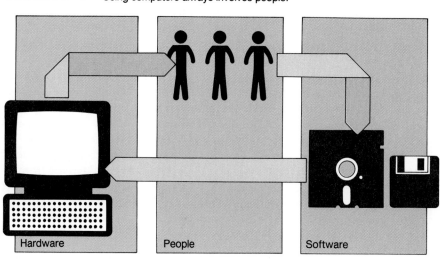

Hardware   People   Software

who works with a computer system to achieve a desired end result. Users may be engaged in solving a business problem, learning more about a particular subject, improving the quality of their personal or professional life, or simply playing a game.

Look at Figure 2–2. As you can see, people play many diverse roles in a typical business computer system. The left-hand column shows the type of work done by computer professionals. Engineers with advanced degrees in computer science design computer systems. Technical specialists design, build, and test the hardware and software elements. Once a computer system design has been shown to work properly, systems analysts and software application designers implement the system. Implementation involves setting up the hardware and tailoring software programs to the specific needs of the system's users. After a computer system is implemented and running, operators make sure the hardware processes run smoothly, while software engineers maintain, or take care of, the system.

The right-hand column shows the many types of users who work with the computer system. This includes people in manufacturing, shipping, warehousing, and other operational areas. Office workers use the computer for tracking inventory, accounting, and a variety of office tasks. Managers use the system to monitor business performance.

Perhaps the most important role people play in the computer system is defining the questions we ask computers to help us answer. In a sense, it is because we are so curious about our world that computer systems even exist. We have been wondering and thinking and asking questions about our world for thousands of years. This intellectual process is often called *analyzing,* or

---

FIGURE 2–2   The primary roles of people, software, and hardware in the computer system.

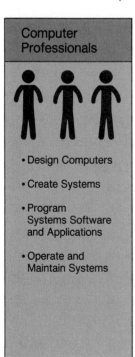

Computer Professionals

- Design Computers
- Create Systems
- Program Systems Software and Applications
- Operate and Maintain Systems

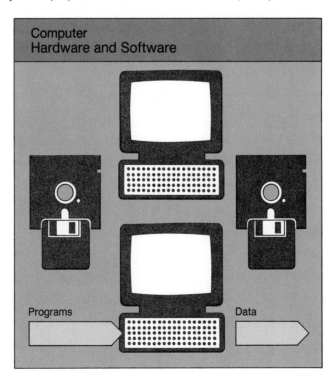

Computer Hardware and Software

Programs   Data

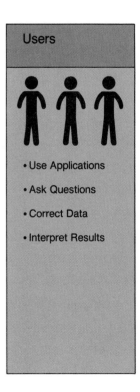

Users

- Use Applications
- Ask Questions
- Correct Data
- Interpret Results

using our mind to make sense of things. The term *systems analysis* is used to describe the process a human uses to determine how best to solve a business problem. For our purposes, it is how to solve a business problem using a computer system. Systems analysis is only one aspect of business problem-solving; we discuss the topic in greater detail in Chapter 7.

FIGURE 2−3   Applications are numerous and diverse in business, education, science, personal, and professional fields.

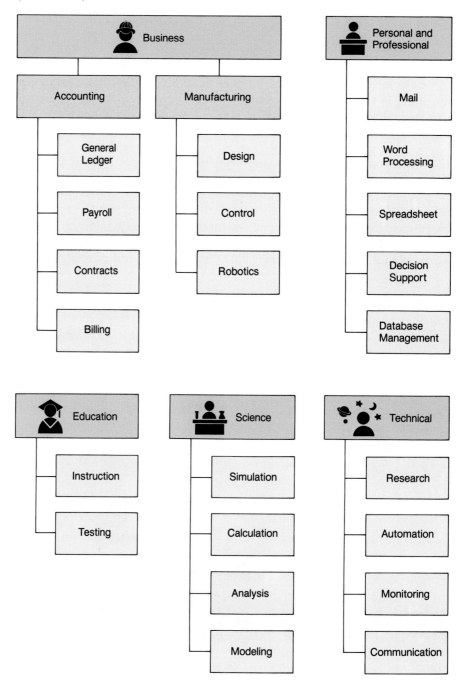

Fifty years ago, computers solved relatively simple mathematical problems. This was due, in part, to the relative simplicity of the software. Today, we have software that allows us to use computers in highly complex ways, such as plotting and guiding space shuttle flights, exploring for the earth's natural resources, or mapping weather patterns. Once people realized the computer could solve a simple problem, they said, "I wonder if it can solve a more difficult one." In other words, we have continually made the computer a more useful and efficient machine.

Software: The Instruction Component

Software provides the instructions that tell computers what to do. Most software is in the form of programs, which contain instructions for particular data processing operations. Programmers are the people who design, write, and test software.

There are two kinds of software. The first, **system software,** includes programs that run the computer system or that aid programmers in performing their work. A common example of system software is DOS. Users only need to use system software occasionally.

The second kind of software is **application software,** which directs the computer to perform specific tasks for the user. A word processing program is an example of application software. Figure 2–3 shows many varieties of software applications.

Figure 2–4 shows the computer system and the relationship between the user, the two types of software and the hardware. Hardware is the primary building block. System software makes it possible for the application software to make proper use of the hardware. The application software facilitates performing a task or solving a problem for the user. The rest of this chapter explains the hardware. In Chapter 3 you'll learn how to use system software, and the chapters in Module II show you how to use popular application software.

People have been engaged in the pursuit of knowledge for a long time. Technology has evolved over hundreds, even thousands of years; for example, Gutenberg's printing press led to electronic publishing, and Leonardo da Vinci's ideas for flight led to the airplane.

FIGURE 2–4   How people use computers. The user interacts with the application software, which interacts with the system software, which sends instructions to the computer hardware.

User   Application   System   Hardware
                        Software   Software

Today, it's safe to say it isn't necessary to "reinvent the wheel." By that we often mean we don't need to find solutions to problems that have already been solved. It also means we have already developed many standard methods for solving problems that have been proven effective and reliable.

Standard methods are a tried and tested form of problem-solving techniques; others have used them and proven that they work. Examples include formulas used in scientific equations and common factors in performing engineering calculations. Today, we have literally millions of these conceptual tools that we use to help us solve all kinds of problems. Over the past four decades, most of these conceptual tools have been adapted for use with computers in the form of software.

Media   You might wonder what software looks like. Software commonly comes on **media,** which is the material on which computer instructions and data are recorded. There are several kinds of media but the one we encounter most often with personal computers is the floppy disk. A **floppy disk** is a flexible plastic disk, coated with a magnetic substance, usually sealed in a plastic sleeve. Most of the software sold in retail stores is on floppy disks, or "floppies." Both system software such as DOS and application software such as a spreadsheet come on floppy disks.

The **mini-floppy** is 5¼ inches in diameter. In this size, the disk is held in a flexible plastic sleeve. Figure 2–5 is a cutaway illustration of a 5¼-inch floppy disk. Many computers sold today use the **micro-floppy,** a 3½-inch disk, as shown in Figure 2–6. Its shell is made of firm plastic but the disk inside is the same flexible material of the 5¼-inch floppy.

Silicon chips are another medium. When used to store instructions, they are called **firmware,** a combination of software and hardware instructions. A silicon chip is a thin piece of silicon on which electronic components are etched. Chips can be used to store program instructions or data. Figure 2–7 shows an example of a printed circuit board with rows of silicon chips. The

FIGURE 2–5   A cutaway view of the 5¼-inch floppy disk.

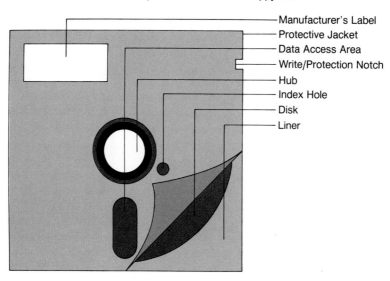

Manufacturer's Label
Protective Jacket
Data Access Area
Write/Protection Notch
Hub
Index Hole
Disk
Liner

chip is mounted in a plastic case with metal "feet" that plug into a **printed circuit board,** a thin insulating board used to mount and connect various electronic components and chips.

There are other kinds of media. Data or instructions can be kept on hard disks, magnetic tapes, cassette tapes, optical disks, or laser disks, similar to CDs. We'll discuss each of these in detail in Chapter 10. The term *software* has become so popular that it is often used to refer to audio and video media as well, such as audio cassettes and videotapes.

Now that we have an idea of the roles people and software play, let's look at hardware.

FIGURE 2 – 6   3½-inch floppy disks.

D. McCoy/Rainbow

FIGURE 2 – 7   Chips perform a variety of tasks; some are used as firmware.

H. Mark Weidman

Hardware: The Processing Component

Hardware is the physical part of the computer system, consisting of electronic and mechanical devices we can actually see and touch. Hardware stores and manipulates the data supplied by the human component and executes the instructions provided by the software component.

Computer hardware falls into two categories: processing hardware, which consists of the central processing unit or CPU; and peripheral devices. The central processing unit, as its name implies, is where data processing is done. Peripheral devices allow people to interact with the central processing unit. Together, they make it possible to use the computer for a vast array of tasks. Let's take a closer look at how they work together.

The CPU: Heart of the Computer

The **central processing unit (CPU)** is the central organ of computer hardware, containing circuitry that controls the interpretation and execution of instructions. With such an important job, you might think a CPU would have to be very large. In fact, the CPU in most personal computers is a single chip, a thin slice of silicon smaller than your little fingernail, as you can see in Figure 2–8. We'll explore chips in more detail later in this chapter.

The CPU consists of three components: the control unit, the arithmetic/logic unit (ALU), and main memory. The **control unit** directs the step-by-step operation of the computer. Like a traffic policeman directing cars, the control unit directs electrical impulses between itself, the ALU, and main memory. It also controls operations between the CPU and the peripheral devices. These electrical impulses consist of the data and instructions being processed. Now let's look at the other two components.

The **arithmetic/logic unit (ALU)** performs arithmetic and logical operations. The arithmetic operations are addition, subtraction, multiplication, and division. The logic operations compare two pieces of data to determine if one is greater than, less than, or equal to the other. Figure 2–9 shows the flow of data within the CPU and between the CPU and main memory.

FIGURE 2–8   Smaller than a human fingernail, the silicon chip that is the computer's CPU.

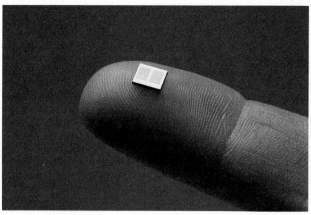

T.J. Florian/Rainbow

Main memory, also called RAM for random access memory, is the storage area directly controlled by the computer's CPU. Main memory assists the control unit and the ALU by serving as storage for the programs being executed and for data as it passes through. Main memory is usually a number of additional chips electrically connected and in close proximity to the CPU. Figure 2–10 shows a typical personal computer **motherboard**, the main printed circuit board, with CPU and memory chips installed.

FIGURE 2–9   The paths data takes between the control unit, ALU, and main memory.

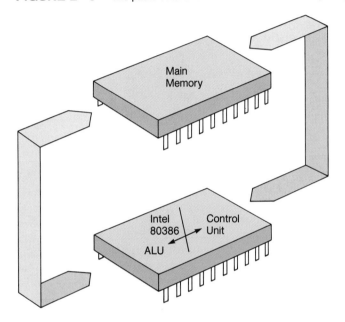

FIGURE 2–10   Motherboards.

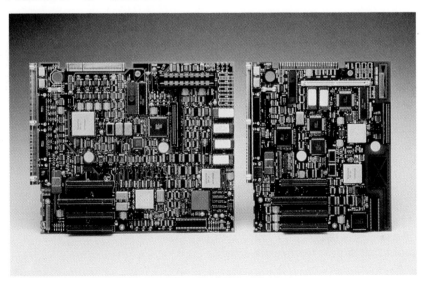

Courtesy of IBM Corp.

The control operations of the control unit, the arithmetic and logic operations performed by the ALU, and storage operations performed by main memory comprise everything the CPU does. These operations alone may not sound very impressive. Yet by combining these simple abilities in a variety of ways computers can perform, in the twinkling of an eye, a task that would take a human weeks or months to accomplish.

Peripheral Devices

Peripheral devices, also called peripherals, are input, output, and storage devices connected to the CPU. Peripheral devices fall into three categories. The first category is **input devices**, which allow us to enter data into the computer. A common input device is the keyboard, which allows us to use our fingers to type data or instructions into the computer. The second category is **output devices**, which allow us to receive data from the computer. A common output device is the monitor or video display. The CPU and some common input and output devices are shown in Figure 2–11. The third category is **auxiliary storage devices**, which are used to store data for an indeterminate period of time. A common auxiliary storage device is the **disk drive**, which reads data from a magnetic disk and copies it into RAM, and which writes data from RAM onto a disk for storage. Understanding how computer memory works is very important and is the next topic we will discuss.

Computer Memory

Memory is the general term used to describe a computer system's storage facilities. Memory's job is to store the instructions, or programs, and data in the computer. In this section, we will discuss several types of computer memory.

Memory can be divided into two major categories: main storage and auxiliary storage. Main memory (also called main storage, internal storage, or primary storage) is associated with the CPU. Some storage operations send the contents of main storage to an output device, such as the monitor or a printer, or to auxiliary storage according to the instructions people issue to the software program. Main memory is short-term, **volatile memory** — its contents are removed when replaced by new instructions and data, or when electrical power to the computer is turned off.

Throughout the remainder of this book we will refer to main storage as **random access memory**, or **RAM**. RAM is sometimes called the "working memory" of the computer because it holds the data and instructions during data processing. RAM is read-write memory: it can read, or receive, data and instructions from other sources; it can also write, or transfer, data to other sources such as auxiliary storage.

There is another kind of memory called **read only memory**, or ROM. ROM is called read only memory because it holds instructions that can be read by the computer, but not written to. These are permanent instructions used to start the computer and direct many of its operations; they cannot be changed.

Auxiliary storage, also called auxiliary memory or secondary storage, is memory that supplements main storage. This type of memory is long-term,

FIGURE 2 – 11   Some common input and output devices.

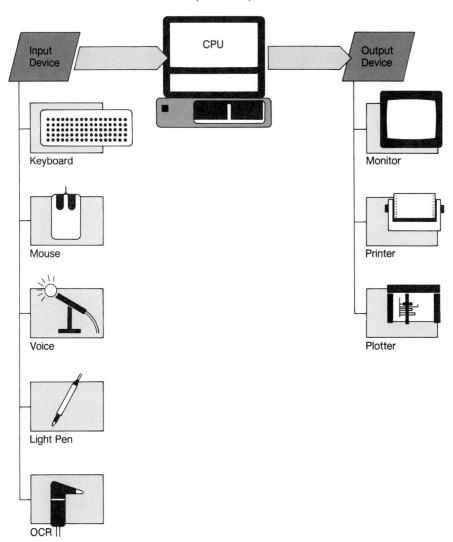

nonvolatile memory. Nonvolatile means it stores and retains programs and data, regardless of whether the computer is turned on or off. The two most common types of auxiliary storage devices for personal computers are floppy and hard disks. Figure 2–12 diagrams computer memory and shows its relationship to hardware in the computer system.

Let's see how the different kinds of memory work together. Say you wrote a short memo that read, "Department meeting at 3:00 P.M. today." It is stored temporarily in main memory or RAM, then you send it to the printer for a paper copy. You decide you don't need to store it for posterity, so it can be removed from memory. However, you do want to save the five-page report on new products you wrote for the marketing manager. This document passes from main memory into auxiliary storage for long-term safekeeping.

FIGURE 2 – 12   Main memory, auxiliary storage, and other hardware devices.

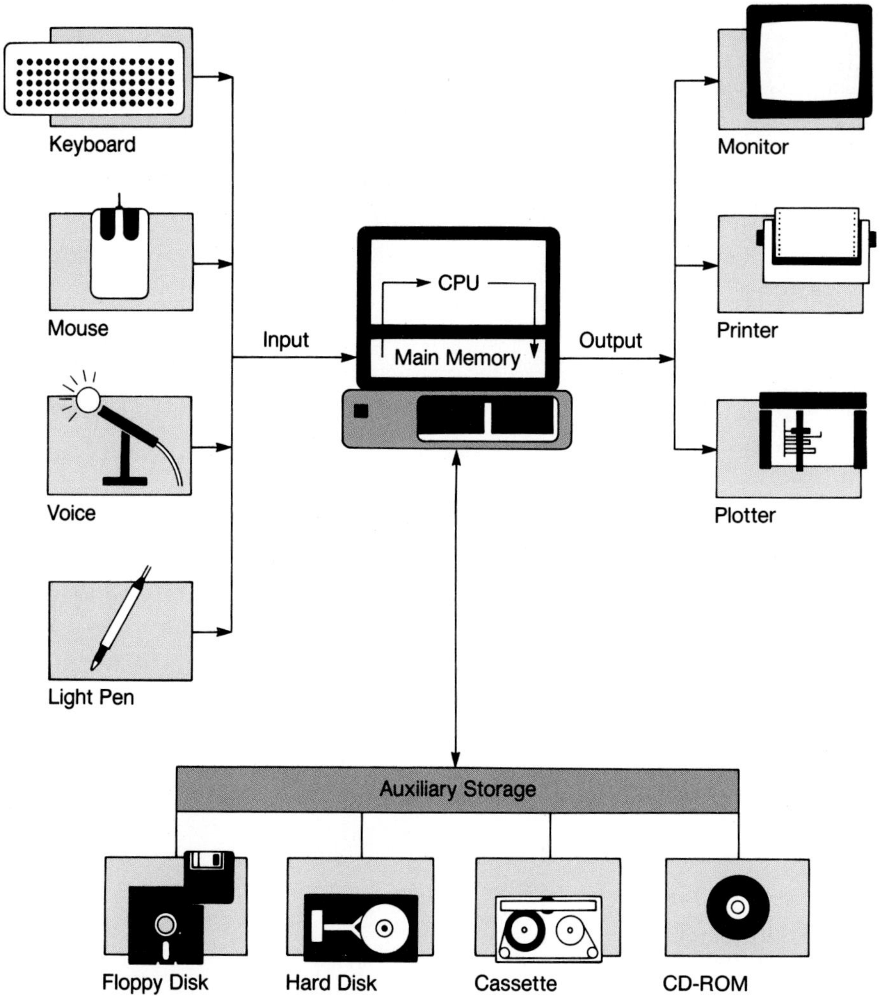

Computers differentiate between main storage and auxiliary storage for the sake of speed and efficiency. The CPU can work faster if the data and instructions it is processing are physically nearby. Main storage is usually on a chip or circuit board along with the CPU. However, auxiliary storage is usually slower because it involves some type of mechanical device. For instance, disk drives must spin the disk to store data. There is also a slowdown when the CPU must send signals back and forth between remote auxiliary storage devices.

The Personal Computer Hardware System

All computers operate in a similar fashion; therefore, if you understand the personal computer hardware system, you can grasp how minicomputers and mainframes operate as well. Standard personal computer hardware includes a system unit that houses the CPU and is connected to a keyboard as an input

FIGURE 2 – 13   A typical desktop and portable personal computer showing system unit, monitor, and keyboard combinations.

Photos courtesy of Compaq Computer Corporation

FIGURE 2 – 14   In this system, the system unit also holds the monitor and floppy disk drive.

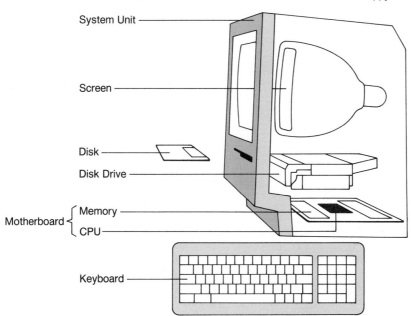

device and to a monitor as an output device. Figure 2 – 13 shows several system unit/keyboard/monitor combinations. In some computers, the system unit and monitor are contained in the same cabinet. Other systems, such as the Macintosh, combine the system unit, monitor, and disk drives all in one unit, as shown in Figure 2 – 14.

FIGURE 2 – 15   Top left: plotter; top right: high-speed LED printer; bottom left: laser printer; bottom right: color dot-matrix printer.

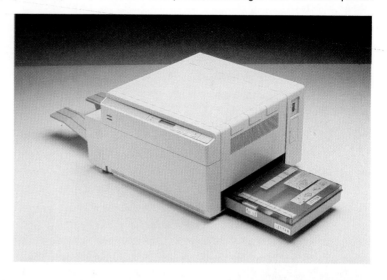

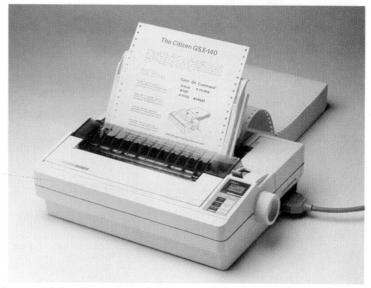

Top left: Courtesy of Hewlett-Packard Company; top right: Courtesy of Fujitsu America; bottom left: Courtesy of Hewlett-Packard Company; bottom right: Courtesy of Citizen America Inc.

Usually, a personal computer will have at least one floppy disk drive or a hard disk drive for storage, and a printer for producing output on paper. Figure 2 – 15 shows several printers and plotters — special types of printers used to produce graphics. Another common input device is the **mouse**, so called because of its shape and long connecting cord that resembles a tail, as shown in Figure 2 – 16. We'll describe these hardware devices and their uses in more detail in Chapter 10. But now, let's review what role hardware plays in the overall working of the computer system. Figure 2 – 17 shows a typical sequence. A person sends input via the keyboard to the CPU. The CPU executes the instructions according to the software program you have selected and returns the results to the monitor or printer.

FIGURE 2–16 Working with a mouse, distinguished by its tail and its shape, which was designed for the human hand.

R. Schleipman/Offshoot

FIGURE 2–17 A typical sequence: Input is sent, via the keyboard, into the CPU. The CPU executes instructions according to the software program selected and returns the results to the monitor or printer.

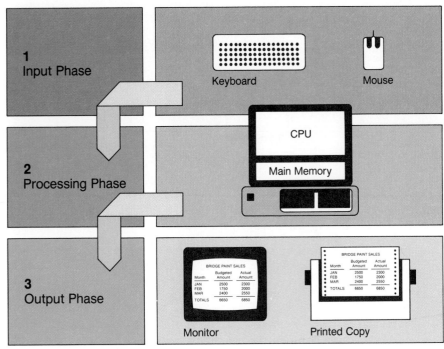

Courtesy of NeXT Inc.

D I S K b y t e

Computers Are Like Stereos

Computers are similar to stereos. Most component stereo systems have an amplifier (or a receiver). Like the computer's CPU, the amplifier is the central component of the system. The amplifier receives input from its own tuner or from a cassette deck, a compact disk player, or a turntable. Likewise, the computer CPU receives input from the keyboard on which you type. The amplifier processes the input, amplifies it, then sends it to output devices, usually speakers or headphones. Similarly, the computer CPU sends output to the monitor or printer.

We can also compare the media used on stereos to computer media. In both systems, we have some devices that can only "read" media. Compact disk players only play CDs but do not record them. Computers have ROM, which can't be changed, either. But both stereos and computers have other forms of media such as tapes and floppies that can be recorded or "written" on.

Although we can see similarities and parallels in the hardware devices and the media stereos and computer systems use, there is a great deal of difference between these two systems. Stereos don't have programs that allow them to perform a variety of tasks; they produce sound but they can't do the payroll. However, the similarities help us understand the concept of a system, and by contrast we can see that computer systems perform a variety of tasks exceedingly well.

The basic physical characteristics of stereos and computers are similar.

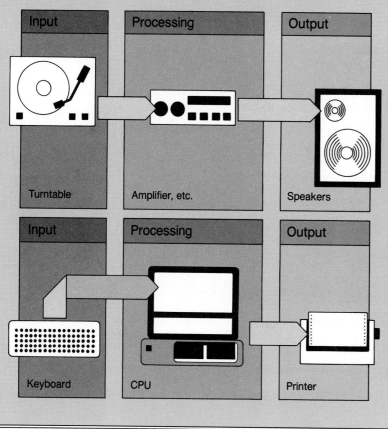

Input — Turntable
Processing — Amplifier, etc.
Output — Speakers

Input — Keyboard
Processing — CPU
Output — Printer

1. Name the three components that comprise a computer system.
2. What are some of the functions people perform in the computer system?
3. Which component of the computer system provides instructions for processing the data?
4. Identify the standard hardware devices that make up a personal computer.
5. What kind of memory is controlled directly by the CPU?
6. Where are data and instructions stored during data processing?
7. What do we call long-term computer memory?

THE COMPUTER SYSTEM IN ACTION: DATA PROCESSING

Data processing is a computer performing one or more operations on data to produce a desired result. The result of data processing is data, which people turn into useful information. In a typical data processing operation, a person has a problem to be solved; for example, adding a list of 42 numbers. The numbers, representing data, are fed into the computer via an input device. Computer software provides instructions to the CPU about how to add the list of numbers. The CPU then processes the data and returns the total to the user: the sum of the 42 numbers. The result, while still data, is of greater use to the person than before processing.

Data and Instructions

Recall from Chapter 1 that we defined data as the raw material of information, ready for processing. When working with computers, we provide data as input and receive data as output. Data can be numbers, such as a scientist's calculations or a business manager's annual sales figures. It can also take other forms, such as written words, photographic images, and even sounds, including the human voice. In Latin, the singular form of data is *datum* but today, *data* is commonly used to refer to both singular and plural.

Instructions are groups of characters, either letters or symbols, that define the operations the computer performs. Software provides instructions, usually in the form of programs, telling the computer what to do with the data. Instructions can request the computer do something as simple as adding two numbers or as complex as comparing images of galaxies.

The Four Data Processing Operations

Computers, regardless of their size or the kind of work they do, perform four basic operations:

- Input.
- Processing.
- Output.
- Storage.

D I S K b y t e

John von Neumann

To many of his peers, John von Neumann was a greater genius than Albert Einstein. Some saw him as a workaholic, his head crammed full of ideas. Indeed, he slept only five hours each night. To his friends, he was Johnny, a fun-loving man.

Von Neumann was born in Hungary, earned a Ph.D. in physics when he was 22 years old, and was soon teaching at the Institute for Advanced Study at Princeton University. By the time he was 31, during World War II, he was a major contributor to the Manhattan Project, which developed the first atomic bomb.

Von Neumann was a technical adviser on virtually every major computer project in the early days of the digital computer. His work

The Babbage Institute

resulted in a paper in which he laid out a new design for the computer. Now called the von Neumann architecture, his design divided the

CPU into three parts: the control unit, the arithmetic/logic unit, and main memory.

He also developed the stored program concept, which said that instructions should be stored along with data in the computer's main memory, so that the instructions can be more quickly accessed and more easily modified. Some computer experts feel this concept is the most important characteristic of the digital computer.

Von Neumann's brilliant synthesis of computer concepts has had a lasting effect. It set the course for decades of further computer development. Forty years later, most computer designs are still based on the von Neumann architecture and the stored program concept.

Each of these four operations involves specific computer hardware. A keyboard typically performs the *input* operation, sending data and the problem to be processed to the CPU. The CPU's control unit and ALU route and process data and instructions to perform *processing* operations. The results of processing are sent to the monitor, printer, or both as the *output* operation. Disk drives or other auxiliary storage media receive the results in the *storage* operation. Figure 2–18 diagrams a sequence of the four computer operations. In business, an event that affects the business is called a *transaction*. Computers process data about these transactions; therefore, we often refer to the work computers perform as transaction processing.

A Data Processing Example

Each time we use a computer to perform data processing, a sequence of steps or operations occurs. The steps vary, depending on the software we use and the requirements of the problem we wish to solve. The four data processing operations reflect this process in general. Let's look at a specific example to get a better understanding of how computers work.

In this example, the computer adds a list of 42 numbers. First, the CPU loads the software necessary for processing the data into RAM. Then the

FIGURE 2 – 18   The four data processing operations: (1) the input operation sends keyboard input to the CPU; (2) interactions between the CPU and RAM execute processing operations; (3) data from RAM is stored on a floppy disk in the memory operation; and (4) the CPU sends data to the printer in the output operation.

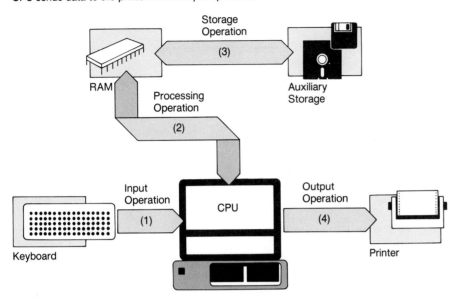

FIGURE 2 – 19   The input operation sends data from the keyboard to the CPU.

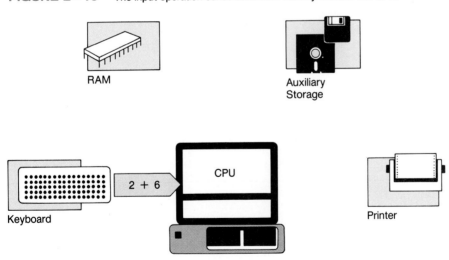

process begins at the keyboard, with the input operation. We enter the data to be processed — the 42 numbers we want added — and indicate that we want them totaled. As we type, the keyboard sends electrical signals representing each letter and number to the CPU. This is the input operation, diagrammed in Figure 2 – 19. The CPU's control unit stores the input in RAM and sends signals to the monitor, causing it to display the input on the screen. This portion of the sequence is diagrammed in Figure 2 – 20.

FIGURE 2 – 20   The CPU stores the data in RAM and sends data to the monitor for display.

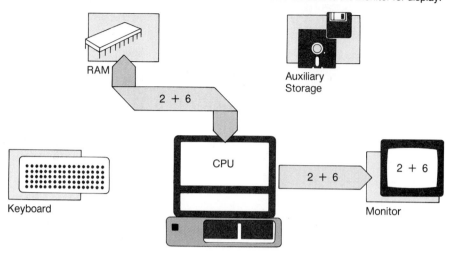

FIGURE 2 – 21   The ALU interacts with RAM to perform the next processing operation.

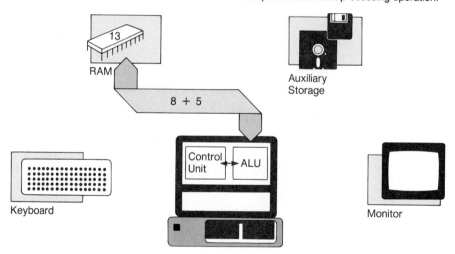

Next, the ALU performs the addition (or the processing) operation. The control unit sends the addition instruction to the ALU 42 times — once for each number — adding the numbers together as it goes. For example, say the first three numbers are 2, 6, and 5: $2 + 6 = 8$ and $8 + 5 = 13$. In a simple calculation of this sort, the ALU adds the numbers in a tiny fraction of a second. Results of the calculation are sent to RAM for temporary storage. This portion of the sequence is diagrammed in Figure 2 – 21.

In the output operation, the control unit obtains the result from RAM and routes the data wherever the software instructs it to. Typical output operations send the result to the monitor so we can see it, or to the printer so we have a printed copy. Output can also be directed to auxiliary storage. This portion of the sequence is diagrammed in Figure 2 – 22.

FIGURE 2−22   In the output operation, the result is sent to the monitor or printer.

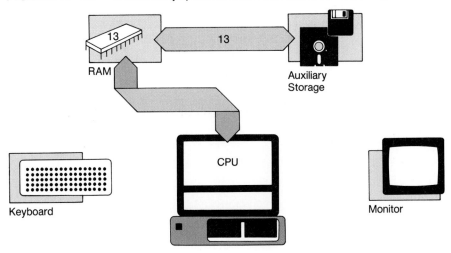

FIGURE 2−23   In the memory operation, the result is sent to auxiliary storage.

Depending on the software instructions, in the memory operation the result is also sent to auxiliary storage, such as a disk drive, for permanent storage. This portion of the sequence is diagrammed in Figure 2–23.

This process has many variations, but this example is typical and shows the role of each device: the keyboard, the control unit, RAM, the monitor, the ALU, the printer, and auxiliary storage. It begins when someone needs to solve a problem. The software issues the instructions to the hardware, which performs the processing. Once finished, the computer system presents its results. If the system has done its work properly, the human should have what he or she needs to solve the problem.

Two Methods of Data Processing

Computers perform the four data processing operations using one of two different methods: batch processing or on-line processing. **Batch processing** means the data is collected in a batch over a period of time, then usually input, processed, and output all at once. Batch processing helps people use the computer more efficiently; the computer can be used for important tasks during the day, then perform the more repetitious and less important tasks overnight. Batch processing is best suited to tasks where there are many transactions to perform, or to tasks that are not particularly time-sensitive. For example, say a steel company only makes concrete reinforcement bars once a week, on Thursday. It accumulates hundreds of orders Monday through Wednesday; the computer batch processes them Wednesday night. The computer tallies the orders and determines how much steel to make on Thursday, then prepares the invoices and shipping forms so the orders can be shipped to customers on Friday.

On-line processing means that data is processed immediately, as soon as it is input. On-line processing is more frequently used as people and businesses require more speed and efficiency in handling transactions. For example, an on-line order entry system at a mail-order sporting goods company allows the operator to enter the transaction immediately, producing an invoice and sending the paperwork to the warehouse for packing and shipping.

The latest advance is *on-line transaction processing,* where the computer system completes the entire transaction as soon as it is entered. This is used in businesses where up-to-date information is critical, such as the airline industry. With on-line transaction processing (OLTP), for example, the computer reserves seat 11B for you the moment your travel agent selects it.

MEMORY CHECK

1. What do we call the raw material of information?
2. What element of data processing is provided by software?
3. Name the four operations a computer performs.
4. What do we call it when the computer performs these operations?
5. What kind of memory receives results in the memory operation?
6. Describe the different kinds of processing.

THE COMPUTER ADVANTAGE

A computer system is a powerful tool. It enhances our problem-solving abilities because it works with great accuracy and at high speed.

Accuracy and Speed

One of the reasons computers have become such important tools for people is that, given proper data and instructions, computers consistently deliver accurate results. Modern computers often execute instructions numbering in the billions, without making an error. This is why our governments, universities,

and businesses rely on computers to provide information on finances, population, national defense, science, and a host of complex, interdependent world
systems.

A counterpart to the advantage of accuracy is the computer's speed. For
example, even today's small computers can perform calculations in a few
minutes that would take a person years to complete. Today, most computers
work so fast that they are measured by how many **millions of instructions per
second (MIPS)** they execute. An instruction, to use our previous example, is
adding two numbers together.

We should also note that computers, unlike humans, work tirelessly, day
and night, weekends and holidays, to complete their tasks. Computers can be
economical, too; they do not require raises (although upgrading the hardware
and software can be expensive!), and once operating properly, they will continue to do so with little maintenance or human attention. This, at least, is the
goal of computer automation.

Chips

You may wonder how computer designers have managed to make computers
so fast. Part of the answer lies in size. By making the electronic components of
computer hardware smaller and smaller, the distance their electrical signals
must travel has become shorter. The result is increased speed. Most of the
advances in speed in the past decade can be attributed to the silicon chip.

Chips are also called integrated circuits or ICs. An **integrated circuit** is a
number of electronic components and their connecting wires that have been
miniaturized. There can be thousands of components on a single chip. As we
saw in our discussion of the CPU, chips are often smaller than the human
fingernail. To give you an idea of the level of miniaturization, a chip can
contain 200 ICs in an area the size of the diameter of a human hair, as you can
see in Figure 2–24. Each chip is made up of grids, somewhat like the layout of
city streets, composed of electronic circuits. Each circuit contains precise
information that directs computer operations. Figure 2–25 offers a close-up
view of the maze of circuits on a chip's surface.

FIGURE 2–24   The grids on the surface of a silicon chip are only 2 microns wide,
compared to a human hair which is 70 microns.

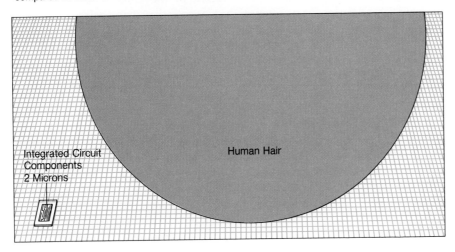

FIGURE 2–25   A close-up of circuit patterns on a chip.

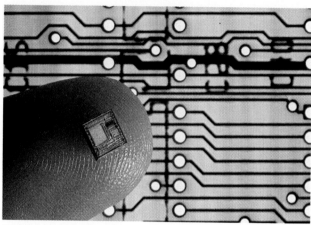

M. Manheim/The Stock Market

A chip can be any of the following, depending on how it is designed:

- A CPU.
- A ROM chip, for read only memory.
- A RAM chip, for random access memory.
- A controller, for routing electrical signals from one place to another.

Bits and Bytes

At their most basic level, computers only understand the language of electricity: positive and negative, or on and off. Since computer hardware is electronic, to communicate with it we must speak its simple language. For this reason, we use the **binary number system**—a system based on just two numbers or digits: 1 (for on) and 0 (for off). Each of these numbers is called a binary digit, or bit for short. A **bit** is the basic unit of data recognized by a computer. (See Appendix A to learn more about the binary number system.)

Computer designers realized that they could make computers work faster by grouping bits together for presentation to the CPU. This is like our language—it's easier for us to speak in words, rather than spelling out each letter as we talk to one another. The term we use for a grouping of bits is a byte. A **byte** is a group of bits that can be operated on as a unit by the computer. The relationship between bits and bytes is shown in Figure 2–26.

Bytes are sometimes organized into **words**, or logical units of information. **Word length** is the term used to describe their size, counted in numbers of bits. However, a word to a computer is not the same as a word in our language. Most bytes represent just one letter, digit, or symbol. It takes several bytes to represent most human language words.

An early standard established a byte as a group of eight bits. So each byte contained exactly eight binary digits, a combination of eight 1s and 0s. We call a computer whose CPU is designed for bytes of eight bits an 8-bit machine. In the early 1980s, most personal computers were 8-bit machines. But larger computers were faster because their CPUs were designed to work with bigger bytes. These machines used 16- and 32-bit bytes. As engineers were able to

DISKbyte

GIGO

Have you ever received a bill from a department store or a receipt in a restaurant with a mistake on it that was later explained as a "computer error"? In all likelihood it was a human error.

The fact is, computers are only as accurate as the people who use and program them. If computers are given poor data, errors may occur. If they are given poor instructions, they may make errors or even fail to produce results.

The term *GIGO* has been coined to describe bad data and/or instructions. GIGO stands for "garbage in, garbage out." In a classic case of GIGO, in the 1960s a computer was programmed to study the earth's population and pollution. The programmer misplaced a decimal point in the program and the computer predicted the planet would choke to death on its own noxious waste fumes. Once the decimal place was moved, the earth regained its health. Clearly, people must ensure that the data and instructions computers work with are correct—*not* garbage.

FIGURE 2–26   Typically, 8 bits equal 1 byte. The byte shown here represents the letter *A*.

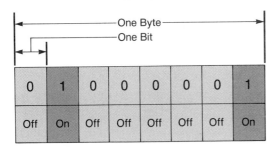

pack more components on a chip, it became possible to build 16-bit and 32-bit computers that fit on a desktop. Supercomputers are at the leading edge of this drive for greater speed; some of their CPUs work with 64- or 128-bit bytes!

Advances in computer speed and accuracy may make us think computers can do almost anything; but the truth is, people are still the most important part of the computer system. No matter how much data is processed, it is still data until a thinking, breathing person turns it into useful information.

Information: The End Result

What is information? **Information** is the end product people obtain from computer systems. In a computer system, hardware and software components store and process data. People collect and interpret this data, turning it into meaningful information by applying it to our world. For example, the computer may hold a company's expense and profit figures. In the computer, it's simply data. The data becomes information when a person uses it to create a financial report.

Joseph E. Izzo, a management consultant and author of *The Embattled Fortress: Strategies for Restoring Information Systems Productivity,*[1] presents this view of information:

> Over the past few years, both business generally and the computer industry specifically have embraced the concept of the Information Age. . . . All this talk has led many to believe that information is an end product of the computer. . . . There is nothing wrong with information; it's just that computers don't produce it. They produce data. It is when a human being takes the computer's data and passes it through a cognitive, mental process that we get information. The human then uses that information to make a decision, hopefully for the good of the firm.

It is important to realize that the process of using computers is a circle, beginning and ending with people. People ask questions and use computers as tools to produce data. Like any tool, computers must be used conscientiously and wisely for the good of all people.

MEMORY CHECK

1. How does size relate to computer speed?
2. What are the two digits that make up the binary number system?
3. What is a byte?
4. Why are people the most critical element of a computer system?
5. Why is it important to distinguish between data and information?

ETHICS

The actor Charles Chaplin wrote in his autobiography that "Man is an animal with primary instincts of survival. Consequently, his ingenuity has developed first and his soul afterwards. Thus the progress of science is far ahead of man's ethical behavior." Sometimes, people employ ethics when it's to their advantage; sometimes they set ethics aside by rationalizing that a greater good must be served. Unfortunately, ethics is not like an immutable law of nature but part of a set of personal beliefs. What constitutes the ethical use of computers? Here is a true story about a computer and a presidential election. No laws were broken; but think about the implications beyond the event itself.

On election night, November 4, 1952, Walter Cronkite announced to the television audience that "an electronic brain" would be used to predict who would become the next president of the United States. Programmers had labored for months, entering data to help the Remington Rand UNIVAC I, the first commercial computer system, make intelligent prognostications. Charles Collingwood, the host, told the viewers, "A few minutes ago, I asked him (UNIVAC) what his prediction was, and . . . he's not ready yet with the predictions." But in fact, UNIVAC had already analyzed the results, and with

---

[1] © 1987 Jossey-Bass, Inc., San Francisco.

only 3 million votes counted, declared a landslide victory for Dwight D. Eisenhower. Eisenhower would take 43 states and 438 electoral votes, UNI-VAC declared; his opponent, Adlai E. Stevenson, would win only 5 states.

Yet political analysts and pollsters had predicted a close race; the "electronic brain" must be wrong! Arthur F. Draper, Remington Rand's director in charge of the election-night show, had the computer program altered, not once but twice, in an attempt to bring the computer's predictions more in line with the experts' anticipated results. At midnight, with the Eisenhower landslide going full tilt, Collingwood asked Draper to explain the disparity between the computer's predictions and the actual results to the TV audience. "We asked UNIVAC to forget a lot of trend information, assuming that it was wrong . . . but it is now evident we should have had nerve enough to believe the machine in the first place," Draper confessed. Eisenhower won by 442 electoral votes, just 4 more than UNIVAC on its own had predicted.

Clearly, this was not wise use of the computer. UNIVAC was manipulated to make its computations agree with the predictions. If the television show's producers hadn't wanted an accurate prediction, then what did they have in mind for UNIVAC? In the hands of unethical politicians, UNIVAC could have been used quite unscrupulously. Indeed, there are many who feel computers should never be used in electoral ballot counting. We need to be concerned about this type of computer manipulation, but decisions in such matters are often out of our hands. Ultimately, the ethical use of computers comes down to the ethical beliefs and principles of each and every individual.

CAREERbyte

Joanne Howell: Combining an Interest in Writing with Computers

Programmers come with a variety of different backgrounds, perhaps because there was no formal education or training for them in the beginning. In fact, the first textbook on FORTRAN, written by Daniel D. McCracken, wasn't published until 1961. The first Ph.D. in computer science wasn't established until the following year, at Purdue University. People came to programming from anthropology, English, mathematics, music, and many other disciplines. They still do today.

Joanne Howell is a course developer for Digital Equipment Corporation, a computer hardware and software manufacturer. She works at the company's software engineering facility in Nashua, New Hampshire. She graduated from Johns Hopkins University with a bachelor's degree in psychology and a minor in creative writing. Joanne began working with personal computers in college, helping other students learn to use them in the university computer lab. Her interest deepened. "I had learned the basics of using personal computer software and hardware, and how using computers can simplify tasks, but I wanted to learn more about how computers work, and how software is created," she says. After graduation, she applied for a job as an entry level programmer at Digital, and got it.

Joanne began her career at Digital working at its regional office in

Courtesy of Jon Rochester

Maryland, outside of Washington, D.C. Her initial assignment was to write programs to generate business reports. Her duties then grew to include designing and creating database applications for Digital's customer service organization. She quickly learned the BASIC programming language and enjoyed using it. "Programming is an extremely creative activity," Joanne says. "This creative aspect is often not discussed because most people think that they have to be mathematical geniuses to program. I think programming is more like writing. Words, as a vocabulary, are the basic building blocks of a story. Programming language statements are the vocabulary used to build an application. As a programmer, you choose the vocabulary that best communicates the actions you want the program to perform. Having a good grasp of a programming

language vocabulary gives you a real sense of accomplishment."

Joanne transferred from Maryland to New Hampshire to become a course developer within Digital's Educational Services division. "I wanted a position in which I could use my programming knowledge and writing experience, and learn more about Digital's software." As a course developer, Joanne is assigned to projects to create course materials used for training. These course materials include written textbooks and programming examples that explain the software concepts and provide hands-on exercises for practice. Digital offers over 500 different courses that train customers and its own employees to use the variety of Digital hardware and software products available.

"My job involves creating materials for specific Digital software products," she says. "For example, I've worked on a course that describes how to use some of the advanced features for one of our most important computer systems. These features are only available to programmers who are creating high-performance systems. This course was very technically detailed, but I enjoyed the challenge of learning about and using these features because it helped me to become a better programmer." Joanne Howell has successfully combined her programming skills with her interest in writing to forge an interesting and challenging career.

SUMMARY

1. *Identify the functions of people, software, and hardware in a computer system.* The computer system consists of three essential components: people, software, and hardware. People use application software, which interacts with system software, which sends instructions to the hardware.

2. *Identify the two types of people who work with computers.* People who work with computers fall into two groups. Computer professionals design, test, build, implement, maintain, and operate computer systems. Computer users work with computers to achieve a desired end result for business or personal purposes. People ask the questions computers help solve.

3. *Define two kinds of software.* Software provides instructions in two forms: system software and application software. System software runs the computer, while application software performs specific tasks for the user. Software is stored on many forms of media, most commonly floppy and hard magnetic disks.

4. *Describe the two categories of hardware components.* There are two categories of computer hardware: the CPU, which does the processing, and the peripherals, which allow people to communicate with the CPU. The CPU is commonly a chip. Peripherals include input devices, such as a keyboard, and output devices, such as a printer.

5. *Name the three components that comprise the CPU.* The CPU is comprised of the control unit, the arithmetic-logic unit, and main memory.

6. *Describe the types of computer memory and their uses.* Main memory is commonly referred to as random access memory or RAM; it is volatile storage. The other kind of memory is read only memory or ROM; it cannot be changed. Auxiliary storage, such as a disk drive, is more permanent storage and is called nonvolatile.

7. *Identify the four operations of data processing.* Data processing is comprised of four operations: input, processing, output, and storage. In the final stage, the data produced by the computer system is presented to people for interpretation as useful information.

8. *Describe the two methods of data processing.* Batch processing means the computer processes data that has been gathered together over a period of time. On-line processing means the data is processed immediately, as soon as it is input.

9. *Define the terms bit and byte.* A bit is a basic unit of data the computer recognizes; it is either a 1 (on) or a 0 (off). A byte is eight bits, which often are organized into computer words or logical units of information.

10. *Describe the difference between data and information.* Data is what the computer processes; it is received in when people use an input device. The output device also produces data, which people turn into useful information.

KEY TERMS

application software, p. 33

arithmetic-logic unit (ALU), p. 36

auxiliary storage, p. 38

auxiliary storage device, p. 38

batch processing, p. 50

binary number system, p. 52

bit, p. 52

byte, p. 52

central processing unit (CPU), p. 36

chip, p. 51

computer professional, p. 30

computer system, p. 30

computer user, p. 30

control unit, p. 36

disk drive, p. 38

firmware, p. 34

floppy disk, p. 34

information, p. 53

input device, p. 38

integrated circuit (IC), p. 51

main memory, p. 37

media, p. 34

memory, p. 38

micro-floppy, p. 34

millions of instructions per second (MIPS), p. 51

mini-floppy, p. 34

motherboard, p. 37

mouse, p. 42

nonvolatile memory, p. 39

on-line processing, p. 50

output device, p. 38

peripheral devices, p. 36

printed circuit board, p. 35

random access memory (RAM), p. 38

read only memory (ROM), p. 38

silicon chip, p. 34

system software, p. 33

volatile memory, p. 38

word (computer), p. 52

word length, p. 52

REVIEW AND DISCUSSION QUESTIONS

1. Why is the human component essential to the computer system?

2. What is the primary purpose in designing software?

3. What are the two kinds of computer software?

4. What are the two things that media is able to store?

5. What are the two categories of hardware components in a computer system?

6. Why do we say the CPU is the "heart" of the computer?

7. Name the three components that make up the CPU.

8. What is the function of the control unit?

9. What does the ALU do?

10. Describe some similarities between computers and stereos.

11. Why is it important to understand the computer as a system?

12. What is the difference between volatile and nonvolatile memory?

13. What are two characteristics of ROM?

14. What are two characteristics of RAM?

15. Identify the four operations of data processing.

16. Why is it important to understand the concept of GIGO?

17. The word *bit* is made up of what two words?

18. What is the difference between a bit and a byte?

19. Explain the difference between data and information.

20. Discuss how computers help us increase or enhance human knowledge.

ISSUES

1. The competition in chips and computers between the United States and Japan is intense. In the 1980s, Japan was charged with "dumping" (selling below cost) their chips in the U.S. market. Sometimes there are chip shortages, which cause prices to skyrocket. Do you think dumping is unethical, or just a clever business strategy? Do you think limiting competition by setting up trade barriers would help or hurt the development of computer technology?

2. Consider these scenarios from your everyday life. One, you buy something at the grocery store with a sticker stating the price is $1.98. However, when the clerk passes the item over the scanner, it rings up $2.49. Two, you believe you have paid your last VISA card bill on time, but this month's statement shows a late charge. Are these examples of a "computer error"? Why do they occur? Who should be responsible for correcting them — the originator of the error or you, the consumer? Do we need to be more alert to computer errors? Should there be more responsive mechanisms in place for correcting computer errors?

3. Our government, banks, and industries rely heavily on computers for nearly all transactions and functions. It is said that if a Fortune 500 company's computer system went on the blink, the company would lose millions of dollars a week. If an enemy set off an electromagnetic pulse (EMP) bomb, banks would lose billions upon billions of dollars in electronic money transfers. Does this dependence on computers make our economy and national security too vulnerable? What can we do about it?

CHAPTER 3

Hands On
Using a Personal Computer

CHAPTER OUTLINE

Tim Paterson: The Man Behind DOS
Mastering Your Personal Computer
Getting Acquainted with Personal Computer
    Hardware
    The IBM PC
    The Apple Macintosh
    Personal Computer Configurations
    DISKbyte: Tips for a Clean and Healthy Computer
The Many Faces of the Human-Computer Interface
    The Command Line Interface
    The Menu-Driven Interface
    The Graphic Interface
DOS, The Disk Operating System
    DOS Files
    The DOS Directory
    The Prompt
    The Command Line
    The Cursor
A DOS Work Session
    Booting DOS from a Floppy Disk
    Issuing Commands
    Commonly Used DOS Commands
    DISKbyte: Issuing Commands on Other Computers
    Using Application Programs
    Ending a Work Session
    *DISKbyte: Tips for Keeping Your Programs and
       Data Safe*
Ethics
    *CAREERbyte: Michael Dell: Starting a
       Computer Business in a College Dorm Room*
Summary
Key Terms
Review and Discussion Questions
Issues

OBJECTIVES

After reading and studying this chapter, you should be able to:

1. Identify the most popular types of personal computers and explain the best way to work with one.
2. Describe different types of personal computer configurations.
3. Identify the characteristics of different human-computer interfaces.
4. Explain the way DOS organizes files and directories.
5. Describe the steps involved in working with DOS.
6. List some of the commonly used DOS commands.

TIM PATERSON: THE MAN BEHIND DOS

"I made my one contribution," says Tim Paterson, the man who created the MS–DOS operating system for personal computers. "I feel like I had an effect on history." Even though we usually attribute MS–DOS to Bill Gates and Microsoft Corporation, it was Tim Paterson, a computer engineer working at Seattle Computer Products in 1980, who really created the personal computer industry's most widely used operating system.

Seattle Computer Products was a hardware company that, by 1979, had created the components for a personal computer using the 8086 microprocessor. "We needed an operating system, and nothing else was available, so we decided to write our own," Tim explains. "In 1980, we shipped the first version of what we called '86–DOS.'"

Courtesy of Tim Paterson

About the same time IBM approached Microsoft, a Seattle-area software company best known then for its BASIC programming language, about an operating system for its soon-to-be-introduced Personal Computer. Microsoft didn't have one, but thought it knew where to get one. Seattle Computer Products had helped Microsoft with its 8086 BASIC; maybe they could help again. A deal was struck to allow Microsoft to adapt 86–DOS for the IBM PC for $40,000.

Although 86–DOS had been shipped to customers, Tim considered it far from ready. He spent several months bringing it up to the specifications he'd established at Seattle Computer. "IBM and Microsoft didn't know what I was doing to it," he says. "They just wanted minor changes, like improving the text editor."

Tim finished his work in 1981, just about the same time he went to work for Microsoft. Then Microsoft bought the full rights to 86–DOS from Seattle Computer for $50,000, prior to IBM announcing the IBM Personal Computer. DOS was the beginning of a long and mutually beneficial relationship between Microsoft and IBM. No one had any idea how phenomenally successful the PC would be, but Tim's operating system became Microsoft's cash cow. To date, over 40 million copies are in use.

Tim has worked at both Microsoft and Seattle Computer Products over the years, mostly on projects unrelated to DOS. For a time he ran his own business, Falcon Technology, and contracted with Microsoft to create a version of DOS for Microsoft called MSX–DOS for Japanese personal computers. He enjoys the group he works with, and says of Microsoft, "The company can't be beat." The same could certainly be said of DOS, which continues to thrive when many said it would not. What's the latest version? "Russian DOS," for the growing number of personal computer users in the Soviet Union.

MASTERING YOUR PERSONAL COMPUTER

One of the most satisfying experiences in life is the ability to master a task, a subject, or the operation of a machine. Whether it's knowing how to cook chicken cacciatore, learning ancient Celtic mythology, or driving a car, we all enjoy that sense of accomplishment and self-confidence that comes from doing something well.

This is certainly true when it comes to mastering the computer. In this chapter, we're going to show you how to use a personal computer. By **personal computer,** or **PC**, we mean a computer system that fits on a desk top, that an individual can afford to buy for personal use, and that is intended for a single user. Today, the term *personal computer* is most often used to refer to this type of computer, regardless of the manufacturer. It doesn't matter whether the personal computer is made by IBM, Apple, or another computer maker; they are all personal computers. The personal computer is intended to help you become more personally productive in your work and your life.

Have you used a personal computer? Whether you have or not, you may have heard someone who is computer literate say, "Using a computer is easy!" We're not going to say that, because learning to use a personal computer takes some *time* and requires some *effort*. But there is a significant payback for your time and effort, for once you know how to use one, you have a real advantage in life. Your work, whether in college or on the job, will be quicker and easier to accomplish. You'll find the personal computer useful in many aspects of your personal life, such as keeping valuable information or managing your personal finances. Equally important, you can list the fact that you're computer literate on your résumé when you apply for a job. Understanding how computers and software work might put you a nose ahead of the competition for that big promotion. Your life will be easier in general because you'll better understand the many computerized activities, transactions, and processes of the Information Age. You'll be in step with — not a step behind — modern times. And once in a while you might even enjoy playing a computer game!

You've already learned the fundamental computer concepts and about the internal components that make up a computer system. Now we introduce you to the personal computer from a "hands-on" perspective. We begin by showing you several types of personal computers, then we explain how the operating system puts you in control of the computer. You'll learn to use some of the actual commands that perform everyday tasks. If you have a personal computer at home, or if there is one in a lab or classroom at your school, you might find it helpful to familiarize yourself with its workings as you read this chapter.

GETTING ACQUAINTED WITH PERSONAL COMPUTER HARDWARE

Learning to use a personal computer is really no more difficult than learning to drive a car or use a VCR. Contrary to popular opinion, it's very difficult to damage a personal computer in normal usage; at the very worst, you might lose something you typed. The two most important things to remember are: (1) take your time, and (2) do things carefully. If you follow these two simple guidelines, you'll have very few problems with your personal computer.

The Flight Check

Before pilots go flying, they check out their aircraft. Let's do a preflight check on the personal computer. Most personal computers, regardless of who makes them, have the same parts and components: a keyboard, a video monitor, a CPU. However, different types or brands operate differently, and a main reason for this is because they use different operating systems. An **operating system** is part of the computer's system software. It controls the execution of computer programs and manages certain computer tasks. We'll discuss the operating system in more detail later in this chapter.

For now, we're going to describe the two most common types of personal computers, so you'll gain a familiarity with them. One is the well-known IBM PC and those computers that operate similarly to it, called PC-compatibles; the other is the Apple Macintosh. There are others, but these are the ones you'll most commonly encounter in business and education.

The IBM PC

In 1981, International Business Machines introduced the IBM Personal Computer, or PC. Soon, other companies such as Epson, Tandy, Compaq, and Zenith introduced computers that worked very similarly to the PC. They are called **PC-compatibles.** (The PC/XT and PC/AT are examples of PC and PC-compatible models.) What IBM PCs and PC-compatibles have in common is very similar operating systems. This is what makes them compatible and enables them to utilize the same application programs. We call this operating system **DOS,** which stands for **disk operating system.** Figure 3–1 shows an IBM PC and a closeup view of the keyboard. DOS is an integrated set of programs that performs three important tasks. First, it lets you gain access to the various operations of the CPU, such as processing and sending data to memory. Second, it controls the peripheral devices, so you can store data on a disk or print it out on the printer. Third, it provides various support services while you work with application programs, such as listing disk contents or telling you how much storage space is available.

In 1987, IBM discontinued making the PC and introduced the Personal System/2, or PS/2. It has many of the attributes of the original PC, as well as a new operating system called OS/2, more RAM, and other features. What's most important to remember is that these are all considered personal computers. Figure 3–2 shows an IBM PS/2.

The Apple Macintosh

The Macintosh is also a personal computer. The Macintosh's introduction to the world in 1984 was quite a media event. It appeared in a television commercial entitled "1984" that was shown one time only during that year's Super Bowl football game. The Macintosh has been improved several times over the years and now a more powerful version, the Macintosh II, is available in several different models. Figure 3–3 shows a Macintosh SE.

The Macintosh was the first widely available personal computer to employ a mouse as an input device. The mouse is one of several features designed to make the Mac a user-friendly computer — one that is very easy to learn and to

FIGURE 3-1   An IBM PC.

Gabe Palmer/The Stock Market

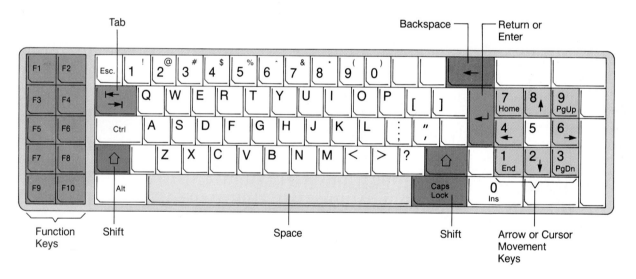

use. Another is its operating system, which makes it easy to issue instructions and obtain information. Apple calls its operating system simply Macintosh System Software, and it has many features not found in other operating systems. We'll discuss human-computer interfaces and operating systems in more detail in the next section.

Personal Computer Configurations

Computer-literate people often use the word *configuration* to describe a computer's attributes. **Configuration** describes the various hardware elements that, together, make up a computer system. This includes the type of monitor or video display (color or monochrome, which may be green, orange, or

FIGURE 3 – 2   An IBM PS/2.

J. Curtis/Offshoot

FIGURE 3 – 3   A Macintosh SE.

Courtesy of Apple Computer, Inc.

black/white), the quality of the video display, the amount of RAM (random access memory), and the number and type of floppy or hard disk drives. It also includes other devices that may be connected either internally or externally. An essential device for any configuration is a printer.

A personal computer can be configured as a desktop personal computer like the Macintosh, or as a lightweight, portable laptop computer, or even as a more powerful workstation. If we were describing the configuration of a stereo or an auto, we'd probably refer to its features or accessories. A full-featured auto is often termed *loaded*. A full-featured personal computer is called *fully configured*.

DISKbyte

Tips for a Clean and Healthy Personal Computer

Nothing is more important to successful computing than taking good care of your personal computer and your disks. Think about the fact that the silicon chips computers use are manufactured in a special "clean room" where a microscopic speck of dust can render a chip unusable, or the fact that a hard disk is sealed in an airtight case, and you get the idea. A glop of peanut butter on a floppy disk can gum up your drive. Spilled soft drinks, cookie crumbs, and cat hair can cause keys to stick. Here are some cleanliness tips for your personal computer.

- Keep the cabinet, keyboard, and monitor clean. Use a spray cleaner on the plastic and a window cleaner on the monitor. A bright and shiny computer makes for a happier, more productive user. A brush will often dislodge cookie crumbs from between keys. Brush the dust and lint away from the fan grille, if your computer has one.
- Use a commercial disk drive cleaner from time to time, to remove bits of plastic and dust from the disk drive.
- Cover your computer, at least the keyboard, when not in use.
- Get a yearly servicing and checkup for your personal computer because invariably it will break down when you need it the most.
- Don't smoke while you're using the personal computer because smoke, dust, and airborne pollution can damage disks and drives.
- Keep your computer out of direct sunlight, which can warp the cabinet and cause cables or circuits to crack. Keep it away from excessive humidity and dryness. Static electricity and strong magnetic fields (as from a stereo speaker) can destroy electronic circuits and damage the contents of a disk!

A Simple Configuration   The basic or least expensive configuration for a personal computer is a monochrome monitor, a minimal amount of RAM, and one disk drive. RAM is measured in thousands or millions of bytes. For convenience, we round off the amount of RAM; for example, what we call 640K is actually 655,536 bytes. Likewise, 1 **kilobyte** or 1K of RAM is actually 1,024 bytes.

Most PC-compatibles come with either 640K or 1 **megabyte** (1MB) of RAM. One megabyte is approximately 1,000 kilobytes (1 million bytes). The Macintosh comes standard with 1 megabyte (1MB). Figure 3–4 shows common RAM configurations.

A Full Configuration   While you may not need a fully loaded car, it is often sensible to have a fully configured personal computer. A full configuration for a state-of-the-art personal computer system includes a color monitor with high-quality screen display, at least 2MB of RAM, at least one floppy disk drive, and one hard disk with at least 30MB of storage capacity. A color display is useful if you plan to use graphics software. In addition, many nongraphic programs, even word processing, are primarily intended for a color monitor, and can be awkward to use on a monochrome display. Figure 3–5 shows how the same program appears on color and monochrome monitors.

FIGURE 3–4   Some common RAM configurations.

Amount of RAM	Typical PC Configuration
64K	Early IBM PC
128K	Early Macintosh
256–512K	PC-compatibles
640K	PC/XT, PC/AT
1MB	Macintosh SE
2–4MB	Mac II, PS/2

FIGURE 3–5   Color often makes it easier and more efficient to use applications.

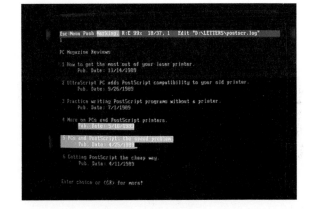

F. Bodin/Offshoot

Many applications have grown more complex and have added more features, requiring more RAM. For example, word processing programs often include a spelling or grammar checker. Large spreadsheets, filled with numbers and calculations, require large amounts of memory, too. Generally speaking, the more RAM, the better. It is not uncommon to use applications that require most of the 640K of main memory.

Likewise, **hard disk drives,** built-in auxiliary storage devices that hold large quantities of data, are getting more common. Remember our discussion of the CPU's access to RAM versus auxiliary storage in Chapter 2? We explained that computer instructions and data are held in RAM but the CPU sometimes must go to the disk drive for additional instructions or data. Think of the difference between RAM and the hard disk as the difference between retaining knowledge in your head versus having to look something up in a book, as shown in Figure 3–6. While not as fast as RAM, you can access programs and data faster from a hard disk than you can from a floppy disk. In fact, some programs require that you have a hard disk drive.

Another way hard disks are more useful is when working with large programs that come on multiple disks. A 20MB hard disk holds the equivalent of about 28 720K micro-floppies or 55 360K mini-floppies. Without a hard disk, you have to swap the floppies in and out of the floppy disk drive when you need to perform different operations. A hard disk allows you to store the entire

FIGURE 3–6   Understanding the difference between random access memory (RAM) and hard disk auxiliary storage is similar to how people retain knowledge. The teacher asks the student for the answer to a mathematical problem. In the left-hand figure, the student knows the answer and speaks from memory, just as data is retained in RAM. In the right-hand figure, the student does not know the answer and must refer to the book, just as the CPU must access the hard disk for data.

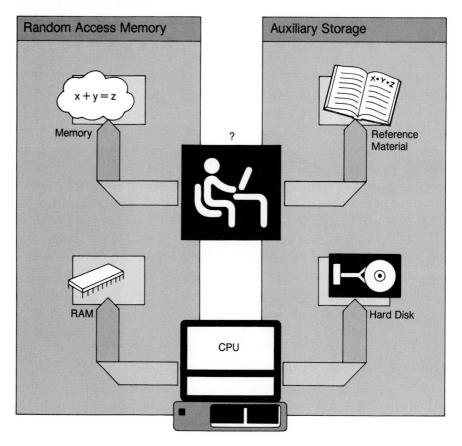

program, with no disk swapping. Programs often run more smoothly from a hard disk. There are other components in a configuration, such as the peripheral devices that can be connected to each other as well as to the printer. But for now, let's see how a fully configured personal computer as we've described it works in actual practice.

MEMORY CHECK

1. What is a computer that works just like an IBM PC called?
2. What input device did the Apple Macintosh popularize?
3. What are the three components that make up a personal computer configuration?
4. When does it make sense to use a hard disk drive?
5. What two guidelines should you always follow to avoid having problems working with your personal computer?

THE MANY FACES OF THE HUMAN – COMPUTER INTERFACE

The operating system also determines how certain things look on the screen. What we see on the screen is called the **human-computer interface,** or the way the computer and its software are presented to the human being who is about to use them. The hardware interface is primarily the monitor and the keyboard, as well as a mouse if one is available. The software interface is the way the operating system, as well as the application program, appear to us on the screen.

The most important aspect of the human-computer interface is how we issue commands to the computer system. A **command** is an instruction issued to perform a specific task or function. We'll discuss the command in greater detail later in this chapter.

When only skilled computer professionals used computers, the human-computer interface was very simple and straightforward. These people understood the computer quite well and wanted a no-frills interface so they could do their programming work quickly. But average users often have different needs, so different human-computer interfaces have been designed. There are three basic types of human-computer interfaces available on personal computers today: the command line interface, the menu-driven interface, and the graphic interface.

The Command Line Interface

The original DOS interface is a good example of a command line interface. The **command line interface** requires that you type a command to make something happen. However, you must already know what that command is. For example, to learn what programs or data are stored on the disk in the floppy disk drive, you must know what command to type. When using DOS, you type a command and then press the Enter or Return key to actually issue that command. The command for displaying the contents of the DOS program disk is:

```
A>dir
```

The Menu-Driven Interface

As more and more people with no prior experience began using computers, they wanted a human-computer interface to help them remember commands or see what to do next. One of the first friendly interfaces was called a *menu* because it presented a list of the commands, tasks, or projects the user most often worked with. The **menu-driven interface** was developed to make the command line interface easier to use. Figure 3 – 7 shows a menu that displays a DOS directory and commands.

The Graphic Interface

The most popular human-computer interface for new users is the graphic interface, popularized by the Macintosh. The previous two interfaces use only text—numbers, letters, and standard keyboard characters. The **graphic interface** uses *images* in the form of drawings, boxes, and characters, in addition

FIGURE 3-7   With a menu, the directory appears on the screen and commands are shown either above or below for easy reference.

```
  Path: C:\                                              7-15-90 10:12:32 am

 C:\                                         │FILE  *.*
  ├─123                                      │
  ├─ADRSBOOK                                 │DISK  C:
  ├─DBASE                                    │ Available
  ├─DOS                                      │  Bytes  12,374,016
  │ └─UTILS                                  │
  ├─HAS                                      │DISK Statistics
  ├─K051                                     │ Total
  ├─NEURLNET                                 │  Files        996
  ├─PCTOOLS                                  │  Bytes  19,929,373
  ├─PZP                                      │ Matching
  ├─SWITCHIT                                 │  Files        996
  ├─WEB                                      │  Bytes  19,929,373
  ├─WP51                                     │ Tagged
                                             │  Files          0
 AUTOEXEC.BAK    COMMAND .COM   LOADHI  .SYS │  Bytes          0
 AUTOEXEC.BAT    CONFIG  .SYS   msdos   .sys │ Current Directory
 AUTOEXEC.SAV    io      .sys   NOEGA   .COM │ C:\
 BUFFERS .COM    LOADHI  .COM   QEMM    .COM │  Bytes      121,885

 DIR        Available Delete Filespec Global Invert Log disk Makedir
 COMMANDS   Print Rename Showall Tag Untag Volume eXecute Quit
 ←┘ file  F7 autoview F8 split    F9 menu  F10 commands    F1 help  ? stats
```

FIGURE 3-8   When you press or click the mouse button twice, the filenames appear.

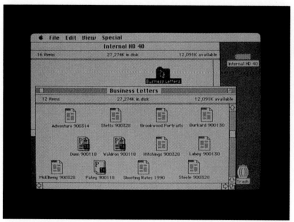

F. Bodin/Offshoot

to text. It commonly employs **icons,** which are pictorial figures or representations designed so that most people easily recognize them. To see what work is stored on a disk, you move the mouse to position the character—usually an arrow—on the icon that resembles a disk. Press or click the mouse button twice and the disk contents appear, as shown in Figure 3-8.

The graphic human-computer interface, sometimes called the graphic user interface or GUI, is becoming more widely accepted as the standard. Many computer companies now offer their computer systems with a graphic interface. The most common ones are the Macintosh interface, Microsoft Windows for the personal computer, and Presentation Manager for the PS/2.

It's important to note that there are trade-offs when using a menu-driven or graphic human-computer interface. For example, using the arrow keys to move through a menu, or moving the mouse to the icon and clicking, is often slower and requires more hand-eye coordination than simply pressing one or two keys to issue a command. On the other hand, the mouse often makes certain tasks easier to accomplish than using commands and arrow keys in combination; what's more, you don't have to remember the command names. Therefore, it's not uncommon for human-computer interfaces to incorporate the best of both worlds. New users often depend on the menu-driven or graphic interface while they're learning, then switch to the command line interface as they grow more proficient.

---

1. What do we call the way the computer hardware and software present themselves to the user?

2. What do we call a human-computer interface where we type in commands?

3. What do we call a human-computer interface where we use a menu?

4. What do we call a human-computer interface where we use graphic images?

5. Why might it be desirable to have a human-computer interface that employs more than one way to issue commands?

MEMORY CHECK

DOS, THE DISK OPERATING SYSTEM

Turning the personal computer on is not enough; it must have instructions for the tasks it is to perform. These instructions come in the form of software. The primary tasks and functions the personal computer performs come from the instructions in systems programs.

You have already learned that there are specific systems software instructions embedded in chips that make up ROM (read only memory). These instructions help the computer give itself a checkup when you switch the power on, to make sure everything is in working order. Most of these instructions occur without our being aware of them. However, one that you often can see when you first turn the power on is the computer checking its RAM.

The other aspect of systems software, the one we can actually interact with, is called the operating system. The operating system for the personal computer is called DOS, for disk operating system. DOS must be loaded into the personal computer's main memory before it can be used. There are also a number of instructions given to the computer by the operating system, as shown in Figure 3–9. As you can see, most are unavailable to you, the user. One that is very important that you can't see is the Basic Input/Output System, or BIOS. It contains instructions specific to the computer you are using; for example, there is a BIOS that only works on an IBM PC.

When you load the operating system into the computer's memory, it is called a **boot,** or booting the computer. The term comes from the old saying, "Pulling himself up by his own bootstraps," meaning someone who is able to do something on his own. Once booting is completed, you can issue DOS instructions and use application programs such as word processing.

FIGURE 3–9   The DOS structure consists of the BIOS or Basic Input Output System, which is stored in read only memory (ROM), and the operating system or DOS, which has two aspects: its internal commands to itself and the commands or functions controlled by the user.

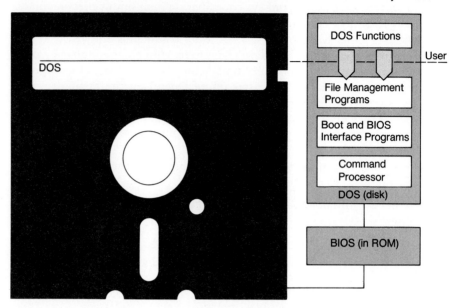

DOS awakens the hardware and allows you to control the personal computer. It is responsible for managing all the input and output tasks, such as assuring that when you type a character on the keyboard, that same exact character appears on the screen and is stored in memory. Think of yourself as the personal computer's manager; DOS makes sure all your instructions are carried out accurately and promptly.

DOS Files

DOS is actually a collection of programs, each of which performs specific tasks. Programs and data are stored in files. The **file** is a group of related records and the primary unit of data storage in DOS-based computers (as well as most others). It is very similar to the file folder in a common filing cabinet. Just as a file folder might contain memos with instructions or informational letters and reports, so a DOS file can contain either program instructions or data. There are files that are unique to DOS; files that both DOS and an application uses; and files created by the user while working with an application. Figure 3–10 shows these types of files. DOS uses files itself, performs operations on applications files, and allows you to create your own files.

Each file in DOS has a unique **filename,** which can be up to eight characters long, followed by an optional period or dot and three-character filename extension. As Figure 3–11 shows, DOS requires an .EXE or .COM extension for a program file, but you can give your files any extension (or no extension) you want. For example, the filename for this chapter is THREE, which may be typed without the dot or extension. However, as we wrote, we needed to keep track of our revisions, so we used the filename THREE.100 the first time, then THREE.101, THREE.102, and so forth, each time we subsequently worked on this chapter.

FIGURE 3 – 10   Types of DOS files.

ANSI.SYS	A DOS file that issues system commands
SORT.EXE	A DOS file that performs a DOS task
WP.EXE	A file that starts word processing application
THREE.100	A user-created data or text file (word processing)

FIGURE 3 – 11   The five types of DOS filename extensions.

.COM	A command file that issues a specific command
.EXE	An executable program file, more complex than a .COM file
.SYS	An operating system file
.BAT	A batch file, which starts other programs
.CPI	A Code Page Information file

DOS Filenames

There are five different types of files used in DOS itself, and they are distinguished from one another by their filename extensions. All five types of filename extensions are shown in Figure 3 – 11. Of the five different types, .COM, .EXE, and .SYS are the most commonly used. Batch (.BAT) files contain instructions that perform a special grouping of commands and are often created by the user. .CPI files are used by skilled programmers.

The two types of files you'll work with most commonly in DOS are .COM and .EXE files because they perform the widest variety of tasks. For example, PRINT.COM will print a file, and DOS executable (.EXE) files are used to start almost all application programs. You'll learn some DOS commands later in this chapter.

The DOS Directory

DOS stores files on a disk in a **directory,** a list of the files stored on a disk or a portion of a disk. The primary directory is called the **root directory.** DOS also allows you to create **subdirectories** under the root directory. Thus you can keep your programs and data well organized and easy to find. For example, you could keep your DOS program in the root directory, your word processing program in a subdirectory, and the files you create in word processing in a subdirectory off the word processing subdirectory. Both floppy disks and hard disks can be organized into directories; Figure 3 – 12 shows the DOS program listing in the root directory of a floppy disk (A:\) and three subdirectories (i.e., WORDPROC) at the bottom.

Loading DOS

Personal computer software, whether it's the operating system or an application, usually comes on a floppy disk. It's from that disk that the personal computer's DOS got its name. The acronym DOS — *disk operating system* — dates back to the early 1970s when it was used to refer to an IBM mainframe operating system. **Loading** is the process of reading software into the

---

FIGURE 3-12   DOS program directory and root directory with subdirectories.

```
COMMAND   COM     23612    6-18-86    5:57p
ANSI      SYS      1651    3-21-86   12:00p
DRIVER    SYS      1102    3-21-86   12:00p
VDISK     SYS      6445   11-17-86   11:11a
ASSIGN    COM      1523    3-21-86   12:00p
ATTRIB    EXE      8234    3-21-86   12:00p
CHKDSK    COM      9819    5-14-86    3:43p
DISKCOMP  COM      4123   11-17-86   11:42a
DISKCOPY  COM      4955   11-17-86   10:53a
DU        EXE      8416    8-09-86   10:24a
FC        COM     14601    9-30-86    2:39p
FDISK     EXE     18252   11-18-86    5:17p
FIND      EXE      6403    3-21-86   12:00p
FORMAT    COM     11138    6-23-86    1:00p
GRAFTABL  COM      8349    5-14-86    3:41p
GRAPHICS  COM     14347    9-26-86    6:45p
JOIN      EXE      9012   11-17-86   11:18a
KEYBFR    COM      4248   11-17-86   10:27a
KEYBGR    COM      4259   11-17-86   10:28a
KEYBIT    COM      4039   11-17-86   10:29a
KEYBSP    COM      4161   11-17-86   10:30a
KEYBUK    COM      4004   11-17-86   10:30a
LABEL     COM      2889    5-14-86    3:42p
MODE      COM     14167   10-09-86    3:35p
MORE      COM       282   11-06-86   12:58a
PRINT     COM      8963    5-14-86    3:43p
RECOVER   COM      4284    5-14-86    3:43p
REPLACE   EXE      4912   10-31-86   11:21a
SELECT    COM      3784   11-06-86    4:08a
SETMODE   EXE      8320    8-08-86    8:49a
SHARE     EXE      8544    3-21-86   12:00p
SORT      EXE      1898    3-21-86   12:00p
SUBST     EXE      9898    3-21-86   12:00p
SYS       COM      4607    6-23-86   10:30a
TREE      COM      8695    5-14-86    3:42p
XCOPY     EXE      5426   10-04-86    4:42p
APPEND    COM      1725    3 21 86   12:00p
TESTBUG   COM       598   10-04-85   12:00p
EPSON     TXT       366   10-04-85   12:00p
WORDPROC         <DIR>     8-19-90    1:09p
SPRED            <DIR>     8-19-90    1:10p
DBMS             <DIR>     8-19-90    1:10p
        42 File(s)      29696 bytes free

A:\>
```

computer. When we load DOS, we do so by copying the DOS disk's magnetic contents into the personal computer's RAM.

The Prompt

Once this process is complete, DOS displays a screen as in Figure 3–13. DOS lets you check the computer's internal clock to date and time stamp your files (Figure 3–12). If the date you see is correct, press the Enter key; if the time is correct, press Enter again. If the date and time are not correct, DOS lets you type in the correct date and time by displaying on the screen "Enter new (date:)." Now you are at the DOS prompt. The **prompt** is a character or message that tells you the computer system is ready to accept a command or input. A command is an instruction you give to the computer. A prompt may be textual, such as "ENTER COMMAND," or a character such as a question mark (?) or a period (.). In DOS, the prompt is a right-pointing arrow or *caret* that looks like this: >.

FIGURE 3 – 13   After successfully booting, DOS displays this screen.

```
Phoenix 80386 ROM BIOS PLUS Version 1.10.10
Copyright (C) 1985-1989 Phoenix Technologies Ltd.
All Rights Reserved

MYLEX Corporation
386

640K Base Memory, 01408K Extended
Current date is Sun  8-19-1990
Enter new date (mm-dd-yy):
```

FIGURE 3 – 14   Two types of cursors: one is a rectangle, the other an arrow.

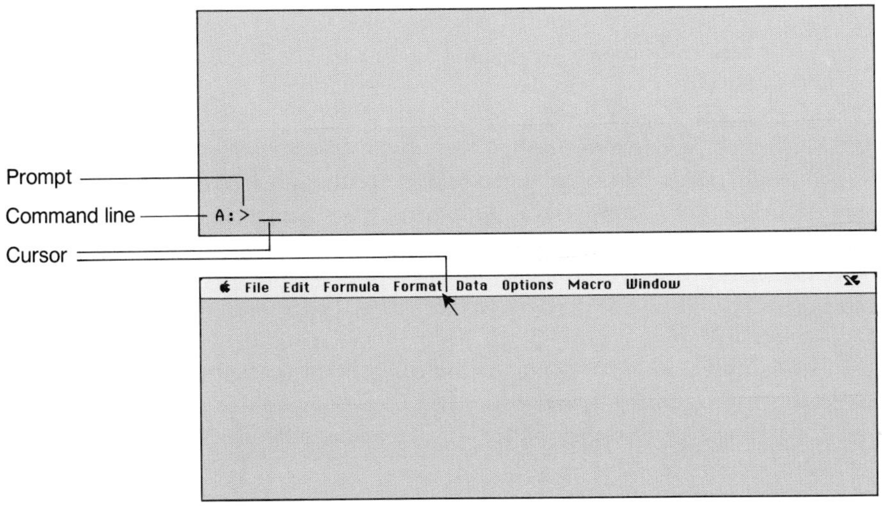

The Command Line

Prompt
Command line — A : >
Cursor

File   Edit   Formula   Format   Data   Options   Macro   Window

The Command Line

The prompt appears on the command line. The **command line,** as its name implies, is the portion of the screen where you issue DOS commands or instructions. Once you have typed the command and reread it to make sure it is accurate, you must press the Enter key to issue the command.

The Cursor

How do we issue commands at the prompt on the command line? By typing them on the keyboard. But first, we need to know if the command line is ready to accept a command. The **cursor** is usually a blinking rectangle or a blinking underline that tells us where the next keyboard character we type will appear on the screen. It appears just to the right of the prompt. Other types of personal computers that use a mouse, such as the Macintosh, often display an arrow for pointing at the menu and issuing commands. Figure 3 – 14 shows screens with rectangle and arrow cursors. Regardless of the type of task we're working at, the cursor is our constant point of reference.

M E M O R Y
C H E C K

1. What does the term *DOS* stand for?

2. What is the term used for loading the operating instructions into the personal computer to awaken it?

3. What is the primary unit of data storage in DOS computers?

4. Where are the primary units of data storage kept by DOS?

5. Describe how a filename is organized and how many characters it contains.

6. Name the device that tells you where you can type the next character. What is the area where they both appear on the screen called?

A DOS WORK SESSION

Turning on a personal computer, or "powering up," as many like to say, is as easy as flipping on the power switch. The only real difficulty is that the power switch isn't always easy to find! If you don't see it on the front panel, look on the side or in the rear, near the power cord. Figure 3–15 shows the location of the Macintosh SE power switch.

One difference between personal computers and larger computers — workstations, minicomputers, and mainframes — is that the larger computers are often left on all the time. Repeated powering up and down causes more wear and tear on sensitive electronic circuits and especially on the spinning hard disk drive. If you plan to use your personal computer off and on during the course of the day, it's a good idea to leave it on all day long; personal computers only consume about as much electricity as a television set. Special screen saver programs blank the monitor display when it is not in use so that the phosphor coating on the inner surface of the monitor's screen does not become burned and scarred.

FIGURE 3–15   The Macintosh SE power switch is located at the back of the system unit.

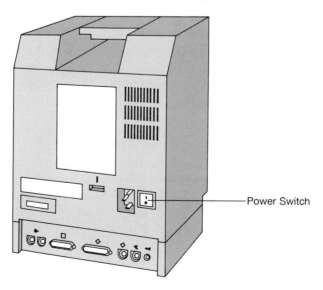

Power Switch

Now we're going to flip the power switch, turn on the personal computer, and start our first work session. Yet switching the power on by itself does little or nothing unless we add the software component. Before we go any further, let's turn our attention to how DOS awakens the hardware.

Booting DOS from a Floppy Disk

As we mentioned, the computer will do nothing until it receives instructions, so let's boot DOS from a floppy disk. When the power has not yet been switched on, this is called a *cold boot*. Switch off your personal computer's power now and locate the A drive. Figure 3–16 shows the most common personal computer disk drive configurations. As you can see, floppy disk drives are usually identified as A and B and the hard disk drive is usually identified as the C drive.

A floppy disk containing instructions for the computer is called a **program disk.** There is a DOS program disk, as well as program disks for the applications you use. Now, insert the DOS program disk, with the label facing up, into drive A. Many disk drives have a switch or a lever that must be pressed or turned, locking the door so the drive motor will be activated properly. Now turn on the power switch. You will probably hear some sounds and see a light begin to glow, indicating that the drive is spinning and reading data from the disk into memory. When the sounds stop and the light goes out, you should see the date and time information on the screen, as described earlier in this chapter. Press Enter twice, or change the date and time if you wish, to move the cursor to the A> on the command line.

There is another way to boot (or reboot) DOS. It is called a *warm boot* because the power is already switched on and the DOS disk is locked in the drive. With a warm boot, some of the basic systems software instructions remain loaded in the computer; with a cold boot, the computer is entirely reset. A warm boot is executed by pressing the personal computer's reset button, or by holding down the Control and Alt keys and simultaneously pressing the Delete key. A warm boot can be performed on a personal computer with either floppy disk drives or a hard disk drive. However, a cold boot on a hard disk drive personal computer is a little different.

FIGURE 3–16 Common floppy disk drive locations.

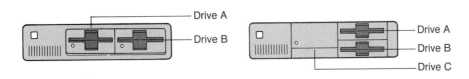

Booting DOS from a Hard Disk

We mentioned earlier that it is easier to use applications with a hard disk; well, so is booting DOS. When the hard disk is initially set up, DOS makes it possible for the computer system to automatically find and load the operating system each time the personal computer is switched on or rebooted. DOS, once loaded, displays the date and time, then takes you to the C prompt on the command line. Remember, the C prompt refers to the C disk drive — the hard disk drive.

We'll now turn our attention to issuing commands.

Issuing Commands

The way we get the computer to perform work and solve problems is by issuing a command, which is then executed by the operating system software. Some DOS commands request information about the computer system, such as listing the files we have stored on a disk. Others perform tasks such as copying the contents of a disk or loading an application.

Commands are issued differently depending on the type of computer, or the commands may have slightly different names, but most personal computers utilize commands that are similar in purpose. DOS commands are issued by typing them at the prompt on the command line, followed by pressing the Enter or Return key. On a Macintosh, commands are listed in menus at the top of the screen and are issued by placing the arrow on the appropriate icon with the mouse and then clicking its button.

The DOS command line provides no menu. It presumes that you already know the command and the proper way to type it, which is called the syntax. Syntax is the formal way elements of language — whether our spoken language or a computer programming language — are put together to make sense. If you make a mistake, sometimes called a *syntax error,* DOS returns a message to you on the screen that says "Bad command or file name." The abruptness of this message and its lack of help for the user are one reason DOS is not generally considered user friendly. Even so, the DOS command line offers great flexibility in using the computer system, as we shall see.

Commonly Used DOS Commands

When we left our personal computer, we had just confirmed that the correct date and time had appeared on the screen, and that the cursor was standing ready at the prompt on the command line. Assuming you are using a personal computer with two floppy disk drives, let's learn to use some DOS commands that will help us understand DOS better and perform some important tasks at the same time. It's extremely important that you type DOS commands precisely, using the correct DOS syntax, or else you will get the "Bad command or file name" error message. DOS requires that you insert blank spaces (using the keyboard's space bar) or certain punctuation marks in many commands; watch for them.

DIR (Directory) One of the most important things we need to know about a disk, whether floppy or hard, is what files it contains. We learn this by using the DIR command, which lists a directory of the disk's contents. With your DOS program disk in drive A, type:

DIR A:

at the prompt and then press the Enter key. The screen will fill with file-names, listed alphabetically, moving from the bottom to the top. This is termed *scrolling*.

What if there are more files than lines on the screen? The directory will continue to scroll filenames up and off the top of the screen until it reaches the end, where it lists the total number of files and amount of free disk space as shown in Figure 3–17. But what if we want to see the files that have already scrolled past?

FIGURE 3 – 17 The directory listing ends by showing the total number of files and amount of free disk space.

Volume in drive A is MS330PP01
Directory of A:\

4201	CPI	17089	7-24-87	12:00a
5202	CPI	459	7-24-87	12:00a
ANSI	SYS	1647	7-24-87	12:00a
APPEND	EXE	5794	7-24-87	12:00a
ASSIGN	COM	1530	7-24-87	12:00a
ATTRIB	EXE	10656	7-24-87	12:00a

DISPLAY	SYS	11259	7-24-87	12:00a
DRIVER	SYS	1165	7-24-87	12:00a
EDLIN	COM	7495	7-24-87	12:00a
EXE2BIN	EXE	3050	7-24-87	12:00a
FASTOPEN	EXE	3888	7-24-87	12:00a
FDISK	COM	48919	7-24-87	12:00a
FIND	EXE	6403	7-24-87	12:00a
FORMAT	COM	11671	7-24-87	12:00a
GRAFTABL	COM	6136	7-24-87	12:00a
GRAPHICS	COM	13943	7-24-87	12:00a
JOIN	EXE	9612	7-24-87	12:00a
KEYB	COM	9041	7-24-87	12:00a
LABEL	COM	2346	7-24-87	12:00a
MODE	COM	15440	7-24-87	12:00a
MORE	COM	282	7-24-87	12:00a
NLSFUNC	EXE	3029	7-24-87	12:00a
PRINT	COM	8995	7-24-87	12:00a
RECOVER	COM	4268	7-24-87	12:00a
SELECT	COM	4132	7-24-87	12:00a
SORT	EXE	1946	7-24-87	12:00a
SUBST	EXE	10552	7-24-87	12:00a
SYS	COM	4725	7-24-87	12:00a

34 File(s)   5120 bytes free

FIGURE 3 – 18   Typing DIR/W, which stands for directory/wide, displays the files horizontally, in rows of five, across the screen.

```
A:\>dir/w

 Volume in drive A is CON_VER200
 Directory of  A:\

COMMAND  COM    ANSI     SYS    DRIVER   SYS    VDISK    SYS    ASSIGN   COM
ATTRIB   EXE    CHKDSK   COM    DISKCOMP COM    DISKCOPY COM    DU       EXE
FC       COM    FDISK    EXE    FIND     EXE    FORMAT   COM    GRAFTABL COM
GRAPHICS COM    JOIN     EXE    KEYBFR   COM    KEYBGR   COM    KEYBIT   COM
KEYBSP   COM    KEYBUK   COM    LABEL    COM    MODE     COM    MORE     COM
PRINT    COM    RECOVER  COM    REPLACE  EXE    SELECT   COM    SETMODE  EXE
SHARE    EXE    SORT     EXE    SUBST    EXE    SYS      COM    TREE     COM
XCOPY    EXE    APPEND   COM    TESTBUG  COM    EPSON    TXT    WORDPROC
SPRED           DBMS
       42 File(s)     29696 bytes free
```

DOS provides us with two options. One, we can type the command DIR/P, for *pause*, and the screen will display the first 25 lines of text. Press the Enter key a second time and another 25 lines are displayed. Two, we can type DIR/W, which stands for *wide,* and DOS will display the files horizontally, in rows of five, across the screen. Try these commands yourself, as shown in Figure 3–18.

FORMAT   All disk drives do not work in exactly the same way; therefore, the blank disks you buy must be formatted for the type of personal computer you use. FORMAT is a command that **formats** or creates an electronic pattern on the floppy disk. This pattern divides the disk into *tracks* and *sectors,* where specific parts of application programs and data will later be stored. Tracks are concentric rings, like growth rings in a tree, while sectors are like slices of a pie. Once a disk is formatted, it can be *read from* and *written to* by your computer. When data is written, it's put on certain tracks within certain sectors; then, when you want to read it, the disk drive searches the appropriate sectors and tracks to find it again. Hard disk drives must be formatted, too, but this has often been done for you by the computer manufacturer or retailer. You should not attempt to format a hard disk drive unless you are very certain you know what you're doing.

Take out a new, unused floppy disk. We will format it so that we can store our work files on it; this is known as making a **data disk.** When using the FORMAT command, it's important to specify the disk drive containing the disk we want to format. Since we have our DOS disk in drive A and don't want to format it, type:

FORMAT B:

Now press the Enter key, and you will see the message, "Insert disk in drive B and strike any key when ready." Insert a brand new floppy disk in drive B and touch a key such as Enter. The disk will be formatted, and when the process is finished, you will see a message telling you that formatting is complete and how much space is available, in bytes.

The FORMAT command both prepares a blank disk for use with your computer system and erases any programs or data already stored on that disk.

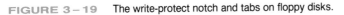

FIGURE 3 – 19   The write-protect notch and tabs on floppy disks.

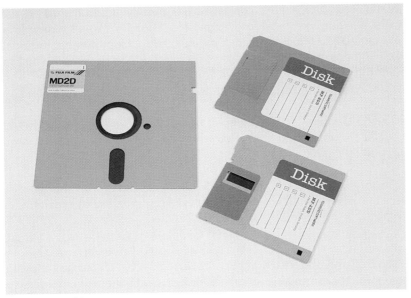

D. Dempster/Offshoot

For that reason, disks come with a write-protect feature. **Write-protect** is a way to prevent a disk or tape from being written to. On a 5¼-inch disk, there is a notch on the right side of the disk, as shown in Figure 3 – 19. When the notch is covered with a tab, the disk cannot be written to. Sometimes, program disks have no write-protect notch to prevent accidental erasure. The 3½-inch disk has a plastic tab that slides open for write-protection.

It is also important that you specify the correct disk drive for the disk you are formatting. If you were to simply type FORMAT, you would erase your DOS program disk in drive A. This is because you didn't specify a drive, so DOS assumes you mean the default drive, which is generally drive A. **Default** means the computer system makes an assumption when no specific choice is given. This is yet another good reason to write-protect your disks. The FORMAT command could erase your entire hard disk just as easily! Both cases underscore the importance of making copies of disks — our next topic.

DISKCOPY   The DISKCOPY command copies the entire contents of one disk to another. Leaving your DOS program disk in drive A and the newly formatted disk in drive B, type:

```
DISKCOPY A: B:
```

and press Enter. The disk in drive A is called the *source* disk, and the disk in drive B is called the *target* disk. The correct DOS syntax is that the first drive designation (A) is the drive you are copying *from,* and the second is the drive you are copying *to.*

Certain hidden files make a disk bootable or able to awaken the personal computer. A **hidden file** contains software information that is the copy-righted property of the computer company; we have no need to gain access to these hidden files. If the disk we were copying from contained the hidden files, they will be copied along with all the others, thus making the new disk bootable as well. The DISKCOPY command has another useful feature. If the target disk has not been previously formatted, DISKCOPY will format it as well. When DISKCOPY is finished, a message asks, "Copy another diskette? (Y/N)." You can make another copy of the same disk in drive A, or you can insert another disk to copy. If you are finished, type N, then press Enter, and you will be returned to the DOS prompt, ready to issue a new command.

Changing Drives   Now is a good time to learn how to change drives. We'll be able to see if the files were successfully copied. Let's change from drive A to drive B by typing:

`B:`

and pressing Enter. You'll see the prompt B> appear on the command line. Now type:

`DIR`

to get the file listing and total number of bytes remaining. If your disk copying was successful, the information about the disk in drive B should be identical to that of the disk in drive A. Now type:

`A:`

and press Enter to return to the A drive.

So far, we've learned some commands that apply to disks. Now let's learn some that apply to files.

COPY   The COPY command is a much more flexible command than DISKCOPY. It allows you to copy a single file, a group of files, or all the files on a disk. Take the copy of your DOS program disk out of drive B and insert a new disk; format it if necessary. Now, let's copy a single file named ANSI.SYS from drive A. Type:

`COPY A:ANSI.SYS B:ANSI.SYS`

and press Enter. You'll hear the disk drives spin and then see the message "(1) file copied."

For the sake of clarity, we've shown you the exact command syntax for copying a file. In actuality, however, you don't have to type the A drive designation; if you do not, DOS assumes you mean the A drive, the default drive. On a hard disk drive system, the default drive designation is the C drive or hard disk. Default drives may be changed but for safety and consistency, the A drive should always be your default floppy drive and the C drive your default hard disk drive. Further, you don't have to retype the filename after B: because DOS assumes you want to retain the same filename. Therefore, we could simply type:

`COPY ANSI.SYS B:`

then press Enter and achieve the same results.

We can copy a group of files quickly and easily by using a special DOS feature called a wildcard. A **wildcard** is a character — either an asterisk (*) or a question mark (?) — that serves as a substitute for one or more characters when working with files with similar or identical filenames. We're going to use the asterisk (*) wildcard to copy all the files that end with the filename extension .SYS. Type:

```
COPY *.SYS B:
```

and press Enter. The asterisk tells DOS you don't care what the filename is, you want to copy all the files with the .SYS filename extension. You'll see "(4) files copied" appear on the screen.

Next, we'll take the asterisk wildcard one step further and copy *all* the files from the A drive to the B drive. Type:

```
COPY *.* B:
```

and press Enter. All the files, with the exception of the hidden files mentioned in DISKCOPY, are copied. This is an important difference between these two copy commands. The COPY command will not copy the hidden files that create a bootable disk.

DELETE Now that we know how to copy, let's learn how to delete files. The DELETE command eliminates an unwanted file from a disk, thereby making room for new file storage. When typing, DELETE can be abbreviated DEL.

The DEL command syntax performs identically to COPY; we can delete a single file or, using the asterisk (*) wildcard, a group of files, or all files. Just for practice, delete all the files on the disk in drive B using the following commands:

```
DEL B: *.COM
DEL B: *.EXE
DEL B: *.SYS
```

Type DIR and press Enter after each deletion to observe the process. DOS has another command, called ERASE, that works the same as DELETE. Use the ERASE command (all you need to type are the first three letters, ERA) to delete the remaining files on the disk in B drive, one at a time. Don't forget to press Enter!

RENAME Since a DOS filename is only eight characters long, we often must abbreviate a name or make it unintentionally difficult to understand. Later, however, we might think of a filename that is easier to remember or that better identifies the file contents. The RENAME command allows us to change the file's filename, its filename extension, or both. The RENAME command can be abbreviated REN; type:

```
REN OLDFILE.301 NEWFILE.301
```

and press Enter. As a general rule, only rename files that you have created, such as word processing data files. It's usually not a good idea to rename DOS files or other application program files. For example, renaming a word processing program's file extension from WP.EXE to WP.XXX would render it a nonexecutable file. In other words, the word processing program would not load and run. Just how does an application program load and run? That is the topic we will explore next.

D I S K b y t e

Issuing Commands on Other Types of Personal Computers

The Apple II personal computer uses an operating system called DOS that is very similar to MS-DOS. It has both command line and menu characteristics.

CATALOG, like DIR, lists the files on a disk.

INIT formats a blank diskette for use; you can create a greeting program at the same time by typing:

```
INIT Welcome to a work ses-
sion with your Apple II!
```

Then, every time you use this disk, you'll see this greeting message.

```
COPY or COPYA are the same
as DISKCOPY.
```

A program called FILEM is used to work with files. Once in FILEM, you type FID and a menu appears:

```
<1> COPY FILES
<2> CATALOG
<3> SPACE ON DISK
```

```
<4> UNLOCK FILES
<5> LOCK FILES
<6> DELETE FILES
```

and so forth.

The RENAME command is the same on the Apple II and DOS.

The Apple Macintosh has a graphic interface that relies on the mouse to issue many commands. Refer to Figure 3–20 as you study the following commands.

The DIR command is a screen filled with boxes or windows that contain graphic file folders (which resemble manila file folders) and files (which resemble a typed piece of paper). Using the mouse, you move the arrow to the folder or file, then press the mouse button (called *clicking*) twice. If you "open" a folder, it shows the files within. If you open a file, you can read what's in it. You can also change the interface from icons to filename, date, and other selections by clicking the View selection on the menu bar.

The ERASE command from the Special menu formats disks.

To COPY a disk, you click on the disk to be copied from and, using the mouse, move it until it covers the disk you want to copy to. Release the mouse button and the disk will be copied. This is often called *click and drag*.

Changing drives is simple; you simply double click on the disk you want to change to.

To COPY a file, you can select the DUPLICATE command from the File menu, or click and drag the file to the disk.

To DELETE a file, you click and drag it to the Trash can icon at the lower-right corner of the screen. (However, if you click and drag a *disk* to the trash can, it ejects the disk from the drive.)

To RENAME a file, you click on the current filename, then hit the Backspace key to delete it. Now, type in the new name and press the Return key or click the mouse. ◼

Using Application Programs

Once the operating system is loaded into the computer's main memory, we can remove the DOS disk and load the application program. In most dual floppy disk systems, the program disk is inserted into the A drive and the data disk, where our files are stored, is inserted into the B drive. On a hard disk drive system, both the program and data files may be stored on the hard disk or C drive. Alternately, programs may be stored on the C drive and data files on a disk in the A drive. Many application programs allow you to create separate directories, one for the program and one for the data files, which often makes it more convenient to find your files. Chapters 4 through 6 explain how to use the most popular personal computer applications: word processing, spreadsheet, and database management systems software.

FIGURE 3 – 20   Using operating systems commands on a Macintosh.

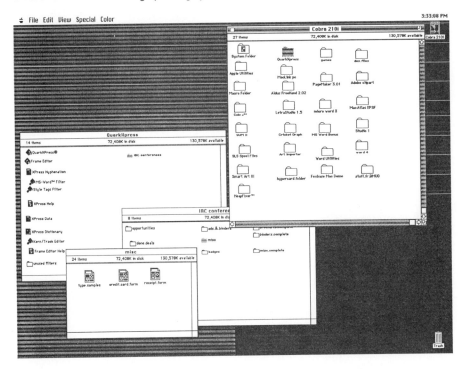

Ending a Work Session

Learning how to properly end a work session with your personal computer is as important as knowing how to begin one. If you are working with an application, you must properly save your files before exiting the program. To **save a file** means to store the data you have created on a disk so that you can work with it again at another time. These procedures are explained in more detail in the applications chapters.

The first and most important step in ending a work session is to make protective copies of your work. The process of making extra, or duplicate, copies of your programs and files for safekeeping is called **backup**. The copy of DOS you made using DISKCOPY is a backup disk. You should apply the adhesive label that comes with your new disks and identify it as a copy of DOS. This becomes your *working copy* that you use every day; put the original away for safekeeping. (See the DISKbyte, "Tips for Keeping your Programs and Data Safe," for more suggestions.)

Whether you are working in DOS or an application, your floppy disks should be removed from the drives before turning off the power. Make sure the disk drive indicator light is off, assuring you that the disk is not in use. If the light is on, you run the risk of harming the disk or corrupting the data stored there. If your personal computer has a hard disk drive, there is a special DOS program you can use to safely shut down the system. Just as we *powered up* when we began our work session, shutting the power off is often called *powering down*.

DISKbyte

Tips for Keeping Your Programs and Data Safe

It's expensive when lack of care results in repairing or replacing your personal computer. It's worse when carelessness means losing your personal computer's data. All the software and all the files you create are extremely vulnerable. Follow our advice and avoid tears!

- Never use the original program disk that the software publisher provides. Make a copy for daily use and store the original in a safe place.
- Never remove a floppy disk from the disk drive if the indicator light (usually red, green, or amber) is on. The light indicates that the drive is using the disk; you could lose or damage data if you remove the disk.
- Make backup copies of everything you create. If you use a hard disk drive, copy your work onto floppies once a day or once a week,

depending on how frequently you use it. If your hard disk fails, you still have all your work. Unfortunately, many people do not become advocates of the backup procedure until they have an accident and lose all their work. We repeat: *Many people do not become advocates of the backup procedure until they have an accident and lose all their work.* A power surge or failure, a solid bump on a disk drive, or an accidental spill may destroy months or years of stored data. Being able to restore it from a backup disk may keep you sane.
- Store backups in a safe place. Some people keep their original program disks and backups in another physical location, such as a safety deposit box, at home (or at the office), at a friend's, or in a fireproof safe. If a fire or flood wipes you out, your

data is still secure. Large banks back up their computers every 12 hours and ship the backups to a remote secure site, such as a concrete bunker, in armored trucks. Clearly, banks take backing up seriously; shouldn't you?
- Print out copies of your files. This is called **hard copy,** and is another way to assure you have a backup. If you lose data on a disk, at least you can retype it. Again, keep your hard copy printouts in a safe place.

No one can guarantee the continued health of your personal computer, nor that you will never lose any data. But you can limit your losses if you (1) take your time, (2) do things carefully, and (3) follow these guidelines. Your authors have sometimes learned all of the above from experience. In your case, we hope a word to the wise is sufficient.

According to computer service and repair technicians, the most common hardware problem people encounter with their personal computers is an unplugged power cord. Often, the plug has wiggled loose from the wall socket or from the socket on the back of the computer. Next most common is circuits that have been burned up by a power surge or electricity brownout. Service and repair technicians advise everyone to buy a high-quality surge protector and line filter power strip that the personal computer, monitor, and printer can all be plugged into.

The technicians say the most common software problems are (1) the disk is inserted into the drive upside down, and (2) the disk is inserted but the drive door latch is not locked in place.

Now you know how DOS works with the personal computer to carry out your commands as well as the basic operations of your personal computer.

You can see how the software and hardware, working under your direction, comprise a computer system. Regardless of their size, all computers use the basic principles you've learned here.

1. What are the two ways you can boot a personal computer?

2. Why is it important to understand the DOS syntax?

3. What is an important difference between the DISKCOPY and COPY commands?

4. What does the wildcard allow you to do?

5. What are the terms DOS uses to identify the "from" and "to" disk drives?

6. When you don't use a disk drive designation, what does DOS assume?

7. What are the names commonly used for the two types of floppy disks used with an application program?

8. What steps should you always take before powering down?

MEMORY CHECK

ETHICS

Computers have brought a new definition of right and wrong behavior, or ethics, to the world. The ethical use of a computer generally means not inflicting harm or loss on another. For example, it is considered unethical to make copies of a software program owned and copyrighted by another. This is called **software piracy.** It is unethical to gain access to other people's computer systems without their express permission. It is unethical to read someone else's files, such as those of a welfare recipient or a doctor's patient, unless it is your job to do so. And it is unethical—and illegal—to damage or destroy programs or data—property—on someone else's computer.

Yet all these things happen, and often without consequence to the perpetrator. Computer "clubs" are often formed so that people can gather and make illegal copies of software programs. There are stories of supposedly brilliant teenagers who use their personal computers to illegally gain access to someone else's computer and destroy files. Several of these people have been tried and convicted for such crimes. Employees, and even students, have read other people's personal files on disks, when they would never think of reading a letter in another person's desk drawer.

All these acts are unethical and, in some cases, illegal as well. Often, there is an "Everybody's doing it, so why don't I?" attitude associated with these acts. Sometimes it's hard to behave ethically when such behavior is neither encouraged nor rewarded. Your own principles must guide you, but when in doubt, ask yourself these questions: Would I steal a book from the library? Would I break into someone's home? Would I read someone's private correspondence? If the answer to these questions is no, then the same should apply in computer situations.

CAREERbyte

Michael Dell: Starting a Computer Business in a College Dorm Room

It is very popular in the computer industry to create a story about the company birthplace—especially if it's in a garage. But Michael Dell, 19 years old, started his computer company with $1,000 in his dorm room at the University of Texas in Austin. Michael sensed a need for low-cost personal computers that retail stores weren't addressing, and it paid off. That was in 1984; today, Michael Dell's office at Dell Computer Corporation is on the top floor of his own building, atop a hill that allows him a view of his old campus. Dell Computer is one of the 10 top personal computer companies in the world, and Michael is one of the 100 wealthiest Texans.

Michael's success was no fluke. He was avidly interested in personal computers and studied the market. He saw that retailers reaped a great profit on each computer but provided few services after the sale—something he believed new users needed. His strategy was simple: buy the parts, assemble the computers, and sell them direct to individuals and businesses.

Courtesy of Dell Computer Corporation

But equally important, Dell offered service and support to every customer. In fact, Dell's service and support are so good that the company has built its advertising campaign around the slogan, "So how come you never call?" But the proof is there, too; Dell computers have consistently ranked number one in corporate customer satisfaction polls. What's more, Dell computers win industry awards for price and performance, year after year.

Once his mail-order business was established, Michael added a telemarketing division to sell computers over the phone. That was followed by a direct sales force, which calls on corporate clients. Dell computers aren't sold only in the United States, either; the company has subsidiaries in Canada, England, France, Sweden, and Germany.

In person, Michael is a quiet but hard-working man, putting in 16 long business hours a day. He keeps his private life very private, and acknowledges the contributions of others in making Dell Computer a success. "This company is 1,200 people; this company is 16 vice presidents; this company is five directors; this company is a quarter-billion dollar company that has a lot of people behind it. It is not a one-person company," he says.

His parents characterize him as "curious, very creative and very determined" as a child. One of his employees calls him "unusual," and says, "Every company talks about taking care of the customer—it's like God, mother, and apple pie. But Michael actually means it."

SUMMARY

1. *Identify the most popular types of personal computers and explain the best way to work with one.* A personal computer system is one that fits on a desk top and is designed to be used by one person at a time. There are several different types, or brands, of personal computers made by companies such as Apple and IBM. Personal computers that work like certain IBM models are called PC-compatibles, and are made by companies such as Compaq, Epson, Tandy, and Zenith.

2. *Describe different types of personal computer configurations.* Personal computers come in different configurations, which determines the complexity and sophistication of the tasks they are able to perform. The hardware elements that change a configuration include the monitor, the quality of the video display, the amount of RAM, the number and type of floppy and hard disk drives, and other devices such as the printer.

3. *Identify the characteristics of different human-computer interfaces.* The way people interact with the computer is through the human-computer interface. There are three kinds of human-computer interfaces: the command line, the menu, and the graphic interface. Each has advantages; some systems allow you to use more than one interface, depending on your proficiency with the computer.

4. *Explain the way DOS organizes files and directories.* The operating system provides the instructions that make personal computers perform tasks.

DOS is an integrated set of programs that provide access to the CPU and the peripherals that allow us to perform a number of important tasks when working with applications. Files are the primary unit of data storage in personal computers. Files have filenames and are grouped into directories, such as the root directory or various subdirectories. DOS must be loaded into the computer; once it is, we can issue instructions at the prompt, which is found on the command line. The cursor shows us where the prompt is located.

5. *Describe the steps involved in working with DOS.* There are several ways to boot DOS and thus begin a work session: the cold boot and the warm boot. Booting works somewhat differently, depending on whether you are using a floppy disk or a hard disk. Commands are the way we issue instructions or perform tasks with the computer system. It is important to enter these commands in the proper syntax, or language, that DOS will understand. The key to working successfully with a personal computer is to take your time and do everything carefully.

6. *List some of the commonly used DOS commands.* DOS commands allow us to perform work and solve problems with the personal computer. Some commands list files; some start application programs; others prepare disks for use. Some commonly used DOS commands include DIR, FORMAT, DISKCOPY, COPY, DELETE, and RENAME.

KEY TERMS

backup, p. 85
boot, p. 71
command, p. 69
command line, p. 75
command line interface, p. 69
configuration, p. 64
cursor, p. 75
data disk, p. 80
default, p. 81
directory, p. 73
DOS (disk operating system), p. 63

file, p. 72
filename, p. 72
format, p. 80
graphic interface, p. 69
hard copy, p. 86
hard disk drive, p. 67
hidden file, p. 81
human-computer interface, p. 69
icon, p. 70
kilobyte, p. 66
loading, p. 74
megabyte, p. 66

menu-driven interface, p. 69
operating system, p. 63
PC-compatible, p. 63
personal computer (PC), p. 62
program disk, p. 77
prompt, p. 74
root directory, p. 73
save, p. 85
software piracy, p. 87
subdirectory, p. 73
wildcard, p. 82
write-protect, p. 81

REVIEW AND DISCUSSION QUESTIONS

1. What makes a PC-compatible compatible?

2. What are the hardware elements that make up a personal computer configuration?

3. When might it be necessary to have a fully configured personal computer?

4. What would provide a clue as to where to locate a difficult-to-find power switch?

5. What specific hardware and software tasks does DOS perform?

6. What is the primary unit of data storage in DOS?

7. What is the name of the place where primary units of data storage are stored on a disk?

8. Name and describe the three types of files DOS uses.

9. Describe two ways of moving the cursor on the screen.

10. When is it wise to write-protect a disk? When would you not?

11. Describe several advantages of the hard disk over the floppy disk.

12. Rank the three human-computer interfaces according to your preference, and briefly explain what you like or dislike about each one.

13. Why is it important to understand DOS syntax?

14. What personal computer does not require that you know its operating system syntax?

15. What key must you always press after issuing a command in DOS?

16. What do you think it would be like if you did not have to press a key on issuing a command?

17. Why is it important to understand default drive designations?

18. When both the program and data files are on a hard disk, how can you keep them separate from one another?

19. When, and under what circumstances, should you back up your disks?

20. Describe how you personally would keep your data private, safe from the scrutiny of others.

ISSUES

1. Ethics is a subject of concern on all levels of society. Is it true when it comes to violating the ethical uses of computers, "everybody's doing it"? Read some current articles on software piracy and unauthorized computer usage, then compile a list of questions concerning ethical computer use. Take a random survey or, if your professor permits it, survey your class on their computer ethics. Is everybody doing it? What is it that they're doing? What is your assessment of today's attitude toward the ethical use of computers?

2. Computers are a significant investment in terms of money. There's the computer, the printer, and the software to buy, plus accessories and other items. But the computer also requires a significant investment of your time, to learn the hardware, the operating system, and the applications. This could be literally hundreds, perhaps thousands, of hours. Yet the personal computer industry is still growing and changing rapidly. Given this investment in time, how would you feel if your hardware suddenly became obsolete? What if the maker suddenly introduced, for example, a new operating system with a significantly changed human-computer interface that you had to learn all over again? What if the software company came out with a new, improved version of your favorite application but you found it was riddled with programming errors that were destroying your files?

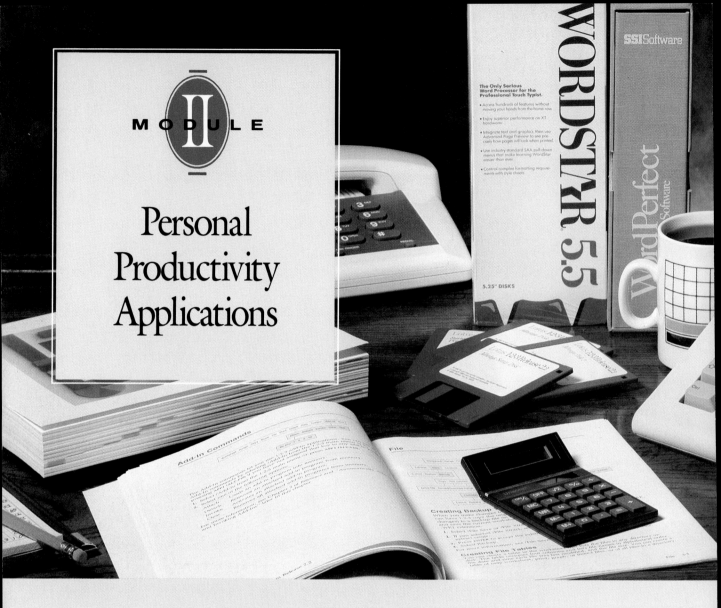

MODULE II

Personal Productivity Applications

Personal productivity means using the personal computer to accomplish tasks and solve problems better and more quickly than you could using conventional means. Personal productivity applications are software programs designed specifically for certain tasks or problems. The next three chapters show you how to use the most popular personal productivity applications: word processing, the spreadsheet, and the database management system.

Chapter 4 discusses word processing, a program that lets you work with *ideas* and *text* to create a variety of documents: memos, letters, reports, poetry, short stories, magazine articles, books, and more. Word processing allows you to write, edit, revise, store, and print documents more effectively than you could using a typewriter. You can make your documents look more attractive, or you can automatically check them for spelling and grammar accuracy.

Chapter 5 discusses the spreadsheet, a program designed to analyze mathematical or financial situations and produce possible solutions in a matrix or table. It combines the accountant's paper ledger

sheet, the pencil, and the electronic calculator. Although the spreadsheet can display text, its principal task is performing calculations. An additional advantage is its ability to present numerical data graphically or in pictures.

Chapter 6 discusses the database management system, a program that allows you to store, organize, and retrieve information stored in a database. The database can be something as simple as an address book or as complex as the personnel records for a huge corporation. A database management system can store both text and numbers but its primary purpose is to add, organize, modify, and display the stored data.

To summarize, word processing lets you create text in the form of documents that others will read. The spreadsheet lets you create financial records and analyses that involve mathematical equations and formulas. The database management system lets you store and maintain records in the form of text and numbers. The following chapters explain each application's uses and advantages in more detail.

CHAPTER 4

Word Processing

CHAPTER OUTLINE

Writing in the Modern World
The Back Pages of Written Communication
What Is Word Processing?
Basic Word Processing Features
   Using Files
   The Word Processing Screen
   Editing Modes
   DISKbyte: Word Processing and Writing
A Word Processing Work Session
   Getting Started
   Entering Text
   Commands
   Revising Text
   DISKbyte: Word Processing Tips
Using Advanced Word Processing Features
   Spelling Checker
   DISKbyte: Spelling Checkers Can Be Deadly
   Thesaurus
   Outliner
   Table of Contents Generator
   Index Generator
Word Processing Applications
   Mail/Merge
   Manuscript Preparation
The Ever-Evolving Word Processing Program
Ethics
   *CAREERbyte: How to Get Rich in the Software
     Industry*
Summary
Key Terms
Review and Discussion Questions
Issues

OBJECTIVES

After reading and studying this chapter, you
should be able to:

1. Explain the advantages of word processing over
   typewriting.
2. Describe how word processing works and how
   it uses files.
3. Explain the steps in entering, formatting,
   revising, saving, and printing text.
4. Describe some of the advanced word processing
   tools and how they are used.
5. Describe some word processing applications.

WRITING IN THE MODERN WORLD

Mark Twain once wrote, "The reports of my death are greatly exaggerated." Similarly, the reports of the death of the printed word are greatly exaggerated. No matter how hard companies try to sell people on reading from a computer screen, most still want a printed page.

Dave Barry is a 20th-century Mark Twain. Before becoming a nationally syndicated newspaper columnist and humorist, he taught business writing in corporations for eight years. This experience may be where he developed his sense of humor; for example, consider this excerpt from one of his articles entitled "Effective Writing, Sort of":

Courtesy Crown Publishers Inc.

> When you walk into a big company, you see all these people peering intently at their little computer screens, and you think, "GOSH! This is so ORGANIZED!" What you don't know is that the reason they're staring so intently at the screens is that the computer has just notified them that they have shipped 60,000 highly sophisticated miniature electric motors to a convent in rural Brazil. They are pounding away at the keyboards feverishly, trying to correct the problem, but in so doing they are inadvertently issuing maternity leaves to every employee whose first name ends in a vowel.

Dave goes on to explain how this is handled with business correspondence:

> These events will cause hundreds, maybe thousands of memos to be generated. Everyone who could conceivably be held responsible will write at least one memo to defend himself, and many people will write several. All these memos will circulate for awhile, until they reach critical mass and clot together in the form of files on the computer.

In another column, Dave offers advice on how to become a writer:

> First of all, you must understand that there's no substitute for talent and plain old hard work. If you want to succeed as a writer, you'll just have to sit yourself down and write a really brilliant novel, such as *Moby Dick,* then sell it to a publisher who doesn't realize it has already been published. This ought to be easy. Nobody has read *Moby Dick* for 60 years. College students still buy it, but only for the purpose of highlighting it with yellow markers and writing traditional college-student notes in the margins, such as "MAN VS. NATURE."

Dave Barry clearly is a funny guy, and he has a lot of fun writing as well. His newspaper columns have earned him a Pulitzer prize for social commentary. You may not have an opportunity to earn your living writing humorous newspaper columns, but it is highly likely you will have to write in your profession. This chapter is intended to help make that task easier by showing you how to use word processing.

THE BACK PAGES OF WRITTEN COMMUNICATION

The history of written communication is very long. It goes all the way back to ancient Egypt, when people painstakingly chiseled the hard surfaces of stones to record the details of their commerce and the facts of their daily lives. We have an expression dating back to those times: "Carved in stone" means that something is set, recorded, meant to last through the ages. Indeed, the Egyptians' toil left us a clear picture of their lives but at a tremendous cost.

Methods of writing evolved through the thousands of years leading up to our time. Eventually, quills replaced chisels and pens and pencils replaced quills. Writing became easier but was still far from easy.

When Christopher Latham Sholes invented the typewriter in the 1860s, he advanced the process of writing considerably. However, he had to keep pace with available technology. Typing too fast caused the typewriter's keys to get tangled up. So Sholes designed the typewriter keyboard to slow down the writing process. Keyboards designed since then, such as the Dvorak design shown in Figure 4–1, allow people to type faster, but so many of us learned on the old typewriter keyboards that they remain the standard.

Until computers came into widespread use, many writers still used pencils to compose their rough drafts. They typed a final draft when they had their work in more polished form. Those with poor typing skills spent hours retyping to produce error-free final drafts. Up until the last decade or so, this was how most of us created our formal written communications. Then came the PC and word processing. In this chapter, we'll show you how computers make writing easier than any tools we've used before.

We'll begin by giving you an overview of word processing application software, beginning with basic features. Then we'll demonstrate how to use a word processing application with a hands-on session. Next, we'll look at advanced tools, the writer's aids developed to enhance our word processing capabilities. We'll also show you some ways people use this popular software program.

Word processing has continued to evolve since the days of the first word processors. Today, there are hundreds of word processing software programs available, for a wide variety of purposes. At the end of this chapter, we'll review the history of, and latest developments in, word processing.

WHAT IS WORD PROCESSING?

Word processing (WP) is using a software application to write, revise, format, save, and print text for letters, reports, manuscripts, and other written documents. Regardless of what you do when you first get your hands on a PC, chances are, sooner or later, you'll find yourself using a word processing application. This is confirmed by statistics: 65 to 75 percent of PC application software sold is for word processing.

The Word Processing Advantage

Word processing is a tool for working with ideas and text. Whether writing term papers or letters, composing the lyrics to a tune or creating a business

FIGURE 4–1 The QWERTY keyboard was designed to work around the limitations of mechanical typewriters. The Dvorak design puts the keys we use most in the "home key" positions.

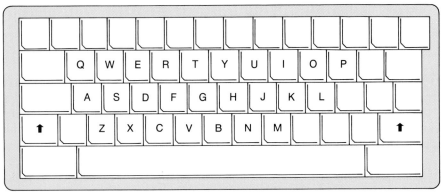

QWERTY Layout

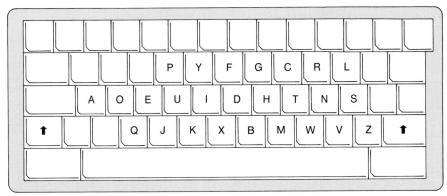

Dvorak Layout

memo, word processing helps us write more easily. This is because it has distinct advantages over other writing tools and methods. Let's examine the advantages of using word processing.

Writing Word processing makes writing easier for us in two ways. First, word processing automates many actions we perform manually on typewriters. For example, we can type continuously without inserting a carriage return at the end of each line of text because word processing automatically performs a word wrap by pushing our text to the next line. Also, we don't have to insert a new piece of paper at the end of each page, as we do with typewriters, because of a feature called scrolling, which continuously feeds us an electronic sheet of paper. We'll look at these and other ease-of-use features in the next section on basic features.

Many word processors give us a second advantage by incorporating writing tools such as spelling and grammar checkers, thesauruses, and outliners. Instead of turning to books for the help these tools can offer, we can use computerized versions of them quickly and easily. We call these tools writer's aids; we'll explore them further later in this chapter.

Revising   Several word processing features make revising, or editing, our writing easier. **Revising** is the process of checking, changing, and modifying text that you have written. It includes:

- Adding text.
- Deleting and undeleting portions of text.
- Searching for or replacing specific characters, words, or phrases.
- Moving and copying blocks of text.

We'll look at each of these features in detail in the basic features section that follows.

Another advantage to revising with word processing is the ability to create any number of **drafts,** a term used to describe successive versions of your document. When you write, whether you create a letter, a poem, or a term paper, you usually edit the material once or twice, making changes and corrections. If you write with a pencil, you may wear out a lot of erasers making changes, winding up with a final draft that's quite hard to read. If you use a typewriter, you may spend many hours typing and retyping to produce a good final draft. With word processing, each draft is an uncluttered version of your work, always available to serve as the final draft.

Formatting   Formatting is the process of emphasizing and arranging text on the screen or the printed page (not to be confused with formatting disks). Word processing allows us to format every element of our written documents. We format *words* by underlining, boldfacing, or italicizing. We format *lines* by centering text and setting margins and tab spaces. We format *pages* by setting line spacing, justification, and page breaks. We format *documents* by setting page numbering, headers, and footers.

We can do most of these things with typewriters; however, the word processing advantage is that many can be done automatically. With word processing, you can choose these format settings in advance and have your text follow them as you write. What makes word processing especially valuable is being able to change these settings whenever you want, so pages can be redesigned and reformatted automatically. Retyping is unnecessary.

Printing   At any point in the writing process, you can print what you have written. Printing lets you easily read your work by providing a printed, paper copy of each draft. When you finish and are ready for others to read it, printing allows you to make your writing look like an excellent typist has typed it.

Other writing tools require that we rewrite or retype the entire document to produce a revised draft. Word processing's printing capability lets us create a revised version of a document by rewriting only those portions we want to change. The longer the document, the greater this advantage can be.

MEMORY CHECK

1. What four writing functions do we perform with word processing?
2. List four actions we take in revising text.
3. What is a draft?
4. What is formatting?
5. Describe the word processing printing advantage.

BASIC WORD PROCESSING FEATURES

Word processing is used by people in many walks of life: architects, doctors, journalists, managers, office workers, and everyday people like you and us. Yet regardless of *what* they write, people use word processing in very similar ways. There are many features that allow us to work both creatively and efficiently with the words we write.

Using Files

We defined files in Chapter 3 as the basic unit of storage in most computers. You saw how files are used to save either programs or data. Like many applications, word processing uses files to save what we write. Each time we write, we create or open a file. Word processing programs often have a sample file on the disk that you can use for practice. If you have a sample file, use it now to help become oriented to the following features. Let's take a look at the word processing screen and examine some basic word processng features.

The Word Processing Screen

Most word processing screens are designed to look like a sheet of paper — with a few electronic improvements, of course! However, most of the screen is blank, waiting for you to fill it with text. The first and most important thing is to locate the cursor, for it tells you where you can begin entering text.

Cursor Movement   You learned about the cursor in Chapter 3. Word processing uses the cursor for the same purpose as DOS. The cursor is the blinking symbol in the work area on your screen that indicates where the next character you type will appear. When you begin working with a new file, it is usually found at the top left-hand corner of the screen.

Refer to the keyboard shown in Figure 4–2. The four arrow keys are used to move the cursor through the text on the screen. Some keyboards have specially designated arrow keys, while others use the numeric keypad keys numbered 2, 4, 6, and 8 for this purpose. The Num Lock key is a toggle key. A **toggle key** is so called because you press it to switch, or toggle, between two modes. The Num Lock key toggles between the numeric keys and the cursor movement keys. To see how this works, press it once and type the down arrow or 2 key; now press it again. Word processing also makes use of other toggle keys on a standard keyboard, such as the Caps Lock key.

Using the arrow keys alone moves the cursor one character at a time. Refer again to Figure 4–2. Word processing programs also use other keys, such as Control (Ctrl) and Alternate (Alt), in combination with the arrow keys. They move the cursor to the next word, sentence, line, paragraph, page, or even to the beginning or end of your document. These keys are very useful when revising text.

Status Line   The **status line** provides information about your word processing session at the top or bottom of the screen. The status line usually includes the name of the file in use and the page, line, column, and space the cursor presently occupies. Figure 4–3 is an example of a status line.

FIGURE 4 – 2   The arrow keys move the cursor one character at a time, and perform other cursor movement functions when used together with the Shift and Ctrl keys.

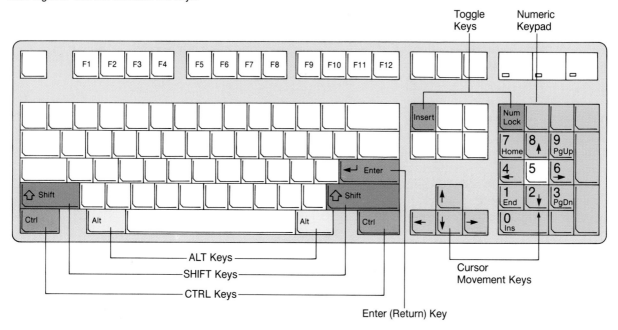

FIGURE 4 – 3   Most status lines show page, line, and cursor position or column numbers. Some add a document number and the name of the file being edited.

```
C:\WP50\FILES\TERM.100                 Doc 1 Pg 10 Ln 33 Pos 16
```

Word Wrap   When using an electric typewriter, you must press the carriage return key at the end of each line you type. **Word wrap** is a feature that automatically moves a word to the beginning of the next line if it will not fit at the end of the original line. This feature lets you type without stopping to look at the screen to decide if the typed line is too long. It saves keystrokes and makes writing a more natural process. However, when you wish to end a line manually — for example, to begin a new paragraph — pressing the Enter key inserts what is called a *hard return.* Then whatever you type next will appear on the following line.

Scrolling   The vertical movement of text on the screen is called **scrolling.** The term was borrowed from ancient days when people wrote on scrolls — long rolls of paper attached to round cylinders at each end. To read scrolls, people unrolled the paper from one cylinder as they rolled it up with the other, leaving text between the rolls exposed for viewing.

Word processing works similarly, as illustrated in Figure 4 – 4. Twenty-five lines are commonly displayed. The remainder of the document either

FIGURE 4 – 4   Scrolling combines an ancient reading technique with modern technology.

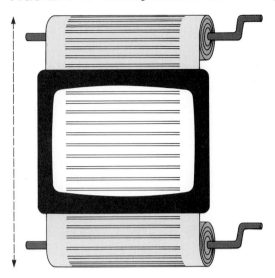

precedes what is shown or follows it. We can scroll through the text using the up and down arrow keys to move a line at a time, or the Page Up and Page Down keys to move a screen or a page at a time. Scrolling occurs automatically when we enter text. When you reach the bottom of the screen the text scrolls up, displaying the newly entered text one line at a time.

Editing Modes

Most word processing programs allow you to use one of two editing modes for entering text. In **Insert mode,** every character you type is placed at the position of the cursor, pushing all the text in front of the cursor ahead. Nothing you wrote before is deleted; new characters typed are inserted into existing text. In **Typeover mode,** every character you type replaces what was there before at the position of the cursor. Typeover mode, sometimes called Overstrike mode, deletes each old character as you type a new character. The Insert key is another toggle key and is commonly used to switch between insert and typeover mode. Figure 4 – 5 gives examples of insert and typeover modes.

Help

Sometimes we get lost, confused, or simply need more information on how to use an application. People who create software know this, so they invented **Help,** which contains instructions, tips, pointers, explanations, and guidance. It is always available while you are using the program, usually by pressing a key such as F1 or by clicking on the word "Help" in the menu. Help often provides information on current format settings, which keys perform specific tasks, detailed instructions on how to use advanced features, and more.

Figure 4 – 6 shows a portion of a word processor Help screen. Read it carefully; in most cases, it explains how to use the Help feature. It is especially important to note how to exit Help. Using Help saves time and helps you avoid frustrations, so it's good to get in the habit of using it.

FIGURE 4–5 These are before and after examples of typing in insert and typeover modes. In both cases, we typed the words *instead of* at the point of the word *or*. In insert mode, word wrap pushes the word *typeover* to the next line. In typeover mode, only the *r* of the word *typeover* remains.

```
Before:
Word processors let you choose between insert or typeover
modes.

After:
 Insert Mode:
 Word processors let you choose between insert instead ofor
 typeover modes.

 Typeover Mode:
 Word processors let you choose between insert instead ofr
 modes.
```

FIGURE 4–6 Help includes definitions of special keys and their functions.

```
Cancel
 Cancel
 Cancels the effect or operation of any function key that displays a prompt
 or menu. It will also stop the operation of a macro or merge before it is
 finished.

 Undelete
 When no other function is active, this key undeletes (restores) up to
 three deletions. A deletion is any group of characters or codes erased
 before the cursor is moved. WordPerfect temporarily inserts the most
 recent deletion at the cursor position. You can then restore the text or
 display the previous deletion.

Selection: 0                                    (Press ENTER to exit Help)
```

MEMORY CHECK

1. How are files used in word processing?
2. How do we move the cursor?
3. What is a toggle key?
4. What does the status line tell us?
5. Define insert and typeover editing modes.
6. Explain how word wrap works.
7. What is scrolling?
8. When and how do we use the Help feature?

DISKbyte

Word Processing and Writing

Robert B. Forest has had a distinguished 34-year career as a computer industry editor and journalist. For 10 years he was editor of *Datamation,* a computer industry magazine, and lived in Europe for 2½ years as a freelance writer. He ran his own public relations firm, Information Age, from a renovated mill in Connecticut, prior to retiring. Before his career in journalism, he was an English teacher. In the following excerpt from an article in *Information Center* magazine entitled "On Writing," Bob discusses writing from the computer perspective and concludes with a few humorous thoughts.

The process of writing is not altogether different from the process of computer programming. Both steps involve different steps or stages.

The first step in programming is to analyze the problem; in writing, that means defining the audience and the article's purpose. Next, the programmer designs the program; the writer creates an outline. Coding, or writing the program, is the same as putting words together or writing the article. The programmer debugs the program for errors, just as the writer edits and proofreads their writing. Finally, the programmer tests the program; the writer lets someone else review or read the article.

Defining the audience and purposes may be the most important step in writing—and the one most often ignored. When you have a writing assignment, give yourself not one deadline, but several. Give yourself at least a week from the time you start consciously considering your assignment and the date you start writing. And give yourself one week from the time you start writing until you have to turn it in.

On the day of the first deadline, you can take 15 to 30 minutes to think about it—maybe write down the salient characteristics of your audience and your purpose.

A week later you can start writing. After you have the first draft, take a day or so for someone else to review it and to incorporate any sensible changes that they suggest.

That's probably a distinct departure from how you approach writing tasks now. Most of us wait until the last minute to accomplish all the stages of the process. You generally don't write a program in one day. And writing, I maintain, is not all that different.

You've been patient—both of you. So I will reward you with some of Forest's Famous Rules of Writing:

- It's kind of important to be precise.
- Don't be negative.
- Passive (verb) voices should be avoided.[1]

A WORD PROCESSING WORK SESSION

Now that you understand word processing's basic features, let's put this knowledge to use. In this section, we'll walk you through the process of creating a simple word processing document. We'll begin by showing you how to get oriented, then we'll look at commands and demonstrate how to use them to perform the basic word processing functions.

There are differences in both hardware and software that determine how each word processing application works. IBM PCs and their compatibles work primarily with commands assigned to various keys. The Apple MacIntosh utilizes icons and a mouse. Despite these differences, both systems have the same basic word processing features.

---

[1] Robert B. Forest, "On Writing," *Information Center* (July 1987), pp. 71–75.

Getting Started

The first thing we do is power up the computer; if necessary, refer to the procedures for booting your personal computer in Chapter 3. Next, load the word processing program. If you are using a computer with two floppy disk drives, insert the word processing program disk in drive A and a data disk in drive B. If you are using a computer with a hard disk drive, follow the instructions for changing to the word processing subdirectory. Now, type the name of the executable file to start the program. In just a few seconds, you'll see the opening screen appear!

Depending on the program you're using, you may see a command line, a menu, or just a blank screen waiting for you to type in text. Some programs ask that you create a filename when you begin, while others don't request it until you have finished your work session. If yours is the former case, simply assign a filename at the prompt and press Enter; then you should have a screen ready to accept text. We're going to learn word processing by creating a term paper on the American Revolutionary War, so let's call our file TERM.100.

Entering Text

Once you have opened a file, you can begin writing, or *entering text* as we say in word processing. Until you choose to exit, everything you write will be stored in this file. Regardless of the nature of your writing, whether it is a poem, a short story, a play, a letter, a business memo, or a book-length manuscript, we call text prepared with word processing a **document.** Now let's take a look at the initial screen in Figure 4–7 and identify what we see.

Most of what you see is a blank screen; this is your work area for entering text. However, you probably see the status line either above or below the work area. As you already know, it contains information pertinent to your document. It shows the cursor location in the file; right now you're at the left

FIGURE 4–7   The word processing opening screen.

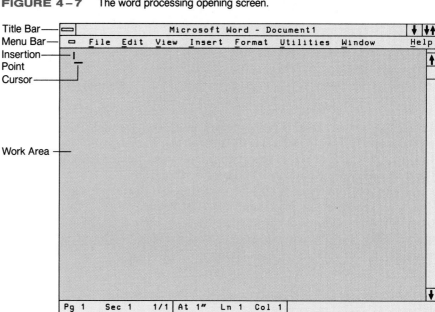

margin on line 1, page 1. Most word processing programs have a default setting of 80 characters across the screen, indented ten spaces or one inch for the left and right margins (to resemble a piece of typing paper). If you press the space bar a few times, you'll see the cursor move from left to right and the character number change, 11, 12, 13, 14, etc., in the status line. If you press Enter, you'll see the cursor move down a line and the line number change to 2.

Let's begin writing that history paper about the American Revolutionary War. To begin, you may want to set down some words and phrases that reflect your understanding of the topic. Some people are most comfortable jotting ideas on a piece of paper first, but another word processing advantage is that you can type in your thoughts and then easily modify or edit them. You don't have to feel like you've made a commitment to keeping things exactly as they first appear. We've done your library research for you, so type in the list shown in Figure 4–8.

Commands

Commands allow us to issue instructions to the word processing progam so that we may work with files or with the text within files. As you will see as you study this and the subsequent chapters on the spreadsheet and database management system, there is a similarity and consistency in commands across different applications. We have found that the best approach when working with a new application is to begin with the basic commands, then build upon them with more advanced commands as the specific need arises. Thus, you'll learn the basic word processing commands in this work session, then we'll explain some advanced commands in the section that follows. These basic commands are:

- *Format* text
- *Block editing* text
- *Delete* and *undelete* text
- *Search and replace* text
- *Save* a file
- *Retrieve* a file
- *Print* a file

FIGURE 4–8   A history paper idea list.

```
American Revolution
French and Indian Wars
Stamp Act of 1765
Restricting Colonial Industry
The Boston Massacre
The Boston Tea Party
Battle of Lexington and Concord
Paul Revere
George Washington
General Cornwallis and the French Army
Treaty of Paris


C:\WP\TERM.100                          Doc 1  Pg 1  Ln 1     Pos 10
```

FIGURE 4-9   Basic and advanced word processing commands.

File Manipulation	Cursor Movement	Deleting and Undeleting	Block Editing	Search and Replace	Formatting	Printing
Create	Arrow keys	Backspace	Move	Find	Appearance	Setting
Edit	Home	Delete	Copy	Search	Format	Setup
Retrieve	End	Insert	Delete	Substitute	Setup	Selection
Include	Page	Typeover	Append	Replace	Layout	Quality
Rename	Screen	Overstrike	Select	Global	Page	Attribute
Move	Up	Undelete	Highlight		Header	Font
Copy	Down	Undo	Cut		Footer	
Save	Left		Paste		Boldface	
Exit	Right		Uppercase		Italic	
Delete file	Word		Lowercase		Underline	
	Line					

Figure 4-9 shows the diversity of both basic and advanced word processing commands.

The keyboard **function** keys are often used to issue commands in word processing, as well as other applications. The 10 "F" keys, as they are often called, perform many or all the basic commands shown above. They are often used in conjunction with the Control, Alt, and Shift keys so they can perform more than 10 commands. Function keys are placed either horizontally across the top of the keyboard or to one side; Figure 4-10 shows the two most common IBM PC and PC-compatible function key layouts.

Format   **Format** is the command we use to organize and design text as it appears either on the screen or as it is printed. An example of simple formatting is indenting a paragraph, using the Tab key. Word processing also permits us to format the left and right margins; for example we normally use *left margin justify* so all the lines are justified, or aligned, on the left but are unjustified or ragged on the right. This is how a document typed on a standard typewriter, such as a business letter, appears. Similary, *right margin justify* aligns the right margin so that text looks just like it does on the textbook page you are currently reading.

Let's use the text we created to practice some additional formatting commands. First, let's use the command to *double space* the text. Press the function key marked Format, then select line spacing. As you can see, it says 1; select 2, then press Enter to issue the command. You may have to press the Enter key again to leave the Format menu and return to the text, so do that now. Your text should be double-spaced. You can triple-space and often quadruple-space as well.

Next, let's make the first line the title of your paper. Make sure you are in insert mode and that the cursor is located on the "A" in "American Revolution" then type the word "The" followed by a space. We'll learn a new cursor movement command now; hold down the Control key and press the left arrow key; you'll see the cursor jump back to the "T" or position 10. Let's *center* this line on the page by pressing the function key for center, then Enter. You should see "The American Revolution" centered on your screen.

FIGURE 4–10   The two most common keyboard and function key layouts.

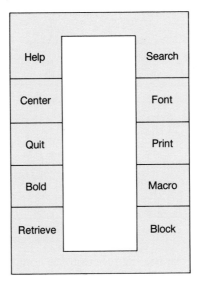

Help F1	Search F2	Center F3	Font F4	Quit F5	Print F6	Bold F7	Macro F8	Retrieve F9	Block F10	Save F11	Format F12

Block Editing   **Block editing** lets you mark a portion of the document so you can perform a number of text manipulation operations upon it. The process involves marking the beginning and end of the text you wish to work with, then issuing the command to perform the task. Block editing is commonly used to:

- Change the text appearance with various format commands.
- Copy or move text to another location in the file.
- Delete text.
- Save text in a separate file.

Block editing is sometimes referred to as **cut and paste,** since we "cut" the block out of the document and then "paste" it somewhere else.

There are two methods for marking, or defining, a block of text. One involves putting a special character at the beginning and end of the block. The other employs **highlighting,** which makes the text stand out either by using a different color or by using *reverse video* to switch the text and background.

We're going to use block editing to format your paper's title in **boldface.** First let's mark the block. Is the cursor on the "T" at the beginning of the line? Press the function key for Block; you'll see the message "Block on" appear on the screen. Use the Control key and right cursor key to highlight all three words. Your screen should look like the one in Figure 4–11. Now, press the function key for Bold and watch what happens. The title is set in boldface, the block message is gone, and our task is finished.

FIGURE 4–11   Examples of formatting for text emphasis.

```
                         The American Revolution
French and Indian Wars
Stamp Act of 1765
Restricting Colonial Industry
The Boston Massacre
The Boston Tea Party
Battle of Lexington and Concord
Paul Revere
George Washington
General Cornwallis and the French Army
Treaty of Paris
C:\WP\TERM.100                              Doc 1 Pg 1 Ln 1      Pos 54
```

We can use the function key commands, either by themselves or in conjunction with block editing, to underline text or put it in *italics*. You can practice formatting different words and text if you like, but it is also important to know how to convert boldface, underlining, or italics back to plain text. Refer to your word processing software reference manual, or use Help, to learn how to do this.

Revising Text

Any time we add text to a document or alter text within a document we are *revising*. At this point in our term paper all we have is a list of topics, so let's do some revising to expand it into some topic sentences and paragraphs. Enter the text as shown in Figure 4–12. Try using the arrow keys to scroll through your text (try them in combination with the Control key as well). This will also give you the opportunity to try out some new keys and commands.

Delete   If you make a mistake, use the Delete key to erase the character the cursor is resting on. The Backspace key erases characters behind the cursor. If you hold down the Control key and press the Backspace or Delete key, you'll erase the *word* the cursor is resting on.

You can also use block editing to **delete** text. This is useful when you have larger portions to delete, such as a line, sentence, or paragraph. Let's try this by pressing the function key to begin block editing, then highlighting the line, "Restricting Colonial Industry." Once it is highlighted, simply press the Backspace or Delete key. A message will appear on the screen asking you to confirm that you wish to delete this text. This is a precaution against accidentally deleting something, which you may come to appreciate in time! Press Y for yes and the line will be deleted.

Undelete   What if you accidentally deleted some text, whether you were using the block editing function or simply one of the deletion keys? Most word processors now have an **undelete,** or **undo,** feature. This allows you to restore portions of deleted text. In some cases, that may be limited to the last deletion; often it will restore deletions prior to that as well. To see how this works, press

FIGURE 4–12   Revising text.

The American Revolution

French and Indian Wars

The English believed the American colonies should help pay for the French and Indian Wars (1754–1763) because they were fought in defense of the colonies.

Stamp Act of 1765

The English were in need of additional revenues, partly because of fighting wars such as the French and Indian Wars. They decided to levy taxes on the colonies for the first time in history. They started with a molasses tax, then a sugar tax, then the Stamp Act, which taxed legal documents, newspapers, and almanacs. The colonists had no voice in these matters, and this became known as ''taxation without representation.''

Restricting Colonial Industry
The Boston Massacre

The Boston Tea Party

Samuel Adams organized the Boston Tea Party in 1773, an act of civil disobedience against the English intended to protest levying a duty on imported tea. Three hundred forty tea chests were tossed overboard into Boston Harbor.

Battle of Lexington and Concord

Paul Revere

George Washington

General Cornwallis and the French Army

Treaty of Paris

the function key for undelete (sometimes this is the same key used to cancel the last command you issued); you will see the line we just deleted reappear on the screen. Now follow the instructions to confirm that you want to undelete the text.

Search and Replace   These are the last commands we'll learn for working with text in a document. **Search** performs the task of finding a specific portion of text we've written. Search can find letters, numbers, or characters such as the @ or , or & and even the hard carriage return when you press Enter, in any combination. For this reason, we often refer to searching for *character strings*. **Replace** inserts a new word in place of the one we have searched.

Search is helpful in several ways. It can find errors in spelling or syntax, it can locate words that need to be capitalized, and it can quickly locate specific words, passages, or references in a large file. Let's search for the word "tax." Press the function key for Search, then at the prompt enter the word "tax" and press Enter. You'll see the first occurrence of the word appear highlighted on the screen; note how "tax" has been highlighted in the word "taxes." Press the Search function key again and again and you'll be taken to each subsequent occurrence.

FIGURE 4–13   Using the Search and Replace command to change "English" to "British."

```
                        The American Revolution
French and Indian Wars
   The English believed the American colonies should help pay for the French and In-
dian Wars (1754-1763) because they were fought in defense of the colonies.

Stamp Act of 1765
   The English were in need of additional revenues, partly because of fighting wars
such as the French and Indian Wars. They decided to levy taxes on the colonies for
the first time in history. They started with a molasses tax, then a sugar tax, then

   Replace with: British
```

Now let's see how the Search and Replace functions work together. Note that we've used the word "English" in our term paper; it should actually be "British," so let's change it. Word processing allows us to use search and replace in two ways: to stop at each occurrence and confirm the replacement, or to perform a global search and replace without our intervention. Since we know there won't be any exceptions, let's use the global function.

Press the function key for search and replace; first you'll have to type in "English" as the search word, then "British" as the replace word, as shown in Figure 4–13. Press the key to start the search and in the wink of an eye, all the changes will be made!

Save   We've learned a great deal about word processing, so let's wrap up our work session. The first thing we want to do is safely save our file. Word processing lets you hold your work in RAM until it is saved. **Saving** stores the contents of RAM on a disk or other nonvolatile, auxiliary storage device. Press the Save function key now; you'll see a message in the status line asking you to name the file you wish to save (if you haven't already done so). We decided to name this file TERM.100, so type that in and press Enter.

Most word processing programs have a Save option that allows you to save your work without exiting your file. This lets you save the file safely on the disk, then immediately return to work on it. Many programs also have an *autosave* feature that automatically saves the file you're working on every few minutes or when you type a certain number of keystrokes. Once you have properly saved a file, you can exit word processing and return to the DOS prompt. *Never* exit word processing until you have saved your work, or all will be lost!

Retrieve   Retrieve, as you might imagine, is the opposite of save: it allows us to recall a file from the disk and so we can revise the document. Retrieve is also useful for working with successive drafts of the same document. Most word processing programs allow you to use the DOS commands to copy,

---

DISKbyte

Word Processing Tips

1. Use word processing to brainstorm and for prewriting exercises. Because you can move, add, delete, and edit so easily, your work will take shape much more quickly. It's tedious — and rather pointless — to write ideas or drafts on paper and then type them into a word processing file.

2. If your word processing software has a window feature, use it. Windows make it easy to view and edit more than one manuscript, or several portions of the same manuscript, at the same time.

3. *Don't* overuse **print features.** <u>Underlining,</u> **boldface,** and *italics,* not to mention TYPE-FACE SIZES, should be used sparingly, otherwise the text becomes <u>**difficult to read.**</u>

4. If you're using software that only allows you to use eight-character filenames, name your documents carefully. Choose words that convey the content, rather than the type of file. For example, it's much easier to remember what's in a file called TOYSTORY than one called FICTION.

5. Save your work frequently. Although this applies to any application you use, most people find it incredibly frustrating to lose their writing. If your word processing software has an automatic Save feature, set it to save every five minutes — or less.

---

rename, or delete files. This often makes it easier to organize information, especially when you work with many documents over long periods of time.

Take our term paper file called TERM.100, which is our first draft. If you want to keep it in its original form when you begin your revision, you can save open a new file and use the retrieve command to "copy" the contents of TERM.100 into it. Now save the new file with the TERM.200 filename as your second draft. This has the benefit of allowing you to mark your progress from draft to draft; it also assures that you have a safe copy of everything you wrote last.

Print   At any point that you'd like to see how your document looks on paper, you can print it. The Print command sends the file to the printer (provided you have one and it's hooked up properly), which provides us with a properly formatted paper copy of our document. Printing is also an effective way to back up, or save, your work in another medium.

Word processing programs usually offer a wide variety of print settings, including options for numbering pages, whether to include page headers or footers (such as the title of the paper or references), typeface styles, and other format characteristics you studied earlier in this chapter. Much of what you can do depends on what kind of output your printer is capable of producing.

You may never come to the end of learning your word processing program's features. You'll discover that the more you learn, the easier it is to use, because many features have been built in at all levels of expertise. As you master some, you'll find yourself curious to learn how to do others. Reading the documentation, using the Help function, and continuing to experiment will be likely to produce additional rewards for you.

**M E M O R Y
C H E C K**

1. What is the word processing term we use to describe the file that we enter text into?
2. Describe several format commands and what they do to text.
3. What tasks do we commonly use Block editing for?
4. What is the term used for adding or altering text?
5. What keys are used to delete characters? To delete words?
6. What is the purpose of undelete?
7. What do we look for with the Search command?
8. What does the Save command do with data?
9. Describe two ways to use the Retrieve command.
10. What additional benefit does printing provide?

USING ADVANCED WORD PROCESSING FEATURES

No matter how easy it is for you to communicate, writing takes effort. It demands almost everything we have to give: concentration, precision, insight, and creativity. To help us write more effectively, we sometimes turn to writer's aids. We use the dictionary to check spelling and clarify word meanings. A thesaurus helps us make word choices. Outlining methods help us organize our ideas. Many advanced word processing programs make these writer's aids available as part of the application.

Spelling Checker

When you want to be sure you spell a word correctly, you probably turn to a dictionary. What a frustrating experience that can be! How do you look up a word you don't know how to spell? A word processing spelling checker can solve this problem for you. This tool requires only that you type the word as closely as possible to how you think it should be spelled and select the spell checking option. If you spelled it incorrectly, most word processing programs highlight the word by calling attention to it with another color, then show you a list of alternatives from a built-in dictionary. You can select a word to replace what you typed, edit it, or ignore it. Figure 4–14 shows one program's spelling checker display.

Various word processing programs check spelling in different ways but all perform the same function. Most will read through every word in your file, comparing with the words in their dictionaries, and note words that don't match. Most allow you to replace your words with those from a list. Some even allow you to do a global replace—replacing every occurrence of your misspelled word with the correct word in the spelling checker.

In addition, some spelling checkers locate duplicate words. For example, if you accidentally type a word twice, like "the the," your spelling checker will highlight this and ask you if you want to make a change.

Spelling checkers can be valuable even to the best of writers and typists, catching mistakes that might otherwise require a good copy editor. They allow

DISKbyte

Spelling Checkers Can Be Deadly

The offbeat Australian magazine, *Computing Australia*, reported that an overzealous computer was responsible for a "potentially lethal error" involving an organized crime loan collector. Apparently, a newspaper writer's original story called the loan collector a *ruthless inforcer* (instead of *enforcer*). A spelling checker substituted the term *informer* for *inforcer* in the printed version of the story. Until they figured out that the computer had made an error, some miffed mobsters considering fitting the loan collector with concrete overshoes. And we thought the worst computer error ever was a bill for $100,000!

FIGURE 4–14   A spelling checker screen. The word *dealeting* was selected for checking. The spelling checker lists alternative words and a menu listing actions the user can take.

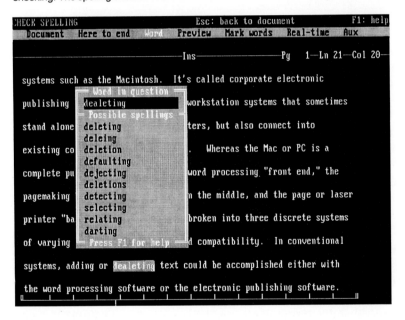

us to write continuously, without pausing to look up words in a dictionary. We can leave the final spelling check and corrections till the writing itself is finished.

Thesaurus

Sometimes when we write, we find that we're using the same word over and over again. When this becomes a problem, writers may turn to a thesaurus to look up synonyms—words with similar meanings. To make this easier and bring all the tools of writing together, some word processing programs have a built-in thesaurus.

FIGURE 4–15   A thesaurus screen. The term *publishing* was selected. The thesaurus displays several synonyms for this term.

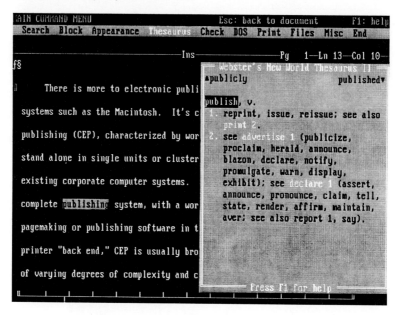

Using a thesaurus is usually as easy and convenient as using a spelling checker. You issue the Thesaurus command, you are asked for the word you want to replace, and a list of synonyms is displayed on the screen. The thesaurus may also suggest similar terms to look up. You can type these words and get more alternative words. Figure 4–15 shows a thesaurus display.

When you use a written thesaurus, you can spend several minutes, even hours, paging through and following up all your options. Much of the value of using a word processing thesaurus lies in its speed; the searching is done quickly by the computer. Your writing flow and momentum aren't interrupted as much when you use this tool.

Outliner

If you've taken an introductory writing course, you know all about outlining. With outlines, you put random thoughts and ideas into organized form. Many word processing programs help you create and edit outlines.

As you probably know, you identify parts of an outline with arabic and roman numerals, and letters in upper- and lowercases. Sorting out the proper form of a formal outline can be as much work as working with the ideas it contains. Word processing is designed to take this part of the burden off your shoulders. Instead of figuring out the right number or letter an outline entry should have, you just have to indicate the level at which an outline entry should occur. If an entry is a major section of a paper or chapter of a book, you use a code to indicate this, and the outliner provides the proper number or letter in the outline.

Some on-line outliners make modifying your outline easier, too. You no longer have to renumber all elements when you insert a new entry. That part is done automatically by the outliner. As with many other aspects of word processing software, outliners do the mechanical work, leaving you free to concentrate on the ideas and content of the writing process.

Table of Contents Generator

Once you've written a long paper or manuscript, you will probably want to prepare a table of contents. Of course, you could do this by using the block functions of your word processor, selecting and deleting large sections of text, and leaving behind all the section titles and subsection heads. Advanced word processing software can do this more simply and efficiently for you. If you identify the elements of your paper or manuscript according to the rules set up by the program, you can issue a command that will automatically choose those parts of your file, separate them from sentences and paragraphs, and store them in another file. The result is a complete table of contents, produced with very little additional work on your part.

Index Generator

A natural complement to a table of contents in a large piece of writing is an index. The words linked to key aspects of your paper or manuscript can be grouped alphabetically and stored together to help people who want to find selected portions of what you have written, by topic, in the index. In the old days—or when we use the technology of the old days—you have to read through your work and note the use of each key term and its page number if you want to compile an index. But if you use full-featured word processing, you can save yourself innumerable hours and produce a superior index.

Some programs that have indexing capabilities require only that you list the terms you wish your index to contain. After you compile the list, the software takes over, searching your document, noting each term and the page where it occurs. Then it compiles an index automatically. Indexing a large document might require weeks of human effort. Advanced word processing can do the same job in less than an hour.

MEMORY CHECK

1. Name four writer's aids.
2. What do we call a word processing version of a dictionary?
3. What advantages do spelling checkers have over dictionaries?
4. What do spelling checkers identify besides misspelled words?
5. What two things do thesauruses that are built into the software provide?
6. Identify an advantage of using a built-in outliner.
7. How does word processing produce tables of contents and indexes?

WORD PROCESSING APPLICATIONS

People use word processing for just about every form of written communication. Whether they want to write formally or informally, for business or pleasure, to communicate facts and statistics or the inner landscape of creative expression, people have found word processing an invaluable tool. Whether you're writing scripts, poetry, speeches, press releases, business correspondence, reports, proposals, or a résumé, word processing's special features are suited to writing, to ideas, and to people.

Word processing's popularity is not hard to understand. As writers, we tend to change our minds and find ways to improve on what we started with. A word processing program is a very forgiving, flexible tool. The convenience word processing lends to the writing experience often makes computers the best tool for writing. Mail/merge and manuscript preparation are two examples of word processing applications.

Mail/Merge

Word processing has changed the way business correspondence is prepared. Before word processing was available in the office, businesses had two choices when it came to mass mailings: either spend a lot of time and labor individually typing each letter, or prepare just one, impersonally addressed to "Reader" or "Occupant."

Word processing offers a third option. Now, one letter can be prepared, with special symbols inserted where the intended reader's name and address should be. Then, with the aid of a **mail/merge** feature, letters are printed, pulling in names and addresses from a separate file, to make each letter unique. Used with a **mailing list program** that prints envelopes or mailing labels, businesses can now speedily make individualized mass mailings without incurring high labor costs. (See Figure 4–16.)

FIGURE 4–16   A mail/merge application.

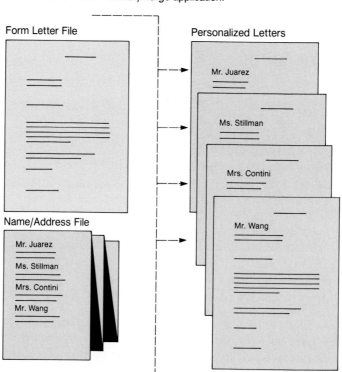

Manuscript Preparation

The word *manuscript* may forever connect the ancient and the modern forms of writing. It's a combination of two terms — *manual* and *script* — and comes from the Latin *manuscriptus,* meaning written by hand. We use it to identify an original work of writing, usually a book. Most manuscripts are one of a kind, typed or hand-written, rather than typeset and printed in quantity for mass distribution. Word processing has changed all that.

First, we throw out the ancient means of writing manuscripts because we don't write by hand or with typewriters. Second, laboring long hours to produce a perfected copy is no longer necessary. Third, we can reproduce multiple copies of manuscripts easily. Using word processing technology and printers, we write more easily, edit quickly, and can print 10, 100, or 1,000 copies of our manuscripts and submit them to anyone who might be interested in our work.

Writing a book is a big project but word processing makes it easier. You can bring all the elements of word processing together to simplify this task. Writing, revising, formatting, and printing features streamline the process. Spelling checkers and an on-line thesaurus help with the writing. Table of contents and index generators help create aids to reading and interpreting your manuscript. How far we've come from the days of chisels and stone!

1. Identify five ways people use word processing.

2. What is a mail/merge utility?

3. What does a mailing list program do?

4. How has word processing changed manuscript preparation?

MEMORY CHECK

THE EVER – EVOLVING WORD PROCESSING PROGRAM

Now let's expand our concept of word processing by looking back to see where its been and forward to see how it's growing.

Derived from data processing, the term *word processing* was coined by IBM to signify using computers to manipulate written words. The first word processing system was created by IBM in 1964. Called the MT/ST (for Magnetic Tape/Selectric Typewriter), it used magnetic tapes to store documents. In 1969, IBM updated it so that it stored information on magnetic cards — and, logically, named it the MC/ST.

In 1976, Wang came out with the WP 55, a highly successful office word processing system. Both IBM and Wang word processors were special, dedicated systems that only performed word processing tasks. When personal computers became popular, MicroPro International Corporation was quick to see the need for a good word processing application program, and came out with WordStar in 1979. WordStar quickly became a best-seller but failed to keep its lead because its developers did not revise and update it to keep pace with new competitors.

Today, there are many excellent word processing software packages available, some very simple for people new to personal computers, some designed for executive use, and others with literally hundreds of features for the more advanced user. For example, one is designed for scholarly manuscripts and even permits typing text in Greek, Hebrew, and Russian.

An "add-on" program is a supplemental program that works with the software—in this case, word processing—to make it even more useful. Grammatik IV evaluates grammar, style, punctuation, and usage, with a twist —it has a phrase editor, based on guidelines set by the National Organization for Women (NOW), that watches for sexist words and phrases. Webster's New World Combo is a dictionary/thesaurus based on Webster's *New World Dictionary*. From the famous Webster's who have brought us dictionaries for more than a century, New World Combo proofreads your work against a dictionary of 114,000 words. Its thesaurus contains 20,000 entries, 330,000 synonym references, and 1 million replacement words.

The newest word processing software programs have a feature called *wizzywig*. It's actually an acronym, WYSIWYG, which stands for "what you see is what you get." WYSIWYG makes it possible to see a page on the screen exactly as it will look on paper, with boldface, italics, underlining, special formatting, and so forth. Some advanced word processing programs incorporate desktop publishing features. Desktop publishing gives you greater formatting capabilities, including merging multiple print typeface styles and graphic images on one page. We'll explore desktop publishing in depth in Chapter 7.

The word processing software you choose will depend on your level of experience with the personal computer, your needs, your hardware, and your pocketbook. You can buy packages for as little as $39 or as much as $499. Most of today's word processing programs have been revised and improved over the years and are fine writing tools. They do their job and they make it much easier for writers to do theirs. And, as your needs change, you can always graduate to more sophisticated word processing programs.

MEMORY CHECK

1. Name two companies that developed early word processing.
2. Identify three features in newer word processing systems.
3. What is a desktop publishing system?
4. What factors will determine which word processing software is right for you?

ETHICS

Plagiarism is the theft and use of another person's original writing. You may have heard discussions at your college about plagiarism, for it has been around a long time. In the past, people would often plagiarize by copying another's writing from a book or a term paper. The Information Age and word processing make it even easier to plagiarize. For example, a student loaned a fellow student the disk containing her bibliography for the class term paper. He used it for his term paper; in fact, he gave it to 10 other students. All received a reprimand for their actions. This means you take more stringent measures to avoid plagiarizing, even unintentionally.

It is common to see all kinds of information distributed on floppy disks and optical disks these days. This includes magazine articles, the works of William Shakespeare, book excerpts — the list goes on and on. In addition, it is not uncommon to obtain information from electronic sources over the telephone lines.

All this information can easily be plagiarized, simply by copying portions of text into a word processor and creating a file. The plagiarist changes a few words, modifies some sentences, adds or deletes a paragraph here and there, and calls it an original work. But the plagiarist knows that he or she has committed an unethical act. And while a short-term goal has been met — that of getting a term paper in on time — the long-term goal of acquiring knowledge through the learning process and disseminating it through the effective use of language has not. Plagiarism, like other unethical acts, really hurts the plagiarist most of all.

A recent college graduate was hired as associate editor of a well-known investment advice newsletter. Key to the newsletter's success was its original insights into the market and unique perspective on how to invest. This young woman worked hard but often ran late on her deadlines. Afraid she would not have her article done in time, she plagiarized an article from a magazine published by an investment services company, typing it into her word processor as an original piece. The editor immediately sensed the lack of insight in the work and challenged its originality. The young woman confessed she had plagiarized the work, and although her editor understood the reason, it was grounds for dismissal. The writer couldn't be trusted to report and write ethically and responsibly again.

CAREERbyte

How to Get Rich in the Software Industry

"What the world needs . . ." are words that we all use to describe what we perceive as a need. Two college professors turned a perceived need and an interest in better software for writers into thriving, successful businesses.

WordPerfect Corporation

Alan Ashton taught computer science at Brigham Young University. He looked at the word processing software available and listened to people's complaints. Each program had certain features but there was always a "but." Something was lacking; it was hard to use; it needed to do something it didn't do. Alan believed there might be a market for a program that didn't have these shortcomings, one that had every "bell and whistle."

So in 1980, Alan formed a business with his best graduate student, Bruce Bastion, called Satellite Software. They recruited programmers

Courtesy Reference Software

from BYU and created a word processing program. People bought it and used it. Then Alan and Bruce did something no one else was doing: They listened to their customers and revised the program accordingly. The software got better and better, and more people used it. By 1988, they had captured 60 percent of the market.

This is the story of WordPerfect, one of the most powerful and popular word processing application programs on the market. Alan and Bruce changed the company's name to WordPerfect Corporation and built an 11-acre corporate campus in Orem, Utah. They treat their employees well: only 5 of the 200 programmers have ever left. They also treat customers well: 475 customer support technicians handle 12,000 calls a day. Every new

SUMMARY

1. *Explain the advantages of word processing over typewriting.* Word processing is a quicker and more efficient way of working with words and ideas than a typewriter. The word wrap feature lets us write continuously. Revising is much easier, since we do not have to retype paper page after page. Formatting allows us to design text and pages for different purposes. Printing gives us a paper copy to read whenever it is convenient.

2. *Describe how word processing works and how it uses files.* The word processing screen is designed to look like a sheet of blank paper. The status line gives us important information about the cursor location; the arrow keys are used to move the cursor through text. Word processing stores text in files; a file may be a poem, a letter, or a term paper, and is usually referred to as a document.

3. *Explain the steps in entering, formatting, revising, saving, and printing text.* The first task we perform in a word processing work session is entering text into the document. Format commands allow us to change margins; use **bold**, <u>underline</u>, and *italics;* center lines; and more. Block editing lets us move, copy, delete chunks of text, or store it in a new file.

WordPerfect release adds features that users want. In 1989, WordPerfect Corp. became the third-largest software company. That's how you build success.

Reference Software

Don Emery taught business at San Francisco State University and was disappointed in the writing his students handed in. As a marketing professor, he realized it wasn't possible to teach all the necessary concepts of grammar, spelling, punctuation, and so forth; perhaps, however, the computer could provide some assistance in these areas.

In 1985, Bruce Wampler, a professor at the University of New Mexico, came up with the idea to develop a writing improvement software program. He created a program called Reference Set that combined a spelling checker and a thesaurus, and "popped up" while you were using the word processing program. Don Emery thought there was a market for Reference Set. With Bob Jackson of San Francisco State and Paul Brest of the Stanford Law School, Don and Bruce formed a company called Reference Software.

The following year, Reference Software released Grammatik II, a word processing document analyzer. It "read" text and suggested improvements in grammar, style, punctuation, and spelling. A marketing expert, Don structured

Courtesy WordPerfect Corporation

Grammatik based on a combination of what users demanded and his unique personal vision of writing improvement tools. The product of advanced computer techniques and the study of linguistics, each new version of Grammatik has evolved and added more features. The current version is capable of sophisticated document analysis. It breaks each sentence into parts of speech, comparing each word and phrase to a complete collection of writing rules.

Grammatik is the leader in its field, as is WordPerfect. Both companies continue to introduce new, more useful versions of their software. Grammatik IV, which works within WordPerfect, makes proofreading a document seem as simple as spell-checking it. Reference Software also offers specialized spelling checkers than can be added to WordPerfect's main spelling dictionary. Both companies demonstrate that success in the software business is a result of listening to customers and providing the features people want.

Search lets us find text, or character strings; replace lets us change words or phrases. A work session ends when we save the file. It can be retrieved to work on it again; the retrieve command can be used effectively to create subsequent drafts of a document. Printing gives us a paper copy and an additional form of backup.

4. *Describe some of the advanced word processing tools and how they are used.* Advanced word processing tools give us additional capabilities. The most common one is the spelling checker, closely followed by the thesaurus. An outliner automatically creates an outline of your document; a similar tool is the table of contents generator. An index generator compiles a list of key terms.

5. *Describe some word processing applications.* Word processing is used in homes and offices, by people from all walks of life. It is most prevalent in business where it is used to write letters, memos, and reports. Mail/merge is a popular application that lets you combine a name and address with a form letter. Writers use word processing for manuscript preparation because it relieves them of so many tedious manual tasks.

KEY TERMS

block, p. 107
block editing, p. 107
cut and paste, p. 107
delete, p. 108
document, p. 104
draft, p. 98
editing, p. 107
Format, p. 106
Function key, p. 106

Help, p. 101
highlighting, p. 107
Insert mode, p. 101
mail/merge, p. 116
mailing list program, p. 116
Replace, p. 109
revising, p. 98
saving, p. 110
scrolling, p. 100

Search, p. 109
status line, p. 99
toggle key, p. 99
Typeover mode, p. 101
undelete, p. 108
undo, p. 108
word processing (WP), p. 96
word wrap, p. 100

REVIEW AND DISCUSSION QUESTIONS

1. What percentage of software sold is for word processing?
2. Describe two ways word processing makes writing easier.
3. Where does the program store the text you write?
4. Identify six basic features found in most word processing programs.
5. What is a draft?
6. Why do we often write several drafts?
7. Name four block editing actions.
8. Identify three writing actions word processing performs automatically.
9. Identify four differences between using a word processing program versus a typewriter.
10. Identify four ways formatting emphasizes text.
11. How can Help orient us to a new application?
12. At what other times would you be likely to use Help?

13. Why is it important to periodically save your work?
14. Describe two ways to save a file.
15. Identify four advanced features found in word processing.
16. How can using word processing make a business more efficient?
17. What should you take into account when you purchase word processing software?
18. Describe how word processing facilitates book-length manuscript preparation.
19. Explain how you would use word processing to store and retrieve consecutive drafts of a document.
20. Discuss plagiarism. Is it possible to monitor and ensure the ethical use of word processing?

ISSUES

1. Science tells us that the average human is able to memorize 10 basic commands or key combinations associated with using an application. There are also certain conventions that are common to the way we use computers, such as pressing the Enter key after issuing a command. How do these apply to the concept of "ease of use"? Should a word processing program have the most important commands on the first 10 function keys? When should a command be on a toggle key, and when should it use the Enter key? What *is* ease of use?

2. Computers are supposed to help us do things better, faster, and cheaper. However, some of the most popular word processing programs require extensive training. How can we evaluate the advantages in using computers and word processing against the human costs, both in time and money, of learning how to use them?

3. Plagiarism is unethical behavior. Is there ever a time when it is OK to use someone else's writing in your documents? How should that be properly done? How would you feel if you saw something you wrote appear in a document another student or co-worker submitted as his or her own original work? Is it plagiarism to use something you previously wrote over again?

CHAPTER 5

The Spreadsheet

CHAPTER OUTLINE

The VisiCalc Evangelist
Working with Numbers
What Is an Electronic Spreadsheet?
   Birth of the Spreadsheet
   The Spreadsheet Advantage
   DISKbyte: Mitchell Kapor and the Road from
      Transcendental Meditation to Computer
      Software
Basic Spreadsheet Features
   The Spreadsheet Screen
   Menu Line and Command Line
   Scrolling Window
   DISKbyte: Paul Funk and the Add-On Market
      for Spreadsheets
A Spreadsheet Work Session
   Creating the Spreadsheet
   Commands
Using Advanced Spreadsheet Features
   Functions
   Recalculation
   Templates
   Macros
   Spreadsheet Graphics
Spreadsheet Applications
   DISKbyte: Spreadsheet Tips
The Ever-Evolving Spreadsheet
Ethics
   CAREERbyte: The Spreadsheet Wizard
Summary
Key Terms
Review and Discussion Questions
Issues

OBJECTIVES

After reading and studying this chapter, you should be able to:

1. Explain what a spreadsheet is and how a spreadsheet program works.
2. Describe the different uses for a spreadsheet.
3. Identify the various characteristics of the spreadsheet screen.
4. Explain the steps in creating and editing a spreadsheet.
5. Name some of the advanced functions and features of the spreadsheet.

THE VISICALC EVANGELIST

Allen Sneider was the first registered owner of VisiCalc, the first electronic spreadsheet program for a personal computer. Allen is a certified public accountant and a partner with the Philadelphia-based accounting firm of Laventhol & Horwath. Having the first registered copy is like having a first edition of a valuable book. He was so excited about the potential for this new type of software that he would take his Apple II computer, printer, and all the accessories with him when he called on clients, so he could show them VisiCalc's capabilities.

Courtesy of Allen Sneider

"That was the most exciting time of my professional career," says Allen. "It made me feel 10 years younger. At the beginning, it was difficult for some people to understand the significance between columnar paper and an electronic spreadsheet. And they couldn't understand how it worked on the Apple II; they thought the so-called personal computer was a toy. So I told them it was called a personal-sized business computer."

Allen became, in his words, a "VisiCalc evangelist," demonstrating the spreadsheet wherever he went. He created an extensive study and visual demonstration called "The use of the personal-size computer to perform accounting, tax, and business consulting services" for the people at Laventhol & Horwath. One of his associates, convinced, used VisiCalc to perform an extensive tourism study for a Caribbean resort island that filled 10 data disks!

Today, Laventhol & Horwath primarily uses PC-compatible personal computers and 1-2-3 from Lotus, the spreadsheet that succeeded VisiCalc. However, Allen says there are still a few Apple IIs with VisiCalc used for smaller jobs. Almost all the firm's professional staff, including CPAs, tax personnel, management advisers, and auditing and accounting people, have their own personal computer and use Lotus 1-2-3. They create forecasts and financial statements, perform many tax services, and create various schedules for business clients. In fact, Allen's office does the accounting and taxes for Mitchell Kapor, the man who created Lotus 1-2-3!

WORKING WITH NUMBERS

Probably the most famous accountant of all time was Bob Cratchit, Tiny Tim's father in the Charles Dickens story, *A Christmas Carol.* Seated at a tall bench, Bob would dip his quill pen into the inkwell and write the results of Scrooge's financial transactions into a large book called an accountant's ledger. Each page in the ledger book was called a columnar page or **ledger sheet** because there were a number of vertical columns running down the page. In addition, lines drawn across the page created rows running from left to right. A typical blank ledger sheet is shown in Figure 5–1.

Bob would write in the names of debtors and the amount of money they owed to Scrooge *(credits),* as well as the amount Scrooge owed to others *(debits),* in the boxes created by the columns and rows. In this way, Bob created what is called a *balance sheet* that told Scrooge whether or not he was making money.

As business grew more sophisticated and complex, columnar or ledger sheets were used for other purposes than just calculating the company's profits and losses. They were used to keep track of manufacturing, advertising, and research and development costs. They were used to calculate interest, taxes, salaries, and sales figures. They were used for tracking a company's current financial picture but also to create projections of what management anticipated would occur in the future.

Over the years, the green-tinted ledger sheet grew in size to accommodate these more complex financial situations. As ledger sheets grew in size, they also became far more complex to work with. People created ledger sheets with pencils and erasers for many years, working with rows and columns of figures they had to total by hand or with an electronic calculator. If an incorrect number was written into one of the boxes, or if projections changed, it meant a great deal of tedious erasing and refiguring. That is, until the electronic spreadsheet came along.

FIGURE 5–1   A typical blank ledger sheet.

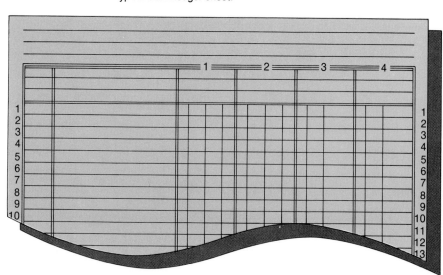

WHAT IS AN ELECTRONIC SPREADSHEET?

An electronic spreadsheet — we'll simply call it a **spreadsheet** — is an application that uses mathematical formulas to perform calculations on data arranged in a matrix or grid. It is the software version of the paper ledger sheet. A spreadsheet has the same columns and rows as a ledger sheet and serves the same purpose as its paper counterpart. The spreadsheet is a very popular application with more than just accountants and auditors. Now anyone, from marketing managers to automobile salespeople to the Flower and Garden Club treasurer, can easily learn to use a spreadsheet program.

The spreadsheet makes it possible to create a visual, mathematical model of a specific financial situation on the personal computer's screen. A **model** is a replica or copy that can be tested or changed without disturbing the original, in the same way an engineer creates a model of an auto or an airplane. The spreadsheet model is financial, thus it involves the use of mathematical numbers and equations.

Consider a model used to compute a company's sales figures. The spreadsheet stores sales by month. At the end of the year, sales are totaled, costs are subtracted, and the resulting figure is profits. Now management can use the spreadsheet to plan next year's sales. If the sales force sells 20 percent more this year than last, what will the company earn in profits? The spreadsheet will quickly calculate the new figures. This is a simple financial model, and it is possible to get all this information and more using a spreadsheet.

The spreadsheet was the first software program originally developed for the personal computer, then adapted later for use on larger computers. Before this, most software was first created for mainframes, then adapted to run on minicomputers, then personal computers. There were other kinds of specialized financial software programs available for mainframes and minis but there was nothing quite like the spreadsheet.

Birth of the Spreadsheet

The spreadsheet story is an interesting example of creating a new kind of software to solve a problem. In 1978, Dan Bricklin was a student in the Master's of Business Administration program at Harvard University. Like the other M.B.A. students, Dan had to use paper, pencil, and calculator to solve problems posed in the case studies. There had to be a better way, he thought. Couldn't a computer help? Dan asked Bob Frankston, a programmer friend, to work with him.

Frankston was fascinated with the idea of creating a new kind of software program. "Our goal was to provide a high-performance tool that would allow financial planners the same kind of flexibility enjoyed by people using word processors," Frankston said. He worked every night, pounding the keys of his Apple II in his attic apartment, then slept all day. By January of 1979, Frankston was done. Bricklin chose the name VisiCalc, for Visible Calculator, and he and Frankston formed a company named Software Arts to market it.

VisiCalc was a success because it helped people do their work more efficiently, quickly, and easily. News of the spreadsheet traveled slowly at first; then, in 1981, VisiCalc took off. Businesspeople flocked to computer stores to buy Apple IIs, just so they could use it. Software Arts' 1981 sales projections (prepared using VisiCalc!) had to be revised from $1 million to $2 million, then to $2.5 million, then to $3 million!

But it wasn't long until another spreadsheet came along called 1-2-3 from Lotus. As its name implies, it was three separate programs that all worked together. This was called integrated software. Integrated software makes it relatively easy to switch from one program to another and to share data between programs; we'll learn more about integrated software in Chapter 7.

In 1-2-3, the primary application program is the spreadsheet. There is a graphics program that transforms spreadsheet data into pictorial representations commonly used by businesspeople. There is also a database management program for keeping track of simple information such as addresses or telephone numbers. Even though it is integrated software, users wanted the spreadsheet more than the other programs. 1-2-3 debuted in 1983, and by this time, corporate America had made the IBM Personal Computer its machine of choice. 1-2-3 ran on the IBM PC and shot to the top of the software best-seller list; it has remained there ever since.

Between VisiCalc and Lotus 1-2-3, the spreadsheet program is generally considered the reason for the personal computer's enthusiastic acceptance in the business world. Even though word processing is still the most widely used application in businesses large and small, the spreadsheet is a very close second.

The Spreadsheet Advantage

The spreadsheet is designed to work with numbers and mathematical formulas. Its principal task is performing calculations, which it does very efficiently. The spreadsheet combines the paper ledger sheet, the pencil, and an electronic calculator to provide several advantages over its paper counterpart. For example, the electronic ledger sheet is much larger. Where the largest paper ledger sheets have about 30 columns and 51 rows, a modern spreadsheet usually has at least 255 columns and 255 rows.

Other advantages include speed and convenience. The spreadsheet's calculator is built in, so it can total a column of figures in less than a second; if you want to correct or insert another number, it will give you the new total just as quickly. All adding, subtracting, multiplying, dividing, and many other mathematical functions are performed automatically. A **function** generates a mathematical result or value. A **value** is simply a number. Therefore, if we add two numbers or values such as $3 + 4$, we arrive at another value, 7. We'll learn more about functions and values later in this chapter.

What-If Analysis   The spreadsheet makes it possible to speculate about the financial future. In the same way we can quickly retotal when a mistake has been made, we can test a variety of financial models. This is called performing a what-if analysis. A **what-if analysis** involves substituting one number for another to see what difference it will make. For example, *what if* the company has a 20 percent increase in sales next year? *What if* we build a new manufacturing facility? *What if* we decide to raise or lower the price of our product by 6 percent? Numerical data can be replaced easily in the spreadsheet to see what would happen in scenarios such as these. The ability to perform what-if analyses and test different speculative financial models is one of the spreadsheet's most useful features. It has provided business with a powerful planning tool that is used extensively. *What-if analysis* has become a common business term.

DISKbyte

Mitchell Kapor and the Road from Transcendental Meditation to Computer Software

Mitch Kapor admits that "having a rather eclectic background, including stints as a radio disk jockey and a psychiatric hospital worker, I tended to view things a little differently from my programming colleagues."

Kapor worked in California, writing software called VisiPlot/VisiTrend, a graphics program that creates charts from VisiCalc spreadsheets. He mentioned to a friend that it would be handy if, while actually using VisiCalc, you could just press a key and make a graph. "He couldn't understand what I was talking about," Kapor recalls.

So Kapor kept the idea to himself, moved to Boston, and used the money he made creating VisiPlot to hire programmers to help him create an integrated software package that combined three applications: a spreadsheet, graphics, and a database. Mitch practiced transcendental meditation, where one sits in the lotus position. So he called the program Lotus 1-2-3.

F. Bodin/Offshoot

Selecting the IBM PC wasn't exactly planned. "We still weren't sure which machine we would release it on. But in August 1982, when IBM introduced its PC with the powerful Intel 8088 processor, we knew this was the machine to go with."

Today, the company Kapor formed, Lotus Development Corporation, is one of the top software publishing companies. It has made him a millionaire many times over. Yet Kapor refuses to gloat egotistically about his success. "It has been suggested that 1-2-3 did for the IBM PC what VisiCalc did for the Apple II, providing a reason for placing these machines on managers' and executives' desks. But the impact just wasn't the same, even though our software has proven extremely popular."

Kapor has resigned his top position at Lotus to explore new possibilities for personal computers. He has said, "Once or twice a week, I get so frustrated that I want to pick [the computer] up and throw it out the window." Underlying everything Kapor does is a consistent philosophical view: to "keep developing software companies until I get it right."

MEMORY CHECK

1. The spreadsheet is the software version of what kind of paper form?

2. What three tools does the spreadsheet combine?

3. What type of model is the spreadsheet used to create?

4. In what way does the spreadsheet's handling of functions and values differ from the calculator's?

5. What type of analysis feature does the spreadsheet employ for speculating about the financial future?

BASIC SPREADSHEET FEATURES

As we've said, the spreadsheet combines three manual tools for working with numbers: the ledger sheet, the pencil, and the calculator, shown in Figure 5–2. The ledger sheet is what you see on the computer screen. The keyboard or mouse takes the place of the pencil. The calculator is actually your personal computer's microprocessor, the arithmetic-logic unit or ALU you learned about in Chapter 2. It's activated by the spreadsheet software when you issue certain commands to the spreadsheet called formulas. A spreadsheet **formula** is a rule expressed as an equation. It is very similar to a mathematical formula, where mathematical expressions are combined to produce an answer. A simple mathematical formula is $32 + 24$; a more complex one is $(5X - 3X) + (32 + 24)$. Spreadsheets use similar expressions, as you shall see.

In this chapter, we'll show you how to create a spreadsheet to track your college expenses and create a budget. First, though, let's see what a spreadsheet looks like. Just as we did in the previous chapter, we discuss the spreadsheet program in general terms; the spreadsheet you use may appear somewhat different, although the concepts are the same.

The Spreadsheet Screen

While sharing some things in common with its paper counterpart, such as columns and rows, the spreadsheet has a slightly different look and feel. A paper ledger sheet is static; the lines are drawn and you can't change them. It's

---

FIGURE 5–2   The spreadsheet combines three manual tools for working with numbers: the ledger sheet, the pencil, and the calculator.

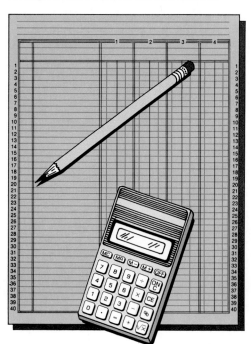

quite another case with the spreadsheet. Let's see why. Refer to Figure 5–3 as we explain the spreadsheet's features.

Columns and Rows   The spreadsheet has a border that runs horizontally across the top of the screen, and vertically down the left-hand margin. The horizontal border displays the **columns**, which are designated with the letters of the alphabet: A, B, C, and so on. Once the columns reach Z, they begin again with AA, AB, AC, and so on. The vertical border displays the **rows**, which are numbered 1, 2, 3, and so on.

Columns are commonly used to create time categories such as months or years. In a spreadsheet for managing a personal college budget, the first column might start with September and end with June. Columns are designed in a uniform width but you can widen them when necessary. People often widen the first column so they can type in words or phrases to identify the columns that follow.

Rows are commonly used for listing entities such as companies the firm does business with, or areas of expenditures such as manufacturing, marketing, shipping, and so forth. In a personal college budget, the rows might list such things as clothing, entertainment, books, supplies, and so on. There is no need to change the size of a row, since the cell content is always typed on a line by itself to the width of the column.

Cells   On the ledger sheet, the vertical columns and horizontal rows form squares on the paper. In the spreadsheet, this square is called a **cell**, indicating a place where we can type in data. Usually, there are no visible lines separating them. Cells are identified by their column-and-row position. For example, when you begin working with a new spreadsheet, the command line shows the pointer is located in column A, row 1, so the cell designation is "A1."

FIGURE 5–3   A typical spreadsheet screen.

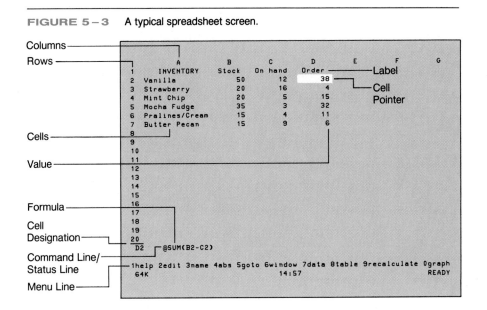

Cell Pointer   The **cell pointer** takes the place of the cursor found in other programs. The cell pointer illuminates the particular cell it is located in, to indicate where data may be entered. If your computer has a green monochrome monitor, the cell pointer glows green as if reminding us of the accountant's green ledger sheet paper and green eyeshade. The arrow keys can be used to move the pointer from cell to cell. Other keys move the pointer to specific locations such as the home cell, A1, or to a particular cell such as B155.

Labels and Values   Cells may contain labels or values. **Label** is the term used to refer to text in a spreadsheet. As you already know, values are numbers and they take two forms. One is the **constant**, the raw number or data we enter for processing. The other is the mathematical formula used for performing calculations on the constants. For example, say the constant 12 is in cell A1 and the constant 24 is in cell A2. Using the formula $+A1+A2$, we can arrive at the answer, 36. Any time the cell contains a constant, that is what we see.

Menu Line and Command Line

Most spreadsheet programs display some type of **menu line**, which lists a description of commands and other valuable information about the spreadsheet. Sometimes it is at the top of the screen; other spreadsheet programs display it below the spreadsheet itself. Some programs show the menu line at all times on the screen; others require that you press a key, commonly the diagonal or / mark, to display it.

The **command line**, as its name implies, displays the commands we use to work with the spreadsheet. It, too, may be either above or below the spreadsheet. The command line is usually easy to recognize because the first item indicates which cell the pointer is in, determined by the column and row identifiers — A1, C3, and so on.

The command line commonly shows the contents of the cell the pointer is positioned in, a label (text) or a value (either a constant or a formula). This is sometimes referred to as the **status line**, whether it is combined with or separate from the command line. The formula is not displayed in the cell itself; it is usually seen only in the command line. You can enter either a label or a value at the command line. If you enter a label or a constant, that is what you will see in the cell. If you enter a formula, the cell will display only the constant that results from calculating that formula. The formula itself may contain constants and/or another formula but not a label. The formula can only act on numbers, not text.

The command line also displays the commands used in creating a spreadsheet — for such tasks as entering data, editing, copying, printing, and saving the completed work. The command line may display other information too, such as the date and time or the status of certain special keys on your keyboard. For example, in some spreadsheet programs, the Number Lock key activates the number keys on the personal computer's numeric keypad and deactivates the cursor movement keys. We'll learn more about commands when we begin creating our own spreadsheet.

FIGURE 5 – 4   The spreadsheet scrolling window.

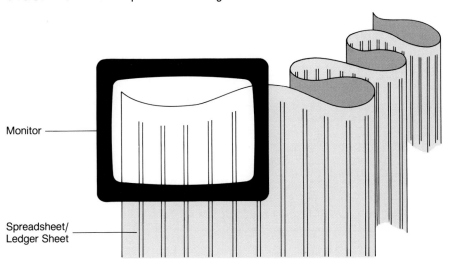

Monitor ——

Spreadsheet/
Ledger Sheet ——

Scrolling Window

You may remember we said there are hundreds of cells in the average paper ledger sheet (30 columns and 51 rows). The average spreadsheet program contains as many as half a million cells; one claims to have a billion! That's great, but how can you possibly see all of them? With a scrolling window, as shown in Figure 5 – 4, you see only a portion of the spreadsheet on the screen. The pointer and page movement keys allow you to scroll from left to right and up and down, moving to the different areas of the spreadsheet as you enter labels or values into the cells. In most cases, you fill the cells in the portion of the spreadsheet visible on the screen, then scroll to the right or downward to continue filling more cells. As your spreadsheet grows larger than a single screen, you can use other commands that shift the spreadsheet an entire screen or permit jumping to a particular cell such as L22 or B55.

1. In the spreadsheet grid, what do the vertical lines form?

2. In the spreadsheet grid, what do the horizontal lines form?

3. What is the box formed by a column and a row called?

4. What is the cursor called in a spreadsheet program?

5. What is the term used to refer to text? To numbers?

6. Where do we see commands and instructions on the screen?

7. What is the purpose of the scrolling window?

**M E M O R Y
C H E C K**

DISKbyte

Paul Funk and the Add-On Market for Spreadsheets

Paul Funk created what is now termed the *add-on* market for Lotus 1-2-3. One of the major problems with 1-2-3 spreadsheets was that they were often wider than the normal sheet of paper. Paul Funk found this out for himself, and was frustrated in his attempts to convince Lotus Development Corporation that it should do something about the problem. That led to his decision to form Funk Software and introduce a program called Sideways. It printed the spreadsheet on its side, down the length of the paper instead of across. It was

Courtesy of Funk Software Inc.

an instant success, and today it's estimated that one of three Lotus 1-2-3 users also uses Sideways.

Next, Funk took a look at the print quality of the 1-2-3 spread-

sheet. Paul believed it could look more professional, so he and his programmers went to work on another add-on product known as Allways. It allows a choice of different type faces, as well as shading for business charts and graphs, creating a more dignified, professional visual appearance. Allways was an immediate success—such a success, in fact, that Lotus decided to package it with its latest version of 1-2-3, at no extra charge. Today, Funk Software is a $10 million business.

A SPREADSHEET WORK SESSION

The key to developing a useful spreadsheet is knowing what kind of information you want, designing the spreadsheet so that it can be easily used and understood, and then creating the formulas that will get the job done for you.

There is nothing particularly difficult about this but it does require some planning. Let's work on that personal college budget we've been discussing, and see how we can turn it into a useful spreadsheet.

Creating the Spreadsheet

What kind of information do you want? The idea behind a budget is living within your means, so primarily you want to know if you are over budget or under budget. That means allocating a certain amount of money to specific expenditures occurring within a specified period of time. Let's say you have a monthly budget of $100 to spend on clothing, books, entertainment, and other things.

Creating a clear and simple design makes a spreadsheet easier to use, so let's create one. You might want to make a sketch with a pencil and a ledger sheet like the one in Figure 5–5 before you begin, to help visualize the spreadsheet.

Once you've created your spreadsheet on paper, let's create one with the computer. As in the previous chapter, you need to load the software first. Make

FIGURE 5-5   A pencil and a ledger sketch helps you visualize the spreadsheet.

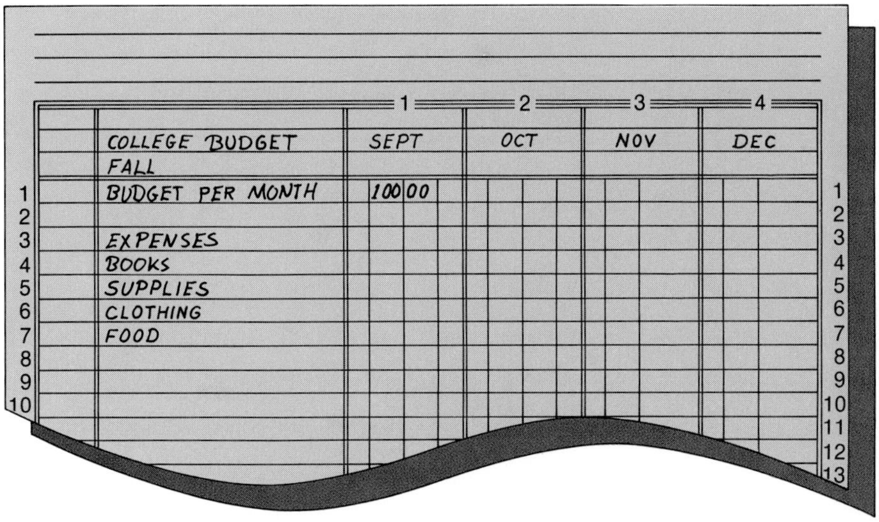

sure your personal computer is turned on and you have DOS loaded into memory. Now, insert the spreadsheet program disk and type the filename that executes the program. When the spreadsheet appears on the screen, the first cell, A1, is illuminated because that's where the cell pointer is resting. Find the command line because that is where we enter the commands, formulas, and constants. Before we start, let's review some commonly used commands we'll be using to prepare our budget.

Commands

Commands issue instructions to the spreadsheet program, to perform tasks or manipulate the design of the spreadsheet itself. For example, **Calculate** is a command built into the spreadsheet's operation. Once you have entered the proper constants and formula (and, with most spreadsheets, pressed the Enter key), calculation occurs automatically. Here are some commonly used commands:

- *Copy,* sometimes called *Replicate,* copies the contents of a cell or group of cells into another cell or group of cells.
- *Delete* removes a column or a row.
- *Insert* adds a row or column, the opposite of delete.
- *Move* takes the contents of a cell or group of cells and moves it into another cell or group of cells.
- *Print* prints your spreadsheet.
- *Retrieve* gets a spreadsheet you have previously created and saved, and puts it on the screen.
- *Save* safely stores on disk the spreadsheet you are currently working on.

Let's use each of these commands to create our spreadsheet.

FIGURE 5–6   Labels across the top of the spreadsheet identify columns.

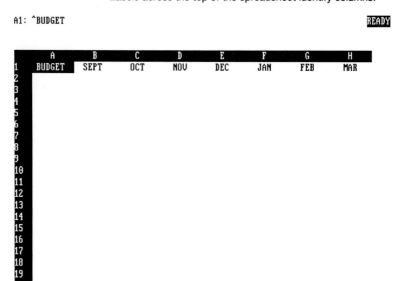

A1: ^BUDGET   READY

	A	B	C	D	E	F	G	H
1	BUDGET	SEPT	OCT	NOV	DEC	JAN	FEB	MAR

Entering Labels   First, let's create the labels that identify our work across the top of the spreadsheet, as shown in Figure 5–6. If you simply type the text, it will be input into the cell flush left. However, it is considered good practice to center labels; it also makes them easier to read. To center your text, type the caret or ^ symbol prior to typing the word and your text will appear centered in the cell. Therefore, type:

BUDGET

in cell A1, then press Enter.

Now, type in the text exactly as shown except for adding the carets, moving the cell pointer with the arrow key. Abbreviate the months. Continue until you have reached June (column K) and watch how the spreadsheet window scrolls. When you've finished, use the Home key to return the pointer to cell A1.

Now, let's create the labels for itemizing expenses down column A. As you can see, the column, only 9 characters wide, won't accommodate the labels. Therefore, we'll use the Column Width command to widen column A. Press the / key to call up the menu line and select Worksheet. *Worksheet* is the term often used to describe a spreadsheet file. In the menu line, it refers to commands *within* the spreadsheet; the other commands you see refer to *external* commands. Now select the Column command. Next, select width. When you see "Enter column width," type 20 and you'll see column A widen. Now type in the text, just as it appears in Figure 5–7. Leaving spaces between various categories makes the spreadsheet easier to read.

Entering Constants   We must enter data, in the form of constants, for the spreadsheet to act on. Let's say you have a budget of $100.00 per month, which is in your checking account. You also have a credit card, but even if you use it, your total expenditures mustn't exceed the $100.00 budget.

Move the pointer to B3, AMOUNT BUDGETED PER MO, and type in 100, for $100.00. Note that all you see is 100. So that we may see all the

FIGURE 5–7   Expense itemizations are listed down the columns.

A17: [W20] 'OVER/UNDER BUDGET   READY

	A	B	C	D	E	F
1	BUDGET	SEPT	OCT	NOV	DEC	JAN
2						
3	AMT BUDGETED PER MO					
4	BALANCE FORWARD					
5						
6	EXPENSES					
7	Books					
8	Supplies					
9	Clothing					
10	Food					
11	Phone					
12	Entertainment					
13	TOTAL EXPENSES					
14						
15	Credit Card Charges					
16						
17	OVER/UNDER BUDGET					
18						
19						
20						

FIGURE 5–8   B3, AMOUNT BUDGETED PER MO, is $100.00. Expenses are entered in each row.

B11: 17.05   READY

	A	B	C	D	E	F
1	BUDGET	SEPT	OCT	NOV	DEC	JAN
2						
3	AMT BUDGETED PER MO	$100.00				
4	BALANCE FORWARD	$100.00				
5						
6	EXPENSES					
7	Books	$8.95				
8	Supplies	$2.25				
9	Clothing	$34.90				
10	Food	$25.00				
11	Phone	$17.05				
12	Entertainment					
13	TOTAL EXPENSES					
14						
15	Credit Card Charges					
16						
17	OVER/UNDER BUDGET					
18						
19						
20						

budget figures in dollars and cents, we must use the Global Format command. First, select the Global command, meaning we wish to change something that affects the entire spreadsheet. Next, select the Format command, which alters the way constants appear in cells. The menu shows that you can make them scientific, currency, percentages, and so forth. Select currency, with two decimal places. You'll see the 100 now appears as $100.00! Move down to B4, BALANCE FORWARD, and type in 100, then continue down the column, entering expenses in each row as shown in Figure 5–8.

FIGURE 5 – 9   The spreadsheet formula is shown in the command line.

B13: +B7+B8+B9+B10+B11+B12

```
                  A              B        C       D       E       F
 1            BUDGET          SEPT      OCT     NOV     DEC     JAN
 2
 3  AMT BUDGETED PER MO    $100.00
 4  BALANCE FORWARD        $100.00
 5
 6  EXPENSES
 7  Books                    $8.95
 8  Supplies                 $2.25
 9  Clothing                $34.90
10  Food                    $25.00
11  Phone                   $17.05
12  Entertainment
13  TOTAL EXPENSES          $88.15
14
15  Credit Card Charges
16
17  OVER/UNDER BUDGET
18
19
20
```

Entering Formulas   To enter formulas properly, you must understand the relationships between the numbers in your spreadsheet. We're going to use a formula to add up the monthly expenses, paid by cash or check, in cells B7 through B12 and get a subtotal in cell B13. The formula is:

+B7+B8+B9+B10+B11+B12

Now you can see how much you spent in September in Figure 5 – 9. As you might imagine, typing formulas like this can get pretty tedious, so there is an abbreviated form. It is called a function, which combines a formula or series of steps to produce a value. Here is an addition function called @SUM that replaces the formula above:

@SUM(B7..B12)

Type it into B13 to see how it works. We'll study functions in more detail in the next section of this chapter.

Calculate   Calculate is the spreadsheet's process of performing mathematical operations, utilizing the computer's ALU. After typing in the formula, you'll see two things happen. One, the status line shows the formula you just created. Two, the spreadsheet calculates the total of the column and puts the answer in cell B13. Any time you create a formula in a cell, you'll see the formula appear in the status line and the answer appear in the cell itself.

Next, let's enter the separate credit card charges, the $20.95 you spent for the football team sweatshirt, in cell B15. Now we're ready to get a grand total, which shows whether you're over or under budget, in cell B17. Move the pointer to B17, the September OVER/UNDER BUDGET column. This is the bottom line, so let's type in a formula using the @SUM function again. Type the formula:

@SUM(B4–B13–B15)

FIGURE 5–10 The spreadsheet automatically calculates and displays the results based on the formula in B17.

B17: @SUM(B4-B13-B15)   `READY`

	A	B	C	D	E	F
1	BUDGET	SEPT	OCT	NOV	DEC	JAN
2						
3	AMT BUDGETED PER MO	$100.00				
4	BALANCE FORWARD	$100.00				
5						
6	EXPENSES					
7	Books	$8.95				
8	Supplies	$2.25				
9	Clothing	$34.90				
10	Food	$25.00				
11	Phone	$17.05				
12	Entertainment					
13	TOTAL EXPENSES	$88.15				
14						
15	Credit Card Charges	$20.95				
16						
17	OVER/UNDER BUDGET	($9.10)				
18						
19						
20						

which subtracts the contents of cell B13, TOTAL EXPENSES, and cell B15, CREDIT CARD CHARGES, from B4, BALANCE FORWARD. As Figure 5–10 shows, you did a fine job creating your spreadsheet but not so well with your budget! You have overspent by $9.10, which is shown as a minus balance in parentheses, ($9.10).

Copy Now let's set up the rest of your spreadsheet to automatically perform budget calculations each month. This is quickly and accurately accomplished using the Copy command, which duplicates the contents of a range of cells in the spreadsheet. That range may be one cell or a number of cells that you specify in the spreadsheet. This includes not only the constant in the cell but formulas as well. First, we'll use the /Copy command to put the $100 figure in each month's AMT BUDGETED PER MO column. Specify B3 as the range to copy *from,* and enter C3..K3 as the range to copy *to.* This is called an *absolute cell reference* because it is copying identical data from one cell (B3) to the others (C3, D3, F3, etc.).

Next, create a new formula for the BALANCE FORWARD row in cell C4. Type the formula +C3+B17, which adds the balance from the previous month to the amount budgeted for the current month. You won't see the formula appear in cell C4, only in the command line; instead, the cell shows the amount you can spend in October and still remain within your budget.

Now use the /Copy command to copy this formula into the subsequent cells: D4..K4. Figure 5–11 shows the formula and the correct balances forward. This is called *relative cell reference* because the cell references change in each successive column. Move the pointer from C4 to D4 and you will see D3+C17; E4 shows E3+D17, and so on.

Two more Copy commands will finish our spreadsheet. First, copy the @SUM formula in B13 to cells C13..K13. Since we haven't registered any expenses here yet, those totals remain at zero. Last, copy the formula

---

FIGURE 5–11   Each month automatically adds $100.00 to the balance forward.

C4: +C3+B17   READY

	A	B	C	D	E	F
1	BUDGET	SEPT	OCT	NOV	DEC	JAN
2						
3	AMT BUDGETED PER MO	$100.00	$100.00	$100.00	$100.00	$100.00
4	BALANCE FORWARD	$100.00	$90.90	$100.00	$100.00	$100.00
5						
6	EXPENSES					
7	Books	$8.95				
8	Supplies	$2.25				
9	Clothing	$34.90				
10	Food	$25.00				
11	Phone	$17.05				
12	Entertainment					
13	TOTAL EXPENSES	$88.15				
14						
15	Credit Card Charges	$20.95				
16						
17	OVER/UNDER BUDGET	($9.10)				
18						
19						
20						

@SUM(B4−B13−B15) in B17 to cells C17..K17. As you can see, it is possible to copy not only the contents of cells — constants or labels — but formulas as well. Figure 5–12 shows in cell C17 how the spreadsheet, utilizing relative cell referencing, automatically readjusts the formulas for the new cells they are copied into.

Move   The Move command moves a cell or range of cells to another location in the worksheet. For example, you can move an entire row. Let's relocate the BALANCE FORWARD row to the bottom of the spreadsheet. Position the pointer in cell A4 and issue the /Move command. When you are asked to enter the range to move from, type A4..K4, specifying the entire row. Now, enter where you wish to move it to: A19..K19. Now move it back to row 4.

Insert and Delete   Insert and Delete commands allow us to add or insert a new row or column, and conversely, to delete or remove a row or column. For example, inserting a row between rows 3 and 4 makes our spreadsheet look neater. The Insert command does this by shifting everything from row 4 down one row, or over one column, automatically readjusting the formulas. The Delete command does just the opposite.

Save   As you learned in the two preceding chapters, it is essential that you save your work. This is accomplished by using the /File selection from the menu, then selecting the Save command. If your spreadsheet program doesn't have an automatic save feature (as discussed in Chapter 4), use the Save command often while you're working in your spreadsheet to ensure you don't accidentally lose all your figures and formulas. Save your spreadsheet now, and give it a filename if you haven't already done so. When you save a file in most spreadsheet programs, all the labels, constants, and formulas remain on the screen so you can continue working.

FIGURE 5 – 12   The spreadsheet shows the cumulative totals of what is left in your budget.

C17: @SUM(C4-C13-C15)   `READY`

	A	B	C	D	E	F
1	BUDGET	SEPT	OCT	NOV	DEC	JAN
2						
3	AMT BUDGETED PER MO	$100.00	$100.00	$100.00	$100.00	$100.00
4	BALANCE FORWARD	$100.00	$90.90	$190.90	$290.90	$390.90
5						
6	EXPENSES					
7	Books	$8.95				
8	Supplies	$2.25				
9	Clothing	$34.90				
10	Food	$25.00				
11	Phone	$17.05				
12	Entertainment					
13	TOTAL EXPENSES	$88.15	$0.00	$0.00	$0.00	$0.00
14						
15	Credit Card Charges	$20.95				
16						
17	OVER/UNDER BUDGET	($9.10)	$90.90	$190.90	$290.90	$390.90
18						
19						
20						

Retrieve   Retrieve is another /File command used to recall a spreadsheet from mass storage or disk. There are several options under the File command. If you're not sure what filename you gave the spreadsheet, you can choose List. The Combine command lets you merge two spreadsheets into one.

Print   The Print command prints your spreadsheet. Once you've safely stored a spreadsheet on disk, it's good insurance to print a copy. That way, if anything happens to the file, you can always rekey your work.

MEMORY CHECK

1. When preplanning a spreadsheet, what helps make it easier to design?
2. What command is used to change column width?
3. What is the feature that performs mathematical calculations called?
4. What command is useful when you want to transfer identical data from one cell to another?
5. What command should you use, not only to close your spreadsheet but to protect it from accidental loss?

USING ADVANCED SPREADSHEET FEATURES

When someone becomes proficient with a particular application and a computer, they are often referred to as a power user. As you learned in the previous chapter on word processing, there are special advanced features that help you work more efficiently with the program and the data. This is also true with spreadsheet software. Let's look at some of the most commonly used power-user spreadsheet features.

FIGURE 5–13   In the personal budget, the Average function shows the average amount you spend on clothing each month.

B20: @AVG(B10..K10)   `READY`

	A	B	C	D	E	F
1	BUDGET	SEPT	OCT	NOV	DEC	JAN
2						
3	AMT BUDGETED PER MO	$100.00	$100.00	$100.00	$100.00	$100.00
4						
5	BALANCE FORWARD	$100.00	$90.90	$109.05	$74.15	$63.70
6						
7	EXPENSES					
8	Books	$8.95	$18.50	$0.00	$4.95	$2.95
9	Supplies	$2.25	$6.60	$0.00	$0.00	$0.00
10	Clothing	$34.90	$22.00	$15.95	$49.80	$32.00
11	Food	$25.00	$11.75	$31.00	$18.50	$5.00
12	Phone	$17.05	$15.00	$18.00	$22.00	$4.00
13	Entertainment		$8.00	$0.00	$15.20	$0.00
14	TOTAL EXPENSES	$88.15	$81.85	$64.95	$110.45	$43.95
15						
16	Credit Card Charges	$20.95		$69.95		
17						
18	OVER/UNDER BUDGET	($9.10)	$9.05	($25.85)	($36.30)	$19.75
19						
20	Clothing Av. per mo	$30.93				

Functions

Functions, as you already know, combine built-in formulas that perform special mathematical tasks for us with a minimum of keystrokes. Functions, like formulas, work with the data in the spreadsheet, as opposed to commands, which work with the spreadsheet itself. In some spreadsheet programs, you type them in at the command line; in others, a special key such as the @ sign is used to activate a function. The following are the five most common functions:

1. *Average (@AVG)* takes the average of a set of constants.
2. *Count (@COUNT)* literally counts or tallies the contents of cells; for example, the number of cells with a dollar amount of $5 or more.
3. *Maximum (@MAX)* gets the greatest number within a range of cells.
4. *Minimum (@MIN)* gets the lowest number within a range of cells.
5. *Sum (@SUM)* totals the contents of a range of cells.

Let's fill out the subsequent months in our budget, as shown in Figure 5–13, so we can try out some functions. Note the credit card charge in November when you had to buy a scientific calculator. Once you've finished, move the pointer to cell A18 and type in "Clothing Av. per mo" as a label. Now let's find out how much you're spending, on average, for clothes. Enter this function in B18:

`@AVG(B10..K10)`

You'll see the formula appear in the status line and the average amount appear in B18. Alternately, you could use the Sum function to see how much you've spent to date. You could also use the Maximum function to tell you what item you spent the most on.

FIGURE 5–14   The automatic recalculation changes the results.

B5: 150   `READY`

	A	B	C	D	E	F
1	BUDGET	SEPT	OCT	NOV	DEC	JAN
2						
3	AMT BUDGETED PER MO	$150.00	$150.00	$150.00	$150.00	$150.00
4						
5	BALANCE FORWARD	$150.00	$190.90	$259.05	$274.15	$313.70
6						
7	EXPENSES					
8	Books	$8.95	$18.50	$0.00	$4.95	$2.95
9	Supplies	$2.25	$6.60	$0.00	$0.00	$0.00
10	Clothing	$34.90	$22.00	$15.95	$49.80	$32.00
11	Food	$25.00	$11.75	$31.00	$18.50	$5.00
12	Phone	$17.05	$15.00	$18.00	$22.00	$4.00
13	Entertainment		$8.00	$0.00	$15.20	$0.00
14	TOTAL EXPENSES	$88.15	$81.85	$64.95	$110.45	$43.95
15						
16	Credit Card Charges	$20.95		$69.95		
17						
18	OVER/UNDER BUDGET	$40.90	$109.05	$124.15	$163.70	$269.75
19						
20	Clothing Av. per mo	$30.93				

Recalculation

Recalculate, or recalc, refigures your spreadsheet whenever you make a change. It is one of the spreadsheet's most powerful features and works in place of an eraser and pencil to make corrections and updates. If you have to change a number for any reason, you don't have to reenter the entire column of constants all over again, one at a time, as you would with a calculator. Instead, recalc totals the column for you. This makes creating what-if analyses easy. As spreadsheet users say, you "plug in" some numbers or constants, and calculate them; then you "plug in" some new numbers that change the scenario and recalculate to get another outcome.

As previously noted, you went over budget in September. Let's use the spreadsheet's what-if ability to recalculate a reasonable budget for you. What if your budget was $150 per month? Enter the new figure in cell B3 and copy it to the subsequent cells in row 3. Change BALANCE FORWARD in B4 to 150 as well. Compare Figure 5–13 with 5–14. The spreadsheet has automatically recalculated the subsequent BALANCE FORWARD, as well as the OVER/UNDER BUDGET figures. That may turn out to be more than you need, so try $125 and see what you get.

In most spreadsheet programs, recalculation occurs automatically. Every time you make a change, recalculate runs through all the constants and formulas, making all subsequent changes for you. That's fine if you are only making one change. However, if we are making many changes, manual recalculation is more convenient. The spreadsheet doesn't have to perform unnecessary and time-consuming recalcs after every change; instead, it is done after we've made *all* changes. Recalculation significantly sets the spreadsheet apart from the ledger sheet.

Three other useful advanced spreadsheet features are templates, macros, and graphics. Let's look at each.

Templates

It's often possible to use a spreadsheet design over and over. A **template** is a spreadsheet with labels, commands, and formulas already created and saved in a file so that you can begin entering data without doing all the other tedious, repetitive work. It is like a blank form, waiting to have data entered into its cells. For example, storing this year's college budget spreadsheet without the expenditures is a template you can use over again next year.

There are templates for everything from accounting to tax preparation to home budgets. Some people create their own templates but you can also buy ready-made templates. Some are in books and magazines, so you must key in the one you want and save it as a file. Often you can find templates on disk, so you don't have to do the keying. Once you are in the spreadsheet program you simply load the template, as you would any other file, then fill in the cells. All the calculations will be performed automatically.

Macros

A **macro** contains commands or formulas that you create, then store in the spreadsheet so that you can use them again and again. Macros help you program your spreadsheet in many different ways, so you can use it more productively. They are also timesaving devices that save you keystrokes on tasks you frequently perform in your spreadsheet work. For example, you could create a macro that totals your monthly expenditures, tells you the least expensive and most expensive things you bought, and shows how much you were over or under budget. Every time you wish to use the macro, you simply type its filename.

Macros are typed directly into a cell as a label. Here's a simple macro that will save your budget spreadsheet and then retrieve the new version. Move to cell A19 (a blank cell), and type

^/FS~R

which is spreadsheet shorthand for ^ (a centered label), / (the menu), F (for File), S (for Save), ~ (a tilde symbol, for Enter), and R (for Replace). Press Enter; now you see the macro in the cell and on the command line. The macro now contains instructions to perform each of those tasks. Next we must save the macro, so return to the menu by pressing the / key, then select R for Range, then N for Name, and lastly C for Create. You'll see "Enter name:" appear at the top of the screen; type \S and press Enter. Now you'll see "Enter range: A19" appear on the same line. Now your macro is complete! Whenever you want to use it, simply hold down the Alt key and press s. Try saving the usual way, with the Save command, and see how much time and how many keystrokes the macro saves you.

Spreadsheet Graphics

Spreadsheet **graphics** are pictorial representations of the numeric data produced by the spreadsheet. A number of spreadsheet programs are able to turn numeric data into business presentation graphics. These pictorial representations are most commonly in the form of a pie chart, a line graph, or a bar chart, as shown in Figure 5–15. Although we discuss graphics software in greater detail in Chapter 7, it's important to recognize the graphics aspect of spreadsheet programs.

FIGURE 5–15 Spreadsheet data can be displayed as a pictorial representation such as a line graph or a bar chart.

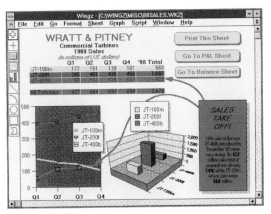

Courtesy of Informix Software Corp.

Spreadsheet data often must be presented to other people; for example, in business meetings. Sometimes it's hard to see the importance of a row of numbers, or to properly grasp their relationship to other numbers. This is where presentation graphics software comes in. Presentation graphics are high-quality graphics used in business plans, proposals, and budgets, which convey numerical data. The graphics program may be a companion program to the spreadsheet, or a separate program capable of accepting and converting spreadsheet data. In either case, the finished presentation graphics can be printed out and displayed on paper, as overhead transparencies, or even as color slides.

MEMORY CHECK

1. What do we call the feature that uses built-in keystrokes to perform mathematical tasks?
2. What is the feature that makes it possible to change figures and perform what-if analyses?
3. What feature makes it easy to store and reuse commands and formulas?
4. What are special files that store commands and keystrokes for reuse called?
5. What do we call pictorial representations of spreadsheet data?

SPREADSHEET APPLICATIONS

The spreadsheet can be used in hundreds of different ways, not only for business applications but for many personal ones as well. The spreadsheet can be used to collect, organize, and calculate many kinds of data into orderly, informative reports. Reports are commonly used in business to share information with management. The spreadsheet is ideal for creating reports because it not only permits organizing and calculating numerical data but also because it lets you use text that identifies the numbers. Here are a few examples of both business and personal spreadsheet applications.

FIGURE 5–16   The balance sheet, income statement, and financial analysis ratios form a common business report.

```
        A        B        C       D       E        F       G      H
                            BALANCE SHEET
 1      ----------------------------------------------------------------------
 2
 3    COMPANY NAME:     XYZ Company        AS OF : December 1982
 4
 5    ASSETS                               LIABILITIES
 6      Cash............    1300             Accounts Pble...   1600
 7      Accounts Rec.....   2600             Notes Pble......   1900
 8      Notes Rec........      0             Interest Pble...      0
 9      Inventory........   7300             Taxes Pble......    300
10      Oth cur assets...    300             Oth Cur Liab....    800
11          Tot Cur Assets.........  11500      Tot Cur Liab.........   4600
12
13      Land............   1200             Bonds Pble......   2000
14      Building........      0             Loan Pble.......      0
15      Equipment.......   5200             Mortgage Pble...    200
16      Less accum dep...  1300             Oth LT Liab.....      0
17      Other assets.....     0
18          Tot Non-cur assets.....   5100      Tot Non-cur Liab......  2200
19                                             Owners Equity.........  9800
20          Total Assets........  16600      Total Liabilities.....  16600
21                   INCOME AND RETAINED EARNINGS STATEMENT
22      ----------------------------------------------------------------------
23    COMPANY NAME:     XYZ Company        FOR PERIOD ENDED: December 1982
24
25    Sales Revenue..............  25900          Tax Rate(.XX)=     40.00%
26    Other Revenue..............    200
27
28              TOTAL REVENUE.....  26100
29    Less Expenses:
30      Cost of Goods Sold........  20500
31      Selling...................   2120
32      Administrative............   1300
33      Interest..................    180
34      Income Taxes..............    800
35          Total Expenses..............  24900
36              NET INCOME........   1200
37    Less:
38      Dividends.........................    600
39          RETAINED EARNINGS........    600
```

Balance Sheet, Income Statement, and Financial Analysis Ratios

These three financial tools—the balance sheet, the income statement, and financial analysis ratios—form a common business report that is prepared at least annually and can often be found in a company's annual report. In the simple spreadsheet in Figure 5–16, you can see each of the three categories. The balance sheet shows the difference between assets and liabilities. The income statement shows how much profit the company made after expenses.

```
        A        B        C        D        E        F        G        H

40
41    PROFITABILITY RATIOS
42    . . . . . . . . . . . . . . . . . . . .
43
44    RATE OF RETURN ON ASSETS                                =     7.88%
45        NET INC+INT EXP(NET OF TAX)/AVG TOT ASSETS
46
47    PROFIT MARGIN RATIO                                     =     5.05%
48        NET INC+INT EXP(NET OF TAX)/SALES
49
50    TOTAL ASSET TURNOVER RATIO                              =   156.02%
51        SALES/AVG TOTAL ASSETS
52
53    INVENTORY TURNOVER RATIO                                =   280.82%
54        COST OF GOODS SOLD/AVG INVENTORY
55
56    PLANT ASSET TURNOVER RATIO                              =   507.84%
57        SALES/AVG PLANT ASSETS
58
59
60
61    LIQUIDITY RATIOS
62    . . . . . . . . . . . . . . . . .
63
64    CURRENT RATIO                                           =   250.00%
65        CUR ASSETS/CUR LIAB
66
67    QUICK RATIO                                             =    84.78%
68        LIQUID ASSETS/CUR LIAB
69
70    SOLVENCY RATIOS
71    . . . . . . . . . . . . . . . . .

      LONG-TERM DEBT RATIO                                    =    18.33%
          TOT NON-CUR LIAB/TOT NON-CUR LIAB+O.E.

      TIMES INT CHARGES EARNED                                =  1211.11%
          NET INC(BEFORE INT&TAX)/INT EXP
```

The financial analysis takes the form of profitability and liquidity ratios that are created with data from the balance sheet and income statement.

Payroll Information

Collecting and calculating payroll information is simple with a spreadsheet. Figure 5–17 shows that once the basic salary and tax information is entered, an employee's number of hours worked is entered and the spreadsheet does the calculating. Changes in withholding tax or a raise are easily entered, with the spreadsheet automatically performing the recalculations.

FIGURE 5–17   Collecting and calculating payroll information is simple with a spreadsheet.

	A	B	C	D	E	F	G	H	I	J	K	L	M	N
1														
2			PAYROLL DATABASE											
3	ASSUMPTIONS: OVERTIME FACTOR(eg 1,5)			1.50			FICA RATE....	0.06						
4	DAILY REGULAR		7.00		8.00			FICA MAXIMUM.37000.00						
5														
6	DATABASE:													
7								TAX %-	TAX%-	TAX%-	PAY $	THIS WEEK'S HOURS WORKED AND		
8	NAME			SS#		MAR-CODE	EXEMPT	FEDERAL	STATE	LOCAL	HOURLY	SUN	MON	TUE
9	SPARKS, BOB			765782343		1	3	0.47	0.05	0.02	15.12	ENTER #	7.00	7.00
10	REINDER, NANCY			234233454		1	2	0.43	0.05	0.00	14.75	ENTER #	7.00	7.00
11	LEWIS, PAULETTE			786903984		0	1	0.27	0.03	0.00	7.56	4.00	9.00	9.00
12	GERMAN, STANELY			447326987		0	1	0.35	0.04	0.00	11.34	ENTER #	7.00	7.00
13	HOWARDS, PETER			132568567		1	1	0.47	0.05	0.02	15.12	ENTER #	7.00	7.00
14	NORMAN, LESLIE			786465876		0	1	0.25	0.03	0.02	7.34	4.00	8.00	9.00
15	PHILLIPS, PETER			396785634		1	4	0.32	0.04	0.02	11.17	ENTER #	7.00	7.00
16	ENTER LAST, FIRST, MI			ENTER #		(1=R/D=S)	ENTER #	ENTER #	ENTER #	ENTER #	ENTER #	ENTER #	ENTER #	ENTER #
17	ENTER LAST, FIRST, MI			ENTER #		(1=R/D=S)	ENTER #	ENTER #	ENTER #	ENTER #	ENTER #	ENTER #	ENTER #	ENTER #
18	DUMMY END RECORD													
19														
20	TOTALS											8.00	52.00	53.00
21														
22														
23	MACRO INSTRUCTIONS FOR UPDATING Y-T-D TOTALS AND DATABASE													
24														
25	THIS IS FOR THE INITIAL STORAGE OF Y-T-D TOTALS:													
26	/FXVTEMPPR·A09.AW17~(Home)/FSPAYROLL~(HOME)													
27														
28	THIS IS FOR THE WEEKLY LOADING OF PREVIOUS Y-T-D TOTALS:													
29	(GoTo)AF9~/FCCETEMPPR~(Home)													
30														
31	THIS IS FOR THE WEEKLY STORAGE OF Y-T-D TOTALS:													
32	(Calc)													
33	/FXVTEMPPR·A09.AW17~R													
34	(GoTo)L9~"ENTER #/·C·L9.R17~(Calc)													
35	(Home)/FSPAYROLL~R/WEY													
36														

Classroom Information

It may come as no surprise that some teachers use a spreadsheet to keep attendance records and student grades. Figure 5–18 shows how each quiz or test score can be quickly entered, with cumulative grades available at any time.

FIGURE 5–18   Each quiz or test score can be quickly entered in the spreadsheet.

STUDENT DATABASE

NAME	WEIGHT= 0.2 GRADE1	WEIGHT= 0.2 GRADE2	WEIGHT= 0.2 GRADE3	WEIGHT= 0.3 GRADE4	WEIGHT= 0.1 ATTEND	WEIGHTED AVERAGE
Berman, Jim	3.6	2.9	2.4	3.5	4	3.23
Brown, Joe	4	3	3.6	4	5	3.82
Carlyle, Mary	2.8	3.5	3.9	2.9	5	3.41
French, Janet	3.4	2.4	4	3.7	5	3.57
Griffith, Jill	4	3.2	3	4	5	3.74
Miller, Sue	2.5	3.7	3.2	2.5	5	3.13
Samson, Bob	3	4	3.1	3.5	3	3.37
Swan, Millie	3	3	4	2.4	4	3.12
Volt, Steve	3.2	3.6	2.7	4	5	3.60
ENTER NAME	ENTER #	ENTER #	ENTER #	ENTER #	5	0.50
ENTER NAME	ENTER #	ENTER #	ENTER #	ENTER #	5	0.50
CLASS AVERAGES	2.681818	2.663636	2.718181	2.772727	4.636363	2.908181

	I	J	K	L	M	N	O	P
1					ATTENDANCE LOG			
2								
3								
4								
5			ENTER	ENTER	ENTER	ENTER	ENTER	
6		STUDENT NAME	DATE 1	DATE 2	DATE 3	DATE 4	DATE 5	TOTAL
7								
8		Brown, Joe	1	1	1	1	1	5
9		Swan, Millie	1	1	0	1	1	4
10		Miller, Sue	1	1	1	1	1	5
11		French, Janet	1	1	1	1	1	5
12		Berman, Jim	1	1	0	1	1	4
13		Volt, Steve	1	1	1	1	1	5
14		Samson, Bob	1	0	1	0	1	3
15		Griffith, Jill	1	1	1	1	1	5
16		Carlyle, Mary	1	1	1	1	1	5
17		ENTER NAME	1	1	1	1	1	5
18		ENTER NAME	1	1	1	1	1	5
19								
20		TOTALS	11	10	9	10	11	51
21								

FIGURE 5–19   Planning a festive occasion is a useful, nonfinancial spreadsheet application.

	A	B	C	D	E	F	G	H	I	J	K	L	M
1													
2				WEDDING/PARTY PLANNER									
3													
4			0 = NO, 1 = YES										
5	# of guests on List:			19	# of responses recv'd:		11						
6	# of invitations req'd:			11	# of guests attending:		8						
7													
8							# INVITED	INVITE MAILED	RESPONSE RECV'D	# WILL ATTEND	GIFT		THANKS SENT
9	GUESTS					ADDRESS							
10	Mr & Mrs John Peters					6 Milltown Rd, Schenectedy, NY 11234	2	1	1	2	Place Setting		0 / 1
11	Mr & Mrs Bill Biler					2314 16th St, Queens, NY 22435	2	1	0 / 1	ENTER #	Silver Setting		0 / 1
12	Mr & Mrs Antoine Goram					43 Sitter St, Darien, CT 03333	2	1	0 / 1	ENTER #	Crystal Goblet		0 / 1
13	Mr & Mrs Tony Newly					12 Waring Way, London, England	2	1	0 / 1	ENTER #	ENTER GIFT		0 / 1
14	Mr & Mrs Paul Newman					Jimminy Rd, Billings, Montana 55439	2	1	1	2	ENTER GIFT		0 / 1
15	Mr & Mrs John Firestone					94 Summer St, Pevers, NM 99654	2	1	1	2	ENTER GIFT		0 / 1
16	Mrs Eunice Engle					1 Abbey Way, Homey, VA 44219	1	1	1	1	ENTER GIFT		0 / 1
17	Mr & Mrs Ron Waters					754 Winsaka Rd, Croton, NY 22310	2	1	1	2	ENTER GIFT		0 / 1
18	Mr & Mrs Glen Keirs					12 Main St, Ossining, NY 11010	2	1	1	0	Place Setting		0 / 1
19	Miss Sandra Keirs					12 Main St, Ossining, NY 11010	1	1	1	0	ENTER GIFT		0 / 1
20	Miss June Keirs					12 Main St, Ossining, NY 11010	1	1	1	0	ENTER GIFT		0 / 1
21	ENTER NAME					ENTER ADDRESS	ENTER #	0 / 1	0 / 1	ENTER #	ENTER GIFT		0 / 1
22	ENTER NAME					ENTER ADDRESS	ENTER #	0 / 1	0 / 1	ENTER #	ENTER GIFT		0 / 1
23	ENTER NAME					ENTER ADDRESS	ENTER #	0 / 1	0 / 1	ENTER #	ENTER GIFT		0 / 1
24	ENTER NAME					ENTER ADDRESS	ENTER #	0 / 1	0 / 1	ENTER #	ENTER GIFT		0 / 1
25	ENTER NAME					ENTER ADDRESS	ENTER #	0 / 1	0 / 1	ENTER #	ENTER GIFT		0 / 1
26	ENTER NAME					ENTER ADDRESS	ENTER #	0 / 1	0 / 1	ENTER #	ENTER GIFT		0 / 1
27	ENTER NAME					ENTER ADDRESS	ENTER #	0 / 1	0 / 1	ENTER #	ENTER GIFT		0 / 1
28	ENTER NAME					ENTER ADDRESS	ENTER #	0 / 1	0 / 1	ENTER #	ENTER GIFT		0 / 1
29	ENTER NAME					ENTER ADDRESS	ENTER #	0 / 1	0 / 1	ENTER #	ENTER GIFT		0 / 1
30	ENTER NAME					ENTER ADDRESS	ENTER #	0 / 1	0 / 1	ENTER #	ENTER GIFT		0 / 1
31	ENTER NAME					ENTER ADDRESS	ENTER #	0 / 1	0 / 1	ENTER #	ENTER GIFT		0 / 1
32	TOTALS						19	11	8	9			0

Wedding or Shower Planner

Planning a festive occasion is a useful, nonfinancial spreadsheet application. Figure 5–19 shows how easy it is to keep track of those invited, who attended, what gifts were given, and if appropriate thank-you notes and other details were completed.

Sports Information

Sports fans can keep track of their favorite player and team statistics with a spreadsheet. Figure 5–20 shows the top hitters in baseball and how their at bats, runs, and hits are calculated to produce their batting average. Using your personal computer and a spreadsheet, you could become a sabermetrician, or baseball scientist.

Scientific Information

The spreadsheet is often used to gather and process data from scientific experiments. It can be used to analyze data in chemistry, physics, or other lab tests, or from various natural occurrences such as the tides, earthquakes, and so forth. Figure 5–21 shows a scientific spreadsheet application.

FIGURE 5–20   Sports fans can keep track of their favorite player and team statistics with a spreadsheet.

	A	B	C	D	E	F
1	Player	Games	At Bat	Runs	Hits	Percentage
2						
3	McGee	125	501	76	168	.335
4	Magadan	142	445	73	147	.330
5	Brett	141	543	82	178	.328
6	R. Henderson	134	482	116	157	.326
7	Dykstra	148	586	106	191	.326
8	Palmeiro	152	589	72	189	.321
9						
10						
11						
12						
13						
14						
15						
16						
17						
18						
19						
20						
21						

51K   (Formula) AVERAGE(C3:D3)

F3 >

FIGURE 5-21   A scientific spreadsheet application.

```
            A       B       C       D       E       F

1
2
3                SOLAR RAYS ON TILTED SURFACE
4
5                ENTER PARAMETERS:
6
7                LATITUDE    35.00
8                TILT        35.00
9                DECLIN      18.00
10
11      *****************************************************
12
13               SIN(L-T)     0.00
14               COS(L-T)     1.00
15               SIN(D)       0.31
16               COS(D)       0.95
17
18                   HOUR    ANGLE
19                 800.00    61.61
20                 900.00    47.74
21                1000.00    34.55
22                1100.00    23.27
23                1200.00    18.00
24                1300.00    23.27
25                1400.00    34.55
26                1500.00    47.74
27                1600.00    61.61
```

MEMORY CHECK

1. What are the two tasks the spreadsheet is good at performing?

2. What are some of the most common spreadsheet applications in business?

3. How does the spreadsheet add value to business reports?

4. What three financial tools does the spreadsheet make use of?

5. How does the spreadsheet make it easy to work with numbers in so many different ways?

DISKbyte

Spreadsheet Tips

1. Plan your spreadsheet on paper before you begin working with the program on the computer. Think through the problem you want to solve, drawing a rough sketch of the data on a sheet of blank paper or a ledger sheet. Jot down the mathematical equations you'll need to come up with answers. This saves you a great deal of time, and you'll make fewer mistakes.

2. Learn to use macros, which is a way to record, save, and reuse formulas, equations, labels, and such. A macro lets you fill a cell with data by tapping a key or two, rather than dozens or hundreds of keystrokes. In addition, macros are a way to customize your keyboard.

3. Use Copy or Replicate when you need to copy data from one place in the spreadsheet to another.

4. When you build a model, even a simple one like your college budget, you have created a template. Save it blank, without any data, and then you can reuse it over and over again.

5. If your completed spreadsheet doesn't work, you'll have to edit it. Make a copy of the spreadsheet and save it under a different filename; then make corrections to the copy and test it. If it works, fine; if not, you can start over again with the original.

6. Spreadsheets take up a great deal of disk space. Make sure you have plenty before you start working.

7. Recalculate your spreadsheet before you print it; otherwise, it may print out the previous version.

THE EVER–EVOLVING SPREADSHEET

The spreadsheet is a product of the personal computer generation of software, and one that has continued to evolve. Today, it is the most widely used productivity tool for managers in business, and it is not uncommon to find people who use it as much as five hours a day. It continues to evolve with such features as the three-dimensional spreadsheet, which allows you to overlay several spreadsheets one on another. Nearly every major software company has a powerful spreadsheet for its customers.

The Apple Macintosh is often used in business now, and a spreadsheet program called WingZ promises to do for the Mac what VisiCalc did for the Apple II and Lotus 1-2-3 did for the IBM PC. WingZ combines the spreadsheet with 3D graphics, charts, and text, then allows arranging each element on the screen to print out on a single page for presentation. What's more, it can do so in color or black and white. WingZ is an example of the next generation in spreadsheet software.

Most software originated on large computers, and later was made available for personal computers. In an interesting reversal, Lotus 1-2-3 is now available in a mainframe version. Clearly, the spreadsheet is a useful tool, one that people are constantly using to find more ways to work with numbers. And making numbers make sense is the most important goal of all.

ETHICS

There is an old saying in business: "Figures do not lie." But spreadsheet users must be careful about trusting the figures they see, for the figures are only as accurate as the person who entered them. It's possible to make errors in formulas, or to slip a decimal place, or forget to recalculate when you change something. People have made errors with pencil and paper, adding machines, and electronic calculators for years. Now they make errors with spreadsheet models, too. A faulty model with incorrect formulas will produce errors in the spreadsheet.

It's possible to make a spreadsheet lie, in the same way *any* numbers can be made to lie. A product manager can simply pluck sales projections out of the air, plug them into the spreadsheet, and project success. Inaccurate data produces inaccurate results: garbage in, garbage out.

Using a spreadsheet program ethically means entering the correct data to arrive at a correct conclusion — and accepting the results. Since it's possible to create what-if scenarios with the spreadsheet, it's easy to keep feeding numbers in until the desired results are produced. This is not a good use of the computer, and it doesn't make sense morally, ethically, or practically — from a business perspective.

It's often hard for humans to own up to their mistakes. It's not uncommon to hear people blaming the computer for errors in many walks of life. In fact, some companies have brought lawsuits against software companies, alleging the program made a mistake that cost them money. Lacking merit, none have been brought to trial. The problem, as might be expected, is garbage in, garbage out.

The spreadsheet needs to be used accurately and sensibly. If that's done, using it ethically should follow.

CAREERbyte

The Spreadsheet Wizard

Jack McGrath is a free-lance writer who found a new career with the spreadsheet. Jack first encountered an Apple II running VisiCalc while researching a business article he was writing. Having worked with paper spreadsheets long before, he was fascinated. In 1981, once it was clear that VisiCalc was an enormous success, Dan Bricklin hired Jack to write a newsletter for the thousands of VisiCalc users. It was called "SATN," for Software Arts Technical Notes, and quickly became known as the best user support newsletter in the software industry. As a result, Jack has made a career out of experimenting with interesting ways to use spreadsheet programs. Jack took ideas and suggestions from VisiCalc users and turned them into useful spreadsheet applications. In the process, he grew familiar with the spreadsheet's vast potential, and began creating applications himself. "SATN's" readership grew to over 10,000. He wrote and edited "SATN" for three years, until Software Arts closed its doors.

But even as he remained loyal to VisiCalc users, Jack was aware of Lotus 1-2-3's success. When SATN ceased publication, he put his knowledge and his newsletter publishing experience to good use by starting his own Lotus 1-2-3

Courtesy of Jack McGrath

newsletter, called "Jack McGrath's @Max." Meanwhile, his reputation continued to grow: "I would be at a CPA [certified public accountant] convention," Jack says. "People would see my name badge and come up to me and say, 'I've been reading your stuff for years!'" His readership grew even more when he began writing a regular monthly spreadsheet applications column in a major financial magazine.

The business press began calling him to ask his opinion about this or that spreadsheet. Once the delays in releasing the updated version of Lotus 1-2-3 began, he was asked if 1-2-3 would be hurt. Jack told *The Wall Street Journal* that "for any product to displace 1-2-3, it will have to cure cancer, taste like chocolate, and cost $1." He was held in such respect in the industry that he was one of the first to be permitted to test the new version of Lotus 1-2-3.

To date, Jack McGrath has written over 2,000 spreadsheet templates and applications, most of them for 1-2-3. Some of the most popular are on the lease-versus-buy decision for large capital expenditures, how to value a small corporation's stock, and cash flow forecasting for business. He's also written numerous personal financial planning applications, such as how to budget and plan for sending a child through college. But he's also written some rather unusual applications, such as the one that planned a Christmas dinner so all the food would be cooked on time for the family to sit down at 4:30.

Jack has collected his best applications in a book called *1-2-3 at Work: The Joy of Lotus,* so named because he says "all spreadsheet books are essentially cookbooks." He is a perfect example of how someone with a particular interest and a good idea can find success in the computer industry.

SUMMARY

1. *Explain what a spreadsheet is and how a spreadsheet program works.* The spreadsheet is an application that allows us to create sophisticated mathematical models for financial and economic planning. It is the electronic counterpart of the paper ledger sheet, the pencil, and the hand-held calculator. The spreadsheet was invented by an MBA student who saw a real need for it in his schoolwork.

2. *Describe the different uses for a spreadsheet.* The spreadsheet can add, subtract, multiply, and divide. However, it can also let us create and test financial models, using its what-if analysis capabilities. The spreadsheet allows us to use formulas, some of them by using built-in spreadsheet functions to perform a series of mathematical operations.

3. *Identify the various characteristics of the spreadsheet screen.* The spreadsheet screen represents the paper ledger sheet. Vertical columns and horizontal rows create cells, which may contain labels (text) and values (numbers) in the form of constants or mathematical formulas. The cursor in a spreadsheet is called a cell pointer, and wherever it is placed is where labels or values will be placed. Spreadsheet programs commonly have a menu line and/or a command line, where commands and other important information are displayed, and a status line, where labels, constants, and formulas are typed and displayed.

4. *Explain the steps in creating and editing a spreadsheet.* We begin by creating a spreadsheet design on paper, then create the labels followed by entering data, or constants. Next, we enter the formulas necessary to perform calculations on the data. The spreadsheet does the calculating for us. We can copy, move, insert, or delete the contents of cells, whether in columns or rows. As with other applications, we save the file when we're finished working with it and can retrieve it to work some more. Printing gives us a hard copy to look at, and also serves as a backup.

5. *Name some of the advanced functions and features of the spreadsheet.* Advanced features help us become power users. Functions, which are often identified by the @ symbol, perform special tasks with a minimum of keystrokes. Recalculate helps us quickly see the results of changing figures or performing a what-if analysis. The spreadsheet normally recalculates automatically, but can usually be set to manual as well. We can create templates for spreadsheet designs we use over and over. Macros store labels, constants, or formulas we use frequently, which can be recalled with just a few keystrokes. There are thousands of business and personal uses for the spreadsheet.

KEY TERMS

calculate, p. 135
cell, p. 131
cell pointer, p. 132
column, p. 131
command line, p. 132
constant, p. 132
formula, p. 130

function, p. 128
graphics, p. 144
label, p. 132
ledger sheet, p. 126
macro, p. 144
menu line, p. 132
model, p. 127

recalculate, p. 143
row, p. 131
spreadsheet, p. 127
status line, p. 132
template, p. 144
value, p. 128
what-if analysis, p. 128

REVIEW AND DISCUSSION QUESTIONS

1. What are the advantages of working with a mathematical model?
2. How do what-if analyses help a business make better decisions?
3. What are the advantages offered by integrated software packages such as Lotus 1-2-3?
4. What three manual tools are built into a spreadsheet?
5. What are the primary features of a spreadsheet?
6. What is the first decision you must make when setting up a spreadsheet?
7. Why is it vital that you understand the relationships between the constants and the formulas in your spreadsheet?
8. Why is recalculate such a powerful spreadsheet feature?
9. How do templates save you time and energy?
10. What do macros help you do more effectively?
11. Why is it important to be able to turn spreadsheet data into a graphic representation?
12. What types of workers do you think get the most benefit from a spreadsheet?
13. What are the risks in using a spreadsheet?
14. Why is it important to check your formulas and the results the spreadsheet produces?
15. What are the advantages of using a spreadsheet in business?
16. Name three ways you could use a spreadsheet.
17. What features would you add to a spreadsheet to make an ideal integrated software package?
18. Why do you think there is such a strong emphasis on using mathematical and analytical computer tools such as the spreadsheet in business planning and decision making?
19. When is it most important to create presentation graphics from the spreadsheet?
20. The electronic spreadsheet was a unique innovation in computer software. Discuss how Dan Bricklin got the idea for the spreadsheet; similarly, is it possible that there are more software innovations in store for us in the future?

ISSUES

1. A construction company used a spreadsheet to create a bid for building a multimillion dollar office complex. One of the line items, overhead costs totaling $250,000, wasn't inserted in a cell that was part of the formula. As a result, it didn't get calculated into the final bid. The company won the bid but found it would lose money because overhead wasn't factored in.

The construction company sued the software developer, claiming the problem was a bug or malfunction of the spreadsheet. Was it? Or was it carelessness? One spreadsheet expert says that formula errors are very common. Do you think the construction company had cause to sue? Should the instruction manual have made special mention of this kind of error? Who, if anyone, is at fault?

2. Imagine you are at your job and your boss comes in with a new project. He is excited; you can tell he hopes its success will earn him a promotion. He asks you to "do up a spreadsheet that'll make it look real good for management." The implication is clear; he wants you to create a false set of numbers that ensure a positive return on investment. What should you do?

3. You have a personal computer that you share with a colleague—let's call her Jane. Jane is an avid sports fan and follows all the team's games. She is using a spreadsheet to record team statistics. One day you walk in and there are two other people in the room, hovering over Jane and the computer. She is performing a what-if analysis on how certain players will perform in Saturday's game. The other two people take out money and begin placing bets. It seems to you that Jane is a bookie! Is this illegal? Is it an unethical use of the computer?

Database Management Systems

CHAPTER OUTLINE

Computer Wins Indy 500

What Is a Database?
 The Database Management System
 The DBMS Advantage

Basic Features of the DBMS
 Types of Database Management Systems
 Data Elements
 *DISKbyte: Wayne Ratliff — Father of the
   Personal Computer DBMS*
 The DBMS Screen

A DBMS Work Session
 Database Design
 Creating a Database
 Saving the Database
 Manipulating Data
 Printing Reports

Advanced Database Management
 Personal Information Managers
 Managing a Corporate Database
 DISKbyte: The DBMS as a Productivity Tool

The Ever-Evolving DBMS
 DISKbyte: DBMS Tips

Ethics
 CAREERbyte: Building a Geoprocessing Database

Summary

Key Terms

Review and Discussion Questions

Issues

OBJECTIVES

After reading and studying this chapter, you should be able to:

1. Explain the difference between a database and a database management system (DBMS).
2. Describe the advantages of a DBMS.
3. Identify the four types of DBMSs and the data elements they use.
4. Explain the steps in creating and editing a database.
5. Describe some features of the modern databaselike personal information manager.
6. Describe how business and government use advanced data management.

COMPUTER WINS INDY 500

A few years ago, the United States Auto Club (USAC) decided there was so much information associated with the famous Indianapolis 500 auto race that it needed a computer to manage all of it. David L. Bowers, a member of USAC, previous race car driver and team owner, and vice president of marketing at Emerald Intelligence, a software company, led the project to computerize the data on the race cars during the month of practice and qualification, as well as during the race itself. Hewlett-Packard, Tandy, and IBM have donated their most powerful personal computers and printers in the past; Micro Data Base Systems (MDBS) provided Guru, its most sophisticated database management system software; and USAC provided the people to gather and store the information in the computer system.

Courtesy of Emerald Intelligence

When they were done, they had a database that held the answers to just about any question anybody might ask. Prior to the race, the system was made available to the press, race officials, and drivers to obtain background on the race, official rules, and profiles of other participants. Many companies sponsor cars and provide their products. The database provides a list of all the cars using Champion spark plugs or B. F. Goodrich tires, for example. According to David, "This data makes it possible to corroborate the statements that product companies make in worldwide advertising campaigns, such as '9 of the last 10 winners of the Indianapolis 500 have used our product.'"

The system was used to compile and analyze complex race data. This was important because there are a number of monetary awards given to drivers, and products used on race cars have to be certified. For example, was a certain part able to perform without failing for the entire race? Using Guru, it was possible to get race results and product certifications much more quickly and accurately. "In recent years we have seen these contingency awards, as we call them, total more than $1 million," says David, "often times with complex legal and contractual issues regarding performance and payout. The database is essential in helping provide accurate and timely reports."

The information in the Indy 500 database has become a valuable resource for the future as well, helping driving teams learn how competitors performed and how to choose the most reliable parts and products. Product manufacturers are using the data to test other products, learning what specifications are necessary, as well as better manufacturing methods. The key is the great degree of flexibility and versatility in ways of examining and analyzing database information that Guru provides. Database management systems have helped businesses make information more useful for many years. Today, people in many other walks of life are discovering how useful they can be.

WHAT IS A DATABASE?

Many people collect one thing or another. How about you? Do you collect anything? If you do, you probably are familiar with some of the problems of managing a collection. One way to keep track of a collection is to create a **database** — a group of related records and files. Libraries are in the business of collecting books, and most have databases to help manage their collections.

For most of this century, libraries used card catalogs as databases to manage their book collections. Card catalogs hold three kinds of cards to represent each book the library owns. First, there is a title index, which has one card for every book in the library, filed alphabetically by book title. Second, the card catalog has an author index, which has one card for every book, filed alphabetically by author name. Third is the subject index, which has a card for each book according to topic. When a book falls into several subject categories, it has several subject cards. Card catalogs file subject cards in alphabetical order, too.

The card catalog is an excellent manual database — it allows library users to search the entire contents of a library book collection by flipping through cards, rather than walking through the library reading book spines. It also allows users to search for books in three ways — by title, author, and subject. But a card catalog has several limitations. It is slow; you often have to flip through many cards to find the one you're looking for. It is a single-user system; if someone else is using the drawer pertaining to the subject you're exploring, you have to wait to use it. And it is limited in its scope. For example, if you want to find all the books written by Isaac Asimov pertaining to Mars, you have to manually search either all the Mars subject cards or all the Asimov author cards, carefully reading each one. Some searches require looking through several dozen (even several hundred) cards.

When computer use became widespread, libraries found that turning their card catalogs into computerized databases, for use with a database management system, could make searches easier and simpler. Let's find out why.

The Database Management System

A **database management system (DBMS)** is application software that lets you organize, store, and retrieve data from a single database or several databases. A DBMS helps you manage data better by excelling at three tasks: (1) it allows you to *design* the way data is organized, then *enter* it in a logical manner; (2) it allows you to *manipulate* this data, modifying, searching, sorting, and organizing it in various ways; and (3) it allows you to *format* and *print* your data as reports. Combining these three tasks — data entry, manipulation, and printing — sets database management systems apart from the other software we've studied so far.

The DBMS Advantage

Managing databases with computers has become very popular. A DBMS allows you to use a database in many ways that aren't possible with traditional paper records. One DBMS advantage is *flexibility*. A DBMS allows you to search for many kinds of data. While a card catalog can only be searched according to title, author, or subject, a computer database can be searched and manipulated by any type or category of data. For example, you could design a library database so that a DBMS searches it by book publication date, or by the

FIGURE 6 – 1   Library card catalogs and database management systems have similar data structures to organize data.

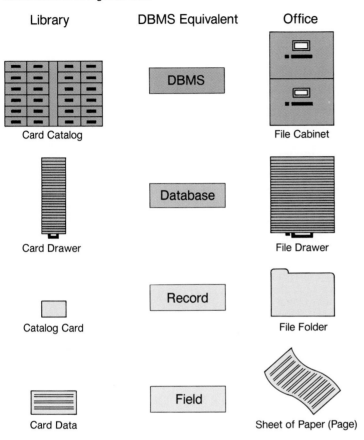

Library	DBMS Equivalent	Office
Card Catalog	DBMS	File Cabinet
Card Drawer	Database	File Drawer
Catalog Card	Record	File Folder
Card Data	Field	Sheet of Paper (Page)

number of pages in its books, or even by the language in which books are written. Figure 6 – 1 shows the relationship between a library card catalog, an office filing system, and a DBMS.

A second DBMS advantage is *discrimination.* A DBMS allows you to search selectively. For example, a DBMS can provide you with a list of all books by Isaac Asimov, written about Mars, before 1979; or a listing of all science fiction novels over 400 pages long.

A third DBMS advantage is *extensibility.* You can often use a DBMS to search many different kinds of databases. For example, you can search through databases in a dozen university libraries from one location, so long as the basic file structure is the same.

The features and advantages of word processing, the spreadsheet, and the database management system overlap to some extent. It is possible to search word processing files for a name and address or a specific phrase, but its strength is in its ability to manage text. A spreadsheet is capable of producing sales or manufacturing reports, but its strength is in its ability to perform mathematical calculations. A database management system is able to draw on the strengths of word processing by sorting through large quantities of text or the strengths of a spreadsheet by tabulating numeric data and making it available in many different ways. Let's learn more about databases and the software — the DBMS — we use to manipulate them.

BASIC FEATURES OF THE DBMS

There are several different kinds of DBMSs. One thing all share in common is data. While all computer applications use data, the DBMS uses it in a very orderly fashion. In this section, we'll learn about the different types of database management systems; next, we'll see how data is used in a database; and lastly, we'll learn how a database is used in a DBMS.

Types of Database Management Systems

As with other applications we have studied, people and hardware, combined with DBMS software, form a computer system that helps us effectively perform database management tasks. People design databases but in the past they were constrained by the available hardware and software technology.

By the late 1950s and early 1960s, many businesses had recognized the value of a computerized database. Meanwhile, computer technology was improving. These events stimulated computer professionals to begin developing different database models to accomplish jobs more efficiently. Let's briefly study the evolution of database management systems.

Flat File   The first computerized databases were simple file management systems; in fact, one was named just that, referred to by its acronym, FMS. The file management system was useful for gathering and storing data but in design it was nothing more than a library card catalog. For that reason, the file management system is often called a **flat file database,** because each file is stacked on top of the previous one. If you wanted to find something, you started at the beginning and looked through each file until you got the right one. There was no way to group similar files together, or to look for files that shared similar characteristics — for example, all the customers who lived in Rockville, Maryland.

The earliest flat file database files were stored on reels of magnetic tape, which we will discuss in more detail in Chapter 10. That meant the data was stored *sequentially,* or one record following another. For example, letters might be stored in chronological order by date or purchase orders might be stored in numerical order. Business quickly outgrew file management systems, and the following requirements emerged:

- The need to quickly retrieve specific data.
- The need to update data only once, in a file used by the entire corporation, rather than having to update multiple copies of the same file located in different databases.

FIGURE 6–2   A bank's DBMS. Note how the same information recurs in different databases.

Savings Deposits	**Quarterly Interest Payments to Account**	**Withdrawals**
account id		account id
data	account id	date
amount	date paid	check serv #
identification	date credited	check issue id
teller id	withholding	
location	begin balance	**Adjustments**
branch location	calculated rate	account id
batch #	calculated	date
sequence id	period	adj type
work request?		reason code
supervisor verify	**Activity**	
IRA?	customer id	**Interest Payment**
	type	account id
CD Withdrawals	amount	date
account id	date	date paid
amount	process date	amount paid
date	teller id	amount withheld
closeout?		
extension	**Deposits**	
branch location	account id	
teller id	date	
location	bank float amt	
domicile	cust float amt	
check #	IRA year	
	mature date	

• The goal of working with all the corporate databases as if they were a single, unified entity.

During this time, business was flourishing. Large companies found it increasingly difficult to keep track of all the data in the computer: personnel files, equipment maintenance files, correspondence files, purchase order files, inventory files—the list goes on and on. Figure 6–2 shows a large bank's database management system. Note the complex interrelationships between the various databases. In business or government, a database of this size and complexity may be located on many computers. The customer file is only one database; others may include the company's payroll, inventory, assets, business correspondence and records, and a host of other stored data.

But the new DBMS requirements were also a response to diversity in the corporate environment. Each department often had its own way of managing files. There was no way to exchange data between departments that used different computer systems or DBMSs except the old way—paper. Managers seeking information on parts, prices, or inventory, for example, had to go from department to department, and from one DBMS to another, to gather all related data.

The advent of the disk drive in the late 1950s, with its ability to access data in *random order* instead of sequentially, made it easier to design databases according to relationships between different data. Now it was possible to quickly find all citizens who didn't pay their income taxes in 1985, or every customer who bought a blue queen-size blanket.

Flat file database management systems are still in use today. The most common ones are used for simple organizing chores on personal computers.

FIGURE 6–3   A hierarchical or inverted tree database.

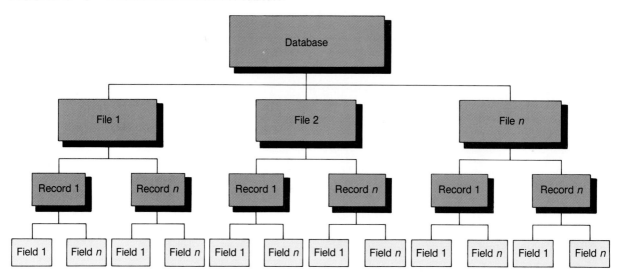

Many are specially designed to perform specific tasks such as creating an address book, a personal belongings inventory, a recipe file, and just about anything that can be logically organized.

Hierarchical   The **hierarchical database** model allows you to create relationships between logical data elements by establishing an inverted or upside-down tree structure from the central root to the branches, as shown in Figure 6–3. Its main limitation is that you have to move from the root to a branch to access one file or record, then back to the root and out to a different branch to access another file or record. Therefore, we say the hierarchical database creates *one-to-many relationships* because you begin with the root, then move to the branches. An example of a hierarchical database is IBM's Information Management System (IMS).

Database designers knew the idea of using many branches was a good one but they needed to solve the problem of having to return to the root every time they wanted to go out to another branch. In database terminology, they needed the ability to establish more relationships.

Network   If the tree was a good model, database designers reasoned, the human cardiovascular system is even better. After all, its branches are interconnected and blood flows anywhere, as long as it passes through the heart. Therefore, the next step in DBMS evolution was the **network database** model. In DBMS terms, this system utilizes what are termed *many-to-many relationships,* as veins intricately intertwine throughout the body. You don't have to enter the network database through the root, as in a hierarchical database; you can enter it anywhere. The most widely used example is IDMS, from Computer Associates. Figure 6–4 shows a network database.

Relational   The network database was a big step forward in database design in the 1970s; but an even more efficient model, the relational database, emerged in the 1980s. A **relational database** allows you to interchange and

FIGURE 6-4   A network database.

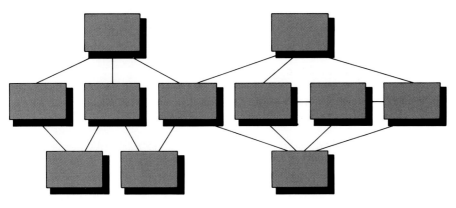

FIGURE 6-5   A relational database table.

Employee		
Name	**Office Location**	**Department**
Doney	Phoenix	Accounting
Black	Denver	Sales
James	Cleveland	Sales
Giles	San Diego	Accounting
Smith	Miami	Accounting
Fink	San Diego	Sales

cross-reference data between different records. The relational database model is the most modern, easiest to understand, and most flexible of the three. In a relational database, all data is viewed as essentially alike; therefore, it creates *any-to-any relationships*. Data is stored in tables, as shown in Figure 6–5. The relational database has become the industry standard.

Figure 6–6 shows all three types of databases and how they would organize the same data. You can see that the relational database avoids creating duplicate data elements and is more flexible in organizing data. Because of this flexibility, you can focus on working with your data, rather than spending time maneuvering through the DBMS. Most personal computer DBMSs use the relational model.

Data Elements

In a DBMS, data is arranged from the smallest to the largest. These are referred to as **data elements** or data items, individual pieces of data that are joined to produce information. Without data elements, we would not have consistent data organization or effective data management. There are two levels of data elements used in the DBMS. One is called physical data representation and the other is called logical data representation.

FIGURE 6–6　　The same data is represented here in each of the three types of databases.

Hierarchical

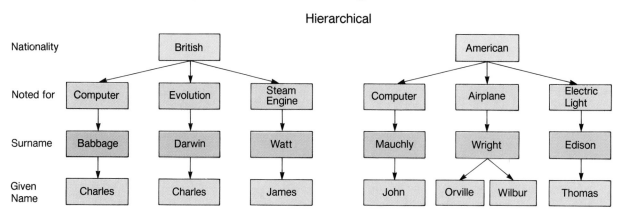

Network

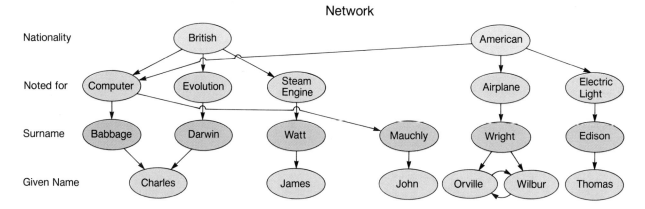

Relational

Surname	Given Name	Nationality	Noted for
Edison	Thomas	American	Electric Light
Babbage	Charles	British	Computer
Wright	Orville	American	Airplane
Mauchly	John	American	Computer
Darwin	Charles	British	Evolution
Watt	James	British	Steam Engine
Wright	Wilbur	American	Airplane

Source: Reprinted with permission, *High Technology* magazine (December 1984). Copyright © 1984 by High Technology Publishing Corporation, 38 Commercial Wharf, Boston, MA 02110.

Physical Data Representation　**Physical data representation** refers to how data is stored and retrieved on the computer system's auxiliary storage devices. Physical data elements include the bit, byte, and word that you learned about in Chapter 2. These elements are stored in files on some form of magnetic media, such as a disk.

Logical Data Representation　**Logical data representation** is an organized method for storing data in a database. For example, a database of customer files may be organized by name, address, phone number, and last order; or it may be organized by credit card number, phone number, ZIP code, address, and name. All logical data may be in one file or it may be in a number of files, depending on the way it was designed and hence represented.

Most people organize things in logical ways. For example, a library card catalog has these data elements: data item, card, drawer, and index. Several data items pertaining to each book are written on a card. Cards are collected in drawers. Drawers are assembled into the title, author, and subject indexes.

Office filing systems use data elements similar to the library card catalog system. Sheets of paper, like data items, are stored in folders. Folders are collected in file drawers. Drawers are components of file cabinets. These are effective manual data management systems and they are used extensively all over the world.

Just as the card catalog and filing system use logical data elements, so does the DBMS. Its logical data elements are called *characters, fields, records, files,* and *databases.* Let's examine them one at a time, to see how they work together. As you read, it may be helpful to refer to the comparisons shown in Figure 6–1.

Characters   A **character** is a single symbol, letter, number, or punctuation mark defined in the database. It is the smallest unit of data manipulated by a DBMS. Characters work together to form meaningful data such as words, social security numbers, and so forth.

Fields   A **field** is a group of characters that represent an **attribute** or characteristic of an **entity.** An example of a field is a person's (the entity) first or last name, their ZIP code, or their hat size (the attribute). In other words, it is a data item that is part of a larger whole. A field is similar to a data item on a library card or a blank line to fill in on an employment application. In a card catalog database, the card is an entity, a book; each field on the card contains an attribute of the book, such as its title, author, subject, publication date, and page count.

Records   A DBMS **record** is a collection of related data items or fields that a DBMS treats as a unit. For example, a record contains all the information about a customer that is needed to process an order. A record holds all the attributes necessary to complete an entity. A record is like a card in a card catalog database. Card catalogs have one card for each book. Office systems may have one folder for each employee or customer.

Files   Within the DBMS, a file is a collection of related records that serves as a unit of storage. The file holds all of the company's customer records. Of course, there are many types of files, and they may be organized however people want. Customers may be grouped into files by state, by alphabetical order, and so forth. As with any other computer files, there can be backup files as well. DBMSs hold related records in a file in the same way all the subject cards, say those for the letter *R*, are kept together in a card catalog.

Databases   The simplest database is a single file; however, DBMSs really shine when they bring large quantities of data together. They do this by grouping many files into a database. A database is a common pool of data — a single, common storage entity used by the DBMS. A database may have dozens, even thousands, of files. In the library, it is the entire card file cabinet. A DBMS can manipulate multiple databases, too.

D I S K b y t e

Wayne Ratliff: Father of the Personal Computer DBMS

The idea of a DBMS for a personal computer seemed farfetched in 1980. Could the personal computer, with its tiny 64K of RAM and floppy disks that held only 241K bytes, ever produce a truly useful database? Wayne Ratliff thought so.

Wayne Ratliff was an aerospace engineer who developed the first DBMS for personal computers using the now-defunct CP/M operating system in the late 1970s. He called it DBMS Vulcan, and it had all the personality of that other Vulcan, Mr. Spock, until George Tate and Hal Lashlee came along. They were business and marketing

Photo by Carolyn Ratliffe

whizzes, and saw Vulcan's potential. Together, the three formed the software company Ashton-Tate. But when it came time to market

the software, they learned another company owned the Vulcan name. An advertising man suggested dBASE II, saying it sounded "hightech." The "II" was added to make it sound like a new and improved dBASE I—which, of course, had never existed.

dBASE II was a success, and when the IBM PC came out, there was a real, improved version of dBASE II—dBASE III. With these products, Ashton-Tate has reigned as the king of DBMS software for personal computers for many years. Wayne Ratliff has continued as an innovator in personal computer software.

The DBMS Screen

In word processing, the screen resembles a blank sheet of paper. In the spreadsheet, the screen is a worksheet, ready for you to enter data into cells. With the DBMS, we work with two basic types of screens. The first is the menu, where we issue commands to create a database and subsequently work with it. The second is the database screen where we actually enter data, or fill in the blanks so to speak.

The DBMS cursor most often appears as a highlighted rectangle, either in color or reverse video, similar to the spreadsheet. You use the arrow keys to move from command to command in the menu, pressing Enter to issue the command. The same is true as you enter data in the database screens. We mentioned before that there is a certain degree of consistency across different applications. Like its counterparts, the DBMS uses the Backspace and Delete keys, the Page Up and Page Down keys, and may use the Function keys as well. Don't hesitate to use Help as you learn about the keys and the program.

Refer to Figure 6–7. Like our other applications, the DBMS usually has a status line to tell us where we are in the task we're performing. The status line may tell you things such as how to perform the task you are currently working on. Often you will see a helpful additional message that describes the purpose of the particular command or function you are contemplating using. Now that you know what the screen looks like, let's begin our work session.

FIGURE 6-7   The opening screen of the DBMS.

Set Up Create Update Position Retrieve Organize Modify Tools   10:00:22 am

```
Database file
Format
View
Query
Report
Label
```

ASSIST   <B:>   Opt: 1/6
Move selection bar - ↑↓. Select - ↵. Leave menu - ↔. Help - F1. Exit - Esc.
                Create a database file structure.

MEMORY CHECK

1. What are the four types of database management systems?
2. What advantage does a relational database model have over the other models?
3. What are the two types of data elements in a DBMS?
4. What are the three types of physical data elements?
5. What are the five types of logical data elements?
6. What are the three main elements of the DBMS screen?

A DBMS WORK SESSION

As with the other applications we've studied, our database management work session presents features and commands in a general way. Our goal is to explain database concepts and applications so that you'll be able to learn a specific software package more easily. As with the spreadsheet program in the previous chapter, the best way to begin working with a DBMS is to carefully plan out what you want it to do in advance. That is our first topic for discussion.

Database Design

As we've explained, a database is a collection of records and files; it may or may not be on a computer. Regardless, the most important first step is **database design,** planning or describing the data that comprises our database and the relationships between the various kinds of data it contains. Our goal is to make the data easy to enter and easy to use.

There are two steps in database design. The first is **data definition,** creating a detailed description of the data. The second is defining **data relationships,** the interaction between various data elements. Once we've built the database using the DBMS software, it's often difficult to go back and change it. A little planning goes a long way, so please resist the temptation to power up the computer. Let's get out pencil and paper to see how we're going to organize our database.

Data Definition   Most of us are familiar with movies, so let's create a videotape film library database. There are many kinds of data we could collect about movies: category, title, director, actors, year made, length, rating, color or black and white, awards won, plot summary, your own review comments — the list goes on and on. In database terms, each movie is an entity; each characteristic is an attribute.

What do you need to know? What are the most important things you want to store about your movie collection? It may be that if you include everything you consider interesting in your database, you might find it too large or impractical to use. One way to determine what you need to know is by thinking about how you'll use the database.

Perhaps you will use your movie database to help decide what movie you want to watch. Let's say you have a few friends over to watch a movie. You ask them, "What would you like to see?" One requests a drama, while another suggests a comedy. Someone else asks if you have any Woody Allen movies. A third would like to see a Steve Martin comedy. Another asks if you have Martin's *The Jerk.* As you can see, there are many attributes involved in organizing this database. When beginning a database design, it's usually best to list as many attributes as you can, then weed out the less-essential characteristics as you progress. Figure 6–8 shows a sketch of our database design.

Data Refinement   **Data refinement** is the condensing and ordering phase in database design. You don't want your database cluttered with data you'll rarely use, so decide which attributes are least important and take them off the list. There is another important reason for data refinement. As you set up the DBMS software to type in movie titles, names of actors and actresses, and so forth, you'll have to allocate a specific number of blank spaces to be filled in. Each is a character, and you'll recall that the character is the smallest unit of data manipulated by the database. If you allow for too many characters, you'll use up memory space on your data disk. On the other hand, if you don't allow for enough space, you won't be able to fit everything in. Therefore, you must be judicious in your character counts. For example, try to settle on an average title length and abbreviate long titles such as *Everything You Always Wanted to Know about Sex but Were Afraid to Ask.*

Creating a Database

Once you have finished your database design and have determined all the attributes, you can begin working with the DBMS to create the database. The first thing to do, of course, is power up the computer. If you need to refresh your memory on how to do so, review the section on booting your personal computer in Chapter 3. Next, when you see the DOS prompt, type in the DBMS program name to load it.

FIGURE 6–8   Database design is a handwritten process. Sketch out the data you need to use beforehand, to make working with the database management system easier.

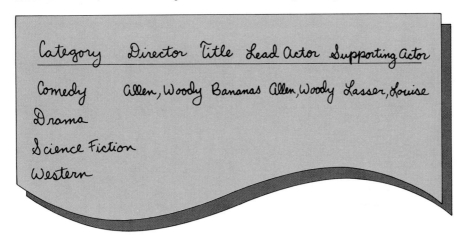

The first thing you'll see is a screen similar to the one in Figure 6–7. Select the command for creating a new database; in this case, move the arrow key to Create and press the Enter or Return key. As you recall, you can create not one but many databases with your DBMS program: one for movies, another for your butterfly collection, or any other data you want to collect. So at this point, when you are prompted to name the database, please do so. We'll keep it simple and call it MOVIES.

Creating Fields   After pressing the Enter or Return key, you'll see the screen for creating fields. Remember how we selected attributes for entities in database design? Now each entity or film will become a record, and each attribute about that entity will become a field. Our task is to create fields of the correct type and size. As you can see on the screen, there are four possible characteristics for each field: name, type, width (in characters), or number of decimal places (for numeric data such as money). Here are some guidelines:

- *Name:* Any characters, including text, numbers, or symbols, may be used.
- *Type:* This defines what kind of data will be entered into this field — characters, numbers, or a date.
- *Width:* A field has a definite limit on the number of characters it can hold, usually 254. As mentioned earlier, do not allocate any more characters than absolutely necessary.
- *Decimal:* This tells the database how many decimal places to assign to numeric data such as dollars and cents.

Now we will see how our planning for database design and specifications pays off. We're going to create all the fields that will be used in the records of our database. We'll see later how the choices we make here can affect how we use our database. For now, let's set up these character fields for our movie database: CAT (category), TITLE, DIRECTOR, ACTOR1, ACTOR2, RATING, TIM (length in minutes), and DATE. Type CAT at the cursor in field 1, then press Enter to proceed to the next field. Refer to Figure 6–9 for the field

---

FIGURE 6–9   Creating fields in the database.

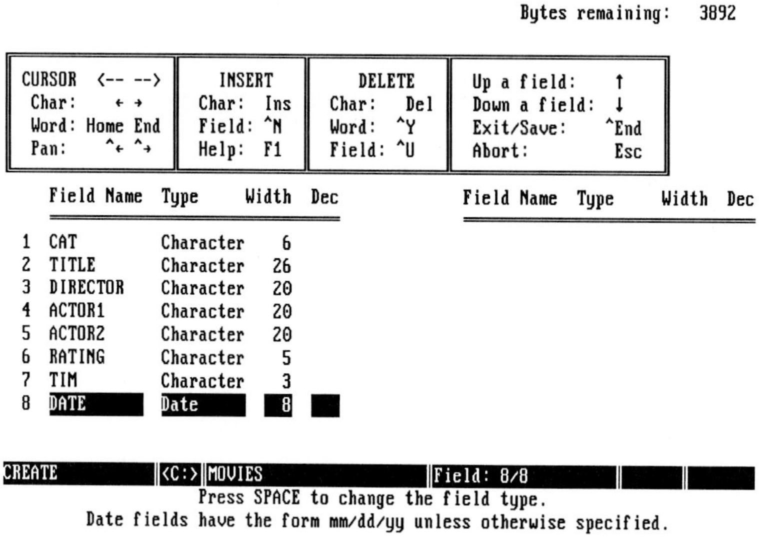

Bytes remaining: 3892

```
┌─────────────────────┬──────────────┬──────────────┬─────────────────────┐
│ CURSOR   <-- -->    │   INSERT     │   DELETE     │ Up a field:      ↑  │
│ Char:     ← →       │ Char:  Ins   │ Char:  Del   │ Down a field:    ↓  │
│ Word: Home End      │ Field: ^N    │ Word:  ^Y    │ Exit/Save:    ^End  │
│ Pan:     ^← ^→      │ Help:  F1    │ Field: ^U    │ Abort:         Esc  │
└─────────────────────┴──────────────┴──────────────┴─────────────────────┘
```

	Field Name	Type	Width	Dec		Field Name	Type	Width	Dec
1	CAT	Character	6						
2	TITLE	Character	26						
3	DIRECTOR	Character	20						
4	ACTOR1	Character	20						
5	ACTOR2	Character	20						
6	RATING	Character	5						
7	TIM	Character	3						
8	DATE	Date	8						

```
CREATE              <C:> MOVIES                  Field: 8/8
```
Press SPACE to change the field type.
Date fields have the form mm/dd/yy unless otherwise specified.

---

types and widths. The eighth field is for the year the film came out. Press the space bar to change the field type from character to date for this entry. We will not use the decimal field. Once you have described all the fields, hold down the Ctrl key and press the End key, which issues the Save command to save your database design. If you're ever in doubt about a command, use the Help key to refresh your memory.

Entering Records   The next command you see asks if you want to begin entering data into the fields of our new database. Select yes and you will see the first blank record (sometimes called a page) appear, with its eight blank fields. Notice how each field is blocked out on the screen to the character width we previously set.

Enter the data exactly as shown in Figure 6–10A and fill in each field. Be careful as you enter data. Press the Caps Lock key and enter all text in UPPER-CASE LETTERS; most DBMS programs recognize the difference between upper- and lowercase, and may fail to recognize words that aren't entered in the proper case. Watch the fields as you enter your data; it's easy to accidentally enter a director's name in an actor field. Establishing your own abbreviation conventions for names or movie titles is important too. For example, be sure you enter all people's names the same. Allen, Woody in one place and Woody Allen in another may mean the same thing to you but not to the DBMS as it does its organizing. Don't categorize an action/adventure movie ACTION in one record and ADVENT in another, unless you want two separate categories.

Use the Backspace and Delete keys, along with the arrow keys, to make corrections. Note that when filling in the date field, it must be entered in the DOS format: month/day/year. Since all we're concerned about is the year, enter 01 for the month, 01 for the day, and the last two digits of the year. When you finish a record, a new blank one will appear. You can scroll back and forth between records by using the Page Up and Page Down keys.

FIGURE 6 – 10A   Entering data into fields in a record.

```
┌─────────────────┬──────────────────┬───────────────┬─────────────────────┐
│ CURSOR  <-- -->  │        UP  DOWN  │ DELETE        │ Insert Mode:  Ins   │
│  Char:   ←  →    │ Field:  ↑   ↓    │ Char:   Del   │ Exit/Save:   ^End   │
│  Word: Home End  │ Page: PgUp PgDn  │ Field:  ^Y    │ Abort:        Esc   │
│                  │ Help:  F1        │ Record: ^U    │ Memo:       ^Home   │
└─────────────────┴──────────────────┴───────────────┴─────────────────────┘
```

```
CAT        COMEDY
TITLE      BANANAS
DIRECTOR   ALLEN, WOODY
ACTOR1     ALLEN, WOODY
ACTOR2     LASSER, LOUISE
RATING     ****
TIM        82
DATE       01/01/71
```

```
APPEND        <C:> MOVIES              Rec: 1/1          Ins      Caps
```

Continue to add the records to your database as shown in Figure 6 – 10B. Remember GIGO? The quality and performance you get out of your database depends on what you put into it. The more you learn about how your DBMS works, the easier it is to use it efficiently. Always take your time and work carefully and thoughtfully. Remember to save your work frequently, after every few records you've entered, using the Ctrl-End Save command.

Append   Each time you use the Save command to save the records you've completed, you are taken back to the DBMS main menu, as shown in Figure 6 – 11. Note that the menu selection is on Update and Append. Update lets you continue working with the same database, and Append lets you append the database or add new records. The status line at the bottom of the screen shows you the database name and the number of records completed. To continue, all you have to do is press Enter or Return. A fresh record screen with blank fields appears, ready for you to begin working again. Go ahead and enter one or two more movies, then save your work. You can also use Append to edit previously created records.

Saving the Database

Thus far, you've learned how to save your database design and database records; now let's see how the entire database is saved. Use the Ctrl-End keys to save the last work you did. You'll be returned to the main menu. Now move the left or right cursor arrow until the Set Up selection is marked, as shown in Figure 6 – 12. Move the Up or Down arrow until Quit is marked, and press Enter or Return. All your work is saved, and you exit the DBMS program as well. This is the proper way to save your work session.

FIGURE 6-10B   Data to enter into our database.

```
DRAMA                      COMEDY                          SCIFI
AMADEUS                    FERRIS BUELLER'S DAY OFF         STAR WARS
FORMAN, MILOS              HUGHES, JOHN                     LUCAS, GEORGE
HULCE, TOM                 BRODERICK, MATTHEW              HAMILL, MARK
ABRAHAM, F. MURRAY         GRAY, JENNIFER                  FORD, HARRISON
**                        **                              *****
158                       103                             121
01/01/84                  01/01/86                        01/01/77

COMEDY                     DRAMA                           COMEDY
EVERYTHING YOU WANT TO KNOW NAME OF THE ROSE, THE          MANHATTAN
ALLEN, WOODY              ANNAUD, JEAN-JACQUES            ALLEN, WOODY
ALLEN, WOODY              CONNERY, SEAN                   ALLEN, WOODY
WILDER, GENE             ABRAHAM, F. MURRAY              KEATON, DIANE
***                      **                              ***
87                       130                             96
01/01/72                 01/01/86                        01/01/79

SCIFI                     DRAMA                           SCIFI
BLADE RUNNER             LOOKING FOR MR. GOODBAR          ALIEN
SCOTT, RIDLEY           BROOKS, RICHARD                  SCOTT, RIDLEY
FORD, HARRISON         KEATON, DIANE                    WEAVER, SIGOURNEY
HAUER, RUTGER          GERE, RICHARD                    SKERRITT, TOM
**                     *                                **
118                    135                              117
01/01/82               01/01/77                         01/01/79

ACTION                  HORROR                           DRAMA
STAKEOUT               JAWS                             INTERIORS
BADHAM, JOHN          SPIELBERG, STEVEN                 ALLEN, WOODY
DREYFUSS, RICHARD    SCHEIDER, ROY                      KEATON, DIANE
ESTEVEZ, EMILIO      DREYFUSS, RICHARD                  MARSHALL, E.G.
***                  *****                              ***
118                  124                                99
01/01/87             01/01/75                           01/01/78

ACTION                COMEDY
NEVER SAY NEVER AGAIN AMERICAN GRAFFITI
KERSHNER, IRVIN      LUCAS, GEORGE
CONNERY, SEAN        DREYFUSS, RICHARD
CARRERA, BARBARA     HOWARD, RON
**                   ***
137                  110
01/01/83             01/01/73
```

FIGURE 6 – 11   The Save command takes you back to the main menu. Pressing Enter takes you back into the database.

Set Up Create **Update** Position Retrieve Organize Modify Tools `04:05:48 pm`

```
                 ┌──────────┐
                 │ Append   │
                 ├──────────┤
                 │ Edit     │
                 │ Display  │
                 ├──────────┤
                 │ Browse   │
                 │ Replace  │
                 ├──────────┤
                 │ Delete   │
                 │ Recall   │
                 │ Pack     │
                 └──────────┘
```

ASSIST   <C:>MOVIES   Rec: 1/1
Move selection bar - ↑↓. Select - ←┘. Leave menu - ↔. Help - F1. Exit - Esc.
         Add new records to the bottom of this database file.

FIGURE 6 – 12   Quitting the database after saving the work.

Set Up Create Update Position Retrieve Organize Modify Tools `04:26:49 pm`

```
┌──────────────────┐
│ Database file    │
├──────────────────┤
│ Format for Screen│
│ Query            │
├──────────────────┤
│ Catalog          │
│ View             │
├──────────────────┤
│ Quit             │
└──────────────────┘
```

ASSIST   <C:>MOVIES   Rec: 17/17   Caps
Move selection bar - ↑↓. Select - ←┘. Leave menu - ↔. Help - F1. Exit - Esc.
         Finish this session of ASSIST and QUIT

Now let's return to our work session. You see the DOS prompt on the screen; type in the name of the program and you'll see the main menu again. Refer again to Figure 6–12. The first line, Database file, should be marked; press Enter or Return and you'll see our database name, MOVIES, appear in a box. Press Enter again and you'll see the MOVIES appear in the status line at the bottom of the screen. Now you can continue adding more records by moving back to Update and selecting Append. However, let's learn some of the different ways the DBMS allows us to work with — *manipulate* — the data we've already stored.

Manipulating Data

Do you recall our discussion about the difference between data and information? The DBMS offers a perfect opportunity to show how data produced by the computer system becomes information in the hands of the user. This is because the DBMS allows us to selectively retrieve and examine the data stored in the database. Let's take a look at some ways we can manipulate our movie database.

List   First, we should make sure all the records we entered are properly stored. The status line shows the total number of records, but it would be nice to see a list of them. Move the cursor across the menu bar, from Set Up to Retrieve. The first selection is List, so press Enter or Return to select it. You'll see another box appear; the first selection is Execute the command, so choose it. You'll be asked if you want to print or not; select no and the list will appear on the screen, scrolling up to the last entry.

Now you know all the records are there. List can show your data in other ways. Select it again but when the second box appears, move down to Construct a field list, which lets you choose different fields to display in the list. Another box appears, displaying all your field categories; press Enter or Return to choose the first three: category, title, and director. Now use the arrow keys to move back to Execute the command in the first box, and this time select the printer. What you get is shown in Figure 6–13. You can list fields in many different combinations.

FIGURE 6–13   Using the List command to display selected fields.

```
Record#   CAT     TITLE                            DIRECTOR
      1   COMEDY  BANANAS                          ALLEN, WOODY
      2   DRAMA   AMADEUS                          FORMAN, MILOS
      3   SCIFI   STAR WARS                        LUCAS, GEORGE
      4   DRAMA   NAME OF THE ROSE, THE            ANNAUD, JEAN-JACQUES
      5   SCIFI   BLADE RUNNER                     SCOTT, RIDLEY
      6   SCIFI   ALIEN                            SCOTT, RIDLEY
      7   COMEDY  FERRIS BUELLER'S DAY OFF         HUGHES, JOHN
      8   COMEDY  EVERYTHING YOU WANT TO KNO       ALLEN, WOODY
      9   COMEDY  MANHATTAN                        ALLEN, WOODY
     10   DRAMA   LOOKING FOR MR. GOODBAR          BROOKS, RICHARD
     11   ACTION  STAKEOUT                         BADHAM, JOHN
     12   HORROR  JAWS                             SPIELBERG, STEVEN
     13   DRAMA   INTERIORS                        ALLEN, WOODY
     14   ACTION  NEVER SAY NEVER AGAIN            KERSHNER, IRWIN
     15   COMEDY  AMERICAN GRAFFITI                LUCAS, GEORGE
     16
     17
```

Index   We didn't enter the movies into our database in any logical or orderly way, so let's use the DBMS to organize them. The command is Index, and it puts data into either alphabetical or numerical order. Move to the Organize menu selection and select Index. When the second box appears, press the F10 key, then the Down Arrow key once. You will see a screen like the one in Figure 6–14. Press the Enter or Return key and the word TITLE will appear in the box. Press Enter until you see another box appear on the screen, asking for a filename. Call it TITLES and press Enter; when the processing is finished, you'll see "100% Indexed" appear above the status line.

Now, move back along the menu bar to Set Up, and select Database file. Select MOVIES.DBF (DBF stands for database file). When you are asked if the file is indexed, reply yes. You'll see the file you created, TITLES.NDX, appear in the box. Press Enter, and the word "Master" appears beside the index filename. Now move from Set Up to Update and then down to Browse. Press Enter again and you'll see your records indexed as shown in Figure 6–15, alphabetically by title.

The Index command is very useful for ordering information. It helps us find what we're looking for more quickly, whether it is customer records stored by invoice number or by customer name. Record numbers are sequential and can't be changed, but an index is organized the way we want it. It's much quicker to find data once it has been indexed, and if two databases have been combined, indexing becomes even more important. However, there is another useful organizing command, Sort, which we will study next.

Sort   The Sort command is used to order and often to separate one or more records in a database. The fields it uses are termed **sort keys;** the first is the primary key, and there may be others. For example, we might do a primary sort for all movies by category, and another that alphabetizes each director by category. Let's see how the Sort command works on a primary sort.

FIGURE 6–14   The menu for creating an Index.

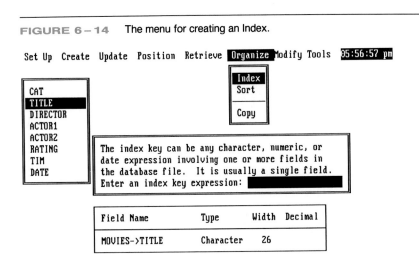

FIGURE 6–15   A partial listing of the movie database, indexed alphabetically by title.

```
┌─────────────────────┬──────────────────┬───────────────┬──────────────────────┐
│ CURSOR   <-- -->    │         UP  DOWN │    DELETE     │ Insert Mode:   Ins   │
│  Char:      ←  →    │ Record:  ↑    ↓  │  Char:   Del  │ Exit:         ^End   │
│  Field: Home End    │ Page:  PgUp PgDn │  Field:  ^Y   │ Abort:         Esc   │
│  Pan:      ^← ^→    │ Help:    F1      │  Record: ^U   │ Set Options: ^Home   │
└─────────────────────┴──────────────────┴───────────────┴──────────────────────┘
```

```
CAT--- TITLE-------------------- DIRECTOR------------ ACTOR1-------------
SCIFI  ALIEN                     SCOTT, RIDLEY        WEAVER, SIGOURNEY
DRAMA  AMADEUS                   FORMAN, MILOS        HULCE, TOM
COMEDY AMERICAN GRAFFITI         LUCAS, GEORGE        DREYFUSS, RICHARD
COMEDY BANANAS                   ALLEN, WOODY         ALLEN, WOODY
SCIFI  BLADE RUNNER              SCOTT, RIDLEY        FORD, HARRISON
COMEDY EVERYTHING YOU WANT TO KNO ALLEN, WOODY        ALLEN, WOODY
COMEDY FERRIS BUELLER'S DAY OFF  HUGHES, JOHN         BRODERICK, MATTHEW
DRAMA  INTERIORS                 ALLEN, WOODY         KEATON, DIANE
HORROR JAWS                      SPIELBERG, STEVEN    SCHEIDER, ROY
DRAMA  LOOKING FOR MR. GOODBAR   BROOKS, RICHARD      KEATON, DIANE
COMEDY MANHATTAN                 ALLEN, WOODY         ALLEN, WOODY
```

```
BROWSE          <C:> MOVIES                    Rec: 9/17              Caps
```

View and edit fields.

Start by pressing the Escape key to return to the main menu, then move to Set Up, select Database file, press Enter on MOVIES.DBF, and select No Indexing. Now move to Organize, down to Sort, and press Enter. As you can see, the menus work the same way they did for Index, so select Category and use it as the filename. Again, you will see the message "100% Sorted" appear above the status line.

Now return to Set Up, select Database file, then select the new file you just created, CATEGORY.DBF, and select No Indexing. Next, follow the same instructions as you used for browsing an indexed file and you will see your database sorted by category. A portion is shown in Figure 6–16.

The Sort command allows you to organize records in either ascending or descending order; indexing only allows ascending. You can also sort across fields, whereas you can only index within a single field. A note of caution: A sorted file is a duplicate of the original file. For that reason, sorted files are usually considered temporary files, created to look at data in a particular way, then deleted.

Modify   By now, we hope you understand what we meant by the need to design your database carefully. But even the best laid plans can go astray, and our DBMS is very forgiving. The Modify command lets us change the width of a field, to redefine it (character, numeric, or date), or even add additional fields. Let's add a last field for your review comments on each movie.

Simply move in the main menu to Modify and press Enter or Return for Database file. The next screen shows you the current record structure. We'll add a field at the end, so press the Arrow key to move down the list; a ninth field will appear. Fill it in as shown in Figure 6–17 and press Ctrl-End to save the changes. Move across the main menu to Update and down to Edit; press Enter. Now you can edit each record and add your own mini review!

FIGURE 6 – 16   A partial listing of the movie database, sorted alphabetically by category.

```
CURSOR   <-- -->            UP   DOWN      DELETE         Insert Mode:  Ins
Char:         ←  →    Record:  ↑     ↓     Char:   Del    Exit:        ^End
Field: Home End      Page:  PgUp  PgDn     Field:   ^Y    Abort:        Esc
Pan:       ^←  ^→    Help:   F1            Record:  ^U    Set Options: ^Home
```

```
CAT--- TITLE------------------- DIRECTOR----------- ACTOR1--------------
ACTION NEVER SAY NEVER AGAIN    KERSHNER, IRWIN     CONNERY, SEAN
ACTION STAKEOUT                 BADHAM, JOHN        DREYFUSS, RICHARD
COMEDY MANHATTAN                ALLEN, WOODY        ALLEN, WOODY
COMEDY AMERICAN GRAFFITI        LUCAS, GEORGE       DREYFUSS, RICHARD
COMEDY FERRIS BUELLER'S DAY OFF HUGHES, JOHN        BRODERICK, MATTHEW
COMEDY EVERYTHING YOU WANT TO KNO ALLEN, WOODY      ALLEN, WOODY
COMEDY BANANAS                  ALLEN, WOODY        ALLEN, WOODY
DRAMA  LOOKING FOR MR. GOODBAR  BROOKS, RICHARD     KEATON, DIANE
DRAMA  AMADEUS                  FORMAN, MILOS       HULCE, TOM
DRAMA  INTERIORS                ALLEN, WOODY        KEATON, DIANE
DRAMA  NAME OF THE ROSE, THE    ANNAUD, JEAN-JACQUES CONNERY, SEAN
```

```
BROWSE          <C:> CATEGORY              Rec: 13/17              Caps
```
            View and edit fields.

FIGURE 6 – 17   Modify lets you change the design of your database by adding or altering fields.

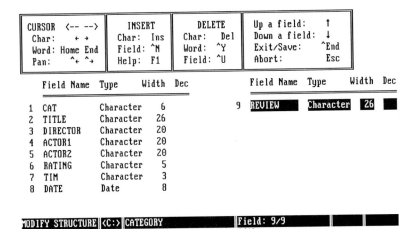

                                   Bytes remaining: 3866

```
CURSOR   <-- -->       INSERT        DELETE        Up a field:      ↑
Char:         ←  →   Char:  Ins    Char:   Del    Down a field:    ↓
Word: Home End      Field:  ^N    Word:    ^Y     Exit/Save:     ^End
Pan:       ^←  ^→   Help:   F1    Field:   ^U     Abort:          Esc
```

	Field Name	Type	Width	Dec		Field Name	Type	Width	Dec
1	CAT	Character	6		9	REVIEW	Character	26	
2	TITLE	Character	26						
3	DIRECTOR	Character	20						
4	ACTOR1	Character	20						
5	ACTOR2	Character	20						
6	RATING	Character	5						
7	TIM	Character	3						
8	DATE	Date	8						

```
MODIFY STRUCTURE <C:> CATEGORY              Field: 9/9
```
                    Enter the field width.
            Character fields are 1 to 254 positions wide.

Delete   Sometimes you want to delete a record. To do so, move to the Update section of the main menu, then to Browse. Use the Page Up and Page Down keys to select the record you wish to delete, then hold the Ctrl key down while pressing the letter *U*. At the right side of the status line you'll see "Del" appear. That record is now marked for deletion. Now, press Esc to move back to the menu, then down to Pack. Press Enter and you'll see a box appear; press Enter again for Execute the command. This two-step operation lets you make sure you want to delete the marked record.

Printing Reports

Like word processing and spreadsheet applications, database management systems provide a means of producing hardcopy output. Sometimes this function is termed a **report writer.** Basic features built into most DBMS report writers allow you to take data you have organized, then attractively format and print it.

Some DBMSs have a report writer with many useful features: the formatting capabilities of word processing, the number processing of spreadsheets, graphics output capabilities, and versatile database search and select features. With such a DBMS, we could design a report that shows the percentage of comedy, drama, action, and horror movies in our database as a pie chart. For now, let's create a simple report.

First, we must use the Create menu and select Report. When prompted for the report name, type FILMRPT and press Enter or Return. Next, you will see a screen to help you design your report's page format. We're going to use the standard settings, so the only thing we'll change is the first entry, Page title. Press Enter and you'll see a box appear. This is the text entry box; you may use up to four lines of text. Type:

```
FAVORITE MOVIES
From The Home Videotape Library
```

and then press Enter twice, to insert two blank lines after your page title. Use the Save command, Ctrl-End, to save the title.

Next, let's make our report more attractive by creating a three-column page. Move the cursor across the menu to Columns and press Enter. Using the first selection, Contents, press Enter; a prompt appears to the right, asking you to enter the name of the field from which the data will be drawn, so type

FIGURE 6–18   The printed report.

```
                        FAVORITE MOVIES
                  From The Home Videotape Library


Favorite Directors         Favorite Movies              Favorite Stars
ALLEN, WOODY               BANANAS                       ALLEN, WOODY
LUCAS, GEORGE              AMERICAN GRAFFITI             DREYFUSS, RICHARD
ALLEN, WOODY               INTERIORS                     KEATON, DIANE
KERSHNER, IRVIN            NEVER SAY NEVER AGAIN         CONNERY, SEAN
SPIELBERG, STEVEN          JAWS                          SCHEIDER, ROY
BADHAM, JOHN               STAKEOUT                      DREYFUSS, RICHARD
BROOKS, RICHARD            LOOKING FOR MR. GOODBAR       KEATON, DIANE
ALLEN, WOODY               MANHATTAN                     ALLEN, WOODY
HUGHES, JOHN               FERRIS BUELLER'S DAY OFF      BRODERICK, MATTHEW
ALLEN, WOODY               EVERYTHING YOU WANT TO KNOW   ALLEN, WOODY
SCOTT, RIDLEY              ALIEN                         WEAVER, SIGOURNEY
SCOTT, RIDLEY              BLADE RUNNER                  FORD, HARRISON
LUCAS, GEORGE              STAR WARS                     HAMILL, MARK
ANNAUD, JEAN-JACQUES       NAME OF THE ROSE, THE         CONNERY, SEAN
FORMAN, MILOS              AMADEUS                       HULCE, TOM
```

DIRECTOR. Now move down to the next line, Heading, and type Favorite Directors. We'll leave the column width at 20, and that's all we'll change. Press the Page Down key to move to the next column. Enter TITLE for Contents and Favorite Movies for the Heading. Change the column width to 26, to conform with the field width. Use Page Down to move to the third column; enter ACTOR1 and type Favorite Stars for the Heading. Save your work with Ctrl-End, then move across the main menu to Exit and choose Save, which saves your report format. Now we are ready to use it.

Move to the Retrieve selection on the main menu and select Report. Press Enter or Return to get the box and select FILMRPT. Press Enter again and you'll see the command box; select Execute the command, and no for the printer selection. You'll see your report scroll up the screen. Now, follow these steps once again but this time select yes for the printer selection. You'll get a printed report like the one in Figure 6–18. Once you've finished printing your report, quit your DBMS work session as you've already learned how to do.

1. What are the two steps in database design?
2. What must you create after you have opened a new database file?
3. When is the List command helpful?
4. When would you use Index? When would you use Sort?
5. What command do you use to alter the record?
6. What printing advantages does the DBMS offer?

MEMORY CHECK

ADVANCED DATABASE MANAGEMENT

Database management systems, like most applications, were born in the business world and migrated to the personal computing world. Today, even though the two areas have some similarity, technological advances are moving in different directions. Here are two examples of advanced database management.

Personal Information Managers

One problem with the traditional DBMS is that data has to be structured — organized by fields, records, and files. But the data people use doesn't always fit neatly into this structure. Several people working with personal computers in the mid-1980s came up against this problem and resolved to do something about it. What has emerged is a new kind of relational DBMS called the **personal information manager (PIM)**. It is actually a product of several different fields of research, combining some traditional desktop tools like the appointment calendar, calculator, and "to do" list, as well as word processing and a DBMS. Figure 6–19 shows the screen of a typical PIM.

PIMs go a step further in the way they organize data. For example, a PIM might associate information by items or topics, and sort through the topics using categories or **keywords**, which are key terms common to several topics. This is effective for keeping small bits of information: phone messages, reminders, names and addresses, or a to-do list.

FIGURE 6–19   A PIM lets you organize and manage less-structured data.

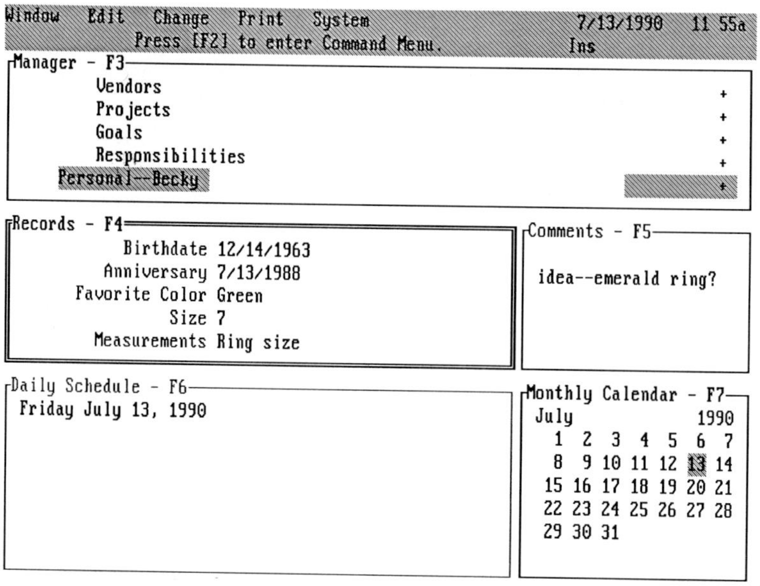

```
┌──────────────────────────────────────────────────────────────────────┐
│ Window  Edit   Change   Print    System              7/13/1990  11 55a│
│               Press [F2] to enter Command Menu.      Ins              │
│ ┌Manager - F3───────────────────────────────────────────────────────┐ │
│ │      Vendors                                                     + │ │
│ │      Projects                                                    + │ │
│ │      Goals                                                       + │ │
│ │      Responsibilities                                            + │ │
│ │      Personal--Becky                                             + │ │
│ └───────────────────────────────────────────────────────────────────┘ │
│ ┌Records - F4════════════════════════┐  ┌Comments - F5──────────────┐ │
│ │      Birthdate 12/14/1963          │  │                           │ │
│ │     Anniversary 7/13/1988          │  │  idea--emerald ring?      │ │
│ │  Favorite Color Green              │  │                           │ │
│ │           Size 7                   │  │                           │ │
│ │   Measurements Ring size           │  │                           │ │
│ └────────────────────────────────────┘  └───────────────────────────┘ │
│ ┌Daily Schedule - F6─────────────────┐  ┌Monthly Calendar - F7──────┐ │
│ │ Friday July 13, 1990               │  │ July              1990    │ │
│ │                                    │  │  1  2  3  4  5  6  7       │ │
│ │                                    │  │  8  9 10 11 12 13 14       │ │
│ │                                    │  │ 15 16 17 18 19 20 21       │ │
│ │                                    │  │ 22 23 24 25 26 27 28       │ │
│ │                                    │  │ 29 30 31                  │ │
│ └────────────────────────────────────┘  └───────────────────────────┘ │
└──────────────────────────────────────────────────────────────────────┘
```

Some PIMs also have special software that lets you make assumptions and create relationships between information. For example, your things-to-do list says get the leaky faucet fixed; there is no listing in your phone book for a plumber but there was a handyman named Jim who did some repair work for you once. A PIM might use the keyword *repair* to help you find his phone number and address.

In some of the newer PIMs, the file structure is superceded by the *information base.* An information base, which resembles a cross between a text file and a free-form database, may contain many kinds of files. It can keep data in many formats. Instead of being organized by filenames, the information base structures data by logical relationships; for example, short text (notes), long text (letters, reports, and book chapters), databases, appointment books, business forms, and so forth. One type of data can be easily linked to another, according to your needs, and changed often. Links can be created for any kind of searching and ordering. These links can be more effective for organizing data than keywords, which have to be in the text somewhere.

For many years, we have had to work with data in ways that conform to the computer's way of data processing. There is a trend toward designing software that guides the computer to do our work the way we do it. PIMs are a step in that direction.

Managing a Corporate Database

When it comes to databases, bigger often can be better. However, the more data we store, the more complex it becomes to manage our database. Business and government utilize hundreds of databases, with the ever-increasing need to share and exchange data between them. A brokerage must report customer profits from stocks and bonds to the Internal Revenue Service. A magazine publisher selling its subscriber mailing list to another business for advertising purposes must deliver it on a compatible disk or tape. In some firms, just managing data for the company itself is an immense task, requiring the skills of specially trained computer professionals.

It is often best if databases are centrally managed, even if they are primarily used by individual departments. Each department has access to the files they need, while common data can be shared between various departments. In a corporate system, there is often a *centralized* database, with accounting, employee records, and other corporate data. Then there are a number of *decentralized* databases, specific to a department or function. Marketing may have its own customer database, for example. Any data that is centralized can be shared with the decentralized databases, so that now everyone in the company sees the single, most current, file. With a DBMS, sharing makes it easier for everyone to use the data, and it is more accurate and current. A well-managed database environment can make a major contribution to the company's success and productivity.

But all this doesn't just happen magically when a DBMS is installed. People who understand the company's line of business, its management structure, and its computer systems must install and maintain a complex database environment. For these reasons, two things are key to success: a database administrator and a data dictionary.

Database Administrator   Try to imagine how much data is stored in the corporate databases at companies like General Motors or Procter & Gamble. Probably about a hundred times more than we can imagine. So much, in fact, that corporate databases have a full-time manager called a **database administrator (DBA)**. The DBA is responsible for maintaining the DBMS, ensuring the accuracy and the integrity of its data. The DBA works with department and corporate managers to decide these key aspects of database usage:

- What data should go into the database.
- What relationships should exist between various data items.
- Who has permission to read database information.
- Who has authority to update the database.

For example, if inventory records are kept in the database, the DBA must find out if the manufacturing manager uses these records to make manufacturing plans. The DBA must find out what the inventory manager needs to know to maintain the records, such as part numbers, quantities, stock levels, and so forth. The DBA also must determine what the purchasing people need to know, such as the part number, description, company of manufacture, and price. The DBA will use all this information to set up a single inventory database that works for all who need to use it.

Data Dictionary   Managing a corporate database can be a complex job, with many relationships to consider and many people to serve. The work would be almost impossible without the aid of a data dictionary. The **data dictionary** is a list of all the fields, files, and commands utilized in manipulating the database. It is like an instruction list or a repair diagram for the system. A simple example is the index we created for the movie database in this chapter. Say we created 15 indexes; the data dictionary would list them all and explain what each did.

DISKbyte

The DBMS as a Productivity Tool

In the past, the computer staff was responsible for creating all new end-user applications. However, as more and more employees became computer users, the demand for applications outstripped the Information Systems (IS) department's ability to supply them. 4GL/DBMSs provide tools that allow end users to create their own databases. They use the 4GL for design, then build their own specialized database from data in the corporate database. This means a number of small databases do daily work, relieving the central database for other tasks. Then the smaller databases send the data they have processed to the central database, updating it and keeping it current.

One of the first companies to do this was the Bank of America in the late 1970s. Using NOMAD, a 4GL/DBMS, with their IBM mainframe, the Bank of America allowed end users to create their own database applications — a real first, since programmers had been responsible for creating new applications in the past. Within three years, NOMAD had 5,000 users who had created 500 new applications to help them do their work more productively.

The data dictionary establishes the rules that govern using the database: data definition rules, database access rules, and data usage rules. The information it contains is essential to the DBA. We might call the data dictionary the DBA's chief assistant. With a well-designed DBMS, a good data dictionary, and effective management from a DBA, corporations can continue to grow and have their databases grow smoothly, right along with them.

Database management systems are critical to both business and government in their day-to-day functioning. DBMS technology has advanced with every passing decade, and is certainly continuing to advance even more rapidly in the 1990s.

MEMORY CHECK

1. What software products comprise a Personal Information Manager?
2. Why must corporate data be managed?
3. What two types of databases are found in large corporations?
4. What are some of the duties of a database administrator (DBA)?
5. What is a data dictionary, and what does it do?

THE EVER–EVOLVING DBMS

The trend in DBMS applications, as in other areas, is toward greater ease of use. New applications continually strive to bring the full power of the computer to the user. As we said earlier, the advance from magnetic tape to disk technology made it possible to design entirely new types of databases. Greater processing speed has improved personal computer DBMS applications. Rapid

DISKbyte

DBMS Tips

1. Design your database carefully and thoroughly on paper before you begin using your DBMS program. Study it frequently, to determine if you've left anything out and to assure that the structure is logical.
2. Create a practical data dictionary. Don't make field lengths longer than they need to be. Define data that you'll want to search for: if you want to search for an area code or ZIP code, be sure you distinguish them as such. Otherwise, the database will stop every time it sees any numbers in sequence.
3. Use your word processor to enter large quantities of existing information into your database. This is accomplished by creating a file in the format the DBMS can read. The specifics for performing this task can be found in the DBMS user manual.
4. Use the DBMS programming language to simplify the ways you commonly retrieve data.
5. Unlike spreadsheet programs, DBMS programs range from easy to learn and intuitive to extremely difficult to learn, almost a programming language. Choose your DBMS carefully; read comparison reviews in publications like *InfoWorld* before you buy.

advancements took RAM from 256K to 640K, and disk storage grew from 140K to 360K to 1.2MB—not to mention hard disk auxiliary storage advances. With these changes, a personal computer could provide an effective DBMS.

But until the mid-1980s, you still had to do some programming to use, or access, the database. One early personal computer DBMS program had no menus, only a blank screen with a period—not even a blinking cursor. To work with a database listing household items for your insurance agent, you typed in a commands like:

`.DISP ALL DESCRIP VALUE`

Now we have much more Englishlike commands for searching a database, called query languages. A **query language** is a type of programming language that allows users to make DBMS inquiries without using programming "codes" or keywords. Instead of the using commands with formal syntax like that shown above, we can simply type:

`LIST ITEMS AND PRICES`

One of the most popular query languages was developed for mainframes and minicomputer relational DBMSs, and is now available for personal computer programs. It's called SQL and was developed by IBM. **SQL** stands for **structured query language,** which has many ease-of-use features that made it instantly popular. Now a number of software vendors have their own SQL products. Query languages are discussed in Chapter 8.

Most DBMSs for personal computers are considered relational and often have their own programming languages to help users design the database more easily. Personal computer DBMSs also continue to grow in data capacity. dBASE II, for example, has been upgraded for the personal computer using DOS to dBASE IV. It is now capable of storing over 1 billion records, each with 128 fields containing 4,000 characters each — if you have enough auxiliary storage, of course.

The next generation of DBMSs allows us to connect personal computers and workstations in a network so they can work with other computers, including personal computers, minis, and mainframes. But the process of giving us easy access to the data we use most often is still under development. Now DBMS designers are striving to make the computer follow human work styles, rather than requiring people to work like the computer.

Ultimately, databases will be connected one to another so that we can have access to any data, regardless of where it is stored. This is called **distributed database management systems.** Large corporations are beginning this process, building a new kind of database called a *repository,* where the entire company's knowledge and information can be stored. In time, we will see government databases and private databases linked across telephone lines, forming a massive, nationwide repository: an electronic library we can access for facts and knowledge at any time. Indeed, the world is becoming a database.

ETHICS

Clearly, we are in the midst of an information explosion. The computer's ability to store and maintain massive volumes of data has greatly expanded the information available to people. Since much of this data is private, relating to individuals and corporations, we have to be concerned with privacy.

Privacy involves boundaries. In earlier times, it was easier to establish those boundaries. Statements such as "one's home is one's castle" were the basis of law. No one had a right to invade the sanctuary of your personal four walls, or disturb your home's contents, without a publicly demonstrated, authorized need.

But today, our personal concerns are extended beyond the home. Personal information is no longer simply recorded on paper and protected by walls. It has become much more elusive, in the form of bits and bytes that can travel over wires and even be beamed to and from satellites.

Now the boundaries of personal information are more abstract. The statement for our times might be "who needs to know?" By this we mean, "for what purpose does the world at large seek information about me that I consider personal and private?" This is pertinent to us all. Here are some questions to demonstrate this fact:

- If you subscribe to a magazine, you have given its publisher your address. Should that publisher have the right to share or sell your address to other publishers without your consent?
- If you allow an insurance company to cover your medical, dental, or psychological services, this company has a legal right to view your records. If your employer is providing your insurance coverage, should it have the right to see your medical information?
- If you use a Visa or MasterCard credit card, your purchases are recorded in the bank's corporate database. Who should be allowed to view this personal information? Should data on your buying habits be used to help companies pursue you as a customer?

These are just a few examples of how our everyday activities can become data items in corporate databases. When the lines among these corporations or the boundaries between corporations and government and the public become blurred, our privacy becomes more than a philosophical matter. How data is interpreted can become misinformation that has a direct impact on our lives.

CAREERbyte

Building a Geoprocessing Database

Kevin Johnson and Allan Schmidt worked at Prime Computer, a company that makes superminicomputers that are used in science, research, and special applications. Kevin's degree was in landscape architecture, and Allan's was in computer graphics. They were part of a team that developed a unique database management system that, when combined with graphic information, became what is termed a Geoprocessing Information System (GIS).

A GIS is used to develop information that can be used to make decisions about many types of natural and human resources. Natural resources include land, forests, and the air; human resources include public safety, social problems, cities, water and sewer systems, and so forth. The GIS combines cartography or mapping with data from databases. The maps may come from printed sources such as the U.S. Geological Survey, from photographs taken by remote sensing devices mounted on satellites, or may already be in computer "digitized" form. The databases come from various government agencies such as the Bureau of the Census or the Department of Agriculture.

The end result is a high-quality workstation that displays a detailed color map, often in several

dimensions, with displays of data and information about that map, as you can see in the accompanying photograph. You can look at the map and ask about a certain area or resource, and the GIS will query the database for information. Alternately, you can query the database to tell you where a certain type of tree grows, and it will display the appropriate maps.

The Prime GIS was put to an interesting use: finding the best location in the United States for a supercollider. It turned out that Illinois was the best choice. Then the state of Illinois used the GIS to plan how to build the supercollider,

checking local zoning codes, availability of building resources, and so forth. Another GIS was used to map crime statistics in a large metropolitan area, so the police could determine trouble spots. This helped them deploy officers more quickly.

The GIS is a very practical and worthwhile way to use maps and database management systems. It is also a computer technology that is rapidly spreading. Architects, cartographers, and urban planners are using GISs every day, but Kevin says that people with GIS computer systems skills are, and will continue to be, very much in demand.

Courtesy of Prime Computer

SUMMARY

1. *Explain the difference between a database and a database management system (DBMS).* A database is a group of related records or files used to keep track of information. A database may be manual, on paper, or on magnetic media for use with computers. A database management system (DBMS) is the application software that lets you organize, store and retrieve data from one or more databases.

2. *Describe the advantages of a DBMS.* Database management systems (DBMS) provide an effective way to use computers to enter, manipulate, and print data that has been organized in specific ways. There are three primary advantages. A DBMS is flexible, allowing us to use or examine data in many different ways. It allows discrimination, or the ability to search very selectively for data. The DBMS's third advantage is extensibility, the ability to use many databases so long as the structure is the same.

3. *Identify the four types of DBMSs and the data elements they use.* There are four major types of DBMSs: the flat file, like a stack of recipe cards; the hierarchical, like a tree, uses one-to-many relationships; the network, like the body's circulatory system, uses many-to-many relationships; and the relational, which cross-references between tables, uses any-to-any relationships. In the DBMS, data is arranged into physical and logical data elements. The three types of common physical data are the bit, byte, and word. The five logical data elements are the character, field, record, file, and database.

4. *Explain the steps in creating and editing a database.* The first step in working with a DBMS is database design, which includes data definition and refinement. This helps plan for creating fields, the first step in creating a database. Once fields are designed, they may be filled with data to form records. Once the database is ready, the data in it may be manipulated in several different ways, using commands such as List, Index, and Sort. The DBMS lets you print data in neat, attractive reports.

5. *Describe some features of the modern database-like personal information manager.* The personal information manager, or PIM, combines a relational DBMS with other desktop organizing tools. It is useful for keeping a variety of different kinds of information, from phone numbers to desktop reminders to an appointment calendar. Some PIMs utilize an information base, which permits organizing data in more useful formats than the conventional file. Then it is possible to find specific information through links.

6. *Describe how business and government use advanced data management.* Business and government heavily depend on the database, and have developed sophisticated ways of working with data. In most cases there are many databases; one is centralized, but many are decentralized. Heavy database use requires the services of a database administrator, who assures data integrity. It also requires a data dictionary, which is like an instruction book that explains how the fields, files, and commands operate. SQL and other query languages are making DBMSs easier for everyone to use. In the future, we will probably see distributed databases, where any data is available to anyone.

KEY TERMS

attribute, p. 167
character, p. 167
database, p. 160
database administrator (DBA), p. 183
database design, p. 169
database management system (DBMS), p. 160
data definition, p. 170
data dictionary, p. 183
data elements, p. 165

data refinement, p. 170
data relationships, p. 170
distributed database management system, p. 186
entity, p. 167
field, p. 167
flat file database, p. 162
hierarchical database, p. 164
keyword, p. 181
logical data representation, p. 166
network database, p. 164

personal information manager (PIM), p. 181
physical data representation, p. 166
query language, p. 185
record, p. 167
relational database, p. 164
report writer, p. 180
sort key, p. 177
structured query language (SQL), p. 185

REVIEW AND DISCUSSION QUESTIONS

1. Explain the difference between a database and a DBMS.
2. What are some advantages of using a DBMS?
3. What are some limitations of using manual databases?
4. Identify the logical data elements common to all DBMSs.
5. Why is it important to organize data in a DBMS so carefully?
6. Discuss the relationship between fields and records, and how that relationship affects the way we can organize and use data in the database.
7. Name the four types of databases.
8. Which type of database is most common in a personal computer DBMS?
9. What are the first steps in creating a database *before* you turn on the computer? What are the first steps *after* you turn it on?
10. Describe several ways you would use the database manipulation commands to extract specific information from our MOVIES database.

Do you foresee any problems working with the data in its present form? How might you redesign it to correct those problems?

11. What is the report writer used for?
12. Why do corporations have special DBMS requirements?
13. What does the database administrator do?
14. Why is a data dictionary necessary?
15. How can a DBMS enhance a company's productivity?
16. Why is it important to be able to access data on a variety of databases? Why not just keep it all in one centralized database?
17. How would a DBMS on your personal computer make your life easier?
18. How is a personal information manager different from a traditional DBMS?
19. How are the concepts of using DBMSs changing?
20. How might DBMSs in business and government affect you?

ISSUES

1. More and more companies have come to the conclusion that information stored in corporate databases can be used for commercial purposes. For example, you belong to an auto club, which you use often because your old car breaks down frequently. The auto club maintains a database of the number of service calls, noting the types of problems encountered as well. Say you have a lot of flat tires; the auto club collects your name with others like you, then it sells the list to a tire dealer, who mails you an advertising brochure offering a discount on new tires. Is this performing a useful service, or is it an invasion of privacy?

2. Data security remains a big issue in business and government. A secretary created phony vendor records in her company's database and paid bills totaling $80,000 to them. Then she and her boyfriend cleaned out the bank accounts and left the country. Estimated losses due to such crimes by insiders total at least $100 million a year, perhaps as high as $3 billion. Nobody knows, because businesses are often reluctant to admit the crimes. They fear the stockholders and the public will think ill of them. Is that the right attitude? How would you feel if, instead of dismissing guilty employees and covering up their crimes, a company that was robbed by employees prosecuted them and made the event public knowledge? Which approach is more likely to prevent future crimes?

MODULE III

Computer Software

Take the word *software*. It's so new that it did not appear in the 1971 edition of the *Oxford English Dictionary*. Yet software has made dramatic changes in society and has created an entirely new industry. Indeed, software has made many people wealthy; Bill Gates, cofounder of Microsoft, the leading personal computer software company, is a *billionaire*.

In the previous chapters, you learned about the three most popular application software packages. Now you're ready to learn more about software, the grey matter of computers. There is great diversity in software. It helps us with tasks that control the machine. More importantly, it does many tasks that we as people think about or use our brains to perform. Indeed, without software, computers would be of little value.

Chapter 7 builds on what you learned in Chapter 3 about operating systems. It presents a complete overview of system and application software. We explore the operating system and its many functions

so that you'll come to appreciate all the things it can do for you. The second half of the chapter explores the diversity of computer software applications, such as graphics and electronic publishing.

Once you know what software is, Chapter 8 explains how software is created. You'll learn about the various computer professionals and their involvement in software development. We explore the various steps involved in creating a new software program. You'll learn about the various tools that developers use, and the important role users play in the process.

One of the great things about the software industry is that anyone with a good idea can develop a software program. Anyone with the desire to learn programming can become a computer professional. And anyone with the entrepreneurial spirit can use a computer and a software application to start a new business.

CHAPTER

7

Software

From Operating Systems to Applications

CHAPTER OUTLINE

Helping Make Software Easier to Use
The Versatility of Software
   Understanding Files
   DISKbyte: The Abstract Industry
System Software
   The Many Faces of an Operating System
   The Servant: Providing Command Languages
      and Utilities
   The Traffic Officer: Controlling Input and
      Output
   The Appointment Secretary: Scheduling
   The Hotel Manager: Storage Assignment
   The Librarian: Data Management
   Personal Computer Operating Systems
   Minicomputer Operating Systems
   Mainframe Operating Systems
   Trends in Operating Systems
Application Software
   Integrated Software
   Computer Graphics
   Electronic Publishing
   Utility Software
   DISKbyte: Multimedia: The Next Great
      Application for Computers?
What Lies Ahead?
   DISKbyte: Tips for Buying Personal Computer
      Software
Ethics
   CAREERbyte: Jackie Willig Silver: A Desktop
      Publishing Pioneer
Summary
Key Terms
Review and Discussion Questions
Issues

OBJECTIVES

After reading and studying this chapter, you should be able to:

1. Explain the various tasks performed by operating systems software.
2. Identify leading personal computer, minicomputer, and mainframe operating systems.
3. Understand the difference between stand-alone and integrated software.
4. Describe some other commonly used applications.
5. Describe the uses for utility software for applications and operating systems.
6. Understand the uses for artificial intelligence and expert systems.

HELPING MAKE SOFTWARE EASIER TO USE

Therese Myers got her start with computers by accident, and ended up one of the most respected woman entrepreneurs in the industry. She attended Carnegie-Mellon University and spent two years working in computer systems development at Citibank between her undergraduate and graduate degrees. Her work took her to California, where she saw a "really hot" workstation that recreated an executive's desktop with applications for in and out baskets, mail, phone messages, a calendar, and more. What excited her even more was the workstation's ability to shift between these applications.

Photo by Susan Young

Over the next few years, Terry built 25 prototypes of such a workstation. "In 1981 the IBM Personal Computer had just been announced," she says, "and people were starting to ask for integration, so I decided to try building software that sits on top of the operating system."

Terry, with Gary Pope, a highly talented software developer, assembled a team of software designers and system integrators to form a new software company, Quarterdeck Office Systems. Gary led the team that worked for the next three years to develop DESQ, a program that allowed users to select the applications they wanted to use from a menu, then switch easily from one to another. The original program was improved again and again, and evolved into today's DESQview.

Terry describes Quarterdeck's mission this way: "To help individual PC users and corporate microcomputer managers protect their considerable investments in PC hardware and software by making existing resources more useful and enhancing people productivity. I believe it's very important that the user gets more power at low cost." That philosophy has helped Quarterdeck grow into a major force in the software industry — almost 2 million copies of DESQview are in use today.

Quarterdeck is an excellent example of how the computer industry has fostered a new set of business values and corporate cultures very different from those based in the industrial revolution. Quarterdeck is a progressive company and has forged a number of business partnerships with personal computer and workstation companies who bundle DESQview with their products. The company also now offers many of the desktop applications, such as a calendar, datebook, and notepad, that Terry saw in the original prototype years ago.

DESQview was the program that launched a new market in the software industry, what we now term the "user interface." Today, there are similar programs available for almost all personal computers and workstations, including the Macintosh, the IBM and IBM-compatible personal computers, and workstations. Indeed, the trend is clearly that no computer should be without the features provided by DESQview or a similar program. And even though many of these programs compete with one another, DESQview's concepts and pre-eminence were confirmed in 1989 when Quarterdeck was awarded a U.S. patent for the DESQview technology.

THE VERSATILITY OF SOFTWARE

Today's computers are designed so they can perform many different tasks. For example, you can use a personal computer to write letters, solve differential equations, play video games, plan a diet, draw a chart or graph, publish a newsletter, and do literally thousands of other tasks.

What gives computers this versatility? In a word, software. Do you recall our comparison between computers and stereo systems in Chapter 2? We would be far less likely to buy a stereo if it only played one song. But since stereos can play many kinds of music, we find them very useful. We program a stereo when we put in the tape or CD, and thus create the kind of output we desire. In some ways, changing the music program on a stereo from jazz to classical is similar to changing software on a computer.

Even before ENIAC (the first full-fledged digital electronic computer) was completed, its inventors were thinking about what other tasks they could use it for. One of the reasons today's computers are so useful is that they are easily changed by programming them for different tasks. Programming is the process of creating a set of instructions that direct the computer to perform specific data processing tasks. When we program computers, we translate methods for solving specific problems into a language that computers are able to understand and work with.

Although we explore programming languages in much more detail in Chapter 8, it is important to understand that programming is used to create software. We introduced you to software in Chapter 2; you learned how operating system software works in Chapter 3. The next three chapters explored three popular applications. In this chapter, you'll learn more about the different types of system software and application software.

Understanding Files

Computer software uses files to store data. The file is a basic unit of storage in a computer. In Chapter 3, we explained how DOS uses files on a personal computer. Well, application programs are written and stored as files. The work you create with an application, as you learned in the three chapters in Module II, is also stored as files. All the software discussed in this chapter is stored in files of one kind or another.

There are many types of files. Some files contain the instructions used for the computer's operating system, while others are for applications. These files are usually not open to inspection or modification by users — as the label on some appliances says, "no user-serviceable parts inside." Files we create in applications such as word processing or spreadsheets are clearly "user-serviceable."

However, in many cases, a file created by one application may not be easily used by another. A file created in, say, WordStar, may not be readable by WordPerfect, and a Lotus 1-2-3 file can't be read by dBase III. This is because each application creates files in its own particular file format. If this is so, then how can we exchange data between applications? In most cases, by converting the file into the ASCII format. **ASCII** stands for the American Standard Code for Information Interchange. Most applications are designed to read and write files in ASCII, so they can be easily exchanged.

DISKbyte

The Abstract Industry

The following essay, "The Abstract Industry," was adapted from *Software Magazine*'s special issue, "A Software Industry Retrospective: 1969–89."[1]

The beautiful thing about the software industry is that it keeps building on itself. Software reproduces like some strange life form. It is like having the gas tank refill itself while you drive. Brick by brick, tap by tap, the software gets built. And all the software that gets built relies on the software behind it, and points to the software that is possible in the future. Where will it end?

People who fear the unknown may have a lot to fear in the software industry. Maybe it is possible to program impenetrable shields of laser patterns in the sky. That is something to fear.

Those who work in the industry know such perfect software is a long way off, and probably impossible to build in any lifetime. A little insight may help allay such fears.

One insight into the software industry is its people. It is a young industry on its second generation. Yet, the number of those who helped to build it is still identifiable. At least, that is what we assert.

Overall, it is a fair industry. Women have a significant presence in the software development community of users, consultants, and certainly marketing professionals. A Bureau of Labor Statistics recent stat: women accounted for 39 percent of all workers in computer programming and software-related fields as of February 1989, up from 38 percent five years earlier.

It seems software is likely to create more of a demand for itself as it grows.

On to 2009.

SYSTEM SOFTWARE

System software runs the computer system, performing a variety of fundamental operations that make the computer available for use. These operations include:

- Booting the computer and making sure all aspects are operational.
- Performing operations such as retrieving, loading, executing, and storing application programs.
- Storing and retrieving files.
- Performing a variety of system utility functions.

System software includes the operating system software, or OS for short, which controls the execution of computer programs. It also controls programming tools, which are used to translate and help improve computer programs. It acts as an intermediary between the user or application programs and the computer hardware to control and manage the operation of the computer. In a sense, the OS is the resident authority in your computer, as portrayed in Figure 7–1. Whatever you want to do has to be done with the help and cooperation of

---

[1] Reprinted with the permission of *Software Magazine,* March 1989 Extra, Sentry Publishing Co., Inc., Westborough, Mass. 01581.

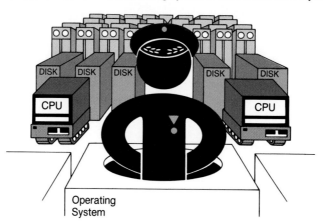

Operating
System

the operating system. The OS provides input/output control, scheduling, storage assignment, data management, and related services. In the next section, we'll explore some examples of what the OS does.

The Many Faces of an Operating System

One way to understand what a computer operating system does is to think of it as a supervisor. Perhaps you've had a job where you worked for a supervisor, or were one yourself. If so, you know that the supervisor is the person who directs your activities according to instructions he or she receives from upper levels of management. Typically, supervisors facilitate interactions between you and your co-workers, assign tasks to you, and direct and monitor your work. These are also an operating system's primary functions. Next, we'll describe five operating system functions in terms of some familiar people we encounter in everyday life.

The Servant: Providing Command Languages and Utilities

> "Open the pod bay doors, HAL."
> Arthur C. Clarke, *2001: A Space Odyssey*

Effective working relationships depend on effective communication, and this is certainly true with computers. Communicating effectively requires that we use a commonly understood set of words and phrases. For example, order takers at fast-food restaurants use codes to quickly and efficiently relay customer orders to the food preparers. Similarly, operating systems have abbreviations and codes that allow us to communicate quickly and efficiently with the CPU. We call these codes a **command language.** The command language codes allow us to give instructions to our servant, the operating system, quickly and effectively.

Operating systems utilize commands that are loaded into the computer's main memory. For example, when you type DIR at the DOS prompt on your

FIGURE 7–2   Typing DIR at the DOS prompt gives a list of the files on the disk in use.

```
.                 <DIR>        1-02-80     3:02a
..                <DIR>        1-02-80     3:02a
4201      CPI     17089        7-24-87    12:00a
5202      CPI       459        7-24-87    12:00a
ANSI      SYS      1647        7-24-87    12:00a
APPEND    EXE      5794        7-24-87    12:00a
ASSIGN    COM      1530        7-24-87    12:00a
ATTRIB    EXE     10656        7-24-87    12:00a
BACKUP    COM     29976        7-24-87    12:00a
CHKDSK    COM      9819        7-24-87    12:00a
COMMAND   COM     25276        7-24-87    12:00a
COMP      COM      4183        7-24-87    12:00a
COUNTRY   SYS     11254        7-24-87    12:00a
DEBUG     COM     15866        7-24-87    12:00a
DISKCOMP  COM      5848        7-24-87    12:00a
DISKCOPY  COM      6264        7-24-87    12:00a
DISPLAY   SYS     11259        7-24-87    12:00a
DRIVER    SYS      1165        7-24-87    12:00a
EDLIN     COM      7495        7-24-87    12:00a
EGA       CPI     49065        7-24-87    12:00a
EXE2BIN   EXE      3050        7-24-87    12:00a
FASTOPEN  EXE      3888        7-24-87    12:00a
FC        EXE     15974        7-24-87    12:00a
```

FIGURE 7–3   Some common DOS commands.

COPY	Makes copies of files
DATE	Sets the date
DIR	Lists the files on a disk
DISKCOPY	Copies an entire disk
ERASE	Removes files from a disk
FORMAT	Prepares a disk for use
PRINT	Prints a file on the printer
RENAME	Changes file names
TIME	Sets the time
TYPE	Displays the contents of a file on the monitor

personal computer screen, the operating system issues a command to the CPU to list the files it finds on the disk or directory you are working in, as we can see with the DOS command and its output shown in Figure 7–2. Each operating system has a collection of these commands, and Figure 7–3 shows some that are common in DOS. The operating system acts as a servant by responding to the commands we issue and performing several key operations for both users and for application programs.

Some commands we issue let us use programs called *utilities* to perform the work we request. We introduced several of these utilities in Chapter 3. For example, it is often necessary to copy files from one disk to another, or make backup copies of important work. Most operating systems have a copy utility. You can be quite specific about what you want to copy, from particular files to an entire disk. Operating system commands and utilities can be quite extensive, filling whole volumes.

The Traffic Officer: Controlling Input and Output

"Would you tell me please, which way I ought to go from here?" said Alice.

"That depends a good deal on where you want to get to," said the Cat.

Lewis Carroll, *Alice's Adventures in Wonderland*

Whether you are using a personal computer or a mainframe, your computer has many input and output (I/O) devices. A typical personal computer uses a keyboard, a monitor, and a printer. Like a skilled traffic officer, the operating system coordinates between these various I/O devices and other peripheral devices such as hard or floppy disk drives, making sure data flows properly between them and sorting out possible confusion.

For example, let's see how the operating system manages the printing process. When you want to print a file, you type the PRINT command. The next thing you know, the printer begins printing. By itself, your command is meaningless to the CPU. The operating system is a vital link to getting the job done. First, it translates your command into the binary language of bits and bytes that makes sense to the CPU. Second, like a traffic officer seeing a car's turn signal, it realizes that you want to produce output on a specific device. Next, it stops whatever the CPU is doing and redirects its attention to the printing function. Fourth, the operating system searches the available peripheral devices, chooses the correct one, translates its name for the CPU, and commands the CPU to send your file to that device. After the file is printed, the operating system tells the CPU the job is done so it is free for the next request.

The Appointment Secretary: Scheduling

"Time is nature's way of keeping everything from happening at once."
Anonymous

Operating systems are master appointment secretaries. Some computers allow only one user to do one thing at a time. Others are designed to meet the needs of several users doing many different things, as if the computer had dozens of minds doing many things at once. In actual fact, this is an illusion. With few exceptions, the computers we work with have but one CPU, and can do only one thing at a time.

How does the single CPU do the work of many while it seems like we are the only user? First, with speed. The CPU works very fast. Processing time is measured in nanoseconds, or *billionths* of a second. Figure 7–4 illustrates some physical comparisons of the speed light (and thus, electricity) travels.

FIGURE 7–4 Electricity travels about 11 inches every 1/1,000,000th of a second. This is like traveling from New York to Los Angeles in .13 seconds, around the earth in .134 seconds, from the earth to the moon in 1.282 seconds, or from the sun to the earth in 8.32 minutes.

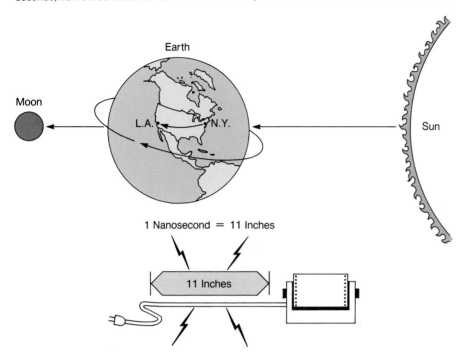

Second, the OS is very efficient at **scheduling** or making maximum use of the CPU by performing tasks in a precise sequence. Scheduling makes it appear as though the CPU is doing many things at once, when in fact it's only capable of doing one thing at a time—albeit very, very quickly.

With effective scheduling, the operating system makes use of a brief pause in one user's activities to perform the requests of other users. It does this by establishing rules and priorities among users and by making use of every fraction of a second to keep the CPU working at maximum efficiency.

Another aspect of scheduling involves **multiprogramming,** or using more than one application at the same time. Most large mainframe and mini-computer operating systems are designed for multiprogramming, permitting many applications to share the CPU so that many users can perform a variety of tasks consecutively.

The Hotel Manager: Storage Assignment

"A place for everything and everything in its place."

Isabella Mary Beeton, *The Book of Household Management*

If you have done any programming, you know that computers must keep track of every bit of information. All data and instructions must be stored and cataloged by the computer. The operating system plays a key role in managing this data. An effective hotel manager keeps track of all the hotel's rooms and their occupants. Similarly, the operating system is constantly assigning and reassigning main memory storage locations for data and instructions.

Not only does the operating system make assignments, it also categorizes what it stores. As you learned in Chapter 2, there are many ways we use memory. Some things that we use frequently, such as input and output instructions, must be kept in main memory. Others that are used less frequently, such as data files, can be temporarily stored on disk. Still others, which are used even less frequently, like backups of a mainframe's database, can be farmed out to mass storage devices. The operating system, aided by application programs, knows where to find every single piece of data, even when there are millions or billions of pieces. That's quite an effective hotel manager!

The Librarian: Data Management

"Tis in my memory lock'd,
And you yourself shall keep the key of it."

William Shakespeare, *Hamlet*

If you've ever visited or used a large library, you are aware of the tremendous volume of information people have at their fingertips. A library is a repository of information in the form of books and periodicals; it is similar to a computer's auxiliary memory where we store data in files. But storing data is only one aspect of its usefulness. People need to know the location, size, date, and composition of the files in the computer. Operating systems are essential in supervising these vast amounts of data.

A librarian knows the organization of the books in the library and can help you find exactly what you're looking for. Similarly, an operating system helps you locate and use the files and programs in auxiliary storage. As the librarian can help you find a book, perhaps by showing you how to use a catalog of the library's books, so can an operating system help you find computer data. One way is by providing the DIR command we showed you earlier in this chapter. The operating system also may know who is using particular files, when they are used, and who is allowed to use each file.

Now that you have a general idea of what operating systems do, let's take a look at some of the most common types. The following sections briefly describe some personal computer, mini, and mainframe operating systems.

Personal Computer Operating Systems

Most personal computers in use today are single user computers; that means one person uses one application at a time. Instead of having to handle the requests of multiple users and sort out the input and output of many devices, the operating systems running these personal computers execute instructions in a very straightforward manner, serving one user and performing one function at a time.

Some personal computers have more advanced operating systems with multiuser, multitasking capabilities. **Multiuser** operating systems process the work of two or more users, working at different terminals or personal computers, at the same time. **Multitasking** operating systems perform two or more functions or tasks simultaneously for a single user. Multitasking is the personal computer equivalent of multiprogramming for minis and mainframes. A multitasking system allows you to write with a word processor while

FIGURE 7-5   Multitasking: Each "window" is an application.

Courtesy of Lotus Development

performing spreadsheet calculations in the background, for example. Figure 7–5 shows multitasking at work. Let's compare several personal computer operating systems.

DOS   The most common personal computer operating system is MS–DOS, developed by Microsoft Corporation of Bellevue, Washington. MS–DOS stands for Microsoft Disk Operating System. PC–DOS is a similar operating system developed for the IBM PC. Today, we simply refer to these operating systems as DOS.

DOS is a simple operating system. It includes several basic utilities but its primary function is telling the personal computer to perform whatever task the application you're using tells it to. The first version of DOS was not very easy to use. For example, if you wanted to enter the date, you had to type it as 12–18–1944. It would not accept a date entered as 12/18/1944 or 12/18/44. A more serious drawback is that DOS makes no provision for an electrical outage or other system failure. Unless you frequently save your work, an unexpected system failure can destroy a lot of effort.

Despite its shortcomings, DOS has been a workhorse operating system for a long line of personal computers. As Figure 7–6 shows, it has been improved and revised extensively over the years and now provides user-friendly features such as a menus. Figure 7–7 shows the menu-oriented version of DOS Version 5.0.

OS/2   The OS/2 operating system was developed by Microsoft and IBM for its PS/2 line of personal computers. OS/2 offers features not found in DOS. It has more RAM capacity, which allows it to run more complicated applications; multitasking capabilities; and a graphic interface. The OS/2 graphic interface, called Presentation Manager, allows you to run several

FIGURE 7–6   DOS versions.

Version	Date	Features
1.0	1981	Original disk operating system
1.25	1982	Support for double-sided disks
2.0	1983	Support for subdirectories (especially hard disk)
2.01	1983	Support for international symbols
2.11	1983	Bug corrections
2.25	1983	Extended character set support
3.0	1984	Support for 1.2MB floppy disk, up to 32MB hard disk
3.1	1984	Support for PC networks
3.2	1986	Support for 3.5-inch micro-floppy disk
3.3	1987	Support for IBM PS/2 computers
4.0	1989	Menu-driven user interface; support for 1.44MB floppy disk, hard disks over 32MB
5.0	1990	Window interface; better memory use

FIGURE 7–7   Improvements in DOS are reflected in its Version 5.0 menus and window.

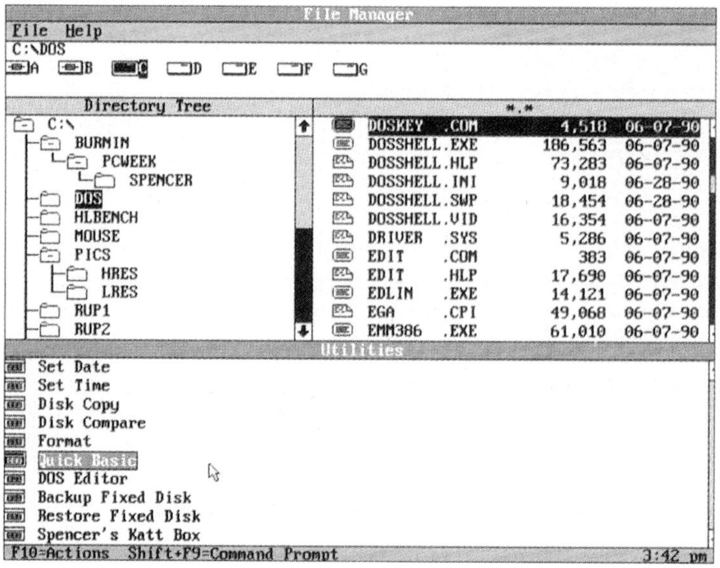

Source: *PC Week,* July 2, 1990, p. 1.

applications in windows—separate boxes displayed on the monitor screen. This makes it possible to, for example, perform word processing in one window while working with a spreadsheet in another. OS/2 is a single user operating system but works much faster than DOS.

Multifinder   Multifinder, the Macintosh operating system, uses icons and graphics instead of the command line common to DOS and OS/2. A file folder holds various documents, which are visually displayed on the screen. The mouse is used to move files and folders from one place to another; a trash can icon is used to erase them from the disk. A menu is displayed across the top of the screen, with "pull-down" menu commands connected to each.

Apple has improved Multifinder many times since its introduction. It permits multitasking, and most recently has added a variety of desktop publishing capabilities as standard features. Additionally, other software companies have introduced programs that make Multifinder even more useful, such as one that permits multiple users.

Minicomputer Operating Systems

Minicomputer operating systems are more complex than those for personal computers. Most are multiuser, multiprogramming systems that control an extensive array of peripheral devices. Mini operating systems are fast, handle large volumes of data, and perform many I/O operations.

UNIX   UNIX is an operating system developed at AT&T Bell Laboratories in New Jersey. UNIX was initially designed to offer a powerful and convenient programming environment for experienced users.

UNIX commands are abbreviated and extremely powerful. Steps required by many simpler operating systems are eliminated to make UNIX faster. Novice users often find UNIX rather unfriendly and unforgiving. A mistake that would be small using DOS can be a big mistake on UNIX!

People who can do many things at once find UNIX especially valuable. UNIX allows you to, in effect, be many users at once. This is accomplished by making it easy to run several subprocesses or user sessions at the same time. Each subprocess can perform several tasks at once.

UNIX use is widespread, in part because it is a more portable operating system than most. **Portable** means it can be used on several different computers, regardless of their manufacturer. Because of its effective use of computer processing capabilities, many UNIX features have been added to some personal computer operating systems. UNIX is the preferred operating system for most workstations and is available for use with some personal computers as well.

VMS   VMS is the operating system Digital Equipment Corporation developed for its family of VAX (Virtual Address Extension) computers. VMS stands for Virtual Memory System. The key to understanding the strengths of VMS is the word *virtual*. Virtual means existing in essence but not in actual fact.

VMS is like the vice president at an important social function like the President's Ball. Imagine a room filled with dignitaries, ambassadors, top businesspeople, and elected officials. Everyone wants to feel like he or she is the president's closest friend or associate. Since the president can't be with everyone at the same time, the vice president makes sure to spend a little time with everyone, giving them the sense that they are among the select few who are most important to the president.

The VMS operating system includes a device called the Swapper that does almost exactly this. The Swapper serves every user of the VAX/VMS system, giving each one access to the CPU. Because the Swapper is very fast and very good at keeping track of all user requests, most users feel they are among a privileged few who have direct use of the CPU. The result is a minicomputer system that often seems as dedicated to the user as a personal computer. Figure 7–8 lists some VMS commands.

FIGURE 7–8   Some common VMS commands.

AUTHORIZE	Allocates system resources to users
COPY	Copies a file from one disk or directory to another
DELETE	Deletes a file
DIFFERENCE	Shows the differences between two files
DIRECTORY	Lists contents of the default directory
EDIT	Edits a file
HELP	Displays help on commands
LOGIN/LOGOUT	Begins/ends a user session
MAIL	Sends/reads mail messages
PURGE	Deletes prior versions of files
RECOVER	Restores a file lost by system failure
RENAME	Changes file names
SET DEFAULT	Sets default disk and directory
SET PASSWORD	Sets a new user password
SHOW PROCESS	Shows use of system resources
SHOW PROTECT	Shows users allowed access to a file
SHOW QUEUE	Lists printer and batch jobs being executed or waiting to be executed
SHOW USERS	Lists current users of computer
SPAWN	Begins a user session within an active user session

Mainframe Operating Systems

One of the advantages of using mainframes is that they permit the most extensive assortment of peripheral devices of all computers. One feature commonly found in mainframe operating systems is the ability to communicate with many kinds of peripherals and auxiliary storage devices. Each printer, disk drive, mag tape reader, and mass storage device can have its own language. Mainframe operating systems effectively communicate with all these parts of the computer system. Mainframe operating systems are typically multiuser, multiprogramming systems with even greater processing speeds than mini operating systems.

MVS   MVS is a well-known operating system in the mainframe world, developed by IBM. MVS specializes in batch processing, which involves collecting several user requests or programs into batches for processing at a later time. Batch processing is used primarily for large, periodic jobs such as corporate billing or payroll.

MVS also has extensive multiuser capabilities. That is because it was created using principles established during Project MAC at the Massachusetts Institute of Technology. Project MAC's goal was to create a time-sharing computer system. **Time-sharing** means it could be used by many people simultaneously for different purposes or applications—thus its name, Multiple-Access Computer. The operating system Project MAC created in 1962 was known as CTSS, for Computer Time-Sharing System, and it was able to serve 200 users.

MVS is a big operating system, containing 520 million 8-bit characters, coded into 13 million instructions. Because it's big, it can do big things: one MIS department has seven interconnected CPUs, with approximately 15,000 terminals in over 450 locations, running under the MVS operating system. Between 500 and 700 users can have access to the CPU at a time, using between 300 and 400 different applications. Figure 7–9 lists some MVS commands.

FIGURE 7 – 9   MVS commands for a mainframe environment are more complex than those for a PC environment.

```
//*       ---------------------------------------------------------   00000010
//*       FORTCLG - FORTRAN COMPILE, LINK, AND EXECUTE.               00000020
//*       ---------------------------------------------------------   00000030
//        PROC DECK=NODECK,SOURCE=,MAP=NOMAP,LOAD=LOAD,LIST=NOLIST    00000040
//FORT    EXEC PGM=IEYFORT,REGION=100K,                              00000050
//             PARM='&DECK,&SOURCE,&MAP,&LOAD,&LIST'                  00000060
//SYSPRINT DD  SYSOUT=A                                              00000070
//SYSPUNCH DD  SYSOUT=B                                              00000080
//SYSLIN   DD  UNIT=SYSDA,SPACE=(CYL,(1,1)),DISP=(,PASS)             00000090
//LKED    EXEC PGM=IEWLF440,COND=(4,LT,FORT),REGION=96K,             00000100
//             PARM=(XREF,LIST,LET)                                  00000110
//SYSLIB   DD  DSN=&&FORTLIB1,DISP=(SHR,PASS)                        00000120
//         DD  DSN=&&FORTLIB2,DISP=(SHR,PASS)                        00000130
//SYSLMOD  DD  DSN=&&GOSET(GO),DISP-(,PASS),UNIT=SYSDA,              00000140
//             SPACE=(CYL,(1,1,1))                                   00000150
//SYSPRINT DD  SYSOUT=A                                              00000160
//SYSUT1   DD  DSN=&&SYSUT1,UNIT=SYSSQ,SPACE=(1024,(100,50),,,ROUND) 00000170
//SYSLIN   DD  DSN=*.FORT.SYSLIN,DISP=(OLD,DELETE)                   00000180
//         DD  DDNAME=SYSIN                                          00000190
//GO      EXEC PGM=*.LKED.SYSLMOD,COND=((4,LT,FORT),(4,LT,LKED))     00000200
//FT05F001 DD  DDNAME=SYSIN                                          00000210
//FT06F001 DD  SYSOUT=A                                              00000220
//FT07F001 DD  SYSOUT=B                                              00000230
//*       ---------------------------------------------------------   00000240
```

Trends in Operating Systems

Personal computer operating systems such as OS/2 are becoming increasingly sophisticated. Not only do they handle the traditional chores of managing memory and controlling peripherals but they now include such features as user-friendly interfaces and networking capabilities. Many features such as multiuser and multiprogramming/multitasking capabilities, previously found only in mainframe and minicomputer operating systems, are appearing in personal computer operating systems.

In the past, computer manufacturers chose to keep the operating systems they developed for their computers **proprietary,** meaning the exact workings of these operating systems were private, protected information. This meant that if you wanted to use a particular manufacturer's hardware, you had to use the operating system designed for it, and you couldn't alter that operating system. VMS is a proprietary operating system; it works only on computers manufactured by Digital Equipment Corporation.

The opposite of a proprietary product is an open system. UNIX is an example of an **open system,** a product that can be altered for use with many manufacturers' hardware. Because the inner workings of UNIX are available to the public, anyone can develop applications to work on this operating system. The result is the first nonproprietary operating system that works with personal computers, workstations, minis, and mainframes.

Operating systems are important in maximizing the potential of computer systems, but most of their functions are invisible to us. Like the engines in our cars, if they work poorly we feel it; if they work smoothly, we appreciate it. Still, what is most visible to us is application software. We'll explore the diverse world of applications next.

MEMORY CHECK

1. What kind of software is the operating system?
2. Identify five functions of an operating system.
3. What is the most common personal computer operating system?
4. What is a multiuser system?
5. Define the term *multitasking*.
6. What is a portable operating system?
7. What is the difference between a proprietary and an open system?

APPLICATION SOFTWARE

Now let's turn our attention to the software you'll be interacting with most: application software. At first, there was only one application: a calculator that solved mathematical problems. Over the years, as Figure 7–10 shows, applications have shifted from the computer "back room" to departmental end users. Today, thousands of applications exist; you learned how to use the three most popular packages in Module II.

When we use applications, we don't see all that's happening between the application and the operating system, nor do we see how the operating system is facilitating interactions between the application and the hardware. But we

---

FIGURE 7–10   Applications have changed over the years to serve less experienced computer users.

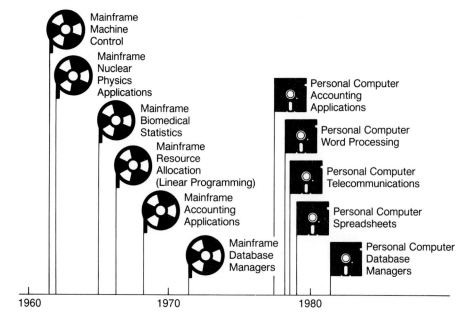

don't need to, just as we don't need to know exactly how CDs work to appreciate the music they contain. What we really want from application software is results.

You will recall from earlier chapters that computers work with data and instructions. At the application level, data is commonly stored in files, and instructions are found in programs such as the applications we'll discuss in this chapter.

Figure 7–11 shows the relationships between various programs and data in a corporate database management system. The diagram shows that many kinds of data such as files, records, and lists provide the input to the DBMS.

FIGURE 7–11 A DBMS uses data and instructions in the form of records and programs to organize and process data.

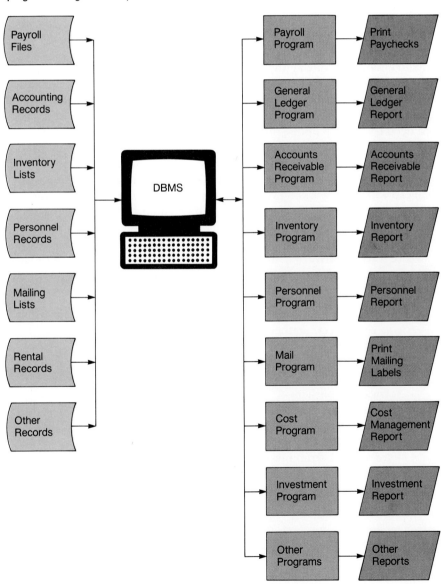

This DBMS works with several associated programs such as a payroll, general ledger, and mail to produce several kinds of output such as checks, a general ledger report, mailing labels, and so on.

This section concerns the evolution of application software: where we are going and what we're going to do when we get there. First we'll study integrated software, a combination of individual applications. Then we'll look at computer graphics software and the world of designing with computers. Next we'll learn about electronic publishing software, which makes everyone a publisher. Then we delve into the world of helpful programs called utilities, followed by special-purpose software for home, education, and special needs. Last, we'll look at the leading edge in software development.

Integrated Software

The application programs for personal computers you studied in the preceding chapters — word processing, the spreadsheet, and the DBMS — are commonly known as **stand-alone programs.** That means they work alone, by themselves. There is nothing wrong with that if you spend a large proportion of your time using one application such as the spreadsheet. But what if you frequently need to write memos to accompany your spreadsheet analysis? What if you want to create a bar chart from the statistical information in your spreadsheet for a presentation? What if you keep your address book in a DBMS and need to look up phone numbers all the time?

It would be nice to switch between applications rather than store the file you're working on, quit the application, return to the operating system prompt, change disks or directories to the new application, then run it. Only then can you begin working with a new file. To return to the previous application or change to another means going through all these steps once again. What's more, if you want to transfer data between two applications, it is either difficult, unlikely, or impossible.

Integrated software combines several stand-alone applications capable of freely exchanging data with each other into a single program. Figure 7–12 shows the versatility of integrated software. There are several advantages:

1. You can switch from one application to another merely by pressing one or two keys, rather than the complicated exit-enter process just described.
2. The applications all work similarly to one another, so it is not as difficult as learning separate applications created by different software publishers.
3. Because the applications work similarly, there is often a user-friendly interface such as a menu bar for selecting functions or switching between applications.
4. Files, or data from files, can be transferred from one application to another; for example, a portion of a spreadsheet can be removed and then inserted into a word processing report.

There are disadvantages in using integrated software, too. One is that a particular application is very good, while others may have shortcomings. For example, the word processing may be excellent but the DBMS may be poor. Another is that transferring data from one application to another may not work properly; for example, when transferring numbers from the spreadsheet

FIGURE 7–12   An integrated software program.

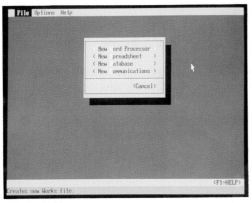

F. Bodin/Offshoot

to word processing, the columns may not line up properly. Over time, most integrated software programs have been revised and improved to overcome many of these disadvantages.

The Evolution of Integrated Software   The first integrated software package, Context MBA, combined word processing, the spreadsheet, database management, and graphics. It was launched in 1982 but wasn't marketed effectively enough to really get off the ground. Lotus 1-2-3 was introduced at a gala party, high atop New York's World Trade Center, a year later. Lotus combined the spreadsheet, graphics, and a database management system into one program. It is easy to switch between them, and it is possible to share data between them as well. Lotus 1-2-3 topped $1 million in sales its first week on the market, so Mitch Kapor is generally credited with introducing the first popular integrated software for the IBM PC. Figure 7–13 shows how Lotus 1-2-3 shares data between applications.

What happened to word processing? Mitch says it was part of the original plan but the programmer quit and they didn't replace him. There is a Lotus 1-2-3 with word processing today called Symphony.

Commonly, integrated packages have four or five applications: word processing, a spreadsheet, graphics, database management, and telecommunications or networking. This is extremely useful. It means you can write a memo in word processing, and with just a few keystrokes send it to another computer. Some integrated packages provide additional utility programs such as a spelling checker, calendar, calculator, or an outliner.

How Integrated Software Works   Integrated software is loaded into your computer and runs like most other programs. However, since it consists of several different applications, it is usually much larger than a stand-alone program. If there is insufficient space in memory to hold the entire program, it is often necessary to switch disks to perform various tasks. A hard disk drive gets rid of this annoyance. Integrated software usually favors one application; for example, Lotus 1-2-3 favors the spreadsheet, while Word-Perfect Executive favors — you guessed it — word processing. Although the other applications work just fine, you might think about which you'll use more often, for that one will have the most features.

FIGURE 7-13   Lotus 1-2-3 allows you to take a calculation made in the spreadsheet, combine it in a database report, then graphically display it.

N141: [W14] 'Week   `READY`

	N	O	P	Q	R	S
141	Week	Agent	Insurance			
142	07/13/90	D. Feldman	293,000			
143	07/13/90	W. Berman	190,000			
144	07/13/90	W. Buckley	140,000			
145	07/13/90	D. Levin	111,000			
146	07/13/90	S. Bayle	103,000			
147	07/13/90	V. Vinopal	48,000			
148	07/13/90	C. Slocum	24,000			
149	07/20/90	D. Feldman	281,000			
150	07/20/90	W. Buckley	173,000			
151	07/20/90	V. Vinopal	164,000			
152	07/20/90	D. Levin	137,000			
153	07/20/90	W. Berman	83,000			
154	07/20/90	C. Slocum	63,000			
155	07/20/90	S. Bayle	11,000			
156	07/27/90	D. Feldman	197,000			
157	07/27/90	S. Bayle	196,000			
158	07/27/90	W. Berman	186,000			
159	07/27/90	W. Buckley	152,000			
160	07/27/90	V. Vinopal	114,000			

CRUSADE.WK1   `NUM`

An insurance agency database in 1-2-3

C29: (F1) [W10] @SUM(C23..C28)   `READY`

	A	B	C	D	E	F	G	H	I
20									
21				Sales Person					
22	Product	|	Sharp	Lake	Gregory	East			
23	Windows	|	10.0	2.8	2.6	8.1			
24	Doors	|	4.0	8.1	5.2	4.4			
25	Jambs	|	2.2	8.3	5.1	2.5			
26	Sills	|	7.0	17.1	3.7	12.1			
27	Trellises	|	11.0	4.7	16.4	9.2			
28			=====	=====	=====	====			
29	Total		34.2	41.0	32.9	28.3			

PIE0.WK1   `NUM`

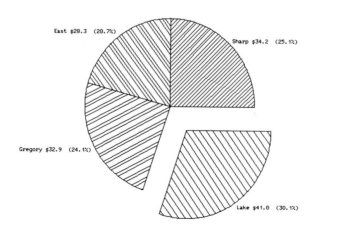

Sales by Representative (000 Omitted)
05/25/92

East $28.3 (20.7%)

Sharp $34.2 (25.1%)

Gregory $32.9 (24.1%)

Lake $41.0 (30.1%)

FIGURE 7–14   The drawing on the right has been "cut" from a graphics file and "pasted" into the word processing document file on the left.

F. Bodin/Offshoot

The ability to share data or files between applications has been one of the most nagging problems besetting personal computer users. Integrated software addresses this problem head on but with varying degrees of success. In computer jargon, some programs are highly integrated, meaning they let you pass data back and forth very easily. Others are loosely integrated, meaning their main advantage is that they enable you to switch quickly between applications. Some software companies let you purchase loosely integrated applications separately.

Even so, exchanging data between files or applications, commonly called *cut and paste,* is extremely useful. You can put monthly sales figures from the spreadsheet into a database of year-to-date corporate revenues. You can insert a name and address from the DBMS into a word processing letter's address heading. Some integrated software programs (and some stand-alone programs as well) also permit opening more than one file in a single application and then switching between them. For example, using the DBMS, you can switch between two different databases, one for your address book and another for company sales figures. Or let's say you wrote an analysis of industrial pollution for your earth sciences class last semester. Now you're taking a political science course and you're writing a paper on environmental politics. In your previous paper, you quoted a Sierra Club spokesperson and want to reuse the quote. All you have to do is open the previous file, cut the quote from it, and past it into the new file. Figure 7–14 shows cut and paste.

---

1. What is a program such as word processing or a DBMS called?
2. What type of software combines several programs into one?
3. Why do we need to switch between applications?
4. Describe a use for the cut-and-paste function.
5. Describe the difference between highly integrated and loosely integrated.

MEMORY CHECK

Computer Graphics

People are visually oriented; therefore, if computers are going to be useful, they should provide visuals, too. **Graphics** are pictorial representations; **computer graphics** are pictorial representations of data. Without graphics, we wouldn't have user-friendly interfaces. Computer graphics used to be reserved for the few, mostly artists and engineers, but the Macintosh changed all that. It demonstrated that the computer was capable of producing high-quality graphics at an affordable price and brought many people flocking to computers who hadn't been interested before.

Types of Computer Graphics

In its simplest form, an image on the computer screen is simply a character: a letter, a number, or a symbol. This is called text. Many applications display text only. Text is contrasted with graphics, which displays shapes, lines, and images. Early, simple graphics programs allowed you to connect lines between points on the screen, say to make a box or a star, and were called **vector graphics.**

But what we commonly call graphics today is **high-resolution graphics,** a sharp, crisp video display that can display curving lines, shading, detail, color, and so forth. Resolution refers to the amount of detail in the graphics display—the higher the better.

To produce high-resolution graphics you must have the right hardware, including internal video circuits and the right video monitor. Personal computer video monitor resolution is rated according to the number of **pixels** or dots of light it can display on the screen. Pixels form a grid on the screen to create graphics. A typical personal computer color monitor displays 640 by 220 pixels, or about 14 million dots. That means the picture can show a great deal of fine detail or resolution. Figure 7–15 shows the difference between vector graphics and high-resolution graphics.

Presentation Graphics

There are several types of graphics software. What we see most commonly is called **presentation graphics,** the computer graphics or visuals used for business. Presentation graphics present numerical, statistical, financial, or other quantitative data in a visual form, usually a pie chart, a bar chart, a line graph, or scatter graph, as shown in Figure 7–16.

FIGURE 7–15   Vector graphics (left) and high-resolution graphics (right).

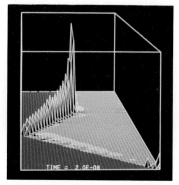

D. McCoy/Rainbow   Courtesy of Apple Computer, Inc.

These graphics are intended to convey information about a situation quickly and clearly, either in a printed report or on a transparency master or slide. As you learned in the preceding section, presentation graphics are a common program component with integrated spreadsheet packages. Presentation graphics can be created with data from either a spreadsheet or a database.

Draw and Paint Graphics Programs   The Macintosh made it possible to create artwork or designs from scratch, using a program called MacDraw as the palette and the mouse as a pencil or brush. Now there are many color draw and paint programs for personal computers. A draw program is designed to create line drawings, which is useful for illustrators, drafters, and designers. A paint program allows more creativity, including changing brush thickness or creating sprayed or spattered designs. Figure 7–17 shows drawing and painting using a mouse.

FIGURE 7–16   Examples of the versatility of presentation graphics.

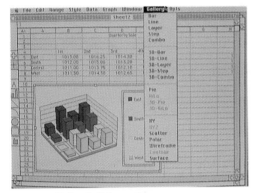

Courtesy of Informix Software Corp.

Courtesy of Hewlett-Packard Company

FIGURE 7–17   Drawing and painting using a mouse.

H. Mark Weidman

The Evolution of Computer Graphics   Philippe Villers was studying for his master's degree at MIT in 1962 when he first saw Sketchpad. The brainchild of Ivan Sutherland, another MIT graduate student, Sketchpad allowed drawing on the face of a video display with a light pen. It was a visionary work, and it inspired Villers to create the first commercial computer-aided drafting system, The Designer Studio. This software combined computer graphics and drawing software for use on a special terminal with a drawing tablet, and set the course from computer graphics to computer-aided design, or CAD.

Computer-Aided Design   CAD is engineering design software that replaces the drafting table, special drafting tools, pencils, and templates, permitting users to create designs in three dimensions. A decade ago, CAD required an expensive terminal, but like many other mini and mainframe applications, there are programs now for the personal computer. Today, CAD is only one phase of the automated process known as **computer-integrated manufacturing (CIM)**. CAD designs are now tested on the computer screen, then revised and refined. The designs are turned into working specifications, both graphics and text, in a process called **document and image processing.** For example, the manufacturing specifications for an aircraft engine accompany the drawing itself. Once the specs are complete, they are sent, as computer instructions, to the manufacturing floor for computer-aided manufacturing (CAM). Therefore, CAD plus CAM equals CIM.

Computer Art   Back when graphics systems were expensive, they were used mostly by engineers designing automobiles, aerospace vehicles, computers, electronics circuits, and the like. Even so, many people were drawn to computer graphics terminals for artistic expression and amusement, and in 1973 the First Annual Conference on Computer Graphics and Interactive Techniques (now called SIGGRAPH) was held. In addition to its speakers, a SIGGRAPH conference is like attending an art opening of the finest, most interesting computer-generated art in the world. Figure 7–18 shows the process of creating computer art.

FIGURE 7–18   A computer graphics system for creating computer art.

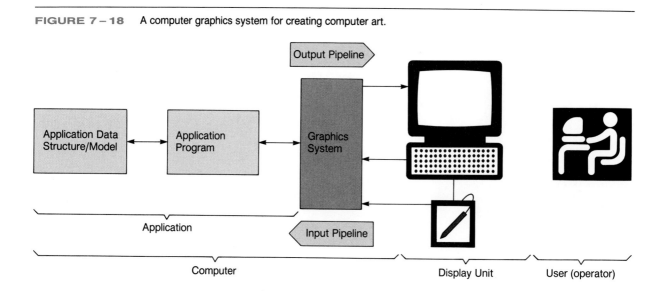

Using Computer Graphics   Today, computer graphics touch many areas of life:

- Designers and special effects technicians use computers for television commercials and movies (Figure 7–19).
- Artists create comic books such as "Shatter," done completely on the Macintosh (Figure 7–20).

FIGURE 7–19   Special effects created on a supercomputer.

Light Scapes/The Stock Market

FIGURE 7–20   "Shatter," a comic book created entirely on the Macintosh.

Permission from First Publishing

FIGURE 7–21   The fourth dimension as visualized by Thomas Banchoff of Brown University.

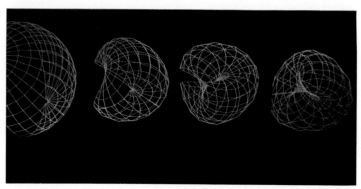

D. McCoy/Rainbow

FIGURE 7–22   Image processing systems allow entry of auto photos for insurance claims.

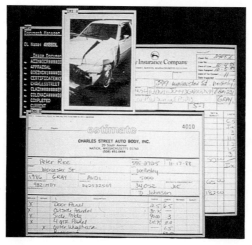

Courtesy of Wang Laboratories, Inc.

- Thomas Banchoff of Brown University experiments with computer graphics and theoretical physics to visualize the fourth dimension (Figure 7–21).
- Wang and other computer companies now offer insurance information systems that capture a photograph of a damaged car or house in the claims database, replacing a text explanation (Figure 7–22).

Computer graphics is evolving into image processing, where information that was once represented in words can now be captured, stored, and manipulated pictorially in the computer. But as CAD applications evolve, so do others. Surgeons can manipulate an image of a diseased organ, captured from a computerized axial tomography (CAT) scan. They can simulate the surgery to see if it will correct the problem without ever touching the patient (Figure 7–23). Computer graphics have certainly come a long way since pie charts.

FIGURE 7–23   Computerized axial tomography (CAT) scans give doctors a cross-sectional view of the human body.

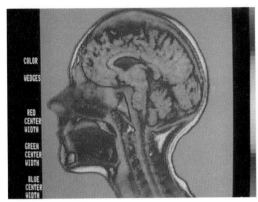

D. McCoy/Rainbow

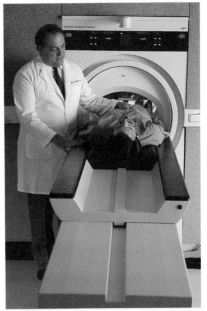

H. Mark Weidman

1. What are some of the most common business graphics?

2. What are the dots of light on the computer screen called?

3. What is the most commonly used type of computer graphics?

4. What has replaced traditional drafting methods and tools?

5. What do we call a computer system that captures and stores visual images and text?

6. What is the process that combines CAD and CAM called?

**M E M O R Y
C H E C K**

Electronic Publishing

Electronic publishing is the process of converting text materials, commonly produced with word processing software, into a more professional, publishable format. Typically, documents include anything from books and instruction manuals to magazines, brochures, leaflets, flyers, advertisements, newsletters, and pamphlets.

Electronic publishing creates *typeset* as opposed to *typewritten* documents. You can change or combine type **fonts,** type sizes and styles, and display boldface, underlining, and italics, as shown in Figure 7–24. Electronic publishing justifies right-hand margins and creates multiple columns on a page. In addition, it lets you alter the space between lines, a process called leading, to make each column exactly the same length. Figure 7–25 shows some examples of electronic publishing capabilities.

FIGURE 7–24 Electronic publishing permits using a wide variety of type fonts in boldface, italics, and with underlines.

Courtesy of Interleaf

FIGURE 7–25 An assortment of documents created using electronic publishing demonstrates its many capabilities.

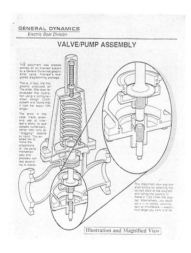

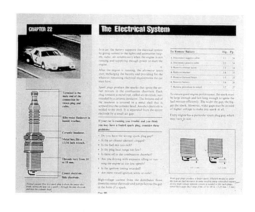

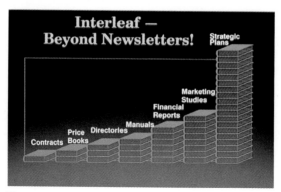

Photos courtesy of Interleaf

FIGURE 7 – 26   The steps in electronic publishing.

1. **Begin with a General Layout**

   The built-in layout tools will help you develop a format for your document. Place text and graphic elements exactly where you want them on each page.

2. **Enter Your Text**

   Enter the text for your document by either typing it in with the built-in word processor, or import your text directly from any other program with an ASCII text format.

3. **Create Your Graphics**

   Use the built-in drawing tools to create your own graphics or import them from your favorite drawing program.

4. **Add Your Finishing Touches**

   The layout and typesetting features allow you to explore different creative options directly on your screen. You can reposition graphics, change a type size, or use other special effects.

5. **You're Ready to Print**

   Once your page looks just the way you want it to, press a key and your document is delivered to you via your dot matrix or laser printer.

Electronic publishing also allows you to insert graphics to dress up the publication. Finally, electronic publishing creates finished or **camera-ready** pages that are printed on a high-quality printer or a Linotronic typesetter, ready for the printer. At this point, the conventional printing process takes over. Figure 7 – 26 shows the steps in electronic publishing.

Types of Electronic Publishing   Today, there are two types of electronic publishing. One is **corporate electronic publishing (CEP),** which companies use for both external documents such as user manuals and advertising brochures, as well as internal use, for example, to publish a company newsletter.

The second type of electronic publishing is **desktop publishing (DTP),** word processing combined with advanced formatting capabilities. DTP is used in many schools for flyers and announcements, in small businesses for advertising, and by entrepreneurs to publish their own newsletters or to offer professional DTP services to businesses in their communities. Personal computers are used for DTP, while CEP may use either stand-alone personal computers or larger workstation- or minicomputer-based electronic publishing systems. Figure 7 – 27 shows some corporate and desktop publishing systems.

The Evolution of Publishing   Printing changed very little from the 11th century to the 20th century. Type was made of lead and printing presses were in the hands of the few: newspapers, book printers, and the like. The computer industry was among the first to perceive a need for internal publishing operations: a typical computer system comes with a shelf of instruction manuals between 6- and 20-feet long! Xerox and IBM were early participants in CEP in the mid-1970s. Today, to quote industry expert David H. Goodstein, "Publishing is every company's second business."

Using Electronic Publishing   In CEP, workstations and software create everything from marketing materials to reference manuals to user documentation. For example, Lotus Development Corporation uses a workstation

FIGURE 7–27   Examples of desktop (left) and corporate (right) publishing systems.

Courtesy of Interleaf

H. Mark Weidman

system to produce its user documentation for 1-2-3 and other software products. Others that use CEP systems include General Electric, Boeing, and the National Center for Health Statistics. Networking now permits sending typeset documents from a personal computer to a satellite system that links a business to its printer, so that the entire photocomposition and pagination process is electronically transmitted. No paper need be exchanged. Both *USA Today* and *The Wall Street Journal* are electronically transmitted to remote printing sites across the country where they are printed, then distributed to readers so that you have today's news first thing every morning.

DTP is used in many different industries and walks of life. Newsletters that used to be typewritten and then typeset are now written using word processing, then typeset, designed, and illustrated using DTP. The owner of a hobby store uses DTP to create his own newspaper advertisements, saving $1,300 per ad that he formerly paid a graphic artist. DTP is not just for small business, either. *USA Today* uses Macintoshes to create many of the simple charts and graphics used in the newspaper—along with a more expensive system for photograph preparation.

DTP shows more and more signs of replacing more expensive workstation- or mini-based corporate electronic publishing systems. At the same time, stand-alone word processing software has more and more DTP capabilities such as page layout, multiple type fonts, and the ability to insert graphics. Perhaps most amazing of all is the fact that there have been more changes in the publishing process in the past 20 years than there were in the preceding 1,000.

1. What is the difference between corporate electronic publishing and desktop publishing?

2. What is a font?

3. What does the term *camera-ready pages* mean?

4. When electronic publishing and networking are combined, what is eliminated?

5. Which shows more growth potential, DTP or CEP systems?

MEMORY CHECK

Utility Software

There are few computer users who couldn't use a little help now and then. That's why we have utility software. **Utility software** performs commonly used services that make certain aspects of our computing go more smoothly.

Types of Utility Software   There are two basic types of utility software:

1. Systems-level utility programs that help us work with the operating system and its functions.
2. Application utility programs that augment and extend the usefulness of our application programs.

These utilities are commonly purchased separately, and in addition to, the operating system or application program.

The Evolution of Utility Programs   Computers have always had utility programs. They accompany operating system software to perform tasks such as printing what's on the screen, formatting a disk, or setting the date and time. We often take these built-in utilities for granted because an operating system just wouldn't be complete without them. Yet sometimes a built-in DOS utility is less than satisfactory: perhaps it's hard to use or doesn't have all the functions we need. That's why there are add-on systems-level utility programs.

Using Systems-Level Utility Programs   EDLIN, the DOS text editor, is an example of a built-in utility. You can use it to create and edit an operating system program such as the AUTOEXEC.BAT file used to customize the way we start programs. However, EDLIN is a line editor, which means you can only work with a single line at a time. Moreover, it's like programming; you have to type a command such as:

```
(n),(m),destM
```

A man by the name of Philippe Kahn thought of a better way to create and edit files like these and created a utility program called Sidekick to do it. But instead of providing just a text editor, Sidekick is a set of integrated utilities: a calculator, calendar, telephone dialer, and an ASCII table to help programmers recall the various keyboard characters.

FIGURE 7 – 28   Sidekick in action.

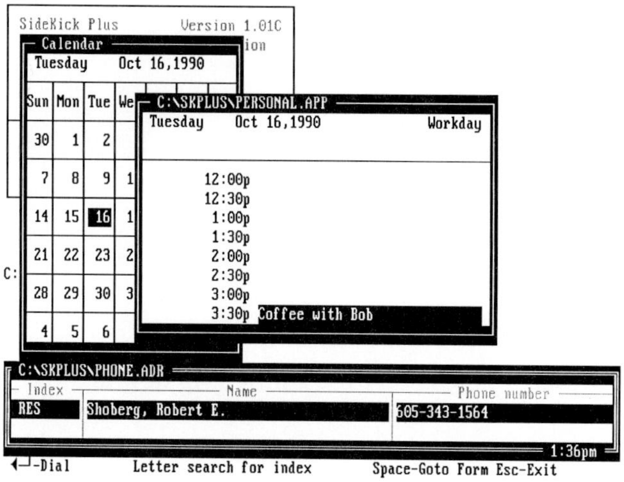

```
SideKick Plus          Version 1.01C
 ┌─ Calendar ──────────────────────┐ion
 │ Tuesday      Oct 16,1990         │
 │                                  │
 │ Sun Mon Tue We┌─ C:\SKPLUS\PERSONAL.APP ─────────────────┐
 │              │ │ Tuesday     Oct 16,1990          Workday │
 │ 30   1   2   │ │                                          │
 │              │ │                                          │
 │  7   8   9  1│ │  12:00p                                  │
 │              │ │  12:30p                                  │
 │ 14  15  16  1│ │   1:00p                                  │
 │              │ │   1:30p                                  │
C:│ 21  22  23  2│ │   2:00p                                  │
 │              │ │   2:30p                                  │
 │ 28  29  30  3│ │   3:00p                                  │
 │              │ │   3:30p Coffee with Bob                  │
 │  4   5   6   └─┴──────────────────────────────────────────┘
 └────────────────────────────────┘
┌─ C:\SKPLUS\PHONE.ADR ──────────────────────────────────────┐
│ ┌ Index ┐────────── Name ──────────── Phone number ──────── │
│  RES    Shoberg, Robert E.            605-343-1564          │
│                                                    1:36pm   │
└────────────────────────────────────────────────────────────┘
◄─┘-Dial      Letter search for index      Space-Goto Form Esc-Exit
```

Sidekick is a **terminate and stay resident (TSR)** type of program. That means it boots up, then waits in the background while you're using your application program until you need it. Say you're busily writing a paper in word processing and need to check your class schedule for tomorrow. You press the Control and Alt keys together and Sidekick pops up, displaying the main menu. You press the key for the calendar. After checking it, you realize you must cancel an appointment with Bob. Since Sidekick uses windows that present each utility in its own box on the screen, you simply press the key for the phone book and it appears on the screen with the calendar. You search for Bob's initials, then hit Return to dial the call. Once it rings, you can pick up the telephone receiver and talk to Bob. When you're through using Sidekick, hit the Escape key and Sidekick disappears until you're ready to use it again. Figure 7 – 28 shows Sidekick.

Other types of systems-level utility programs include:

- DOS shell (Figure 7 – 29), a program that helps you manage and view the contents of a hard disk. It arranges directories and files in a graphic display on the screen, and provides many DOS functions such as copy, delete, rename, and create a new directory.
- Windowing programs (Figure 7 – 30) that allow you to run more than one application at a time, much like an integrated software program. Instead of simply switching between programs, however, you can have more than one on the screen at a time in variously sized windows.
- Disk maintenance utilities (Figure 7 – 31) that restore accidentally erased files, help you recover from an emergency such as a power outage, reconstruct the hard disk when it "crashes" or fails to operate properly, and offer other utilities for easier operating system maintenance.

FIGURE 7 – 29   XTree ProGold, a DOS shell program that shows directories, filenames, and disk statistics.

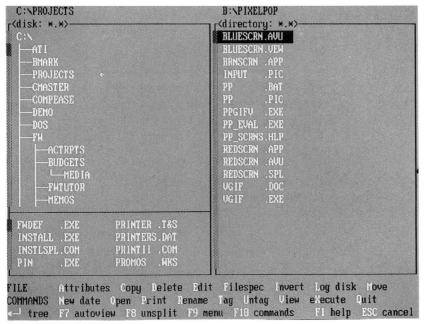

Courtesy of Executive Systems, Inc.

FIGURE 7 – 30   How Microsoft Windows is used.

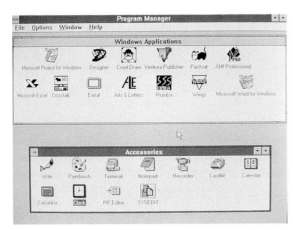

Courtesy of Microsoft Corp.

FIGURE 7–31   The Norton Utilities disk maintenance utility.

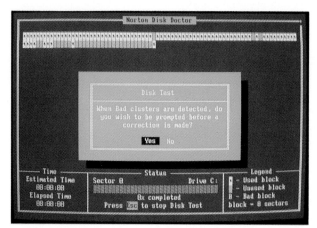

F. Bodin/Offshoot

Using Application-Level Utility Programs   Application programmers don't always think of everything users would like to have in their programs. There are probably more utilities for word processing than any other application. These include the outliner, thesaurus, spelling checker, grammar checker, syntax and usage checker, and print spooler, which allow you to print a file while continuing to enter text into another.

Other utilities for any kind of application include:

- Keystroke managers that create macro keys for various applications or the operating system, like those you learned about in the spreadsheet chapter.
- Envelope or label printers that capture a name and address then print them on the envelope.
- Text finders that search for any file, regardless of the application in which it was created, locating it by name or by key word search.
- Formatting programs that make spreadsheet and DBMS reports more attractive and informative.

HyperCard™: The Future of Utilities   HyperCard is a concept that often defies definition. Perhaps it's like human powers of intuition. **HyperCard** is a Macintosh software program that falls between a utility and an application. HyperCard is a way to informally organize many kinds of information. That might include words, pictures, and even sounds. You put your information on an electronic note card, then HyperCard gathers related notecards into stacks of information. You are permitted to find information by free-form associations between any notecards in any stacks. You can instantly jump from one concept or picture or sound to another, like Han Solo throwing the switch to jump the *Millennium Falcon* through hyperspace. For example, you are listening to the song, "I Heard It through the Grapevine" on your Macintosh, which reminds you to put raisins on your grocery shopping list, which also reminds you that you're supposed to bring snacks to the party Friday night, so you put this on your calendar. HyperCard lets you find your own uses for it, instead of forcing you to follow set patterns like most programs (Figure 7–32).

FIGURE 7–32   Apple Macintosh HyperCard™. The public library screen display shown here illustrates an information application for higher education offering both directed search and exploratory browsing.

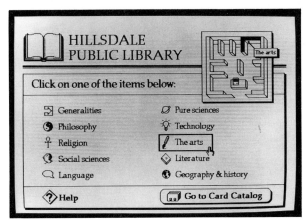

Courtesy of Apple Computer, Inc.

DISKbyte

Multimedia: The Next Great Application for Computers?

Multimedia is the next step toward becoming totally conversant with the computer, as if it were a friend joining you for a stimulating conversation. Multimedia is sometimes referred to as interactive, which means it lets you and the computer engage in an ongoing exchange or presentation of information.

Let's say your computer is in a den and a friend has come to visit you. In that den are books, audio and video equipment, drawings and photographs, and your knowledge. You strike up a conversation about, say, 1960s music. You discuss the philosophy behind certain songs, playing excerpts, showing video clips from concerts, reading passages from rock group biographies, looking at posters and album covers. You can relive your favorite memories or learn more about early rock groups—whatever you want to do.

That's multimedia. Except the computer has stored all that information, from film clips to text to graphics, in its database. Multimedia employs networking tools to extract information from databases or tunes and film clips from CD-ROMs, and whatever you contribute in certain types of files. On the Macintosh, multimedia uses HyperCard tools. When perfected, multimedia lets you find and display anything—*anything*—in a matter of seconds. No more thumbing through books or fast-forwarding the VCR.

MEMORY CHECK

1. What are the two types of utility software?
2. Why would you need a utility program?
3. What does TSR stand for?
4. Why would you use a windows program?
5. Why would you use a keyboard macro program?

WHAT LIES AHEAD?

Where is software taking us? Clearly, operating systems are becoming more useful and graphical. They are making it easier for us to work with applications, which are growing ever more powerful. On the leading edge of both systems software and application software is a software technology called **artificial intelligence (AI).**

The term *artificial intelligence* describes a computer system that has the property of intelligence with the ability to reason, understand relationships between objects, and in general think like a human being. Machine intelligence is a more accurate description, although it is infrequently used. How can we tell if a computer is as "smart" as a human? In 1950, an Englishman

—
D I S K b y t e
—

Tips for Buying Personal Computer Software

People commonly buy their application software in a retail store such as Egghead Software, or from a mail-order software company. Both retail stores and mail-order houses offer discounts and guarantee software; but how do you know what's best? There is a bestseller list, but that doesn't tell you if the software fits your expertise level or needs. Therefore, you may find this checklist useful in making your selection:

1. List the tasks you would like the software to perform.
2. Determine whether the features of a particular application match your task list.
3. Some software is designed exclusively for particular brands of personal computers and operating systems. Make sure the application runs on the hardware and operating system you use.
4. Check how much memory the software requires and make sure your personal computer has adequate memory space.
5. Try it out! Determine whether the application is easy to use. Many retail software stores permit you to return software.
6. See if the application includes good documentation. If it doesn't, sometimes book publishers provide good user manuals.
7. Check for on-line help built into the application and try it out for ease of use.
8. Some applications offer technical support you can call when you have problems. Is this true of the application you are considering? Is there an additional charge for this support? Is it a toll-free 800 telephone number?
9. Is the software copy-protected? Most is not these days. If it is, does the copy-protection make it hard to install on your personal computer or awkward to use? Does the publisher provide backup disks? Is there a charge for them?
10. How long has the software been available? Look at reviews and advertisements in trade publications. Is it highly regarded? Are there user testimonials? Applications are updated, so be sure you get the latest version. Mail in your warranty card so you will be notified when a new version is available.

One last consideration: If you haven't yet purchased your personal computer, conventional wisdom suggests you choose the application(s) you like, then buy the appropriate computer system. In many cases, there are compromises you must make between software and hardware; just try to make as few as possible. If you're like most people, the investment means you'll probably have to live with your system for quite a while.

named Alan Turing devised the Turing Test. It asks a panel of human judges to read two sets of typewritten responses to questions and see if they can determine which was written by a human and which by a computer. So far, no computer has passed the Turing Test.

Raymond Kurzweil, a leading proponent of artificial intelligence, says, "I believe that by the end of this century, AI will be as ubiquitous as personal computers are today. The majority of software will be intelligent, at least by today's standards." However, Hubert and Stuart Dreyfus disagree: "There is almost no likelihood that scientists can develop machines capable of making intelligent decisions. . . . AI has failed to live up to its promise, and there is no evidence that it ever will." The debate—as well as the research—continues.

AI has produced computer systems capable of humanlike feats. Computers can play chess: Against most of us they win; against grand masters, they lose. Computer systems are able to store and randomly retrieve information, approximating how a human would do so, and it is here that AI has achieved the most success. These are called expert systems.

An **expert system** offers solutions to problems in a specialized area of work or study, based on the stored knowledge of human experts. Expert systems have been developed for medicine, oil exploration, civil engineering, food preparation, monitoring plant operations, and hundreds of other applications. For example, MYCIN is an expert system that can diagnose blood and bacterial infections based on the knowledge of many doctors stored in its knowledge base, then recommend antibiotics for treatment. In another example, when the chief cook at Campbell's soup decided to retire, his recipe preparation knowledge was stored in an expert system. In a sense, that cook will live on through the computer!

Can we ever create a computer system that would think as well as a human? One wonders if such a thing is even a good idea. Hamlet, in Shakespeare's great tragedy, says, "There are more things in heaven and earth, Horatio, than are dreamt of in your philosophy." This is surely true with software. Perhaps it is better, at least for the time being, to simply have smarter programs.

---

1. Identify five common software applications.

2. In applications, what form do data and instructions take?

3. How do applications use files?

4. Identify two personal productivity applications.

5. Identify a common business application.

MEMORY CHECK

ETHICS

Illegal or unauthorized software copying used to be called *software piracy,* perhaps in part to alert people to the seriousness of the act. It is a problem that plagues the software industry because it is so widespread. People who would never think of photocopying a book so they could read it will often make a copy of someone else's software program without giving it a second thought.

Software copying hurts both software publishers and computer users. It hurts publishers by taking revenues they would otherwise have earned that could have been used to develop new and better software. It hurts users because they do not usually copy the documentation manuals, so they often don't learn to take full advantage of the program. In addition, they can't take advantage of technical support or obtain new versions of the program.

In the past, many personal computer software publishers used copy-protection programs embedded in the disk that either did not permit copying or only allowed one or two copies, say to a hard disk and for an extra backup copy. But many people resented copy-protection, for it made it awkward to use the program; for example, even if the program would copy to the hard disk, you still had to insert the original program disk (sometimes called a key disk) in its drive before the program worked.

The software industry finally bowed to consumers; very few programs are copy-protected these days. Large corporations purchase a site licensing agreement to obtain multiple copies for office workers. But individuals still copy office software and then use it at home, and that is still software piracy.

The software publishers have said to us, in effect: "All right, we trust you to buy our program, and not to make unauthorized copies of it." Each and every individual should strive to live up to that trust.

CAREERbyte

Jackie Willig Silver: A Desktop Publishing Pioneer

Jackie Willig Silver used to be an executive for a large public relations firm in Tampa, Florida. In addition to her normal job duties, she also managed the publication of specialty newletters for many of her client companies. The newsletters were great publicity for the clients and a great source of revenue for the PR firm. Jackie saw an opportunity to start her own business writing, producing, and publishing newsletters and other printed materials. In 1984, she resigned to start her own firm, Newsletters, Etc.

Jackie set up office in her townhouse, where she wrote and edited client newsletters on a typewriter for the first few months. Her time was filled coordinating between designers, graphic artists, typesetters, and printers. "It seemed like all I did was drive from one to the other," she says. Then a friend told her about the recently introduced Macintosh personal computer and its desktop publishing capabilities. Jackie saw a demonstration and fell in love with it.

Her first job was producing a four-page newsletter, using Page-Maker desktop publishing software. It took her eight frustrating hours to design her text into the proper format, but as a learning process it was time well-spent. The entire process took only two days, but she says, "If I had used an artist and a typesetter, the same job

Courtesy Jackie Willig Silver

would have taken two weeks. I not only saved time, but I didn't have to pay the artist or the typesetter, so that profit was mine to keep."

Jackie thus became one of the first desktop publishers. It didn't take long for the word to get around: Jackie can save you hundreds of dollars a month on your advertising and public relations. Eventually she was producing about 15 newsletters a month, although there were a number of "Etc." assignments as well. One was a client who wanted a 100-page catalog produced for his boat shop, displaying many marine parts and accessories. She desktop-published a 32-page color magazine and 250 playing cards for a trivia game called "The Wine Connoisseur."

"Using desktop publishing increases a newsletter's profits about 200 percent," Jackie says, "because it replaces so much hand work. It

eliminates 7 out of 11 steps involved in producing a printed brochure or newsletter—even more, probably."

Over time, Jackie upgraded and improved her Mac system, and was one of the first individual entrepreneurs to own a laser printer. Newsletters, Etc., was very successful. "Well, sometimes it's tight deadlines and long hours, but I love the work. It's very satisfying to design a handsome newsletter and make all the text and graphic elements work well together." She became widely known for her pioneering efforts in desktop publishing. Articles were written about her in magazines such as *Publish!,* and she began giving speeches at conferences. Her notoriety led to a job as a traveling emissary for a desktop publishing software company, but in time she wearied of the travel. Today, Jackie is semiretired but remains active as an authorized trainer for Aldus Corporation, publisher of Page-Maker, the world's most widely used desktop publishing program. "My training is very individualized," she says. "I ask, 'What are you working on today?' and teach the user how to do that. To me, that's the key to good training." She still loves her Macintosh but is thinking about another career. Jackie says, "So far, I haven't seen anything as exciting as desktop publishing."

SUMMARY

1. *Explain the various tasks performed by operating systems software.* Software is the link between people and computer hardware. It provides two types of tools that bridge this gap: system software and applications. System software runs the computer and provides tools that assist application programmers. The operating system controls the computer's basic functions. It does so by providing command languages and utilities, controlling input and output, scheduling, managing data and instructions, and maintaining libraries.

2. *Identify leading personal computer, minicomputer, and mainframe operating systems.* There are many operating systems. The most common personal computer operating systems are DOS and Multifinder. The most common minicomputer operating systems are UNIX and VMS. The most common mainframe operating system is MVS. Some operating systems are proprietary, meaning they work on one brand of computer only; others are called portable, meaning they work on computers from different manufacturers. Portable operating systems make it possible to have open systems, which permit connecting different computers together.

3. *Understand the difference between stand-alone and integrated software.* A stand-alone application program works solely by itself; the applications in Module II are stand-alone. An integrated program combines four or five (or more) stand-alone applications that work similarly to each other. You can easily switch from one to another and exchange files or data between them. The main disadvantage is that one application tends to be very good, while the others have shortcomings.

4. *Describe some other commonly used applications.* Computer graphics programs that can draw, paint, or create three-dimensional drafting are in wide use. Most common are presentation graphics and computer-aided design (CAD). Electronic publishing combines word processing with advanced formatting capabilities, including adding graphics, to produce high-quality documents.

5. *Describe the uses for utility software for applications and operating systems.* Utility software provides commonly used services and specific tasks that make our computing work easier. There are systems-level utility programs, such as DOS shells and windowing programs. Examples of application-level utility programs include text finders and formatting programs. HyperCard is an emerging new type of utility program.

6. *Understand the uses for artificial intelligence and expert systems.* Artificial intelligence (AI) is software that attempts to replicate the human thinking and reasoning processes. The goal in AI research is to create computer systems that think similarly to people. The most advanced AI techniques are found in expert systems, which are used to offer solutions in specialized areas of knowledge, from science and medicine to various business uses.

KEY TERMS

artificial intelligence (AI), p. 226
ASCII, p. 194
camera-ready, p. 219
command language, p. 196
computer graphics, p. 212
computer-integrated
  manufacturing (CIM), p. 214
corporate electronic publishing
  (CEP), p. 219
desktop publishing (DTP), p. 219
document and image processing,
  p. 214

expert system, p. 227
fonts, p. 217
graphics, p. 212
high-resolution graphics, p. 212
HyperCard, p. 224
integrated software, p. 208
multimedia, p. 225
multiprogramming, p. 199
multitasking, p. 200
multiuser, p. 200
open system, p. 205

pixels, p. 212
portable, p. 203
presentation graphics, p. 212
proprietary, p. 205
scheduling, p. 199
stand-alone program, p. 208
terminate and stay resident
  (TSR), p. 222
time-sharing, p. 204
utility software, p. 221
vector graphics, p. 212

REVIEW AND DISCUSSION QUESTIONS

1. What role does system software play in the computer system?
2. What is the difference between system software and the operating system?
3. Name the five "faces" of the operating system, and what each does.
4. What is a command language?
5. What advantages does multitasking offer? How is it distinguished from multiprogramming?
6. Why would a multiuser system be useful?
7. What advantages does UNIX offer?
8. What is a primary advantage with VMS?
9. What are the advantages with MVS?
10. Why are there so many different operating systems? Would it be beneficial to have just one, or have all compatible with one another?
11. What are the roles of records, files, and programs in application software?
12. What would be your most important criteria in choosing an application software package?
13. When would it be preferable to use a stand-alone application over integrated software?
14. Describe multimedia applications and discuss different ways you would use them.
15. What utility software takes the place of integrated software?
16. What determines how clear graphic images are on the video monitor?
17. What other skills or talents might be useful in using applications such as graphics or desktop publishing?
18. What do you see as the advantages to electronic publishing?
19. Does HyperCard's method of organizing information more closely resemble the way a human thinks than a DBMS's method?
20. Discuss some ways you think artificial intelligence will change the way we use software.

ISSUES

1. A major headache in selecting software is making sure it runs on your computer. There are many factors that must be considered: is your computer an IBM PC or PC-compatible, or a PS/2? What model of Apple II or Macintosh? Does it have the proper operating system and enough RAM? In the name of free enterprise, computer makers make their hardware distinct, while software publishers must adapt their products to specific hardware types. Should computer manufacturers conform to standards so that any software could be used with any hardware?

2. Many computer users "swap" copies of software, whether it is the latest operating system upgrade or an application. This is properly termed *software pirating* and when it happens, neither the programmer who wrote the program nor the software publisher that produced and promoted it are rewarded for their work. Do you feel software pirating is ethically proper or morally correct? Is it stealing? What if the programmer or the software company only intended to cover their costs in the price of the update?

3. Are application developers coming up with software that you find useful? If you had to critique an application you are familiar with, would you have more complaints than praise for it? Do you think application developers listen carefully enough to their users?

4. Many businesses now use expert systems as counselors when making business decisions. Would you have confidence in a decision your stockbroker made, knowing it was based on an expert system? Do you feel expert systems should be allowed to make important decisions?

CHAPTER

8

Software Development

CHAPTER OUTLINE

The First Programmer
The System Development Process
Analyzing Problems and Designing Solutions
    Structured Techniques
Coding and Debugging the Program
    Writing Source Code
    DISKbyte: Programming Errors Can Be
        Expensive!
    Debugging the Program
    Testing and Acceptance
Writing the Documentation
The Evolution of Programming Languages
    Machine Language
    Assembly Language
    DISKbyte: How to Motivate Programmers
High-Level Programming Languages
    Statements and Syntax
    Compiling High-Level Languages
    FORTRAN: A Scientific Language
    COBOL: A Business Language
    DISKbyte: Grace Murray Hopper
    BASIC: A Personal Computer Language
    C: A High-Level Language
Advanced Programming Languages
    Fourth-Generation Languages
    Object-Oriented Programming
    CASE: Computer-Aided Software Engineering
Ethics
    CAREERbyte: Clark Gee, Systems Analyst
Summary
Key Terms
Review and Discussion Questions
Issues

OBJECTIVES

After reading and studying this chapter, you should be able to:

1. Identify the steps in the system development life cycle.
2. Define the features of structured programming.
3. Define the types of computer documentation.
4. Describe some of the various programming languages used to write software.
5. Describe some of the advanced programming tools and techniques.

THE FIRST PROGRAMMER

When you hear the word *programming,* you probably think of people writing programs for computers. However, programming traces its roots to the textile industry in the year 1801. People then as now appreciated fabrics and tapestries with various colors and patterns, whose creation required the talents of skillful weavers, with keen minds and nimble fingers. Creating fabrics with complex patterns was time-consuming and expensive. A Frenchman named Joseph-Marie Charles Jacquard is considered the first programmer. He was a weaver who dreamed of a machine that would help do his weaving more quickly, inexpensively, and with fewer mistakes.

Jacquard studied the weaving process and its machinery, the loom. Displaying the analytic qualities of a good programmer, he designed a loom

The Jacquard loom, one of the first programmable machines.

Brown Brothers

that could be programmed to create patterns and designs using something called a punched card. Jacquard's punched card was a wood slat with holes punched in it, shown here. It was an invention that would continue to be used for over 180 years.

Jacquard's loom was complex yet straightforward in design. Inside the loom, threaded needles pressed upward against the punched cards. If a needle passed through a hole in the card, it pushed up a thread to be woven into the fabric. If there was no hole, the thread remained unwoven below the card. Thus, different patterns were generated by different hole patterns in the cards. Cards were fed into the loom in sequence, allowing many operations to take place automatically.

Jacquard's loom demonstrated two important ideas. One, we can translate complex designs into codes or programs that machines can understand. Two, in so doing, machines can be instructed to perform repetitive tasks. This principle was the basis for early computers. In addition, the practicality of punched cards led to their widespread use with digital electronic computers.

THE SYSTEM DEVELOPMENT PROCESS

As you know, *people* working with *software* and *hardware* create *computer systems*. This process is called system development. As this chapter explains, the majority of the work entails creating software—either systems software or application software. Software is created by programmers; their work is called programming. Programming is the process of creating instructions that direct computers to perform specific data processing tasks. Whether for looms or computers, programming involves using instructions the machine being programmed understands. Punched cards instructed Jacquard's loom mechanically, as did the early computer punched card shown in Figure 8–1. Today's software instructs computers electronically.

Programmers write many types of programs, from systems software to application software. The task has grown increasingly complex and sophisticated over the years. Today, many people, with differing skills and job titles, are involved in creating computer programs. As a result, this process has been given a name: the **system development life cycle.** The life cycle's complexity and the steps involved varies, depending on the size of the company, the number of people on the development staff, the size and complexity of the problem that must be solved, and the programmers' skills and experience. But in general, the system development life cycle is comprised of these steps:

1. *Analysis*—identifying and defining the problem.
2. *Design*—planning the solution to the problem.
3. *Coding*—writing the program.
4. *Debugging*—correcting program errors.
5. *Testing and acceptance*—making sure the system works properly and turning it over to the users.
6. *Maintenance*—keeping systems working properly and improving them when necessary.
7. *Documentation*—writing software, user, and reference documentation.

In this chapter, we'll discuss each step in the system development life cycle and demonstrate the process with a programming example. We'll begin by defining a problem and then design the sequence of steps that solve that problem.

FIGURE 8–1   An IBM punched card.

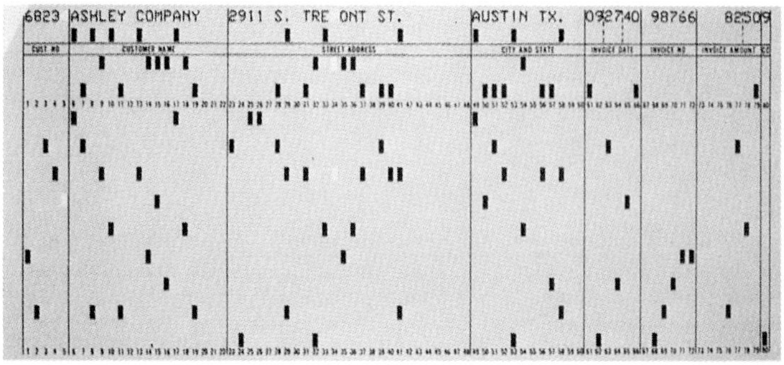

Courtesy of IBM Corporation

Then we'll turn our attention to coding — creating instructions with programming languages. We'll give an overview of coding and explain program debugging. Finally, we'll look at documentation and how it is written.

Tools have been developed to help people create programs. Manual aids called flowcharts and diagrams help define problems and shape solutions. Text editors make it easier to write programs and documentation. System software programs translate programs and help programmers find their errors. We'll survey a number of programming languages. Integrated programming tool sets and computer-aided software engineering (CASE) help programmers make the most of their time and efforts. We'll explore these advanced tools after we study the program development process.

ANALYZING PROBLEMS AND DESIGNING SOLUTIONS

Let's begin our discussion by looking at the first steps in the system development process: systems analysis and design. **Systems analysis** is the study of an activity, a procedure, even an entire business, to determine what kind of computer system would make it more efficient. **Systems design** is the activity of planning the technical aspects for the new system. This activity is usually triggered when a user requests a new system; for example, your teacher might ask the college's programming staff to write a program to keep track of class grades, or a company's telemarketing department might ask for a program that keeps track of customer ordering information. Systems analysis and systems design are the planning steps, and they are the most important of all. They are usually done manually; at this point in the program development process, the computer we need to use is the one on our shoulders.

Creating a new application can be as difficult or as easy as writing an essay or a term paper. In the same way you would do some research before you begin writing, systems analysis and design requires research and planning. Large software development companies have found that effective early planning can cut the overall program development time and costs by as much as 60 percent.

The **systems analyst** is responsible for systems analysis and design. The analyst gathers and analyzes the data necessary to develop the new application. Systems analysts and other computer professionals work in businesses of all types and sizes, in government agencies, and in computer hardware and software companies — to name a few. The CAREERbyte at the end of this chapter tells the story of a systems analyst developing a new application. Depending on the organization and its size, a systems analyst might also be called a systems consultant, a systems engineer, an information analyst, or a business analyst. Whatever the title, the systems analyst:

- Analyzes the problem.
- Determines what people, software, and hardware resources are necessary to solve the problem.
- Designs and specifies the computer system and the methods for the information system to solve the problem.
- Guides or manages the project to a successful conclusion.

A beginning analyst spends about one third of his or her time in analysis and design, versus two thirds in actual programming. A lead analyst spends three quarters of his or her time in analysis and design and the balance managing several ongoing design projects. Regardless of their position, analysts must begin by analyzing the problem.

Analyzing the Problem

Sometimes the hardest part of problem solving is the first step: clearly analyzing or defining the problem. Taking time to precisely define the problem we want to solve greatly increases the likelihood that we will produce an effective program.

Systems analysis or defining the problem often involves asking three questions:

1. Will the computer be an effective tool for providing solutions?
2. What will we send to the program as input?
3. What will we receive from the program as output?

The system development process may be clearer if we demonstrate it, so let's look at an example.

Most of us use checking accounts to pay our bills. Often, we wind up paying several of the same bills every month. Would a personal computer help us with this chore? Well, first we could use the personal computer to print checks. We probably would have fewer arithmetic errors if we let the computer do our adding and subtracting. The personal computer could also resolve our difficulties with balancing our checkbooks.

So the answer to question 1 is yes, we could use the computer to help us in this area. As to questions 2 and 3, we will provide deposit and payment information as input. We will get printed checks and account balances as output. We could represent this in a simple diagram, like that shown in Figure 8–2.

In this case, defining the problem is rather simple. If we were programmers or systems analysts working on a satellite communication system, the problem would be more complex. The process, however, would be the same.

At this point in the system development process, it is appropriate to determine whether an application already exists to solve our problem. It may be faster, cheaper, and more effective to buy an application program that's already been designed, coded, debugged, and documented, than to perform the following steps ourselves. If not, we'll proceed with designing our own checkbook program.

Designing the Program

Once we've determined that we want to solve a problem with the computer, and that the best way to proceed is by creating our own system, the next step is systems design. The simple part of systems design is selecting the computer hardware; the more complex decisions have to do with conceiving and designing the software program. As with other human endeavors, we can proceed in two ways. The first we might call the "seat of the pants" method. It means we jump right into the task, using only our own wits, experience, and a lot of intuition. This was the most common approach taken to programming in the early days of computing. The second is the systematic approach, utilizing tools and methods that people have developed through years of experience.

FIGURE 8–2   A simple input/processing/output diagram.

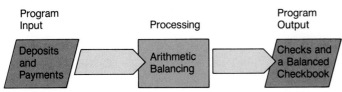

In the early days of programming, the seat of the pants method was the only way to design and write a program. This may have been exciting but the programs took a long time to write and often had major flaws. They were frequently too complex, difficult to test, and very difficult for others to correct and improve. If a programmer went on to other endeavors, leaving his or her work to successors, new programmers were often unable to figure out the organization and logic of the programs they were required to maintain. In addition, these programs weren't always easy for users to work with.

Structured Techniques

By the mid-1960s, government institutions and corporations were floundering in a sea of programming problems. Programs written in many individualistic styles led to chaos in software development and maintenance. In response, people such as Edsger Dijkstra, Corrado Bohm, and Guiseppe Jacopini developed and advocated a variety of **structured techniques.** Structured means a technique that is orderly and that can be understood by others in addition to the program creator.

There are a number of structured techniques, including structured programming or coding, structured analysis, structured design, and so on. Structured techniques often result in reduced program development time, increased programmer productivity, less testing and debugging, and programs that are simpler and easier to maintain. We'll look more closely at structured coding techniques in the next section. Here, we'll explore a few of the more commonly used structured analysis and design techniques.

Structured Analysis   Structured analysis uses data flow diagrams to chart a system's progress. The concept is that of a logical system, showing how data moves from one point to another. Structured analysis requires the analyst to logically think through what the system should do, before determining how it should be done. The emphasis is on the end result—what the user needs from the system—rather than on sophisticated programming techniques. Interestingly, the logical base of structured analysis often allows the analyst to come up with more creative solutions to problems.

Structured Design   Structured design commonly utilizes a method called the *top-down approach,* which breaks the problem into parts and arranges these parts in a hierarchy, according to their size and level of detail. The result is a hierarchy or series of steps, beginning with the overall problem to be solved and continuing down in a series of increasingly more detailed parts of the problem.

FIGURE 8 – 3   Structure charts arrange program modules in a hierarchy: The lower the level, the more detailed the operation.

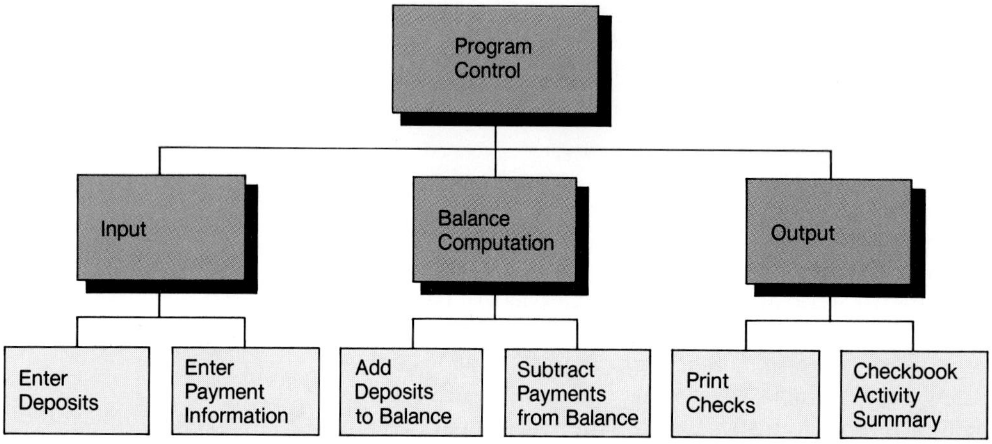

Computers work by performing tasks in step-by-step fashion. For this reason, they are good at working with algorithms. An **algorithm** is a limited set of step-by-step instructions that solve a problem. Once the steps are well defined, programmers can easily go on to write code in **modules** — distinct, logical parts of a program.

Five tools have been developed to assist us when using structured techniques: structure charts, HIPO charts, system flowcharts, program flowcharts, and pseudocode. Structure charts and HIPO charts help us break the problem down into parts and then arrange the parts according to how they will work together. Two kinds of flowcharts — system and program — help us establish the methods and procedures we'll use to design the hardware and software, respectively. The system flowchart shows the methods and procedures used in a system at a very general level. In contrast, the program flowchart shows the logic of each program depicted in the system flowchart. Pseudocode lets us describe our program design in Englishlike terms that can then be translated into a formal programming language, moving us one step closer to producing a finished program. Let's take a closer look at these tools and see how they work.

Structure Charts   A tool commonly used by programmers is the **structure chart.** It is a graphic representation of top-down programming, showing program modules and their relationships in increasing levels of detail. The structure chart establishes the program hierarchy, beginning with the overall problem to be solved, then showing the problem broken down into modules, submodules, subsubmodules, and so on. It also shows each module's purpose in solving the problem. Boxes represent modules. The lines that connect the boxes show how the modules are related. Figure 8 – 3 is a structure chart that shows how we expect our checkbook program to work.

HIPO Charts   **HIPO** (Hierarchy plus Input Processing Output) **charts** take structure charts to a greater level of detail, showing program input, how processing the data should proceed, and the output desired at the end. HIPO charts can be set up in hierarchies or layers so that you have a HIPO chart for

FIGURE 8-4   HIPO charts are created for each module in the structure chart. This HIPO chart reflects the Program Control module from Figure 8-3.

Input	Process	Output
Open Checkbook File	1. Receive deposits	Updated Checkbook File
Open Check-Print File	2. Add deposit information to Checkbook file and Summary file	New Check-Print File
Open Summary File	3. Receive payment information	New Summary File
	4. Add payment information to Checkbook file, Check-Print file, and Summary file	
	5. Store Checkbook file, Check-Print file, and Summary file	
Enter Deposits	6. Print checks	Printed Checks
	7. Print summary	
Enter Payments		Printed Summary

the overall program and additional HIPO charts for each program module. Figure 8-4 is a HIPO chart representing the top-level box from the previous structure chart.

Flowcharts   Another tool programmers use is the **flowchart,** a diagram that shows how a computer system's components will be used to solve a problem, or the steps used to solve a problem. A **system flowchart** typically contains symbols that represent hardware and media components, and their roles in solving the problem. A **program flowchart** diagrams the solution from the software perspective, showing the data processing actions to be performed. The American National Standards Institute (ANSI) has established standard system flowchart symbols, shown in Figure 8-5.

Figure 8-6 shows our checkbook program's system flowchart. The program and its output will be retained in on-line storage. Deposit and payment data will be entered via the keyboard. Checks and the summary file will be documented—in this case, printed on the printer.

ANSI has also established program flowchart symbols, shown in Figure 8-7. We used these symbols to produce the diagram in Figure 8-8 of our checkbook program's step-by-step processing operations. Note that this chart parallels the hardware operations from our system flowchart in Figure 8-6 and the modules in the structure chart in Figure 8-3. A flowcharting template, like that shown in Figure 8-9, can be a handy tool in preparing system and program flowcharts.

FIGURE 8–5 The American National Standards Institute (ANSI) standard system flowchart symbols.

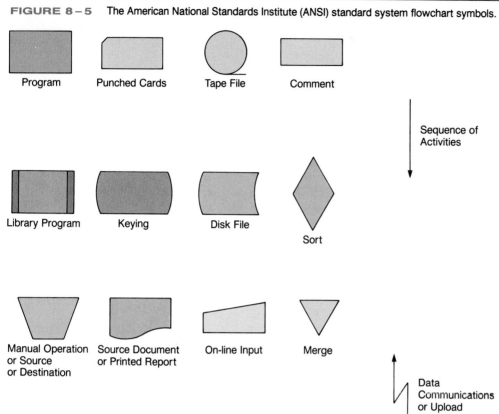

FIGURE 8−6 This systems flowchart shows the hardware components used by a sample checkbook program.

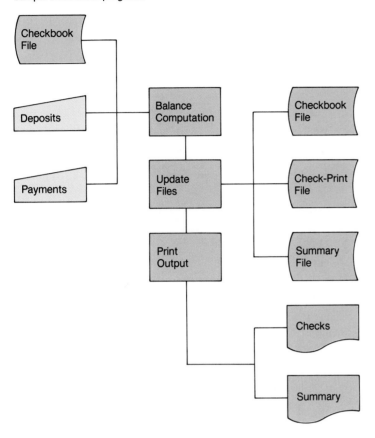

FIGURE 8−7 ANSI has established these standard program flowchart symbols.

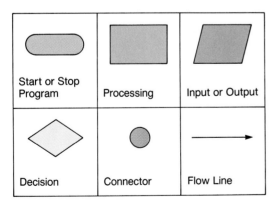

FIGURE 8 – 8   This program flowchart brings us one step closer to outlining the source code of the checkbook program.

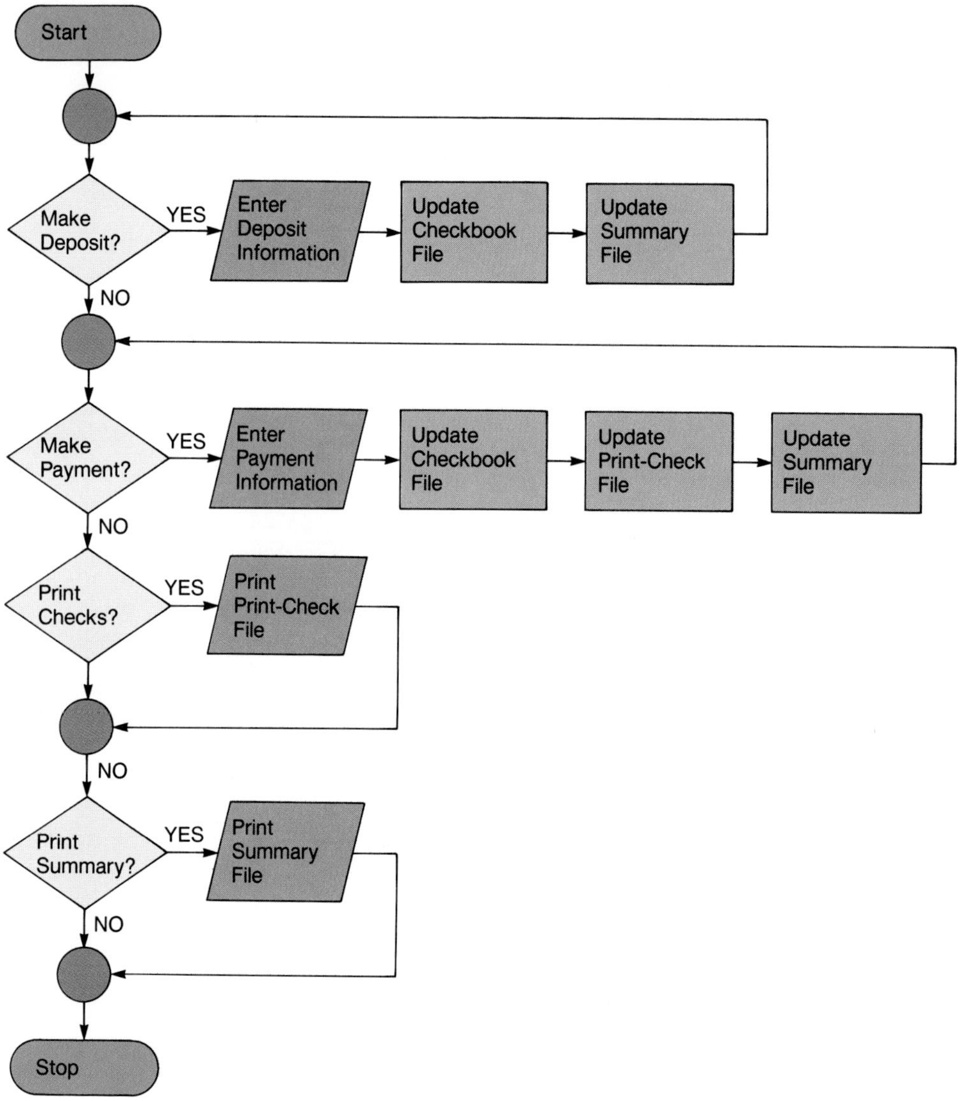

Pseudocode   **Pseudocode** is another handy tool. It consists of English phrases that describe the processing steps to be performed by a program or module. It's an intermediate form of program instructions, written in familiar terms instead of a programming language. Pseudocode moves us one step closer to actually writing the program code. Figure 8 – 10 shows a sample of our checkbook program pseudocode.

Structured techniques help us understand what we're doing before we begin writing code. They provide several kinds of road maps, in various levels of detail, to serve as guides in coding, which is the next step in the system development process. Now that we have defined the problem and designed the algorithm we will use to solve it, we can confidently proceed with coding the program.

FIGURE 8–9 Flowchart templates are often used in creating system and program flowcharts.

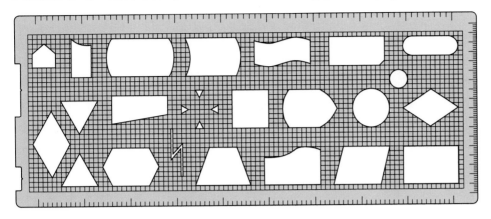

FIGURE 8–10 This checkbook program pseudocode allows us to outline source code without having to adhere to the rules of an actual programming language.

```
BEGIN
     DEPOSIT PROMPT
     DO WHILE ANSWER=Y
          READ DEPOSIT
          ADD DEPOSIT TO BALANCE
          UPDATE SUMMARY FILE
          DEPOSIT PROMPT
     END-DO

     PAYMENT PROMPT
     DO WHILE ANSWER=Y
          READ PAYMENT
          SUBTRACT PAYMENT FROM BALANCE
          UPDATE SUMMARY FILE
          UPDATE PRINT-CHECK FILE
          PAYMENT PROMPT
     END-DO
  END
```

1. Which two program development steps are the most important?

2. What three questions do we ask when defining the problem?

3. What is an algorithm?

4. What is a module?

5. How do we arrange modules in structure and HIPO diagrams?

6. What does the acronym HIPO stand for?

7. How does pseudocode help us write a better program?

MEMORY CHECK

CODING AND DEBUGGING THE PROGRAM

Analyzing and designing programs involves manual tasks, easily performed without computers. Coding and debugging are the opposite—now we put away the pencil and take up the keyboard. By coding we mean programming—actually writing the program using a programming language. Next, using system software, we compile or translate the program code into the language the CPU understands. The compiler also helps us find errors, so we can debug or correct our programs. Let's look more closely at writing, compiling, and debugging programs.

Writing Source Code

Source code is the actual computer program, written in a specific programming language, that will be sent to the computer for processing. It is somewhat like shorthand in that it replaces ordinary language. Using source code makes programming a little easier for the programmer. For example, when writing with a programming language, rather than saying *divide,* we simply type /. Once the program is written, it will be translated into the 0s and 1s by the system software. *Writing source code, programming,* and *writing computer instructions* all mean the same thing. We call it **coding** for short.

Before we begin coding, we must decide which programming language we want to use. Today, there are many to choose from but the decision is made easier because most programming languages are designed for specific kinds of problems. FORTRAN is often the preferred language for scientific programming, COBOL for business, Pascal for structured coding, and BASIC for programming education. We'll look more closely at these and other programming languages later in this chapter.

By the time we begin coding, the program planning stage should be finished. If we have defined the problem well and created a good design, coding will take less time than the other steps in the system development process. Even though our checkbook program may contain up to 1,200 lines of code, the structure and HIPO charts we created should make coding quick work.

Text Editors   A **text editor** is an essential tool for the coding step in the system development process. It is a program that allows you to write, erase, and manipulate words on the monitor screen. A text editor is very much like a word processor but without many of the formatting features.

Programming languages require certain formalities, just like your professors insist on a particular style when writing term papers. Advanced text editors help programmers stick to the proper forms. For example, if a programming language asks that each line of source code be indented a certain number of spaces and end with a period, you can set up a text editor to automatically begin each line with a tab and end with a period. Other functions like search, cut and paste, automatic word wrap, and automatic line spacing also make coding a little easier.

Structured Coding   **Structured coding** or **programming** was the first structured technique, borne of the need for a more organized way to write programs. Structured coding states that all programs can be written using

FIGURE 8 – 11   The three primary control structures used in structured programming.

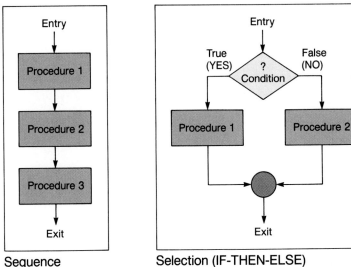

Sequence   Selection (IF-THEN-ELSE)

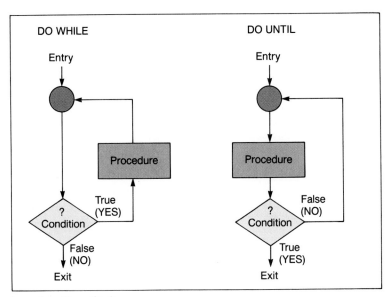

Looping (iteration)

three basic constructs: sequence, selection, and looping, as shown in Figure 8 – 11. Programs written using structured coding techniques are easier to read, understand, and maintain. Note, however, that structured coding is distinct from other structured techniques. You can use structured coding whether or not you use structured design techniques.

Source code is the product of the coding step. Using text editors, programmers create files consisting of instructions written in a programming language. Figure 8 – 12 shows a portion of our checkbook program in one version of BASIC. But as we mentioned earlier, these instructions must be translated before the application can be run for the CPU. Let's look at how this translating is done.

FIGURE 8-12   A portion of the checkbook program in BASIC.

```
PROGRAM checkbook
    !+
    ! Local Variables
    !-
    DECLARE STRING          answer
    DECLARE DECIMAL (14, 2)      balance, &
                                 deposit, &
                                 payment

    answer = "Y"
    balance = 0.0
    UNTIL answer = "N"
        INPUT "Do you want to enter deposits (Y/N)"; answer
        answer = SEG$ (answer, 1%, 1%)
        answer = EDIT$ (answer, 32% )
        IF answer = "Y"
        THEN
            INPUT "Deposit amount"; deposit
            balance = balance + deposit
            ! Update Summary file here
        END IF
    NEXT
    answer = "Y"
    UNTIL answer = "N"
        INPUT "Do you want to enter payments (Y/N)"; answer
        answer = SEG$ (answer, 1%, 1%)
        answer = EDIT$ (answer, 32% )
        IF answer = "Y"
        THEN
            INPUT "Payment amount"; payment
            balance = balance - payment
            !   Update Summary file here
            !   Update Print-check file here
        END IF
    NEXT
    PRINT "Your balance is ";balance
```

Translating Source Code

We could say the computer's CPU understands everything we send to it. Obviously, when we type a letter on the keyboard, the CPU recognizes it. But when we type a word, even a simple one like ADD, to the CPU it's only an A and two Ds. In this form, it's not an instruction the computer can carry out.

Similarly, our computer can't run our application until the source code is translated into instructions in binary form: 0s and 1s. Translation is done by special system software tools called compilers, assemblers, and interpreters. All these tools turn source code into object code. **Object code** contains **executable instructions** that can be read and operated on by the CPU. There are slight differences among these system software tools. Let's take a closer look at each one.

DISKbyte

Programming Errors Can Be Expensive!

Programming can be costly work. A programmer may only be able to write 50 or 60 error-free source code lines a day, at a cost to the company of about $15 a line. A simple, single-function program may contain about 200 lines of code, while a typical application program has about 50,000 lines.

American business has spent over $2 trillion on programming since the computer was invented. Between 60 and 80 percent of most programming budgets are spent on maintenance, or finding errors, updating, and revising existing programs.

Finding and correcting errors is extremely important. However, all too often, attempts to remove or correct program errors result in introducing new errors. This happened to American Airlines' SABRE reservation system in 1987. A program was revised so that American could make more profit by automatically adjusting the number of discounted seats on certain flights. But the program erroneously reported no discounted seats at all on many flights. Rather than buy a more expensive seat, passengers booked flights on other airlines with discounted seats instead. This programming error resulted in American Airlines losing an estimated $50 million in a three-month period. 💾

Compilers   A **compiler** is a special type of program that translates entire files of source code into object code, which in turn becomes an executable file. The executable file then can be read and run by the CPU.

On personal computers, source code is translated directly into executable code. These files are easily recognizable in a personal computer's disk directory because their filenames end in .EXE. On minis and mainframes, source code is usually translated into object files, which must be linked together to create executable files.

Some advanced compilers also produce other kinds of files, like analysis and program error files. These can be very useful to programmers because they contain important information about how clearly the computer understands the source code as written.

Assemblers   An **assembler** translates **assembly language**—a programming language that uses mnemonics such as letters, numbers, and symbols instead of numeric instructions—into **machine language**, the 0s and 1s the CPU understands. We will explore these two languages in more detail later in this chapter.

Interpreters   An **interpreter** translates source code one line at a time for immediate execution by the CPU. Like the compiler, an interpreter translates from the language the programmer used to write the program. However, an executable file is not created in the process. As a result, the program runs slower. And unlike the compiler, there is no analysis and program error correction; serious errors cause the program to simply stop running. Interpreters were widely used on early personal computers, which lacked the memory capacity to run larger compiler programs.

FIGURE 8 – 13   In 1945, this moth caused the Mark I computer to quit temporarily and was duly recorded in a log book. The first "bug" is on display in the U.S. Naval Museum in Dahlgren, Virginia.

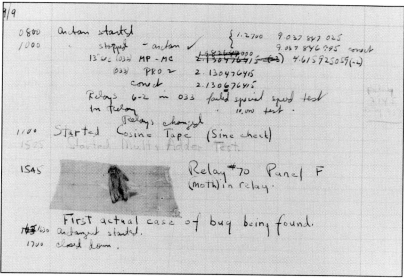

Courtesy of Naval Surface Welfare Center, Dahlgren, Virginia (1988).

Debugging the Program

In the early 1940s, a programming team found a moth in a computer, which caused the computer to malfunction. Ever since that incident, the term *bug* has been used to describe a program or hardware problem. Figure 8 – 13 shows the naval record of that first bug.

Software bugs are common in programming. Detail and precision is required, almost to the point of perfection, to make a program run successfully. Without debuggers, programmers must carefully comb through their code, searching for mistakes. A **debugger** is a system software program that identifies program errors. For example, the debugger is used when a program runs but fails to produce correct output. A debugger reports problems as error messages. Programmers use error message listings, like those shown in Figure 8 – 14, to track down bugs. Debugging can be a costly process, consuming as much as 50 percent of program development time.

Testing and Acceptance

No system is truly worthwhile unless it meets the needs of the users it was designed for. Therefore, once a system is debugged, it goes into testing, which lets people see how the program works. There are two types of testing: system tests and user tests. System testing involves entering various kinds of data to see how the program reacts under different conditions. In our checkbook program, we might want to try to write a check for more than our current balance, to see what happens. If such a condition destroys our database, we'll know we have a major bug in the program!

User testing, as its name implies, means letting the users test the system under actual working conditions. Users can look not only for system malfunctions but for such things as ease of use, how quickly the system performs its

FIGURE 8–14   An early attempt to compile our checkbook program produced these error messages because some BASIC statements were incorrect.

```
Diagnostic on source line 16, listing line 16
source file: CHECKBOOK.BAS;1
               IF answer = "Y"
%BASIC-E-INSERTB,          assuming THEN before end of statement

Diagnostic on source line 17, listing line 17
source file: CHECKBOOK.BAS;1
          WHILE
%BASIC-E-FOUND,          found end of statement when expecting an expression

Diagnostic on source line 21, listing line 21
source file: CHECKBOOK.BAS;1
          THEN
.................1
%BASIC-E-FOUND, 1:       found keyword THEN when expecting one of:
                                    an operator
                                    end of statement
                                    "("

Diagnostic on source line 30, listing line 30
source file: CHECKBOOK.BAS;1
          THEN
.................1
%BASIC-E-FOUND, 1:       found keyword THEN when expecting one of:
                                    an operator
                                    end of statement

Diagnostic on source line 35, listing line 35
source file: CHECKBOOK.BAS;1
          END IF
%BASIC-E-MISMATFOR,       missing NEXT for UNTIL at listing line 25

%BASIC-E-ENDNOOBJ, CHECKBOOK.BAS;1 completed with 5
diagnostics - object deleted
```

tasks, and a number of design characteristics. Using our checkbook program as an example, the programmers may have designed the system to accept the date only if it is typed 02–14–1992. Users might ask that it be modified to also accept dates that are typed in as 2/14/92 or Feb. 14, 1992.

Maintenance

Once the users have accepted the system, it goes into production, which means it is in daily use. That does not mean, however, that it is perfect. Most systems are constantly changed, modified, and improved. This is called *maintenance,* an ongoing process during the life of a system. The users' needs might change, or certain business procedures might require updating or modifying the system. Figure 8–15 shows the relationship between the work involved in systems design and systems maintenance. As you can see, developing the system is only the tip of the iceberg!

FIGURE 8–15   The relationship between the work involved in systems design and systems maintenance can be likened to how much of an iceberg floats above the water's surface.

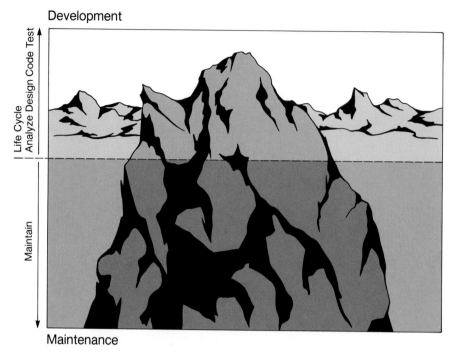

Development

Life Cycle
Analyze Design Code Test

Maintain

Maintenance

1. What is coding?

2. How does a text editor help a programmer?

3. Identify two aspects of structured coding.

4. What is the difference between source code and object code?

5. What do compilers, assemblers, and interpreters do?

6. What is debugging?

7. Why is maintenance so important?

WRITING THE DOCUMENTATION

Now let's explore the final step in the system development process: the **documentation,** or instructions that accompany the software. There are three kinds of documentation: software, user, and reference documentation. They are differentiated by the people who use them. **Software documentation** is chiefly for programmers who will maintain the program. **User documentation** and **reference documentation** are for the people who will use the program. Software documentation explains how a program works. User and reference documentation explains what a program does and how to use it.

Writing the documentation is the final step in the system development life cycle but ideally it is a *process* that continues throughout development. Even though the final details cannot be written until the programming is finished, waiting until the end of the project to begin writing often results in poor documentation. Likewise, once the project is complete, the developers are

FIGURE 8-16   A BASIC program showing comments listed as REM. REM comments are ignored when the program is compiled.

```
 10   REM  *****************************************************
 20   REM          Program:  Average Scores
 30   REM          Author:
 40   REM          Date:     August 9, 1989
 50   REM
 60   REM      This program prints and averages student test
 70   REM      scores.
 80   REM  *****************************************************
 90   REM              Data Definitions
100   REM
110   REM          TOT.SCORE = total score
120   REM          AVG.SCORE = average score
130   REM  *****************************************************
140   REM
150   PRINT "Student Name", "Score"
160   PRINT
170   PRINT "Abrahms, H.", 88
180   PRINT "Beaudelieu, M.", 85
190   PRINT "Eastman, P.", 95
200   PRINT "Fernandez, F.", 86
210   PRINT "Stein, G.", 70
220   PRINT "Telemachos, V.", 72
230   PRINT Valbonne, A.", 73
240   LET TOT.SCORE = 88 + 85 + 95 + 86 + 70 + 72 + 73
250   LET AVG.SCORE = TOT.SCORE / 7
260   PRINT
270   PRINT "The average score for this exam was", AVG.SCORE
280   END
```

anxious to get the software installed or out to market, and the documentation process is rushed. Good documentation is no accident; it is the result of careful planning and development, just like the software itself. Let's look at each type of documentation.

Software Documentation

When you write a program for your computer, as its author you know what it's for. But what if some other programmer wants to understand your program? Unless you explain it to them, the only way they can understand it is to sort through all the lines of code and try to figure out what you intended the program to do. For this reason, professional programmers always write software documentation.

Software documentation describes the purposes and organization of a program for other programmers. It is usually written as **comments.** Comments are notes written in English that are interspersed with source code, explaining aspects of the program to other programmers. Special symbols tell compilers to ignore these comments; they are there only to explain what a program does. For example, any line in a BASIC program that begins with REM (for remark, or comment) is software documentation and won't be read as part of the program. Figure 8-16 shows an example of a BASIC program with comments.

Comments are often written before each part of the program, telling what the programmer intended that part to do. Software documentation should not be confused with user documentation, which is written in manuals and explains how to use the program, not how it was written.

User Documentation

No program is complete until its purposes and functions are described in written form for its intended audience. User documentation, or user manuals, explain how to use system software and applications. As we'll see, there are many levels of users, with corresponding levels of documentation.

User manuals are the mainstay of user documentation. For example, user documentation for Apple Macintosh MacPaint explains how to draw faces, maps, logos, or whatever you choose. It doesn't tell you how the underlying program makes this happen.

User documentation usually describes program functions according to what you see when you use an application. It explains menu choices and symbols, defines commands, and gives examples of the way you might use the program. Of course, more complicated software requires more detailed documentation.

Audience   Good user documentation carefully targets its audience. If children are going to use the application, the documentation will be written in terms children understand. If advanced computer users are more likely to use it, the documentation will be written in their language.

Tutorials   Another feature of good user documentation is teaching how the application works in step-by-step fashion, like a tutor. Instead of trying to convey the overall purpose with a few sentences, tutorials carefully walk you through a hands-on session, with examples and explanations that build on each other, until, at the end, you see all the application's facets. We used this tutorial method in Chapter 3 to show you how to get started with your personal computer, and in Chapters 4, 5, and 6 to demonstrate word processing, spreadsheet, and database management systems applications.

Reference Documentation

Some people master just enough of a program to get their primary work done. However, they may want to learn additional features or functions when the need arises. These advanced functions usually aren't described in a manual's tutorial section. Instead, they are often cataloged in reference manuals. For this reason, reference documentation is often more detailed than user manuals.

Reference manuals document features, commands, and functions, usually in alphabetical order. They briefly define or explain how to use each function, such as Save, "@" commands, or Global Search and Replace. A reference manual may contain a set of pictures showing what each graphic symbol in your graphics application is used for. Once you learn how the reference manual is organized, it also becomes a useful tool.

FIGURE 8–17   This quick reference fits in pocket or purse, yet covers all the word processor's commands.

/Worksheet Column

Description: The /Worksheet Column command allows you to change the characteristics of the worksheet columns. You can use the command to change the column width and to hide and display columns.

Options: After entering /Worksheet Column, you will be presented with four options.

Set-Width: After choosing this option, you have two alternatives: Either use the RIGHT ARROW key and the LEFT ARROW key to change the column width of the current column, or type in the exact width desired for that column. With Release 1A, you can choose any width between 1 and 72. With Release 2, you can choose any width between 1 and 240. If you choose a column width narrower than the width of your data, numeric data will display as asterisks.

Reset-Width: This option returns the width setting for the current column to the default setting — that is, either the initial setting of nine characters or the setting established with /Worksheet Global Column-Width, if you used that command.

Hide: This option affects the display and printing of worksheet data. You can hide one or many columns, depending on the range you specify for

87

Courtesy of Osborne/McGraw-Hill

Quick-Reference Guides

Quick-reference guides are condensed versions of full-size reference manuals. Often small enough to carry in your pocket, this type of user documentation contains very brief summaries of features, functions, and commands. When you have become well acquainted with the software, you may find you refer primarily to this type of user documentation, just to refresh your memory. Figure 8–17 gives an example of a quick-reference guide.

1. Which kind of documentation explains how a program works?
2. Which kind of documentation explains what a program does and how to do it?
3. What is a comment?
4. Why is user documentation written for a specific audience?
5. What is a tutorial?
6. What is a quick-reference guide?

MEMORY CHECK

THE EVOLUTION OF PROGRAMMING LANGUAGES

Programming has been with us for over 40 years but it wasn't born at the same time as the first computers. When ENIAC and other early computers were built, there were no programming languages. ENIAC was initially programmed by flipping toggle switches and changing cables. Needless to say, this was a slow, awkward process. People quickly began searching for a better, faster way to issue instructions to the computer.

The result was what we now call programming languages. The first language closely resembled the toggle-switch method, issuing 0s and 1s to the computer by simply substituting software for hardware. As programming languages evolved and improved, they became more Englishlike. Let's take a closer look.

Machine Language

As we learned in Chapter 2, electronic digital computers understand only machine language — the language of the 0s and 1s that make up bits and bytes. Machine language requires no translation. From ENIAC to today's most sophisticated digital computers, machine language is the same. Machine language is directly understood or executed by hardware. Electronic circuitry turns these 0s and 1s into the operations the computer performs. The problem was that it was extremely tedious for a person to sit at a keyboard and enter the instructions in long sequences of 0s and 1s.

Assembly Language

The first way this programming problem was addressed was by assembly language. You'll recall that an assembly language uses letters, numbers, and symbols to represent individual 0s and 1s. For example, whereas in machine language multiply is set as 001011, in an assembly language you just write M, which is translated by an assembler into the 001011 of machine language. This greatly simplifies programming.

Assembly languages are powerful programming tools because they allow programmers a large amount of direct control over the hardware. They offer programmers greater ease in writing instructions but preserve the programmer's ability to declare exactly what operations the hardware performs.

Assembly languages are machine-specific, or machine-dependent. Machine-dependent means the instructions are specific to one type of computer hardware. Assembly languages are still provided by most computer manufacturers — they can't be translated and used on another computer. Assembly code for a Prime mini won't work on a Digital mini. Assembly code can't even be transferred between some machines built by the same manufacturer. For the most part, assembly languages are used by systems programmers to develop operating systems and their components. Thus, one early programming problem was solved but another one remained: how to make programming languages portable or transferable from one computer to another. The answer was, in theory at least, high-level programming languages, which we turn our attention to next.

DISKbyte

How to Motivate Programmers

J. Daniel Couger, Distinguished Professor of Information Systems and Management Science at the University of Colorado, Colorado Springs, has been studying what motivates computer professionals for many years. One thing that has remained consistent in his studies is that the work itself is the most powerful motivator. Analysts and programmers are more productive when the task requires using a variety of skills, when they can work on one project from beginning to end and see the results, and when the assignment is meaningful. They like their independence and freedom but they also like to be told when they've done a good job by their superiors. "Today, the field is attracting people with an even higher need for professional and personal development and achievement," says Dr. Couger.

A case in point: Carl Alsing of Data General was an outstanding systems programmer. He wrote the operating system code for many early computers Data General produced. His most remarkable feat was writing the operating system for Data General's first supermini-computer in just two weeks, a task that would have taken anyone else many, many months. He did it by isolating himself at home on his back porch, which he called "the microporch," where he wrote what he called his "microcode." Perhaps for Carl Alsing an important aspect of motivation was working outdoors with plenty of fresh air!

---

1. How were the first computers programmed?

2. What is the language of machine language?

3. What is an example of assembly language?

4. What does the term *machine-dependent* mean?

5. What is an assembly language primarily used for?

MEMORY CHECK

HIGH-LEVEL PROGRAMMING LANGUAGES

Assembly languages were the first bridge between our native tongue and the computer's binary language. However, it wasn't long before programmers realized they could take programming one step further. The creation of high-level programming languages followed. **High-level languages** are a method of writing programs using Englishlike words as instructions.

High-level programming languages combine several machine language instructions into one high-level instruction. So, as we move up the ladder from machine language to high-level languages, *less is more;* fewer program instructions have a greater effect on the computer. Where a programmer had to correctly write a string of 0s and 1s in machine language, assembly language required only a single letter or a short *mnemonic,* a term or word that is easy to identify, such as ADD for addition. And where several instructions are required to program an operation in assembly code, a high-level language requires just a single statement.

Statements and Syntax

Human and computer languages have two major similarities: (1) a set of words and (2) a set of language usage rules. In human language, we construct sentences in a specific way—subject, predicate, and so on. Likewise, when using a computer language, we write instructions using statements and syntax.

A **statement** is an expression of instruction in a programming language. For example, PRINT FILE.TXT is a statement. A statement translates into one or more instructions at the machine language level. Each programming language includes a set of statements and a syntax. *Syntax* is the set of rules governing the language's structure and statements. To write a program in any programming language, we have to use its statements and strictly abide by its syntax rules. These syntax rules may include how statements are written, the order in which statements occur, and how sections of programs are organized.

For example, in the following BASIC statement, you must include the quotation marks around the letter Y, or the compiler will not correctly translate it:

```
answer = "Y"
```

Also, BASIC requires that you must terminate each control structure. So when you use an IF statement, at some point you must have an END IF statement. Again, if you don't, the compiler will determine the program has an error and won't produce an executable program.

Some high-level languages also require that you organize programs in sections. A typical first section identifies the program and the programmer. This may be followed by a declaration section and then by a program section. Whatever the language requires, you must abide by its rules. As with other aspects of computing, close is not good enough!

Compiling High-Level Languages

High-level source code must be translated before it can be read by the CPU. Each language has a compiler or interpreter to convert its Englishlike expressions into machine language.

High-level languages provide benefits by utilizing statements but they give up something in the process. Programmers no longer have the direct control over the hardware that they have with assembly languages. When high-level languages are compiled, statements are translated into specific machine instructions determined by the compiler. Programmers can't alter these translations without rewriting the compiler—a large task.

Portability

An additional problem high-level languages were meant to address was portability. You'll recall from Chapter 7 that portable refers to using one form of software, such as an operating system or an application, on several different kinds of hardware. Programmers hoped they could use the same version of a language like BASIC no matter what manufacturer's hardware they were working with. This didn't come to pass. To try to ensure customer fidelity, most computer manufacturers developed their own versions of the major high-level languages specifically for their own hardware. This means code for a particular language often must be modified before a program written for a Honeywell computer will run on a Hewlett-Packard computer, for example. Nevertheless, code written in a high-level language is much more portable than assembly code. High-level source code can usually be easily modified to work on different hardware than it was written for, unlike assembly code.

We divide high-level programming languages into two categories: structured and unstructured. Here, we encounter yet another use for the term *structure,* which is distinct from either structured design or structured programming. A structured high-level programming language requires the programmer to write source code in well-defined sections, which are compiled in sequence. Unstructured programs allow the programmer to create programs in a more random fashion.

High-level languages are used for all kinds of programming but are especially valuable to application programmers, who create specialized software. There are over 200 general- and special-purpose high-level languages in use today. Let's look at four widely used high-level programming languages, examining the features that make them powerful and effective tools for programming computers.

FORTRAN: A Scientific Language

One of the first high-level languages was **FORTRAN,** for FORmula TRANslator. It was created in 1954 by John Backus, one of IBM's most respected scientists, for developing scientific and engineering applications. FORTRAN allows programmers to calculate complex formulas with a few source code instructions. Like a wise mathematician, it readily understands and executes the language of numbers.

FORTRAN is an unstructured language. FORTRAN was patterned after the CPU: it reads and executes instructions, one after another, without much regard to categories and classes. If you want to define a data item, you can do so at any point in the program. Other languages such as COBOL and Pascal require that each major program element reside in one place, all together. FORTRAN doesn't have that requirement.

As with most high-level programming languages, FORTRAN has been revised and refined over the years. Even John Backus has been trying to write a "better" FORTRAN. Standardized versions, approved by the American National Standards Institute (ANSI), were released in 1957, 1958, 1962, and 1978. Computer manufacturers who adopt these standards make it possible to use the same version of FORTRAN on nearly any computer hardware. Figure 8–18 shows a sample FORTRAN program.

COBOL: A Business Language

About the same time FORTRAN was invented, **COBOL** was developed by the COnference on DAta SYstems Languages (CODASYL). COBOL was issued by the U.S. Government Printing Office in 1960. COBOL stands for COmmon Business-Oriented Language. Its developers represented a cross-section of computer users in business, industry, government, and education. Among the COBOL developers was Grace Hopper, a pioneer in computer programming. Working for the U.S. Navy, Hopper was a driving force behind COBOL, working to ensure it would become a standard across the industry.

FIGURE 8-18   A FORTRAN program that produces the average of 10 numbers.

```
C   COMPUTE THE SUM AND AVERAGE OF 10 NUMBERS
C
        REAL NUM, SUM, AVG
        INTEGER TOTNUM, COUNTR
C
        SUM = 0.0
C   INITIALIZE LOOP CONTROL VARIABLE
        COUNTR = 0
        TOTNUM = 10
C
C   LOOP TO READ DATA AND ACCUMULATE SUM
    20 IF (COUNTR .GE. TOTNUM) GO TO 30
        READ, NUM
        SUM = SUM + NUM
C       UPDATE LOOP CONTROL VARIABLE
        COUNTR = COUNTR + 1
        GO TO 20
C   END OF LOOP - COMPUTE AVERAGE
    30 AVG = SUM / TOTNUM
C   PRINT RESULTS
        PRINT, SUM
        PRINT, AVG
        STOP
        END
```

COBOL is a structured programming language. This means that COBOL "has a place for everything" and requires programmers to "put everything in its place." COBOL programs are separated into four sections, called divisions:

1. The Identification Division documents the program name, the programmer's name(s), dates, and any other important identification information.
2. The Environment Division names the computer hardware, including the CPU and I/O devices.
3. The Data Division identifies all associated files and working storage sections of the program.
4. The Procedure Division contains all the instructions in the COBOL program.

COBOL divisions are further divided into paragraphs and sections. This structure helps programmers write code efficiently and with a minimum of repetition and confusion. COBOL programs are self-documenting; simplicity of structure and expressions make them almost self-explanatory.

COBOL is almost a standard in business programming in the United States. Over the years, one programming language after another has threatened to displace COBOL but so many COBOL programs have been written for large computer systems that it would be very costly to change now. The American National Standards Institute (ANSI) standardized COBOL in 1968

DISKbyte

Grace Murray Hopper: A Computer Science Pioneer

Few individuals can be said to have changed the world, yet one for whom this might be considered an understatement is Admiral Grace Murray Hopper. This feisty, colorful, and brilliant woman has truly gained a measure of immortality through her many accomplishments.

It would be hard to imagine a more distinguished career than hers. Consider these achievements. She:

- Graduated from Vassar, Phi Beta Kappa.
- Earned M.A. and Ph.D. degrees from Yale.
- Anchored Harvard's Mark I programming team.
- Joined the Eckert-Mauchly Computer Corporation as senior mathematician in 1948.

Courtesy of Digital Equipment Corporation

- Served as senior programmer on UNIVAC I project.
- Developed one of the first program translators at the University of Pennsylvania in 1952.

- Created the programming language Flow-Matic, which was the basis for COBOL.
- Wrote the compiler that made it possible for COBOL to run on almost any computer.
- Won first Computer Sciences Man-of-the-Year in 1969.
- Served 43 years in the Naval Reserve, retiring as a Rear Admiral at age 79.

Today, Grace Hopper is still serving in the vanguard of the computer field. She's moved on, from academia and the military to industry. In 1988, at 81 years of age, she began a new career as a senior consultant and industry spokesperson with Digital Equipment Corporation.

and issued a revised form in 1974 called ANSI–COBOL. After long years of industry debate, COBOL 85 was approved. Today, COBOL is among the most standardized high-level programming languages. Figure 8–19 shows a sample COBOL program.

BASIC: A Personal Computer Language

BASIC, or the Beginners All-purpose Symbolic Instruction Code, was developed over a period of years by professors John Kemeny and Thomas Kurtz and students in the computer science program at Dartmouth College. It was released in 1965. Although originally developed on mainframe computers, BASIC is the most popular programming language used by personal computer owners. In most versions, BASIC is an unstructured language. Its creators intended that it teach programming concepts as students wrote programs. It is sometimes called conversational because it uses terms such as START, READ, INPUT, and STOP.

FIGURE 8—19   A COBOL program that produces the average of 10 numbers.

```
         IDENTIFICATION DIVISION.
         PROGRAM-ID.     AVERAGES.
         AUTHOR.         DEB KNUDSEN.
         DATE-COMPILED.
         ENVIRONMENT DIVISION.
         CONFIGURATION SECTION.
            SOURCE-COMPUTER. HP-3000.
            OBJECT-COMPUTER. HP-3000.
         INPUT-OUTPUT SECTION.
         FILE-CONTROL.
            SELECT NUMBER-FILE ASSIGN TO "NUMFILE".
            SELECT REPORT-FILE ASSIGN TO "PRINT,UR,A,LP(CCTL)".
         DATA DIVISION.
         FILE SECTION.
         FD  NUMBER-FILE
             LABEL RECORDS ARE STANDARD
             DATA RECORD IS NUMBER-REC.
         01  NUMBER-REC                  PIC S9(7)V99.
         FD  REPORT-FILE
             LABEL RECORDS ARE STANDARD
             DATA RECORD IS REPORT-REC.
         01  REPORT-REC                  PIC X(100).

         WORKING-STORAGE SECTION.
         01  END-OF-NUMBER-FILE-FLAG     PIC X(3) VALUE SPACES.
             88  END-OF-NUMBER-FILE               VALUE "YES".
         01  SUM-OF-NUMBERS              PIC S9(7)V99.
         01  AVERAGE-OF-NUMBERS          PIC S9(7)V99.
         01  NUMBER-OF-NUMBERS           PIC 9(5).

         01  WS-REPORT-REC.
             05  FILLER                  PIC X(2)    VALUE SPACES.
             05  FILLER                  PIC X(17)   VALUE
                                         "Sum of Numbers = ".
             05  WS-SUM-OF-NUMBERS       PIC Z,ZZZ,ZZZ.99-.
             05  FILLER                  PIC X(3)    VALUE SPACES.
             05  FILLER                  PIC X(15)   VALUE
                                         "# of Numbers = ".
             05  WS-NUMBER-OF-NUMBERS    PIC ZZZZ9.
             05  FILLER                  PIC X(3)    VALUE SPACES.
             05  FILLER                  PIC X(21)   VALUE
                                         "Average of Numbers = ".
             05  WS-AVERAGE-OF-NUMBERS   PIC Z,ZZZ,ZZZ.99-.
             05  FILLER                  PIC X(8)    VALUE SPACES.
```

The original BASIC was easy to learn, allowing novice computer users to write simple programs within a few minutes. Today, many manufacturers have developed varieties of BASIC that are as complex as other high-level programming languages.

BASIC uses five major categories of statements:

• Arithmetic statements allow users to use BASIC like a calculator. Typing PRINT 2 + 2 programs your computer to display the result, 4.
• Input/Output statements, including READ, DATA, INPUT, and

```
PROCEDURE DIVISION.

100-MAIN-PROGRAM.
    OPEN INPUT  NUMBER-FILE
         OUTPUT REPORT-FILE.
    MOVE SPACES TO REPORT-REC.
    MOVE ZEROS TO SUM-OF-NUMBERS.
    MOVE ZEROS TO AVERAGE-OF-NUMBERS.
    MOVE ZEROS TO NUMBER-OF-NUMBERS.

    READ NUMBER-FILE
        AT END MOVE "YES" TO END-OF-NUMBER-FILE-FLAG.

    IF END-OF-NUMBER-FILE
      NEXT SENTENCE
    ELSE
      PERFORM 200-PROCESS-NUMBER-FILE
          UNTIL END-OF-NUMBER-FILE.

    PERFORM 300-COMPUTE-AVERAGE.

    PERFORM 400-PRINT-RESULTS.

    CLOSE NUMBER-FILE
          REPORT-FILE.

    STOP RUN.

200-PROCESS-NUMBER-FILE.
    ADD 1 TO NUMBER-OF-NUMBERS.
    ADD NUMBER-REC TO SUM-OF-NUMBERS.

    READ NUMBER-FILE
        AT END MOVE "YES" TO END-OF-NUMBER-FILE-FLAG.

300-COMPUTE-AVERAGE.
    DIVIDE SUM-OF-NUMBERS BY NUMBER-OF-NUMBERS
        GIVING AVERAGE-OF-NUMBERS.

400-PRINT-RESULTS.
    MOVE SUM-OF-NUMBERS TO WS-SUM-OF-NUMBERS.
    MOVE NUMBER-OF-NUMBERS TO WS-NUMBER-OF-NUMBERS.
    MOVE AVERAGE-OF-NUMBERS TO WS-AVERAGE-OF-NUMBERS.

WRITE REPORT-REC FROM WS-REPORT-REC.
```

PRINT, program fundamental data flow functions.
- Control statements, including GOTO, IF–THEN, FOR, NEXT, and END control the sequence of instructions executed by the computer.
- Other statements, including REM and DIM, help document BASIC programs and set up data dimensions, respectively.
- System Commands tell the operating system how to work with BASIC programs. For example, RUN means execute a program; LIST directs the computer to display a BASIC program.

FIGURE 8-20   A BASIC program that produces the average of 10 numbers.

```
10  REM COMPUTE SUM AND AVERAGE OF 10 NUMBERS
20  LET SUM = 0
30  FOR I = 1 TO 10
40    INPUT N(I)
50    LET SUM = SUM + N(I)
60  NEXT I
70  LET AVG = SUM / 10
80  PRINT "SUM = ",SUM
90  PRINT "AVERAGE = ",AVG
999 END
```

BASIC fundamentals are standardized and available as Standard Minimal BASIC, released in 1978. Today, there are many popular implementations of BASIC. One is Microsoft BASIC, which many computer makers offer along with their operating system. For example, IBM offered it with its PC–DOS. Another is TrueBASIC, a structured version developed by Kemeny and Kurtz. It was developed in response to criticism of unstructured BASIC, and is available for many computers. In addition, ANSI issued a standard for structured BASIC in 1987. Figure 8–20 shows a sample BASIC program.

A BASIC statement was used to name a 1982 cult movie about computers. The movie was called *TRON*, the command that means "turn on trace" to print program line numbers. How to turn it off? TROFF, of course.

C: A High-Level Language

C is a relatively new programming language developed by Bell Laboratories. It gives programmers a larger measure of control over the hardware, like an assembly language, but incorporates many of the statement features of high-level languages. C is a structured language that can be used effectively for almost any kind of programming. Figure 8–21 is an example of a C program.

A World of Programming Languages

There are many high-level programming languages that we haven't discussed here. Figure 8–22 shows several high-level languages and some of their characteristics. The following list gives some additional facts about these specialized programming languages:

- Ada: named for Augusta Ada Lovelace Byron, the first female programmer (1816–52), Ada was developed by the Department of Defense for military programming.
- APL: for A Programming Language, it is best suited for writing mathematical programs.
- PL/1: developed by a committee especially for the IBM System/360. Originally it was to be called NPL, for New Programming Language,

FIGURE 8-21   A C program that produces the average of 10 numbers.

```c
#include <stdio.h>
main ()
   {
      int i, num;
      float sum;

      printf("Enter numbers \n");
      sum = 0;
      for (i = 0; i < 10; i++)
        {
           scanf("%d",&num);
           sum = sum + num;
        }
      printf("Sum = %3.1f\n",sum);
      printf("Average = %3.1f\n",sum / 10.0);
   }
```

FIGURE 8-22   This chart summarizes the characteristics of several high-level programming languages.

Language

Feature	Ada	APL	BASIC	COBOL	FORTRAN	Pascal	PL/1	RPG
Scientific		✓	✓		✓	✓	✓	
Business			✓	✓		✓	✓	✓
Problem Oriented								✓
Procedure Oriented	✓	✓	✓	✓	✓	✓	✓	
Standardized	✓		✓	✓	✓	✓	✓	
Englishlike			✓	✓		✓	✓	
Highly Used			✓	✓	✓			✓
Interactive		✓	✓			✓		

but the acronym was already being used by the National Physics Laboratory in England.

- Pascal: designed as a teaching language, it helps students learn structured programming and good programming habits.
- RPG: Report Program Generator is especially useful for creating reports.

Next, let's look at even higher-level languages.

1. What is a statement?
2. What is syntax?
3. Explain what is meant by an unstructured language and identify one.
4. Describe three of the most popular programming languages, and the specific purposes for which each is used.
5. Explain what is meant by a structured language and identify one.

ADVANCED PROGRAMMING LANGUAGES, TOOLS, AND TECHNIQUES

Many businesses have an application backlog or waiting list of systems to develop for users, which the programming staff doesn't have time to get to. In some companies, the backlog is over six years! One response to the problem is programming languages that users can quickly learn so they can create their own applications. An example is fourth-generation languages. Another response is advanced tools and techniques for the programming staff that help them work more productively, such as computer-aided software engineering, or CASE. In this section, we examine some of these advanced programming languages, tools, and techniques.

Fourth-Generation Languages

You may have heard the cliche, "If you want it done right, you have to do it yourself." Many computer users have come to feel this way about the applications they request from the computer information systems department. Unfortunately, marketing directors, order processors, inventory managers, and purchasing agents are rarely programmers as well. That leaves them at the mercy of the computer department's backed-up scheduling for new applications and hoping they can accurately communicate what kind of application they want. Another solution is to allow users to create their own applications using a fourth-generation language.

A **fourth-generation language (4GL)** is a language that uses Englishlike phrases and sentences to issue instructions. The 4GL lets users express *what* they want the system to accomplish, rather than having to issue detailed instructions as to *how* to do it. 4GLs are programming languages that allow nonprofessional computer users to develop software. 4GLs make it possible for users to write many of their own applications. They make programming easier by bringing the language syntax even closer to English. They also make programming easier by using menus and questions-and-answer sequences to create instructions instead of strings of programming language procedures. Hence, 4GLs are often referred to as nonprocedural languages. Fourth-generation languages make it possible for just about anyone to become a programmer. Figure 8–23 shows a typical screen created with a 4GL.

Before we explore some common 4GLs, let's look at their features:

● Emphasis on end results. With 4GLs you ask for information and the computer supplies it. Since you may know better what you're looking

FIGURE 8–23   A typical screen created using a 4GL.

PC/FOCUS release 5.5; Information Builders, Inc., New York, NY

for than the computer's standard way of producing it, you specify the problem you want to solve rather than the means of arriving at a solution. Sophisticated underlying software does the rest.

- Limited training is required. 4GLs don't require that you learn a traditional high-level programming language. Sometimes you have to know what certain terms or symbols mean but you won't spend weeks learning a language and its syntax, as with COBOL or even BASIC.
- Interactive dialogue replaces writing source code files. With 4GLs, you simply type your request, such as SHOW RESULTS OF MARKETING PROMOTION. Instead of writing programs, you interact directly with the computer by typing Englishlike phrases or by selecting symbols or menu choices on the monitor. 4GL software translates your instructions into high-level programming code and automatically carries out your requests.
- Increased programmer productivity. 4GLs are powerful! This means they provide an even greater ability to perform instructions than high-level languages. Shorter statements and fewer total hours spent programming produce more results.
- Increased memory requirements. It's not all rosy. 4GLs do cost something: they require about 75 percent more memory than high-level languages.

These are the basic features common to most 4GLs. Like high-level languages, different fourth-generation languages have been created to accomplish specific tasks. These include very high-level or nonprocedural languages, database query languages, and application generators. Let's examine each.

Nonprocedural Languages   **Nonprocedural languages** (very high-level languages) fall into two categories. One is often referred to as **natural language** and is designed for users, people without a programming background. These include a special version of APL, mentioned earlier, and NOMAD, which usually works in conjunction with a database management system. The other category is languages designed for MIS professionals. The list includes languages such as FOCUS, IDEAL, and MANTIS, again usually used with a DBMS.

There are several nonprocedural languages that perform specific tasks. One is SIMULA, used to create simulations such as testing aircraft wing strength. Another is HOS, or Higher Order Software, a language that automatically checks and verifies source code as it is created so that it is mathematically correct. HOS is designed to remove programming and maintenance errors from code.

Query Languages   Query languages simplify searching computer memory for information. Query languages are good examples of business-oriented 4GLs. They let you program computers without knowing programming. They give you access to computer data without requiring that you execute COBOL or FORTRAN source code. Query languages produce excellent information. For example, if everyone in the company got a 6 percent raise, the query language could update all payroll files at once. SQL, which stands for structured query language, is the standard query language for relational database management systems for both IBM mainframes and PCs.

Application Generators   Another 4GL is called an application generator, more commonly referred to as a 4GL/DBMS, or fourth-generation language/database management system. It allows you to create custom applications used specifically in a database management system, hence the appended DBMS. The 4GL/DBMS is most commonly used by companies where large mainframe computers are used to manage a huge corporate database. Personnel needs access to worker records, finance needs its numbers, manufacturing needs materials inventories; the 4GL/DBMS allows these workers to design their own applications.

One interesting use of a 4GL/DBMS took place at a company that produces frozen dinners. Government regulations and the company's own requirements for nutrition and calorie counts led to a need for monthly quality control reports. The company's chief chemist wanted to take sample dinners, analyze them, and determine if they were meeting the regulations and requirements. If the dinner didn't pass inspection, she wanted to know what was wrong, what plant produced the dinner, and on what day.

The chemist went to the MIS department and asked if they could create this application, which was basically analyzing data from the corporate database. She was told they had an enormous application development backlog, and it would take several years before they could get to it. She began exploring alternatives and learned about a 4GL/DBMS called NOMAD2. Although she was not a computer expert, she decided to give it a try. Within two weeks, she had her application up and running, without any help from the MIS department. All the chemists in the department learned NOMAD2, and it is used constantly. It is a time-saver, too; the caloric content of a glazed chicken used to take over an hour to analyze manually. Now it only takes one or two minutes.

Users often create their own applications using a 4GL/DBMS. According to James Martin, a computer industry expert, "A 1,000 percent increase in productivity in data processing is possible . . . and the key is application development without conventional programming—putting some of the development in the hands of end users, rather than programmers."

Many years ago, as telephones proliferated, AT&T put dials on phones so "users" could become their own operators. Fourth-generation languages are doing the same thing for computers, effectively making users into programmers but without the tedium of learning complicated languages. As this happens, users are able to get more useful data from the computer. Data begets information, and information begets knowledge.

It is important to remember that there are many definitions and interpretations of fourth-generation languages in general and nonprocedural languages in specific. It is a new field that is growing and changing.

Object-Oriented Programming

OOP, object-oriented programming, is a tool both programmers and users alike can use. Bits of code are put together into objects; the objects are fitted together to form a program. OOP is similar to building a modular house, where parts are prefabricated and fitted together according to the buyer's desires. Another advantage with OOP is creating modules that can be reused in other programs. In addition, software created with OOP can be modified and revised by adding or subtracting modules.

OOP makes programming much easier for professionals but it also opens the door for users to create software they need without having to learn a formal language. An application can be created by simply selecting objects, or, as shown in Figure 8–24, icons from a menu.

CASE: Computer-Aided Software Engineering

An interesting new set of software tools emerged in the 1980s: **computer-aided software engineering (CASE).** CASE tools help programmers make the most of their time and effort, and are used in three ways. The first is program design, including analysis, design, and documentation. CASE dramatically lowers these so-called front-end development costs by automating many manual operations and tasks. The computer itself replaces paper, pencil, and the flowchart template.

Excelerator is a CASE tool developed for the personal computer that designs, validates, and prepares specifications for applications and information systems. The systems analyst can create a system design, show it to the end users, work with them to tailor it to their needs, then create the program specifications used in coding. Figure 8–25 shows Excelerator.

The second way CASE tools are used involves coding, debugging, and maintenance tools—the back end of development. These tools streamline and automate many programming tasks, and include text editors with built-in language templates, source code management libraries, and program performance and efficiency analyzers. Many companies have at least one enormous database that has become increasingly expensive or difficult to maintain and update. One CASE activity called *reengineering* adapts these older applications to current business requirements.

FIGURE 8-24   Two sets of objects used in object-oriented programming (OOP). The first row shows Macintosh objects, the second DOS objects.

  Dialog - Assign this step whenever you want two-way communication between end-user and computer to occur. It is the only step that allows end-user participation.

  Display - This step is designed for one-way communication. Use it when you want the computer to display a message to the end-user that does not require a response (e.g., a "Please Wait" message).

  Report - You will assign this step when you want to give the end-user an option to print report information.

  Compute - Assign this step when the program requires that the computer perform a mathematical computation.

  Decision - Use this step when you want the program to choose between two conditions (e.g., if the customer has a balance then print an invoice; if not, then go on to the next customer.)

  File - The system will automatically arrange all like records in a file. Use the File step when you want to delete or compact a file or to import and export information from other files.

 Record - Assign this step at all places in the program where it is necessary for the program to work with a record (e.g., to set up a new record, find an existing record, etc.).

  Cancel - Add this step to tasks the end-user may wish to abandon (e.g., a lengthy print routine).

  Safety - The Safety is a safeguard against data loss in the event of a recoverable error in the program. Add it to your program to allow the end-user to get out of the program and minimize damage if such an event should occur.

  End - Use this step to take the end-user out of the program.

Courtesy Maxem Corporation

For example, if a company started using a database 30 years ago, many of its early departments may no longer exist. Accidentally using a portion of the database designed for these departments can cause a malfunction or even a failure. A reengineering CASE tool such as the Bachman Data Analyst will clean up existing files and redesign the database to bring it more in line with the company's current and future needs. It also paves the way for migrating from the old database to a new one. Figure 8–26 gives a view of a Bachman Data Analyst screen.

FIGURE 8 – 25   Excelerator CASE tools.

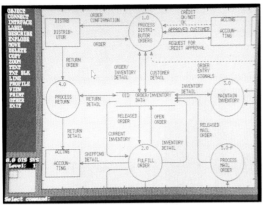

Jon Goell/Index Technology

FIGURE 8 – 26   A Bachman Data Analyst screen.

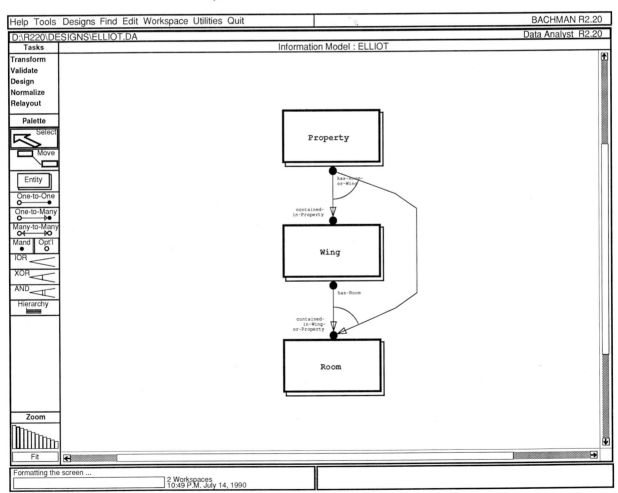

Courtesy Bachman Information Systems, Inc.

FIGURE 8–27   Integrated CASE, a tool for complete system development, permits designing systems from block diagrams. Texas Instruments' Information Engineering Facility (IEF) for OS/2 lets you design, build, and test business applications from diagrams, all at the OS/2 workstation. The iterative design/generate/test development process is shown here, with design work on an Entity Relationship diagram in the full screen, Diagram Testing of the application in the lower window, and actual application execution in the upper window. Today, complete mainframe applications can be designed, generated, and tested on a single OS/2 workstation.

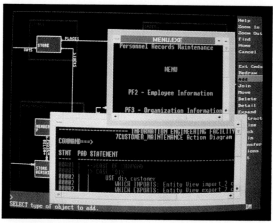

Courtesy Texas Instruments

The third type of CASE tool is called Integrated CASE or I–CASE. It is a tool for complete system development and is being used in many large corporations to create more flexible systems and to create systems more quickly. I–CASE permits designing systems from block diagrams, as shown in Figure 8–27. This allows people to focus more concretely on who should get what information. TWA used I–CASE to design a system that monitors its frequent flier program. In the past, it took three working days to make changes in the system; now it takes half an hour.

Once the system is designed using I–CASE, it is often possible to use a code generator, a special software program, to create a large portion of the source code. The code generator writes code faster and more accurately than programmers, and once this code is written, it maintains itself. Blue Cross/ Blue Shield of North Carolina used a code generator for a large health-care system. Only 16,000 lines of code were written by programmers; the code generator wrote the remaining 194,000. A system that could have taken several years to complete was ready and working within six months.

MEMORY CHECK

1. What makes a 4GL easier for nonprogrammers to use?
2. Describe the three different types of 4GLs.
3. Identify a disadvantage to using a 4GL.
4. What is SQL, and what is it used for?
5. What is object-oriented programming?
6. Describe the concept behind CASE, and several ways in which CASE tools are used.

ETHICS

As we've seen, programming involves a degree of creativity. As a means of solving problems, we can accurately state that programs are creations or inventions. To underscore this fact, consider that in recent years, many companies and individuals have sought U.S. government patents on programs. Of course, any time individual origination is concerned, ownership often becomes an ethical issue.

Many computer corporations feel that they own the programming ideas of their employees. They insist that while an employee is on the payroll, any and all programming output is the property of the corporation. This includes both the programs themselves and even "intellectual property" — ideas. If we examine their perspective, we can see why they take this stance. Employees work together, attend meetings and seminars, and generally discuss programs under development. The problem solving they do is valuable and has the potential to create profitable products. If an employee turns this information into a product he or she sells outside the corporation, we might consider this a form of theft. To prevent this, the ideas of the individual are usurped for the group's advantage.

The line between ethical and unethical behavior in this type of situation is often drawn on the basis of monetary gain or loss. Has the programmer used company resources such as computer time or corporate data? Did the company authorize using the computer for work on an individual's project on personal time? Has the employee agreed that all work he or she does belongs to the company? Was the project originally intended for company use? These and many more issues must be clarified.

Many companies now have a set of ethical guidelines for employees to follow; failure to do so often results in immediate dismissal. When systems people are found breaking the rules, it is not uncommon to see them escorted out of the building by the security guards. This ignominy is prompted by fear that they will take programs or software with them, or even possibly cripple the system with bugs.

Clearly, ethical behavior means not breaking company rules. However, the rules must be clear. If the programmer is hired on a free-lance basis, he or she may be entitled to retain ownership. If the company wishes to keep its system development private, it must inform employees of this fact. You can see that when it comes to programming, discretion plays a big part in determining what's right and what's wrong. Most important, it means developing and adhering to a strict set of personal ethical guidelines.

CAREERbyte

Clark Gee, Systems Analyst

The systems analyst plays a very important role in many companies. He or she is the person who makes a new computer system a reality, guiding, shaping, and creating it every step of the way. Clark Gee is a systems analyst with Thomson Financial Networks, an international firm specializing in delivering financial information electronically via computers to brokers, traders, and analysts. Clark studied computer science and economics at Tulane University. He took a year off from college to work in a computer department, to make sure it was what he wanted as a career. Convinced, he resumed his computer science studies but also took business and economics courses so he would understand "the real world," as he calls it. He gained that real-world experience at several companies before joining Thomson.

In 1989, Clark was put in charge of a very important project in the Global Markets Group at Thomson. The group wanted an information product that would track the value of various foreign currencies — the yen, the Deutsche mark, the British pound, the French franc — against the American dollar. These foreign exchange rates vary constantly, and the program Clark was to create would have to gather data 24 hours a day from the American, European, and Asian markets. Once the data was gathered, the program had to present it to currency traders in a meaningful way on a computer screen. They called it GFI Forex Chartist, for Global Financial Information Foreign Exchange.

Photo by Andrew K. Howard

Clark followed the system development life cycle approach you learned about in this chapter. In the analysis phase, the group gave Clark a thumbnail sketch of what the product should do and how it should look to the user — the trader. From this meeting, Clark wrote an outline describing where the data would come from and what kinds of technical analysis the program would have to perform on that data. He selected the tools he would use to create the program: a personal computer and a version of the BASIC programming language.

Clark also wrote a memo to the group explaining how he would actually develop the product and what it should look like when he was done. He wanted to make sure that he understood what the group wanted. He presented his outline and memo to his manager, who

made a few changes, approved it, and let him get started.

In the design and development phase, Clark used his analysis to figure out how to design the computer system and write the software program. Of central importance was the screen presentation; it had to be easy for the traders to quickly spot the information they needed. Clark divided this phase into two tiers. One was designing and writing the program as described. The second was when he showed it to the group, "who now, once they actually saw it, could then tell me what it was they really wanted," Clark says wryly. Tier two was revising and rewriting accordingly.

In the third phase, implementation, Clark put the new system to work. At first, he let people in the group use it, to get their feedback. He monitored its data collection, to make sure everything went smoothly. The system collects data as frequently as every five minutes, and a problem could mean getting garbled data or perhaps none at all.

The final phase, support, was pretty simple for this system. The users are highly experienced traders, so they didn't require training. The system is almost totally automatic, so it does not need much maintenance. The database is backed up three times a day and the system automatically resets itself after a power outage.

Thomson regards GFI Forex Chartist as a successful computer system and product. It only took a few months to create and the product was introduced on schedule. Clark was pleased that his first big project at Thomson went so well.

SUMMARY

1. *Identify the steps in the system development life cycle.* The programming process for creating systems or application software is characterized as the system development life cycle. The steps include analysis (of the problem), design (planning the solution), coding (writing the program), debugging (correcting errors), testing and acceptance (prior to turning the system over to users), maintenance (keeping it working properly and improving it), and documentation (writing the necessary manuals).

2. *Define the features of structured programming.* In the early days, programming was a matter of personal style, reflecting the methods and styles of individual programmers. Structured techniques evolved in the 1960s, including structured coding, structured analysis, and structured design. They provide an orderly way to write programs so they can be understood by other programmers.

3. *Define the types of computer documentation.* Written documentation is used to aid programmers and users alike. Software documentation describes the purpose and organization of a program. User documentation explains how to use the program. Reference documentation explains all the program's features and functions in detail. Quick reference guides provide a simple introduction to basic features and functions.

4. *Describe some of the various programming languages used to write software.* Programming languages have evolved over time. Early programming involved direct control of the hardware through machine language to assembly languages. Later, high-level languages such as FORTRAN and COBOL were invented, making programmers more productive. The variety of programming languages and methods has grown; BASIC is a popular personal computer language. There are literally hundreds of programming languages available for both general and specialized programming.

5. *Describe some of the advanced programming tools and techniques.* There are many programming languages, tools, and techniques available to help the professional programmer and the average user. Both can use fourth-generation languages to create new applications, most commonly for a DBMS. Nonprocedural, or natural, languages and query languages are commonly used. Object-oriented programming is a new technique that uses objects, or modules, of prewritten code and links them together like building blocks. CASE tools are designed for professional programmers and are used to speed application development.

KEY TERMS

algorithm, p. 238

assembler, p. 247

assembly language, p. 247

BASIC, p. 259

C, p. 262

COBOL, p. 257

coding, p. 244

comments, p. 251

compiler, p. 247

computer-aided software engineering (CASE), p. 267

debugger, p. 248

documentation (reference, software, user), p. 250

executable instruction, p. 246

flowchart (system, program), p. 239

FORTRAN, p. 257

fourth-generation language (4GL), p. 264

high-level language, p. 255

HIPO chart, p. 238

interpreter, p. 247

machine language, p. 247

module, p. 238

natural language, p. 266

nonprocedural language, p. 266

object code, p. 246

object-oriented programming (OOP), p. 267

pseudocode, p. 242

source code, p. 244

statement, p. 256

structure chart, p. 238

structured coding (programming), p. 244

structured techniques, p. 237

system development life cycle, p. 234

systems analysis, p. 235

systems analyst, p. 235

systems design, p. 235

text editor, p. 244

REVIEW AND DISCUSSION QUESTIONS

1. List the steps in the system development life cycle.
2. Identify two program design methods.
3. What parallels can you draw between designing and creating a software system and other endeavors?
4. What is pseudocode?
5. Identify two aspects of structured coding.
6. What do we call the output file produced by a compiler?
7. What is the difference between a compiler and an interpreter?
8. How do debuggers assist programmers?
9. What two aspects of programming do CASE tools serve?
10. Why do you suppose that, despite numerous attempts, there has never been a single, universal programming language?
11. What is the difference between software documentation and user documentation?
12. What is the difference between user documentation and reference documentation?
13. How can software documentation help save new programmers time and effort?
14. Evaluate two or three different user and reference documentation manuals for their strengths and weaknesses, then develop a profile of the ideal documentation.
15. Which programming languages allow programmers direct control over the hardware?
16. Which level of programming language is more portable?
17. Identify the two elements common to both human and computer languages.
18. Which language is considered best for writing scientific programs?
19. Which language is most commonly used for business programming?
20. What makes C a different kind of programming language?

ISSUES

1. Gerald Weinberg, an expert on programmers and programming, says that programming is a complex human activity. Programmers would agree; most feel that their work is a form of artistic expression and don't want to be disturbed when they are "creating." Business managers want programmers held accountable for their work productivity just like other employees, to avoid project delays and the application backlog. Is it possible to strike a happy medium between the two? Is it possible that tools such as 4GLs and CASE will eventually replace the programmer?

2. Despite the advances in computer hardware, many industry observers feel there have been relatively few innovations in software. They cite the spreadsheet and desktop publishing as the only applications developed during the 1980s. In addition, critics often contend that programmers design systems that are easy to create but quite often difficult or awkward to use. An example is an order entry system that asks for the customer's ZIP code, phone number, catalog number, credit card number, and item number, rather than following the more natural way people convey personal information: name, address, phone number, catalog and item number, and credit card number. In your experience, have computers made any real progress in meeting people's needs or work styles, rather than making us conform to the way they work?

3. Intellectual property or the right of ownership, is a serious ethical and legal concern in the software industry. Employers asked programmers to sign away all rights to their work while on the company payroll, while some programmers feel any code they write is an original creative expression, no different than a novel or a painting. What's more, software publishers have sued each other for copying what is termed the *look and feel* of a program. The lawsuit Lotus Development Corporation brought against two competitors for its Lotus 1-2-3 spreadsheet competitors, Paperback Software and Mirror Technologies, was decided in favor of Lotus, confirming the right to copyright look and feel. How will the advent of attorneys and litigation affect creativity and innovation in software development?

MODULE IV

Computer Hardware

The earliest computers were so large that they filled entire rooms the size of a basketball gymnasium. It was easy to think of the computer in terms of something similar to a power generating plant. Is it any wonder that people thought the world would only need a few such machines? As you know, computers today come in many sizes. Now that you understand how a computer works and have a good idea how to use one, we'll take a closer look at the physical characteristics of the machine.

Chapter 9 explores processing hardware. You'll learn about the many sizes, shapes, and varieties of computers. You'll see everything from the desktop personal computer to the newest laptops, special-purpose minicomputers, the workhorse mainframes, and the elegantly designed supercomputers.

When trying to understand computer peripherals, described in Chapter 10, one is reminded of the humorous story of the blind men trying to describe an elephant. The man who touches the elephant's tail describes something quite different than the one who touches its ear or leg. Peripherals make

it possible for people to use the processing hardware, which without peripherals is like a brain without a body. You'll learn all about input devices, which provide a variety of ways to put the CPU to work, the output devices that give us the results of that work, and the storage devices we use to save our work.

Key to understanding developments in computer hardware is the human factor, termed *ergonomics*. The people who design processing hardware and peripheral hardware are constantly searching for ways to make their products easier for people to use, and thus make the computer system itself more useful.

CHAPTER

9

Processing Hardware

Computer Power to the People

CHAPTER OUTLINE

Better, Faster, Cheaper Computers
Processing Hardware
  Computer Systems
  General-Purpose and Special-Purpose
    Computers
The Personal Computer
  The Personal Computer System
The Desktop Personal Computer
  IBM PCs and PC-Compatibles
  Types of PC-Compatibles
  The IBM Personal System/2
  The Apple Macintosh
The Laptop Personal Computer
  Portables and Laptops
  DISKbyte: The Incredible Shrinking Computer
The Workstation
  Workstation Characteristics
  DISKbyte: Reduced-Instruction-Set Computing
The Minicomputer
The Mainframe Computer
The Supercomputer
  DISKbyte: A Chilly Supercomputer
  Parallel Processing
The Ever-Evolving Computer
Ethics
  CAREERbyte: Computer Architects
Summary
Key Terms
Review and Discussion Questions
Issues

OBJECTIVES

After reading and studying this chapter, you should be able to:

1. Define processing hardware and describe the hardware components that are common to all computer systems.
2. Describe the difference between general-purpose computers and special-purpose computers.
3. Name the four types of computers.
4. Describe the different types of personal computers and how each is used.
5. Describe the characteristics and uses of the minicomputer, mainframe computer, and supercomputer and how each is used.
6. Name some of the computer pioneers and companies that have led the computer industry.

BETTER, FASTER, CHEAPER COMPUTERS

Early computers were plagued by problems associated with the glass vacuum tube. These large, fragile devices generated excessive heat and were relatively unreliable. Many scientists and engineers were at work seeking solutions that led to the silicon wizardry we call a chip. John Bardeen, William Shockley, and Walter Brattain earned a Nobel Prize for developing the transistor. A British radar engineer proposed the idea of creating an entire electronic circuit on a block of semiconductor material. Jean Hoerni, Federico Faggin, Robert Noyce, and others made significant contributions. But engineers at two companies, Texas Instruments and Intel, were largely responsible for the advances in integrated circuits and microprocessors.

Jack St. Clair Kilby
Courtesy of Texas Instruments

Ted Hoff
Courtesy of Intel Corporation

Jack St. Clair Kilby was an engineer at Texas Instruments in Dallas, an electronics firm working on what they termed "Micro Modules," or miniaturized circuits, for the military. While at work Jack says he "realized that, since all of the components could be made of a single material, they could also be . . . interconnected to form a complete circuit." This breakthrough discovery meant that the three main components in a circuit — the transistor, the resistor, and capacitor — could all be made simultaneously, or *integrated,* on a single slice of silicon. Kilby created the first integrated circuit or IC in 1958. Texas Instruments demonstrated it in a computer for the U.S. Air Force that used 587 ICs in a space of only 6.3 cubic inches. The circuitry it replaced required over 150 times as much space. And because electricity didn't have to travel as far, the circuits were faster. Clearly, ICs were practical and had great potential.

Ten years later, a microelectronics firm named Intel was starting up near Palo Alto, California, an area that has come to be known as "Silicon Valley." Marcian E. "Ted" Hoff, a Stanford University graduate and an engineer at Intel, was asked to design a set of 12 chips for electronic calculators, each of which would perform certain functions. Ted thought that was rather inefficient, so he redesigned them into four chips sharing a single processor that could be programmed to perform many tasks. This was exactly what mainframe computers did, using far more circuits. Ted's creation was named the Intel 4004 and the company often referred to it as "a computer on a chip," or what we call a *microprocessor* today. It was the first in a family of Intel microprocessor chips that led to the IBM PC. Today, there are microprocessors in cash registers, videogames, toys, automobiles, stereos, and appliances, to name just a few uses. Jack Kilby and Ted Hoff dramatically changed the world we live in. Table 9–1 depicts the evolution of microprocessors. The photo essay shown in Figure 9–1 shows the process of manufacturing integrated circuit chips.

TABLE 9–1   The evolution of microprocessor chips.

Chip Manufacturer	Micro-processor	Word Size (bits)	Clock Speed (MHz)	Used In
Mostek	6502	8	1	Apple IIe
				Atari 800
Zilog	Z-80A	8	4	Radio Shack TRS-80
				Model 1
				Epson QX-10
Intel	8086	16	4.77	Leading Edge XT
Intel	8088	16	4.77–10	IBM PC and PC/XT
				Compaq Portable
Intel	80286	16	8–12	Toshiba T1600 Laptop
				IBM PS/1
Intel	386SX	32	16–20	Zeos 386SX
				Ergo Brisk
Intel	80386	32	16–33	Compaq Deskpro 386
				IBM PS/2 Model 70-A21
Intel	80486 (I486)	32	25–50	IBM PS/2 Model 90
				AST Premium 486/25
Motorola	68000	32	8–12	Apple Macintosh
Motorola	68020	32	12–33	Macintosh LC
Motorola	68030	32	16–50	Macintosh II models
				Commodore Amiga 3000
Motorola	68040	32	25–	NeXT workstation
				Hewlett-Packard
				workstations

PROCESSING HARDWARE

Hardware is the term we use to describe the computer's physical components — the machine itself. That includes the chips, circuit boards, and components you learned about in Chapter 2 but it is also more than that. Hardware is any and all the components or physical devices — those things we can touch and feel — that make up a computer system. This chapter focuses on processing hardware: the CPU aspect of various types and sizes of computers.

Chapter 3 explained the personal computer from a hands-on perspective. Component for component, the personal computer is the equivalent of its larger predecessors. If you understand how a personal computer works, you can understand how all computers work. Whether a personal computer, a minicomputer, a mainframe, or a supercomputer, all utilize the same components.

Once upon a time, we were able to say that the larger the computer, the more powerful it was. Soon we will have the power of a supercomputer in a desktop computer. In fact, we can look at the computer industry as one long, continuous drive to create smaller, more powerful, less expensive computers. Indeed, significant advances in this respect have occurred with every passing decade.

In this chapter, we explore the world of processing hardware, from the smallest briefcase and laptop computer to the largest mainframe and supercomputer. We'll describe the differences between these various types

FIGURE 9–1   Manufacturing the chip.

Stages of integrated circuit creation (photo inserts of each stage).

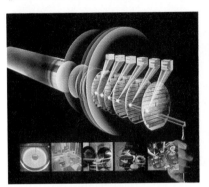

Courtesy of Texas Instruments

Crystal growing in furnace containing molten silicon.

Courtesy of Texas Instruments

Photolithography patterning process.

Courtesy of Texas Instruments

Silicon wafers baking in a diffusion furnace.

Courtesy of Texas Instruments

Etching operation.

Courtesy of Texas Instruments

Assembly bonding and packing phase.

Courtesy of Texas Instruments

of computers and explain how they are used. Along the way, we'll tell you some stories about the people who created some of them and in the process made the computer industry great. In the next chapter, we'll discuss the various kinds of peripheral hardware that work with the CPU: the monitor, input and output devices, storage devices, and so forth.

Computer Systems

Let's quickly review the computer system. A computer system is comprised of people, software, and hardware. Some computer systems have more hardware components, and thus are more complex, than others. The simplest computer system is a personal computer since it has only four or five components that take up a small space on a desktop. It's like a stereo boom box: all the components (usually excepting the printer) are contained within the system unit. The most complex computer is a mainframe, which can have hundreds of components that literally fill rooms.

Computer Components   All computer systems, regardless of their size, have these four hardware components or devices:

- A processor—the CPU—where the data input is processed according to the program instructions.
- Input/output devices or peripherals such as the keyboard and printer, which receive data from people and enter it into the computer for processing, then send it back to people so it can be used.
- Storage components or devices such as disk drives or tape drives to keep data for later use.
- Routing and control components, which direct the instructions and/or data from one component to the next, making sure each does its task properly.

General-Purpose and Special-Purpose Computers

Computers are generally classified as general-purpose or special-purpose machines. A general-purpose computer is one used for a variety of tasks without the need to modify or change it as the tasks change. A common example is a computer used in business that runs many different applications—payroll, order entry, inventory control, and computer-integrated manufacturing.

A special-purpose computer, on the other hand, is designed and used solely for one application. The machine may need to be redesigned, and certainly reprogrammed, if it is to perform another task. Special-purpose computers can be used in a factory to monitor a manufacturing process; in research to monitor seismological, meteorological, and other natural occurrences; and in the office, for dedicated word processing. Figure 9–2 shows several special-purpose computers. We'll discuss general-purpose and special-purpose computers throughout this chapter.

Types of Computers

Now that you know what all computers have in common, let's see how certain computers differ from one another. These differences often have to do with the way a particular computer is used; therefore, we can say there are different types of computers that are suited for different kinds of work or problem solving. In this chapter, we discuss these types of computers:

- *Personal computers,* including desktops, laptops, and workstations. As you already know, a personal computer is a computer system that fits on a desktop, that an individual can afford to buy for personal use, and that is intended for a single user.
- *Minicomputers,* powerful computers the size of a dishwasher or refrigerator, that permit many people to use the computer simultaneously. Minicomputers tend to be used in special-purpose applications, though they are also used as general-purpose computers.
- *Mainframes,* even more powerful and complex computer systems capable of running all the applications needed in a business or governmental agency, often with hundreds of users working simultaneously. Mainframes are usually general-purpose computers.
- *Supercomputers,* the most powerful computers, commonly used in special-purpose applications where vast amounts of computer power is required.

FIGURE 9—2   Some special-purpose computers.

Computer-controlled precision manufacturer.

Mark Segal/Click-TSW

NASA control room.

H. Mark Weidman

Turbine troubleshooting.

General Electric Research and Development Center

Electrical power and steam plant control room with touchscreen monitors.

Charles Thatcher/Click-TSW

Computerized control room of cerium (lanthanide, rare earths) plant.

Bob Thomason/Click-TSW

Since you're already familiar with the personal computer, that's where we'll begin our discussion.

1. What do we refer to when we use the term *computer hardware?*
2. What are the three characteristics of computers that the industry has continuously strived for?
3. Is it still true that the largest computers are always the most powerful?
4. All computers have what four components?
5. Name the four types of computers.

THE PERSONAL COMPUTER

In Chapter 3, you learned the personal computer basics; now we'll expand our discussion. In the early days, the personal computer was called a microcomputer, reflecting the fact that it was smaller than a mainframe or a minicomputer. Even though *microcomputer* is a perfectly acceptable term, today we use the term *personal computer* generically to refer to several different types of computers. Figure 9–3 shows two of the earliest personal computers, the Altair 8800 and the Processor Technology SOL-20. The personal computer has evolved a great deal since its introduction in the mid-1970s.

The Personal Computer System

A personal computer is a complete computer system just like its larger counterparts, the mainframe and the minicomputer; it is just more compact. The CPU, routing and control components, and storage devices such as disk drives, are usually housed in a single, compact cabinet or system unit that fits on a desktop. The video monitor, keyboard, and printer are usually separate components, connected by special cables to the system unit.

FIGURE 9–3　The Altair 8800 was a kit computer, introduced in 1975. The Processor Technology SOL-20 was designed for word processing.

Jack Rochester

Jack Rochester

There are different ways to configure personal computers. Configuration refers to the choice of various components that make up the computer system. You may recall we explained two configurations of the desktop personal computer in Chapter 3. Now we are going to study the three basic *types* of personal computers to see how each is unique. We'll find out how each came into being, then take a look at some configurations to see how they lend themselves to different uses.

Types of Personal Computers

Personal computers can be classified by *type,* or the way they are designed. There are three basic types of personal computer: the desktop, the laptop, and the workstation. Each type of personal computer shares many characteristics in common with its counterparts, but people use them in different ways. Desktop personal computers tend to be used by office workers in offices. Laptop personal computers tend to be used by businesspeople who travel in their jobs or by people who work both at an office and at home. Workstation personal computers tend to be used by scientists, engineers, programmers, and other technical specialists.

1. What is the older, less commonly used term for personal computer?
2. What components are generally considered separately when referring to a personal computer system?
3. What are the three primary types of personal computers?

MEMORY CHECK

THE DESKTOP PERSONAL COMPUTER

A **desktop personal computer** is a computer that:

- Fits on a desktop.
- Is designed for a single user.
- Is affordable for an individual to buy for personal use.

Desktop personal computers are commonly used for education, running a small business, or, in large corporations, to help office workers be more productive. Some of the more common desktop personal computers are:

- The IBM PC and PC-compatible.
- The Compaq Deskpro 386.
- The IBM PS/2.
- The Apple Macintosh.

While there are many other desktop personal computers, such as the Commodore, Atari, and Amiga, their use is not as widespread. People tend to choose a personal computer based on the software they want to use. Software developers, hoping to sell as many copies of their programs as possible, write applications for the personal computers they believe will be widely used for a long time—in other words, they try to bet on the winner. In this way, the software industry actually can make a new personal computer either a success or a failure. Let's look at the characteristics of the three most popular personal computer families.

FIGURE 9 – 4   The IBM PS/1 uses an 80286 microprocessor and is intended for home use.

Courtesy of IBM Corporation

IBM PCs and PC-Compatibles

The IBM Personal Computer or IBM PC was the most widely used — and widely copied — personal computer. Originally, IBM considered its PC a home computer. However, corporate America was quick to recognize the PC's usefulness in boosting office worker productivity. Up until this time, when office workers needed to use a computer, it was usually a mainframe or a minicomputer. However, often, not everyone who needed to work on the computer could be accommodated. In addition, applications suited to an individual worker were limited. Today, IBM offers a home computer called the PS/1, shown in Figure 9 – 4.

The IBM PC was designed as an **open architecture** machine. That means that certain aspects of its design were made available to software developers outside IBM so they could write software for the PC, thus enhancing its acceptance. In this respect, the idea was successful. Hundreds, then thousands of personal computer software programs were soon available. Even though the IBM PC was designed as a single-user computer that performed one task at a time, those tasks or applications were just what office workers wanted. Sales took off: in 1981, IBM sold 35,000 PCs; the next year, 190,000 were sold.

However, the open architecture philosophy also made it possible for other computer companies to design personal computers that worked almost identically to the IBM PC. In 1983, PC-compatibles eclipsed IBM PC sales — 670,000 to 590,000 — and IBM never caught up again.

Types of IBM PCs

The original IBM PC came with 64K bytes of memory and either one or two floppy disk drives. Personal computers didn't have hard disk drives yet; in fact, IBM offered a cassette drive with its first model! When IBM did introduce a hard disk drive model two years later, it was called the PC/XT.

In 1984, a faster PC was introduced: the IBM PC/AT, which stood for Advanced Technology. This was the last model in the IBM PC line.

FIGURE 9–5   The Compaq Deskpro 386/20 and the Compaq Portable 386, a significant technological step forward.

Courtesy of Compaq Computer Corporation

Types of PC-Compatibles

The PC-compatibles gave IBM stiff competition in the personal computer business it had created by selling nearly identical machines at far lower prices. Companies such as Compaq, Tandy/Radio Shack, Zenith, Epson, and NEC built PC-compatibles with the same types of microprocessor. They used the MS–DOS operating system, which was nearly identical to IBM's PC–DOS. This made it possible to use almost any software for the IBM PC on a PC-compatible.

These companies followed in IBM's footsteps, introducing an XT-compatible and then an AT-compatible shortly after IBM's machines debuted. But in 1986, Compaq decided to take a chance and beat IBM to market with a personal computer that used the newest and fastest microprocessor, the Intel 80386. It was called the Deskpro 386/20 and was followed shortly by the Portable 386. Figure 9–5 shows the 386 computers that made Compaq the leader in PC-compatibles. Compaq went on to set the record for reaching the Fortune 500 faster than any other company in history.

Today, the 386 microprocessor is becoming the standard for most personal computers in the office. However, Intel has already announced its successor, the 80486 (usually designated the I486), and plans to introduce the 80586 in 1995 and the 80686 in 1997. These microprocessors bring even greater speed and efficiency and represent the promise of the desktop super-computer.

Using PCs and PC-Compatibles

PCs and PC-compatibles are used in organizations of all sizes. For example, Harvey Rosenfeld bought an IBM PC for Public Citizen, Inc., Ralph Nader's public interest group in Washington, D.C. Their PC was an office time saver, allowing the staff to write press releases and legislative testimony, perform accounting tasks, and prepare mailing lists more quickly. Harvey says it also paved the way for the Nader organization to compete more effectively with other public interest groups. Today, over 80 percent of Public Citizen's employees use PC-compatibles. Word processing has replaced typewriters, hard disk drive storage has reduced the amount of paper kept in filing cabinets, and laser printing has cut their outside printing costs dramatically.

The IBM Personal System/2

In 1987, IBM launched a new line of personal computers that were technologically more sophisticated. They are called the Personal System/2 or PS/2 computers. IBM chose to make the PS/2 a **closed architecture,** meaning a competitor would need specific permission to duplicate it; this time, IBM hoped to keep the market to itself. PS/2s are smaller, sleeker machines that use the 3½ inch micro-floppy and are capable of utilizing some advanced internal components that enhance speed and make the machine more versatile.

Types of PS/2s

IBM offers many different models of PS/2s, including one that works just like the original PC, a PC/AT, and several 386 models. The 386 and 486 models have a feature called the Micro Channel Architecture, which permits connections to other larger IBM computers. (See Figure 9–6.)

A new operating system called OS/2 came with the 386 model PS/2s. It provided advantages over DOS such as utilizing more random access memory (RAM) and multitasking, and the ability to use two or more applications at the same time. It was also intended to encourage the development of entirely new applications, but few are currently available. Even so, many industry experts predict PS/2s using OS/2 will continue replacing personal computers using MS–DOS and will become the standard desktop personal computer within a few years.

FIGURE 9 – 6   IBM PS/2 386 and 486 models include the Micro Channel, which offers certain advantages to companies using other larger IBM computers.

Courtesy of IBM Corporation

Using PS/2s

Banks have traditionally used the latest computer technology to automate their own operations but First New York Bank for Business found a way to use personal computers to improve customer service. In the past, when a customer wanted to cash a check, the signature card had to be compared to verify identity. That meant looking through a card file or contacting central book-keeping, which could take as long as 30 minutes.

New York Bank for Business installed PS/2s with special graphics capabilities and software called Signet to perform this task. Now, when tellers retrieve customer account information from the computer, they see the authorized signatures appear right on the screen. The system also tells them what other signatories are permitted on the account or if two signatures are required to cash a check. The bank says the main reason customers change banks is due to bad service. Using the powerful PS/2s and Signet, they can cash a customer's check in a minute or less. Now, that's service!

The Apple Macintosh

Apple computers enjoy a strong and loyal following. The Apple II, introduced in 1977, is still in wide use in homes and schools. It was also the first personal computer to gain widespread use in business because VisiCalc, the first spreadsheet program, was written for it.

Apple is also the company that created the Macintosh. Steven Jobs conceived the idea for the Mac while visiting the Xerox Palo Alto Research Center, a think tank and laboratory for extending the frontiers of technology. There, he saw the Xerox Star, a computer with color graphics and a mouse that moved the cursor around the screen, touching graphic symbols to issue commands.

The Star was a commercial product but its $18,995 price tag posed a problem. Jobs knew that Apple had to bring this advanced technology to the public but in a more affordable version. The ideas were tested on a machine called the Lisa and finally culminated in the introduction of the Macintosh in 1984. Today, Macs are widely used by people who work in publishing and graphic design but they are used in a wide variety of business environments as well.

Types of Macintoshes

The Macintosh was designed to have a closed architecture, like the IBM PS/2 computers, allowing Apple to maintain a strict degree of quality control over software and accessories developed by other companies. The Macintosh configurations follow a pattern similar to the IBM PC. There is the Macintosh Classic, a basic personal computer without a built-in hard disk drive. Next is the Macintosh SE130, with the hard disk drive built in. Both are designed as complete systems, which means you aren't expected to add a monitor or internal electronic devices.

The Macintosh LC and II series are more modular personal computers; you can put a system together with a number of options such as color versus monochrome monitor. The LC uses the 68020 microprocessor and the IIsi, IIci and IIfx models use the more powerful 68030.

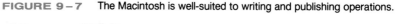

FIGURE 9−7   The Macintosh is well-suited to writing and publishing operations.

F. Bodin/Offshoot

Using the Macintosh

The Macintosh II is a popular personal computer with employees of E. I. duPont de Nemours, working at the Savannah River nuclear power plant in Aiken, South Carolina. Engineers use them for engineering design and drafting and office workers use them for traditional word processing and spreadsheet analysis. These office workers found two other interesting uses for the Macintosh. Since it lends itself to high-quality graphics, they began designing their own slides and overhead drawings for speeches and presentations. And since it has a variety of type fonts (styles), they began designing new office forms and redesigning old ones that needed updating. Not only did they end up with better forms, they saved a great deal in graphic design charges and printing costs. Figure 9−7 shows Macintosh models at work in an office.

Although there are three different types of personal computers commonly in use, there is a strong drive in business for connectivity, the ability to share data between machines of different types. Computer makers prefer to have customers buy all one brand—theirs—but certain types of machines are better suited to different tasks. In addition, different people prefer different types of computers. When many types are used throughout an office, connectivity becomes essential. We discuss this topic in more detail in Chapter 11.

MEMORY CHECK

1. What are the three most common types of personal computers?

2. What do we call a personal computer that works just like an IBM PC?

3. Name some of the personal computers we refer to when we use the term generically.

4. What is the difference between an open architecture and a closed architecture?

5. Name one or two differences between a personal computer system and a mainframe or minicomputer system.

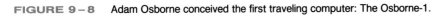

FIGURE 9–8   Adam Osborne conceived the first traveling computer: The Osborne-1.

The Computer Museum/Photographic Archives

THE LAPTOP PERSONAL COMPUTER

While desktop personal computers are designed for a desktop, the laptop is a computer you can take with you. Like a desktop computer, a **laptop** is used by a single individual but can be used in many different places; it is not confined, by its size or weight, to a desktop. It has the same components as a desktop machine but in most cases the monitor is built in. The printer is usually separate. What sets the laptop apart is that all its components, including its special monitor, are self-contained in a very small package. These factors contribute to making the laptop somewhat more expensive than a desktop. However, cost has done little to dim their popularity.

Portables and Laptops

The first traveling computer was the Osborne-1, introduced in 1981 (Figure 9–8). The Osborne was termed a portable or "luggable" computer, and it changed the way people used computers because now they could be taken to any place of work. People didn't particularly enjoy toting a 20- to 25-pound computer through airport terminals but most felt it was worth the effort to have the portability. The portable computer market took off when Compaq Computer Corporation introduced the luggable PC-compatible.

In 1982, Epson introduced a true laptop, the HX-20. It weighed only a few pounds and used the same liquid crystal display (LCD) as digital watches but could only display six lines of typing. Many others followed but it wasn't until laptops could offer an easy-to-read, full-screen display that they came into wide use.

There are many portables available today; some weigh as much as 15 pounds, while others weigh as little as 3 pounds. There are laptops so small they fit in the palm of your hand. There are laptops that fit in a briefcase, called *notebook computers*. There are laptops that can be plugged into a desktop monitor and other equipment, called *docking laptops*.

Managers and employees who travel frequently use laptops to keep in touch with their office. Sales representatives keep company information on their laptops to show prospective clients, and send electronic orders into the company computer. Writers use laptops so they can work on their manuscript no matter where they are. Let's look at the various types of laptops people use.

DISKbyte

The Incredible Shrinking Computer

Even though computers have come a long way from their gigantic beginnings, the keyboard remains the most common input device for machines large or small. Executives have shied away from using computers for just this reason, but many people who work outside of offices would use a computer quite efficiently were it not for the keyboard's awkwardness. These people include: salespeople who must collect data in the field or at the job site, for example, in grocery stores; construction site supervisors, who must evaluate drawings and reports; equipment maintenance, public utility, or safety workers; and a variety of data collectors, such as census takers.

Enter the GriDPad from Grid Systems, the first computer that uses a pen as an input device. It's designed to replace the paper business form, clipboard, and pencil. Now, instead of writing data on a sheet of paper which must be sent to the company's data entry

Courtesy of Grid Systems

department, in a single step it's computer-ready data. GriD estimates there are more than 10 million workers and professionals who could use a computer they can *write* data into.

The team that created the GriD-Pad was headed by Jeff Hawkins, who had done work in neurobiology that helped him develop software to recognize handwriting.

The 4.5-lb. computer was built around a standard PC-compatible microprocessor and uses DOS as its operating system. What makes it unique is its 10-inch diagonal display screen and the electronic pen on a tether. You can choose between graphics and business forms. You draw lines or print block letters on the screen and the computer recognizes them. If a letter is somehow illegible, the GriDPad asks you to write it again more clearly.

Tenneco Gas Transmission field engineers use the GriDPad to complete reports on their 18,000 miles of natural gas pipelines. They must constantly complete field inspection reports on corrosion, repairs, and service interruptions, and using the GriDPad allows them to transfer these reports almost instantaneously to the corporate mainframe computer. The GriD-Pad has made their work far easier to accomplish, and has eliminated paperwork in the bargain. ◼

Types of Laptops

Laptops fall into the same three general categories as desktop personal computers: PC-compatibles, IBM PS/2 and PS/2-compatibles, and the Apple Macintosh portable. Let's look briefly at each.

PC-Compatible Laptops   PC-compatible laptops are the downsized equivalent of PC-compatible desktop computers. They commonly use 3½-inch floppy disk drives and 2½-inch hard disk drives to reduce size and weight. Laptops usually do not have all the keys that a desktop computer has, such as the numeric keypad. Some laptops have a rechargeable battery pack, while others must be plugged into a wall outlet for use. A laptop with a liquid crystal display (LCD) takes less power and can run on batteries. However, a laptop with the brighter, sharper gas plasma display requires wall current. The same is often true of the more powerful laptops using the 386 microprocessor. Figure 9–9 shows several different PC-compatible laptop configurations.

FIGURE 9 – 9   Several different PC-compatible laptop configurations.

Courtesy of Dynabook Technologies

Courtesy of Kurt Strand

Gini McKain

Courtesy of Darius Corp.

PS/2-Compatible Laptops   As the business world begins using the PS/2 more widely, the market for PS/2 compatibles will grow. Since the PS/2 uses the Micro Channel architecture, it is possible to add more functions such as a cellular telephone that will transmit both voice conversations and computer data, as shown in Figure 9 – 10.

The Macintosh Portable   Macintosh users had to wait a long time for the Apple Macintosh portable, a large but technologically advanced machine. Apple substituted a track ball for the mouse and gave the new machine an *active-matrix display,* which means the monitor is basically a large integrated circuit that switches tiny points of light on and off. Figure 9 – 11 shows the Macintosh portable.

FIGURE 9 – 10   A PS/2 compatible that combines a computer and cellular telephone into one system, capable of transmitting both voice conversations and computer data.

Courtesy of Canon

FIGURE 9 – 11   The Macintosh portable.

Courtesy of Apple Computer Inc.

Using Laptops

People use laptops for many of the same tasks that they use desktops — and more. Here are a few examples.

Tom Temple, a resident of Seattle, Washington, uses his laptop to aid him in competition sailing with his boat, the *Argonaut*. On a race from Victoria, British Columbia, to Maui, Hawaii, he used his Toshiba laptop to navigate and track the other boats he was competing with. "I wouldn't go off shore without the computer," says Tom. "I can't imagine not using it. To be competitive, you have to use methods other than the old pencil and paper."

Pat Meier heads Pat Meier Associates, a public relations firm in San Francisco, California. She writes press releases for her clients and articles for journals and magazines with her laptop. She communicates with clients and members of the press electronically on a daily basis. Pat takes her Zenith laptop with her wherever she goes, from home to the office and whenever she travels.

Once, in Las Vegas, it saved her from near disaster. It was the day before a trade show when her client suddenly announced they would be unveiling a new product. Pat had to have a press release, and she had to have it now. She quickly wrote it on her laptop in her hotel room and sent it via electronic mail to her office. There, her editorial assistant formatted it on the proper stationery, printed it on the laser printer, then sent it via facsimile back to Pat. The client made a few corrections and approved it. Pat phoned in the corrections. Her assistant printed out the final, then had it duplicated and shipped in time for the trade show opening the next day. "That's why I never leave home without my laptop," says Pat, who toted her Zenith through Europe so she could keep a travelogue of her vacation.

The laptop is just one more step forward in the computer industry's drive to create better, smaller computers. Laptops have made working with computers much easier for businesspeople. Now it is possible to transfer the data stored in your desktop to a laptop. And when you return, all the data on the laptop can be transferred back to the desktop machine. It may not be long before we see the desktop computer replaced altogether by desktop docks for our laptops.

1. What's the main difference between a desktop and a laptop?

2. What were the first traveling computers called?

3. What was the most important factor in making laptops popular?

4. Name two factors that make it necessary to run a laptop on wall current instead of a battery.

5. Name at least two different types of laptop monitors.

MEMORY CHECK

THE WORKSTATION

A **workstation,** like its personal computer counterpart, is a computer that fits on a desktop. It is most commonly used by a single individual but it may also be shared among users. The workstation combines the ease of use and convenience of a personal computer with some of the power and functions of larger computers. Workstations differ in costing more than most individuals can afford for personal use.

Workstation Characteristics

Workstations have three main characteristics: (1) they use powerful microprocessors, often with special operating system software and commonly with special application software; (2) they have an easy-to-use interface; and (3) they are capable of multitasking. While these three characteristics used to be unique to workstations, they are being adapted to the more powerful 386 and 486 personal computers over time. Let's take a closer look at each characteristic.

The Microprocessor   In the 1980s, four companies became well known for their workstations: Sun Microsystems, Hewlett-Packard, Apollo Computer (now part of H-P), and Digital Equipment Corporation. These companies manufacture their own proprietary microprocessors. Proprietary means the chip is made exclusively by or for a certain manufacturer. In fact, Hewlett-Packard pioneered ultrapowerful microprocessors when it created the *superchip* in 1981. This chip was so complex that it took a team of engineers 18 months to design it.

Similarly, Sun developed its own SPARC microprocessor chip for its workstations. Then, contrary to prevailing industry practices, Sun decided to make the SPARC chip nonproprietary. Sun offered other workstation makers the opportunity to license the chip for use. The idea was to create a Sun-compatible standard, just as MS–DOS is a standard. Another emerging standard is based on the RISC microprocessor (see the DISKbyte titled Reduced-Instruction-Set Computing on page 299).

The Interface   Workstations were the first computers to make the friendly user interface of prime importance. The interface was intended to make it as easy as possible for users to get their work done, rather than having to spend time manipulating the computer system. A Datapro report published in 1981 said, "the integrated workstation is meant to represent a natural technological extension of a person's mind. (It) comes the closest to setting the pace for future information systems."[1]

Multitasking   You learned about multitasking—the ability of the computer to run two or more applications at the same time—in Chapter 7. Figure 9–12 shows a video display on a NeXT workstation computer with several applications running concurrently. The workstation also makes it possible to have a small multiuser computer that can be shared by others. These were significant benefits that, over time, have led to new and innovative ways for people to utilize computers.

FIGURE 9–12   The NeXT workstation video display showing multitasking.

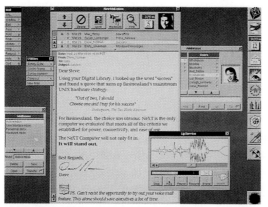

Courtesy of NeXT, Inc.

---

[1] "All about Executive and Professional Workstations," © 1981 Datapro Research Corp., p. 101.

Types of Workstations

Workstations were first used by engineers for computer-aided design (CAD). But in the late 1970s, Allen Michels saw an emerging need among office workers and business executives for a computer more powerful than a personal computer, with many different software functions. He founded Convergent Technologies, based in Silicon Valley, and introduced the Integrated Work Station in 1979. Today, workstations are designed for three markets: scientific and engineering, office automation, and education.

Scientific and Engineering Workstations   Workstations are used to design everything from gears and pulleys to microchips and telephone networks. Workstations not only permit drawing and designing in two and three dimensions, but testing and simulation as well: an aircraft designer can create a computer simulation to test wind shear, or an electrical engineer can test a new chip design in a simulated circuit. Models of microscopic molecules can be viewed in three dimensions, rotated, and even animated using graphics *superworkstations*. Figure 9–13 shows such a workstation.

Office Automation Workstations   Workstations are used for a variety of tasks throughout the office. People who perform similar jobs, or who perform tasks in cooperative work groups, often use personal computers and workstations that are connected to one another. Senior management and executives use workstations with special executive information systems software to keep their fingers on the company's pulse. Doctors often have a workstation in their office that is connected to the hospital where they practice. When a patient needs to be admitted, the file and proper forms can be transmitted to the hospital admissions office in a matter of seconds, shortening the paperwork process and assuring that the patient obtains speedy and proper care.

FIGURE 9–13   A graphic designer's workstation.

Courtesy of Hewlett-Packard Company

Educational Workstations   Many colleges and universities make workstations available for engineering students, or for general use with a variety of personal computers in computing labs. Steve Jobs, who co-founded Apple and created the Macintosh, introduced the first personal workstation for students, the NeXT Computer System. Although it is more expensive than a personal computer, it offers many more features. The NeXT has highly detailed graphics, sound, and even music. It has many built-in applications and special tools such as a library containing a dictionary, a thesaurus, a book of famous quotations, the works of William Shakespeare, and more.

From the beginning, Allen Michels envisioned a workstation that would integrate many tasks and functions in an easy-to-use computer. This would come about through the marriage of a variety of hardware and software technologies, combined with new insights into **ergonomics,** the study of how to create safety, comfort, and ease of use for people who use machines such as computers. As computer engineers learn more about how we think and work, workstations will just keep getting more useful.

Using Workstations

Astrophysicists at the Harvard-Smithsonian Center for Astrophysics use Sun Microsystems workstations for their engineering work. They routinely sketch graphs and diagrams on the screen using computer-aided drafting software, as well as sophisticated calculation software to test mathematical equations. They also exchange ideas and information with each other in electronic messages. One project they have worked on in cooperation with NASA is the Advanced X-Ray Astrophysic Facility. It is an observatory in space that will measure cosmic X-rays, which are invisible on earth. The astrophysicists hope that the information provided will help them understand better how the universe was formed and what its eventual fate will be.

The Sun workstation performed an additionally important task: helping gather visual and textual information into a comprehensive report for NASA to explain how an X-ray telescope would function aboard the observatory. Using electronic publishing software, they combined graphics screens, mathematical equations, and textual explanations into a document that took just six hours to prepare. Previously, it would have taken two days. Equally important, the report was so professionally prepared that it was much easier for the NASA people to understand.

While most workstation applications are oriented to science and engineering, here is one that is designed for creative people. The William Morris Agency has installed an "interpersonal network" of NeXT workstations at its offices in Beverly Hills, New York, London, and Nashville. William Morris's clients are people in the entertainment business, including motion picture and television stars, directors, writers, producers, news anchors, musical performers, and recording artists. It's important that the agents — creative but very busy people — share ideas and information throughout the organization. The NeXT workstation was chosen because its graphical interface and advanced design makes using the database and exchanging electronic messages from one workstation to another extremely easy. The agents can send each other client information and look at talent profiles on the screen. In addition, using a special application called "Who's Calling?", they can schedule

DISKbyte

Reduced-Instruction-Set Computing

Today, we have personal computers that are based on many different microprocessors and operating systems. Yet one thing almost all microprocessors have in common is the manner in which they process instructions. **Complex instruction-set-computing (CISC)** is a microprocessor or CPU architecture and operating system design that allows it to recognize 100 or more instructions, enough to carry out most computations. Most people feel CISC computers are adequate for our computing needs; besides, all our application software is based on the CISC instruction set and operating system. Do we need yet another CPU architecture? Proponents of reduced-instruction-set computing, or RISC, seem to think so.

Reduced-instruction-set computing (RISC) is a microprocessor or CPU architecture that uses a condensed set of instructions for its operating system. RISC microprocessors have the advantage of simplicity and elegance over CISC microprocessors. They are also extremely fast. The increased performance and lower price of RISC microprocessors has had a profound effect on the computer industry, prompting companies such as IBM to introduce an entire line of RISC workstations.

However, older technologies are kept alive by the huge investments individuals and companies have already made in them. Users who have invested heavily in CISC, for example, are reluctant to purchase incompatible RISC machines. The abundance of existing software for CISC machines is also a factor in the continuing support of that technology. Many questions concerning the RISC versus CISC remain unanswered.

The debate over reduced-instruction-set computing versus complex-instruction-set computing typically focuses on which architecture is better, rather than which architecture best handles a specific set of problems. RISC is fast; but simple applications such as word processing do not require greater speed. CISC computers offer a wide diversity of applications; but these applications are often constrained by fundamental limitations in the CPU (or microprocessor) design. RISC is well suited for applications requiring great power, complexity, and diversity such as computer-aided design (CAD).

Both architectures probably have a role in today's computing environment. Yet, as with any decision regarding the "best" computer to purchase, the first criterion is the software application.

meetings with other agents and clients and track previous phone calls. They can also work with multimedia project material that includes text, visual images (including full-motion video), and high-fidelity stereo sound recordings. When completed, the system will have 250 NeXT workstations in five countries.

MEMORY CHECK

1. What is the primary difference between a personal computer and a workstation?

2. How were the first workstations used?

3. What are the three markets or uses for workstations?

4. Name two ways workstations can be used in the office.

5. What is the study of human factors in the use of computers called?

THE MINICOMPUTER

The minicomputer, or mini, is a versatile special- or general-purpose computer designed so that many people can use it at the same time. Minis operate in ordinary indoor environments; some require air conditioning while others do not. Minis also can operate in less hospitable places such as on ships and planes, in manufacturing shops, and so on. Minis cost more than personal computers, typically $20,000 to $500,000, but they are also more powerful. Up to 200 people can use the minicomputer at the same time.

Like all computers, the minicomputer is designed as a system. CPUs, terminals, printers, and storage devices can be purchased separately. Mini systems are more mobile, easier to set up and install, and more versatile than mainframes. It is common to see a minicomputer system combined with specialized equipment and peripherals and designed to perform a specific task. These are called original equipment manufacturer or OEM systems, and are used in publishing, brokerage houses, hospitals, manufacturing, and hundreds of other ways.

A notable event in computer history occurred on a sunny fall day in 1957—the founding of Digital Equipment Corporation by Kenneth H. Olsen in an abandoned woolen mill in Maynard, Massachusetts. He created the minicomputer and grew a company that is the second largest computer company in the world, with annual revenues in excess of $12 billion. Olsen has helped make computer history; in 1986, *Fortune* magazine featured him on the cover as "the most successful entrepreneur in history."[2]

Types of Minicomputers

In 1959, Digital introduced the PDP-1 (for Programmed Data Processor). At a time when typical computer systems sold for over $1 million, the PDP-1's price tag of $120,000 shocked the industry. Of course, it was not able to perform all the tasks of a mainframe but it was a true computer nonetheless. It was followed by several other PDPs, the last of which, the PDP-11, led to the VAX, which is now the most widely used family of minicomputers in the world.

The VAX, introduced in 1975, was a success. Digital ensured its success by making it possible to connect together all computers in the VAX family and some from the PDP family as well. This was done through special circuits that also make it possible to link many other computers, from Apples to IBMs, to the VAX. This strategy, coupled with a wide variety of minis from the desktop MicroVAX to the supermini, as well as its own VAX 9000 mainframe computer, has given Digital an advantage in the computer market. Figure 9–14 shows a Digital minicomputer system.

Today, there are many minicomputer makers such as Data General, which was started by ex-Digital employees. Some, such as Prime Computer, specialize in scientific and engineering systems. Banks use special Tandem "nonstop" systems with two complete CPUs, so that if one fails, the other immediately takes over. Wang has created entire office automation minicomputer systems. IBM, best known for its mainframes, introduced a mini called the AS/400 in 1988, which is widely used in business.

---

[2] *Fortune,* October 27, 1986, vol. 114, no. 9, p. 24.

FIGURE 9–14   A Digital minicomputer; this cabinet houses the CPU.

Courtesy of Digital Equipment Corporation

Using Minis

Minis are often used as small-business computers. Companies whose data storage and processing needs are smaller than those of large banks or government agencies find they can do the job with one or perhaps a few minis. In these situations, the minicomputer works much like a mainframe, although the volume of usage is lower. Company sales, inventory, and financial records are stored on disks. Terminals give people access to the data, and specially designed software allows executives to translate data into reports, charts, and graphs.

Special-purpose minis can be used in places mainframes would find inhospitable. One such use is atop Mount Kilauea in Hawaii. The Hawaiian Volcano Observatory uses two minis to collect and analyze volcanic and seismic data. In this location, 4,000 feet above sea level, hundreds of tiny earthquakes occur daily as a result of volcanic activity.

The minis collect data from dozens of sensors throughout the active areas of the island at the rate of 100 samples per second. The minis then analyze the data showing the effects of ground movement, temperature changes, electromagnetic variations, gravitational fields, and the chemistry of volcanic gases and lava. Telecommunication links allow the resident geologists to share the data they collect with other geological research stations all over the world. Networking with other minis allows this research site to play a vital part in understanding and predicting geologic events in the Pacific.

The mini has become a valuable, versatile computing resource over the years. The extremely powerful **superminicomputer,** a supercomputerlike mini, is used in science research. Even though the trend is toward smaller computers, minis will be around for a long time.

1. Name two ways the minicomputer is different from the mainframe.
2. What is a minicomputer that is fitted with special devices to perform a specific task called?
3. Who is considered the creator of the minicomputer?
4. What is the most successful minicomputer family called?
5. Describe several ways in which the minicomputer is versatile.

THE MAINFRAME COMPUTER

The mainframe is the largest general-purpose computer. It is designed to be used by hundreds — even thousands — of people. Mainframes generally cost at least $700,000 and must be housed in special rooms where temperature and humidity are carefully maintained within certain limits. Most mainframes are used when there is continual, heavy processing and many users.

Mainframes consist of the basic building blocks of a computer system: the CPU, various I/O devices, and external memory. The main difference is that these building blocks are considerably larger than, say, a personal computer's. In some cases, mainframes are so large that there is more than one CPU. There might be a small cluster of CPU cabinets, forming a very powerful mainframe that requires so much main memory that it, too, takes several cabinets to house. In almost all mainframe systems, the controller is in a separate cabinet as well. Figure 9–15 shows a mainframe system.

An extensive array of peripheral equipment is connected to the mainframe: terminals, a variety of printers, many different kinds of storage devices, and communications equipment. A mainframe uses the same peripherals you

FIGURE 9–15 An IBM mainframe system.

Courtesy of IBM Corporation

will find with a minicomputer or a personal computer. What sets the mainframe apart from other types of computers is its powerful CPU, its vast memory and storage capabilities, and the number of terminals that can be connected. For example, Pillsbury, the food products company with headquarters in Minneapolis, has built an entire underground building the size of a football field to house its mainframe computer equipment.

Types of Mainframes

In Chapter 2, you learned that John Atanasoff built the Atanasoff-Berry Computer or ABC, the first electronic digital computer. It was a special-purpose computer, designed for a single task: solving simultaneous differential equations. But the ABC was also the basis for ENIAC, the world's first electronic, digital, general-purpose computer.

Most mainframe computers are general-purpose machines. One of the earliest and most effective uses of general-purpose computers in business was the Prudential Insurance Company's application of ENIAC's descendant, the UNIVAC computer system. The enormous amount of accounting Prudential required, together with the need to calculate complex actuarial tables for risks and premiums, gave the UNIVAC just the test it needed to prove its usefulness. It wasn't long before other large American corporations were clamoring for their own computers.

Today, general-purpose computers play a major role in virtually every aspect of business and organizational life. IBM, formed by Thomas J. Watson, Sr., in 1914, is largely responsible for this. IBM devised many accounting, calculating, and automatic tabulating machines and the first successful electric typewriter.

After World War II, Tom Watson, Jr., joined his father in the firm and was appointed president after his father's death. Watson, Jr., was mostly responsible for IBM's aggressive pursuit of the computer market. "By 1958, 1959," he said, "I realized that I had water in relatively large quantities and I had a dry sponge for a market. And if I could just learn to introduce that water into the sponge in acceptable form, there was no limit to where this business could go."[3] In 1964, after investing four years and $5 billion, IBM introduced the System/360 mainframe computer. It became the most popular mainframe in computer history, and the standard for the industry. It was named the 360 because a perfect circle has 360 degrees. Figure 9–16 shows the IBM 360.

Using Mainframes

In the past, mainframes were used in large companies to perform nearly all computing tasks. As the company grew or as new applications were added, more CPU power or terminals were added to the system. In the 1970s, many companies learned that it was less expensive and often more efficient to install a minicomputer in a department or division than to expand the mainframe. In the 1980s, companies learned this same lesson again with personal computers and workstations.

---

[3] Jack B. Rochester, "An Interview: Thomas J. Watson, Jr.," *Computerworld,* June 13, 1983.

FIGURE 9–16   The IBM 360: Computing in the round.

Courtesy of IBM Corporation

As a result of these changes, computers are assuming different roles in the 1990s. Now, the mainframe is commonly used for applications that affect the entire company, such as accounting or maintaining the corporate database. Minicomputers are used as departmental systems in marketing or manufacturing. Workstations and personal computers are used by individuals or small work groups within departments. The notion that a single computer can satisfy an entire company's needs has been overturned. In the same way that a carpenter or a mechanic chooses the right tool for the job, there are a variety of computers to choose from.

Whitbread & Company PLC is a large English food and drink company. It brews Whitbread beer, distills Beefeater's gin, operates 6,000 pubs, and owns Pizza Huts, TGI Fridays, as well as a number of hotels and inns. In 1983, Whitbread reorganized 10 divisions into 4: breweries, trading, inns, and retail. Ten large mainframe data processing centers were reduced to two, and Whitbread began installing new computer systems.

Whitbread's five breweries each has its own computer system for manufacturing. The pubs have a special terminal used to place orders with the mainframe computer and to file weekly sales reports to the bank. At London headquarters, a manager in the inns division can use a personal computer connected to the centralized mainframe database to learn which inn had the highest sales on, say, Fridays and Saturdays. Whitbread has diversified its computer facilities and in the process has gained what it calls *flexible systems* that help the company solve problems — not create new ones.

MEMORY CHECK

1. What special conditions do large mainframe installations require?
2. In terms of its components, what makes a mainframe different?
3. What was the first general-purpose computer called?
4. What company developed the System/360, the most successful mainframe computer?
5. How are computers being used differently in the 1990s?

FIGURE 9–17   A Cray-2 supercomputer.

Paul Shambroom/Courtesy of Cray Research, Inc.

THE SUPERCOMPUTER

A supercomputer is a very, very fast special-purpose computer designed to perform highly sophisticated or complex scientific calculations. Supercomputers are large and quite expensive. They start at around $5 million and can cost as much as $20 million. They often contain state-of-the-art circuitry and require special installation because of their complexity, power requirements, and the need for their own specially designed cooling systems. Figure 9–17 shows a supercomputer.

Types of Supercomputers

In 1957, William Norris and some other engineers formed a new company, Control Data Corporation in Minneapolis, to build supercomputers. In 1963, CDC introduced what was then the most powerful computer on earth, the CDC 6600. It was designed by a man named Semour Cray.

Seymour Cray is probably the most brilliant but eccentric supercomputer architect of our times. He left CDC in 1972 to start Cray Research, Inc., and built his own supercomputer. Cray likes to wear cowboy boots and string ties and is extremely reclusive. He has a secret lab that he often won't leave for weeks at a time.

Each Cray computer has its own installation platform, plus thousands of dollars worth of air-conditioning plumbing. It must be tested for months before it can be used. Once ready, the entire setup is put in a semitrailer truck and moved to the site. Each Cray comes complete with two engineers to maintain it.

Today, Cray Research is the leading supercomputer maker and CDC is no longer in the supercomputer business. IBM has entered the market, and Japan's Fujitsu is a major competitor. Seymour Cray has gone on to form Cray Computer Corporation, where he and a team of engineers are building the next-generation supercomputer, the Cray-3. The market for supercomputers has grown beyond the research laboratory, as many businesses have found uses for supercomputers as well.

DISKbyte

A Chilly Supercomputer

In 1962, an English computer scientist named Brian Josephson came up with an idea for a way to make electronic circuits work faster. The circuit, called the Josephson Junction, takes advantage of a weird property electrons have when they get very cold: They move through circuits much faster than they ordinarily would. The Josephson Junction is similar to an integrated circuit but with a difference: It is cooled to 4 degrees above absolute zero. At this *superconducting* temperature, the circuit uses one ten-thousandth the energy of a regular circuit and operates at speeds 10 to 100 times faster than the fastest computer in existence. Fujitsu has built logic circuits using Josephson Junctions. Research is underway at IBM to create a Josephson supercomputer the size of a baseball that will consume no more electricity than a 60-watt light bulb.

Using Supercomputers

Supercomputers are known best for their sheer power and massive storage capabilities. Their task is to process large, complex problems at high speed. All the other computers we've discussed in this chapter operate at speeds measured in millions of *instructions* per second; a supercomputer performs billions of *operations* per second. An **operation** is a set of instructions or a programming statement. With supercomputers, an operation is often a complex mathematical equation called a *floating point operation*. Therefore, we often refer to supercomputer performance in FLOPS, for floating point operations per second. A supercomputer that can perform at 2 billion floating point operations per second is referred to as having 2 gigaflops performance. To give you an idea how fast a supercomputer is, compare how long it took each of the following computers to perform a particular calculation:

- IBM PC: 35 hours.
- VAX mini: 7 seconds.
- Cray: less than 2 seconds.

Supercomputers are often used to solve complex mathematical problems; for example, calculating a prime number (one that is divisible only by 1 and itself), or the distance between planets. But computers permit turning many other problems into numbers, such as molecular modeling, geographic modeling, and image processing.

A Cray X-MP supercomputer was used to help make a movie called *The Last Starfighter*. Computer animation isn't new but using the X-MP added a whole new dimension of sophistication. Its most remarkable accomplishment was creating the entire bridge of the alien's starship, complete with animated aliens walking around next to real actors. Because the Cray could process the image in incredibly fine detail, the average viewer would think it looked absolutely real. The X-MP allowed animators to make illusion as convincing as reality itself.

FIGURE 9–18   The Connection Machine. Each red LED represents a CPU.

Courtesy of Thinking Machine Corporation

Parallel Processing

Over the past few years, a new kind of supercomputer has emerged. Instead of having a single powerful CPU, this machine has many microprocessors working together so that many programs, operations, or transactions can be processed simultaneously. This is called **parallel processing.** One of the first commercial successes is the Connection Machine, created by MIT graduate Danny Hillis. It has 65,096 microprocessors all working together. The Connection Machine was used to simulate the airflow around helicopter blades, critical to the aircraft's stability, at United Technologies. It was able to perform the computations five to six times faster than the most powerful Cray supercomputer. Figure 9–18 shows the Connection Machine. Even more powerful parallel processor computers are being developed, using hundreds of thousands of microprocessors. This is termed *massively parallel processing.*

Supercomputer research has been on the forefront of new computer technology for some time. Even so, Neil Lincoln, who worked with Seymour Cray designing supercomputers at CDC, once defined a supercomputer as "a machine that is one generation behind the problems it is asked to solve." That problem, at least in processing hardware, remains striving to create ever smaller, faster, cheaper computers.

1. How does the supercomputer differ from the general-purpose mainframe computer?
2. Who is the foremost supercomputer architect?
3. What are the two main characteristics of the supercomputer?
4. How does a supercomputer's speed compare to that of other computers?
5. What types of processing does a supercomputer like the Connection Machine perform?

MEMORY CHECK

THE EVER–EVOLVING COMPUTER

The human race doubled its technological knowledge — which is another way of saying the creation of new technology tools — from the year A.D. 1 to the year 1750. But then, in just 150 years — by 1900 — that technological knowledge doubled again, and once again between 1900 and 1950. Yet in just the past 50 years, we have made more progress than in the preceding 10,000.

The computer is part of our expanding technological knowledge but it is also a tool used to advance our technological knowledge. One reason is because the computer, unlike a plow or an airplane, can be used for many different things. Back in the 1940s and 1950s, no one imagined we would have computers in wristwatches or cash registers. No other technology has grown so fast, nor provided us with so many benefits, as the computer.

It's easy to look at a computer and perceive only its external cabinetry, the keyboard, the monitor screen, without comprehending all the ingenuity that went into creating a successful, functional computer system. Sometimes it's easy to slip into thinking about computers, or even cars or toaster ovens, as machines that somehow simply exist. Yet each was devised or developed by people. Someone saw a problem, then sat down and figured out a way to solve it.

The computer industry has produced some of America's greatest thinkers, entrepreneurs, corporate leaders, and — yes, mavericks. They share a vision centered on three goals: better, faster, cheaper computers. In the social context, the purpose is to provide more computers for people to use, and in the process, improve the quality of life for all.

Computers have the power to be great tools of democracy. St. John said "The truth shall make you free," and gaining access to knowledge and information is essential to learning the truth. The Japanese government has launched a program to make computers as common as pay telephones so that its citizenry can be better informed. The introduction of personal computers in the Soviet Union has played a significant role in that country's moving toward democracy. Indeed, one of the world's most popular computer games, Tetris, was created by a Russian. In the United States, many colleges and universities are developing exciting new ways to integrate personal computers with traditional education. Truly, the personal computer has given "power to the people."

ETHICS

How can we determine when computers are being used ethically? Is it ethical to create nuclear missiles or nuclear power plants? Is it ethical to use computers in business to outmaneuver or outperform a competitor? Is it ethical to break into or disable a computer system that belongs to someone else, regardless of the reason?

In the 17th century, Dutch factory workers kicked their wooden clog shoes, called *sabots*, into factory machines, causing them to break down. This act became known as *sabotage*. In 1987, a young woman named Katya Komisaruk broke into the NAVSTAR satellite control computer complex at Vandenberg Air Force Base, California, and sabotaged a $1.2 million mainframe computer. "I used my crowbar to haul out all the chips," she said. "I piled them on the floor, jumped up and down and did a dance over them." A peace activist, Komisaruk claimed the act was an expression of her commitment to help the United States avoid nuclear war.

The NAVSTAR computer serves several purposes. In addition to pinpointing the locations of Soviet missile silos, it is used by aviators and sailors as a navigation system to plot their courses. At her trial, Komisaruk's defense was that she destroyed the computer to prevent a greater crime. "It's better to destroy a few machines than to let those machines destroy millions of people," she claimed. The prosecuting attorney responded by saying, "That's like calling a typewriter a weapon of destruction because it can be used to write the attack order." The judge sentenced Komisaruk to five years in prison and ordered her to pay $500,000 in restitution for the computer. She considered her actions ethical and moral, intended to save lives. Yet, what if she had cost the lives of people on board an airplane or a ship?

CAREERbyte

Computer Architects

What does it take to design a computer? First of all, a degree in electrical engineering helps. Second, a curiosity about how tiny, invisible electrons whisk here and there, at the speed of light, on a slice of silicon. And third, a lot of energy. But the sense of accomplishment is incredible, akin to designing and building a skyscraper. Here are a few examples.

Photo by Tresca

A Personal Computer

Lee Felsenstein designed an innovative computer that was not only a success but stood for his political beliefs as well. It was the Osborne-1, the first portable computer. It was made with inexpensive parts, came with software so it was ready to use, and could be carried from place to place. When he first encountered computers, Felsenstein thought they were tools of the "Establishment." The Osborne-1 gave him the chance to design a "Volkscomputer," or people's computer. When it was introduced in 1981, the Osborne-1 was a success but it was gradually supplanted by the IBM PC and PC-compatibles.

Today, Lee Felsenstein is applying his expertise—and his politics—to the issue of robots.

Courtesy of Convex Computer

A Mini

When Data General needed a new superminicomputer, the man Tom West wanted for the job was Steve Wallach. Wallach was a seasoned engineer who had designed several computers but none that had made it into production—"got out the door," as they say. He was also a perfectionist, sure of what a computer system should be like. So when he was first asked to design the Data General Eclipse MV-8000, he refused. He wanted assurance that it would get out the door. It took a meeting with Edson deCastro, Data General's president, to convince him. "Are you sure? If we do this, you won't cancel on us? You'll leave us alone?" DeCastro answered, "That's what I want." Wallach designed the Eclipse and Tracy Kidder wrote a Pulitzer Prize–winning book about it, *The Soul of a New Machine*. Today, Wallach heads his own supermini company, Convex Computer.

Courtesy of Andor Systems

A Mainframe

When Gene Amdahl was in college, he was given an assignment to solve a problem. In the process, he ended up designing his own computer, the Wisconsin Integrally Synchronized Computer, which was more sophisticated than anything IBM had yet produced. He joined IBM in 1952 as a chief engineer, and designed several of the company's most successful computers, including the IBM System/360 discussed in this chapter. In 1970, Amdahl started his first computer company, Amdahl Corp., the first mainframe plug-compatible manufacturer (PCM). Then, a decade later, he started Trilogy, a company with a revolutionary design for a new circuit chip. When it turned out that Amdahl was too far ahead of his time, he promptly started Andor Systems and, in 1989, created a desk-size computer that—you guessed it—works just like an IBM mainframe.

Does a career designing computers or computer-controlled devices interest you? If so, you can rest assured there is a career awaiting you.

SUMMARY

1. *Define processing hardware and describe the hardware components that are common to all computer systems.* Processing hardware is that part of the computer where the CPU resides. All computer systems have a processor, or CPU, input and output devices or peripherals, storage devices, and routing and control components.

2. *Describe the difference between general-purpose computers and special-purpose computers.* A general-purpose computer is one that can be used for many different tasks without the need to modify or change it each time. General-purpose computers are commonly used in business. A special-purpose computer is one designed to perform a single task and no other. It may be redesigned or reprogrammed for another application, however. Special-purpose computers may be used for process control or monitoring purposes.

3. *Name the four types of computers.* There are four major types of processing hardware: personal computers, minicomputers, mainframe computers, and supercomputers. If you understand how a personal computer works, you can understand how other types of processing hardware works.

4. *Describe the different types of personal computers and how each is used.* There are three types of personal computers: desktop personal computers, laptops, and workstations. Desktop personal computers fit on a desktop, are affordable for an individual, and are designed for a single user. Laptops travel with you and are designed for single users. Workstations are often too expensive for individual purchase, but can be shared by several users. They are also capable of multitasking.

5. *Describe the characteristics and uses of the minicomputer, mainframe computer, and supercomputer and how each is used.* Minicomputers can be used in a wide variety of indoor and outdoor locations. Mainframes are large computers, commonly used in business. Like minis, they can have a vast array of peripheral equipment connected to them.

Supercomputers, unlike general-purpose minis and mainframes, are special-purpose computers commonly used in scientific applications. Newer, more powerful parallel processing supercomputers are becoming popular.

6. *Name some of the computer pioneers and companies that have led the computer industry.* IBM is credited with developing the most widely used personal computer, the IBM Personal Computer. Today, companies such as Compaq, Zenith, Epson, and Tandy dominate the PC-compatible market. Apple, under the guidance of Steve Jobs, introduced several of the most popular personal computers such as the Apple II and the Macintosh. Some of the most popular laptop computers are made by Toshiba and Zenith. Some of the most popular workstations are made by Sun Microsystems and Hewlett-Packard.

Kenneth H. Olsen invented the minicomputer and started Digital Equipment Corporation, the world's second largest computer company. IBM is the leading mainframe supplier and rose to a position of preeminence in computers under the leadership of Thomas J. Watson, Jr. Seymour Cray is the most respected supercomputers designer and Cray Research, the company he founded, is the leading company in the field.

KEY TERMS

closed architecture, p. 288

complex-instruction-set computing (CISC), p. 299

desktop personal computer, p. 285

ergonomics, p. 298

laptop, p. 291

open architecture, p. 286

operation, p. 306

parallel processing, p. 307

reduced-instruction-set computing (RISC), p. 299

superminicomputer, p. 301

workstation, p. 295

REVIEW AND DISCUSSION QUESTIONS

1. How have advances in integrated circuits given us better, faster, less expensive computers?

2. How does the number and complexity of hardware components affect the type of computer system?

3. Name the different types of computers.

4. Personal computers continue to grow more powerful; when they are as powerful as large computers, what will happen to mainframe industry leaders such as IBM, or minicomputer industry leaders such as Digital?

5. Describe the different ways in which you would use the three types of personal computers.

6. Describe three of the more common desktop personal computers.

7. Describe how you felt about computers used in business and government before you began using a personal computer, compared to how you feel about computers now.

8. Name an open architecture and a closed architecture computer. What are the advantages and/or disadvantages to each?

9. What are the two major differences between a laptop and a desktop?

10. What are three of the most important characteristics of a workstation?

11. Name a proprietary and a nonproprietary microprocessor standard.

12. What is the acronym for a very fast microprocessor?

13. What are the three primary uses for workstations?

14. What makes the minicomputer different from the personal computer?

15. Making better, faster, less expensive computers has put the minicomputer and mainframe computer industry at risk. Clearly, not everyone can survive in the business. What do you think this will mean to these firms' thousands of users?

16. What makes the mainframe different from the personal computer?

17. What is the difference between a general-purpose and a special-purpose computer? Name one of each.

18. Who is considered the leading supercomputer architect?

19. What do you think about the fact that most supercomputers are used for secret government research, for example, weapons systems?

20. What is the newer kind of supercomputing called?

ISSUES

1. How do you feel about the fact that there are so many different standards for personal computers? If you buy a PC-compatible, you can't use software created for the Macintosh. If you buy a PS/2 type of machine, you are limited in the number of applications available. Why do computer makers create differing standards? From your perspective, what are the advantages and disadvantages of each? Which standard would you choose? Should all computer makers be required to adopt the same standard?

2. The business press is prone to sensationalize downturns in the computer industry. Over the years, companies such as IBM or Digital Equipment Corporation occasionally have a poor quarter or perform less well than expected. The press tends to exaggerate this news, suggesting the demise of the mainframe or mini, or that the company may be about to go out of business. For instance, in 1989, a front-page story in a leading business newspaper said, "Today, Digital is nearly dead in the water." What do you think of this kind of reporting? What are its effects on stockholders? Ask your economics professor what it means when a multibillion dollar company has a flat quarter, and try to assess the real impact.

3. You walk into a friend's room or a colleague's office. The personal computer is on but no one is around. On the screen is the text of something that appears to be extremely personal. You're curious; should you read it or not? You glance at it, not sure; the last sentence on the screen says something that makes you want to read what follows. That means touching the keyboard to scroll the screen up. What if you touch the computer? What if you don't? Is reading the screen ethical, whereas touching the keyboard to read more unethical? Is there any difference between the two?

CHAPTER

10

Peripheral Hardware

Input, Output, and Storage Devices

CHAPTER OUTLINE

Herman Hollerith and the First I/O Device
Peripheral Devices
  The Interface
Input
  Input Devices
  DISKbyte: Great Moments in I/O History
  Input Devices for the Disabled
Output
  Types of Computer Output
  Output Devices
  The Video Monitor
  Printers
  Computer-to-Machine Output
  DISKbyte: Cyberspace: The Ultimate I/O?
  Voice Output
Storage
  Direct Access Storage Devices
  Sequential Access Storage Devices
  DISKbyte: CD–ROM: The New Papyrus
What Lies Ahead?
Ethics
  CAREERbyte: Robert Solomon: A Talent for Innovative Peripherals
Summary
Key Terms
Review and Discussion Questions
Issues

OBJECTIVES

After reading and studying this chapter, you should be able to:

1. Define the peripheral device and explain the purposes of the different kinds of interfaces.
2. Identify the methods of data entry and the different types of input devices used.
3. Describe the different types of output devices and the uses for various output technologies.
4. Explain the uses and purposes for direct access and sequential access storage methods.

HERMAN HOLLERITH AND THE FIRST I/O DEVICE

Herman Hollerith had a problem to solve: trying to count the 1890 census data in less than the seven years it took to do the 1880 census. Aware of Jacquard's work, Hollerith applied **punched card** technology to mechanical tabulating machines. His card, called the Hollerith card, was the same size as a dollar bill. By 1884, Hollerith had developed an electro-mechanical tabulating machine. It used some of the same technology as an electric telegraph and had the same mechanical counters as an adding machine.

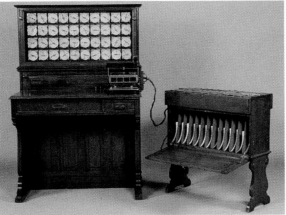

To read the cards, electrical contact was

Courtesy of the IBM Corporation and Neuhart-Donges-Neuhart Design

made by a pin passing through holes in the card, touching a bath of mercury below. The machine could read between 50 and 80 cards a minute. Counting the census involved tabulating data on 62,622,250 citizens. That amounted to 2 billion holes in punched cards. Hollerith's machine did it in just over two years. An article in a magazine of the time said, "This apparatus works as unerringly as the mills of the gods, and beats them hollow as to speed."

Hollerith leased his equipment to the U.S. government and to other countries as well. In 1896, he formed the Tabulating Machine Company. That company became International Business Machines, and the punched card became known as the IBM card. Billions and billions of punched cards have been used for storing both programs and data over the years. But now, other forms of input and output have replaced the punched card. The last IBM punched card plant closed its doors in 1986. Today, the Bureau of the Census uses the most modern VAX computers from Digital Equipment Corp. Yet it took as long to process the census in 1990 as it did in 1890, primarily because the population has grown so much.

PERIPHERAL DEVICES

A peripheral is a device that performs input, output, or storage functions and is connected to the CPU. Without peripheral devices, the CPU is of no use to people. Figure 10–1 shows a variety of peripherals connected to a personal computer. As you can see, some are externally connected, while others are installed inside the cabinet.

In Chapter 2 we explained the four basic data processing operations:

- Input operations.
- Processing operations.
- Output operations.
- Storage operations.

Each of these operations is performed by specific hardware devices — often assisted by software — that allow us to use the computer to get our work done. We also explained that computers commonly process various types of transactions. The primary transaction processing methods are batch processing and on-line processing.

In Chapter 9, you learned about processing hardware, the various CPU devices. In this chapter, we take what we've learned about computer systems concepts, combine it with our understanding of processing hardware, and put it all together with peripheral devices. We explore the three types of hardware peripherals that permit us to utilize processing hardware. They are known as input, output, and storage devices.

An input device such as the keyboard in Figure 10–1 permits us to enter data or problems into the computer for processing. An output device such as the printer in Figure 10–1 provides us with the results of that processing in a form we can perceive with our senses. When discussed together, we often use the acronym I/O to refer to input and output devices. In this chapter, we'll explore the many kinds of input and output devices and how they have evolved over the years.

The third type of peripheral is the storage device. A **storage device** is used to save the data or information that the computer has processed. In Chapter 2, you learned there are two types of storage: main memory and secondary storage. Figure 10–1 shows a main memory printed circuit board and several types of drives used for secondary storage. In this chapter, we'll concentrate on the peripherals used for secondary storage, where we save data for later use.

The Interface

Input, output, and storage devices are designed for specific types of processing hardware. Devices for a Macintosh generally don't work with a PC-compatible or a mini. The term *interface* is used to describe the point where either a peripheral device or a human meets the computer. Let's look at each.

Whether we can use a particular peripheral device with a particular processor also depends on the availability of the proper physical interface. The *physical interface* is a connection on the system unit that permits connecting the peripheral device. A cable or wire is often needed to plug the peripheral into the interface. The two most common physical interfaces are called serial and parallel. The keyboard has its own special interface. All three are shown in Figure 10–2.

FIGURE 10 – 1   A PC showing the variety of peripheral devices that can be connected. The keyboard and video monitor are the most common input and output devices, respectively. A number of storage and other devices may be installed internally.

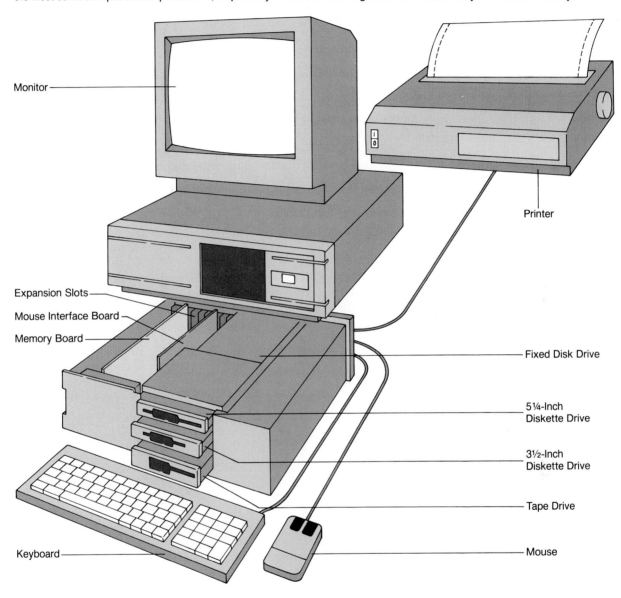

FIGURE 10 – 2   Several common physical interfaces.

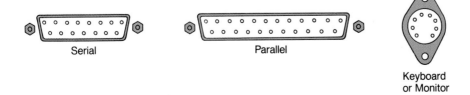

The *serial interface* is used to connect a variety of devices, such as the mouse and modem (you will learn about the modem in Chapter 11). Serial means the data passes through the interface sequentially. The *parallel interface* is commonly used to connect the printer. Parallel means the data passes through the interface simultaneously, or all at once. Both interfaces have been standardized and given names. Serial is usually referred to as RS-232, while the term Centronics is used to describe parallel. In some cases, special software is required in order to use a peripheral; such software is called a *logical interface*.

The point at which people use input and output devices is referred to as the human-computer interface. One goal for many designers is to provide the most humanlike interface possible between human and machine; in other words, we would like to be able to communicate with a computer as simply as we do another person. In the simplest terms, that means designing keyboards that respond well to the touch of fingers or video monitors that are easy on the eyes. As you learned in Chapter 3, the human-computer interface also extends to software such as the GUI (graphic user interface).

Therefore, we have three types of interface: the physical interface and the logical or software interface between the computer and the peripheral, and the human-computer interface between the peripheral and you. In this chapter, we'll look at all the different kinds of peripheral devices; then we'll show examples of how they are commonly used with particular processing hardware. We begin our discussion with the first and most important aspect: input.

MEMORY CHECK

1. What are the three functions performed by peripherals?
2. Name the two ways peripherals are connected with computers.
3. What are the names of the two devices we call I/O?
4. What is a peripheral-to-computer connection called?
5. What is a human-to-peripheral connection called?

INPUT

We use input devices to perform the two most basic computational tasks, **data entry**, the process of entering data into computer memory, and issuing commands. Nothing happens in the CPU until there is data for it to process. Once data is available, we must give the CPU instructions for what to do with it. For many years, people have entered data manually into computers, usually by means of typing it on a keyboard. This method is slow and prone to typing errors. Therefore, developing faster, more accurate—better—data entry or input devices has been a high priority.

Input Devices

Most input devices depend on people using their limbs, in conjunction with their senses, to perform data entry. In most cases, that means our fingers and our eyes—although, as we shall see, that too is changing.

FIGURE 10 – 3   The Switchboard keyboard lets you design your own layout.

Courtesy Datadesk International

The Keyboard   The most widely used input device is the keyboard, which was adapted from the typewriter. Computer keyboards use the standard QWERTY alphanumeric keys. This convenient and familiar layout makes it possible for typists to quickly learn word processing. In addition, many keyboards have a numeric keypad to aid people who work with numbers. Spreadsheet users find the numeric keypad especially useful. Most computer keyboards also have a set of function keys and keys to control cursor movement. Figure 10 – 3 shows the latest advancement in keyboards.

Pointing Devices   There are several types of **pointing devices** that are used to move the cursor, usually working in conjunction with a keyboard. The most common pointing device is the mouse, so named because it slides over your desktop and has a wire or "tail" attached to the computer. A mouse commonly has two or three buttons that are used to issue commands and provide input to the computer. Using the mouse to move the cursor to the menu and pressing a button, commonly called *clicking,* issues the command to open or close a file. The mouse can also be used to highlight a block of text you wish to move or delete. The cursor is placed at the beginning of the text, a button is pressed and held down, and then the cursor is *dragged* to the end of the block. Then the button is released and the block can be moved or deleted.

There are two common types of mice: electromechanical and optical. Usually the electromechanical mouse has a hard rubber ball in its base, which turns movement into electrical signals. The optical mouse projects a beam of light downward and must be used on a special metallic pad. Some tasks such as drawing lend themselves to efficient use of a mouse. However, tasks such as word processing would be awkward, extremely tedious, and time-consuming without a keyboard.

Another commonly used pointing device is the **trackball,** which performs like a stationary, upside-down mouse, as shown in Figure 10 – 4. Many people prefer the trackball over the mouse because it does not require as much hand-eye coordination, nor does it require the extra desk space necessary to move the mouse. The Macintosh portable has a built-in trackball.

FIGURE 10 – 4   The trackball, an alternative to the mouse.

Courtesy of Kensington

FIGURE 10 – 5   Joysticks employ advanced technology to emulate the actions of the mouse.

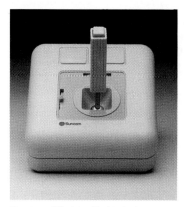

Courtesy of Suncom Technologies

The joystick is another pointing device, one that is usually associated with playing computer games. Joysticks used to produce jerky movement and were awkward to hold; however, newer models such as the one shown in Figure 10 – 5 use advanced technology for smooth movement; some are ergonomically designed to fit the hand.

Writing and Drawing Input Devices   There are several ways to use a device similar to a pen for entering data. One is the light pen, used to draw, write, or issue commands when it touches the specially designed video monitor screen. For example, a circuit designer can draw the interconnecting wires in electronic circuits with a light pen. The light pen was originally developed for computer-aided drafting at MIT in 1964.

Even simpler than the light pen is your finger, which can be used as an input device on a video monitor with a touch-sensitive screen. You may have used a touch-sensitive screen to obtain information at an airport or the grocery store.

DISKbyte

Great Moments in I/O History

Father of the Mouse

Douglas Englebart pioneered the input device known as the mouse. His first model, built in 1963, was made of wood and used two wheels for movement. "We were experimenting with lots of types of devices at the time," Englebart recalls. Indeed, he and his colleagues at Xerox's highly respected Palo Alto Research Center were also exploring such futuristic concepts as the workstation, graphic user interfaces, and networking, to name a few. "I felt until something better came along, the mouse would definitely remain the best pointing device for computer users."

Son of EP

The first dot-matrix printer for a personal computer was created by the Japanese company, Epson, which in Japanese means literally, *son of EP*. The EP stands for electronic printer, which was part of an extremely accurate timing device that Seiko, Epson's parent company, built for the 1964 Summer Olympics in Tokyo. It was used to clock various events and print out the winning times. The timing device became the quartz watch, and the electronic printer became the dot-matrix printer.

FIGURE 10–6   Skip Morrow, cartoonist, uses a digitizing tablet to produce his work.

Courtesy of Kurta Corporation

Did you ever play with an Etch-a-Sketch or Magic Slate when you were younger? A drawing tablet or digitizer is similar and makes a good input device. Some have a form overlay that the data entry clerk fills out with a light pen or stylus. Others have more sophisticated stylus or pointing devices that are useful for designers, architects, artists, desktop publishers, or map makers, to name a few. Skip Morrow, the cartoonist shown in Figure 10–6, uses a digitizing tablet to produce work such as *The Official I Hate Cats Book*.

Video Input   Images from video cameras, camcorders, VCRs, and optical disc players can be input into computers as static "snapshots" with a video digitizer peripheral, then used in many different ways. A series of snapshots can describe a process such as assembling a machine or an athlete's movements. A single snapshot can be used to illustrate text, as in Figure 10–7.

FIGURE 10 – 7   Video digitizers permit capturing moving video "snapshots."

Diana Lyn/Shooting Star

FIGURE 10 – 8   Two types of scanners: the overhead desktop (left) and the hand-held (right).

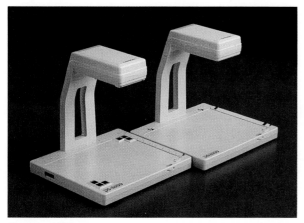

Courtesy of Chinon

Courtesy of Logitech, Inc.

Text Input   One of the most tedious data entry tasks is to retype printed or previously word processed or typewritten text. A scanner uses a light-sensitive device to enter text (and, depending on the software, graphics) into the computer. Early scanners were only able to recognize text that was printed in a specific type font called **OCR**, for **optical character recognition.** Today, scanners can read just about any type font. Figure 10 – 8 shows two types of scanners. A third type, the flatbed, allows you to feed in sheets continuously. The hand-held scanner is able to capture images from source material such as a soft drink can label that can't be conveniently fed through a flatbed scanner.

FIGURE 10 – 9   With the Voicesystem, the spoken words appear on the screen.

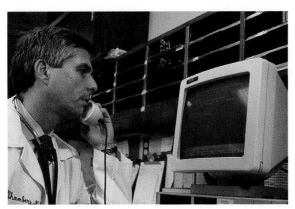

Martin L. Schneider/Associates/Ben Casey

FIGURE 10 – 10   MICR on checks and magnetic stripes on the back of credit cards and bank debit cards are used to enter account information.

D. Dempster/Offshoot

Voice Input   Perhaps the easiest way to enter data into a computer is by speaking; this is called voice input or **voice recognition.** However, since everyone pronounces words somewhat differently, and because of regional accents, the user must teach the computer to understand his or her voice. Raymond Kurzweil has led voice recognition research with his Voicesystem, which can understand over 5,000 words. Doctors, notorious for bad handwriting, have successfully used the Voicesystem when evaluating patients and diagnosing illnesses. As Figure 10 – 9 shows, the spoken words appear on the screen, and can then be printed out as patient records.

Source Data Input   **Source data input** refers to data fed directly into the computer without human intervention. Commonly, three types of media are used, which require special readers. One is **magnetic ink character recognition (MICR),** which allows the computer to recognize characters printed using magnetic ink. MICR is used by banks for processing checks. Another is the magnetic strip, used on the back of credit cards and bank debit cards, that allows readers such as an automated teller machine (ATM) to read account information. Figure 10 – 10 shows MICR and magnetic strip source data input.

FIGURE 10–11   Three different types of POS scanners: the wand, the counter scanner, and the handheld scanner.

Wand scanner.

Russ Schleipman

Counter scanner.

Courtesy of NCR Corporation

Handheld scanner.

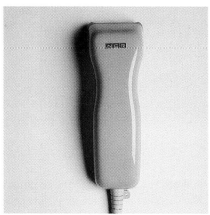

Courtesy of NCR Corporation

Many retail businesses and grocery stores use the third type of source data input, bar codes, or Universal Product Codes (UPC), to scan merchandise as it is sold. The reader is commonly attached to a point-of-sale terminal (POS). Figure 10–11 shows three different types of POS scanners.

Facsimile   Facsimile, or FAX machines, have been in use for many years. Recently, however, we have seen a marriage of computers and FAX, so facsimile has become a type of source data input. A printed circuit board peripheral is installed inside the computer, which translates the computer's bits and bytes into the pattern of dots transmitted via FAX. Computers and facsimile are now being used to deliver information via FAX. The Special Request system lets callers listen to a recording that lists such things as sports information, product prices, investment tips, and interest rates; whatever callers select will then be FAXed to them.

FIGURE 10-12   This input device lets you "read" the screen with your fingertips.

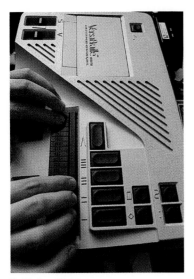

D. McCoy/Rainbow

Input Devices for the Disabled

Some interesting advances in input devices have come from small computer companies to aid the disabled. Voice recognition is one of these techniques but not the only one. Stephen Hawking, the brilliant physicist who suffers from amyotrophic lateral sclerosis, wrote his best-selling book, *A Brief History of Time,* using a mouthstick to press his computer's keys. Special keyboards have been developed for people with cerebral palsy and muscular dystrophy. For the blind, there is a special braille keyboard that translates phrases into conventional letters and words.

   People who can't move their limbs but have some head movement can use special pointing devices that attach to their heads. One such device is a small camera that projects a beam of light at a simulated keyboard. By holding the beam of light on the selected key for a moment, the character is sent as input to the computer. Research is under way at the IBM National Support Center for Persons with Disabilities to create a brain wave scanner. By reading electrical brain waves, the scanner would be able to sense when the person thought about an object such as a baseball, causing the word to appear on the screen. Figure 10-12 shows an input system for the disabled.

1. What is the most common input device?
2. What is a scanner commonly used for?
3. What advantages does voice recognition offer?
4. Name three different kinds of input.
5. Describe two kinds of source data input.

**M E M O R Y
C H E C K**

OUTPUT

As the acronym I/O implies, you don't have much use for input if you can't have output. Output refers to the product of data processing, delivered in a form that people can understand or that can be read by another machine. Today, most output is visual in nature, produced by two devices: a video display screen or a printer.

Types of Computer Output

Most computer output comes in two forms: text and graphics. Text output is, simply, the characters that make up our language. Text output appearance ranges from typewritten to typeset quality. Graphic output includes line drawings, presentation business graphics, computer-aided design, computer painting, and photographic reproduction. As input or data entry methods improve, so do forms of output. As we shall see, sound output is growing more sophisticated and useful. Let's take a look at the devices that provide us with the output we need.

Output Devices

Text and graphic output devices fall into two categories: soft copy and hard copy. **Soft copy** refers to output we cannot touch, such as video or audio. The most common soft copy output device is the video display. **Hard copy** is output we can hold in our hand, such as a printed sheet of paper. The most common hard copy output device is the printer. We shall look at each in detail, as well as several other forms of output.

The Video Monitor

The **video monitor** or display provides soft copy output. The most common video monitors, such as those used with personal computers, are very similar to a television screen; both use a cathode ray tube (CRT) to project an image. Video displays come either in monochrome or color. A monochrome display is a single color displayed against a background, such as green on green, amber on black, or white on black. A color display is able to show a variety of colors.

Types of Video Displays   *Resolution* is the term used to describe the degree of detail in a video display. The higher the resolution, the sharper and crisper the characters or images formed. For example, a conventional television display is **low-resolution,** because you can see lines and graininess in the image. The newer, high-definition (HDTV) or **high-resolution** sets display a picture as sharp and crisp as a film image in a Hollywood movie. The same is true with computer displays. The Macintosh has a monochrome, bit-mapped display that is extremely high-resolution. This makes it good for graphics.

Many other personal computers, whether monochrome or color, have character-mapped displays, which are not as high in resolution as a bit-mapped display. To overcome their grainy display, successive generations of personal computers have employed improved video technologies. The first color display, called CGA or color graphics adapter, could display up to 16 colors. The EGA or enhanced graphics adapter had better resolution and a palette of 64

FIGURE 10 – 13   Monochrome and color resolution.

F. Bodin/Offshoot

FIGURE 10 – 14   Some computers use a gas plasma display.

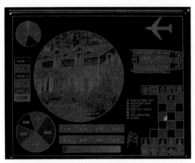

Courtesy of IBM Corporation

colors. That was followed by the VGA or video graphics array, which is even sharper than HDTV and has a palette of 256 colors. Another popular color graphics adapter was the HGC or Hercules Graphics Card, which became the standard for displaying graphics in Lotus 1-2-3. The new 8514/A technology for IBM PS/2s with the Micro Channel has almost twice the resolution of VGA, a palette of 262,000 colors, and the ability to display 256 colors on the screen at a time. Figure 10 – 13 shows both monochrome and color resolution.

Special Video Displays   Some computers require special display technology, either because of power requirements or the needs of special application software. Here are a few examples.

The gas plasma display (Figure 10 – 14) is easy to recognize, since it is a deep orange. It is a flat-panel display composed of three sheets of glass with plasma, an illuminant gas, between them. When electricity is applied, the screen glows. The gas plasma display has several distinct advantages. One, it is very thin, so it could be hung on a wall. Two, there is no limit to its size; one could be as large as a movie screen. Three, it is extremely easy to view. Some laptop computers use a gas plasma display, making it possible to view the screen from any angle and in any light.

The **liquid crystal display (LCD)** is also a flat-screen display commonly used with laptops. To make LCD screens easier to read in dim or bright light, they are backlit—lighted from behind the screen. Some use what is termed *supertwist* technology that also enhances visibility. Some laptops now have a color LCD display.

Terminals   Computer video displays are found on all types of computers, not just personal computers. Mainframes and minicomputers use terminals that commonly consist of a video display and a keyboard for input. These terminals can be used for anything from data entry to computer-aided design (CAD). There are two basic types of terminals. One is the *dumb* terminal, which performs the simplest input and output operations but no processing. A bank ATM is a dumb terminal. The other is the *intelligent* terminal, which has its own CPU or processing capabilities built in. A point-of-sale (POS) cash register and a personal computer are examples of an intelligent terminal.

Printers

A printer provides hard copy output on paper. There is a printer for every need and every pocketbook. The basic criteria for evaluating printers are the quality of the output and the speed, although the sound level is often a consideration. Printers fall into two primary categories: impact and nonimpact. **Impact printers** strike characters on the paper. The most common types of impact printers are the dot-matrix and letter-quality printers. **Nonimpact printers** form a character by other means, most commonly using laser technology or by spraying ink. Different types of printer output are shown in Figure 10–15. Let's look at the most common printing technologies today.

Dot-Matrix Printing   **Dot-matrix** output is produced by printers that utilize wires in the print head. These wires extend out in different patterns, pressing against the ribbon to print the characters on the paper. For this reason, dot-matrix printers can produce both text and graphics. Early dot-matrix printers had nine wires in the print head and were very fast, but the print quality was often unacceptable for professional or business documents. To improve quality, printer makers created 24-pin print heads, which produce **near-letter-quality (NLQ)** output. The primary disadvantages with dot-matrix printers are that they are noisy and their print quality is often insufficient to meet business standards.

Letter-Quality Printing   **Letter-quality** printers are most similar to typewriters and produce the same high-quality output. The two most common letter-quality technologies are the daisy wheel and the thimble, as shown in Figure 10–16. The daisy wheel resembles a daisy; a print hammer strikes each "petal" against a ribbon to form the impression. The thimble resembles the IBM Selectric "golfball," but like the daisy wheel, it utilizes a print hammer. Letter-quality printers offer a wide selection of interchangeable type fonts; however, they cannot print graphics. The impact printer's major disadvantages are noise and slow speed.

Laser Printing   **Laser printers** provide high-quality nonimpact printing. Output is created by directing a laser beam onto a drum, creating an electrical charge that forms a pattern of letters or images. As the drum rotates, it picks up black toner on the images and transfers them to paper.

FIGURE 10–15   Different types of printer output.

Dot-matrix output.

```
     "I don't 'think them up,' to use your phrase.  They

come from some other place, really, it's hard to tell you

where it is, but I can feel it right there and it makes me

think of Montana, Big Sky Country.  When I'm a cowboy on

that range, nothing can stop me."
```

Near-letter-quality (NLQ) output.

```
     "I don't 'think them up,' to use your phrase.  They

come from some other place, really, it's hard to tell you

where it is, but I can feel it right there and it makes me

think of Montana, Big Sky Country.  When I'm a cowboy on

that range, nothing can stop me."
```

Letter-quality output.

```
     "I don't 'think them up,' to use your phrase.  They

come from some other place, really, it's hard to tell you

where it is, but I can feel it right there and it makes me

think of Montana, Big Sky Country.  When I'm a cowboy on

that range, nothing can stop me."
```

Laser output.

```
     "I don't 'think them up,' to use your phrase.  They

come from some other place, really, it's hard to tell you

where it is, but I can feel it right there and it makes me

think of Montana, Big Sky Country.  When I'm a cowboy on

that range, nothing can stop me."
```

Laser printers have the advantages of speed and a wide selection of type fonts, as well as high-quality graphics. A variety of fonts allow you to create any size type, as well as italics and boldface text. Laser printers for personal computers can print up to eight pages per minute; commercial laser printers, such as those that produce bank statements, can print 400 to 500 pages per minute.

Laser printing offers the highest quality text and graphics printing for the desktop. Color laser printers promise to be the next great advance. Although

FIGURE 10–16   The two most common impact printers are the daisy wheel and the thimble.

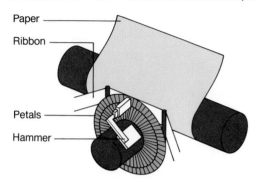

A Single Petal

D. McCoy/Rainbow

Courtesy of NEC Technologies

laser printer prices have fallen dramatically over the past few years, the primary disadvantages are expensive maintenance and the high cost of toner cartridges. A recent advance employs a liquid crystal display (LCD) shutter, like a camera, instead of a laser beam, offering greater reliability and longer life.

Inkjet Printing   Inkjet printers were first used for high-volume printing, such as direct mail brochures. They transfer characters and images to paper by spraying a fine jet of ink. Like laser printers, they are able to print many different type fonts and graphics. In recent years, inkjet printing has come to the personal computer, offering the same high quality as a laser printer but at a more affordable price. Inkjet printers are slower, and their output may smear if it gets wet.

Plotters   **Plotters** use inkjet technology to create scientific and engineering drawings, as well as other graphics, often in color. Color plotters use ink pens that switch on and off according to instructions from the computer and software. Plotters can create very large documents; for example, a chip designer created a schematic drawing of an integrated circuit 7 by 9 feet. Figure 10–17 shows plotter printing.

FIGURE 10–17   This plotter is capable of creating large color images.

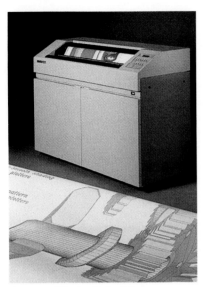

Courtesy of Hewlett-Packard Company

Thermal Printing   As the name implies, **thermal printers** use heat to form a nonimpact image on chemically treated paper. Thermal printing combines high speed with a low-maintenance printing technology; however, the paper is expensive and not as desirable as plain bond paper. Thermal printing is mostly used for low-cost calculators or high-quality color printing.

Computer-to-Machine Output

Computer output can also be sent to another machine, device, or computer. For example, computers are used for process control in factories, buildings, and even the home. With **computer-to-machine output,** the I/O process controls machine operations, maintains heating and cooling, and turns lights on and off at prescribed times. At a Panasonic factory in Japan, computer-controlled robots make vacuum cleaners without any human help (unless something breaks!).

It is possible to produce high-quality color slides directly using computer-to-machine output. Using a cameralike device connected to the computer interface, the image on the screen, whether text, graphics, or both, is output to 35mm film, which is exposed just as it would be in a camera. The film is then developed normally.

Another interesting computer-to-machine output task involves micrographics. **Micrographics** uses miniature photography to condense, store, and retrieve data on film. The two most common micrographics media are microfiche, which are 4 by 6–inch sheets of film, and microfilm, which comes in rolls. Both are used with special readers that magnify the information and display it on a screen. Micrographics holds up well under sustained usage.

Computer output such as newspaper copy, canceled checks, or invoices is sent to a special machine that reduces it in size and then records it 10 to 20 times faster than printing. The film is developed and copied for distribution.

DISKbyte

Cyberspace: The Ultimate I/O?

Imagine one of these computer-created graphics: a protein molecule, the surface of Mars, a depiction of life on Earth 2 million years ago. Now imagine yourself within—actually part of—that graphic! This is *cyberspace,* a three-dimensional graphics system that creates the optical effect of walking through a 3-D image. NASA's Ames Research Center, Autodesk International, and other companies

are developing computer-aided design tools that create a *virtual reality.* Cyberspace travelers wear a stereoscopic headset and "smart gloves" that enable them to control their journey. The traveler sees images displayed on a pair of miniature color CRTs or LCDs, while the gloves make it possible to move through or grasp objects anywhere in the field of view. There is a virtual reality scenario that allows two

persons to play games in a phantom playground.

Early travelers report that the experience is disorienting and unlike anything they've previously experienced. For this reason, excursions are limited to 45 minutes or less. But if the idea of cyberspace catches on, as it's sure to do, there should be one at a nearby video arcade before long.

For example, book distributors prepare weekly microfiches listing books by title, author, price, and number in stock. A single sheet of microfiche holds almost 1,000 sheets of standard paper.

Voice Output

Voice output or speech synthesis is the machine's ability to "speak" like a human. Some computers already talk to us. The soft drink machine thanks us for our purchase. Autos tell us to buckle our seat belt. But when will computers talk to us like the HAL 9000 in the movie *2001: A Space Odyssey?*

Raymond Kurzweil, the man who created the Voicesystem mentioned earlier, thinks we will have very natural-sounding speech synthesis by the first decade of the next century. He describes a very practical use for speech synthesis: a translating telephone system. It uses three technologies: automatic speech recognition for voice input; language translation performed as real-time processing; and speech synthesis for voice output. Then two people, regardless of their native language, can speak to each other over the telephone, or understand one another during meetings of the United Nations, as if they were both speaking the same language.

MEMORY CHECK

1. What are the two types of output copy called?
2. Give examples of low-resolution and high-resolution monitors.
3. What are the two types of terminals?
4. What are the two common categories of printers?
5. List the different types of printers, from the highest to the lowest quality output.
6. What is a main advantage of micrographics?

STORAGE

Storage is the critical link between input and output. In Chapter 2, you learned that storage or memory is where we keep instructions and data after they are entered, during processing by the CPU, and when they are needed for output. Main memory, which you learned about in Chapter 2, is random access memory (RAM). It is temporary storage that utilizes a set of integrated circuit (IC) memory chips, mounted on a printed circuit board installed inside the computer. The CPU microprocessor and RAM chips may be on the same board. When you want to add more RAM to your computer, you either install new chips or install a memory upgrade board.

Auxiliary storage or secondary storage is permanent storage. Once data is safe in auxiliary storage, it can be recalled again and again. A report can be revised and printed again; new figures can be inserted in a spreadsheet and recalculated; an address book database can be updated when someone moves. Auxiliary storage is our primary interest in this chapter.

There are two methods for storing and accessing instructions or data in auxiliary storage. One is direct access, and the other is sequential access. **Direct access,** sometimes called random access, means the data is stored in a particular memory location with a specific address so that any data can be found quickly. This is similar to selecting a song on a CD–ROM; it doesn't take the player any longer to find and play selection 8 than selection 3. Direct access is the most widely used auxiliary storage method; the most common direct access storage medium is the disk.

Sequential access storage means the data is stored in a particular order, perhaps alphabetically or by date and time. Just as you must search sequentially for a particular song on a cassette, so the computer must sequentially search for data. The most common sequential storage medium is magnetic tape, on reels or cassettes. Today, sequential access storage is mostly used to make protective or backup copies of data stored on direct access devices.

As you recall, we use the term *backup* to describe the process of making copies of data and instructions for safekeeping. Backup is the best insurance against loss should the computer or hard disk crash. The simplest backup process on a personal computer is copying from one floppy disk to another. When you purchase an application software package, the publisher recommends you make backups or working copies of your original disks. It is essential that you back up all your data often.

Storage technology has improved dramatically over the years. In many cases, what was once a primary storage medium is today a backup medium. In this section, we'll examine the types of auxiliary storage peripherals most commonly used today.

Direct Access Storage Devices

Direct access storage devices, or DASD, are magnetic disk drives used for auxiliary storage. They may use floppy disks or hard disks; Figure 10–18 shows several different types of DASD drives. We have Alan Shugart of IBM to thank for inventing magnetic disk storage. He built the first hard disk drive for the RAMAC computer in 1957, then invented the floppy disk in 1961.

DASD devices employ a moving read/write head that scans the magnetic surface of the disk. We say it is reading the disk when it searches for data or instructions, and that it is writing to disk when it is storing data or instructions. Figure 10–19 shows the read/write window on a floppy disk; this is

FIGURE 10 – 18 Large computer systems need vast amounts of storage space. The DASD cabinet (top left) contains multiple disk platters.

Courtesy of Amdahl Corp.

Courtesy of IBM Corporation

Courtesy of IBM Corporation

Courtesy of IBM Corporation

FIGURE 10 – 19 Anatomy of a floppy disk.

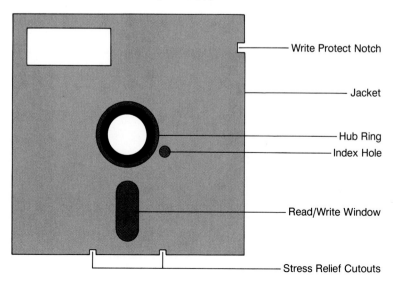

FIGURE 10–20 The head floats very closely above the spinning disk surface on a cushion of air. Note the relative size of disk pollutants.

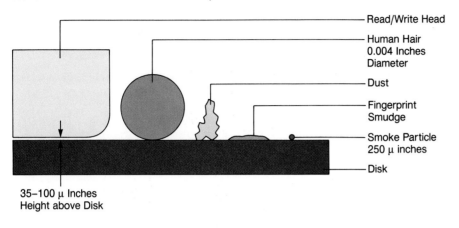

- Read/Write Head
- Human Hair 0.004 Inches Diameter
- Dust
- Fingerprint Smudge
- Smoke Particle 250 μ inches
- Disk

35–100 μ Inches Height above Disk

FIGURE 10–21 One floppy disk format, showing tracks and sectors. Format design and the number of tracks and sectors affect disk storage capacity.

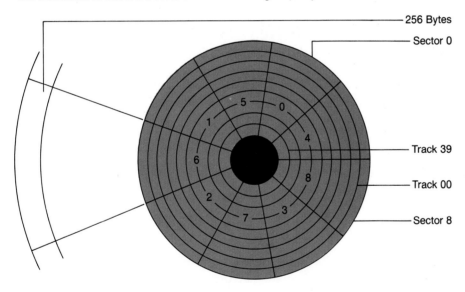

- 256 Bytes
- Sector 0
- Track 39
- Track 00
- Sector 8

where the head moves back and forth. The head floats above the spinning disk surface on a cushion of air. As you can see from Figure 10–20, this cushion is very thin; think of a Boeing 747 flying an inch above the ground at 3,000 miles per hour and you get an idea of the close tolerances. Figure 10–20 also illustrates why it's so important to keep disks clean. When the head encounters a particle of foreign matter that causes it to fail in either reading or writing to the disk, it is termed a *head crash*.

Figure 10–21 shows how a disk is magnetically laid out into tracks and sectors. **Tracks** are concentric circles on which data is recorded. **Sectors** are pie-shaped wedges that compartmentalize the data into the addresses for the head to locate. In addition, some disks organize tracks into **cylinders,** vertical stack of tracks that, again, make it easier to locate data. Let's take a closer look at the various DASDs.

FIGURE 10–22   3½″ disks hold between 720K and 1.44MB; 5¼″ disks hold between 360K and 1.2MB.

D. Dempster/Offshoot

The Floppy Disk   Floppy disks come in two popular sizes: 5¼-inch mini-floppy and 3½-inch micro-floppy for most computer systems. The first floppy disks were 8 inches in diameter but over the years floppy disks have become smaller, while increasing in data capacity. One technique was developing double-sided disks that could be written to on both sides; another was developing high-density disks that doubled and quadrupled the number of tracks. Today, a 5¼-inch disk can hold as much as 1.2MB, and a 3½-inch disk can hold as much as 1.44MB. Figure 10–22 shows various disks and their capacities.

The floppy disk drive begins to spin when it senses a disk is present, timing the speed of rotation very precisely. Some disk drives have a lever or button that locks the disk in and starts it spinning, while others are activated whenever the disk is inserted. The mini-floppy drive head moves within the read/write window; the micro-floppy moves the metal shutter aside to gain access to the disk inside. Then the head moves out to the edge of the disk, a process called *indexing,* which is essential to finding the data in its various locations. Then the head scans the sectors for data or program instructions.

The floppy disk is the primary means of delivering a personal computer software program from the publisher to the user. With the prominent use of hard disk drives on personal computers these days, programs are often copied to the hard disk and then used. The original program disks are stored for safekeeping. Conversely, hard disk drives are most commonly backed up on floppy disks. Therefore, floppy disks are both direct access storage devices and backup storage devices.

The Hard Disk   Hard disk drives operate in a similar fashion to floppy disk drives. Where a floppy disk is made of mylar plastic, a hard disk is made of aluminum; both are coated with a magnetic material. Hard disks are sealed in a metal case to prevent smoke, dirt, or other contaminants from entering. Figure 10–23 shows an early hard disk drive. Today's personal computer uses either 5¼-inch or 3½-inch hard disk drives, and the 2½-inch drive is becoming more common on laptops. Mainframes and minis commonly use 14 inch disk drives that hold several disks or platters. Each has its own head but all move together to read and write to the disk. Figure 10–24 shows a typical multiple-disk platter.

An early hard disk drive, jukebox style.

Charles Babbage Institute/Walter Library

A typical multiple-disk platter, commonly called a disk pack.

Courtesy of IBM Corporation

For many years, the hard disk was referred to as a fixed disk because it was fixed in place. That, however, is no longer always true. Today, we have the convenience of removable hard disk drives for personal computers, such as the one shown in Figure 10 – 25. Removable drives offer several advantages. One, your data is secure because you can take it home with you. Two, removable drives make it easy to copy data from one drive to another. Three, storage capacity is expanded because you can remove a drive that is full and replace it with a fresh one.

FIGURE 10-25   A removable hard disk drive.

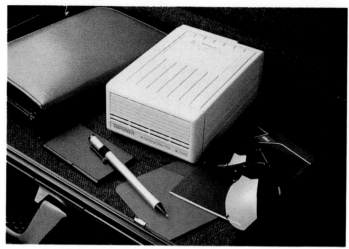

Courtesy of Tandon Corp.

A common hard disk for a personal computer holds 30 megabytes (30MB) or 30 million bytes. A common hard disk drive for a mainframe holds 10 times that or 300MB; some range up to the billions of bytes. However, personal computers are increasingly utilizing larger hard disks. It is not uncommon to see personal computers using the 386 microprocessor with hard disk capacities from 40MB up to 650MB! Large system disk drives utilize disk packs. The average disk pack contains 11 disks, each 14 inches in diameter, and fits into the top of the disk drive.

In addition to its higher storage capacity, the hard disk drive provides much faster access to data than a floppy disk drive. This is extremely important in large businesses, where there may be dozens or hundreds of DASDs that reside together in an area called a disk farm, each holding nearly half a billion bytes of data.

Optical Disc Storage   Even though magnetic disks have great storage capacity, it's still never enough. Sidney Diamond, the vice president of information systems at Black & Decker, says, "You can't just add (new disk drives), or you'd be building new data centers all the time." This means the search for new and better storage technology goes on continuously.

Optical disc (or laser disc) **storage** holds some promise. Optical discs come in several sizes and formats. One is the 12-inch laser video disc, which is also used in home videodisc players and holds a billion bytes, or 1 gigabyte. Another is the optical disc, which can be written to and read from and holds 256MB. A **compact disc-read only memory (CD-ROM)** disc holds 600MB, the equivalent of 1,600 mini-floppies. A CD-ROM, just like its musical counterpart, is written to once, and primarily used to distribute information in much the same way as book publishers do. The write once, read many (WORM) CD-ROM disc can be written to by the user but cannot be erased. A WORM disc holds 200MB. Even better is the erasable optical disc,

FIGURE 10−26   These cartridges contain 3-inch wide magnetic tape; each holds 700 MB. A robot arm removes them from their storage cells, loading the data in just seconds.

Courtesy of Masstor Systems

which can be used just like a magnetic disc to store and then dispose of data at will. WORM discs and drives are becoming inexpensive enough for the average personal computer user but it will be a few more years before erasable CD–ROM discs are affordable.

Although optical discs hold a great deal more data, they are slower than magnetic disks. This is the major reason they are not in wider use today. However, there is no reason to think problems with speed and erasability won't be overcome in time. By the mid-1990s, optical discs will likely be standard equipment on most personal computers.

Sequential Access Storage Devices

Today, sequential access storage devices are most commonly used for backup purposes. No one wants to wait for data that is stored sequentially on tape these days! Here are the commonly used sequential access media and drives in use today.

Reel-to-Reel Tape   Reel-to-reel tape was once a primary means of storage for mainframes but now is commonly used as a backup storage medium. It probably won't be used much longer. There are several reasons for this. One, tape cartridges are falling in price and much easier to work with. Two, loading and unloading reel-to-reel tapes requires a person (often called a "tape hanger") and personnel are growing scarce.

Tape Cartridges   Early tape cartridges were simply the Philips compact cassette most people use to listen to music. Over time, a higher quality tape was used but slow speed was a problem. This led to specially designed tape cassettes or cartridges and special streaming tape drives. Figure 10–26 shows one type of tape cartridge.

D I S K b y t e

CD-ROM: The New Papyrus

Papyrus is the name the ancient Egyptians gave to a product created from the bullrushes that grew alongside the Nile River. The Egyptians created long sheets of this material, called *scrolls,* and wrote on it with pen and ink. Today, we call it *paper.*

Microsoft, a leading software publisher, has dubbed the CD-ROM "the new papyrus." Indeed, much of the information that we traditionally turned to books for is now available on CD-ROM. You can find everything from a dictionary or encyclopedia to Shakespeare and Sherlock Holmes on disc.

Perhaps the most ambitious CD-ROM library project is "The American Memory," undertaken by the U.S. government's Library of Congress in Washington, D.C. There are thousands of priceless and irreplaceable manuscripts, books, photographs, and recordings in the Library that have been deteriorating over time. They are being transferred to CD-ROM in a six-year-long project that will cost over $6 million.

Interestingly, the material is not simply being copied but reorganized into multimedia discs. Words, images, and sound are combined where appropriate, to give a more complete feeling for the material. These multimedia presentations focus on such topics as ethnic groups, presidential campaigns and elections, a specific period in history, geographic regions of the world, and the achievements of specific individuals such as Thomas Alva Edison, who invented the light bulb and the phonograph.

In the past, you would have to visit the Library of Congress if you wanted to see or hear any of these materials. But in a very progressive move, the CD-ROMs of "The American Memory" will be available to schools across the country. And as the price of CD-ROM players and discs continues to fall, more and more of us will be able to have the Library of Congress in our own homes.

Tape cartridges offer several other distinct advantages. They have greater capacity than reel-to-reel tape, 200MB compared to 180MB, and they are considerably more compact. Cartridges come in a library system, with a robot arm that loads and unloads them. The robot has an eye that searches for a cartridge by reading the bar code serial number on the tape cartridge. It is able to find and load a cartridge in 10 seconds. No more tape hangers.

At the Harvard-Smithsonian Astrophysics Laboratory, CD-ROM is being used to back up reel-to-reel tape. Satellites collected celestial images and data, transmitting it for many years back to earth where it was stored on reels of magnetic tape. Now that tape is growing old and subject to deterioration, data could be lost. Thus, the tapes are being copied onto CD-ROMs and sent to scientists at observatories all around the world. What once could only be used by an institution with a large computer system with the proper software, capable of handling the tape reels, is now available on a $5 optical disc.

There are many other types of peripherals for computers. Some are internal peripherals. They are designed as printed circuit boards and are inserted into an **expansion slot,** a type of interface connection in the system unit. These include add-on main memory or RAM, mentioned earlier, or a coprocessor, which is a more powerful CPU. For example, a coprocessor can speed up mathematical operations or upgrade a PC/AT to a 386, and a 386 to a 486.

1. What are the two types of storage?

2. What is the difference between direct access and sequential access?

3. Name several types of direct access storage devices (DASD).

4. What is a major disadvantage of optical storage?

5. What is a major advantage of tape cartridges?

MEMORY CHECK

WHAT LIES AHEAD?

The human-computer interface is central to understanding the evolution of input, output, and storage devices. Think of your brain as a CPU, and your nervous system as the interface to your peripherals — eyes, ears, voice, limbs. It's a great interface; we can control our senses and our bodies effortlessly. There is little doubt that computer engineers would like to develop a human-computer interface that makes communicating with the computer just as easy for us.

But where are these advances leading us? Toward a computer that we can touch or talk to; one that has unimaginably vast amounts of data storage; one that provides any type of output we feel in the mood for. This is just on the horizon, and it's called *multimedia* (discussed in Chapter 7) where text, images, and sound merge with computer data to open a whole new world to us. You might walk down a Paris street with a guide that points things out, speaking a word in French as you see it displayed on the screen. You repeat the word to the computer, and your guide helps you with the correct pronunciation. In another multimedia scenario, an annual report is displayed to a company's board of directors on a wall-size gas plasma display. A voice explains the company's performance while highlighting sales figures. Board members ask questions while touching points on the graph, and the voice answers them.

Multimedia is possible because of advanced input, output, and storage devices. Scanning devices allow us to enter text, photographs, and more. We can enter moving video images, and even connect an electronic piano keyboard to record our own compositions. Optical storage will hold video, sound, text, and computer graphics, in any combination. Advanced video displays will provide more colors and clarity than the best high-definition television (HDTV). Audio output will be digital stereo — music, voice, and computer-generated sound effects. Clearly, peripheral devices are vital to making computers more and more useful.

ETHICS

What promises to provide us with the most dramatic steps forward in making computers more useful also holds an inherent danger: altering facts and reality. A scanner could be used to enter the letterhead of the president of the United States, adding text that declares war on China. Anything from a business card to a birth certificate could conceivably be falsified.

Similarly, a photograph can be entered and then doctored to either re-move or insert images that were previously not there. We have seen this occur at computer trade shows by people demonstrating the powers and features of their products. In one instance, a photograph showed a building and an American flag. The image was scanned into the computer, and using a graphics program the flag was literally erased from the photo.

There is nothing particularly new about falsifying documents but the computer makes it easier; there is less need for expensive, specialized equip-ment. What's more, the computer makes it seem like fun or entertainment. The demonstrator at the trade show did not exhibit feelings of guilt or remorse over falsifying or altering the photograph; on the contrary, she seemed to feel that it was a technological achievement to be able to do so. It is this attitude that the average computer user must recognize and avoid. There is a sense of accomplishment associated with performing computer tasks. That is all the more reason we must be careful to constantly ask ourselves if we are acting prudently, ethically, and legally with our computers.

CAREERbyte

Robert Solomon: A Talent for Innovative Peripherals

Robert Solomon represents the new breed of entrepreneur that the computer industry, in ignoring the old rules and business attitudes, has fostered and nurtured. Educated as a solid fuel rocket scientist, he's a guy whose interests range from sports cars to computers to serious running—he's run in the Boston Marathon three times. In his work, Robert has taken the time to understand how customers think and to hear what they are asking for in a product. He knows that, in his own words, "form follows function." Otherwise, how could anybody start a thriving business selling something as straightforward as a keyboard?

Solomon founded Datadesk International in 1985 in Chatsworth, California. When Microsoft was planning to release Word 3.0, its word processing program for the Macintosh, they wanted to utilize function keys. Apple Computer didn't want function keys; their philosophy was that the mouse should be used instead. So Microsoft asked Datadesk to design a keyboard with function keys, which they did, and business took off.

In the process, Robert realized that a keyboard is *not* just a keyboard. "The power user is not the hacker. The power user is, for example, the legal secretary. And for people who use a computer

Courtesy Miller Communications

keyboard all day long, the keyboard represents their interface to their machine—that's how they control the computer. So all the issues about how does it feel, how does it look, is it heavy enough, does it slide around on your desk, can you use the keys to do what you want to do, become real important issues to these people."

Solomon learned that keyboards are designed differently. Some have keys that are intentionally squishy or firm, quiet or loud. Some are so poorly thought out or inadequately designed that they make people feel the computer is difficult to use. He felt certain he could design a keyboard that was truly superior to what was available and which

truly met the user's needs. He set to work on the problem and today Robert Solomon's prize keyboard is the Switchboard (see Figure 10–3), which he designed himself. It allows the user to custom-configure the keyboard so the function keys, cursor keys, the numeric keypad, and even a trackball, can be moved into six different positions. You can have two sets of function keys, a vertical set and the set that runs horizontally across the top of the keys, so you can have it either way. The Control and Caps Lock keys can be swapped. The Switchboard can be used either with a PC-compatible or a Macintosh simply by flipping a switch; it can also be used as an IBM terminal keyboard. It can even be configured as a Dvorak keyboard!

There are more features, many more. Robert Solomon left no ergonomic aspect unattended, and people are flocking to trade their old keyboards in for a Switchboard. Why? "The Switchboard is the result of hearing what people want, day in and day out," Solomon says, modestly. Its success is no accident; it's the product of careful thinking, thoughtful listening, and understanding the market. It's also proof that you don't have to invent something totally unheard of; simply do whatever it is you do better than the competition.

SUMMARY

1. *Define the peripheral device and explain the purposes of the different kinds of interfaces.* Peripherals allow us to communicate with the CPU. Input, output, and storage devices are connected to the CPU with a physical interface, a mechanical connection most commonly made by plugging a cable into connections. Sometimes a peripheral needs a software, or logical, interface as well. The connection between a human and a peripheral is called the human-computer interface.

2. *Identify the methods of data entry and the different types of input devices used.* The most common input peripheral is the keyboard. Its most common purpose is data entry. Other input peripherals include pointing devices, writing and drawing devices, video, OCR, and voice. Source data, or machine-to-machine input, is another way to enter data into the computer.

3. *Describe the different types of output devices and the uses for various output technologies.* Output devices for human use fall into two main categories: video displays and printers. Video displays may be monochrome or color, high-resolution or low-resolution. High-resolution color monitors are best suited to graphics. Liquid crystal displays (LCD) are used on laptops. Minis and mainframes use both dumb and smart terminals, which combine a keyboard and display. Printers may be dot-matrix, impact, laser, or inkjet; a special type of inkjet printer, called a plotter, is used for large drawings and graphics. As with input, computers can be used for machine-to-machine output; for example, to control processes or to produce micrographics output.

4. *Explain the uses and purposes for direct access and sequential access storage methods.* In addition to main memory, there is auxiliary storage. There are two types of storage peripherals, direct access and sequential access. Direct access, or random access, stores data in a particular location for quick retrieval. Sequential stores data sequentially and is slower than direct access; it is mostly used for backup. Today's primary storage media is magnetic disk, both hard and soft. Primary sequential access devices use tape cartridges, which are replacing reel-to-reel tape for backup purposes. Optical discs may supersede both magnetic disks and tape as the storage medium of the future. They also make it possible to move toward multimedia.

KEY TERMS

compact disc-read only memory (CD–ROM), p. 338
computer-to-machine output, p. 331
cylinder, p. 335
data entry, p. 318
direct access, p. 333
dot-matrix, p. 328
expansion slot, p. 340
hard copy, p. 326
high-resolution, p. 326
impact printer, p. 328
laser printer, p. 328

letter-quality, p. 328
liquid crystal display (LCD), p. 327
low-resolution, p. 326
magnetic ink character recognition (MICR), p. 323
micrographics, p. 331
near-letter-quality (NLQ), p. 328
nonimpact printer, p. 328
optical character recognition (OCR), p. 322
optical disc storage, p. 338
plotter, p. 330
pointing devices, p. 319

punched card, p. 315
sector, p. 335
sequential access, p. 333
soft copy, p. 326
source data input, p. 323
storage device, p. 316
thermal printer, p. 331
track, p. 335
trackball, p. 319
video monitor, p. 326
voice output, p. 332
voice recognition, p. 323

REVIEW AND DISCUSSION QUESTIONS

1. What is the purpose of input, output, and storage devices?

2. What are the two types of interfaces called, and what is the purpose of each?

3. Explain the different kinds of physical interfaces.

4. Describe aspects of the human-computer interface you personally find important.

5. What is the task we perform with an input device?

6. What type of input media has been used longer than any other?

7. Describe three types of input devices and what tasks each is best suited to perform.

8. When do we use source data input methods? Name several examples.

9. Why do you think there have been so many improvements in input devices, and where might these developments be heading?

10. Explain the difference between low-resolution and high-resolution displays. When is high-resolution more useful? Give an example of a high-resolution display.

11. Classify the different types of printers according to print quality.

12. When do we use computer-to-machine output? Name several examples.

13. What are the two common forms of micrographics?

14. What are the two types of computer storage?

15. Explain the two types of access to auxiliary storage. What is each best suited for?

16. What is the main advantage of DASD devices?

17. How is data stored on magnetic media?

18. How will optical disc storage change the way we use computers?

19. What media are most commonly used for backing up data and instructions stored on a DASD?

20. What do you think it will be like to work with computers that understand your voice as input and speak back to you as output?

ISSUES

1. Auxiliary storage, whether it is a hard disk, floppy disk, or optical disc, is expensive. A concern in business, government, or your own personal work is having enough storage — in other words, enough room to store all the data you want to keep. As mentioned in the text, there never seems to be enough disk space; but how much of the data people store really needs to be retained? For example, is every memo announcing an office meeting kept? Do you keep letters and notes you wrote to friends that you won't ever read again? Does it make more sense to simply keep paper copies of only some of your documents? How do you decide what should be deleted? How would a company or a governmental agency formulate such a policy?

2. Over the past few years, a debate has grown up over fact versus fiction on television news and documentaries. Reenactments of actual events have been filmed using actors, often with hypothetical scenarios of what really happened. Many people feel it is neither ethical nor proper to present recreations as actual events; however, television executives seem to feel that this technique is a valid method of depicting events as close to the way they actually occurred as possible. Computers can be used — and misused — in the same way. A computer simulation could show a warplane attacking an American ship. A journalist's video image could be altered so that she appeared to be reporting on a fictitious event. If these and similar events occurred, where — and how — could we draw the line between appearance and reality? What do you suppose we should do about this?

MODULE V

Computer Systems Applications

When U.S. President Rutherford B. Hayes was first shown a telephone back in the 1880s, he commented that it looked like an interesting device but what would anyone ever do with one? However, there were uses for computer systems from the very beginning, even though they were primarily based on efforts to win World War II. Once the war was over, however, a cornucopia of commercial uses for computers emerged. The three chapters in this last Module explore the diversity of computer systems applications or uses in the world today.

Chapter 11 demonstrates what a good idea it was to merge computers and telephones, producing what we call networking. Computers are being connected to each other at a fierce pace around the globe; it seems that everyone wants to exchange data. This chapter explains how you, too, can connect your computer to the phone lines and thus to many other computers. We show a wide variety of networking applications and how they are changing the way people use computers.

Chapter 12 takes you from the early days of business data processing to the brave new world of management information systems—MIS for short.

Business would be lost without computers; indeed, trillions of dollars are shuttled between bank computers every working day. The number of people working in large companies who use computers of every size and shape grows daily. In all likelihood, you are one of them or soon will be, so we explain what MIS means and how it works.

Chapter 13 explores office automation, where computers are used for business decision making. Although other functions such as engineering or manufacturing are automated with computers, office automation is, to quote management consultant and futurist Stafford Beer, "the brain of the firm." It is here that we see computer systems utilized to the fullest: *people* using *software* with *hardware* to turn data into information and information into knowledge.

This book concludes with an Epilogue, exploring what the future of computing holds in store for us. The 1990s promise great leaps forward over the way we've used computers for the past 20 years, but the new millennium — well, that's going to knock your socks off. If you've read any of William Gibson's high-tech science fiction novels such as *Neuromancer,* you know what we mean.

CHAPTER

II

Networking

Connecting Your Computer to the World

CHAPTER OUTLINE

Dennis Hayes and the Personal Computer Modem
What Is Computer Networking?
Network Components
    Telecommunications Hardware
    Telecommunications Software
    Telecommunications Management Software
An On-line Work Session
Telecommunications Networks
    Public Networks
    Private Networks
    DISKbyte: Networking Tips
    The Next Wave in Networks
Using Networks
    Information Services
    Interactive Services
    DISKbyte: Telecommuting: Working from Home
    Business and Governmental Networks
Network Security
    Protecting Networks
    DISKbyte: Radio Modems Fight Credit Card
        Fraud
The Ever-Expanding Network
Ethics
    CAREERbyte: The Networking Professional
Summary
Key Terms
Review and Discussion Questions
Issues

OBJECTIVES

After reading and studying this chapter, you should be able to:

1. Define networking and identify the necessary hardware and software components.
2. Describe the difference between analog and digital signals and their role in networking.
3. Explain the difference between public and private networks and their uses.
4. Name three network topologies and identify the three common types of private networks.
5. Identify several kinds of network services.
6. List several methods of maintaining network security.

DENNIS HAYES AND THE PERSONAL COMPUTER MODEM

Dennis Hayes started his personal computer networking business in his dining room in Norcross, Georgia, one evening in 1977. Dennis, with his partner, Dale Heatherington, soldered electronic parts together to make a personal computer modem, the hardware peripheral device that makes it possible for a computer to send messages over telephone lines.

Modems existed before Dennis started Hayes Microcomputer Products but they were large, expensive, and difficult to operate. The Hayes Smartmodem required little more attention than switching it on, and it set the standard for personal computer modems. In fact, that standard for personal computer networking is now referred to as "Hayes compatible," similar to (IBM) "PC-compatible."

Courtesy Hayes Microcomputer Products, Inc.

Dennis Hayes is notable for three reasons. First, he saw the market for a personal computer modem before anyone else did — even as the first Apple and Radio Shack personal computers were appearing on the market. He saw the market so early, in fact, that people started creating networking services just so personal computer users would have something to do with their modems!

Second, he was a smart businessman. He bought out his partner and kept his business as a private corporation, which he still owns and controls. Dennis decided early on to make a high-quality product in his own American factory, using American workers. That decision created respect for Hayes modems and built Dennis a company with sales estimated at more than $100 million a year.

Third, Dennis has continued to develop newer, faster modems. A hundred years ago, the automobile usurped the horse and buggy and as a result, the buggy whip became useless and obsolete. Now, as the 1990s bring changes to our telephone networks and threaten to make modems obsolete, Dennis Hayes won't let his Smartmodem turn into the buggy whip of the 21st century. He is always at work on new telecommunications devices that make it even easier for computers to communicate.

WHAT IS COMPUTER NETWORKING?

In this chapter, we're going to explore one of the most versatile personal computer applications: computer networking, or more simply, networking. **Networking** allows us to connect two or more computers and exchange programs and data. Networking is also called telecommunications or data communications. But as you will see, networking can be much more than simply transmitting data.

One of the first communications networks was the telegraph of the 1840s. It greatly sped the transmission of information and is still used today. But its use of Morse Code was inconvenient and restricted both speed and content. When the telephone was invented in the late 1870s, many more people participated.

The telegraph and telephone didn't resolve all communications problems. Time and distance still took their toll. For example, the time it took to receive a letter that was sent through the mail could mean a lost business opportunity. Computer networking addressed many of these problems by delivering many kinds of information quickly and accurately. Today, it's not necessary to wait 10 days for a check deposit to clear at the bank. Networked computers make it possible to release the funds overnight.

Today, our networking options are numerous. In addition to the telegraph and telephone, we can use facsimile machines to, in effect, copy whole sheets of paper long distance. But by far the most diverse of our communications options is linking our personal computers into networks that span the globe. With a personal computer, a modem, and a telephone line, we can send and receive electronic mail, read the news, shop for merchandise, manage investments, converse with friends, meet new people, conduct international teleconferences, and browse in vast, electronic information libraries. As Figure 11–1 illustrates, personal computers can be linked to host computers offering various services via networks to share many kinds of information.

In this chapter, we'll explore several facets of networking. First, we'll discuss the hardware and software necessary to communicate with a computer, then we'll demonstrate using a personal computer and networking in an "on-line" session. We'll explore many kinds of computer networks and a number of networking applications. We'll also look at network security problems and learn how people use networks to invade and damage computer systems. Finally, we'll explore the future of networking.

NETWORK COMPONENTS

In general, a network is any system that connects two points by a communication channel. Each point is called a **node.** When you tie a string between two tin cans, the string is the communication channel and the tin cans are nodes; taken together, they form a network. Telephones are nodes in a voice communication network. Computer networks are similar. They consist of interconnected computers or terminals. A node in a data communications network can be a PC, a mini, a mainframe, or a terminal.

To create a network — and to connect our personal computer to one — we need special telecommunications hardware called a modem, and telecommunications software. Let's look at each of these network components.

FIGURE 11 – 1   Personal computers, linked to host computers via networks, are able to use a variety of services.

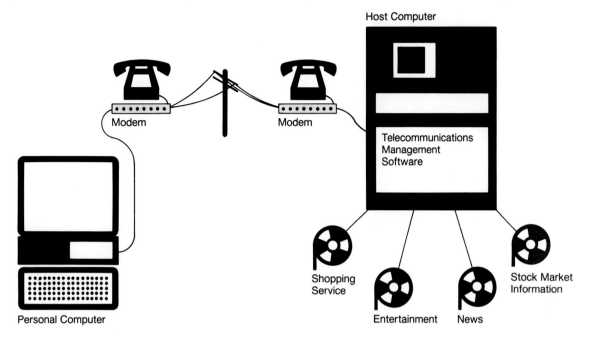

FIGURE 11 – 2   Connecting a terminal to a modem and the modem to a telephone line gives us full networking capabilities.

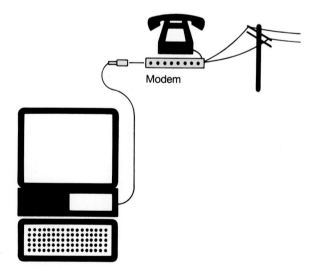

Telecommunications Hardware

A **modem** is a hardware device that allows computers to communicate via telephone lines. You connect a terminal or personal computer to a modem, and the modem to a telephone line, as shown in Figure 11 – 2. Modem is an

FIGURE 11–3   Modulated, digital computer signals and demodulated, analog signals.

Voice Communication—Analog Signals—Continuous

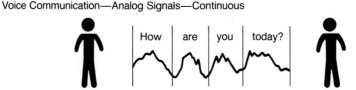

Data Communication—Digital Signals—Discrete

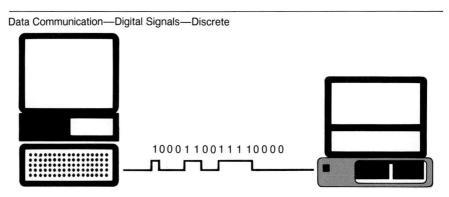

acronym of the terms *modulator* and *demodulator*. Figure 11–3 shows the modulated, digital signals that computers use and the analog signals that telephone equipment understands.

Analog and Digital Communications   Why is modulation/demodulation necessary? Because telephone systems were designed to carry analog, not digital, signals. An analog signal is continuous and changes in tone, pitch, and volume, like our voices. A digital signal is discrete—a steady stream of pulses that does not change. At the sending end, the modem converts or modulates the computer's digital signals into the analog signals used by telephone equipment. At the receiving end, the modem reconverts or demodulates analog telephone signals back into the digital signals the computer understands.

A series of digital signals makes up a data transmission, like a series of letters makes up a word. When you connect to a computer with a modem, you'll hear a high-pitched squeal. This is a carrier signal. It indicates that the computer is available. After connection, the carrier signal is modulated to convey the computer's binary information over the telephone line.

Types of Modems   Modems come in many shapes and designs. The earliest modem, which had two cups the telephone receiver fit into, was called an acoustic coupler. Acoustic couplers can be unreliable, in part because noise can enter the system. However, acoustic couplers allow us to connect almost any phone, anywhere, including pay phones, to network computers, as illustrated in Figure 11–4.

Another kind of modem is the external modem. It is enclosed in a case and connects to the computer with a cable; it has a receptacle for a modular phone plug. One, designed for use with laptop computers, is the size of an audio cassette!

FIGURE 11 – 4   Acoustic couplers make networks as close as the nearest phone.

F. Bodin/Offshoot

FIGURE 11 – 5   Internal modems are mounted on a printed circuit board that fits into an expansion slot inside the computer.

Courtesy of Compaq Computer Corporation

An internal modem is mounted on a printed circuit board that fits into an expansion slot inside your computer. Internal modems usually require no adjustments and are the least expensive. Figure 11 – 5 shows what internal modems look like.

Speed   Modems are also classified by data transmission speed, measured as baud rate. One **baud** is equivalent to 1 bit per second (bps). Early personal computer modems could only transmit at 300 baud, but the rate soon rose to 1200, 2400, then 9600 baud. Larger mainframe computer modems can transmit at speeds of 19,200 to 1.25 million baud.

Since a character is represented as 8 bits, we can determine the speed of a modem by dividing the baud rate by 8. So at 300 baud, 37.5 characters are transmitted per second. A 1200 baud modem transmits 150 characters per second.

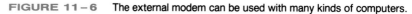

FIGURE 11-6   The external modem can be used with many kinds of computers.

D. McCoy/Rainbow

The Smart Modem   Smart modems can automatically dial a number or answer the phone. They can also redial a busy number over and over, and set baud rate to that of the remote computer. External smart modems have lights that tell you what the modem is doing: the baud rate, when it has made the connection, when it's sending or receiving data, and more. By contrast, consider the first modems of the 1960s. They had to be taken apart and rewired to dial a different telephone number. Figure 11-6 shows one of the external smart modems.

Telecommunications Software

The modem provides the physical link between the computer and the communications network; but without software issuing commands to the computer, nothing will happen. Telecommunications software routes signals to and from the modem, dials telephone numbers, and transmits data between remote computers.

Telecommunications software packages work just like any other application. Usually you insert a program disk and type the program's name. The software can be programmed with telephone numbers that dial the modem and connect to another computer. Once connected or on-line, you can send or receive communications. On-line means, literally, on the phone line, or connected to the other computer.

File Transfer   A common network activity is transferring files. This is called **uploading** when files are sent from a small, remote computer such as a personal computer to a larger, central computer — a mini or mainframe. Its opposite is **downloading,** or receiving files. File transfer lets you send or receive data very efficiently, since you don't have to type it in while you are on-line. This saves time and money.

The ASCII Format   Applications such as word processing and spreadsheets format data, making it appear correctly in the documents you create. Telecommunications software has the ability to transmit just about any kind of data; however, it must be in a standardized format. The most commonly used one is called ASCII (pronounced askey).

ASCII stands for the American Standard Code for Information Interchange and applies to all aspects of networking. ASCII data interchange requires that all the special codes and formats from the application program be stripped from a file. This is the only aspect of the ASCII standards that you control, and it is very simple to do. Most applications offer the option of storing your work as an ASCII file as well as, say, a standard word processing file.

Communications Parameters   Computers and telecommunications applications differ. It can be difficult to get two to "talk" to each other. But we can adjust these differences by setting communications parameters, which include baud rate and other important details that permit the two computers to exchange data. Most telecommunications software programs have a feature that allows you to store these parameters, along with each computer's telephone number and the information you need to connect online, in what are called script files.

In most cases, where one computer is directly connected to another (for example, two personal computers), their communications parameters must match. Synchronizing two telecommunicating computers using a set of standard procedures called protocols is called **handshaking.** Some telecommunications applications are designed to work on many different brands of computers, to overcome hardware incompatibility and expand communications capabilities.

Telecommunications Management Software

Our software discussion thus far has centered on the single user calling a host computer. Now let's look at telecommunications management software or *dialup software,* which controls host computers that receive calls from a number of single users. Like an airport traffic controller, this software determines which computers can participate in a network and the proper paths for communications to take.

When a network becomes overloaded, dialup software decides which computers have priority and which have to wait. This software also keeps track of who is using the network, keeping records and charging accounts when services are used.

Commonly, all telecommunications software performs error checking and security procedures. Dialup software is no exception. Error checking is the process by which networked computers assure the accuracy and integrity of data transmissions. Often, when errors are found, the dialup software tells the transmitting computer to resend the data.

Security procedures are used to prevent someone from intruding in a network without proper authorization. The software requests that potential users identify themselves and prove they are authorized to use the computer before they are actually granted access.

We've seen that networking begins with hardware: connecting a computer or terminal to phone lines via a modem. Next, we load software: a telecommunications application. Then we are connected over phone lines to host computer using telecommunications management software. With this basic knowledge of networking in mind, let's apply what we know in a hands-on session.

M E M O R Y
C H E C K

1. Define the term *network*.
2. What do we call a point on a network?
3. Identify several devices that can be computer network nodes.
4. Modems convert what two kinds of signals?
5. What do we call the signal that is modulated to convey binary information over the telephone line?
6. Identify three types of modems.
7. List three telecommunications software operations.
8. What is the standard format for file transfer?

AN ON-LINE WORK SESSION

There are many things we can do on-line. Here are a few ways we can network:

- Connect to electronic mail services.
- Obtain printed or published information.
- Get the current news and financial reports.
- Exchange programs or data with other personal computers, minis, or mainframes.
- Connect to computerized bulletin boards.

For our first excursion, let's do something simple and easy: send an electronic mail (often called E-mail) message to a friend.

Let's assume that your modem is properly connected and you have already created a script file to call a network mail service. Enter the command to dial up this service. First, you'll hear the dial tone through the speaker in the modem, then the electronic chirps as the modem dials the number. Once the call is connected, you'll hear the carrier signal and then a beep as the telecommunications software takes over.

The two computers now begin the handshaking process, comparing parameters to make sure they understand one another. If they don't, you may see something like this on your monitor:

```
əəə{ { } { }$$$${${ə{ }əə}
```

However, if they handshake properly, you'll see the mail service's main screen. Next, you'll be prompted for your user name and password. These are standard security measures networking services require. If your script file is set up correctly, it will send your user name and password automatically for you. Then you'll be logged on!

We're going to write a message, so next we enter a Create Message command. This menu usually takes the form of a memorandum. The mail service will prompt you for this information: To: (addressee of message); CC: (who to send copies to); and Subject: (optional line for message topic). Next you are prompted to enter the message text itself. Now, type your message as you would in word processing. You may have to press Enter at the end of each line; electronic mail often lacks the word wrap feature.

When you're ready to send the message, issue the command to end the message (usually shown in the command line). You may also have an option to preserve a copy for yourself. Once the message is sent, the E-mail service will probably respond by telling you the date and time it was sent to its electronic destination. All that's left for you to do to finish your work session is log off. The command is usually "EXIT" or "LOGOFF" and is often shown in the command line. This terminates the modem and phone connection; now you can quit your telecommunications software application as well.

One of the remarkable things about network mail services is they allow you to send messages almost anywhere in the world, so long as your addressee has a computer and an account on the same service. Another remarkable thing is the speed that electronic mail travels; the message is usually in the recipient's mailbox in a matter of minutes or seconds.

Let's look at an example. A computer industry journalist in Chicago wrote an article about a corporate CEO, a world traveler. This journalist went to New York to interview the CEO. But by the time he had a draft of the article completed, the CEO had left on a long business trip to Japan. Fortunately, he had taken his laptop computer and modem with him. The journalist transmitted the draft to the CEO's electronic mailbox; once he arrived in Tokyo he read it and transmitted his corrections back to the journalist. The journalist finished the article and sent it, again via electronic mail, to the magazine editor. She downloaded it to a file, edited it, and forwarded it for typesetting and publication. At no time was a paper copy exchanged, nor was the post office used. Can you imagine how long this same process would have taken using U.S. and international postal systems? Figure 11–7 shows the most popular electronic mail systems in use today.

FIGURE 11–7   Electronic mail services are growing rapidly. The number of mailboxes went from 430,000 in 1980 to over 10 million in 1990.

Name	Number of Mailboxes	Number of Messages per Month	Audience
AT&T Mail	290,000	11 million	Business
BITNET	500 + institutions	Unknown	Academic and scientific in US, Mexico, Canada, and Europe
CompuServe Mail	550,000	4 million	Personal, business
Internet	100,000 computers	Unknown	Government agencies, defense department, research and academic institutions (2,000 worldwide)
MCI Mail	110,000	2 million	Business
Prodigy	160,000	4 million	Personal
US Sprint Telemail	180,000	5 million	Business

MEMORY CHECK

1. Identify three things you can do with a networked personal computer.
2. To whom does a mail service allow you to send electronic mail?
3. How do you log on via a modem?
4. What is a script file?
5. What does the term *handshaking* mean?

TELECOMMUNICATIONS NETWORKS

In the days of the telegraph, a network consisted of wires strung on poles, from one sending/receiving station to another. Today, networks are far more complex. They consist of computers, telephone lines, microwave relay stations, satellite dishes, and satellites, all intricately linked, as Figure 11–8 illustrates. Satellite communications utilize microwave relay stations and satellite dishes to extend our communications lines into space, as Figure 11–9 shows. There are many different types and sizes of networks, each designed for a different purpose. Let's take a look at them.

Public Networks

A public network is an *open* communications network available for use by anyone, usually on a fee basis. The U.S. Sprint, MCI, and AT&T telephone networks are examples of public networks. They span the United States and the world. Even though initially designed for voice messages, these telephone networks carry a large volume of computer communications today.

In France, the telephone network was intentionally turned into a computer network by a project called Teletel. Teletel was launched in 1981, when the French telephone and post office department put a terminal called "Le Minitel" in every home in France. Initially, Teletel was to replace printed phone books by giving people on-line directory assistance.

However, enterprising companies soon realized they could provide other on-line services to the public. The program was a success: By 1986, the number of on-line services in France had jumped from 200 to over 2,000. One popular service is called Dialog, which allows people to form groups and have typed, on-line conversations.

Telecommunications-Only Networks In the United States, some networks are used exclusively for computer communications. These are called **packet-switching networks,** which send data in blocks called packets. The two most prominent are Tymnet and Telenet in the United States and Datapac in Canada.

There are two advantages to packet-switching. One, it is more economical to send data in packets. Two, packets are less prone to errors and corruption. Packets are routed to their destination very quickly—in just a few milliseconds. For example, on a packet-switching network you could send the entire text of the novel *Moby Dick*—220,000 words—in less than 30 seconds.

FIGURE 11 – 8   Today's computer networks utilize computers (1,5), telephone lines and microwave relay stations (2), satellite dishes (3), and satellites (4).

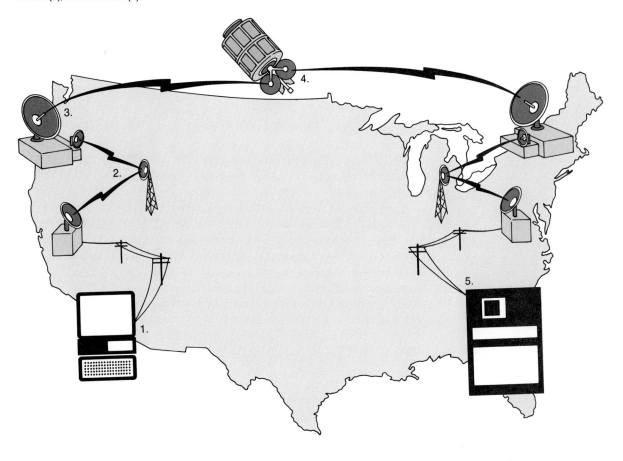

FIGURE 11 – 9   Space-based satellites (like the one on the right) orbit 22,300 miles above the earth, relaying messages between ground-based microwave relay stations.

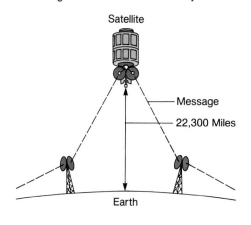

Courtesy of NASA

ARPANET   The first packet-switching network was ARPANET, created in 1968 by the U.S. Department of Defense Advanced Research Projects Agency. It links various government agencies, research labs, and universities. Today, hundreds of locations and thousands of computers are connected to ARPANET which is now one of the many networks on Internet, which is comprised of a number of interconnected global networks (see Figure 11-7).

Private Networks

In addition to public networks, many private networks exist in the United States. A private network is a *closed* communication system, usually confined to a particular company, governmental entity, or other group. An example is DECnet, the electronic mail and messaging system for over 100,000 Digital employees worldwide.

Another private network is American Airlines' SABRE reservation service. SABRE stands for Semi-Automated Business Research Environment. Developed by IBM in the mid-1960s, SABRE now has more than 68,000 terminals that connect 8,000 reservation operators and 14,000 travel agents around the world. Over 470,000 reservations are made on SABRE every day.

Several types of private networks exist to serve a variety of user needs. These are categorized in two ways. One is by topology — the physical layout of network devices and nodes. The other is by the proximity of network nodes and devices. Let's look at these types of networks and examples of how they are used.

Network Topology   **Topology** defines the layout of computers and other devices in a network and how they are connected. Figure 11-10 illustrates the three most common topologies: star, bus, and ring networks. Star networks give many users access to central files and system resources through a host CPU. Bus networks have no central computer but share other network resources such as printers, the same as star networks. In a ring network, individual computers are connected serially to one another. This arrangement is somewhat more expensive but has the advantage of providing many routing possibilities.

LANs   One type of private network is the local area network or LAN. As the name suggests, LANs are set up to allow a group of users in the same geographic location, such as an office or a small company, to share data, programs, and hardware resources. Figure 11-11 illustrates a LAN.

The terminals and computers in LANs are usually hard-wired — physically connected to each other with cables. Hard-wired LANs don't require modems. The cabling is often telephone wiring, called twisted-pair. More commonly, coaxial cable is used. However, fiber optic cable is being used more and more in LANs because it can handle more data and transmits it much faster. Figure 11-12 shows these types of cabling.

The editorial department at Richard D. Irwin, the publisher of this textbook, uses a LAN for cooperative work group computing. The Irwin LAN has seven Apple Macintosh computers. One is a file server whose large-capacity

FIGURE 11 – 10   The three most common local area network topologies: star, bus, and ring networks.

Star Topology

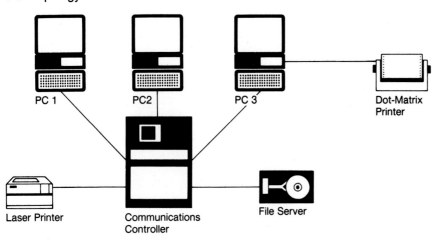

Bus Topology

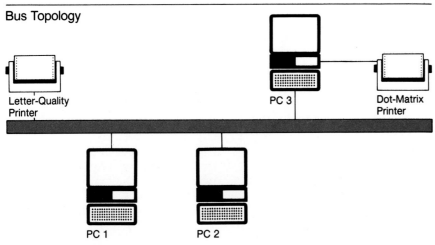

Ring Topology

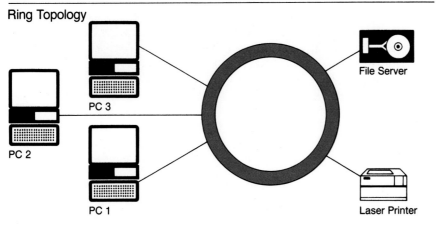

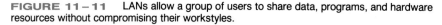

FIGURE 11-11   LANs allow a group of users to share data, programs, and hardware resources without compromising their workstyles.

Lou Jones/The Image Bank

FIGURE 11-12   Cable artistry.

Coaxial cables within a data transmission line.

Optical fibers: a single strand carries more data than all the coaxial cables combined.

Courtesy of Bell Labs

Jon Feingersh/The Stock Market

hard disk stores programs and files. The other six Macs each have one floppy disk drive, so files can be copied and stored. The LAN also has two printers that everyone shares: a dot-matrix for rough drafts and a laser printer for professional-looking correspondence, reports, and proposals.

The LAN gives Irwin's editorial staff several advantages. Sharing the file server and printers means buying less hardware. Storing programs on the file server means only one copy of an application needs to be purchased. Also, master copies of correspondence and manuscript preparation documentation

FIGURE 11-13   This corporate WAN allows the company to send voice and data transmissions between its computer centers at greatly reduced cost (see legend).

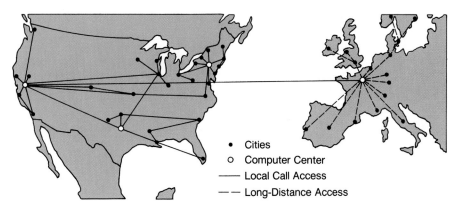

• Cities
○ Computer Center
—— Local Call Access
— — Long-Distance Access

are available in an "everyone folder." These shared files can be downloaded from the file server to any Macintosh and edited to suit individual needs.

MANs   The metropolitan area network or MAN is a network that links computer systems located in different buildings but all within close proximity. Some universities have MANs, as do banks with several offices located in New York. Rockwell International uses very sophisticated computer systems and networks to support its engineers. Its corporate network is called CONSORT, and within it are three MANs. One is at company headquarters in Seal Beach, California; the others are in Cedar Rapids, Iowa, and Richardson, Texas. Each MAN or node serves a number of different sites. Ted Sickles, Rockwell's data network manager, says, "The idea is that any terminal talks to any computer." This is particularly important at Rockwell because the computer could be a Digital mini, an IBM mainframe, or even a Cray supercomputer.

WANs   The wide area network or WAN is another type of private network. WANs use phone lines, microwave relaying stations, and satellites to connect computers located many miles apart. WANs allow users to do the same things as LANs. Even over great distances, WANs allow users to send electronic mail, share data and programs, and use the printers and memory devices linked to the network. Figure 11-13 is an example of a WAN.

Digital Equipment Corporation is an international company that both manufactures and uses the latest networking technology. It has its own WAN that allows employees in every part of the world to log on and communicate with any other individuals in the company. It is the largest corporate WAN in the world.

Digital is structured in layers, and that layering is reflected in the way it uses the computers and networks its manufactures. Corporate management levels need to know the activities of groups and subgroups to plan and monitor the company's growth and fiscal health. Engineering, manufacturing, marketing, and sales people must continually coordinate their efforts to design and build the products Digital's customers want. Individuals need to know the strategies and ongoing projects within their groups. The result is that a corporation as large as Digital, with over 100,000 employees in 62 countries, can function as one company—and as one community.

DISKbyte

Networking Tips

1. Buy a smart modem. They are often preset to work on specific personal computers. Buy either a 1200 baud or 1200/2400 baud modem, the standard operating speeds for most personal network services.
2. Choose an easy-to-use software program. Evaluate the program carefully for ease of setup, entering phone numbers and communications parameters, and redial features. Make sure you can program the software to dial and log into on-line services with ease.
3. When selecting on-line services, ask if there is an additional surcharge for using a 2400 baud modem; if there is, make sure to set your software to dial at 1200.
4. Check the hourly rates for on-line services; some are less expensive at night or on weekends. Watch the clock while you're on-line; it's easy to run up big charges, fast.
5. Plan on-line database searches before you dial. Use the manual to plan the keystrokes to find the information you want. Otherwise, you could spend expensive time pondering what you should be searching for.
6. Do not use a modem on a telephone line with the call waiting feature. If someone calls while you are on-line, call waiting may disconnect you.

Digital is fully networked to facilitate communication. As a result, inter-office memos are now electronic mail. Corporate, departmental, and individual data can be shared among all levels. Many employees are permitted to have terminals at home. This allows them connect to office systems and work any time of day or night.

Digital also provides many network services to its employees. The network stores electronic bulletin boards where employees can discuss corporate as well as personal interests. Topics include reading, sports, baby care, foreign languages, consumer issues, plants, pets, cars, and many more.

The Next Wave in Networks

As more and more people and companies use networking, the importance of being able to connect networks to one another grows. This is true both in the United States and internationally. And as twisted-pair wire and coaxial cable are replaced by fiber optic cables, more and more networks are becoming digital.

Digital networks have three advantages. One, voice transmissions work just fine on digital networks, which makes it possible to leave stored messages, as if an answering machine was built into the network. Two, in an all-digital network, modems are unnecessary. And three, many more services can be added. Regional Bell Operating Companies are experimenting with on-line telephone directories, along with special circuits that do call screening to identify incoming calls before you pick up the phone. Most also offer a variety of push-button audio services such as "900" information numbers.

ISDN   The culmination of this drive for new, improved networking is called the **ISDN,** or Integrated Services Digital Network. The goal for ISDNs is to make every network digital, whether voice or data, and compatible with every other network in the world. An ISDN would make it possible to send video images from one computer to another, without translation. One line could then be used for telephone, computer, facsimile, and television, or teleconferencing when it's used for business.

---

1. What is a public network?
2. What is a telecommunications-only network?
3. What is a private network?
4. Identify the three network topologies.
5. Describe the differences between a LAN, a MAN, and a WAN.
6. What do the letters ISDN stand for?

MEMORY CHECK

USING NETWORKS

Today, networks provide a wide range of personal, business, and governmental services. In general, these network services fall into two categories: information services, which allow us to read local and remote databases; and interactive services, which allow us to exchange information via networks. Here are some examples of these two kinds of network services.

Information Services

Information services are services that maintain and provide access to data repositories. They offer a wide variety of information. You subscribe to an information service as you would to a magazine. When you become a subscriber, you're given a telephone dial-up number that allows you to connect to the service. Many information services require an initial fee and then bill you for usage on a monthly basis.

Information services are one-way services; you can read their data but cannot add to their databases. There are two general categories into which information services fall: news and database services. Let's begin by looking at news services.

News Services   As the name implies, news services provide the latest news, including general interest, business, and financial news. You can read *The New York Times, Forbes, USA Today,* and many newsletters on news services.

The Dow Jones News/Retrieval (DJN/R) service is an example of a news service. DJN/R provides financial information, stock quotations for over 6,000 companies, and other investment information. Since it is owned by Dow Jones, it also offers the full text of articles from *Barron's* and *The Wall*

FIGURE 11-14   This touch-screen program lets you easily use Dow Jones News/
Retrieval.

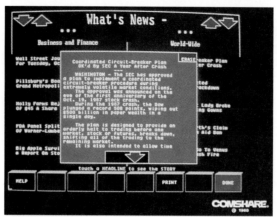

Courtesy of Comshare, Inc.

FIGURE 11-15   A portion of a database search.

* * * * INVESTEXT * * * *

Enter Industry Name, Symbol, or LIST,
<M>ain, <P>revious, <Q>uery, <H>elp: telecm

Industry   : TELECOMMUNICATIONS 55503 pgs 13132 rpts

Enter Text Search Command, <M>ain, <P>revious,
or Help: electronic mail

Number : 935618
Title : Telephone Lines - Industry Report
Date   : Oct-17-1989
Source : DONALDSON, LUFKIN & JENRETTE, INC.
Author : Gross, J.
Length : 35 PAGES

AT&T TO ACQUIRE ISTEL

   On September 26, in an announcement originating from London, AT&T revealed that it will
acquire Istel, Ltd., an electronic mail systems integration and specialty network firm for 180 million
or $291 million. Istel was once a subsidiary of Rover Group PLC, the British car manufacturer,
prior to a management buyout in 1987. Istel still derives approximately 38% of its revenues from
Rover in return for managing Rover's computer systems. Reportedly, Istel ranks second in the
U.K. in electronic data interchange (EDI), a rapidly growing segment of the market that enables
companies to pass documents such as purchase orders to each other without using the post
office.

Street Journal. But DJN/R doesn't confine itself to financial information. It
also provides film reviews, a college selection service, an encyclopedia, and a
medical and drug reference. (See Figure 11–14.)

Database Services   A database service is an information service
whose primary purpose is to provide comprehensive information. These services store very large amounts of data on large-capacity hard disk drives.
Database services allow you to connect your personal computer to a host
computer and read this data. You can also download data to your computer.
Writers, students, lawyers, medical practitioners, and others use database
services to research topics of interest. The U.S. government has hundreds of
specialized databases for such topics as agriculture, population, jobs, health,
and science. In some ways, subscribing to a database service is like having the
Library of Congress in your own home. (See Figure 11–15.)

FIGURE 11–16   A Boston Computer Society electronic bulletin board.

Welcome to the Boston Computer Society IBM User Group
Bulletin Board System

Main Phone   (617) 332-5584

300-9600 BPS, 8 data bits, no parity, 1 stop bit
Now Operating 4 Phone Lines at 2400 BPS

Chief SysOp   Reed Butler
Main SysOps   Doug Chamberlin, Dan Harrington, James Prentice

F. Bodin/Offshoot

Interactive Services

Where information services are one-way streets, interactive services can be two-, four-, six-, and more-way streets. Interactive services allow you to connect your personal computer to a community of computer users to both obtain and exchange information. You can interact with other users in the same way you would over the telephone but with added dimensions. In effect, you and your information become part of the service, to whatever extent you choose.

Electronic Bulletin Boards   One of the most popular interactive services for personal computer users is the electronic bulletin board, sometimes called a BBS or a CBBS, for computerized bulletin board system. An electronic bulletin board allows you to read and post messages for other subscribers. Bulletin board messages are topic-specific or personal, depending on the type of bulletin board. (See Figure 11–16.)

For example, a bulletin board might specialize in bringing buyers and sellers of personal computers together, like classified ads. However, you may also read and post personal messages on any of thousands of topics, from dating to drawing, politics to pets, and sports to spincasting. There are bulletin boards for just about any and every interest.

EFT and Consumer Services   Probably the most common example of an interactive service is Electronic Funds Transfer (EFT). EFT means making financial transactions using a network. EFT often involves using a bank card to make withdrawals and deposits via an ATM. Consumer shopping networks such as Prodigy and the Electronic Mall are also growing in popularity. These services allow you to shop worldwide for many kinds of products or services, from dry cleaners that pick up and deliver to large volume auto sales dealers.

Information Utilities   A third type of on-line service called information utilities combines elements of information and interactive services. Utilities such as CompuServe and Delphi, both give subscribers access to news, exten-

---

DISKbyte

Telecommuting: Working from Home (or Somewhere Else)

Many people take work home from the office. But some employees work at home all the time. In some cases, they are self-employed entrepreneurs; others are employees of government or a company. They work at a personal computer or a terminal, connected to a central computer doing data entry, programming, word processing, accounting, and other tasks. Because they use networks to connect to the office, their work is described as telecommuting.

Perhaps the most intriguing telecommuter is Steven Roberts,

Photo by travel companion Maggie Victor

whose office is the Winnebiko III, a 54-speed bicycle he invented with state-of-the-art computing and communications built in. He uses both a Macintosh portable and a DOS computer that he controls with a special keyboard built into the handlegrips, as well as an ultrasonic mouse fitted to his helmet. Steven has ridden 16,000 miles of American highways, writing about his adventures and using E-mail to submit his articles. He has also written a book about his first 10,000 miles on the road entitled *Computing Across America.*

FIGURE 11–17   The opening menu of Delphi, an information utility.

```
Happy Halloween!  Join the costume party in the Micro Artists Network (MANIAC)
tonight, October 31.  Unmasking at midnight!  Type GR MIC.


MAIN Menu:

Business & Finance    News-Weather-Sports
Conference            People on DELPHI
DELPHI/Regional       Travel
Entertainment         Workspace
Groups and Clubs      Using DELPHI
Library               HELP
Mail                  EXIT
Merchants' Row        BOSTON Services

MAIN>What do you want to do?
```

sive databases, bulletin boards, and shopping services, all for a very reasonable fee. Typical start-up subscription packages cost $25–$30. (See Figure 11–17.)

Business and Governmental Networks

Business and government have found that networks improve communication among workers, help them provide new or better services, and enhance productivity. Let's see how.

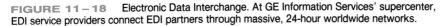

FIGURE 11–18 Electronic Data Interchange. At GE Information Services' supercenter, EDI service providers connect EDI partners through massive, 24-hour worldwide networks.

Jon Feingersh

EDI Electronic Data Interchange (EDI) is using networks to transfer forms such as invoices, purchase orders, shipping notices, and even payments between computers. The data is entered into the appropriate form in the order entry software. Then the data *only* is extracted and transmitted, via EDI software, computer-to-computer using compatible hardware and software, or via a private network such as the one shown in Figure 11–18.

Many accountants and individuals use EDI technology to submit federal income tax returns. The Internal Revenue Service now allows many people to use their personal computers to file tax returns. To do so, you use an income tax preparation software program. You collect the electronic forms that comprise your tax return and electronically transmit them to IRS computers.

EMISARI The U.S. government has used networks to serve the public for quite some time. The EMISARI program is one example.

Back in 1971, inflation was getting out of control in the United States. Wages and prices seemed to be chasing each other, zooming to levels that began to make the U.S. economy very unstable. A crisis developed, and President Nixon declared a 90-day national wage/price freeze.

EMISARI, for Emergency Management Information System And Retrieval Index, was a network created by a computer science professor named Murray Turoff to help the U.S. government communicate about the freeze. It served two purposes. First, it allowed national and regional level policymakers to discuss and coordinate all aspects of the freeze. Second, it gave people access to information they needed to handle local emergency situations.

EMISARI proved to be an outstanding service. The information in the database evolved, and as new problems were identified, isolated, and solved, EMISARI became an on-line library that showed both the history of the freeze and the current state of this new program. By collecting questions and answers, and by showing the history of policy making, EMISARI was a living history and documented itself.

Innovations that made EMISARI especially responsive to the needs of that time have been incorporated into many modern database teleconferences. EMISARI's menus allowed you to retrieve particular varieties of information such as messages, tables, files, and contracts. Other menu options let you update or explain messages. Keywords are used to search for topics throughout the database. For example, if you need data on rent freezes, you could request all the messages that contained the word *rent*.

EMISARI was a strategic tool in designing and implementing the wage/price freeze. Today, there are thousands of similar databases used by federal, state, and local governments, corporations, special interest groups, and dozens of other institutions in the United States. Like any good means of communication, these databases pool ideas so that resources, history, and information can be made available to anyone.

MEMORY CHECK

1. What is the difference between an information service and an interactive service?
2. Identify two types of information services.
3. Identify two types of interactive services.
4. What is an information utility?
5. What does EDI stand for?

NETWORK SECURITY

We talked a little about computer security and the need to physically protect data in Chapter 3. This is true in networking as well, for whenever a computer is connected to a phone line, it is extremely vulnerable to unauthorized people gaining access to the data stored there. We'll explore some of the problems and their remedies, then discuss the ethics of networking.

Protecting Networks

Because networks can make computer systems vulnerable to intrusion, security systems exist to protect them. One such system employs user names, account numbers, and passwords to differentiate between authorized users and intruders. To make this system work, users must keep their passwords confidential.

Another method of ensuring network security is the callback system. In this system, you begin by connecting to the computer via telephone line and modem. Next, the computer prompts you to enter your user name and password. At this point, the computer terminates the connection. The computer verifies your user name and password, then calls your computer back at your preregistered phone number to establish the connection for your work session.

Intruders   People who intrude or break into computer systems are sometimes inappropriately called hackers. A true **hacker** is someone who demonstrates great skill in programming and working with computers; for that

DISKbyte

Radio Modems Fight Credit Card Fraud

When a credit card is stolen, it's likely to be used for only about 48 hours, then thrown away. The thief knows that by the time two days have passed, the word—in this case the number—is out and he or she could be nabbed in the act. But now, a new networking technology that utilizes FM broadcasting promises to shorten two days to two hours—maybe even two minutes.

This new technology is called a Personal Information Network, and it works like this. A credit card company such as Visa or Master-Card keeps all its cardholder records in a database. When you call to report a lost card, the information is extracted from the database and beamed, just like a radio signal, to the merchants. Each merchant has a special FM modem that receives the signal, which is then stored in a personal computer. The merchant can either read the

message on the screen or print out a report.

Merchants used to get a printed booklet of bad credit card numbers that was mailed every two weeks. Sometimes it took a week for it to arrive through the mail. But now, using FM modems, merchants can get a bad card notification in as little as 10 minutes. This means fewer merchants get burned by fraud, and the credit card company can dramatically cuts its losses.

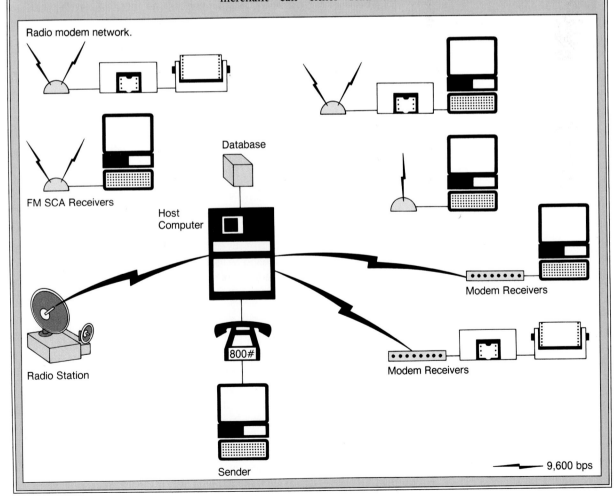

Radio modem network.

FM SCA Receivers

Database

Host Computer

Radio Station

800#

Sender

Modem Receivers

Modem Receivers

9,600 bps

reason, we need to make a distinction between the hacker and the **intruder**, a person who deliberately gains access to a computer system that is the property of another party. Intruders gain access to computer systems by circumventing user name/password security. Some use an automatic telephone dialer to find the numbers of computer systems. When they locate a number, their computer attempts to guess user names and passwords by trying every possible combination of letters and numbers.

To thwart intruders, systems use lockouts — software that only lets you have three tries at entering a user name or password. After three incorrect attempts to enter a correct user name and password, the phone connection is broken. This can certainly slow down the efforts of an intruder. Another security measure requires that authorized users change passwords at assigned intervals. Yet another is the callback system, discussed on page 370.

The latest technology uses keycards, fingerprints, voiceprints, and retinal eye scans to secure multiple-user systems. Although these require additional sophisticated hardware and software, many military, government, corporate, and private institutions often feel their information security is worth the extra cost and effort.

There are many other ways to break into computers and networks. To try figuring out the loopholes before intruders do, some computer owners attempt breaking into their own systems. For example, the U.S. Air Force employs experts from Mitre Corporation to look for weaknesses in its computer security.

Encryption   Encryption is another technique of protecting computer communications. **Encryption** involves putting coding devices at each end of the communication line. Before sending out a message, one computer encodes the text by substituting what appears to be gibberish characters for real letters. At the other end, the message is decoded by the receiving computer. This makes it very hard for transmissions to be read by unauthorized people even if they are intercepted.

File Protection   File protection is now common on personal computers, whether they are used by one person or connected in a network. Individual workers can lock personal files so others cannot read them. In addition, entire disks, whether floppies or hard drives, may also be protected. Figure 11–19 shows a program used to lock disk drives. The first screen shows the password protection; the second shows how the program lets the user know there has been an unauthorized attempt to read the disk files.

The Computer Virus   In recent years, computer systems have been plagued with an insidious program called a virus. A **virus** is a software program that enters computer systems via other programs or through communications networks, then hides itself. It can go unnoticed for long periods as it infects the computer and then causes it to crash.

Viruses are often created by an employee who has been fired and wants to strike back at the company in anger; by young computer "geniuses" who want to demonstrate their computer skill; by programmers with antisocial tendencies or a perverted sense of humor. We have had many virus attacks over the past few years, and although they can be stopped, there does not seem to be a way to prevent them. One such attack occurred in 1988. A graduate com-

FIGURE 11–19   Disk protection program.

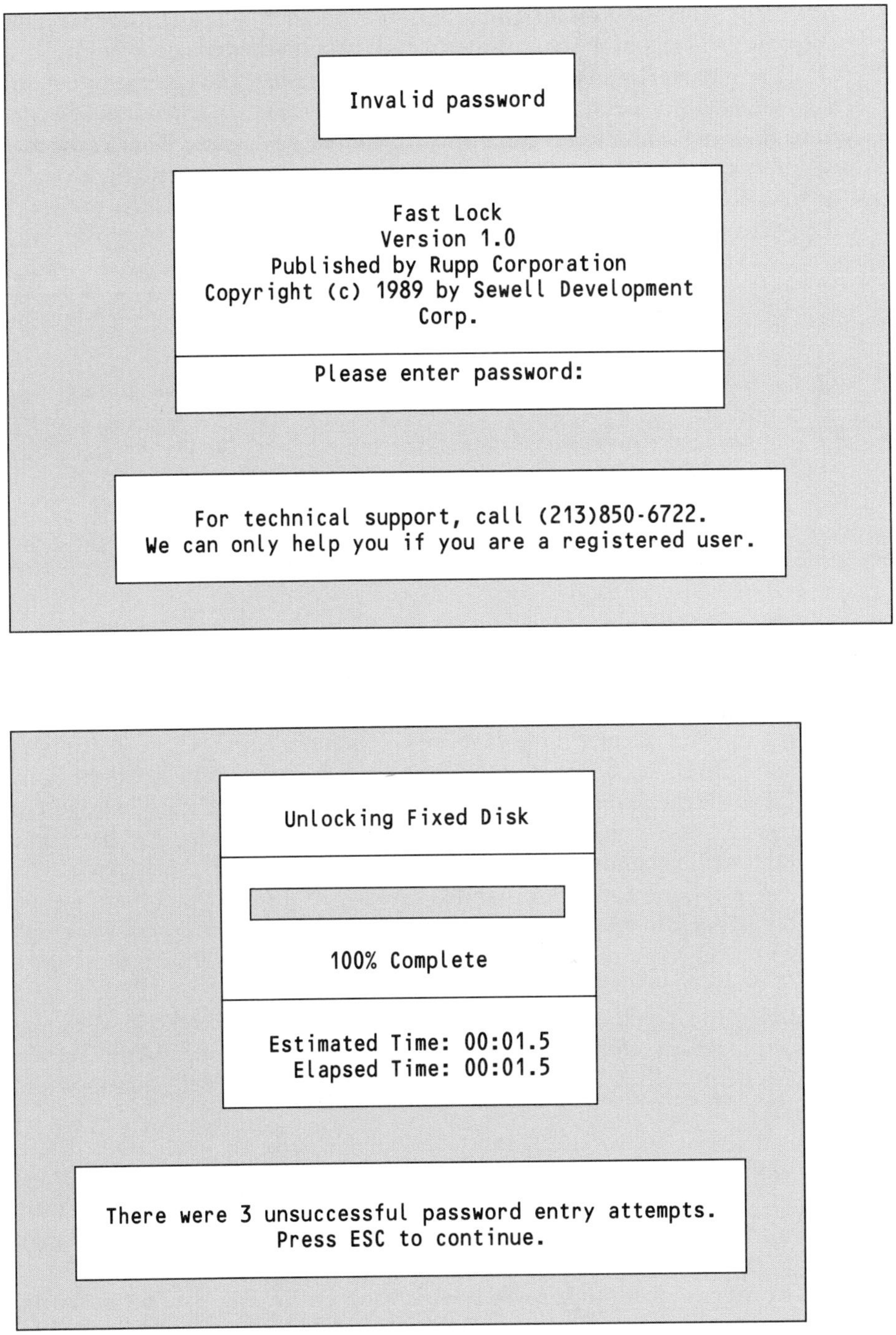

```
                        ┌─────────────────────────────┐
                        │      Invalid password       │
                        └─────────────────────────────┘

              ┌──────────────────────────────────────────────┐
              │                 Fast Lock                    │
              │                Version 1.0                   │
              │         Published by Rupp Corporation        │
              │   Copyright (c) 1989 by Sewell Development    │
              │                    Corp.                     │
              ├──────────────────────────────────────────────┤
              │           Please enter password:             │
              └──────────────────────────────────────────────┘


         ┌────────────────────────────────────────────────────────┐
         │      For technical support, call (213)850-6722.        │
         │   We can only help you if you are a registered user.   │
         └────────────────────────────────────────────────────────┘
```

```
              ┌──────────────────────────────────────────┐
              │           Unlocking Fixed Disk           │
              ├──────────────────────────────────────────┤
              │       ┌──────────────────────────┐       │
              │       │██████████████████████████│       │
              │       └──────────────────────────┘       │
              │             100% Complete                │
              ├──────────────────────────────────────────┤
              │       Estimated Time: 00:01.5            │
              │       Elapsed Time: 00:01.5              │
              └──────────────────────────────────────────┘


         ┌────────────────────────────────────────────────────────┐
         │   There were 3 unsuccessful password entry attempts.   │
         │              Press ESC to continue.                    │
         └────────────────────────────────────────────────────────┘
```

puter science student at Cornell University placed a computer virus on AR-PANET. It brought 6,000 computers to a halt. He was tried, convicted, fined $10,000, and sentenced to 400 hours of community service and 3 years' probation.

Aaron Haber, who teaches at Harvard University, has written that as a society, we must link computer files with the realization that this material often represents the life work and innermost thoughts of a person and is highly confidential. It is more than property and must be treated accordingly.

[The intruder] is an example of how we have failed, and his example is one that will be followed until we change society, says Haber. Intruders will continue breaking into systems and implanting viruses as a game. They know they would not physically ever harm someone, yet do not comprehend the violence of their seemingly benign actions. They rarely see, in person, the results of their activities and this distance promotes their insensitivity.

MEMORY CHECK

1. Identify some of the problems that have led to the creation of computer security systems.
2. What is a lockout?
3. In computing, what is an intruder?
4. Describe how encryption provides computer security.
5. What is a computer virus?

THE EVER-EXPANDING NETWORK

In 1844, Samuel F. B. Morse tapped in dots and dashes with a metal key, sending the first telegraph message from Washington, D. C., to Baltimore, Maryland. By 1871, the Western Union telegraph company eclipsed the Pony Express as the means of moving messages fast. But just five years later, patent number 174,465 was issued to Alexander Graham Bell for the harmonic telegraph — today known as the telephone.

The telephone network expanded rapidly. In just 25 years there were 6 million phones in the United States. American Telephone & Telegraph (AT&T) acquired a controlling interest in Western Union. By the 1980s, AT&T dominated the U.S. communications industry, so in 1983, federal judge Harold Greene ordered a divestiture. This separated AT&T, the long-distance company, from its seven local operating companies: Pacific Telesis, Southwestern Bell, U.S. West, Ameritech, Bell South, Bell Atlantic, and NYNEX.

By this time networking was established, fulfilling the predictions of two early global thinkers. One was Marshall McLuhan, who envisioned a "global village." He saw that modern communications, television, and radio were tying all the peoples of the world together — as if we all resided in one small village.

The other global thinker was Buckminster Fuller, who saw the potential for computers being used to share information, helping nations disperse resources and receive help when they needed it. The international response to the famine in Africa in the mid-1980s proved that Fuller's vision of the future was accurate. We saw starving people and responded to their needs as would members of one village.

Computers play a key part in global dynamics. They have an important role in linking other communications technologies such as television. They control satellites and the innumerable systems that route and control data transmissions of all kinds. We can see this operating on a large scale in international business and relief operations.

Soon, you're also likely to see a networked personal computer at the center of your home, the controller of your personal information and entertainment system. It may answer your phone when you're away and take messages. When you're home it can screen your calls, telling you who is on the other end before you answer. It might become the receiver for all your radio and television signals.

Your personal computer may also take the place of your VCR and tape recorder. You'll be able to set it up to record TV broadcasts and store them digitally until you're ready to view them. We may even see on-line libraries that allow us to "borrow" more video programming than the corner video store could ever supply, as well as all the latest global news, weather, culture, and sports information. These are just a few of the possibilities. The potential of networks to serve us has continually grown for more than 100 years, and appears likely to continue to do so.

ETHICS

It is unethical to gain access to someone else's computer system without his or her express permission (in other words, without a legitimate user name and password). It is unethical to read the files of a welfare recipient, a doctor's patient, or an employee unless it is your job to do so. And it is unethical to damage or destroy programs or data — considered proprietary — on someone else's computer.

Yet all these things happen, and often without consequence to the perpetrator. There are stories of supposedly clever teenagers who crack into a computer and order cases of soft drinks. Stewart Brand, a leading thinker, computer user, and author of *The Whole Earth Catalog* and *The Whole Earth Software Catalog,* says this of people who are challenged to crack into computers: "When you are linked into such computer power, you are no longer a mensch. You are an ubermensch [superman]. . . . What they know is that they are outside the law. The information technology that they are moving with is going so fast that they're ahead of the law. It's like we've come upon a vast new continent, we've just spent a couple of years on the shore — and the closest thing to native dwellers are the intruders."

Others do not take such a poetic view of intruders. Our government has responded to the problems we have with computer security and begun to get tough. The Computer Fraud and Abuse Act of 1986 makes it a felony to cause more than $1,000 in damages by breaking into computers across state lines, or by maliciously trespassing into banking and security dealers' computers. The FBI investigates these cases. In addition, most states have similar laws either on the books or pending. To some, intruders used to be heroes. Now, like the Cornell student, they may also be felons. In 1990, the Secret Service culminated a two-year investigation called Operation Sun Devil that resulted in seven arrests along with the seizure of some 40 computers and 23,000 disks of data. Law enforcement officials say that Operation Sun Devil and other investigations are a response to a dramatic rise in computer crime that threatens personal privacy and the security of government and corporate computers.

Mitchell D. Kapor, founder of Lotus Development Corp. (see Chapter 5), became concerned that the civil and legal rights of computer users are being threatened. He specifically cited freedom of speech and illegal search and seizure. Kapor and Steven Wozniak, co-founder of Apple Computer, Inc., formed the Electronic Frontier Foundation to promote computer education and fund legal efforts to extend First Amendment protection to electronic media.

"Our mission is not to defend people who break into computer systems," said Kapor, "but rather as a response to the government overemphasizing the dangers posed by hackers." The Electronic Frontier Foundation's first action was to award a $275,000 grant to the Computer Professionals for Social Responsibility, a Palo Alto, California-based public advocacy group. The two-year grant will be used to sponsor educational and policy-setting efforts to protect computer users' civil liberties. The foundation will also support the development of tools, such as computer games that teach about computers and software and makes them easier to use.

CAREERbyte

The Networking Professional

The U.S. Bureau of Labor Statistics says that employment throughout the 1990s looks bright, especially for professional workers, technicians, managers, and executives. Engineering, health, and computer occupations are expected to account for over half the growth in the professional occupations. What's more, 2 out of every 10 jobs in the year 2000 do not even exist today.

What that means is incredible opportunities, especially for the enterprising person interested in working in the networking field. To get an idea how important networking is, Georgia State University offers a master of science degree in Business Information Systems, which requires that the student take a full year of communications or networking courses. Why this heavy emphasis? "Because the wrong network could cost a manager his job," says the department chairperson.

Networking has already created new jobs in electronic publishing and research. Here are descriptions of two such occupations: the electronic editor and the on-line librarian or researcher.

H. Mark Weidman

The Electronic Editor
Massive encyclopedic databases such as DIALOG, Nexis, Lexis, and Bibliographic Retrieval Services provide on-line summaries of articles and other published materials. They list the article title, author, publication information, and a brief summary or synopsis of the article's content. That summary must be clearly and concisely written to properly convey the article's contents. An electronic editor reads the articles and writes the bibliographic entry. As more and more of the world's information is published electronically, the importance of electronic editorial skills will grow as significant as those of a newspaper editor, a magazine editor, and even a book editor. And as editors read and study a subject area, their knowledge and expertise grows, expanding their skills and career opportunities.

The On-Line Researcher or Librarian
Learning to use and master on-line encyclopedic databases is not only challenging, it's a profession. Large companies often employ several on-line librarians, responsible for doing all the information searches for others. Many people have started telecommuting jobs at home, doing the same thing for businesses of all sizes. Search information is used to explore new business opportunities, to see what the competition is doing, or to learn what kinds of research may be underway in special fields of interest. On-line information has become a valuable competitive tool, and the people capable of retrieving it are equally valuable to their employers and clients. Sometimes there is enough business to start one's own on-line search company with a substantial list of clients.

SUMMARY

1. *Define networking and identify the necessary hardware and software components.* Networking, also called telecommunications or data communications, expands computer capabilities by tying together computers and communication systems. We use computers, telephone lines, modems, and telecommunications software to obtain information and gain access to many different network services. There is telecommunications software for the user's computer and telecommunications management, or dialup, software for the host computer. ASCII file formats, communications protocols, system settings, script files, and error checking all play an important role in networking software.

2. *Describe the difference between analog and digital signals and their role in networking.* Analog signals vary in tone, pitch, and volume like our voices. A digital signal is a steady stream of pulses that does not change. Modems are used to connect computers to telephone lines; modulation turns digital signals to analog on the sending end and demodulation turns analog signals back into digital on the receiving end.

3. *Explain the difference between public and private networks and their uses.* Public networks offer open communication channels and private networks offer closed communication channels to serve diverse networking needs. Public networks permit access to networking services, such as electronic mail, for a fee. Private networks are used by businesses or other nonpublic entities, such as government agencies.

4. *Name three network topologies and identify the three common types of private networks.* Network topologies have been developed for specific purposes. They include the star, bus, and ring configurations. They are used in designing local area, metropolitan area, and wide area private networks. Local area networks (LANs) connect computers in close proximity. Metropolitan area networks (MANs) link computer systems located in different buildings within a short distance of each other. Wide area networks (WANs) utilize cables, microwaves, and satellites for linking nodes into large and complex computer networks.

5. *Identify several kinds of network services.* There are network services for entertainment, news, business, and governmental uses, to name a few. Information services offer subscribers access to news and database services, a more in-depth information resource. Interactive services allow users to exchange information via electronic bulletin boards, electronic data interchange, and bank and consumer network services. Information utilities provide people with electronic mail, news, and many shopping and entertainment services.

6. *List several methods of maintaining network security.* Hackers are people with highly developed computer skills. Intruders, on the other hand, are people who deliberately gain access to computer systems that don't belong to them. Sometimes they create destructive programs, such as a computer virus. To keep these people out we use passwords, lockouts, callbacks, positive identification techniques, encryption programs, and file protection schemes.

KEY TERMS

baud, p. 353
downloading, p. 354
encryption, p. 372
hacker, p. 370
handshaking, p. 355

intruder, p. 372
ISDN, p. 365
modem, p. 351
networking, p. 350
node, p. 350

packet-switching networks, p. 358
topology, p. 360
uploading, p. 354
virus, p. 372

REVIEW AND DISCUSSION QUESTIONS

1. Why might we say networking has made the world smaller?

2. Dennis Hayes invented the modem before there were many services available for which to use it. Can you think of similar developments in the computer industry?

3. What three components are necessary for networking?

4. Can you identify areas other than banking where the speed of modern telecommunications systems serves you?

5. What is the difference between an ordinary modem and a "smart" modem?

6. What does telecommunications software do?

7. How does a script file simplify networking?

8. Today, we have telegraph, telephone, television, radio, and computer networks. How might it serve us to ensure that these still exist separately 25 years from now?

9. How did networking computers affect the momentum of the Information Age?

10. Why do we need both public and private networks?

11. Why do we have LANs, MANs, and WANs instead of just one network?

12. What advantages do electronic news services have over their traditional counterparts? What disadvantages?

13. What networking services might help you with your college course work?

14. What are some reasons why a corporation without a communications strategy is at a great disadvantage?

15. How might FM receivers play a part in bringing down credit card interest rates?

16. How might EDI improve a company's profitability?

17. What would have taken the place of EMISARI if we didn't have computers? What would we have lost/gained?

18. Describe several uses of the computer security methods currently in use.

19. Can you think of a foolproof method for ensuring the security of a computer system?

20. Do current laws sufficiently protect the rights and interests of computer users?

ISSUES

1. One of the great principles of democracy, applied to modern communications, maintains that access to information is a public right. Yet recent intrusions on networks have seriously disrupted their operations and threaten even more extensive, permanent damage to software and data. In light of these issues, do you think we should restrict access to public networks? Do you agree with Aaron Haber? With the government? With Kapor and Wozniak?

2. Network integration and the Integrated Services Digital Network (ISDN) are evolving into a worldwide network. Considering the financial, political, and information resources such a network would control, could this concentrate too much power in the hands of its owners?

3. With networks carrying confidential information such as credit, law-enforcement, and IRS records, have we as citizens lost control of our personal privacy?

CHAPTER 12

Management Information Systems

The Strategic Advantage in Business

CHAPTER OUTLINE

Richard Nolan: Creating a Vision of MIS
Living in a Systems World
  MIS: A Definition
  Why Use a Management Information System?
  Who Uses MIS?
  A Business Perspective
  A Government Perspective
  The MIS Concept
MIS: Three Components
The People Component
  The MIS Organization
  DISKbyte: Three Top MIS Executives
  End-User Computing
The Software Component
  Distributed Computing
  MIS as a Corporate Resource
  DISKbyte: IBM's Top 10 Customers
The Hardware Component
  Systems Integration
  DISKbyte: Facilities Management: Don't-Do-It-
    Yourself MIS
  New Computer Architectures
  Information Providers
What Lies Ahead?
  The Changing Role of the MIS Executive
Ethics
  CAREERbyte: The PC Manager
Summary
Key Terms
Review and Discussion Questions
Issues

OBJECTIVES

After reading and studying this chapter, you should be able to:

1. Define the term MIS and explain how it is used.
2. Describe the people components of MIS.
3. Explain the ways MIS makes the software component available.
4. Describe how the hardware component is changing the way computer architectures are used in business.
5. Discuss how the MIS organization and its leadership are changing and evolving.

RICHARD NOLAN: CREATING A VISION OF MIS

In the 1970s, Richard L. Nolan, then an associate professor at the Harvard Business School, was studying data processing departments in a number of large companies. He developed what he termed the "stages theory" about why some DP departments were doing better with information systems than others. In 1974, he and a colleague published an article in the *Harvard Business Review* entitled "Managing the Four Stages of EDP Growth." (EDP stands for electronic data processing.) Five years later, Dr. Nolan published a second article in the *HBR* called "Managing the Crises in Data Processing," which added two stages to his earlier model. Nolan identified these stages:

1. *Initiation.* Beginning to use computer technology and experiencing early successes, which in turn leads to increased interest and more experimentation.
2. *Contagion.* The factors in stage 1 lead to widespread interest and new applications and services for users. Information systems usage rapidly proliferates.
3. *Control.* Management begins to feel uneasy with this rapid growth and associated costs and begins to curtail proliferation. Some data processing (DP) projects are deemed impractical; attempts at integrating various applications and systems proves difficult, since each was independently developed without planning for how it would work harmoniously with others at a later date. Users "give up on data processing."

Courtesy of Richard Nolan

4. *Integration.* DP has reorganized itself and started activating new applications and providing high-quality service to users.
5. *Data administration.* Applications are beginning to be integrated, and DP begins exercising tighter control over data and systems.
6. *Maturity.* Full applications integration occurs, and the structure and organization of DP is complete. Information flows duplicate the organizational structure of the company, which results in high-quality utilization of information systems.

Nolan's idea that there were life stages struck a powerful chord in DP managers and has had a profound influence on many information systems departments. Once they recognized a stage they were stuck in, these managers were able to guide the operation into the next, more productive, stage.

This fact has been largely responsible for the growing DP has assumed in the modern corporation and governmental organizations. Due to its increasing importance, we now commonly use the term *management information systems,* or *MIS,* to refer to data processing.

Today, Dr. Nolan is chairman of the consulting firm he cofounded with David P. Norton in 1973: Nolan, Norton & Company. Nolan, Norton is one of the most respected information technology consulting firms in the world; in 1987, it became a division of Peat, Marwick, a major accounting firm.

LIVING IN A SYSTEMS WORLD

The computer has had a dramatic impact on many facets of modern life, lending a high-technology aspect to many things once considered commonplace. We have everything from kitchen appliances controlled by a microprocessor to high-tech thermal underwear. The proliferation of computer systems has created a systems world. There are stereo systems, video systems, ski rack systems, even garden hose attachment systems. Today, the computer pervades every aspect of business procedures, as well as transforming each operation it touches into a system of some sort or other: accounting systems, payroll systems, and office systems, to name only a few.

There are good reasons for this. Just as our natural environment is segmented into various ecosystems, we have a business environment grouped into logical, functional systems. Business groups each have their own tasks to perform but they also interact with other groups. The computer provides the linkages between them, as shown in Figure 12–1. Generally when we talk about the computer in business and the various tasks it performs, we refer to management information systems or MIS. The term MIS, sometimes shortened to just IS, has different meanings, each of which we'll examine next.

Just as there are various hardware components in a computer system — for example, the CPU, main memory, and peripherals — there are various business processes such as order processing, accounting, manufacturing, and

FIGURE 12–1   The computer provides essential links throughout the company. A sales order triggers a series of interrelated processes that utilize many aspects of an Information system to produce the finished product or service.

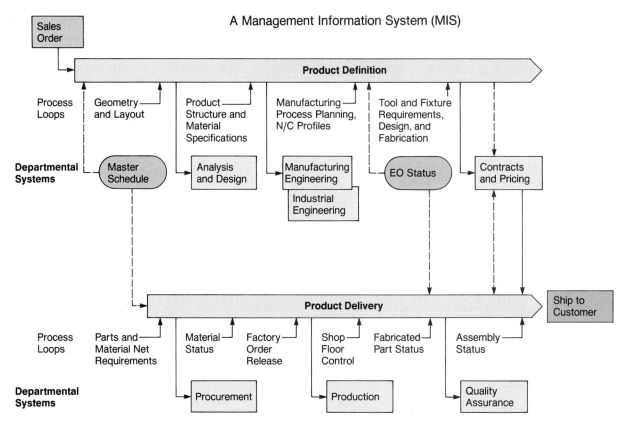

shipping that form a system for managing a business. Working together, these processes assure that the work gets accomplished properly so the business achieves its goals—producing a service or product, satisfying customers needs, creating a profit, and distributing dividends to shareholders.

MIS: A Definition

The term **management information system (MIS)** refers to the computer system, working together with the business organization, to achieve the business goals. Figure 12–2 shows a typical business system; with its human input, processing resources, and products or services output, you can see the resemblance with a computer system. You can also see that the computer system, like the business system, must be managed: standards must be maintained and resources balanced to consistently produce the end product or service.

The computer system provides data that various people in the business use as information to solve problems, plan strategies, and make decisions affecting the health and livelihood of the business. In most cases these people are considered managers, charged with decision-making responsibilities. Generally, as shown in Figure 12–3, managers are categorized into three levels:

- Top-level or senior management.
- Middle or line management.
- Operational or supervisory management.

This is true whether we are discussing corporate management or departmental management, including MIS. Figure 12–4 shows a typical management hierarchy at a Fortune 500 company. In such an organization, the director of MIS reports to the vice president of finance and thus is more of a middle manager.

FIGURE 12–2   The MIS department uses computer systems to create products and services in the same way as the business system.

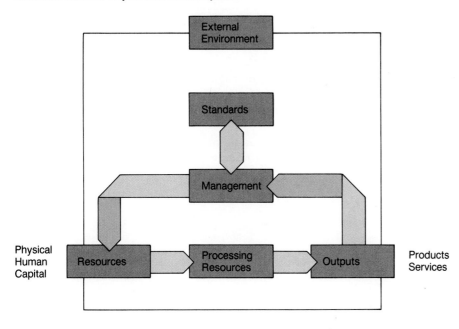

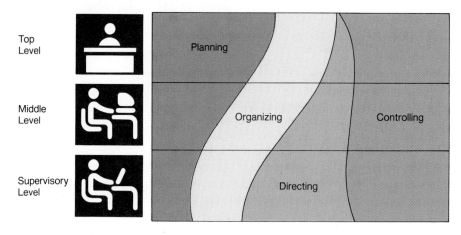

FIGURE 12−3   Management activities in business and MIS. Top management spends most of its time organizing and planning, middle management motivating and developing, and operational management directing and controlling.

However, the MIS organization's role is changing considerably. There is a greater need for MIS to be able to respond to the company's changing priorities. As a result, many progressive companies have promoted the MIS director to a vice president or top-level position. Figure 12−5 shows an organization poised to make those changes.

Why Use a Management Information System?

Let's study the acronym MIS to determine why we should use a management information system.

M   Regardless of the business function, it is essential there be some form of *management* to plan, organize, direct, control, and staff. Management accomplishes objectives through the efforts of many people. Lack of management is responsible for more failures than any other single aspect of business.

I   We must have *information* for management decisions, for planning strategic directions for the future, for improving business performance, and for developing or sustaining a competitive advantage in the marketplace.

S   We need to develop and maintain *information systems* and applications that help make workers more productive and contribute to achieving the business' goals.

Who Uses MIS?

Who uses MIS? There are two answers to this question. First, MIS is primarily used in business, in government, and in the information industry. Even though individuals using personal computers in their home businesses could

FIGURE 12–4 An organization chart for a typical Fortune 500 company. Central MIS serves the various functions; each geographic division may have its own MIS.

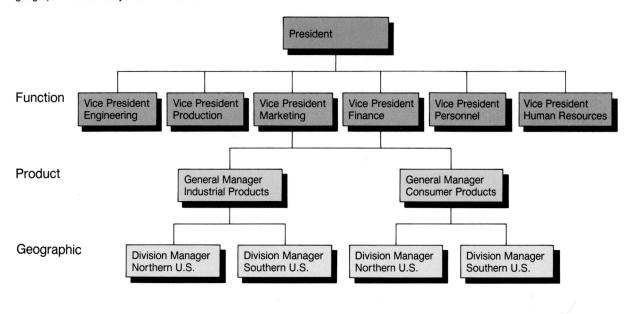

FIGURE 12–5 An organization chart for an MIS organization in transition. Today's systems chart reflects a primary focus on technology issues. Tomorrow's systems chart shows a shift to an organization focused on people and business needs.

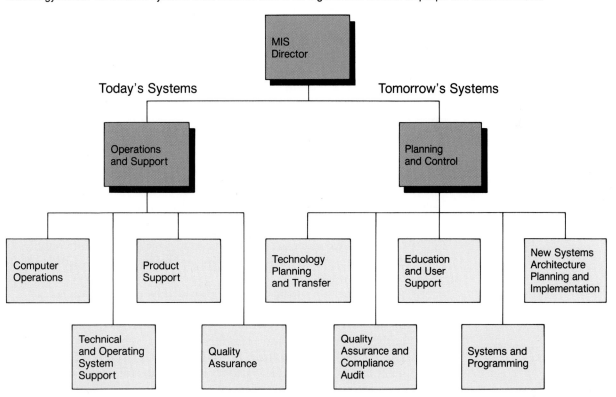

be considered MIS users, in this chapter we are primarily interested in corporate MIS environments. *InformationWeek,* a magazine for information systems professionals, ranks the top 100 MIS organizations in business each year. The smallest of these MIS organizations has an annual budget of $100 million; the largest is in excess of a quarter of a billion dollars!

Second, management information systems are used by managers at the three levels we discussed earlier—top-level, middle, and operational management—to plan, organize, direct, control, and staff MIS operations and projects for users. A project is an assignment for MIS to create an application for users in a business function. The project might be to find a way for a fast-food chain to gather the daily receipts from its many restaurants, or to set up a customer database for a division that is introducing a new product. Let's take a look at how MIS is used.

MIS is not just for large firms. Happy Dan's is a chain of five convenience stores located in Mankato, Minnesota. The stores rent out a combined total of over 1,000 videotapes that must be accounted for at all times. A paper system was used at first but was quickly abandoned; there was no communication between the stores, so a renter had to have a separate membership at each location.

Happy Dan's installed a 386-based personal computer at company headquarters, and installed a terminal, with a bar code reading wand attached, in each store. The terminals are connected via phone lines to the 386. Members are given adhesive bar code labels, which they can attach to a piece of identification such as their driver's license. Each videotape also has a bar code. When a member rents a tape, the clerk scans his or her personal ID bar code to verify membership, then the videotape bar code to indicate that this videotape is checked out. The MIS database software keeps track of how long and how often the tape has been checked out. That allows management to gauge the videotape's popularity; if all the copies are out all the time, they buy more. If no one seems to be renting a videotape, they put it up for sale. Happy Dan's MIS may be small but it manages a great deal of valuable inventory—and information.

A Business Perspective

Management information systems are most widely used in business, where they are often considered a "strategic weapon" in "corporate combat." Management collects business data and turns it into strategic information. This data collected in MIS comes from three sources:

- *Outside sources* such as sales rep surveys, magazines or trade publications, on-line database information, and informal human communication networks or "grapevines."
- *Inside sources* about the company provided by operational management concerning its productivity, resources, staffing, etc., or by middle management regarding opinions or analyses of short-term goals, opportunities, and accomplishments.
- *The information system itself,* by feeding specific data into the computer in order to produce analyses or scenarios for senior management to set future goals, plan strategic directions, or create new competitive advantages. These are often customized information systems called decision support systems (DSS) or executive

information systems (EIS), designed especially for top-level managers without extensive computer skills. We will study these systems in greater detail in Chapter 13.

MIS in Business   A typical large company has many types of information systems in use. While some are designed to assist customers, such as an automated teller network of ATMs at a bank, most are for internal use. Each of the divisions shown in the Figure 12–4 corporate organizational chart requires its own information systems, some of which are centralized and shared by other divisions, and some that are unique to that organization. For example, central MIS provides sales figures that are used by finance to determine the firm's profitability, by marketing to set quotas and measure the sales staff's performance, and by human resources — in this case, payroll — to pay salaries and sales commissions. An organizational MIS for distribution might keep track of local inventories at half a dozen regional warehouses.

From a management perspective, the sales information helps the operational manager know how much product to manufacture and how many workers are required. It also helps the middle manager set goals for new products or an increased market share, and it helps senior management decide on plans for expansion or growth in the future. So in a sense, anyone who is involved in managerial decisions uses management information systems.

Mrs. Fields Cookies   Consider Mrs. Fields Cookies, a company that owns over 500 Mrs. Fields cookie store outlets, the La Petite Boulangerie chain of bakery-cafes, and some combination stores. Senior management — in this case, Randy Fields, the chief executive officer — wanted information that pinpoints what is going well and what is not, so that corrective measures can be taken. He wanted to know anything that might affect the company's plans for the future. His primary interest was in developing a corporate strategy to ensure the company's success. For example, there were signs that the gourmet cookie business may be a fad. If the public grew bored, Randy Fields wanted to be prepared to diversify into other fast-food or restaurant businesses. His ability to do so depended in large part on the quality of information he received.

To accomplish this, Paul Quinn, the vice president of MIS at Mrs. Fields, designed and installed an information system. He was considered part of senior management. Each store had a personal computer to collect data and electronically transmit it to the computer at company headquarters in Park City, Utah, each night. This data included inventory reports, time cards, work schedules, sales figures, and bank deposits. The transmitted store data was captured in the company's minicomputer system, where it was analyzed to determine what was going smoothly and what could go wrong. For example, a store may be having trouble hiring new help and could soon be understaffed. Perhaps it was not providing enough free samples to entice customers.

Middle management at corporate headquarters needed to analyze how all the retail operations were performing on a daily basis, based on reports from each store. This data was analyzed and interpreted by store controllers, middle managers who promptly sent electronic mail messages to retail store managers, alerting them to potential problems. The store managers were part of operational management, and worked with the store controllers to solve problems.

Operational management—the store managers—needed to know baking schedules, worker schedules, and personnel hiring policies. The software Paul Quinn designed for them provided all this information and more in a sophisticated system called ROI, for Retail Operations Intelligence. ROI provided inventory control to maintain supplies and ingredients, and showed the manager baking schedules, such as "6:30 A.M.: Bake 87 oatmeal muffins, 23 fruit muffins." If customers suddenly developed a taste for a certain cookie or muffin, the software noted it and adjusted the baking schedule accordingly. And there was a diagnostic program to help determine why an appliance wasn't working.

Prospective employees filled out an employment application on the personal computer. The ROI software, which utilized an expert system, analyzed the application and created a set of questions for the manager to ask in the face-to-face interview. It also provided skills testing to ensure that employees were properly trained.

Paul Quinn's management information system provided information that helped redirect some of Mrs. Fields growth, specifically recognizing the need to diversify into the La Petite Boulangerie bakeries. It has also created an entirely new business: selling the Retail Operations Intelligence software to other multilocation retail chains. Fox Photo, with 230 stores, bought it, as did some other restaurant chains.

As you can see, the management information system at Mrs. Fields Cookies is many things to each different manager. It is an example of how a good information system provides many data resources and makes a measurable contribution to the manager's decision making.

A Government Perspective

Management information systems are used in almost every aspect of city, county, state, and federal government. At the federal level, they are used to provide census data, research and reports for the legislative bodies, files on taxpayers and medicare recipients, and much more. In fact, there are so many systems and databases in the federal government—many of which are available to the public—that entire books have been written listing them. (See Figure 12–6.)

U.S. Navy MIS   Did you know that the armed forces use MIS as well? The man responsible for the success of the Navy's Naval Supply Command is retired Rear Admiral James B. Whittaker (see Figure 12–7). Admiral Whittaker, who earned a Ph. D. at the University of Michigan and wrote a book on strategic planning for MIS, took the helm of the supply command MIS operations in 1980. He was responsible for a number of successful information systems that have earned the respect of both the government and private industry.

Whittaker's was an important job, for NSC is charged with providing all the Navy's supplies, from toilet paper to nuclear submarine parts. Admiral Whittaker reduced the time it took to obtain mission-critical parts from 20 days to 13 days or less. And he developed information systems that provided information for naval "senior management" as well as the Government Accounting Office (GAO), which oversees all governmental expenditures.

One MIS project, Inventory Stock Point, was aimed at improving operations and inventory at 40 stock points or warehouses. These stock points

FIGURE 12–6   A partial list of available government databases.

Government Databases
ABLEDATA—Rehabilitation
ASIAC (Aerospace Structures of Information Analysis Center)
AGNET—Agriculture
Agricultural Market News Service (Market News)
AFDB (Alternative Fuel Data Bank)
AMB (Antarctic Meteorite Bibliography)
AIC (Arthritis Information Clearinghouse)
AITS (Automated Information Transfer System)
AMIS (Automated Minerals Information System)
Bibliographic Data Base on Glaciology
BIOETHICSLINE
Biological Data/Information System
Bird Banding Data Base
BADB (Boating Accident Data Base)
Breeding Birds Survey Data Base
Bureau of Labor Statistics Electronic News Releases
BDRS (Business Development Report System)
Cancer Information Clearinghouse
CCDB (Carbon-Carbon Data Base)
CBIS (Carcinogenesis Bioassay Data System)
CPIA (Chemical Propulsion Information Agency)
CRGS (Chemical Regulations/Guidelines System)
Clearinghouse on Child Abuse & Neglect Information
Clearinghouse on Health Indexes
Climate Assessment Data Base (CADB)
Coastal Engineering Information Analysis Center (CEIAC)
Coastal Zone Color Scanner Data Base
COMPAT/HAZARD-FAILURE—Chemical compatibility
Computer-aided Environmental Legislative Data System (CELDS)
Computerized Management Network for Agricultural Cooperative Extension Service
    Education (CMN)
Computer Retrieval of Information on Scientific Projects (CRISP)
Conservation and Renewable Energy Inquiry and Referral Service (CEIRS)
Consumer Education Research Network Bibliographic Data Base (CERN I)
Consumer Education Research Network Directory Data Base (CERN II)
Cooperative National Plant Pest Survey and Detection Program (CNPPSDP)
CRF (Current Research File)—Occupational health and safety
Crude Oil Analysis Data Bank (COA)
Data Resources Directory Publications Subsystem (DRD)
Defense Mapping Agency Hydrographic/Topographic Center (DMAHTC)
Defense Pest Management Information Analysis Center (DPMIAC)
Defense Technical Information Center Collection (DTIC On-Line, DROLS)
Dental Research Projects
Development Information System (DIS)
DIDS (Document Information Directory System)
Digestive Diseases Education and Information Clearinghouse
Directory of Persons Interested in Technology Transfer
DOE/RECON (Department of Energy's Remote Console Information System)
Earthquake Data File
Earthquake Effect File
Economic Impact Forecast System (EIFS)
Economic and Social Data System (ESDS)

Source: Matthew Lesko, *The Computer Data and Database Source Book* (New York: Avon Books, 1984).

handle over 3 million parts, valued at $77.5 billion. The MIS project cost $2.3 billion to complete but replaced an antiquated system installed during the 1960s that used punched cards and batch processing. The new system operates in real time, so that inventories are updated much more quickly. **Real time,** as its name implies, means that processing a transaction occurs at the moment it

FIGURE 12-7   Admiral Whittaker, former Navy MIS chief.

Tallat Mohamed

is input into the computer system. Using batch processing, it would take at least six days to get a new part into the inventory system; now, using real-time processing, it only takes one day.

Admiral Whittaker had a large staff of Navy MIS managers, most with M.B.A. degrees and at least five years' experience. He also contracted with Electronic Data Systems (EDS) for systems development and maintenance (see the DISKbyte "Facilities Management: Don't-Do-It-Yourself MIS" on p. 399). Upon retiring, he left in place an MIS organization that functions with much greater efficiency. Today, it serves as a model for others in the military and government to follow. One of Admiral Whittaker's favorite quotes, from the British statesman Benjamin Disraeli, sums up his spirit, hard work, and accomplishments: "The secret of success is constancy to purpose."

The MIS Concept

There are many ways to manage a business. In the study of management, there are various schools of thought: classical management, scientific management, behavioral management, and so forth. There is even "seat of the pants" management, or trying to figure things out as you go along. Most management experts agree that managers usually make decisions based on acquired experience and personal judgment, sometimes backed up or verified by empirical evidence.

The idea or concept behind MIS is *information systems that work in conjunction with the business system,* like an overlay that helps conceptually chart and verify the business plans, directions, and strategies. It does this at three levels of information management:

- Record-keeping, the simplest (and earliest) use for information systems.
- Operations control, improving such things as order entry and processing or inventory control.
- Strategic planning, for such things as increasing market share, outperforming the competition, and in general, gaining a competitive advantage.

These three levels roughly correspond to the three levels of business functions and management, as you will recall from Figure 12–3. To illustrate, let's return to our case study of Mrs. Fields Cookies. The store manager uses the computer information system for record-keeping and other light management tasks. The operations manager uses the system to keep track of retail stores, make operational changes, and assemble data for management reports. The chief executive officer uses the system for planning the company's business directions. In this context, MIS provides a management information system that acts as a model for conducting and managing the business.

---

1. What is the name given to computer systems used in business to achieve business goals?

2. What are the three levels of management?

3. Describe what the three letters in the acronym MIS stand for.

4. What is another acronym commonly used in place of MIS?

5. What are the three sources of data used for strategic or competitive information?

6. Explain the purpose behind the MIS concept.

MEMORY CHECK

MIS: THREE COMPONENTS

In the early days, a business had a computer that kept track of accounting data and records. It was considered an office machine or just a large calculator that helped speed up manual processing. Today, computer information systems are essential to *every* aspect of a well-run business. A company would literally grind to a halt without MIS. Even when the computer function is lost or "goes down" for just a short period of time, the losses quickly add up.

Throughout this book, we've stressed that the computer is a system made up of people, software, and hardware. The same is true of MIS. There are many people to consider in MIS: managers, staff, and end users. MIS software takes many forms; MIS hardware is often complex and ubiquitous. Let's take a closer look.

THE PEOPLE COMPONENT

MIS is unique in that it touches just about everyone in the company. MIS is a department or organization itself, with all its own internal computing needs. Yet it is also an organization providing services to other departments. Within those departments are many people who use computers.

The MIS Organization

Just as business has its organizational chart, so do individual departments throughout the company. MIS is no exception. It takes many different people to run a large MIS organization.

In years past, data processing functions were loosely managed; the atmosphere was fraternal. Projects often ran over budget and past the scheduled completion date because programmers tended to write and rewrite code ("tweak") to make it better. Often, the improvements were barely noticeable to the user and a waste of time and money. In other cases, the application was a programming marvel but was difficult to use or did not provide the information managers needed.

Without firm management controls, MIS often ran afoul of other business departments and gained a reputation for being difficult to work or communicate with. On the other hand, more and more functions and departments wanted information systems, creating a work overload in MIS. As a result, an application backlog grew; in large companies, some estimated there would be a lag time of five to six years before an information system could be completed! An improved management structure has helped get MIS better organized and able to accomplish its tasks in a more businesslike fashion.

MIS Management   At the head of the MIS organization is the senior executive, sometimes known as the vice president, general manager, chief information officer (CIO), or director of MIS. In most cases, this individual has worked his or her way up through the ranks over a period of 10 to 20 years. Many have an undergraduate degree in computer science or MIS, and often an M.B.A. to go with it. They are highly paid individuals with a great deal of authority and responsibility (see the DISKbyte "Three Top MIS Executives"). They often report directly to the executive vice president or even the president of the company. They spend a great deal of their time in planning meetings, helping chart directions for the company, and determining the role of MIS in corporate strategies. It is not uncommon to find them in a corner office, sitting at a large walnut desk—often with no computer in sight!

Reporting directly to the MIS executive is the middle manager, commonly known as the manager of MIS. This is a senior person as well, but one with day-to-day responsibilities. His or her job is to make sure the director's wishes are carried out and implemented by the operational or supervisory managers. For example, if the company decides to begin its fiscal year with a new reporting system, the director must orchestrate the operational managers and their staff to make sure the necessary hardware is purchased, the programming completed, the debugging finished, terminals installed on desks, and so forth.

The operational managers oversee such things as software maintenance, new application development, user training, and a number of other functions. These managers often appoint a project manager to head a team of programmers working on a specific application or project. They are given specific instructions and schedules for completing portions of the projects, some of which take years to complete.

MIS Staff   The MIS staff is made up of people with many different skills, in much the same organizational tasks as the business itself. There are systems analysts who are responsible for analyzing and designing new applications, as well as complete systems. For example, the head of manufacturing might ask a systems analyst to create a system, from hardware to software, to manage the entire manufacturing process of a new product.

Programmers write software using programming languages. They can be found working at terminals or personal computers in conventional office

DISKbyte

Three Top MIS Executives

The top person in MIS is an important member of senior management. According to a MIT study, the position has gained much greater visibility and respect over the past 15 years. Here are three profiles of success.

Courtesy of East-West Center

Raleigh Awaya is administrator for management and computer services at the East-West Center, Honolulu, Hawaii. The East-West Center is a nonprofit educational institution established by the U.S. Congress to promote better relations and understanding among the nations of Asia, the Pacific, and the U.S. through cooperative study, training, and research. "Our emphasis is on how to capture and reuse information for the benefit of the enterprise," he says. "In traditional systems, the computer is the

primary driving force. Here, we start with the end user, say a secretary. We place a high priority on the user interface, training, and good documentation. All this with a staff of 14. In a regular organization it would take 40 people."

Courtesy of Eastman Kodak

Katherine Hudson is vice president and director of corporate information systems for Eastman Kodak. Ms. Hudson worked in systems, new products, and public relations before becoming head of MIS, which has a budget of over $100 million a year. But Kodak, the world's leading photography products company, is also becoming a technology company, and Kathy Hudson's fresh viewpoint is seen as an asset: "I started out with a clean sheet of paper. . . . In one sense, it's been good for me to start out a new job without knowing

what I was doing." But make no mistake; she is an experienced, highly respected MIS executive.

Courtesy of John Hancock Advisors, Inc.

Edward J. Boudreau, Jr., is president and CEO of John Hancock Advisors, the mutual funds division of John Hancock Mutual Life Insurance Co. Mr. Boudreau worked in finance, then successfully managed a three-year project to improve systems and standards — completing the work in only two years. He attributes his success with MIS in part to getting "the IS professionals to speak English. I made it a point not to get mired in the technology; I was always looking at the best interests of the business." It paid off; Mr. Boudreau was promoted from head of MIS to president, then chief executive officer, of John Hancock Advisors.

---

environments. In a Fortune 500 firm, there might be several hundred programmers working on various projects. Some are systems programmers, meaning their work involves expanding, improving, or maintaining the systems software or the existing software applications, such as the accounting system or the manufacturing resource planning (MRP) system.

Others are **applications programmers,** who are assigned to work with various departments in the company, such as customer service, or helping users develop new applications. For example, a company planning to implement electronic data interchange (EDI) might have several systems programmers working in the MIS department, while assigning application programmers to order processing, inventory, and shipping to set up and install the EDI applications.

Still others are **operations technicians,** responsible for maintaining the hardware. Some are responsible for installing terminals and setting up personal computers, while others troubleshoot malfunctioning equipment. Some are in charge of backup systems, such as changing disk packs, tapes, and tape cartridges.

End-User Computing

The IBM PC, introduced to corporate America in 1981, truly changed the way the world computes. Its proliferation was spurred by users' growing frustration with MIS and its inability to provide them with computing services. The reaction to this became known as **end-user computing**, placing personal computers where individuals could easily use them to be more productive in their work. This was due to several factors: the application backlog, noted earlier in this chapter; a purported lack of CPU power to add an infinite number of new terminals; and a general reluctance to let the unsophisticated novice user gain access to the corporate mainframe. At first, personal computer users were not interested in using central MIS services, preferring to use the personal computer simply as a stand-alone computer.

Information Center   As more and more users began working with computer systems for the first time, it became clear that they needed training and assistance. To aid them, IBM devised the concept of the **information center,** which created a bridge between the computer professional in the MIS department and the computer novice in the user department. The IC staff—most of whom came from MIS—trained users, showing them how to create their own applications using software tools such as 4GLs, and taught them to use personal computers. Some ICs are being closed now, having served their purpose. However, users still need help from time to time, so in this office area of MIS there is usually a help desk, where several computer professionals are on duty to take calls from users who need help. Sometimes, user departments have a **PC (personal computer) manager,** who takes time from his or her own work to help others learn personal computers or new software packages.

**M E M O R Y
C H E C K**

1. What is the senior MIS manager called, and who does he or she report to?
2. What is the second-in-command manager called?
3. Name several staff positions that report to the second-in-command manager.
4. Identify three factors responsible for the growth in end-user computing.
5. What department or function helps end users learn to use computer systems?

THE SOFTWARE COMPONENT

MIS is responsible for keeping many, many applications running on a daily basis. These include order processing, accounting, inventory control, computer-aided drafting, manufacturing, database management, and more. Remember, large computer systems are multiuser, multitasking machines; there can be hundreds of applications running at once. These applications must be kept up-to-date, and must be "fixed" if they go down. For that reason, many systems programmers are responsible for **software maintenance,** a term that does not do justice to the importance of the task. In the 1980s, software maintenance accounted for 75 percent of the software budget.

You've already learned about the different types of systems and applications that have evolved up until now. Next, let's see where MIS is heading in the 1990s.

Distributed Computing

For many years, all MIS functions were **centralized,** or kept in the central MIS facility. Eventually, there was more to do than MIS could handle. For that and other reasons, many computers and applications are used in a **distributed computing environment,** placed in different geographic locations but linked functionally to one another in a network where they are most effective. (See Figure 12–8.)

FIGURE 12–8   Distributed computing makes computer resources available throughout the organization.

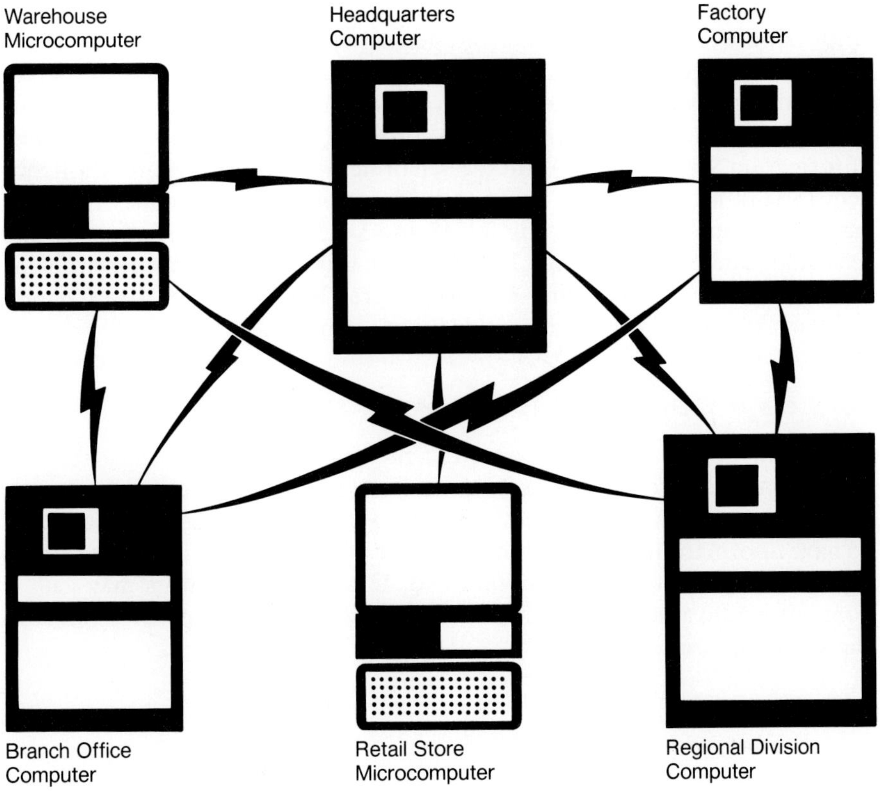

Warehouse
Microcomputer

Headquarters
Computer

Factory
Computer

Branch Office
Computer

Retail Store
Microcomputer

Regional Division
Computer

George P. DiNardo, chief of information management and research at Mellon Bank in New York, after spending 30 years in two highly centralized MIS operations, reorganized his MIS department to reflect a decentralized or distributed computing environment. Over half of the applications are now developed in the user department; Mr. DiNardo says, "The totally centralized systems shop can — if it is a quality shop — build systems better, but the business unit (users) can build better systems. Application programming really belongs under the control of the business units that use that application. How do I feel about this transformation? I feel very good, thank you!"

Enterprisewide Computing   Systems integration, which you will learn about in more detail in the next section, makes it possible to connect all kinds of computers together. It paves the way for **enterprisewide computing** systems, which encompass the entire business and all its operations (the enterprise). The ultimate goal is to provide systems integration on the application level; that is, to make it possible for any application to share data with any other.

How Not to Do It   NASA, the National Aeronautics and Space Administration, had a less-than-successful MIS strategy that got the organization in trouble in the 1980s. Congress funds NASA on a project-by-project basis, which has led to a mess of incompatible systems. NASA has no central MIS organization to oversee or help develop these systems. That means there is no information flow between them, something the scientists and researchers need. This demoralizes workers, and has meant delays in assessing the results of NASA missions. In one case, it took 18 months to obtain flight data. Researchers have waited years to get the computer data they need to evaluate and write about their findings. The result is what researchers call "islands of information," preventing users from getting what they need.

In the past few years, NASA has taken steps to correct the situation. While some contend that NASA should always exist as a scientific laboratory with no centralized management controls, two projects, the Technical Management Information System (TIMS) and the Scientific Applications Information System (SAIS), are attempting to build bridges between the islands. Unfortunately, the same problems recur: TIMS and SAIS are incompatible and can't exchange data or information. Experts agree this is not a computer problem but one that involves getting people to agree how they want to exchange information — and a management decision to implement it.

MIS as a Corporate Resource

As information systems have evolved, the manner of collecting data and transforming it into information has itself become a strategic tool, with true value. Just as a manager becomes more valuable as he or she gains experience, so have information systems. Companies are often reluctant to discuss certain aspects of their information systems, for fear that competitors may gain a competitive advantage by employing the same strategies. That's how valuable these systems are.

DISKbyte

IBM's Top 10 Customers

IBM has dominated the MIS business since the late 1950s. Today, over 70 percent of all American companies are "IBM shops." *InformationWeek* magazine, in conjunction with the market research firm Computer Intelligence, determined the following top 10 IBM shops in the United States.

Company	Annual MIS Expenditures	Comments
Sears Roebuck	$775 million	Also AT&T's largest customer
American Express	Over $300 million	Over 40 mainframes
IBM	$3,581 billion	Over 3,000 mainframes
General Electric	Approximately $275 million	Over 100,000 personal computers
American Telephone & Telegraph	$1,800 billion	Declining number of mainframes in favor of networked minis and personal computers
United Telecommunications	$43 million	US Sprint has 65 networks
Prudential Insurance	$700 million	Bought first IBM in 1955
General Telephone and Electric (GTE)	Approximately $190 million	Has four MIS "superhubs"
NYNEX (New York-New England Telephone)	$600 million	Owns over $150 million worth of IBM equipment
Dun & Bradstreet	Approximately $150 million	Has over 1 terabyte (a trillion bytes) of information stored on IBM equipment

Source: *InformationWeek*, June 12, 1989, pp. 4–22.

For that and other reasons, many corporate information systems use a security system that restricts access to certain types of information. For example, access to the data center is restricted to key personnel by use of passwords and special locks. Security systems create passwords and security levels, so a clerk cannot read memos exchanged between senior executives that discuss a new product introduction. Programmers are often asked to sign employment agreements stating they will not divulge details about the projects they are at work on or the contents of programs they write. For example, an expert system might contain proprietary details about a product's ingredients or proprietary manufacturing techniques that would cause great loss if it fell into a competitor's hands.

Often, computer-generated information, and in some cases proprietary programs, have demonstrated a usefulness that does not conflict with the company's strategic goals. Smart companies realize this material can be sold to others, providing a return on the investment made in developing it and perhaps even a profit. Mrs. Fields ROI system is one example. It has generated millions of dollars a year in additional revenues. Mailing lists are another profitable information resource. Banks and insurance companies often sell specialized programs they have developed in-house. Clearly, MIS is a valuable corporate resource in many different ways.

1. What kinds of applications is MIS responsible for running?
2. What is the most important job in software?
3. Describe the two different ways in which MIS can be organized.
4. What are the advantages in distributed computing?
5. Why is enterprisewide computing desirable?
6. What do we mean when we say MIS is a corporate resource?

THE HARDWARE COMPONENT

In Chapters 9 and 10, you learned about mainframe and minicomputer installations. In medium- to large-size companies, such an installation is the command control central for what is commonly called the MIS department or MIS
organization. In the beginning, the computer was kept in a separate room. By
the late 1950s, most businesses had IBM computers, so they called the computer site "The IBM Room." Over the years, the names data processing (DP)
and electronic data processing (EDP) became fashionable. By the mid-1970s,
the term MIS was commonplace; in the 1980s, it was shortened to information systems (IS). Now we sometimes hear information technology (IT).

These changes reflect the information systems professional's desire to
provide the kinds of computer services the enterprise seeks. There is still a
computer room today but more often it is an area, perhaps an entire floor in
the building, designed to house the computer equipment. There is usually a
shift supervisor and several operations people on duty, monitoring the system,
backing up hard disk drives on tape, and performing maintenance tasks. But
MIS extends throughout the business. There are minicomputers in manufacturing, workstations in engineering, and personal computers in offices everywhere. This is why there is so much interest in distributed computing, enterprisewide computing, and systems integration.

Systems Integration

From the beginning, computer systems from different vendors have been
incompatible with one another. This is true at the hardware level, the systems
software level, and the application level. **Systems integration** is a way of
interconnecting hardware, system software, and applications from many manufacturers into one system. Trade groups have been formed to begin solving
the problem of connectivity, and great strides have been made. Another frequently used name is cooperative processing.

A great deal of systems integration is occurring with personal computers,
and networking companies are leading this field. It is estimated that about 15
million personal computers will need to be integrated in the first part of the
1990s. This is because some users need access to the corporate mainframe's
database, for example, to perform analyses and projections using current
figures. MIS grew concerned that the data passed back from the personal
computer may have been "corrupted," and for several years there ensued the
battles and problems of micro-mainframe connections, or trying to connect
personal computers to the central computer.

DISKbyte

Facilities Management: Don't-Do-It-Yourself MIS

In the 1960s, many companies wanted to install data processing equipment but lacked the staff or the expertise to do it themselves. So they contracted with **facilities management** companies, who came in and ran the whole show for them. Electronic Data Systems (EDS) was formed by H. Ross Perot, a Texan with firm convictions about himself, his employees,

and his company. Perot is most famous for singlehandedly organizing a military-style strike force that rescued EDS employees who had been imprisoned while on assignment in Iran. That adventure was chronicled in the book, *On Wings of Eagles,* by Ken Follett.

Today, EDS is a $5 billion company, with employees in 26 foreign countries. The photo shows the

EDS MIS facility in Dallas, Texas. EDS buys more computers than any other corporation on earth, installing and operating them at customer sites. It has created management information systems for insurance companies, banks, the federal government, and agencies of the armed forces. In the 1980s, it had contracts with the U.S. Army, First City Bancorp of Houston, and Blue Cross/Blue Shield, each representing well over half a billion dollars. In 1984, Ross Perot sold EDS to General Motors, which was to help GM enhance its computer operations and develop sophisticated factory automation systems. Perot became a significant investor in Steve Jobs' NeXT computer, and went on to form Perot Systems, a more specialized counterpart to EDS.

Courtesy of Electronic Data Systems

The problem was solved in two ways. One was by appointing a database administrator in MIS whose job was to maintain database integrity. The other was by using local area networks, where a local file server maintained secure copies of files, and careful methods of transfer and updating were instituted. The file server was connected to the mainframe through another corporate network.

Personal computers thus have gone from stand-alone computers, operating independently of the central computer, to acting as intelligent terminals connected to the mainframe. MIS still has an important and responsible role in the process, and users are happy because they have the best of both worlds: computing power on the desktop and access to the corporate database.

Thus the process has come full circle, except that information systems are far more useful today. Gerry Belcher, the vice president of systems and procedures at the Los Angeles branch of Security Pacific Bank, puts it this way. "In the beginning of my DP career here at the bank, I would get stand-alone time on the mainframe and go down and run and debug programs right at the console. As the computer system got larger and larger, it required a bigger staff and a more structured approach. It started to take much longer to develop applications . . . and we no longer had the reward of quick turnaround.

[Now] we tend to do things [on the personal computer] which are smaller and quicker and bring more satisfaction [than mainframe systems]." Systems integration will take a long while but it is essential. The trend is toward true compatibility at the applications level for data and information exchange.

New Computer Architectures

Like nature and its systems, the evolution of computers and management information systems in the past hasn't always been logical or carefully planned. A **computer architecture** is the design and implementation of computer systems, and the relationship among those system components, in an organization. A computer architecture is quite similar to a building architecture, in that it determines how best to use physical facilities to help people get their work done efficiently. Many businesses have devised their own, while others are promoted by computer vendors. For example, IBM promotes what it terms Business System Planning (BSP) for this purpose.

With the wide variety of terminals, personal computers, peripherals, and separate systems that must connect to the centralized computer, new computer architectures have emerged. These architectures are an aspect of systems integration, or cooperative processing, and utilize both hardware and software interfaces that make it possible to interconnect systems from various manufacturers as shown in Figure 12–9. When coupled with the appropriate

FIGURE 12–9   New computer architectures are designed to take maximum advantage of all types of computer systems.

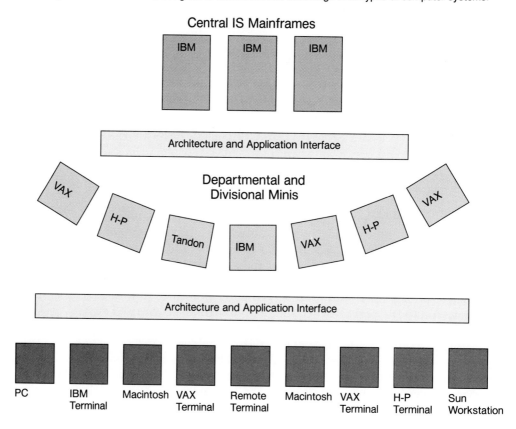

application interfaces, users can work with any application regardless of the computer on which it resides. In addition, utilizing a graphical user interface, the applications appear to work identically to one another—therefore, the user only has to learn how one works to be able to use them all.

Information Providers

The Information Age has created a new type of business: information providers. In the past, we obtained information from libraries and published materials. Now we can obtain it from computers, which have the ability to store and retrieve many more kinds of information, from film reviews to corporate performance reports to competitive intelligence. Dow Jones & Company, Inc., sees itself as an information provider, using computers to do so and also using computers—and MIS—to maintain its product.

Dow Jones is no stranger to selling information; it has done so for over 150 years, starting with credit reports. *The Wall Street Journal* has been published for over 100 years. All Dow Jones services make extensive use of MIS but it is Dow Jones News/Retrieval (DJN/R), the on-line, electronic source of information, that is on the leading edge.

As more users logged on DJN/R, the more it slowed down the conventional, single-processor mainframes and minis. And as more data was added to the database, it became more difficult—and took longer—to find things. "The bigger we got and the more precise the individual wanted to be in his search, the more complicated the search mechanism had to be," explained Bill Dunn, the director of MIS at DJN/R.

A few years ago, Dunn bought two Connection Machines from Thinking Machines, Inc., of Cambridge, Massachusetts. It was the first business (rather than scientific) use for the powerful computer. The Connection Machine is a state-of-the-art parallel processor, with over 65,000 microprocessors all working at once. Now, using the Connection Machine, DJN/R users can very quickly obtain any tidbit of information they need. But that's all users need to care about; from their perspective, who cares what kind of computer does it? Even so, the Connection Machine is beautiful to behold (Figure 9–18, p. 307). What Bill Dunn and Dow Jones seem to understand quite well is that management must provide the linkages between strategy and technology, and that channels of communication must be wide open and available for the users.

MEMORY CHECK

1. Why do we say there is a computer "room," but MIS extends throughout the business?
2. Describe several ways personal computers are being used in business today.
3. What is the goal of systems integration?
4. Describe the purpose of a computer architecture.
5. What do we mean when we use the term *information provider*?

WHAT LIES AHEAD?

The term *management information systems* gained wide acceptance in 1968, when the Society for Management Information Systems (now the Society for Information Management) was founded. The Society is made up of executives, information systems professionals, and academicians who meet to explore the latest trends and ideas in MIS.

As we move into the 1990s, the nature of MIS is changing rapidly. In addition to the push for systems integration and enterprisewide computing, we see that the large mainframe computer has been surpassed in speed and flexibility by desktop computers. Even so, mainframes will not leave us soon; they represent a significant investment, and will act as database machines and file servers for many years to come.

Furthermore, as computing power and information systems are distributed throughout the business more and more, so will MIS people move away from the centralized department and into user departments. As the mainframe becomes a database storage bank, the centralized operation will require less staff; however, the users will need more help maintaining their systems and building new applications. This bodes well for all concerned.

The Changing Role of the MIS Executive

The MIS executive is evolving along with the systems. Every few years, Andersen Consulting surveys several hundred of these executives in Fortune 500 companies to learn their current concerns. This is significant because these companies and their MIS organizations often indicate future trends and directions for the rest of the business world. Increasingly, these executives express a concern with human issues more than technological ones. They want to help create enlightened users and provide better training and education for managers and senior executives. They are also interested in continuing to help improve business through information systems that enhance competitiveness and increase sales. It is also clear that MIS executives are spending a great deal more time with upper management, playing an important role in planning and decision making for the company.

John J. Donovan, an MIT professor and head of Cambridge Technology Group, an educational and consulting company, sees the MIS executive becoming a network manager in the increasingly decentralized computing and business environment. In such an environment, the computer is literally the network. He writes:

> I believe the 1990s will witness the emergence of a new breed of senior information executive — the network manager — whose priorities and challenges will differ in many important respects from the CIO's. Unless CIOs successfully transform themselves into network managers, they will be ill-equipped to confront user dissatisfaction, organizational squabbles, and technological roadblocks invariably triggered by the advance of decentralized computing.
>
> What's the difference between a CIO and network manager? Network managers understand that in a world of accelerating decentralization, the most effective way to oversee a company's computer resources is to relinquish control of them and instead focus on the networks that connect them. Network managers won't merely accept the inevitability of decentralized computing. They will encourage it by surrendering author-

ity over hardware purchases and software development while seizing control of communications systems and policies. The transition from CIO to network manager will be neither immediate nor easy. But it must be made if senior executives want lower costs and enhanced strategic advantage from their computer systems. The CIO who faces the challenges of network management head-on can overcome the perils of decentralized computing and tap its vast potential.[1]

ETHICS

Corporate data security is every employee's business. Corporate computer crimes demoralize employees and make the company look bad. According to the experts, most computer crimes are committed by insiders. Here are three true stories:

- A secretary created phony vendors in a computer database, then authorized $80,000 in payments to them — and took the money herself.
- A chemical company salesman programmed the computer to pay himself double commissions.
- A commodities broker skimmed $1.5 million off his trading pool.

Experts advise that the best defense is an offense — a corporate policy and set of guidelines. Here are five ways to create a sense of computer ethics and prevent computer crime:

1. Top management must be educated about computer crime and its consequences. Studies show that when the president or chief executive understands use and abuse, and takes a public stand against computer crime, employees are less likely to commit such crimes.
2. Managers should warn employees that the company takes a hard line on computer crime, whether it's theft of a floppy disk or stealing information from a database. Offenders will be prosecuted.
3. There should be a company code of ethics, and every employee should receive a copy. It should state explicitly what the company considers a computer crime, and what is ethical or unethical. It should also tell employees what actions are grounds for dismissal and/or prosecution.
4. Employees should have a contact person to notify if they suspect there has been a computer crime.
5. Data security systems must be instituted that require employees to use passwords or other security systems. Passwords should be changed every 30 days. There should be a corporate director of security to investigate possible crimes and make sure employees are protecting their passwords.

It may seem odd, but people will often do things with the computer without thinking it is unethical or illegal. Therefore, most experts agree that educating employees is the first step in computer security. This weeds out the true criminal from the accidental rule breaker by assuring that those who violate the rules are doing so with full knowledge of what the company deems ethical and unethical.

---

[1] John J. Donovan, "Beyond Chief Information Officer to Network Manager," *Harvard Business Review*, September–October 1988, pp. 134–40.

C A R E E R b y t e

The PC Manager

Educating and training users has become a primary objective for MIS departments, taking precedence over acquiring new computer technology. Quality people are needed to use information systems effectively in the future. Some of the concerns businesses have voiced are:

- How have job descriptions changed?
- What types of people or skills do we need now?
- Are we finding these people?
- Where will we find these people in the future?
- Do we need to retrain people who have lost their jobs due to departmental computing, attrition, or downsizing?

Due to these increased training needs, a new occupation has emerged in many large companies: the PC (personal computer) manager. This person is commonly from a user group, someone who has grasped computer technology and intuitively understands application software programs. At first, it was an ad hoc position; that is, the PC manager unofficially helped fellow employees learn to use personal computers and software.

In time, the position became more or less official; while most PC

Mike Antonucci

John Thoeming/Richard D. Irwin, Inc.

managers continue to do their regular work, their training role is sanctioned by management. In some cases, training is their only job. In Chicago, PC managers are such a powerful force that one named Julian Horwich formed the Chicago Area Microcomputer Professionals, which is now over 10,000 strong.

PC managers are a diverse, self-reliant group. Few use the technical support help telephone lines provided by software companies, preferring to learn application programs on their own time or at independent training seminars. Most say it's a full-time job staying ahead of users' needs.

One way Julian Horwich helps his users is by inviting software vendors to meetings, where they provide formal training seminars for PC managers. Many vendors are now providing videotapes as learning tools.

Whatever the tools or techniques, it is clear that many more PC managers will be needed in the future. How do you become a PC manager? Often it's by serendipity. Richard D. Irwin, the publisher of your textbook, equipped all its sales representatives with laptop personal computers a few years back. Someone had to train the representatives. One of those trainers or PC managers, Mike Antonucci, came from the sales staff. He had the interest, the motivation, and the experience working with personal computers to share his knowledge with his fellow sales reps. "I got to help choose the laptops and the software. We had to install an integrated software package, some custom Irwin applications, and telecommunications software so people could exchange electronic mail all over the country. Then I got to help train all my fellow representatives in how to use the system! It was a lot of extra work, but it was also one of the most rewarding experiences I've had at Irwin."

SUMMARY

1. *Define the term MIS and explain how it is used.* MIS stands for management information systems. The term refers to a computer system working together with the business to help it achieve its goals. The same business systems and management structure that work in the company are used in MIS as well. MIS works on three levels: record-keeping, operations control, and strategic planning. MIS management provides information for the company with computer systems. People, software systems, and hardware make up a MIS.

2. *Describe the people components of MIS.* The people component includes MIS management, staff, and end users. There are usually three tiers of MIS management: top, middle, and operational. MIS's role is to aid the end user in obtaining the most productivity from information systems. Two ways MIS does this is through information centers and the personal computer manager.

3. *Explain the ways MIS makes the software component available.* The software component provides systems that make various applications available on a wide variety of computers, throughout the company. This falls into two categories: distributed computing, where applications are developed in the end user department, and enterprisewide computing, where applications for the entire company are developed. Some MIS departments have developed information systems that have commercial value

and are sold to other companies. Software maintenance is the most costly aspect of the software budget.

4. *Describe how the hardware component is changing the way computer architectures are used in business.* The hardware component includes the physical location of the computers; some are centralized, while others are in various departments. Most companies want consistency in computer use, so they strive to interconnect hardware; this is called systems integration. When hardware and software are all integrated so that data and applications can be used everywhere, it is often referred to as cooperative processing. Often, new hardware architectures must be designed to accomplish this.

5. *Discuss how the MIS organization and its leadership are changing and evolving.* We are steadily moving away from a centralized MIS environment to enterprisewide computing; however, mainframe computers will not be departing soon; they still play an important role in maintaining the database. One of the more advanced uses of MIS systems is as information providers, who collect and organize data and then offer it to business and the public. In the future, we can expect to see networking play a more important role in all MIS functions. As the idea of the computer system as a network gains broader acceptance, the MIS manager will likely be a network manager.

KEY TERMS

application programmer, p. 394

centralized computing, p. 395

computer architecture, p. 400

distributed computing, p. 395

end-user computing, p. 394

enterprisewide computing, p. 396

facilities management, p. 399

information center, p. 394

management information
  systems (MIS), p. 383

operations technician, p. 394

PC manager, p. 394

real time, p. 389

software maintenance, p. 395

systems integration, p. 398

REVIEW AND DISCUSSION QUESTIONS

1. What do you think of Richard Nolan's stages of EDP growth? Is it possible to categorize all organizations this way?

2. What is the primary role of computers in business?

3. Name three ways Mrs. Fields Cookies utilizes computers.

4. How can a good computer system ensure the survival of a business?

5. Name the three key components of an effective MIS department.

6. What are two responsibilities of the MIS executive?

7. What talents and achievements do you think an MIS executive would have to demonstrate in order to become the company CEO?

8. What do middle managers do?

9. Name two responsibilities of operational managers.

10. Why did MIS become mired in application backlogs?

11. Name the three levels of information management.

12. How do the three levels of information management apply to MIS business functions and management?

13. Why do companies carefully guard their MIS capabilities?

14. How does the government use MIS?

15. Discuss ways to assure that MIS does not develop an application that generates too much or too little information.

16. What element was missing in NASA's MIS systems?

17. Compare and contrast the key strengths of centralized computing and decentralized computing.

18. Discuss the key strengths of distributed processing and cooperative processing.

19. Do you agree with the philosophy that scientific laboratories should not have a centralized computing system?

20. Think about an office at your school or in the company where you work that is not currently computerized. Using what you know about computer hardware, software applications, and MIS concepts, describe how an information system could be built for this office of function.

ISSUES

1. In the past, we had corporate MIS departments run by computer professionals. When the company needed a new application or system, the professionals designed it. But over the years, computers have grown easier to program and use. Now, many users can create their own applications or systems. In the process, the need for MIS professionals is declining. In many companies, cutbacks in the corporate MIS department and decentralization are resulting in layoffs and firings. Do you feel this is a fair way to treat the people who have maintained computer systems over the years? Can you think of better ways to handle MIS personnel whose jobs are becoming obsolete?

2. It is not uncommon to hear about companies using computer technology to gain a "competitive advantage" in their industry. These firms utilize the computer in some innovative way that the competitors haven't yet thought of, and thus are able to sell more products or services. Yet sooner or later, the competitors figure out the technique; pretty soon, the entire industry uses it. Can you foresee a day when there are no "competitive advantages" to be gained through computers? What happens to competitive business practices if that happens?

3. In the movie *Jumpin' Jack Flash,* an employee discovers she has a talent for stealing small amounts of money using the computer system. Before long, she has enough to buy a fancy sports car. The idea that she is stealing does not seem to cross her mind; rather, she is quite proud of her ability to manipulate the computer so effectively. Discuss reasons why some people behave without scruples or ethics when using a computer.

CHAPTER OUTLINE

The Evolution of the Office
The Office Automation Challenge
    Office Automation: A Definition
    People: The Most Important Element
    Office Systems: Software and Hardware
Office Automation Systems
    Text Management Systems
    DISKbyte: The Evolution of the Typewriter
    Business Analysis Systems
    Document Management Systems
    DISKbyte: Backing Up the Vatican Library
    Network and Communication Management
        Systems
Office Automation Technologies at Work
    The Integrated Desktop
    Large System Integration
    DISKbyte: Two Views of the Office of the Future
What Lies Ahead?
Ethics
    CAREERbyte: Amy Wohl, Office Automation
    Consultant
Summary
Key Terms
Review and Discussion Questions
Issues

OBJECTIVES

After reading and studying this chapter, you should be able to:

1. Define office automation and explain its relationship to other information systems in business.
2. Name the four types of office automation technologies.
3. Explain and describe several management decision-making systems.
4. Describe the importance of the knowledge worker in the modern office environment.
5. Describe the trends in integrated systems and identify some examples.

THE EVOLUTION OF THE OFFICE

In the opening scene of the 1947 film, *The Shocking Miss Pilgrim,* Betty Grable graduates from the Packard Business College in New York. The date is June 10, 1874. Miss Pilgrim is a member of the first class trained to use a newfangled device called the typewriter. In fact, the graduates *themselves* are called typewriters. A representative from the Remington Typewriter Company is present, happy that the 18 typewriting machines his company has already sold will soon have operators.

Miss Pilgrim's new job is at a shipping firm. The office employees are all men, sitting on high stools at tall desks, dipping their pens into inkwells. Their resentment is immediately apparent to Miss Pilgrim, perhaps because she and her machine represent automation, which may take their jobs and livelihoods away from them. Right from the start, Miss Pilgrim and her typewriter—a woman and a machine—are put on notice that they'll have to prove themselves.

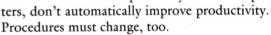
The office in the 1800s.

Brown Brothers

More machines and more women entered the office during the next hundred years but work procedures changed very little. One environment in which office work was done was called a typing pool. Then, with the advent of computers in business, more machines cluttered the office landscape but with an added difference: now, owners and managers wanted workers to be more productive and more efficient, while reducing paperwork at the same time. Yet work procedures didn't change, and there was even more paper. Business had to learn a lesson the hard way: more machines, and specifically more computers, don't automatically improve productivity. Procedures must change, too.

THE OFFICE AUTOMATION CHALLENGE

Today, in the early 1990s, genuine efficiencies in the office are occurring because there are better procedures to accompany the machines. Where the computer once simply replicated the previous manual task, now it more fully automates it. For example, a sales letter must be sent to 20 customers. Before computers it was typed 20 times, once for each name, address, and salutation. Later, using a conventional word processor, the letter was created with special codes programmed into the blank spaces left for names, addresses, and salutations, which were created in a separate file. Finally, the word processor merged the names and the letter for 20 printouts. This was often almost as much effort as simply retyping the letter 20 times, except that each word-processed letter would be perfectly typed and error-free.

Now, in the modern office, all the names and addresses of everyday business correspondents are stored in a database. The codes for the name, address, and salutation are already programmed into the word processing software. The entire process is accomplished with just a few simple keystrokes. The procedures have improved.

The lesson business has learned is that computers alone do not improve productivity. In fact, as noted above, early, less-sophisticated hardware and software sometimes retarded productivity. The equipment was often difficult to learn; many hours were spent trying to master it. Over time, hardware and software was designed to more closely resemble actual work processes — in other words, the way people do their work, rather than a convenient way for the computer to do the work. Then real productivity improvements began occurring.

Office Automation: A Definition

Office automation (OA) is using computer and communications technology to help people better use and manage information. Office automation technology includes all types of computers, telephones, electronic mail, and office machines that use microprocessors or other high-technology components. Figure 13–1 shows a state-of-the-art office.

The people who use office automation are often called **knowledge workers:** senior executives, managers, supervisors, analysts, engineers, and other white-collar office workers. In most offices, information — often in paper form — is the end product, and is essential for conducting the company's business. OA systems keep track of the information originating in various other processing operations throughout the company, such as order processing, accounting, inventory, manufacturing, and so forth. Office automation provides knowledge workers with information-producing systems to collect, analyze, plan, and control information about the many facets of the business, using text, voice, graphics, and video display technologies.

The term *office automation* was first used in 1955 to describe computer-automated bookkeeping, an adjunct of data processing. The term — and to some extent, the entire notion of automating the office — fell into disuse as the emphasis turned to management information systems. There was renewed interest toward the end of the 1970s, when futurists such as Alvin Toffler envisioned the "office of the future." By the mid-1980s, office automation was a popular concept again. The road to OA has been a bumpy one, from being a poor cousin to data processing to finding its own identity in text and information processing.

FIGURE 13-1   Office technology for the 1990s.

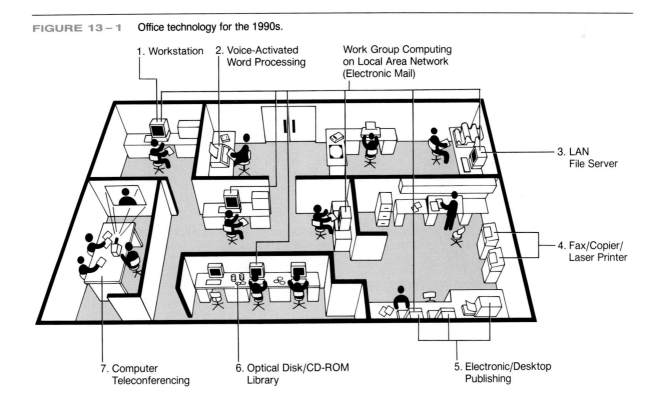

1. Workstation   2. Voice-Activated Word Processing

Work Group Computing on Local Area Network (Electronic Mail)

3. LAN File Server

4. Fax/Copier/ Laser Printer

7. Computer Teleconferencing

6. Optical Disk/CD-ROM Library

5. Electronic/Desktop Publishing

In this chapter, we explore the modern office, which has changed more in the past 10 years than it has in the last hundred. We'll see the incredible transformation of the most populous workplace into one that is lively, innovative, and technologically sophisticated. As we have seen throughout this book, and as we shall see in this chapter, it is the computer system — people, software, and hardware developing new work processes — that truly enhances productivity.

People: The Most Important Element

The office requires skilled workers, just as any other department or division of the company does. For many years, knowledge workers were victims of office technology, forced to use equipment that was not designed to enhance their work. For example, the original typewriter keyboard layout was designed to slow typists down; if they typed too fast, the keys would collide and jam! Office workers were thought of as factory workers, as if they were operating a lathe or a drill press. Business soon learned that the office could not be automated in the same way the factory was, and the field of ergonomics began to emerge.

Ergonomics   Office tasks involve a great deal of thinking and decision making. As a result, hardware and software engineers understand that office systems must be flexible and versatile. Moreover, they must be designed so that any knowledge worker, regardless of background, can easily use them. This is called *ergonomics,* the study of how to create safety, comfort, and ease of use for people who use machines. It is not a new field of study; in fact, it has existed for over a hundred years. With the advent of computers, ergonomics engineers became particularly interested in OA systems, furniture, and environments for the knowledge worker.

Computer ergonomics developed most rapidly in Europe, where standards committees insisted on common electrical connections and ease-of-use criteria. Intensive studies determined the best designs for keyboards, set eye fatigue levels for monitors, and specified desk and seating designs that alleviate physical stress. These standards were adopted by the U.S. computer industry, which in many cases enhanced and improved them. Office furniture companies soon introduced ergonomically designed chairs and equipment. Ergonomics has played a significant role in helping people better utilize office technology.

Office Systems: Software and Hardware

Office automation utilizes computer-based systems to provide information to help knowledge workers make decisions that benefit the business. You have already studied software and hardware separately; in this chapter, we see them functioning together in office automation systems. Several distinct technologies or systems comprise OA:

- *Text management systems,* including electronic typewriters, word processing systems, and electronic publishing.
- *Business analysis systems,* including spreadsheet analysis, decision support systems, and executive information systems.
- *Document management systems,* including database management, document storage, and micrographics.
- *Network and communication management systems,* including the telephone, electronic mail, voice messaging systems, teleconferencing, and **facsimile (FAX).**

In the following sections of this chapter, we'll see how knowledge workers put these four types of office systems to use.

MEMORY CHECK

1. What is the end product of office automation?
2. What are people who use office automation often called?
3. Describe how office automation is essential to the business as a whole.
4. What is the purpose behind ergonomics?
5. Describe the four systems that comprise office automation, and the goals they serve.
6. What are the four primary technologies in office automation systems?

OFFICE AUTOMATION SYSTEMS

As we mentioned earlier, office automation systems are used to collect, analyze, plan, and control information in order for the business to thrive. Order processing, inventory management, manufacturing resource planning, and distribution are distinct systems unto themselves, and are not considered part of office automation.

The four primary technologies used to manage information in office automation — text management systems, business analysis systems, document management systems, and network and communication management systems — are used to manage these various types of information:

- *Text,* or written words.
- *Data,* as in numbers or other nontext forms.
- *Graphics,* including drawings, charts, and photographs.
- *Video,* such as captured images, videotapes, or teleconferencing.
- *Audio,* such as phone conversations or dictation.

In the past, each of these forms of information was created using different technologies. Text was either typewritten or created using conventional typewriters or, more recently, word processing. Data such as sales reports was provided by the central computer. Charts and graphs were either hand drawn or created using 35mm slide photography, and videotapes were used for training. The telephone was the primary audio medium. It wasn't possible to intermix these forms of information.

Today, the computer combines or integrates these different media and others as well. Data, sound, and images can all be entered into a computer, stored, and translated into the kind of output we need. At the center of this integration are networking and communications systems. Let's look at the four office technologies of information management and some of their applications.

Text Management Systems

A **text management system** includes all kinds of typewriters, word processing systems, PCs with word processing, desktop publishing, and text editing systems, and even computerized typesetting equipment. Text management systems are used for:

- Writing memos, notes, letters, and other short documents requiring little if any revision.
- Printing envelopes and labels.
- Preparing preprinted forms such as invoices or purchase orders.
- Composing longer documents, such as proposals and reports, that involve several reviews and revisions.
- Retrieving and editing reusable documents such as form letters and contracts that contain standard replaceable (boilerplate) text.
- Creating display documents, from advertising brochures to in-house or client newsletters.

DISKbyte

The Evolution of the Typewriter

1714 An anonymous British inventor claims to be working on "An artificial machine or method of impressing or transcribing of letters singly or progressively one after another, as in writing, whereby writing whatever may be engrossed in paper or parchment so neat and exact as not to be distinguished from print." No such machine is forthcoming.

1857 W. A. Burt, an American, builds the first working typewriter and types this message to his wife: "Dear Companion, I have but jest got my second machine into operation and this is the first specimen I send you except a few lines I printed to regulate the machine."

1867 Another American, Christopher Sholes, develops the first commercial typewriter. In 1873, he sells the rights to Remington. IT COULD ONLY TYPE UPPERCASE LETTERS.

1872 Thomas Edison creates an electric typewriter. However, it is so crude that it is converted into a ticker tape printer.

1874 Mark Twain becomes the first author to buy and use a Remington typewriter.

1935 First commercially successful electric typewriter is introduced by IBM.

1961 First IBM Selectric typewriter using interchangeable "golfball" typing elements introduced. The golfball was developed by happenstance by Kenneth Iverson of IBM, who was looking for a suitable way to type the characters for his new programming language, APL.

1964 First IBM stand-alone word processing system called the MT/ST. It was a combination of two technologies, magnetic tape (MT) to record and store keystrokes, and the Selectric typewriter (ST) for playback. (See Figure 13–2.)

1969 IBM MC/ST, a system that used a plastic magnetic IBM card to store data, rather than the more cumbersome reels of magnetic tape.

1972 First electronic memory typewriters appear; they can store up to a full page in their tiny memory.

1976 The Wang multiuser Word Processing System (WPS) introduced. Within two years, it becomes the most popular word processor in the world. (See Figure 13–3.)

1979 "Intelligent" electronic typewriters are introduced; they can store documents on floppy disk and are capable of acting as printers in computer systems.

1981 Typewriters with dedicated word processing built in are introduced.

1986 Portable dedicated word processing typewriters introduced.

1990 IBM sells its typewriter business to the investment firm Clayton & Dubilier for an estimated $2.5 billion.

In the modern office, everyone becomes a text creator. The keyboard again becomes a tool of democracy because secretaries do not always have to take dictation or type from handwritten copy produced by managers; often, managers do their own typing. Although many managers have resisted the keyboard for years, this attitude is changing. The secretary, if one is involved at all, spellchecks and formats the document for final printing and distribution. When each person does his or her own text creation, both time and money (wages) are saved and there is little wasted effort. The computer has broken down many traditional, and often artificial, office hierarchies. For example, Linda Dale was once a secretary in the insurance division at Meeker Sharkey Financial Group in Cranford, New Jersey. She took dictation from her boss, an insurance agent, did the typing, and left the decisions about individual policyholders to him. A few years ago, her company installed PCs and trained the secretaries in their use. They were soon able to call up policyholder data on the screen, which helped the agents obtain information more quickly.

FIGURE 13-2   The IBM MT/ST: the first word processor.

Courtesy of the IBM Corporation

FIGURE 13-3   The Wang WPS brought power and user-friendliness to word processing.

Courtesy of Wang Laboratories Inc.

Soon it became clear that there were many routine decisions that the secretaries could make without having to consult the agent. They learned how to renew policies and upgrade benefits. They were able to determine how much the customer could borrow against a life insurance policy and approve a loan up to that amount. Before long, Linda and others in secretarial positions became decision makers and working partners with the agents. This allowed the agents to spend from 25 to 50 percent more time selling insurance.

Linda is now called an administrative sales assistant. The agents consider her a partner in the operation, and she now earns commissions and bonuses on policies she helps sell. "It's like investing in my own business instead of working for someone else to get rich," says Linda. Clearly, the computer has proven to be a job enhancement, as well as a democratizing influence.

Business Analysis Systems

Managers or executives need solid data from which to extract the information necessary to make good decisions for the business. In the past, these knowledge workers had to rely on their experience and other personal factors to make decisions. A **business analysis system** provides data that, when used with the proper software, aids in business analysis and decision making. The spreadsheet is routinely used by corporate "power users" for such things as cost-benefit analyses and creating budgets. Yet there are other computer-based software tools for performing business analyses. Two that are commonly used are decision support systems and executive information systems.

Decision Support Systems Since its introduction in the late 1970s, the **decision support system (DSS)** has evolved in its usefulness and the tasks it performs. A decision support system, as its name implies, helps a manager extract information from various MIS databases and reporting systems, analyze it, and then formulate a decision or a strategy for business planning. The DSS does this by collecting data, then analyzing it with special modeling software.

For example, the manager can see what would happen if a product's sales skyrocketed or if a division were closed down. The software creates charts and graphs from the data, showing how expenses, profits, and other financial factors would be affected. Some DSSs have an artificial intelligence component to help formulate decisions and analyze outcomes.

Executive Information Systems The **executive information system (EIS)** is designed for top managers who often want nothing to do with a computer. Typically, the EIS is a personal computer with brilliant color graphics and extremely easy-to-use software that can present data with just a keystroke or two, as shown in Figure 13–4. It is an executive tool that isn't technologically intimidating. The EIS replaces conventional reports such as a thick stack of computer printouts containing only a few things of interest to

FIGURE 13–4   This mainframe-based EIS utilizes a touch screen.

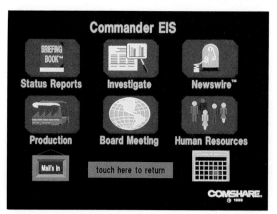

Courtesy of Comshare, Inc.

the executive. The EIS has access to the corporate mainframe and is able to project most of the information in graphical form. Using the EIS, the executive can evaluate the company's performance and track product lines, create scenarios for future product introductions, plot emerging trends in the industry, or plan new directions in which to take the company.

Robert Kidder, chief executive officer of Duracell, once used his EIS to compare U.S. and European sales staff productivity. The EIS captured the data from the corporate mainframe and displayed it on his screen as multicolored graphics. It showed the U.S. salaried sales staff producing more sales than the Europeans. Kidder tapped the mouse button a few more times and learned that in Germany, too many salespeople were calling on small shops that did not generate sufficient revenues. Kidder corrected the problem by licensing distributors to service the small shops instead of having more highly paid salespeople call on them.

Document Management Systems

Document management systems aid in filing, tracking, and managing documents, whether they are paper, computer-based, micrographics, or purely electronic. Over the years, elaborate systems have been created for storing and managing documents; it seems as though no scrap of paper must ever be thrown away. Unfortunately, that same mentality has been passed along to electronic, or computerized, filing systems. We can only guess how much disk space is taken up with documents filled with useless or outdated information.

Nevertheless, OA demands that data be immediately accessible and instantaneously retrievable. For that reason, we are slowly moving away from paper and toward document forms that can be stored on the computer. Briefly, here is how office automation is addressing document management.

Paper   Paper must be filed in such a way that it is easy to locate when necessary but avoided whenever possible. Increasingly, interoffice correspondence and letters are stored on personal computers, often organized into subdirectories that make it easy to review them.

Computer-Based Data   Managers are finding it is easier to extract specific computer-based data from the corporate mainframe, as with an EIS, rather than work with large computer printouts. Increasingly, mainframe data is being distributed to office automation systems, where the people who need it have ready access. This is leading to office image and data management systems like the one shown in Figure 13–5.

Micrographics   Micrographics, which was discussed in Chapter 10, is a convenient, inexpensive way to store bulky documents. It is commonly used in libraries to retain back copies of newspapers and magazines, and by businesses for keeping copies of paper-based transactions — for example, canceled checks at a bank. Computer output microfilming (COM) provides a way to take data stored on tape or disk and transmit it directly to microfilm. For example, a mail-order company can process the many thousands of orders it receives each day on the computer, then record the day's transactions on microfilm instead of printing and filing paper documents.

FIGURE 13–5   An image/data management system. Note the variety of image sources available across the network.

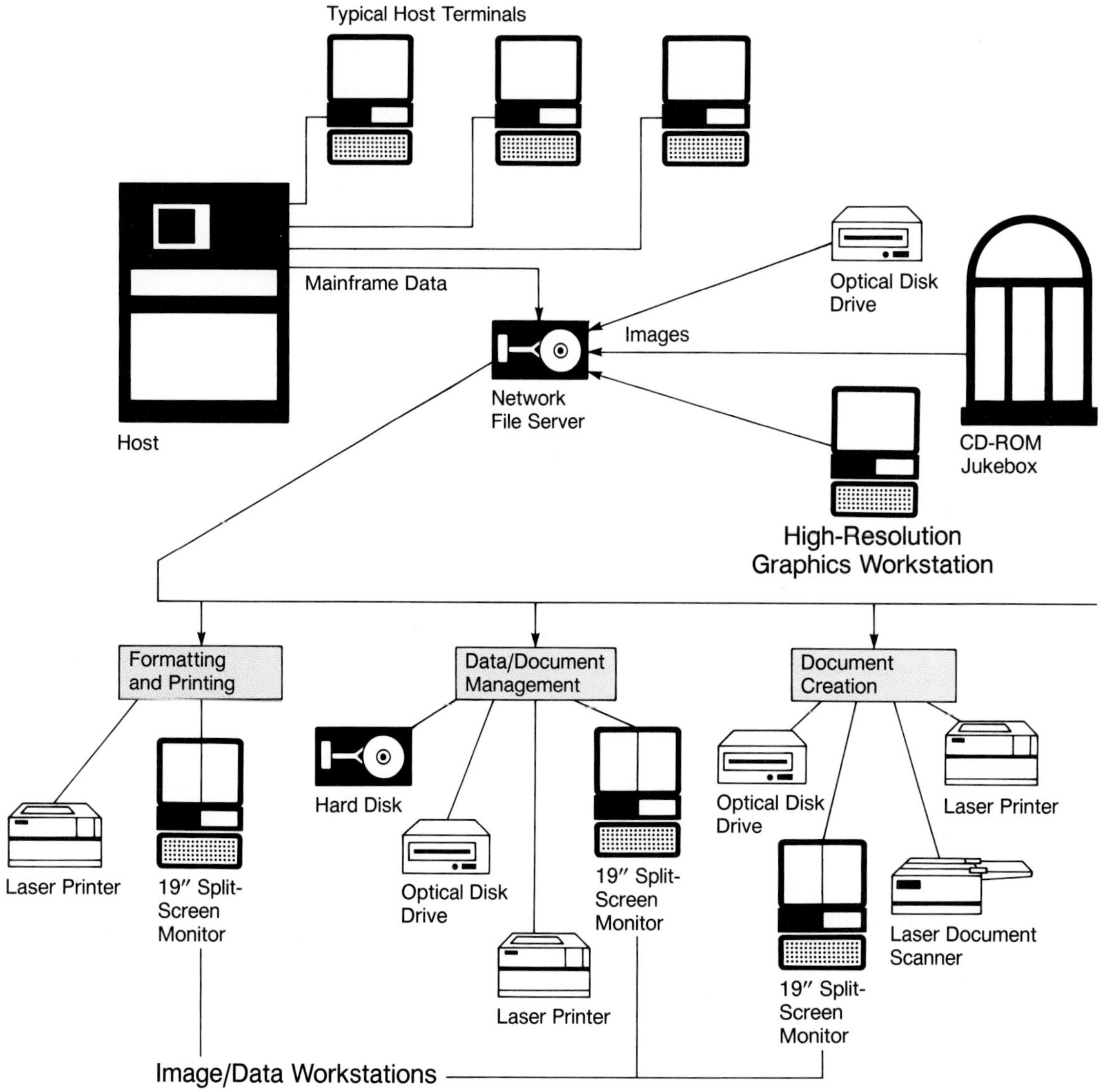

Typical Host Terminals

Mainframe Data

Host

Network File Server

Optical Disk Drive

Images

CD-ROM Jukebox

High-Resolution Graphics Workstation

Formatting and Printing

Laser Printer

19″ Split-Screen Monitor

Data/Document Management

Hard Disk

Optical Disk Drive

Laser Printer

19″ Split-Screen Monitor

Document Creation

Optical Disk Drive

Laser Printer

19″ Split-Screen Monitor

Laser Document Scanner

Image/Data Workstations

Electronic Documents   **Electronic documents** are those captured from on-line databases, as discussed in Chapter 11. These databases are often used to obtain current stock market information and information about competitors for analysis. Raw data is downloaded, then edited and stored in special files or databases. This information becomes readily available for EIS applications. Here is an example of a unique electronic document retrieval system.

Dr. Paul Jacobs and Lisa Rau, a husband and wife team at General Electric, have created an information retrieval system that embodies many human characteristics. It is called System for Conceptual Information Summarization, Organization, and Retrieval (SCISOR), and it uses artificial intelligence, natural language, and sophisticated database management techniques to perform on-line information searches without human intervention. The knowl-

DISKbyte

Backing Up the Vatican Library

How do you make sure a library with manuscripts from before the birth of Jesus Christ and books dating back to the year 1305 isn't destroyed by wars, natural disaster, or just plain old age? That question troubled Pope Pius XII in the 1940s, after seeing the damage caused during World War II. In times past, scribes would likely have sat down with quill pens and hand copied all the Vatican Library codices, books, illuminated manuscripts, and documents, a library so vast that no one is sure how many documents it contains.

But in 1951, a microfilming project sponsored by the Knights of Columbus and St. Louis University began. Its purpose was not to record all the documents but primarily those of interest to Western scholars. Over 3 million feet of microfilm was shot, and 4,000 color slides of illuminated manuscripts were taken. The project took six years but the Vatican's most prized materials are now safe on microfilm and, for the first time, available to scholars around the world.

FIGURE 13 – 6   SCISOR and its creators.

Courtesy of GE Research and Development Center

---

edge worker "teaches" SCISOR a number of key words to search for; then SCISOR "learns" other associated words as it actually searches.

Once so programmed, SCISOR can be turned loose to search through the Dow Jones News/Retrieval databases for any topics or items you are interested in. Once it has completed its search, you can ask it for specific types of information, without having to pore over reams of information. SCISOR has a vocabulary of 10,000 words and can even understand some slang words.

SCISOR, shown in Figure 13 – 6, is not only useful for searching on-line databases but has many useful applications in office automation, searching archived databases for a lost contract, a missing report, or other information that is hard to isolate or identify. It's like having all the data at your fingertips.

FIGURE 13–7   Each window on the Open Desktop screen is a separate application.

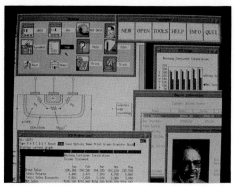

Santa Cruz Operations

New solutions to document management, such as the Open Desktop (see Figure 13–7), are emerging. Open Desktop, as its name implies, makes it possible for knowledge workers to gain access to the information they need without worrying about technological obstacles. The Open Desktop consortium was created by Digital Equipment Corporation (large VAX-based corporate databases), Tandy Corporation (80386-based personal computers), Santa Cruz Operation (the UNIX and DOS operating systems), Locus Computing (special networking software), and Relational Technology (database software). Again, it is an example of how OA technology has been designed to meet people's real needs.

Network and Communication Management Systems

In 1936, an advertisement appeared in magazines across the country that read, "Throw YOUR VOICE into the shipping room. Here is a trick . . . and it is not Ventriloquism . . . that busy executives are doing dozens of times every day." This amazing device, called the Telematic, was the simple intercom system. Today, knowledge workers have many ways to communicate with one another: voice, video, and electronic mail. They can communicate right now, in real time, via phone or computer. And they can also communicate at some point in the future, using the computer-controlled PBX telephone system, to record a digital message and leave it in the recipient's electronic mailbox. These systems are called **network and communication management systems.**

Computers in the modern office are connected in local area networks or LANs, which you learned about in Chapter 11. The LAN has made it possible to easily exchange files and data, as well as send electronic mail messages, between computers. It has also helped people develop new ways to work together. Let's see how.

Desktop Banking   NMB Bank is in the Netherlands, and its network connects 6,000 personal computers located at over 400 bank branches. This system came about because the bank found it had seven different, incompatible computer systems. Departments within the bank could not share data or information, and branches often used different computers altogether. What the bank needed was a system that allowed employees to share information, allowed customers to easily use any branch, and brought the entire computer system up-to-date. Their ambitious project was termed *desktop banking* by Ruud Pruijm, the systems manager.

Each branch has its own local area network, and that LAN is linked to the corporate mainframe. In this way, a branch manager has access to any information stored anywhere else — either at the bank's headquarters or at another branch. Say a customer has moved from Rotterdam to Amsterdam. In Rotterdam he had taken out a loan, and now he wants another one. The Amsterdam branch manager can ask for the customer's files from Rotterdam, and they are sent over the network in a "folder." It is just as though a folder was taken from a file cabinet. In Rotterdam, the electronic folder is reported as out, date- and time-stamped, and sent to Amsterdam. When it is returned, it is logged back in.

Previously, the file would have been sent via a bank messenger or the postal system, which might take days. Now it takes seconds. The new system not only helps improve internal bank procedures but has given the bank many ideas for new financial services it can offer its customers.

Work Group Computing   Many office workers enjoy their work more, and are more productive, when they can work together in small groups. **Work group computing** is a number of people, each of whom has different job duties or tasks, but all of whom are working toward a common goal. **Groupware** is a software product designed to help them accomplish their work together on a local area network. Lotus Development Corporation uses its own product called Notes for group work. Notes helps people share information, both text and graphics, between their personal computers and workstations. It helps them track ideas, analyze data, create continuing dialogues with one another, and present results.

Notes has reduced the time a work group spends in live meetings by providing the members with a 24-hour-a-day forum. People can log on or off the system from their office, from a personal computer at home, or from a laptop on the road. They read the meeting dialogue and add their comments; the group works on the project until everyone agrees on a decision or course of action. People say they feel freer to say what's really on their minds in an on-line forum.

Notes is used by a group of Lotus executives to plan corporate strategies and make decisions — for example, acquiring a new application program from a software developer. Notes collects information in a database assigned to the product, which is assigned to a manager in charge of the evaluation. Others can leave messages registering their thoughts or opinions. Notes, using artificial intelligence techniques, organizes the information efficiently, which helps managers make better decisions. Fewer opportunities are overlooked, and there is less duplication of effort than in other types of group projects. Groupware such as Notes helps knowledge workers present textual or graphic ideas, organize information, create brainstorming sessions, obtain feedback, and solve problems within work groups.

Again we see how the Information Age has changed the way we communicate. In the 1990s, we can expect to see our most important communications relayed via computer, using electronic mail or electronic data interchange. Routine correspondence containing a signature or graphics will be FAXed, but long documents, reports, and highly confidential material may still be printed on paper and sent via overnight express delivery services.

1. What five types of information do OA systems manage?
2. What has changed with respect to the people using text management systems?
3. What is the primary purpose behind an executive information system?
4. Why do we need sophisticated document management systems?
5. What technology is essential for exchanging information in office automation systems?

OFFICE AUTOMATION TECHNOLOGIES AT WORK

Three technology trends have created today's office automation environment. One is the rise of the personal computer, because it is perfectly suited to many routine office tasks. Knowledge workers who did not have access to the corporate computer now are able to do their own computing. Second is the local area network, which makes sharing information possible. Third, since it is now possible to do either stand-alone computing or work group computing, the corporate mainframe assumed a new usefulness in distributed computing.

In a truly distributed computing office, you can have access to the data on any computer, whether it is another personal computer, a mini, or a mainframe. All systems are integrated; that is, we can enter data with any device, store data anywhere in the system, and produce output in a variety of ways, as shown in Figure 13–8.

In this environment, we can say "everything is everywhere," or "the network is the computer." This is the ideal OA environment. Issues such as **data integrity**, or how to ensure data has not been tampered with in an unauthorized manner, as well as system security and some technical issues, must be addressed. Yet there is little doubt that this is the optimal office automation environment. Here are several examples of integrated office environments.

The Integrated Desktop

Software makes it possible for today's knowledge worker, using a personal computer or workstation, to have an integrated electronic desktop. In such an environment, all the various functions are available at the touch of a key, appearing in various windows on the screen. Programs can exchange data with other programs. The simplest example of an integrated desktop is integrated software such as Microsoft Works (Figure 13–9). Another is WordPerfect Office (Figure 13–10), which is a "shell" program that encompasses word processing, a database management system, and a spreadsheet, and allows the cut-and-paste exchange of data. It also offers a calendar, a scheduler, a calculator, a notebook, and other features such as electronic mail. The E-mail feature permits workers in an integrated environment to exchange anything with anyone. This integrated desktop becomes a multiuser, multitasking environment.

FIGURE 13 – 8 This chart shows how data is identified throughout the corporation in a distributed computing environment.

Subject Databases

Locations	Planning	Budgeting	Financial	Product	Product design	Parts master	Bill of materials	Open requirements	Vendor	Procurements	Materials inventory	Machine load	Work in progress	Facilities	Shop floor routings	Customer	Sales	Sales territory	Fin. goods inventory	Orders	Payments	Costs	Employee	Salaries
Head office	M	M	M	M	M				M					V		M	T	T		M	M	M	P	P
Warehouse																			M	R			P	P
District office	T	T	T													R	M	M			T		P	P
Branch office																P	P	P		R	T		P	P
Factory A		T	T	S	S	P	V	V	S	P	P	V	V	V	V	R				T	T		V	P	P
Factory B		T	T	S	S	P	V	V	S	P	P	V	V	V	V	R				T	T		V	P	P
Factory C		T	T	S	S	P	V	V	S	P	P	V	V	V	V	R				T	T		V	P	P

Key: M = Master data: Unique in one location.
V = Variant: Different schema version on different locations.
P = Partitioned data: Same schema, different values.
R = Replicated data: Identical data in different locations.
S = Subset data.
T = Teleprocessing: Data not stored at this location.

FIGURE 13 – 9 Microsoft Works lets knowledge workers custom-tailor their integrated desktop.

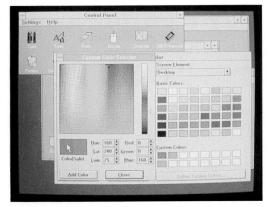

F. Bodin/Offshoot

Another example is Wang Freestyle, which connects a personal computer with a digitizing tablet, light pen, telephone, FAX, and scanner with electronic mail communications. You can send a document to a co-worker, who can write notes, using the pen and tablet, right on the electronic document. Voice comments can be recorded into the document, using the phone. Once the work is completed, your colleague can send the document back to you electronically or print it out and FAX it to you. Voice messages can be sent from computer to computer at any time.

FIGURE 13–10   The calendar and scheduler in WordPerfect Office.

```
Calendar: GUY:CALENDAR          Wednesday, September 30, 1987        11:25am

1987                September              1987      To-Do
Sun   Mon   Tue   Wed   Thu   Fri   Sat      Wednesday, September 30, 1987

                    1     2     3     4     5        1 Send Pricing to IBM
      6     7     8     9    10    11    12          2 pick up dry cleaning
     13    14    15    16    17    18    19
     20    21    22    23    24 > 25    26
     27    28    29 * 30

                  v Memo    > Appt    * To-Do

M   Anniversary tomorrow order flowers
e
m
o

1 Appointments/To-Do; 2 Memo; 3 Date; 4 SetUp; 5 Print; 6 Schedule: 1
```

Courtesy of WordPerfect Corporation

Large System Integration

Office automation in large systems expands on the multitasking, multiuser concept. In large systems, it is not always necessary that every knowledge worker use the same brand of application, such as WordPerfect; sophisticated software interfaces make it possible to exchange data between PC, mini, and mainframe applications. This additional functionality makes it possible to create standards for applications that apply across the company, so the emphasis is on the business benefits, not on trying to make the technology work properly. The ideal situation is to make the entire computer system transparent to the knowledge worker, whose sole concentration can then be on obtaining and properly utilizing information to make decisions.

Digital Equipment Corporation's All-in-1 integrated OA software runs on VAX minicomputers but can be used with other types of computers as well. It offers word processing and text management, electronic mail, facsimile, database management, a calendar, an appointment scheduler, computer teleconferencing, and many other features. When one worker sends another an E-mail message, the recipient's terminal or personal computer beeps to signal an incoming message. With All-in-1, if a meeting time or date is changed, each attendee automatically receives an electronic message.

IBM also offers an integrated system called OfficeVision. It provides electronic mail, text processing, text and graphics merge capabilities, a library filing system, an address book and voice telephone dialer, and a decision support system. These features are available in a multitasking environment and presented on an IBM PS/2 graphical user interface called Presentation Manager. Even though it uses OS/2, DOS applications can be run; as you can see in Figure 13–11, OfficeVision is intended to integrate all IBM computers, from the largest mainframe to the PS/2. Key to OfficeVision is the AS/400, a midrange or minicomputer made by IBM. The AS/400 makes it possible to network various IBM computers that use any of IBM's four major operating systems.

OfficeVision is important because it makes it possible for knowledge workers using a personal computer to access data from large IBM mainframes

FIGURE 13 – 11   IBM's Presentation Manager is the GUI for OS/2.

Courtesy of IBM Corporation

FIGURE 13 – 12   OfficeVision lets you use applications from IBM's PC, minis, or mainframes.

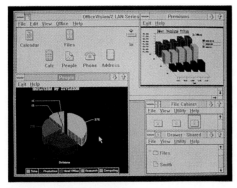

Courtesy of IBM Corporation

in many different ways. It makes a much wider variety of information available to knowledge workers and managers, including inventory control, manufacturing resource planning, financials, and human resources as shown in Figure 13 – 12. Most important, it integrates these applications with the office automation applications into a single architecture for better management planning and control—which is the ultimate goal.

1. What is distributed computing and why is it desirable?
2. What concerns arise with distributed computing?
3. Describe two characteristics of the integrated desktop environment.
4. What additional function makes large systems integration desirable?
5. What is the ultimate goal of office automation?

MEMORY CHECK

D I S K b y t e

Two Views of the Office of the Future

There has been much ado about the office of the future, but the question remains: What has taken it so long to arrive? We've been waiting for over 100 years! Two future thinkers present their views of the office of the future — in both cases, well into the 21st century. The first is Charles P. Lecht, president of Lecht Sciences, a Tokyo-based think tank. The second is Arthur C. Clarke, a highly respected scientist and well-known author who envisioned the first satellite in 1946.

Charles P. Lecht

The environment in the cockpit of the space shuttle is an embryo of our future office. It is the command and control center of a flying cyborg. It is a mission-oriented space in which interpenetrating levels of cooperation between person and person, person and machine, and machine and machine express a dynamic, functional axiom, requiring

no additional explanation or encouragement. In the corporate plan, our pilot becomes president and our co-pilot becomes executive vice president. The duties of the flight engineers are shared by the comptroller, plant manager and marketing manager. Remote facilities are linked via ISDN

Courtesy Charles P. Lecht

technology, with various devices for successful execution of corporate mission, committed in a kaleidoscopic scenario of master/slave relationships orchestrated by "mission control," the boardroom. Occupying our office of the future is the executive of the future, a graduate of our school of the future. Our intrepid future executive will work his way (up?) to the corporate pilot's seat, from which he will guide the operation of the corporate network.

Participation and loyalty will have to replace legislated obedience as the guiding principles of business before the office of the future can fully emerge. But when it does — and it will — the benefits and the gratifications will be so apparent, so accessible, that the idea of a place of work will be consigned to oblivion, where it will remain, unlamented. In its place, a seamless

WHAT LIES AHEAD?

The document is truly the center of OA, as witnessed by the many supporting technologies. It is common to see photocopy machines, facsimile machines, micrographics recorders, and optical scanners, as well as various incoming information sources such as stock market tickers or business news wire services. Each has emerged as a separate technology; however, the computer is emerging as the center of **integrated office systems.**

What office could survive without a photocopy machine? The basic technology, xerography, originated in the mid-1940s. Today, the line between a copy machine and a laser printer is blurring; many feel there is an unneeded step in printing a document, then passing it through a copier for multiple copies. The answer is the intelligent laser printer/copier, which combines the two operations.

Furthermore, the tasks a facsimile machine or FAX performs are not so different from copying or printing. Why not one machine that combines the laser printer, copier, scanner, or FAX? Even as we were writing this book, Xerox announced a machine similar to this.

counterpoint of technological, political, psychological and economic harmony will make itself heard. At that point, we can readily begin to visualize our spaceship Earth as an office of the distant future in the unbounded network of galactic things to come.

Arthur C. Clarke

The office of A.D. 2019 seems like a perfectly ordinary office of the late 20th century except that there are no human clerical or secretarial workers in it. Routine chores—keeping files, setting up appointments, keeping track of schedules, bookkeeping and accounting, and the thousands of details that used to be carried out by human beings—are now in the far more capable hands of computers. The machines are directed by artificial intelligence (AI) and coupled to intelligence amplifiers (IA), computer-like devices capable of linking directly with the human nervous system and extending human mental power, even projecting human images . . . into the wearer's mind.

There are no human security guards, receptionists, personal secretaries or paralegals in today's offices. Every one of these jobs has been assigned to a computer with a very large memory and the ability to link with other computers for even greater power. Sophisticated software gives it the artificial intelligence required for tasks that must otherwise be handled by human workers.

There are few personal office spaces, only cubicles with IA terminals. After all, if the intelligence

Copyright © Charles Adams

amplifier can project human images into your mind, why not let it surround you with whatever office decor pleases you? You can have any furniture, window, or view you want. And you can change it at will, because it costs absolutely nothing; it's only a series of binary numbers in the office computer's memory circuits.

Because face-to-face meetings remain important . . . most offices have at least one conference room with IA interfaces, a few separate computer terminals, and multimedia facilities. . . . In well-equipped offices, your image is picked up by holographic television and sent to your conference partner's office. You sit before each other in three full-color dimensions.

The plushest offices are not as openly computerized and IA-ized as the more workaday environments. When cost is no factor and sheer conspicuous image is the goal, even today's top managers retain their desks, windows, and human secretaries. That is the ultimate one-upmanship in the office world of 2019.

Now, if we were to combine these three technologies with a personal computer with a hard disk drive, we would be able to do many things. Let's say we create and store a magazine advertisement, with text, graphics, a photograph, and the company logo. Now, using mail merge, we address it to each of the people on the distribution list who must approve it; the printer produces an original for each party. There are three managers who are to get a copy, so the copier produces those. Two other managers are in different cities, so we FAX copies to them. All this could be accomplished in just a few keystrokes, saving a great deal of time.

The computer plays an increasingly important role in office systems integration, as more and more office machines are linked. Today, computers large and small, file servers, mass storage, and peripherals such as modems, microfilm copiers, and laser printer/copiers are linked in networks. When a laser printer/copier is linked into the computer system so that a letter can be electronically sent to it and then copied, it is called an intelligent copier. When a number of complementary machines are linked together in an office, we call that an intelligent network. As this happens, the computer and the network become the same; the network is the computer. We have true office automation; we have put it all together.

It seems safe to say the computer is responsible for changing the way we work, from Miss Pilgrim, to Linda Dale, to you, tomorrow's knowledge worker. A U.S. government study states that by the year 2000, three out of five jobs that people will need to be trained and educated for do not exist today. These new jobs are a result of technologies that are emerging as industries. Furthermore, there is an increasing need for people to enter the computer industry in a wide variety of occupations. We hope you have gained an interest in the field from reading this book and might consider a computer career for yourself.

ETHICS

Human beings tend to be competitive and to want to get ahead in life. For many years, people have used war terminology and metaphors to describe business practices. It's no secret that certain people will do unethical — even illegal — things to make money or boost their careers. But can we say, "All's fair in love and war — and business"? This is an issue of particular concern in the office, where so many people can easily gain access to your computer and the data stored in it.

Work group computing is founded on the premise that people work together to achieve common goals. There should be respect for others' rights, privacy, and data in such an environment. However, it is likely that in the real world, unethical people will read other peoples' private files; in fact, some might even sabotage a colleague's work to make him or her look bad. To some extent, security systems should take care of this, but as the old saying goes, locks only keep honest people honest.

What can you do? Don't create temptations. Keep your computer secure; conceal your password and follow the company's security precautions. Keep your personal data on a floppy disk; lock it in your desk or take it home with you at night. Be sure that all your important work is backed up and stored in more than one physical location — on more than one computer system, or on a disk you keep with you.

Finally — and this is the hardest part — realize that you are part of the problem as well as part of the solution. Encourage your fellow employees, through polite conversation and example, to behave ethically. Find mutually shared values and beliefs and discuss them; people who are basically moral and honest find it difficult to wrong those they know personally. And when you see illegal or unethical things occurring, discuss them with your superior. To do otherwise makes you an accomplice to wrongdoing, and it also makes it easier to look the other way the next time it happens.

Kenneth R. Andrews, a former professor of management and editor of the *Harvard Business Review* for many years, writes in the Introduction to his book *Ethics in Practice: Managing the Moral Corporation,* "Commitment to quality objectives — among them compliance with law and high ethical standards — is an organizational achievement. It is inspired by pride more than by the profit that rightful pride produces."[1] Everyone must work together for an ethical workplace.

---

[1] Kenneth R. Andrews, *Ethics in Practice: Managing the Moral Corporation* (Harvard Business School Press, 1989).

CAREERbyte

Amy Wohl, Office Automation Consultant

Amy Wohl was once asked when there would be a paperless office. "The paperless office will arrive about the same time as the paperless toilet," she replied. Amy has kept the business world thinking realistically about the world of office automation for over 15 years. After receiving a master's degree in economics from Temple University, she began her work in the OA field at Datapro Research Corporation, where she was director of office automation consulting and executive editor of the office systems group.

As her knowledge and experience grew, Amy began speaking at industry conferences and seminars, and soon the business and computer press began quoting her. She formed Advanced Office Concepts Corporation; then, in 1984, she started Wohl Associates, the premier office automation consulting

Courtesy Wohl Associates

firm in the United States. She and her associates advise computer hardware and software vendors on product design and marketing, and also help end-user organizations plan and design OA systems. Amy writes a column for *Computerworld* newspaper, and is editor of "The

Wohl Report on End-User Computing."

Amy Wohl saw an emerging market in word processing and office systems in the 1970s, and she capitalized on it. Today, she is one of the most respected consultants and commentators in the field, commanding a fee of $3,000 a day for consulting and speaking engagements. One reason she is so highly regarded is because of her down-to-earth perspective: "Desktop computing today involves buying real computers for doing real work at real prices." Most of the talk in the press is about fanciful systems that users won't need for another five years or more, she says. She is living proof that spotting a trend, then applying oneself to learning the field through direct experience, can lead to a rewarding career—and even renown.

SUMMARY

1. *Define office automation and explain its relationship to other information systems in business.* Office automation is the marriage of computer and communication technologies that bring a variety of office machines together to serve the knowledge worker. The goal is to more efficiently manage information, so that the company can steer other systems—accounting, manufacturing, and so on—toward specific goals. We see people, software, and hardware truly come together in office automation.

2. *Name the four types of office automation technologies.* OA is four systems: text management, business analysis, document management, and network and communication management. The four systems are used to manage text, data, graphics,

video, and audio. Text management includes typing, word processing, and electronic publishing. Business analysis includes decision support systems and executive information systems. Document management may be paper, computer data, micrographics, or electronic documents captured from on-line services. Network management may involve a bank's ATMs or a company's work groups; local area networks are widely used. Work group computing is the wave of the future in OA.

3. *Explain and describe several management decision-making systems.* Office automation systems funnel upward into management decision-making systems. Two common examples are decision support systems, which can be as simple as a

spreadsheet, and executive information systems, which use a personal computer to extract data from corporate mainframe computers.

4. *Describe the importance of the knowledge worker in the modern office environment.*   The knowledge worker is the person using office automation technology either to make decisions or to support the business. For over a hundred years, there were no improvements in the way we accomplished office work; today we realize that to increase productivity we must do more than simply replace typewriters with computers. We must change procedures, and

knowledge workers are doing that themselves with such systems as work group computing.

5. *Describe the trends in integrated systems and identify some examples.*   Distributed computing brings various computer systems together so they may share data and programs. When it is complete, we call it an integrated environment, from an integrated desktop to a large integrated system. An integrated desktop may reside on a single computer or on many workstations across a local area network. A relatively sophisticated large integrated system is the image/data management system.

KEY TERMS

business analysis systems, p. 416

data integrity, p. 422

decision support systems (DSS), p. 416

document management systems, p. 417

electronic document, p. 418

executive information system (EIS), p. 416

facsimile (FAX), p. 412

groupware, p. 421

integrated office systems, p. 426

knowledge worker, p. 410

network and communication management systems, p. 420

office automation (OA), p. 410

text management systems, p. 413

work group computing, p. 421

REVIEW AND DISCUSSION QUESTIONS

1. How does office automation help people make better decisions?
2. Name some of the machines used in office automation.
3. What are office automation workers called?
4. What is the end product of office automation?
5. How is office productivity different from other types of business productivity?
6. Why is ergonomics important in OA?
7. Why is it important to integrate text, data, graphics, video, and audio in the office?
8. How have text management systems changed the way people work with words?
9. How does a decision support system differ from an executive information systems?
10. What is the main purpose behind document management systems?
11. Name the different forms a document can take.

12. Discuss how work group computing will change the way people work, the way their performance is evaluated, and the way they are rewarded.
13. Explain the concept of distributed computing.
14. What are the advantages to an integrated desktop?
15. Why is it important to have large system integration?
16. Ideally, what should the office automation system do for the company as a whole?
17. How can office machines be improved?
18. Discuss ethical office practices with other students, and make a list of ethical practices that people who work in offices should follow.
19. Explain the importance of the LAN in office automation systems.
20. Discuss the ways people have influenced, and will continue to influence, office automation systems and applications.

ISSUES

1. Women have, for many years, been discriminated against in the workplace. Can you think of some examples, either from your own experience or from books, movies, or TV? How do you feel about this form of discrimination? Do you think office automation technology can, as in the case of Linda Dale, have a positive impact on reducing this discrimination?

2. A debate concerning the harmful effects of radiation from the computer's video monitor display has raged for many years. Some claim that it causes illness and can have a detrimental effect on pregnant women and their unborn children. Others claim there is no conclusive evidence, and that sitting in front of the television is more harmful than using a video monitor. See if you can find a recent article that discusses this issue. Do you think a public institute such as the American National Standards Institute, or a governmental agency such as the Occupational Safety and Health Administration, should undertake a study to resolve this issue?

The Future of Computing

—

HAL

—

The final result was a machine intelligence that could reproduce — some philosophers still preferred to use the word "mimic" — most of the activities of the human brain, and with far greater speed and reliability. It was extremely expensive, and only a few units of the HAL 9000 series had yet been built; but the old jest that it would always be easier to make organic brains by unskilled labor was beginning to sound a little hollow.

Hal had been trained for this mission as thoroughly as his human colleagues — and at many times their rate of input, for in addition to his intrinsic speed, he never slept. His prime task was to monitor the life-support systems, continually checking oxygen pressure, temperature, hull leakage, radiation, and all the other interlocking factors on which the lives of the fragile human cargo depended. He could carry out the intricate navigational corrections, and execute the necessary flight maneuvers when it was time to change course. And he could watch over the hibernators, making any necessary adjustments to their environment and doling out the minute quantities of intravenous fluids that kept them alive.

J. Bond/Shooting Star

Source: Arthur C. Clarke, *2001: A Space Odyssey* (New York: New American Library, 1972).

THE 21ST CENTURY

The previous 13 chapters have explained how to use the computers we have available to us today, and how these computers came to be. Now we turn our attention to the future of computing. The computer industry is about 50 years old, but look at how dramatically it has changed in half a century. What will it be like as we enter the next century?

In keeping with our theme, we'll explore the future from the people, software, and hardware perspectives: How will people use computers in the future? What will software be like? What forms will tomorrow's processing hardware and peripherals take? As we examine these three aspects of the computer system, we'll share with you some visions of the future of computing. Finally, we'll turn to the subject of computer systems themselves to see how they will evolve in the next millennium.

PEOPLE

The world of the 1990s is a world where information has a high value. That will be even more true as we enter the next century. People, whether individuals with a family computer or knowledge workers in business and government, will continue to demand easier access to the information computers can provide.

The home computer will be connected to the wall telephone outlet, where it will capture news, information, and entertainment and disseminate it to the appropriate output device — the television or stereo, for example, or to the computer's mass storage device disk for later use. Each member of the family will program the computer, using menu selections, to search for and store items of interest in much the same way we program VCRs.

Today, we must use most media such as radio and television programs sequentially, like the tape storage media we discussed in Chapter 10. Tomorrow, it will no longer be necessary to be in front of the television at 7 o'clock for the news; the computer will make it available when you want it. The same is true for movies, sports, and specials. Instead of searching sequentially, we'll be able to search *heuristically,* on the basis of content or meaning. Suppose you are watching a news story about Brazil and a reference is made to an historic incident you don't understand. You will be able to punch a key and the computer will obtain the relevant background material for you.

No less dramatic, the computer will become the family librarian. Students will program it to collect research for a term paper. Working parents will use it to gather articles of interest, instead of subscribing to a dozen magazines and randomly browsing through them. Today, we can search on-line databases for key topics — providing we know the topic. We get descriptive listings in return. Tomorrow, we will be able to search for facts but they will be *in context with other information.* We can learn not only about Brazil but its relationship to the Pan American States, or its role in earth environmental studies, or its authors in relation to world literature.

V I S I O N S

Raymond Kurzweil

Raymond Kurzweil was the principal developer of the Kurzweil Reading Machine, the first print-to-speech reading machine for the blind.

Through the application of personal computing technology, I am confident that the handicaps associated with the major sensory and physical disabilities can largely be overcome during the next decade or two. In the world of the early 21st century, I believe the lives of disabled persons will be far different than they are today. For the blind, reading machines will be credit-card–sized devices that can instantly scan, not only the pages of text, but also signs and symbols in the real world. Blind persons will carry computerized navigational aids that will perform the functions of seeing eye dogs, only with greater intelligence than today's canine navigators. The deaf will have hearing machines that can display what people are saying. Those without use of their hands will control their environment, create written text, and interact with computers using voice recognition. Artificial hand prostheses will restore manual functionality, controlled by voice, by head movement, and, eventually perhaps, by direct mental connection.[1]

Courtesy of Raymond Kurzweil

Computers will be essential for education on all levels. In the late 1980s, students at various campuses of the University of California used an electronic library card catalog set up by the university to find books, periodicals, and research. They also discovered a "chat" feature, a type of electronic mail that allowed them to form groups within which they sent each other messages. In the future, we will find chat groups by the thousands on all kinds of computer systems. People will join chat groups or electronic grapevines formed around topics of interest such as parenting, gardening, philosophy, old cars, and so forth. So there will be formal information retrieval systems and informal ones as well.

V I S I O N S

Tom Snyder

Tom Snyder is the author of many award-winning educational software programs, as well as books about technology in education.

2009: The Smart Blackboard Drama Driver

Today's history class play: *Napoleon is Blind*.

In Ms. Kemmer's classroom 12 students chatter a bit too energetically — evidence of good old-fashioned stage fright. A student named Molly says, "Ms. Kemmer, PLEASE tell me who I'll be playing today." Molly always loves to get the part of strong, long-suffering women. As usual, Ms. Kemmer's casting remains secret to the last minute.

The play begins. On the big screen, a scene comes to life, silent but rich in color and direction. An old man, perhaps a French farmer, is leaning against a

Courtesy of Tom Snyder Productions

[1] *Boston Computer Society Update* magazine, November 1988, p. 54.

blanket-covered cart, apparently talking to someone or something under the blanket. Across the room, a student named Nick touches the image of the old man on his flat screen. A thought bubble appears over the man's head. Nick twitches, realizing he's in the scene. Nick silently reads the old man's thoughts from the screen: "I'm OK. This soldier doesn't want trouble."

Meanwhile, Molly touches the left edge of her screen, which scrolls backward to a scene in Paris where a crazy-looking street woman mutters to herself. The scene fades to where the old man bursts into a small rustic kitchen. A woman, perhaps his wife, looks at him and puts her hand to her mouth in fear. That's me for sure, thinks Molly as she reaches to touch the old woman.[2]

Knowledge workers will see the effects of the previous decade's national priority on education. Recent graduates will know enough about computers to more quickly learn how to use them in business. By this time, the idea of information as an asset—something a company owns—will have become passé. Information will be viewed as a shared resource, a tool with which workers do their work. Using the new, sophisticated skills, workers will feel a sense of accomplishment, even ownership, for the products and services they create. This in turn will lead to a rebirth of pride in one's job and higher-quality products.

These people will, by and large, be found in work groups; there will be few large factory-type work environments left because they tend to pace themselves according to the slowest. People in work groups can go at their own pace without interfering with each other.

Knowledge workers will become experts in a narrowly defined specialty. As a result, their work will be modular—one component of the entirety produced by their work group—and rewards will be based on quality of performance and timely completion. No one will be an expert in one specialty for long; as the workers' interests change, so will their job descriptions and their work group.

Managers will find their attention turning more and more toward seeking out the entrepreneurs, innovators, and people who are most interested in getting work done better, faster, and cheaper. Computer technology, in taking over many menial aspects of business, will free the spirit and creativity in people. It will help them excel at their work and perform for the greater good of the company.

Computers will also be far more efficient than they have been. In the past, it was often a lot of work to use the computer; by the year 2000, computers will be intuitively easy for people to use, as simple to operate as a household appliance. In business, computers will be helpmates that provide better customer service, speed the product development process, and show people how to avoid making mistakes. We will finally realize the productivity gains we have been seeking for the past 50 years.

---

[2] *Boston Computer Society Update* magazine, May 1989, p. 46.

V I S I O N S

Mario Ruiz/Picture Group

Isaac Asimov

Isaac Asimov is one of the most prolific science fiction writers of our century, and is credited with defining the basic principles and rules of robotics. He has written hundreds of novels and works of nonfiction.

There could be a decentralization of society. People won't have to conglomerate themselves in offices and factories and they could do much more of their work from home. I don't foresee it (technology) being dehumanizing or anything like that; it's just the reverse. I think the computer is a great humanizing factor because it makes the individual more important. The more information we have on each individual, the more each individual counts.[3]

SOFTWARE

Today, most software is oriented toward work. Tomorrow, we will have software that helps us enjoy life more. Instead of simple entertainment such as games, we'll have software that helps us explore our interests and our inquisitiveness. Instead of passive activities and media such as television, 21st-century software will take us places and allow us to participate as though we were actually there. When we watch a soccer game on a screen, we will be able to zoom in on a play or stop the action. When we ask a question, the expert system software will answer it for us.

V I S I O N S

Courtesy of Microsoft Corporation

Bill Gates

Bill Gates is the chairman of the board of Microsoft Corporation, the largest software company in the world. Gates created the first version of the BASIC programming language for a personal computer in 1975.

In 20 years the Information Age will be here, absolutely. Take one example: You're sitting at home. You'll have a variety of image libraries that will contain, say, all the world's best art. You'll also have very cheap, flat-panel display devices throughout your house that will provide resolution so good that viewing a projection will be like looking at the original oil painting. It will be that realistic.

The dream of having the world database at your fingertips will have become a reality. You'll even be able to call up a video show and place yourself in it. Probably all this progress will be pretty disruptive stuff. We'll really find out what the human brain can do, but we'll have serious problems about the purpose of it all. We're going to find out how curious we are and how much stimulation we can take. I can't think of any equivalent phenomenon in history.[4]

---

[3] *InfoWorld*, January 2, 1989, p. 38.
[4] *OMNI*, January 1987, p. 38.

Software naturally follows the procedures people create to do their work, which means that we will still use many of the same *kinds of applications* in the 21st century that we use today. Many, however, will have artificial intelligence components, in much the same way as programs like the Grammatik text analyzer, mentioned in Chapter 4. We'll use "smart" word processors, spreadsheets, and database management programs that learn our working styles and adapt to us. These programs will be able to "sense" when we change printers and "know" when we finish working and it's time to save our work.

Today's programs make us adapt to the way they work; what's more, each program performs a preordained task. You can't balance your checkbook using a word processor. These limitations led to integrated software and windowing or multitasking environments. Tomorrow's individual applications will change more dramatically. There will be many new types of applications that we teach *our* work habits and that perform any number of personal tasks for us.

For example, knowledge workers will have software that creates a virtual electronic desktop, just like the old-fashioned real desktop. The software lets you choose the features you want, then learns to perform tasks according to your work habits. You might want a bulletin board to post electronic notes on, or a telephone dialing directory. Perhaps you need an electronic organizer, or have a shelf of books you refer to often. You may read the daily newspaper, or wish to check televised news or stock quotations at a particular time of day. All these functions and more will be available on your computer screen as fully realized multimedia software reaches maturity.

Such a system will be possible because of several software advancements. One, the human interface will have matured; it will be fully functional, not just a pretty screen. Many of the functions we activate by pressing a sequence of keys will be accomplished by touching a single icon on the screen. Through improved graphic design, our electronic tools will look like their real counterparts: a sheet of paper, an address book, a Post-it note, a book. Hypertext software will allow us to turn pages, clip articles, and store information in ways very similar to the way our human brain works. In short, computer systems will offer more random, unstructured ways to work with data.

Ted Nelson

Theodor Nelson originated the concept of Hypertext and Hypermedia in the 1960s. Since then, he has headed Project Xanadu, whose goal is to create an on-line library system for "hyperintellectuals."

By "hypertext" I mean nonsequential writing.

Ordinary writing is sequential for two reasons. First, it grew out of speech and speech making, which have to be sequential; and second, because books are not convenient to read except in a sequence.

But the *structures of ideas* are not sequential. They tie together every which way. And when we write, we are always trying to tie things together in nonsequential ways.

However, in my view, a new day is dawning. Computer storage and screen display mean we no longer *have* to have things in sequence; totally arbitrary structures are possible, and I think that after we've tried them enough people will see how desirable they are.

Courtesy of Eric Butler

I still don't know why it took so long. I first published the term *hypertext* in 1965, and for the last 20 years have been giving speeches and writing articles about how we need hypertext for education, scholarship, archiving and "the office of the future"—not to mention poetry.[5]

It is in the first decade of the 21st century that we will see the promise of neural networks or neurocomputing unfold. Neural network software re-creates processing as the brain does it. The brain uses millions of neurons; a neural network uses multiple processing elements that act just like neurons. A neural network, or neurocomputer, is a computer system that solves problems and makes decisions in a manner that mimics the human brain. It uses the same mental traits as a human mind: trial and error, fuzzy logic, hit-or-miss reasoning. In these traits, neural network software differs from expert systems, which rely on logical instructions such as If-Then, or > (greater than) and < (less than). You might say that von Neumann computers are left-brain, while neural nets are right brain.

Most neural networks are networks that are created within the software residing on a computer. Each neuron is called a node, just as you learned about in Chapter 11. In a neural net, each node effectively becomes a CPU. There-fore, hundreds, even thousands, of individual nodes work on the data, process-ing, filtering, finally arriving at an answer.

In Chapter 7, we mentioned MYCIN, the expert system that performs medical diagnoses. A neural network developed by Owen Carroll at the State University of New York at Stony Brook can actually evaluate electrocardio-grams (ECGs). The average human's heart beats almost 100,000 times a day; the neural network is trained to "listen" to normal versus abnormal beats. Once it can distinguish the difference, it can detect abnormal heartbeats in an ECG and provide a diagnosis. The expert system, on the other hand, might only be able to infer from a body of expert opinions that a heart condition exists; it would not be able to learn as the neural net does. Neural networks are not greatly different from expert systems; however, they are more accurate and provide greater detail.

To demonstrate the learning abilities of a neural network, Terrence Sej-nowski of Johns Hopkins University demonstrated his Netalk neural network at a conference in 1987. Netalk took standard computer ASCII text and began translating it into speech. At first, the computer babbled like an infant, yet within 16 hours it was talking like a 6-year-old.

In *Svengali*, a classic film from the 1930s, Svengali says, "There are more things in heaven and on earth than are dreamt of in your imagination." This is surely true with software. For many years, people were forced to use the computer in exactly the way the software dictated. Computers and users both proliferated; the market became more competitive, and soon software was being designed more to meet users' needs. Eventually, user groups were formed and the computer industry solicited comments and feedback in order to improve software. Often, individuals couldn't find software that met their needs, so they created it themselves.

Hardware development has proceeded apace, but with software we can see true innovations. Software is created from necessity; often, though, that ne-

---

[5] *Computer Lib-Dream Machines: You Can and Must Understand Computers Now!* rev. ed. (Redmond, Wash.: Tempus Books, 1987).

cessity is born from a creative or innovative spark that, somehow, comes from beyond our imagination. Indeed, perhaps this is why we must continue to explore the outer reaches of software, with artificial intelligence and neural networks, to answer that fundamental question: Can we create a computer system that can think as well as a human?

HARDWARE

Poor hardware: what is it to do except get smaller, faster, cheaper, better? And it will do so; in this decade, we'll watch the Intel family of microprocessors spawn the 80586, 80686, perhaps the 80786, while the Motorola microprocessors go from 68040 to 68050, 68060, each orders of magnitude more powerful than its predecessor. In the new millennium, we will see the first true wrist computers. Some exist today but they lack the power as well as the memory of a laptop or desktop computer. We may also begin to see computer chip implants for the handicapped; already, a chip with image processing capabilities has proven it can help the blind see again.

Most families will have a computer. It will be a 386 machine or a Macintosh with 8 megabytes of RAM, a read/write optical disk, or CD–ROM, and a built-in modem. It will have fiber-optic interfaces to the stereo and the television, as well as to household appliances and the security system. Consumer electronics products will have a label saying "Computer-Compatible."

David J. Waks

David J. Waks is director of technology at Prodigy home network services.

V I S I O N S

Many of us have shared a vision of the next evolution of the home personal computer: the "multimedia home PC," or MHPC. It combines the best features of today's TV set, personal computer, and CD player to provide a medium far richer than any of its predecessors.

What will the MHPC be used for? We see exciting applications for every member of the family. Some examples:

- New versions of today's popular home software, enhanced with pictures and sound.
- New forms of interactive entertainment — "arcade games in the home," with a heightened sense of reality from pictures and sound.
- New and far more effective educational applications. Imagine a personal language tutor that uses pictures, text, and audio to teach you a spoken language; then remembers on a disk what you've already learned so it can focus the next lesson on what you really need help with.
- Personal creative applications, such as home decorating, gardening, physical fitness, and travelogues.
- Catalogs featuring entertaining interactive ads and automatic order entry based on the stored profiles of each family member.

The MHPC could well be the first major change in home computers.[6]

Courtesy of Prodigy

---

[6] *Boston Computer Society Update* magazine, March 1989, p. 46.

Large computer system development will also continue to advance because the need for these machines will not soon go away. Danny Hillis, creator of the Connection Machine, led the way in developing commercial parallel processing machines, computers with hundreds or thousands of simple microprocessors working together. As engineers learn more ways to utilize this complex architecture, their use will grow.

Is the next wave of computers based on light? Alan Huang, an engineer at AT&T Bell Laboratories, thinks so. He has been working for many years on an optical computer. It uses photons of light instead of electrons of electricity to perform processing tasks. A conventional computer appears as a circuit board with integrated chips. An optical processor is a collection of lasers, lenses, prisms, and photonic devices that transmit signals without wires, thousands or even millions of times faster than today's computers. Imagine computers that could operate literally at the speed of light!

The technology to improve peripherals, particularly input devices, is already with us. We have light pens and microphones to make written or spoken input; processor speeds and new software techniques will help advance these methods.

But we can look for other innovative new peripherals as well. In Chapter 10, you learned about cyberspace and the data glove. Well, another peripheral we may see by the year 2000 is the Sensor Frame, invented by Paul McAvinney. It looks like a deep picture frame that mounts over the computer monitor. When the user reaches into it, the sensor frame detects movement and reproduces it on the computer screen. It allows an engineer to manipulate spatial images with three-dimensional accuracy, such as moving the planets into perspective. With peripherals like the data glove and the Sensor Frame, can it be long until we actually step inside the computer display, becoming part of a holographic reality?

V I S I O N S

John Scully

John Scully is chairman and chief executive officer of Apple Computer, Inc.

A future-generation Macintosh, which we should have early in the 21st century, might well be a wonderful fantasy machine called the Knowledge Navigator, a discoverer of worlds, a tool as galvanizing as the printing press. Individuals could use it to drive through libraries, museums, databases, or institutional archives. This tool wouldn't just take you to the doorstep of these great resources as sophisticated computers do now; it would invite you deep inside its secrets, interpreting and explaining — converting vast quantities of information into personalized and understandable knowledge.

Imagine the Knowledge Navigator having two navigational joysticks on each side, like a pilot's controls, allowing you to steer through the various windows and menus opening galleries, stacks, and more. You might even be set free from the keyboard, entering commands by speaking to the Navigator. What you see on the large, flat display screen will likely be in full color, high-definition, television-quality images, full pages of text, graphics, computer-generated animation. What you hear will incorporate high-fidelity sound, speech synthesis, and speech recognition. You will be able to work in

Courtesy of Apple Computer, Inc.

several of these windows at any time, giving you the possibility to simulta-neously compare, for example, the animated structural system of living cells with the animated network of a global economy.

What the Navigator looks like is not as important as what it does. . . . Indeed, within the next decade, the most powerful personal computer avail-able today will be "invisible," like a motor; it will fit into a machine the size of a pocket calculator.

. . . Of far greater importance is how this new tool may change the way we learn, think, work, communicate and live, how it will dramatically change the computer industry from a producer of hardware or software to a producer of mass-personalized knowledge systems.[7]

SYSTEMS

As you can probably see by now, in the 21st century it is becoming more difficult to distinguish the people aspect from the software aspect from the hardware aspect. In the early days, the computer was given a task: calculate an equation, run the payroll, record names and dates. Push a button, then leave the machine to do its work.

In the early 21st century, we will use the computer much more often in our daily lives. It will control our home security system, it will connect with the bank computer for services, it will be our watch, our phone, our calculator, our calendar, our appointment book, our address book, and more. We will use a pen to write on the screen; some of the more expensive units will allow us to use our speech as input.

We will drive smart cars that ride on smart highways; chips built into the auto will guide it down the lane and maintain speed with other traffic. The first, Prometheus, is already in use in Europe. We will work in smart buildings.

Business and industry will rejoice that true systems integration is finally a reality. Through the development of intelligent operating systems and net-working, any computer will be able to exchange data with any other. Large corporations will have "lights out" data centers, where large mainframes conrol vast disk farms 24 hours a day, seven days a week, without human intervention. In the office, a similar integration will have occurred; most office machines will be intelligent and capable of exchanging any kind of text, graphic, video, or audio data, preprogrammed to do their work 24 hours a day.

Our computer will travel with us just about anywhere we go; there will be convenient jacks in pay phones so we can go on-line with ease. We begin to see that as our personal wants and needs change, the interactive software changes too, so that the hardware produces the output we desire. And in the midst of all this, the network has become an information and services cornucopia; we "jack in" whenever we want, to order pizza, send voice or data messages, pay bills, or get news and entertainment.

---

[7] John Sculley, *Odyssey* (New York: Harper & Row, 1987).

We begin to see that, as we learned in Chapter 13, "the computer is the network," and that slowly but surely, we are getting "everything from everywhere." It is awesome to behold at times; it boggles the imagination to think of the effort of so many human minds and their accumulated knowledge making this possible.

As more and more computers are networked, we should see the promise of the computer as a democratizing influence emerge. We have seen the notion of trading partners and multinational companies spearhead the movement toward a world economy; computers enhance this, and make it all the more possible for us to get to know our neighbors around the globe. The best example of this is the electronic mail system that allows American and Russian scientists, politicians, businesspeople, and others to communicate with each other. A service provided by a private firm, San Francisco/Moscow Teleport, it promises to ring the world with "electronic glasnost."

ISSUES FOR THE NEW MILLENNIUM

As computers become a more important and pervasive aspect of our lives, we will certainly all fall prey to the many dilemmas posed throughout this book. What's more, many more await us: What, for instance, are we to make of the *bionic computer,* one that is grown from living tissue, much like the human brain? We can switch off a mechanical-electrical computer without it being an ethical or moral issue; can we say the same for disconnecting a "living" computer?

Our day-to-day problems in the 21st century won't be quite as daunting. Most of us will probably try to cope with the ever-increasing amounts of information that people and computers make available. It has been said that more information has been produced in the last 30 years than in the previous 5,000 years; is it any wonder we have trouble retaining everything we need to know?

Author Richard Saul Wurman calls this *information anxiety* and has written a book of the same name about it. In it, he writes:

> *Information anxiety* is produced by the ever-widening gap between what we understand and what we think we should understand. *Information anxiety* is the black hole between data and knowledge. It happens when information doesn't tell us what we want or need to know.
>
> Almost everyone suffers from *information anxiety* to some degree. We read without comprehending, see without perceiving, hear without listening. It can be experienced as moments of frustration with a manual that refuses to divulge the secret to operating a video recorder or a map that bears no relation to reality. . . . It can also be manifested as a chronic malaise, a pervasive fear that we are about to be overwhelmed by the very material we need to master in order to function in this world.[8]

---

[8] Richard Saul Wurman, *Information Anxiety* (New York: Doubleday, 1989).

The most difficult question we may have to answer in the next century is whether we are information's master or its slave. You recall our discussion of the difference between data and information in Chapter 1; think of how Wurman warns about the gap between data and information, and how information leads to knowledge. If that is so, we must be very careful about the kind and quality of information we process, whether in our brains or in our computers, for indeed, each of us must strive for the highest-quality knowledge attainable.

Computers are certainly powerful tools when used for this purpose. They have helped us make incredible strides in our pursuit of knowledge. Arthur C. Clarke, HAL's creator, has said that any sufficiently advanced technology can barely be distinguished from magic.

The magic continues.

APPENDIX

A

Number Systems

APPENDIX OUTLINE

What Is a Number?
  What Is a Number System?
  The Egyptian Number System
  The Decimal Number System
  Comparing Number Systems
Number Systems for Computers
  George Boole + Claude Shannon = The Binary
    Computer
  The Binary Number System
  Why Computers Use Number Systems
  The Octal Number System
  The Hexadecimal Number System
Number Systems and Computer Codes
  EBCDIC
  ASCII
  Using Number Systems and Computer Codes
Summary
Key Terms
Review and Discussion Questions

OBJECTIVES

After reading and studying this appendix, you should be able to:

1. Define a number.
2. Explain the purpose of a number system.
3. Understand how number systems are used for different purposes.
4. Understand the number systems unique to computers.
5. Describe the two common types of computer codes and their relationship to number systems.

WHAT IS A NUMBER?

The *Oxford English Dictionary* defines a **number** as a "particular mark or symbol, having arithmetical value, by which anything has a place assigned to it in a series." Strictly speaking, a number is a *concept* associated with a numeral. For example, we look in our hand and see a number of pennies, three to be exact; the numeral **3** appears in our mind. A **numeral** is a symbol that represents a value in a specific number system. In common, everyday language, we use the term *number* to refer to a *numeral,* as we shall do in this appendix.

What Is a Number System?

We use numbers to keep track of things, to place a value on things, to measure and compare things, and for many other purposes. No one can accurately say when the human race began using numbers, but it's assumed the first number systems derived from counting on our fingers. A **number system** is a set of symbols or numbers combined with *rules* for how those numbers are used.

The Egyptian Number System

The ancient Egyptians created a number system around 2850 B.C. based on *hieroglyphics* or representational characters. They were no different than our 1 or 2 or 3, but perhaps more interesting to look at:

Our Numeral (decimal)	Egyptian Numeral	Descriptive Name
1	I	Stroke
10	∩	Heel bone
100	ꝯ	Scroll
1000	𓆼	Lotus flower
10,000	𓂭	Pointing finger
100,000	☋	Polliwog
1,000,000	𓁨	Astonished man

Try writing the year you were born in the Egyptian number system.

The Decimal Number System

The number system we use most commonly today is the Hindu-Arabic or **decimal number system,** which is also referred to as a **base 10** number system. That means it is based on 10 numbers (fingers!). The number symbols 1 through 9 appear to have originated in India around 300 B.C. The decimal system did not use the 0 (zero) at the time, although the 0 is believed to have predated the Hindu-Arabic numbers.

FIGURE A – 1   Base 10 system of powers.

Numbers	1	9	9	2
Base 10	(Thousands) 1,000	(Hundreds) 100	(Tens) 10	(Ones) 1
Powers	10^3	10^2	10^1	10^0

FIGURE A – 2   Hindu-Arabic and Roman number systems.

Arabic	Roman	Arabic	Roman	Arabic	Roman
1	I	16	XVI	90	XC
2	II	17	XVII	100	C
3	III	18	XVIII	200	CC
4	IV	19	XIX	300	CCC
5	V	20	XX	400	CD
6	VI	21	XXI	500	D
7	VII	22	XXII	600	DC
8	VIII	23	XXIII	700	DCC
9	IX	24	XXIV	800	DCCC
10	X	30	XXX	900	CM
11	XI	40	XL	1,000	M
12	XII	50	L	2,000	MM
13	XIII	60	LX	3,000	MMM
14	XIV	70	LXX	4,000	$M\overline{V}$
15	XV	80	LXXX	5,000	$\overline{V}$ (or 𝄞)

The decimal or base 10 number system places values on numbers according to their position. The lowest values are to the right, the values increasing as they move to the left, each position raising the value by 10. We refer to these increments of 10 as **powers** or exponents, which means the number is multiplied by itself. For example:

$10^1 = 10$
$10^2 = 10 \times 10 = 100$
$10^3 = 10 \times 10 \times 10 = 1,000$
$10^4 = 10 \times 10 \times 10 \times 10 = 10,000$

Another very famous example is the mathematical equation demonstrating Einstein's theory of relativity, which looks like this:

$E = mc^2$

The ^{2} means the number is taken to the second power. Figure A – 1 shows how the base 10 system of powers works, using a calendar year as an example.

Comparing Number Systems

By way of comparison, there is another base 10 number system we still see in use today. It's the Roman system, which uses letters of the alphabet as numbers. Figure A – 2 shows how it compares with the Hindu-Arabic number system.

FIGURE A–3   Development of the decimal number system.

Do you see the structure in the Roman number system? It changes symbols at 5 and 10, but the numbers preceding each combine the previous number. Once you grasp the logic, when you watch old movies you can tell what year they were made. For example:

Hindu-Arabic   **Roman**
1992   MCMXCII

Try writing the year you were born in Roman numbers.

Interestingly, there was a battle in Europe over which number system to use that went on for hundreds of years. The "algorists" favored the decimal system and the "abacists" favored the Roman (and performed their math on the abacus, hence their name). The decimal number system has only been in wide use since about the year 1500. Figure A–3 shows the development of the decimal number system; notice when the zero appears.

NUMBER SYSTEMS FOR COMPUTERS

There have been many calculating and computational machines designed to use the decimal or base 10 number system. Yet none have proven to work as fast as the modern electronic digital computer that we have studied in this book. The computers we are familiar with use the binary number system. The story of how the binary number system came to be used for computers is the story of pioneering research in mathematics by two men who lived a century apart from one another.

George Boole + Claude Shannon = The Binary Computer

George Boole (1815–1864) proved that logic could be expressed in simple algebraic equations. Over time, this became known as Boolean algebra. His concepts provided the foundation for a number of experiments in building mechanical counting devices. In the 20th century, those same concepts were applied to the study of electronics.

In 1937, Claude Shannon was a student at the Massachusetts Institute of Technology, studying for his master's degree. The title of his master's thesis was "A Symbolic Analysis of Relay and Switching Circuits," and in it he applied Boolean logic, or binary arithmetic, to the circuits that comprise a computer.

Shannon's ideas were first put into use by AT&T's Bell Laboratories, to speed telephone call connections and later to reduce noise. However, his contribution to electronic digital computer technology is equally if not more significant. For his work in switching circuits and information theory, he was awarded the Nobel Prize.

The Binary Number System

The binary number system, as you already know from Chapter 2, uses just two numbers: the 1 and the 0 (zero). Therefore, we call it a **base 2** number system. Modern electronic digital computers use the binary number system for internal processing. This is because the two numbers, 1 and 0, easily represent the two electrical states, *on* and *off*. This simplicity enables computers to perform mathematical operations with incredible speed.

Numbers, letters, and symbols are represented as a series of 1s and 0s. For example, people enter decimal numbers into the computer; a special translation program in the computer converts decimal into binary. This same translation program converts binary into decimal output. Figure A–4 shows the binary equivalents for decimal numbers.

In the decimal system, we count by powers of 10: 1, 10, 100, and so on. In the binary system, we count by powers of 2:

$2^1 = 2$

$2^2 = 4$

$2^3 = 8$

$2^4 = 16$

If you recall, computer memory is incremented by powers of 2. Early personal computers had 64K of RAM, which then grew to 128K, doubling 256K, doubling 512K, then 640K (512 + 128), and so forth.

Why Computers Use Number Systems

Machine language, which you learned about in Chapter 8, uses the binary number system to provide instructions for the CPU. It is the most basic language for the computer; it requires no translation to be understood.

FIGURE A – 4   Binary equivalents for decimal numbers.

Decimal Place		
100	**10**	**1**
		0
		1
		2
		3
		4
		5
		6
		7
		8
		9
	1	0
	1	1
	1	2
	1	3
	1	4
	1	5
	1	6

Binary Place					
32	**16**	**8**	**4**	**2**	**1**
					0
					1
				1	0
				1	1
			1	0	0
			1	0	1
			1	1	0
			1	1	1
		1	0	0	0
		1	0	0	1
		1	0	1	0
		1	0	1	1
		1	1	0	0
		1	1	0	1
		1	1	1	0
		1	1	1	1
	1	0	0	0	0

Therefore, the people most interested in number systems and how they translate one into another are programmers. As you can imagine, it would be extremely tedious to write every character and instruction in binary or machine language; that's why programming languages evolved.

However, it is sometimes necessary for programmers to work with the computer at or near the machine language level. Even so, there are two number systems that have helped make their work easier: the octal and hexadecimal number systems. These number systems have been used as a kind of shorthand so that the programmer does not have to write programs in 0s and 1s. As you read about these systems, refer to Figure A – 5, which compares decimal and binary number systems to octal and hexadecimal.

The Octal Number System

The **octal** number system is a **base 8** system that uses eight symbols, the numbers 0 through 7. Like the decimal system, the octal system places values on numbers according to their position. In this case, numbers are raised by the power of 8. When converting octal numbers to binary, the equation is $8 = 2^3$. This means that a set of three binary digits equals one octal digit. Octal was the first programming language (as opposed to binary or machine language) that programmers actually used to write instructions for the earliest computers.

The Hexadecimal Number System

The **hexadecimal** number system is a **base 16** number system that uses 16 symbols. This means using additional, distinct symbols after we reach 9. Thus, hexadecimal uses letters of the alphabet: A for 10, B for 11, through F for 15, and 10 for 16. Again, symbols have value according to their position. When converting hexadecimal symbols to binary, the equation is $16 = 2^4$. Today, hexadecimal is more commonly used in computers than the octal system.

FIGURE A – 5   Comparison of decimal and binary to octal and hexadecimal number systems.

Decimal Place

100	10	1
		0
		1
		2
		3
		4
		5
		6
		7
		8
		9
	1	0
	1	1
	1	2
	1	3
	1	4
	1	5
	1	6

Binary Place

32	16	8	4	2	1
					0
					1
				1	0
				1	1
			1	0	0
			1	0	1
			1	1	0
			1	1	1
		1	0	0	0
		1	0	0	1
		1	0	1	0
		1	0	1	1
		1	1	0	0
		1	1	0	1
		1	1	1	0
		1	1	1	1
	1	0	0	0	0

Octal Place

64	8	1
		0
		1
		2
		3
		4
		5
		6
		7
	1	0
	1	1
	1	2
	1	3
	1	4
	1	5
	1	6
	1	7
	2	0

Hexadecimal Place

256	16	1
		0
		1
		2
		3
		4
		5
		6
		7
		8
		9
		A
		B
		C
		D
		E
		F
	1	0

In the past, it was useful for programmers to know how to convert from binary to octal or hexadecimal. In fact, expert programmers could perform conversions in their heads while they wrote programs! Yet in time it became possible to use special software programs to perform these tasks automatically so that few today use these number systems extensively. However, systems programmers still find occasions when it is necessary to "crawl under the hood," so to speak, and rewrite or revise portions of the computer system code using these basic tools.

NUMBER SYSTEMS AND COMPUTER CODES

In the same way that number systems are used to represent *instructions* sent to the CPU, computer codes are used to represent *data* sent for processing. **Computer codes** are a set of symbols and rules that assure that the characters we send to the computer system are consistently and accurately represented. There are two computer codes in common use today: EBCDIC and ASCII. Refer to Figure A – 6 for a comparison of these two computer codes and the binary number system.

EBCDIC

EBCDIC stands for Extended Binary Coded Decimal Interchange Code, and it was developed by IBM for its mainframe computers. It is now used by most IBM computers. EBCDIC can represent 256 different letters, numbers, and characters.

FIGURE A–6 Comparison of EBCDIC and ASCII.

Character	EBCDIC	ASCII
0	11110000	00110000
1	11110001	00110001
2	11110010	00110010
3	11110011	00110011
4	11110100	00110100
5	11110101	00110101
6	11110110	00110110
7	11110111	00110111
8	11111000	00111000
9	11111001	00111001
A	11000001	01000001
B	11000010	01000010
C	11000011	01000011
D	11000100	01000100
E	11000101	01000101
F	11000110	01000110
G	11000111	01000111
H	11001000	01001000
I	11001001	01001001
J	11010001	01001010
K	11010010	01001011
L	11010011	01001100
M	11010100	01001101
N	11010101	01001110
O	11010110	01001111
P	11010111	01010000
Q	11011000	01010001
R	11011001	01010010
S	11100010	01010011
T	11100011	01010100
U	11100100	01010101
V	11100101	01010110
W	11100110	01010111
X	11100111	01011000
Y	11101000	01011001
Z	11101001	01011010
Special Characters		
!	01011010	01000001
"	01111111	01000010
#	01111011	01000011
$	01011011	01000100
%	01101100	01000101
&	01010000	01000110
(	01001101	01001000
)	01011101	01001001
*	01011100	01001010
+	01001110	01001011

ASCII

ASCII stands for the American Standard Code for Information Interchange. It was developed so that computer systems made by a wide variety of different companies could exchange data with ease, especially with respect to computer networking and communications. Like EBCDIC, ASCII can represent 256 characters.

Using Number Systems and Computer Codes

Needless to say, there are times when non-IBM computers must communicate with IBM computers; then it is necessary to convert from ASCII to EBCDIC and vice versa. Again, this is similar to converting between the number systems we studied previously, and is primarily accomplished by special software programs.

It would be difficult to use computers without numbers and number systems. If you compare what you've learned in this appendix with what you learned about bits and bytes in Chapter 2, you can now understand how the concepts of the bit and byte are based on the binary number system. You can also understand the translation process between the characters — both as programs and as data — we type into the computer and the way they are represented to the CPU.

SUMMARY

1. *Define a number.* A numeral is a symbol that represents a value in a specific number system, such as the V in the Roman system or the 5 in the Hindu-Arabic system. We commonly refer to a numeral as a number.

2. *Explain the purpose of a number system.* A number system is a set of symbols or numbers used according to specific rules. We use number systems to keep track of things or to place a value on things.

3. *Understand how number systems are used for different purposes.* Both Roman and Hindu-Arabic number systems are decimal, or base 10, systems which we are most familiar with.

4. *Understand the number systems unique to computers.* Computer number systems are used to represent instructions sent to the CPU. The computer uses the binary, or base 2, system which evolved out of research by Claude Shannon, based on George Boole's algebra. It is tedious for programmers to work with the instructions sent to the CPU in binary, so two shorthand methods have evolved to make their work easier. One is the octal number system, which is called base 8; the other is hexadecimal, or base 16, the more popular of the two.

5. *Describe the two common types of computer codes and their relationship to number systems.* Computer codes are used to represent data being sent to the CPU. The one common to IBM computers is EBCDIC. The one common to almost all other computers is ASCII, which can be used to communicate between IBM and non-IBM computers.

KEY TERMS

ASCII, p. 452

computer codes, p. 450

number system, p. 445

base 2, p. 448

decimal number system, p. 445

numeral, p. 445

base 8, p. 449

EBCDIC, p. 450

octal, p. 449

base 10, p. 445

hexadecimal, p. 449

powers, p. 446

base 16, p. 449

number, p. 445

REVIEW AND DISCUSSION QUESTIONS

1. Explain the difference between a number and a numeral.

2. Discuss the reasons why there are different number systems.

3. What are the advantages to using the binary number system for computers?

4. Try taking a number that has a relationship to distance, such as the miles from your home to school, out to as many powers as you can. Discuss the significance to the powers of 10.

5. Create an exercise in working with the binary number system, such as spelling your name or creating your date of birth. Discuss the patterns that the 1s and 0s form.

6. Learn more about George Boole and his special algebra. What kind of man was he? Do you think he realized the importance of his algebra at the time he created it?

7. Learn more about Claude Shannon. What is the special relationship between Boolean algebra and electronic theory?

8. Discuss why it might be easier to use another rather complex number system, such as octal or hexadecimal, as a shorthand for the binary system.

9. Identify the most common number system used for sending data to a wide variety of computer systems.

10. During what computer activity are you most likely to encounter a number system used for representing instructions? For representing data?

APPENDIX B

The Computer Generations

APPENDIX OUTLINE

Introduction
A Brief History of Electronics
   The Vacuum Tube
   The Transistor
   The Integrated Circuit
The First Generation
   Circuit Technology
   CPU Speed
   I/O Devices
   Memory and Storage
   Programming Languages
   Software
The Second Generation
The Third Generation
The Fourth Generation
   Mainframes
   Minicomputers
   Personal Computers
The Fifth Generation
What Lies Ahead?
Summary
Key Terms
Review and Discussion Questions

OBJECTIVES

After reading and studying this appendix, you should be able to:

1. Understand how computer technology has evolved throughout the four generations.
2. Describe the various electronic devices that have driven computer technology from one generation to the next.
3. Understand the most significant advances in circuit technology, CPU speed, memory, programming languages, and software for each generation.
4. Characterize some of the advances we can expect to see in the fifth generation.

INTRODUCTION

The best way to understand where we are going is to understand the events that have led us to where we are. In the same way we want to understand how human society has evolved, it is important that we understand computer evolution. Indeed, computer evolution has had a dramatic impact on human society, and will surely continue to do so in the future.

The **computer generations** are the stages in the evolution of electronic circuitry, hardware, software, programming languages, and other technological developments. These generations help us measure the progress of computer technology. They are an artificial schema people have superimposed on computer history in order to understand events and advancements. You won't find the generations beginning or ending exactly on schedule; some developments overlap from one generation to the next, while others just don't fit neatly into one generation or another. Yet what the computer generations help us do is find a frame of reference with which to measure progress and evaluate advances in computer technology.

We briefly described how computers evolved in Chapter 1. In this appendix, we explore the four generations of progress we have made in greater detail, and we characterize some aspects of the emerging fifth generation. This should be of particular interest to students who are interested in studying the evolution of the computer industry, who plan to pursue a career in computer science or information systems, or who are seeking background material for a term paper or class project.

This appendix begins with a brief survey of the field of electronics, which paved the way for the computer. Then each of the five generations is discussed. The following topics are covered: circuit technology, CPU speed, I/O devices, memory and storage, programming languages, and software, which includes operating systems and application software.

A BRIEF HISTORY OF ELECTRONICS

Perhaps the best way to begin our discussion is to give credit to Benjamin Franklin for flying a kite in a rainstorm, demonstrating how to harness and use electricity. Ben was truly a Renaissance man; he was interested in statesmanship, writing, printing, and science. In the 1750s, he tied a key to a kite string and sent it up in a rainstorm. Lightning struck the key and magnetized it.

Around the same time, a French physicist named Francois du Fay determined that there are two types of electricity. He termed them vitreous and resinous; they later became known as positive and negative. Electricity flows from the negative to the positive. By controlling this flow, in much the same way a water faucet controls water flow, scientists eventually learned to manipulate electricity's two states: on and off. As we shall see, this is essential to how computers operate.

The Vacuum Tube

In the latter part of the 19th century, American Thomas Edison invented the incandescent light bulb and Italian Guglielmo Marconi developed the wireless telegraph. But it wasn't until John Fleming, an Englishman, invented the first vacuum tube in 1904 that people were able to control electricity. A **vacuum tube** is a device for controlling the flow of electrical current. It is composed of metal plates and wires sealed in a glass enclosure. It performs special tasks such as receiving radio signals, amplifying sound, and switching electrical signals on and off. In the early days, the vacuum tube, like its water-controlling counterpart, was called a valve.

The first vacuum tube was a **diode,** which permits electricity to flow in only one direction. Then in 1907, an American named Lee DeForest invented a better vacuum tube, the **triode.** Instead of just controlling the flow of electricity, the triode can amplify it, like raising or lowering the volume on your stereo, or completely switch it on or off. The triode and the more advanced tubes that followed it led to the invention of the radio, radar, television, and ultimately the computer. DeForest was truly the father of modern electronic communications.

Necessity is the mother of invention. This was certainly the case with the vacuum tubes, for they drew vast amounts of electrical power and generated a great deal of heat. It was said that when ENIAC was first switched on, the lights of Philadelphia dimmed. The tremendous heat ENIAC's vacuum tubes generated made them burn out at the rate of one an hour. Computer scientists had to overcome these obstacles to make computing less expensive and more efficient.

The Transistor

The **transistor** is a device that performs the functions of a triode vacuum tube but with a great deal less heat and much higher reliability. It is also much, much smaller. The transistor is made from **semiconductor** materials, usually germanium or silicon, that can achieve electrical potential.

The first transistor was invented at AT&T's Bell Laboratories in 1947 by William Shockley, Walter Brattain, and John Bardeen. They were awarded the Nobel Prize for their discovery, which changed the course of electronics. Over time, transistors grew more versatile and powerful, while growing smaller as well.

The Integrated Circuit

> To see the world in a grain of sand
> And heaven in a wild flower,
> Hold infinity in the palm of your hand
> And eternity in an hour.

These words, written by the poet William Blake some 200 years ago, eloquently describe the silicon chip or integrated circuit. For it is from that most humble and plentiful stuff we call beach sand that the silicon miracle, the heart and mind of the computer, is created. Complex computer circuitry that once filled entire rooms now rests in a sliver of silicon you can hold on the tip of your finger. ENIAC was composed of 18,000 vacuum tubes that made up 100,000 circuits. Now, a single chip, a mere quarter of an inch square, contains over 1 million circuits. Is it any wonder we call it a miracle?

The integrated circuit (IC) is comprised of many transistors, diodes, and other electronic circuit devices. The more devices in an IC, the more complex

FIGURE B – 1   The evolution of integrated circuits and their uses.

Type	Circuits	Used for
Small scale or SSIC	10s	Switching
Medium scale or MSIC	100s	Memory
Large scale or LSIC	1,000s	Digital watch
Very large scale or VLSIC	10,000 – 100,000s	Early CPU
Very high speed or VHSIC	1,000,000s	Microprocessor
Ultra high speed or UHSIC	500,000,000 +	Smart machine

it is. **Integration** is the term used to refer to this complexity. Integration, and thus integrated circuits, have evolved over the years, as shown in Figure B – 1. As a point of reference, we compare each stage of integration according to the number of on/off switches or circuits it could place on one chip.

As you learned in the introduction to Chapter 9, Jack Kilby of Texas Instruments is credited with creating the first integrated circuit or IC. Gary Boone, another engineer at Texas Instruments, was granted the first patent for a microprocessor, or, to quote from the U.S. Patent, for "a computing system including a central processing unit integrated on a single chip." A microprocessor is one particular type of integrated circuit; as you learned in Chapter 2, ICs can be used for many different purposes. Today, the most widely used microprocessor chips for personal computers are manufactured by Intel and Motorola.

Let's look at electronic circuitry in terms of the computer generations. The vacuum tube was first generation; the transister was second generation. Refer again to Figure B – 1. The SSIC and MSIC chips were third generation; the LSIC and VLSIC were fourth generation. We are now beginning to see the first VHSIC and UHSIC chips that could be called fifth generation. With this understanding of electronics, let's take a closer look at the computer generations.

THE FIRST GENERATION

Computers that used vacuum tubes are considered part of the first generation. Yet the ENIAC, developed at the University of Pennsylvania, and the Mark I, developed about the same time at Harvard University, were early noncommercial computers. They were developed by research teams in an academic setting, mostly to see if the machine could be built, not necessarily to sell it on the open market. Therefore, it is more practical to refer to first-generation computers as the commercial machines made from approximately 1951 to 1958.

When we use the term *commercial,* we mean computers that were sold to businesses or research institutions. The UNIVAC I was the first commercial computer sold. In 1951, the U.S. Bureau of the Census bought two, and the Prudential Insurance Company of Boston bought one. IBM was not long in offering its first commercial computer, the 701, in 1953. In 1955, IBM introduced the 704, the most powerful computer of its time. Both were scientific computers but complementary models, the 702 and 705, were developed for business data processing. By this time, computers were somewhat smaller than ENIAC, only filling a room the size of a gymnasium instead of an entire building.

Circuit Technology

Vacuum tubes were the electrical switching devices of the first generation. Early tubes were quite large, some as big as a soft drink can. Due to the heat they generated, their life span was rather short. Over time, they became more reliable, faster, cooler — and smaller. Yet as we have seen, the search for better reliability and better switching components was on from the start.

CPU Speed

First-generation computers were quite slow by today's standards, performing an average of 39,000 operations per second. Just to refresh your memory, operations refers to arithmetic operations such as adding and subtracting. ENIAC could perform only 5,000 calculations or operations per second. Yet it was able to analyze in just two hours a problem that would have taken 100 mathematicians a year to figure out. What an incredible savings in time! Within 10 years, computers were almost eight times faster than ENIAC.

There's an old saying in the computer industry that if automobile technology had advanced at the rate of computer technology, you could buy a Rolls-Royce for $25.00, and it would get 2 million miles per gallon. The saying illustrates Grosch's Law, put forth by Herbert R. J. Grosch in the late 1940s, that computing power increases by the square of its cost. According to Grosch, every time you buy a new system, you obtain four times the computing power for just twice the cost. Grosch's Law has never produced less, but it has produced more.

I/O Devices

Early first-generation computers didn't have keyboards for input operations. Instructions and data were usually fed in using paper tape or punched cards. Punched cards were fine for recording and storing data, but people also needed a convenient way to read computer output. For that purpose, electric typewriters, programmed to type by a paper tape or punched card reader, were used for printing reports.

The punched card was an extremely significant tool throughout the history of computers. Originally devised and patented by Herman Hollerith, it has been in use for over 100 years. During the first generation, it was used for both program and data input and output. IBM perfected the punched card machines, also called unit record equipment, because each punched card was a unit with a complete set of data recorded on it. The punched card became known as the "IBM card."

Memory and Storage

In Chapter 2, you learned about computer memory and that it is measured in bytes. One kilobyte or 1K is 1,024 bytes. First-generation computers had between 1K and 4K of RAM. On the early computers, programs and data were stored first on punched paper tape and punched cards, and then electronically on devices such as mercury delay lines and special tubes. First-generation computers used magnetic drums or cores.

The **magnetic drum** was used as random access memory or RAM, and it was just that: a slowly rotating drum. That was a major problem, since promptly storing and retrieving data is central to a computer's usefulness. An Wang, an engineer at the Harvard Computation Laboratory in 1948, was a pioneer in developing **magnetic core** for memory. He figured out a way to make the magnetic core memory from little magnetic donuts electrically charged to store data. This was used for auxiliary storage. Wang worked with Howard Aiken on the Mark IV, a successor to the Mark I computer mentioned earlier. The idea was picked up by Jay Forrester at MIT and further developed, creating grids with the cores that made it easier to locate data. IBM, which provided support to MIT, was the first to introduce magnetic core memory on its 704, one of its most popular and profitable systems.

Wang's magnetic core memory was used in computers for many years. It was much faster and more reliable than anything else available at the time. An Wang went on to start his own company, Wang Laboratories.

Programming Languages

There were no programming languages as we know them today for first-generation computers. The computer received its instructions in machine language, or as electrical on/off signals. On the early computers, these signals were "programmed" into the computer by flipping switches. On first-generation computers, these instructions were typically fed into the machine on punched cards or punched paper tape.

Software

A typical application during this time was **tabulating,** which means totaling figures or organizing data into tables (that we now term a *spreadsheet*). Insurance companies performed accounting and statistics, and the Bureau of the Census maintained statistics, files, and records. Because the data and instructions were loaded all at once, and since computers could only perform one task at a time, computer work was done in batches, like baking a batch of cookies. As you learned in Chapter 1, this is called *batch processing*.

For example, the computer might be given the job of totaling all the claims processed at an insurance company. Once the job was loaded into the computer, it would run until the job was finished (or until it hit an error, which stopped the computer!). Once finished, the computer was available for another job. For that reason, the operating systems of the 1950s were simply called *batch processing systems*.

THE SECOND GENERATION

Resting in The Computer Museum in Boston is the TX-0, the first all-transistorized computer. It was an MIT Lincoln Labs project that was finished in 1958, heralding the second generation (1958–1964). TX-0 was a test to see how well transistor circuitry worked, and the test proved that it worked very well indeed. It was also one of the first computers with a video display, a

12-inch round CRT. Once completed, the TX-0 was installed at MIT's main campus and remained in use until 1975.

Meanwhile, work was underway at IBM on a new, all-transistorized computer. Its purpose was to perform relatively simple business tasks. When it was introduced, the IBM 1401 was an instant success: it set the standard for business computing and outsold every other computer on the market.

Second-generation computers were much more reliable than first-generation machines. The industry coined a term, **mean time between failures (MTBF)**, to describe reliability. Second-generation machines would go days instead of just minutes or hours between failures, in large part due to replacing many of the less reliable vacuum tubes with transistors. As a result, they were smaller as well, occupying just a large room instead of a gym.

Circuit Technology

Transistors replaced vacuum tubes in the second generation, which covered 1958 to 1964. The transistor performed the same function as a tube but was much smaller, cooler, and more reliable because it was made of a crystalline substance.

The transistor was about the size of a pea, with wires that attached it to an electronic circuit. It generated very little heat, did not require a glass enclosure, and was far less expensive to manufacture. Equally or more important, on an electrical level it was far more efficient and reliable than a tube.

Bell Labs introduced the junction transistor, an improvement on the original, in 1951. Then in 1952, Bell gave the transistor to the world, gratis. This was a rare occurrence, since inventors or companies usually require royalty payments when others use their technology. Bell had spent millions of R&D dollars on the device, but apparently thought there was more to be gained by letting others find new uses for the transistor. Which they did.

CPU Speed

The 1401 wasn't the fastest business computer available. Honeywell offered a machine that was faster, but the IBM was more popular — over 14,000 were put into use. However, processing speeds had improved by this time, by a factor of five; on average, computers could process 200,000 instructions per second.

I/O Devices

The second-generation computers utilized keyboards and video display monitors. It was during this period that the first light pen was used as an input device for drawing on the face of the monitor. High-speed printers came into use, and the first computer that could produce output for a typesetting machine was developed.

Memory and Storage

During this period, RAM grew from 4K to 32K, making it possible for the computer to hold more data and instructions. Magnetic tape was developed in the early 1950s for audio recording, and was adapted to computers as a storage medium for programs and data. "Mag tape" was wider than audio tape and came on large metal spools. You have probably seen a computer's tape drives spinning away in a movie at some time or other. That's because it's often the only way to show that a computer is doing anything.

There were also great advances in auxiliary storage, led by the hard disk drive. One of the first was about four feet in diameter and stood upright, looking very much like a blacksmith's grinding stone. But most significant was IBM's RAMAC (Random Access Method of Accounting and Control) in 1957. The IBM disk drive was refined and improved; within a few years it resembled a jukebox, with six 14-inch disks stacked one atop the other. This disk drive was first used on IBM's 1400 series computers. All together, the disks held 3 million bytes or 3 megabytes (MB). Compare this with today's personal computer hard disk drive, a mere 5 inches in diameter, which commonly holds 20 to 30 MB. The emerging 2½-inch hard drives can hold as much or more as their 5-inch predecessors.

Programming Languages

The IBM 1401 didn't have an operating system; instead, it used a special language called the Symbolic Programming System or SPS to create programs. SPS was an assembly language, the second-generation form of computer programming language. As you already know, earlier computers were programmed with switches and cables, then punched cards, that sent either positive or negative electrical signals — machine language — directly to the machine's circuits. Assembly language permitted using *mnemonics* or special symbols that were in turn translated into machine language — 1s and 0s.

Although there were two high-level languages available, FORTRAN, developed in 1954, and COBOL, developed in 1959, the 1401 had its own language called Autocoder. FORTRAN was created as a scientific language, and COBOL as a business language, in hopes that many programmers would use them and create what are known as standards. **Standards** mean many different manufacturers agree to use specific rules and procedures so that software and/or hardware are compatible. For example, when Philips introduced the first compact cassettes, cassette deck manufacturers all agreed to use it as the standard. Otherwise, there could have been 20 different cassette formats! The same was true of compact discs.

Software

At this time, programmers were writing complete application programs in assembly language, or in FORTRAN or COBOL, for a specific computer. The most significant application software developed during this time was records management, which held many of the most important files and records for a business. These might be an employee's personnel files or inventory records for a product. Another was manufacturing control systems.

Almost every computer had its own unique operating system, programming language, and application software. Standards were slowly adopted over the years, but as you learned in Chapter 9, most large system manufacturers still prefer to make their computer systems proprietary to retain their customers. For example, the original IBM PC was developed as an open system, so any software developer can write applications for it, but Apple Computer systems are proprietary. In the past few years, standards foundations and consortiums have helped make this less of a problem than it was 30 years ago.

THE THIRD GENERATION

Fortune magazine's cover story in September 1966 was entitled, "IBM's $5,000,000,000 Gamble." Its topic was the IBM System/360, introduced in 1964, which heralded the third-generation computers (1964–1971). The article quoted Bob Evans, the project manager, as saying, "We called this project 'you bet your company.'" The $5 billion cost of developing the 360 was far more than IBM's annual revenues at the time. The gamble paid off, for the 360 was an enormous success. It was the first IBM computer to use the integrated circuit, which, as you know, is a number of electrical components on a single slice of silicon.

The 360 was so named because there are 360 degrees in a perfect circle (see Figure 9–16), and IBM wanted its customers to think of it as the perfect computer for all their needs. It apparently worked, because IBM took orders for over $1 billion worth of 360s in the first month. The first one was installed at Globe Exploration Company, Midland, Texas, in May of 1965.

The 360 series and its successor, the 370 series, set real standards for the first time. Other companies introduced computers that worked like the 360, such as RCA with its Spectra computers. In fact, most of the mainframe computers in use today are modeled after the 360/370 machines. Even IBM's top-line 3090 series of computers is based on the 370 system.

As you might expect, third-generation computers were even more reliable than their predecessors. A study of electronic component failure once showed that circuits such as the ones used in the 360 had an MTBF of 33 million hours — that's over 545 years! The computer would have problems from time to time, of course, but at last it could be depended on to run for weeks and months at a time without component failures. And the shrinking computer continued to shrink; now it was the size of a refrigerator, filling a large cabinet or set of cabinets in a room. The IBM 360 wasn't the only family of computers. By 1968, Digital's PDP-8 had spawned several models and was by far the most popular minicomputer.

Circuit Technology

The IBM 360 utilized what was termed *hybrid integrated technology,* where separate transistors and diodes were inserted into circuits. Thought was given to using fully integrated circuits, but IBM felt the new technology was too risky. Thus, IBM established a technology policy of using solid, proven methods rather than pushing the state of the art. Just a year later, in 1965, General Electric introduced a computer using all integrated circuits. Within the next few years, many computers began employing ICs in various circuits. In 1971, Intel introduced the first commercial microprocessor chip, the 4004.

CPU Speed

Even though the IBM 360 wasn't the fastest computer introduced in 1964 — the CDC 6600 supercomputer wears that crown — processing speed increased from the second to the third generation by a factor of five. By 1971, computers were able to process nearly 1 million instructions per second, and thus gave us another acronym: MIPS. What comes after a million? When do you think processing speed will cross that threshold and give us a new acronym,

BIPS (billion instructions per second)? Chances are that could occur before the year 2000.

I/O Devices

The third generation marked the full shift from punched cards to magnetic storage media. Now it was possible to type data on the keyboard and have it stored on tapes or disks. This was called interactive data processing, what today we term on-line transaction processing. This meant that tasks were performed while you actually worked with the computer. Another new way to enter data was called optical character recognition or OCR. An OCR scanner would "read" a document typed in the special OCR characters. Networking equipment allowed sending and receiving data between a remote terminal and the computer, and between computers as well. The IBM Selectric typewriter was used for printing word processing letters and reports.

Memory and Storage

Hard disks and magnetic tape made an interesting flip-flop in the third generaion. RAM took giant strides as it became possible to use hard disks for main memory. Some computers had up to 3 megabytes of main memory. On the other hand, computers began using magnetic tape for auxiliary storage, primarily as backup, to make an additional copy of data stored on auxiliary storage hard disk drives for safety.

Programming Languages

During the third generation, software really flourished for the first time. One reason was because FORTRAN and COBOL were more widely used to write application programs. This made writing programs much easier. Many high-level programming languages were developed during the third generation, among them BASIC and Pascal.

Software

Another reason software flourished was that operating systems had matured. Multiprogramming, discussed in Chapter 7, was in use. In order to make all the 360 series computers compatible (and to make its earlier 1401 compatible as well), IBM created the OS/360 operating system. And since other computer companies were making computer systems that worked just like an IBM — termed **plug-compatible machines (PCM)** — they had to emulate the 360's operating system as well as its hardware.

Yet another reason for software's growth was due to something called **unbundling,** or selling the software separate from the hardware. In the past, if you purchased a computer from, say, Sperry Univac, you also purchased your software from them. If you didn't like that software, or if it didn't meet your needs, you had to hire a custom programmer to modify it. But in the early 1960s, Charles Lecht (see p. 426) started an independent software company called Advanced Computer Techniques and stimulated the industry into unbundled software; in other words, made it possible to buy software from someone other than the computer manufacturer.

ACT and other software companies sold what is called *third-party software*. If a program was written for one machine and was popular, it could be modified and rewritten for another machine. Personal computer software has always been unbundled, except for IBM's proprietary PC–DOS and OS/2 operating systems (although Microsoft offers versions for non-IBM machines), and some other IBM programs such as the Presentation Manager.

Two of the most significant applications of the third generation were networking communications and word processing. The advent of computer-to-computer communications made it possible for a number of people, using terminals, to use a single computer, even different programs, at the same time. This was called *time-sharing* and it led multiprocessing. IBM introduced word processing to the world in 1964, in a machine called the Magnetic Tape/Selectic Typewriter, or MT/ST.

THE FOURTH GENERATION

The fourth generation (1971–1988) brought us many different innovations, several as a result of advances in chip technology. The integrated circuit of the third generation, considered a marvel in its time, now seems rather simple when compared to microprocessor chips. Large-scale integration, a technique for packing more and more circuitry on a single chip, has given us microprocessors as powerful as an entire mainframe computer. The fourth generation brought major advances in second-generation mainframes, in third-generation minicomputers, and added a brand new category of machine: the microcomputer or personal computer.

Mainframes

Mainframes continued to grow more powerful, but there was another interesting development. IBM introduced its successor to the 360, the 370, which was *compatible* with the older series. That meant that, for the first time, operating systems and applications software from 360s would work on 370s. The PCM industry continued to expand. Although RCA failed in its attempt (to the tune of almost half a billion dollars) to successfully market its 360 PCMs, Gene Amdahl, a former IBM engineer and architect who designed the 704 and was on the 360 team, started several successful PCM companies.

Minicomputers

Edson de Castro, a computer designer at Digital Equipment Corporation, left DEC to form Data General and began building minis that competed with Digital's. Other notable mini companies are Hewlett-Packard, Prime Computer, Tandem Computer, and Wang. Hewlett-Packard and Prime have concentrated more on scientific and engineering machines. Tandem came up with an innovative idea: two complete CPUs within one computer, so that if one failed, the other would immediately take its place. Tandem called this "nonstop computing" and has been very successful selling its computers to banks and other businesses that can't afford to have the computer "go down." Wang, having built on its reputation with word processing systems, now markets a complete line of office automation minis for business.

But Digital's VAX is probably the biggest success story in minicomputer history. Begun in 1975, the VAX (which stands for Virtual Address Extension) was an improvement over the PDP-11 mini. The design team was led by Gordon Bell, one of Digital Equipment Corporation's most brilliant engineers. The goal was to create a new, faster 32-bit machine that was compatible with the older, and very popular, 16-bit PDP-11. This was counter to IBM's strategy, which was to introduce a new and improved computer about every five years, one that was incompatible with older models. This, of course, meant that companies would have to replace their old computers and buy the new ones, and then hopefully convert the old software. Often, this was neither practical nor necessary, since the MTBF for fourth-generation computers had grown to months, if not years.

Personal Computers

The personal computer's growth and development is nearly identical to that of the mainframe computer. It started out as a hobbyist's kit, an experimental machine, but people quickly found many uses for it. What is dramatically different is that the personal computer has evolved about four times faster than the mainframe. Today, we have personal computers and workstations with as much processing power as a mainframe or a VAX. Larger computers often have more RAM and are designed to work with dozens, even hundreds, of disk and tape drives. They also permit hundreds of users, working at terminals, to use the computer at the same time. But personal computer memory is growing larger, and now small work groups can use personal computers that are connected together in networks. The picture is rapidly changing in favor of the smaller, easier-to-use personal computer and the more powerful workstations.

Circuit Technology

Curiously, the company that initiated commercial development of the microprocessor—which heralded the fourth computer generation—went out of business. Busicom was a Japanese electronic calculator company that asked Intel, a California electronics firm, to create an advanced integrated circuit for a programmable calculator. Marcian E. "Ted" Hoff was the engineer in charge. He pioneered the 4004, a four-chip microprocessor, in 1969, although it was never used for its intended purpose. The advanced process of packing more circuits on a chip is termed large scale integration, or LSI. The fourth generation brought us VLSI, or very large scale integration.

The 4004 was a breakthrough. Even before it was finished, Intel engineers were working on the next chip, the 8008. It was introduced in 1971; Texas Instruments, Fairchild Semiconductor, RCA, and other electronics firms were introducing competing chips soon after. In 1974, Intel introduced the 8080, which was 10 times faster than the 8008 and had four times the memory capacity. This microprocessor literally launched the personal computer industry. It has been superseded by the 8086, 8088, 80286, the 80386, the 386SX, and the fastest microprocessor to date, the 80486.

Meanwhile, companies specializing in manufacturing memory chips were working to pack more circuits—and thus more memory capacity—on an individual IC. In 1969, memory chip capacity was 256 bits; by 1976, it had risen to 64K bits, or 64,000 bits. By 1983, it had quadrupled to 256K bits.

CPU Speed

The fourth generation gave us a dramatic increase in processor speed. In the early 1970s, processing speed was 1 million instructions per second (MIPS). By the late 1980s, that had increased to 4.77 MIPS in the standard personal computer, and up to 12 MIPS in the PC/AT models. In 1988, some 80386-based personal computers and workstations ran at 20 MIPS; today, speeds reach 33 MIPS.

Grosch's Law was broken in the fourth generation; doubling the speed no longer costs twice as much. Often, it doesn't cost any more at all. Throughout the late fourth generation and as the fifth generation begins to emerge, it's almost impossible to keep up with microprocessor and memory chip advances. Chip manufacturers announce improved performance every few weeks, and, as Figure B–2 shows, we can expect to see this continue well into the late 1990s.

I/O Devices

The keyboard and video monitor have become standard I/O devices, but in the fourth generation, the mouse began playing a major role. The mouse is especially useful for issuing commands to the operating system or the software, which formerly required pressing several keys. Some still find keys or control commands quicker and easier, while others wouldn't trade their mouse for anything.

There were three major fourth-generation printer advances. The first was the Diablo daisy wheel letter-quality printer, the first automatic printer for computers. The second was the incredibly fast inkjet printer, often used for printing bulk mail promotions. Dot-matrix printers have also improved, offering high speed and print quality almost as good as a letter-quality printer. Most in demand is the laser printer, with its variety of professional, printer-quality typefaces, superb graphics, and multiple printing formats.

Memory and Storage

VLSI has also allowed us to progress from computers with only a few kilobytes of memory to personal computers with 2, 4, and often 16 *megabytes* of memory. This additional memory makes it possible to use multitasking operating systems and more complex or graphically oriented applications.

In the early 1970s, an IBM engineer named Alan Shugart invented the floppy disk. The first one was 8 inches in diameter, but floppy disks have now shrunk from 5¼ inches to the popular 3½-inch disk used in Macintoshes, 386-based personal computers, and PS/2s. Floppy disk storage capacity has increased dramatically as well, as discussed in Chapter 10.

Hard disk drives have also grown in capacity; mainframes and minis now have disk drives that hold data in quantities known as gigabytes. Alan Shugart also invented the Winchester hard disk for personal computers. Early models held only 5MB, but that quickly increased to 20MB. Personal computers now have hard disks capable of holding over 600MB.

Programming Languages

The fourth generation introduced fourth-generation languages, more Englishlike languages that nonprogrammers could use to design their own applications. Fourth-generation languages are commonly used with a database

FIGURE B-2   Projected advances in microprocessor and memory chips for the 1990s.

Intel Microprocessors

Year	Model	Speed	Number of Transistors
1989	80486	25–50 MHz	1 million
1992	80586	75–100 MHz	4 million
1995	80686	150 MHz	22 million
1999	80786	250 MHz	100 million

American DRAM Chips

Year	Memory Size	Number of Chip Components
1989	1 megabit	More than 1 million
1991	4 megabits	More than 10 million
1994	16 megabits	More than 10 million
1996	64 megabits	More than 100 million

management system program, on all classes of computers. The fourth generation also saw the development of new languages for artificial intelligence, including Prolog, which was developed in England. As the fifth generation emerges, object-oriented programming (OOP), or using previously created programming modules to assemble new programs, are gaining favor.

Software

Operating systems made it easier for users to work with computers by creating a more friendly user interface. The most notable example is the Macintosh graphical interface, which allows the user to point at images on the screen with a mouse, rather than memorize keyboard commands. Microsoft Windows for DOS and IBM's Presentation Manager for OS/2 were responses to creating a more friendly user interface. Today, most personal computers offer an improved user interface, or a DOS shell program that makes it possible to issue commands from a graphical screen.

Application software likewise became easier to use, with many programs offering "pull-down" or "pop-up" menus that display a list of commands or actions on the screen. Many programs that were only available on mainframes or minis migrated to the personal computer environment; for example, database management systems and accounting programs. The spreadsheet was a new and original application for the personal computer, as was desktop publishing.

THE FIFTH GENERATION

With each passing generation, computers have grown more powerful and sophisticated. In the early days, only people with special training were able to use or operate computers. Today, just about anyone can learn to use a computer. In the past, applications often required designing both computer hardware and software from scratch. Today, we are approaching a time when computer systems will automatically create new applications without any human help or intervention.

We are embarking on the fifth generation of computing (1983–??), where we will have personal computers as powerful as mainframes and software that performs certain thinking functions only our brains could do. One sign of fifth-generation activity was the recognition of legitimate expert systems research around 1983. Another was the fifth generation government-funded research project that Japan formally launched in the early 1980s. The goal was to develop computer systems that combine advances in speech recognition, vision systems, database technology, and the telephone booth so that the average citizen would have extraordinarily easy access to computer power and information. The Japanese project is still underway but today, fifth-generation projects are in development around the world—especially in the United States.

Circuit Technology

One fifth-generation goal is to develop VHSIC and UHSIC (see Figure B–1) chips, more commonly called superchips. Early superchips are two to three times faster than the fastest personal computer microprocessor chip. The first uses for these superchips are in military applications, but scientists say they'll be widely used in consumer products such as digital television sets. Not only will superchips be fast, they'll be self-repairing, too. They'll be able to diagnose their own malfunctions and substitute spare transistors on the same chip.

Chip development is truly at the center of the fifth generation. Other research is underway in the following areas:

- New materials such as gallium arsenide to replace silicon.
- New techniques such as superconductivity or operating in extremely low temperatures that speeds the flow of electricity.
- New applications such as the neurocomputer or neural computing chip.

First developed by Drs. Carver Mead and Federico Faggin, the neural chip works very similarly to the neurons in our own brains. The chips can be linked into massive, complex circuits that scientists hope will eventually lead to "thinking" computers.

CPU Speed

No matter how powerful today's computer, there are still times when we must sit and wait for an operation to be completed. This is because the CPU can only process one instruction at a time, and even though it may be processing at 20, 25, or even 33 million instructions per second, we still end up staring at the screen for what seems like hours.

Fifth-generation computers will overcome the problem of speed in several ways. One is the new generation of reduced instruction set computers, or RISC machines. They take advantage of the traditional von Neumann CPU architecture by utilizing, as the name implies, fewer instructions. Another is the parallel processing architecture that allows many CPUs to share the processing work. Perhaps the most promising is the optical computer, which uses light instead of electricity. Such a computer would be able to process instructions at *nearly the speed of light.*

I/O Devices

Touch screens will be in common use for simple tasks in the fifth generation. Instead of typing, we'll be able to give these computers voice instructions. In time, they will reply vocally, or by more conventional means if we prefer. As the manner in which the computer inputs and outputs changes, so will the user interface — to a point where it will be entirely transparent, as it should be.

Memory and Storage

Memory chips will acquire vast storage capabilities; economies of scale in manufacturing will drop so dramatically that they will be able to hold tremendous amounts of mass storage. Optical storage devices, based on today's CD – ROM and videodisc technologies, will largely replace magnetic disks. Gradually, we will be able to store data on networks as well, so we won't have to pay for our own storage devices at all.

Programming

Object-oriented programming (OOP) and computer-aided software engineering (CASE) tools will be in routine use for developing applications in business. Indeed, many users will be able to utilize OOP for creating personalized applications. This will be a dramatic advance; applications can be designed to one's own personal needs and tastes. No longer will it be necessary to learn how to use a program; the computer will "learn" how to perform a particular task exactly as you want it done. In time, the "programming language" will be our own spoken language, which the computer interprets into its own machine language. The instructions themselves will be programmable, so that computer "crashes" will be a thing of the past: programs will be self-repairing.

Software

The fifth generation will bring us intelligent interfaces that learn to respond to our personal workstyle or lifestyle. For example, the computer knows that you like to wake up in the morning to the morning news headlines, then you like to read your electronic mail. It will alert you when you need to attend a meeting or write a report. As you change between types of data, it will automatically switch between the spreadsheet and database applications. Image processing and voice recognition will be an important part of fifth-generation systems. We will be on-line continuously as the computer searches for and retrieves data we have previously programmed it to find for us.

WHAT LIES AHEAD?

The computer has made advances that are unparalleled by any other invention or achievement of the human race. Yet many believe its greatest contributions are yet to come. The fifth generation is leading us into an age where the computer will be our sidekick, companion, and extension of our brain. We will not have to spend so much time learning how to use it or manipulating its hardware and software to get what we need from it. In this exciting new generation, the computer will become a genuine productivity tool. As it does so, we will find that the fifth generation is bringing us computer systems capabilities we can scarcely imagine.

Yet are *people's* attitudes changing and advancing along with improvements in machines such as the computer? We have seen great resistance on the part of people to change, especially with respect to learning how to understand and use a computer. However, whether we are ready or not, the computer will begin making dramatic changes in our lives over the next 30 years.

We will see much of our daily activities automated by computers. Those who hold jobs will be those who make business decisions or those who work in entertainment and the creative arts: business and government leaders, salespeople, artists, composers, sports players. There will be a vast explosion in creativity, but also a huge leisure class. The quality of life will improve for everyone—but at the same time, the world's population will continue to grow at a rapid pace.

Meanwhile, we will enter the sixth, and perhaps the seventh, computer generations. Computers will be ubiquitous, everywhere and invisible. We will issue instructions to walls, sidewalks, autos, appliances. Robots will tend to our personal needs, and all information and entertainment will be delivered to us, automatically, via fiber-optic networks.

Can we effectively deal with all this change? Author-adventurer Laurens Van der Post said, "Life is its own journey, presupposes its own change and movement and one tries to arrest them at one's eternal peril." We must begin learning how to develop our capacity to change, and expanding our mental and human potential now, in order to prepare for this new world. It is ours and we must be its master, not its slave.

SUMMARY

1. *Understand how computer technology has evolved throughout the four generations.* Advances in electronics in the early part of the 20th century made it possible to develop electronic digital computers. We call the stages in the evolution of computer electronic circuitry, hardware, software, and programming languages the computer generations.

2. *Describe the various electronic devices that have driven computer technology from one generation to the next.* Early computers used vacuum tubes, but they proved unreliable for computing purposes. Real progress in reliability began with transistors and was fulfilled by integrated circuits. ICs evolved into microprocessors and are also used for computer memory and other purposes. We describe the amount of electronic circuitry that can be packed on an IC as integration; for example, very large scale integrated circuit (VLSIC).

3. *Understand the most significant advances in circuit technology, CPU speed, memory, programming languages, and software for each generation.* The first generation (1951–58) mainframe computers used vacuum tubes; CPU speed was measured in thousands of instructions per second. I/O was primarily punched cards and paper tape. Magnetic drum and magnetic core were used for memory and storage. There were no languages, and typical applications were tabulating or maintaining files.

The second generation (1958–64) saw the introduction of the minicomputer. Transistors began to be used; speed was about 200,000 instructions per second. I/O devices were keyboards and video displays; memory and storage devices were magnetic tape and large disk drives. Programming languages were mostly machine-specific, but FORTRAN and COBOL were introduced. Records management was the primary software application.

The third generation (1964–71) used integrated circuits; speed increased to nearly 1 million instructions per second. I/O included improved keyboard techniques and optical character recognition. Hard disks and magnetic tape drives made memory and storage advances. High-level programming languages flourished, and through unbundling, many new applications were introduced.

The fourth generation (1971–88) heralded the personal computer. Speed increased to 20 million instructions per second. The mouse was a preeminent I/O device. Memory and storage capacity increased dramatically, especially with personal computers. Programming languages became more Englishlike, and thousands of new applications were developed in business, education, entertainment, and personal improvement.

4. *Characterize some of the advances we can expect to see in the fifth generation.* The fifth generation (1983–??) promises the ubiquitous computer, everywhere but rarely seen. Current chip technology will make dramatic improvements and new chip technologies will be introduced. Speed will approach that of light. Touch screens and the human voice will be common I/O devices. Users will write their own tailor-made applications in object-oriented programming modules — or software will write itself. Applications will continually adapt to user needs.

KEY TERMS

computer generations, p. 455
diode, p. 456
integration, p. 457
magnetic core, p. 459
magnetic drum, p. 459

mean time between failures (MTBF), p. 460
plug-compatible mainframe (PCM), p. 463
semiconductor, p. 456
standards, p. 461

tabulating, p. 459
transistor, p. 456
triode, p. 456
unbundling, p. 463
vacuum tube, p. 456

REVIEW AND DISCUSSION QUESTIONS

1. What were the major problems with using vacuum tubes in computers?

2. What is the basic material used in transistors and integrated circuits?

3. What electronic components are found in ICs?

4. Why weren't the computers of the 1940s considered first-generation machines?

5. Explain how Grosch's Law works, and how it has changed over the years.

6. Why do you think the punched card was used for almost 100 years?

7. Describe the advantages of third-generation over second-generation computers.

8. What generation has produced the most significant advances for users?

9. What should our greatest concerns be for the future computer generations?

10. Discuss the historical significance of the Information Age (see Chapter 1 DISKbyte, "Understanding the Information Age") and the computer generations. How do they complement one another? Where are they leading us?

GLOSSARY

A

acoustic coupler   The earliest modem, it connects to a telephone handset with rubber cups.

algorithm   A limited set of step-by-step instructions that solve a problem.

analog   As in analog computer, which does not count in two digits but continuously measures and compares changing values instead.

application   A practical use of a computer. Applications let us perform a variety of tasks, such as play games, create a diet, read an astrological chart, or land an airplane.

application programmer   A computer programmer who develops application programs.

application software   Software which directs the computer to perform specific tasks. A word processing program is an example of application software.

arithmetic-logic unit   One of the three components of the CPU; performs arithmetic and logical operations.

artificial intelligence (AI)   Software that attempts to replicate human thought processes, such as reasoning, learning, self-improvement, and associative learning.

ASCII   The American Standard Code for Information Interchange, a standard code adopted to facilitate the interchange of data among various types of data processing and data communication equipment.

ASCII text   Text that conforms to the American Standard Code for Information Interchange standard.

assembler   System software that translates assembly language into executable code.

assembly language   A programming language that uses mnemonics such as letters, numbers, and symbols instead of numeric instructions.

attribute   A characteristic quality of a data type, data structure, element of a data model, or system.

auxiliary storage   One of two types of storage; long-term, nonvolatile storage that supplements main storage; also called auxiliary memory or secondary storage.

auxiliary storage device   One of three kinds of peripherals; used to store data for an indeterminate period of time, for example, a floppy disk.

B

backup   The process of making extra, or duplicate, copies of your programs and files for safekeeping.

backup storage   Peripheral devices, such as reel-to-reel tape drives, used to store copies of data and software.

base   The radix of a number system.

BASIC   Beginners All-purpose Symbolic Instruction Code; a relatively easy-to-learn, easy-to-use programming language widely used in programming instruction and by personal computer users.

batch processing   A technique by which programs to be executed are collected for processing groups or batches; see **realtime**.

baud (bps)   A unit for measuring signal speed, roughly equivalent to one bit per second (bps).

binary arithmetic system   The basis of operation for digital electronic computers. Binary arithmetic uses only two digits — the 0 and the 1.

bit   A binary digit; the basic unit of data recognized by a computer.

block   A portion of data that can be cut, moved, and manipulated.

block editing   Working with a set of characters, words, sentences, paragraphs, or pages of text selected as a block; also referred to as cut and paste.

boot   The process of loading the operating system into a computer's memory.

business analysis systems   One of several technologies that comprise office automation; includes spreadsheet analysis, decision support systems, and executive information systems.

byte   A group of bits that can be operated on as a unit by the computer.

C

C   A programming language that gives programmers a large measure of control over the hardware, like an assembly language, but incorporates many of the statement features of high-level languages.

calculate   The process of performing mathematical operations in an electronic spreadsheet, utilizing the computer's ALU.

camera-ready   Finished pages that are printed on a high-quality printer or a Linotronic typesetter, ready for the printer.

carrier signal   A telephone tone that indicates the computer is available for networking.

cell   A square on a spreadsheet application screen, indicating where to enter data.

cell pointer   A pointer that illuminates a cell in a spreadsheet program, to indicate where data may be entered; takes the place of the cursor found in other programs.

centralized computing   A computing strategy where all MIS functions are kept in a central MIS facility.

central processing unit (CPU)   The central component of computer hardware, containing circuitry that controls the interpretation and execution of instructions. The CPU consists of three components: the control unit, the arithmetic/logic unit (ALU), and main memory.

character   (1) Any symbol, digit, letter, or punctuation mark stored or processed by a computer. (2) A DBMS logical data element; a single symbol, letter, number, or punctuation mark defined in a database, the smallest unit of data manipulated by a DBMS. Characters work together to form meaningful data such as words.

chip   A thin piece of silicon on which electronic components are deposited.

closed architecture   A computer design that requires manufacturers to obtain specific permission from the originator to duplicate it.

COBOL   COmmon Business-Oriented Language; a high-level programming language developed for business data processing applications.

coding   Programming; writing a program using a programming language.

column   The vertical axis for cells on a spreadsheet matrix, usually designated with a letter of the alphabet.

command   An instruction issued to perform a specific task or function.

command language   A language used to give instructions to an operating system.

command line   The portion of the screen where you enter instructions.

command line interface   An interface that requires you to type a command to issue instructions to the computer; one of three types of human/computer interfaces.

comments   Notes written in English that are interspersed with source code, explaining aspects of the program to other programmers.

compact disc-read only memory (CD-ROM)   Optical disc (or laser disc) storage medium that holds 600MB.

compiler   System software that translates source code into executable, object code.

complex-instruction-set computing (CISC)   An operating system design that offers a wide diversity of applications, however often constrained by fundamental limitations in the CPU design.

computer   A device that accepts data, then performs mathematical or logical operations to produce new results from that data.

computer-aided design (CAD)   Using computers in design. CAD allows us to design products (from the curve of an auto's fender to the intricate working of the engine, suspension, and instrumentation) simulating the components in three-dimensional detail.

computer-aided manufacturing (CAM)   Using computers to manage, operate, and control the manufacturing process. CAM computers identify, refine, and produce raw materials; control the machines that form materials; and direct robots that assemble, weld, and finish products.

computer-aided software engineering (CASE)   Computer-based tools and methods that help programmers make the most of their time and efforts.

computer architecture   The area of study that deals with the structure of computer systems and the relationships among system components.

computer code   A machine code for a specific machine.

computer generations   The technical progression of computers in five phases, from the earliest, vacuum tube-based computers (first generation) to knowledge systems capable of understanding spoken and written words and graphics (fifth generation).

computer-integrated manufacturing (CIM)   Computer-aided design integrated with computer-aided manufacturing.

computer literacy   Being knowledgeable about the computer and how it works in our daily lives; also being able to operate and use a computer, at least to do basic tasks.

computer professional   A person who designs, operates, or maintains a computer system.

computer system   A system that consists of people, working together with software and hardware components, used for processing data into useful information.

computer-to-machine output   Using the computer I/O process to control machine operations.

computer user   A person who works with a computer system to achieve a desired result.

configuration   The various hardware elements that, together, make up a computer system; includes the type of monitor, the quality of the video display, the amount of RAM, and the number and type of floppy or hard disk drives. Configuration also includes other devices connected either internally or externally.

constant   (1) A value that does not change during the execution of a program. (2) The raw numbers or data entered on a spreadsheet for processing.

control unit   One of three components of the CPU; directs the step-by-step operation of the computer by directing electrical impulses between itself, the ALU, and main memory and between the CPU and the input and output devices.

corporate electronic publishing (CEP)   The business use of in-house publishing for both external documents, such as user manuals and advertising brochures, and internal use, such as a company newsletter.

cursor   Typically a blinking rectangle or underline that indicates where the next keyboard character we type will appear on the screen.

cut and paste   Block editing that involves selecting a block of text, moving it, and replacing it in a new location.

cylinder   A vertical column of tracks that makes it easier to locate data on a hard disk pack.

D

data   The raw material of information. Data includes facts and numbers suitable for communication or interpretation.

database   A DBMS logical data element: a group of related records and files.

database administrator (DBA)   A full-time corporate database manager responsible for maintaining the DBMS and ensuring the accuracy and the integrity of its data.

database design   Planning the data that comprises a database and the data relationships between various data.

database management system (DBMS)   A computer system which lets you organize, store, and retrieve information from one or more databases.

data definition   A detailed description of the data that comprises a database.

data dictionary   A list of the fields, files, and commands utilized in manipulating a database.

data disk   A floppy or hard disk used for data storage.

data elements   Individual pieces of data joined to produce information.

data entry   The process of entering data into computer memory.

data integrity   The accuracy, consistency, and completeness of data maintained by a computer system.

data processing   The process of utilizing specific procedures that turn data into useful information for people.

data refinement   The condensing and ordering phase in database design.

data relationships   The interaction between various data elements.

debugger   System software program that identifies program errors.

decimal number system   A number system in which each numeral is based on the radix of 10.

decision support system (DSS)   A system that helps managers extract information from various MIS databases and reporting systems, analyze it, and then formulate a decision or a strategy for business planning.

default   An assumption made by a system or language translator when no specific choice is given by the program or user.

delete   Removing data.

desktop personal computer   A small computer designed to fit on the top of a desk.

desktop publishing   Word processing combined with advanced formatting capabilities, including merging multiple print typeface styles and graphic images on one page.

digital   A computer that uses the binary arithmetic system to perform arithmetic and logical operations on data.

diode   An electronic device that can inhibit electrical current flow in one direction and permit current flow in the opposite direction.

direct access   A data storage method that locates data without needing to scan surrounding data, also called random access; contrast with sequential access.

directory   A list of files stored on a disk or a portion of a disk.

disk drive   An auxiliary storage device that reads data from a magnetic disk and copies it into RAM, and that writes data from RAM onto a disk for storage.

distributed computing   A computing strategy where computers and terminals in various geographic locations are linked functionally in a communications network.

distributed database management system   Databases connected one to another to provide access to any data, regardless of where it is stored.

document   Text prepared with word processing.

document and image processing   A process which takes computer-aided designs and turns them into working specifications, both graphics and text.

documentation (reference, software, user)   Written materials that describe computer hardware and software and explain their purposes.

document management systems   One of several technologies that comprise office automation; includes database management, document storage and micrographics.

DOS (disk operating system)   The major PC operating system; an integrated set of programs that perform three important tasks: providing access to the various operations of the CPU, controlling the peripheral devices, and offering various application program support services.

dot-matrix   Output produced by printers that utilize wires in the print head that can include both text and graphics.

downloading   Files transferred from a large, central computer to a small, remote computer.

draft   A version of a document.

E

EBCDIC   Extended Binary Coded Decimal Interchange Code; an 8-bit code used to represent data in computers.

editing   Changing or revising data or text.

electronic   Pertaining to the flow of electricity through components such as vacuum tubes, transistors, or silicon chips.

electronic data interchange (EDI)   A computerized method of sending orders and invoices between a manufacturer and its suppliers.

electronic document   Captured from on-line databases.

electronic funds transfer (EFT)   Using a computer to transfer funds, such as when a manufacturer pays the suppliers' invoices via computer.

electronic mail service   Using computer networks and telecommunications facilities to send and receive textual messages.

encryption   A technique for protecting computer communications, involving coding data so that it is unintelligible without the key to decryption.

end-user computing   A computing strategy that places personal computers where end-users can use them easily and effectively.

ENIAC   The Electronic Numerical Integrator and Calculator, the world's first electronic digital computer; it was completed in 1946.

enterprisewide computing   A computing stategy that encompasses the entire business and all its operations. The ultimate goal is to provide systems integration on the application level, making it possible for any application to share data with any other.

entity   A single item in a database.

ergonomics   The study of how to create safety, comfort and ease of use for people who use machines such as computers.

executable instructions   Instructions which can be read and operated on by the CPU.

executive information system (EIS)   Typically, a personal computer with brilliant color graphics and extremely easy-to-use software that can present data with just a keystroke or two, designed for top managers.

expansion slot   A slot or space in the system box used to connect circuit boards (cards) to the main circuit board (motherboard) used to increase memory capacity or for expanding a computer system's functionality.

expert system   Computer systems, able to store and retrieve data with special problem-solving expertise.

F

facilities management   A computing strategy using an independent service organization to operate and manage a data processing installation.

facsimile (FAX)   Transmission of pictures, maps, letters, and so on via telephone lines from a sending facsimile machine to a receiving facsimile machine.

field   A DBMS logical data element: A group of characters representing an attribute or characteristic of an entity, a data item that is part of a larger whole.

file   A group of related records; the primary unit of data storage in computers, similar to the file folder in a common filing cabinet.

filename   A unique name used to identify a file. In DOS, a filename can be up to eight characters long, followed by an optional period (or dot) and an optional three-character filename extension.

file server   A personal computer whose large-capacity hard disk stores programs and files.

firmware   A combination of software and hardware: instructions stored in ROM devices.

flat file database   A file management system; a database where each file is layered on top of the previous one.

floppy disk   A flexible plastic disk, coated with a magnetic substance, usually sealed in a plastic sleeve.

flowchart (system, program)   Diagrams using symbols and connecting lines to show: (1) the logic and sequence of program operations (program flowchart), and (2) systems of processing to achieve objectives (system flowchart).

font   A family or collection of printing characters of a particular size and style.

format   The pattern in which data is stored on a disk; a word processing command used to organize and design text as it appears on the screen or as it is printed.

formula   A rule expressed as an equation, useful for calculating.

FORTRAN   FORmula TRANslator: one of the first high-level languages, used for developing scientific and engineering applications.

fourth-generation language (4GL)   A language that uses Englishlike phrases and sentences to issue instructions.

function   A process or program that generates a mathematical result, or value.

function key   A keyboard key that performs special functions assigned by the application in use.

G

graphic interface   One of three types of human-computer interfaces that uses images in the form of drawings, boxes, and characters, in addition to text, to allow users to issue instructions. Often graphic interfaces employ a mouse to position the cursor.

graphics   Pictorial representations of data produced by data processing, from simple line or bar graphs to detailed images.

groupware   A software product designed to help accomplish work among many users on a local area network.

H

hacker   Someone who demonstrates great skill in programming and working with computers.

handshaking   Using procedures and standards to establish communication between two computers or between a computer and a peripheral device.

hard copy   Printed copies of computer data in readable form, such as reports or listings.

hard disk drive   An auxiliary storage device utilizing a metal disk coated with magnetic film for data storage.

hardware   The computer's physical components — the machine itself, including chips, circuit boards, keyboard, disk drive, monitor, and other components.

Help   On-line information that gives the user additional information about how an application or system works.

hexadecimal   Pertaining to a number system with the radix of 16.

hidden file   A file that contains software information that is the copyrighted property of the computer company.

hierarchical database   A database where relationships between logical data elements resemble an inverted tree structure, from the central root to the branches.

high-level language   A computer language that uses Englishlike words as instructions, combining several machine language instructions into one high-level instruction.

highlighting   A method for defining a block of text by using a different color or by using reverse video to switch the text and background.

high-resolution   A sharp, crisp video display, well suited for graphic representations.

high-resolution graphics   Graphics which display curving lines, shading, detail, and color with a high degree of detail.

HIPO chart   Hierarchy plus Input Processing Output chart; these take structure charts to a greater level of detail, showing program input and output.

human-computer interface   The way the computer and its software are presented to the human being who is about to use them.

human interface   The point of meeting between a computer and an external entity, whether an operator, a peripheral device, or a communications medium.

HyperCard   A Macintosh software program that falls between a utility and an application that informally organizes many kinds of information, including words, pictures, and sounds into "stacks" which are manipulated to create applications.

I

icon   Pictorial figures or representations displayed on a computer screen, designed to be easily recognizable by most people.

impact printer   One whose printing device come in contact with the paper to form a character; see **dot-matrix** and **letter quality.**

information   Data made meaningful through interpretation by people.

Information Age   The "postindustrial society," a term introduced by Daniel Bell, a Harvard University sociologist, in 1956, meaning an information-based, white-collar worker, service-oriented economy. In the Information Age, information used for decision making and forecasting is increasingly important.

information center   An organization that bridges the gap between the computer professional in the MIS department and the computer novice in the user department.

input device   A hardware component used to enter data into a computer. The keyboard is a common input device.

Insert mode   an editing mode where every character typed is placed at the position of the cursor, pushing all the text in front of the cursor ahead.

instruction   A group of characters, bytes, or bits that defines an operation to be performed by a computer. Instructions are often in the form of programs, telling the computer what to do with data.

integrated circuit (IC)   A complex electronic component that performs key functions in computers and other devices; also called a chip.

integrated software   A group of individual software applications, capable of freely exchanging data with each other; typically a combination of word processing, spreadsheet, DBMS, and graphics.

integration   The process of combining several elements to form a complete, complex system or device.

interpreter   A language translator that translates source codes one line at a time for immediate execution by the CPU.

intruder   Someone who deliberately gains access to a computer system that is the property of another party.

ISDN (Integrated Services Digital Network)   An all-digital network that connects computers directly to one another.

K

keyboard   A hardware component used to enter data and instructions into computer memory.

keyword   Categories or key terms common to several topics used to make searching and sorting data easier.

kilobyte   1,024 bytes, abbreviated K.

knowledge worker   Senior executives, managers, supervisors, analysts, engineers, and other white-collar office workers.

L

label   Text in a spreadsheet cell.

laptop   A small personal computer, often powered by batteries or rechargeable cells, that is easily transported and used in remote locations.

laser printer   An output device that prints by directing a laser beam onto a rotating drum, creating an electrical charge that forms a pattern of letters or images.

ledger sheet   A page in a ledger book, also called a columnar page.

letter-quality   Output of the same high quality as typewriters produce.

liquid crystal display (LCD)   A flat-screen display commonly used with laptop computers.

loading   The process of reading software into the computer.

local area network (LAN)   A type of private network, interconnected by dedicated communication channels, that allows a group of users in a small area (such as a room, building, or site) to share data, programs, and hardware resources.

logical data representation   An organized method for storing data in a database.

logical operations   Computer operations that test and make decisions by comparing values.

low-resolution   Video output similar to a conventional television display showing lines and graininess in its images.

M

machine language   The basic language of computers; the 0s and 1s executed by the CPU.

macro   Two or more commands or formulas created and stored for easy, frequent use.

magnetic core   Tiny iron oxide rings strung on wires, widely used as a storage medium in early computer systems.

magnetic drum   A circular cylinder with a magnetic surface on which data is stored.

magnetic ink character recognition (MICR)   The recognition by machines of characters printed with special magnetic ink.

mailing list program   A program that prints envelopes and mailing labels.

mail/merge   The process of automatically printing form letters, pulling in names and addresses from one file and text from another file.

mainframe computer   A large computer most commonly used in business, made up of many cabinets filled with electronic gear and connected to the main computer cabinet.

main storage   Storage controlled directly by the CPU, used to hold programs and data during data processing. One of two types of storage; short-term, volatile memory. Also called internal storage or primary storage.

management information system (MIS)   A computer system designed to supply organizational managers with the data necessary to achieve business goals.

mathematical operations   Adding, subtracting, multiplying, and dividing.

mean time between failures (MTBF)   A measure of computer reliability: the average time between occurrences of problems which result in system failure.

media   The material on which computer instructions and data are recorded, such as floppy disks, magnetic media, and paper.

megabyte   Actually 1,024 kilobytes; roughly one million bytes. Abbreviated 1MB.

memory   A computer system's storage facilities. Memory stores instructions and data in the computer.

menu-driven interface   One of three types of human-computer interfaces, presenting a list of the commands, tasks, or projects the user most frequently works with, developed to make the command line interface easier to use.

menu line   A list of commands and other valuable information about a software application, typically displayed on the screen.

metropolitan area network (MAN)   A network that links computer systems located in different buildings, but all within close proximity.

microcomputer   A personal computer designed for use by a single individual, usually small enough to fit on a desktop.

micro-floppy   A 3½-inch floppy disk.

micrographics   The use of miniature photography to condense, store, and retrieve graphics information on film, such as microfilm and microfiche.

microprocessor   An integrated circuit used to perform arithmetic, logic, and control functions in a microcomputer CPU; or used as a control unit in a variety of electronic devices.

minicomputer   A medium-sized computer, introduced as an alternative to the mainframe, is used for a variety of tasks. Also called a mini.

mini-floppy   A 5¼-inch floppy disk.

MIPS   A measurement of computer speed based on instructions executed by the CPU: millions of instructions per second.

model   A replica or copy that can be tested or changed without disturbing the original, for example, a mathematical model of a specific financial situation.

modem (modulator-demodulator)   A hardware device that allows computers to communicate via telephone lines by translating digital computer signals into analog signals for telephone transmission.

module   A distinct, logical part of a program.

monitor   A hardware component consisting of a video display screen where the computer displays input and output.

motherboard   The computer's main circuit board, holding CPU and memory chips.

mouse   A small pointing device used to effect cursor movement, so named because it slides over the desktop and has a wire or "tail" attached to the computer.

multimedia   An interactive form of application which lets people and the computer engage in an ongoing exchange or presentation of information.

multiprogramming   (1) Simultaneous execution of two or more programs by multiple CPUs in a computer. (2) Multitasking performed on a mainframe computer.

multitasking   The ability of a computer to perform two or more functions or tasks simultaneously for a single user.

multiuser system   A system that processes the work of two or more users, working at different terminals, at the same time.

N

natural language   A kind of programming language, utilizing Englishlike statements, designed for people without a programming background.

near-letter-quality (NLQ)   Pertaining to output produced by some printers (dot matrix) that does not look as readable as that produced by letter-quality printers (daisy wheel or laser).

network and communication management systems   One of several technologies that comprise office automation; includes the telephone, electronic mail, voice messaging systems, teleconferencing, and facsimile.

network database   A type of database organization that utilizes many-to-many relationships. Access to a network database can be from many points, not just the top.

networking   Linking computers through telecommunications hardware, software, and media to share resources and data.

node   A device connected to a network.

nonimpact printer   One whose printing device forms characters without striking the paper; see laser printer and plotter.

nonvolatile memory   Memory which stores and retains programs and data, regardless of whether the computer is turned on or off.

number   A symbol or symbols representing a value in a specific number system.

number system   A set of symbols and rules for number representation.

numeral   Conventional symbol representing a number.

O

object code   Output from an assembler or compiler that is executable, or is suitable for further processing to produce executable machine code.

object-oriented programming (OOP)   Programming methods and tools that combine bits of code together into objects; the objects are fitted together to form a program.

octal   Pertaining to a number system with the radix of 8. Octal numerals are frequently used to represent binary numbers, with each octal digit representing a group of three binary digits (bits).

office automation   Using computer and communications technology to help clerical and management office workers better use and manage information.

on-line   Connected to, or in direct communication with, a computer.

on-line transaction processing (OLTP)   Data processing wherein the computer system completes the entire transaction as soon as it is entered, used in businesses where up-to-date information is critical.

open architecture   A computer design, part of which is made available by its originator to other hardware and software developers.

open system   A product that can be altered for use with many manufacturers' hardware.

operating system   Part of a computer's system software that controls the execution of computer programs.

operation   A set of instructions or programming statement.

operations technician   Technician responsible for maintaining computer hardware.

optical character recognition (OCR)   A technology developed for reading data such as characters, bar codes, optical marks, and handwriting from hardcopy form into computer memory, using light-sensitive devices.

optical disc storage   A storage method that utilizes lasers and optical disks to store large amounts of data.

output device   A peripheral device that produces the results of data processing in a form we can perceive with our senses. Common output devices include the monitor and printer.

P

packet-switching networks   A method of digital communication that increases efficiency by sending data in blocks, called packets.

parallel processing   Concurrent or simultaneous execution of two or more processes in multiple devices. Performed by advanced computers utilizing many processing units, clusters, or networks.

Pascal language   A structured high-level programming language, widely used for teaching programming.

password   A special term used to identify a computer user and authorize use of a computer system or account.

PC-compatibles   Microcomputers that share certain characteristics with IBM PCs, including very similar operating systems that can utilize the same application programs.

PC manager   A person who takes time from his or her own work to help others learn personal computers or new software packages.

peripheral devices   Input, output, and storage devices connected to a computer CPU.

personal computer   A computer designed for use by a single individual, usually small enough to fit on a desktop; also called a microcomputer, reflecting the fact that it is smaller than a mainframe or a minicomputer.

personal information manager (PIM)   A relational DBMS combining several desktop tools including an appointment calendar, a calculator, word processing, and a DBMS.

physical data representation   The way data is stored and retrieved on the computer system's auxiliary storage devices.

pixel   A picture cell. Shortened version of "picture element." The monitor screen is divided into rows and columns of tiny dots or cells, each of which is a pixel. When stimulated electrically, pixels emit light to form characters and other images.

plotter   An output device that produces drawings and graphs on paper using automatically controlled pens, usually in a variety of colors.

plug-compatible mainframe (PCM)   A mainframe that requires no modification to work together with a mainframe produced by another manufacturer.

pointing device   A peripheral device that moves the cursor, usually used with a keyboard.

portable   Software which can be used on several different computers, regardless of their manufacturer.

power   A symbolic representation of the number of times a number is multiplied by itself, the process of exponentiation.

presentation graphics   Computer graphics used by business, typically presenting numerical, statistical, financial, or other quantitative data in a visual form such as a pie chart, a bar chart, a line graph, or a scatter graph.

printed circuit board   A thin insulating board used to mount and connect various electronic components and chips.

printer   A hardware component that provides a copy of a computer's output on paper.

program   A series or set of instructions that causes a computer to perform data processing.

program disk   A disk containing instructions for the computer.

programmer   A person whose job it is to design, write, and test computer programs.

programming   The process of translating a problem or task into a language the computer understands.

prompt   A character or message that tells you the computer system is ready to accept a command or input.

proprietary software Software that is owned by an individual or business, copyrighted, or not released to the public. One cannot legally use or copy this software without permission.

protocol A set of rules or standards governing the exchange of information between computers.

pseudocode An intermediate form of program instructions, written in English phrases, that describe the processing steps to be performed by a program.

public network An open communications network available for use by anyone, usually on a fee basis.

punched card A cardboard card used in data processing in which tiny holes denote numerical values and alphabetic codes.

Q

quality control Using computers for testing.

query language A type of high-level natural language that allows the user to make inquiries of a computer system using Englishlike phrases instead of programming codes or keywords.

R

random access memory (RAM) Read-write memory, the "working memory" of the computer, into which application programs are loaded and executed.

read only memory (ROM) Memory permanently programmed with one group of frequently used instructions that can be read by the computer, but not written to; is not lost when the computer is turned off and cannot be changed by the user.

real time Processing a transaction at the time it is input into the computer system; see **batch processing.**

recalculate A function that recomputes values on a spreadsheet after data is changed.

record A DBMS logical data element—a collection of related data items, or fields, which a DBMS treats as a unit.

reduced-instruction-set computing (RISC) An operating system design whose limited (reduced) instruction set increases the computer's speed of operation, but limits the range of applications it may run.

relational database A database that allows you to interchange and cross-reference data between different types of records.

Replace A program or feature that searches for words specified and replaces them with alternatives.

report writer A program that converts computer data into a printed report, organized for a specific purpose, typically part of a DMBS application.

revising A word processing feature that allows you to check, change, and modify the text you have written.

root directory The primary, highest level directory, often containing one or more subdirectories.

row The horizontal division of cells on a spreadsheet program, which, together with columns, form the spreadsheed matrix.

S

save Storing the contents of main memory on a disk or other nonvolatile, auxiliary storage device.

scheduling A means of making maximum use of the CPU by sequencing tasks.

scrolling The vertical movement of data on the monitor.

searching A program or feature that searches through a document, noting each term and the page where it occurs.

sector A pie-shaped wedge that compartmentalizes data into addresses for the disk drive head to locate.

semiconductor The material from which integrated circuits are made; this material conducts electricity poorly, but forms circuits when other substances are added to it.

sequential access A storage method that stores data in a particular order, perhaps alphabetically or by date and time, so that files must be searched serially to find a particular record.

silicon chip A thin piece of silicon on which electronic components are etched.

soft copy Output we cannot touch, such as video or audio.

software Computer programs and instructions.

software maintenance The ongoing process of detecting and removing errors from existing programs.

software piracy Copying a proprietary software program without the permission of the originator.

sort key A field used to order and separate one or more records in a database.

source code A program, written in a programming language, that can be translated by an assembler or compiler into object code.

source data input Data fed directly from its source into a computer without human intervention.

spreadsheet An application that uses mathematical formulas to perform a variety of accounting and mathematical calculations. Also, calculations on data arranged in a matrix or grid; the software version of the paper ledger sheet.

standard A rule established to improve quality and/or provide uniformity between various aspects of computer systems and their operation.

statement An expression of instruction in a programming language.

status line A portion of the screen that provides information about an application. The status line usually includes the name of the file in use and the page, line, column, and space the cursor presently occupies; or, in a spreadsheet application, where labels, constants, and formulas are typed and displayed.

storage device A peripheral device used to store computer data, such as a floppy disk, hard disk, or magnetic tape.

structure chart A graphic representation of top-down programming, showing program modules and their relationships in increasing levels of detail.

structured programming Also called structured coding; where programs are written using three basic constructs: sequence, selection, and repetition. Programs written using structured coding techniques are easier to read, understand, and maintain.

structured query language (SQL) A query language developed by IBM, with many ease-of-use features.

structured techniques Techniques that are orderly and can be understood by people other than the program creator.

subdirectory A directory under the root directory.

supercomputer The largest, fastest, and most powerful mainframe computers often used in governmental and science research facilities that require extraordinary amounts of computing power.

superminicomputer A faster, more powerful version of a minicomputer.

system development life cycle An ordered process for software development including several phases: analysis, design, coding, debugging, testing and acceptance, maintenance, and documentation.

systems analysis and design The study of an activity or procedure to determine what kind of computer system would make it more efficient, and planning the technical aspects for the new system.

systems analyst A person responsible for systems analysis and design, who gathers and analyzes the data necessary to develop new applications.

systems integration The process of connecting several kinds of computers together to provide enterprisewide computing.

system software Programs that run the computer system or that aid programmers in performing their work.

system unit The main system cabinet in a personal computer, typically housing the power supply, the motherboard, and one or more storage devices.

T

tabulating To print totals or form data into tables.

template A spreadsheet with labels, commands, and formulas already created, or another type of application already set up for ease of use.

terminal A combination monitor/keyboard, usually connected to a mainframe or minicomputer.

terminate and stay resident (TSR) An application that is booted, then waits in the background until needed.

text editor A program that allows you to write, erase, and manipulate words on the monitor screen.

text graphics An image on a video screen that is simply a character—a letter, number, or symbol.

text management system One of several technologies that comprise office automation; includes electronic typewriters, word processing systems, and electronic publishing.

thermal printer A nonimpact printer that uses heat to form an image on chemically treated paper.

time-sharing A technique of using a computer system by many people simultaneously for different purposes.

toggle key A key pressed once to turn a function on and a second time to turn it off; for example, the Caps Lock key.

topology The physical layout of network devices and nodes.

track A path along which data is recorded on a continuous medium, such as a magnetic tape or disk.

trackball A commonly used pointing device which performs like a stationary, upside-down mouse.

transaction processing A form of business data processing in which transactions are processed as they occur.

transistor A semiconductor device that controls current between two terminals by variations in current flow between them and a third terminal.

triode An advanced electronic device that not only controls the flow of electricity, but amplifies it or completely switches it on and off.

Typeover mode An editing mode where every character you type replaces what was there before at the position of the cursor. Also called overstrike mode.

U

unbundling Selling software, services, and training separately from hardware.

Undelete Replacing previously deleted text.

Undo A command or function that reverses the last action taken by an application.

uploading   Files sent from a small, remote computer to a larger, central computer.

utility software   Software that provides commonly needed services, such as copying data from one storage device to another.

V

vacuum tube   A device for controlling the flow of electric current, used extensively in first-generation computers.

value   A number. In spreadsheet applications values take two forms. One is the constant, the raw numbers or data entered for processing. The other is the mathematical formula used for performing calculations on the constants.

vector graphics   Simple graphics programs that connect lines between points on the screen.

video monitor   The most common soft copy output device, very similar to a television set, uses a cathode ray tube (CRT) to project an image.

virus   An insidious program that enters computer systems via other programs or through communications networks, hides itself, infects the computer, and causes it to crash.

voice output   An audio response device that allows the computer to produce output similar to human speech.

voice recognition   Using the human voice as an input device for the computer.

volatile memory   Memory which stores and retains programs and data only when the computer is turned on.

W

what-if analysis   A means of testing a variety of models, usually involving substituting data or other factors for currently existing ones, to see what difference these may make.

wide area network (WAN)   A type of private network that uses phone lines, microwave relaying stations, and satellites to connect computers over a wide geographic area.

wildcard   A character, usually an asterisk (*) or a question mark (?), that stands as a substitute for one or more characters when working with files with similar or identical filenames.

window   A portion of the video screen dedicated to a specific purpose.

word (computer)   A logical unit of information; a group of bits, bytes, and characters considered as an entity and capable of being stored in one storage location.

word length   The number of bits in a (computer) word, usually 8, 16, or 32.

word processing   A software application that lets users write, revise, format, and print text for letters, reports, manuscripts, and other written documents.

word wrap   A word processing feature that automatically pushes text to the next line when the current line is filled.

work group computing   Several people, each of whom has different job duties or tasks, all working toward a common goal.

workstation   A powerful personal computer that combines the ease of use and convenience of a personal computer with some of the power and functions of larger computers; often used by scientists, engineers, programmers, and other technical specialists.

write-protect   To prevent a disk or tape from being written to.

INDEX

A

Abacus, 12
Ada, 262
AI, 226–27, 467
Algorithm, 238
All-in-1 (OA software), 424
Amdahl, Gene, 310, 464
American Memory, 340
American Telephone and Telegraph; *see* AT&T *and* Bell Laboratories
Analog computers, 11
Animation, computer, 5
APL, 262, 414
Apple Macintosh; *see* Macintosh
Apple II, 84
Application generators, 266–67
Applications of computers, 7, 32; *see also* Database management systems; Spreadsheet; *and* Word processing
Applications programmers, 394
Arithmetic/logic unit, 36, 37, 48
ARPANET, 360
Artificial intelligence, 226–27, 467
ASCII, 194, 355, 452
Ashton, Alan, 120–21
Asimov, Isaac, 436
Assemblers and assembly language, 247, 254, 461
AT&T, 12
Atanasoff, John V., 29, 303
Attribute (in DBMS), 167
Autocoder, 461
Automobile industry, effect of computers on, 18
Auxiliary storage, 38; *see also* Storage

B

Babbage, Charles, 12
Bachman Data Analyst, 268, 269
Backups, 85–86
Backus, John, 257
Barry, Dave, 95

BASIC, 246, 251, 259–62
Batch processing, 50
Baud, 353
Bell, Daniel, 10
Bell Laboratories, 203, 456, 460
Binary arithmetic, 11, 12
Binary number system, 52, 448
Bit, 52–53
Block editing, 107
Bohm, Corrado, 237
Boole, George, 448
Boone, Gary, 457
Booting, 71
Bricklin, Dan, 127, 155
Bugs (in programming), 248
Business analysis systems, 416–17
Byte, 52–53

C

C (programming language), 262, 263
CAD, 18, 19, 214
Calculate (spreadsheet command), 138–39
Calculating machines, early, 12
CAM, 18, 19, 214
Camera-ready copy, 219
Card catalog, 160–61
Careers in computing
    consulting, 25, 155, 429
    hardware design and manufacture, 88, 310, 343
    with networks, 377
    software, 5, 56, 120–21, 187
    systems analysis, 272
    technical writing, 56
CASE, 267–70
CAT scans, 216, 217
CD-ROM, 338–39, 340
Cell pointer, 132
Cells (in spreadsheets), 131
Central processing unit (CPU), 36–38
Centralized MIS, 395
CGA, 326

Character (in DBMS), 167
Chips; *see* Silicon chips
CIM, 214
CISC, 299
Clarke, Arthur C., 427
Closed architecture, 288
COBOL, 257–59, 260–61, 461
Code generator, 270
Coding, 244
Columns (in spreadsheets), 131
Command language (for operating systems), 196
Command line (in spreadsheets), 132
Command line interface, 69, 75
Comments (in programs), 251
Compact disc-read only memory, 338–39, 340
Compaq, 287, 291
Compilers, 247, 256
Complex-instruction-set computing (CISC), 299
Computer animation, 5
Computer architecture, 400–401
Computer codes, 450–52
Computer crime, 23
Computer Fraud and Abuse Act of 1986, 375
Computer literacy, 6–7
Computer output microfilming, 417
Computer professional, 30
Computer user, 30
Computer-aided design (CAD), 18, 19, 214
Computer-aided manufacturing (CAM), 18, 19, 214
Computer-aided software engineering (CASE), 267–70
Computer-integrated manufacturing (CIM), 214
Computer-to-machine output, 331–32
Computers, 6, 11; *see also* Future of computing; Hardware; History of computing; Mainframe computers; Minicomputers; Personal

Computers—*Cont.*
    computers; Software; *and*
    Supercomputers
  common service problems, 86
  ethical use of; *see* Ethics
  generations, 454–71
  limitations, 20–21
  as systems, 30–44
  types, 11, 282
Configurations of PC's, 64–68
Connection Machine, 307, 402
Constant, 132
Control Data Corporation, 305
Control unit, 36, 37
COPY (DOS command), 82–83
Corporate databases, 182–84
Corporate electronic publishing, 219–20
Counting and calculating machines,
  early, 12
CPU, 36–38
Cray, Seymour, 305
Cray X-MP (supercomputer), 306
Cray Y-MP (supercomputer), 15
Credit card fraud, 371
Cursor, 75
Cut and paste, 107
Cybernetics (Weiner), 21
Cyberspace, 332
Cylinders (on disks), 335

D

DASD, 333–39
Data, 11
Data definition, 170
Data dictionary, 183–84
Data disk, 80
Data elements, 165–67
Data entry, 318
Data General, 300
Data integrity, 422
Data management (by operating system),
  200
Data processing, 11, 45–50
  batch and on-line, 50
Data refinement, 170
Data relationships, 170
Database administrator (DBA), 183
Database management systems (DBMS's,
  13, 158–89; *see also* Application
  generators
  advanced applications, 181–84
  advantages over manual systems, 160–
    61
  applications, 159
  basic features, 162–68
  in integrated software, 211
  recent trends, 184–86
  tips for using, 185
  work session, 169–81
Database services, 366
dBASE II, 168, 185–86
DBMS; *see* Database management systems
Debugger, 248
Decimal number system, 445–46
Decision support systems, 416
Default, 81
DeForest, Lee, 456

DELETE (DOS command), 83
Dell Computer, 88
Desktop banking, 420
Desktop personal computers, 285–90
Desktop publishing, 219–20, 229
DESQview, 193
Difference engine, 12
Digital computers, 11
Digital Equipment Corporation
  All-in-1, 424
  course development, 56
  minicomputers, 16, 465, 300–301
  use of networking, 363–64
  VMS (operating system), 203, 205
Dijkstra, Edsger, 237
Diode, 456
DIR (DOS command), 79–80
Direct access storage devices, 333–39
Directories, 73
Disk drive, 38, 461; *see also* Storage
Disk Operating System; *see* DOS
DISKCOPY (DOS command), 81–82
Distributed database management
  systems, 186
Distributed MIS, 395–96
Document, 104
Document and image processing, 214
Document management systems, 417–20
Documentation, 250–53
DOS, 71–86
  booting, 71–72, 77, 78
  commands, 78–83, 196–97
  files and directories, 72–73
  general remarks, 63, 72, 201, 202, 287
  written by Paterson, 61
Dot-matrix printers, 328
Dow Jones News/Retrieval, 365–66,
  401–2
Downloading, 354
Drafts, 98

E

EBCDIC, 450
EDI, 18, 369
EFT, 18, 367
EGA, 326
8514/A, 327
Electronic, 11
Electronic bulletin boards, 367
Electronic data interchange (EDI), 18,
  369
Electronic Data Systems (EDS), 399
Electronic documents, 418
Electronic editor, 377
Electronic Frontier Foundation, 375
Electronic funds transfer, 18, 367
Electronic Numerical Integrator and
  Calculator; *see* ENIAC
Electronic publishing, 217–20
Electronic spreadsheet; *see* Spreadsheet
Electronics, 455–57
Emery, Don, 121
EMISARI, 369–70
Encryption, 372
End-user computing, 394
Englebart, Douglas, 321
ENIAC, 14, 29, 303, 456, 457

Enterprisewide computing, 396
Entity (in DBMS), 167
Epson, 321
ERASE (DOS command), 83
Ergonomics, 411–12
Ethics, 22
  accuracy of data, 54–55, 154, 341–42
  copyright, 87, 118–19, 227–28, 271
  in the office, 428
  privacy of data, 186–87
  property rights, 87, 227–28, 271,
    308–9
  sabotage, 308–9, 375–76
  security, 375–76, 403
Excelerator, 267, 269
Executable instructions, 246
Executive information systems, 416–17
Expansion slot, 340
Expert systems, 227

F

Facilities management, 399
Facsimile (FAX), 324, 412
Felsenstein, Lee, 310
Field (in DBMS), 167
Files, 72–73, 194
Financial statements, 146–47
Firmware, 34
Flat (sequential) files, 162–64
Floppy disks, 34, 336, 466
  formatting, 80–81
  parts, 34, 35, 334–36
Flowcharting template, 239, 243
Flowcharts, 239–42
Fonts, 217
FORMAT (DOS command), 80–81
Formatting disks, 80–81
Formatting text (in word processing), 106
Formulas (in spreadsheets), 130
FORTRAN, 257, 258, 461
Fourth-generation languages, 264–67
Fujitsu, 305, 306
Fuller, Buckminster, 374
Function keys, 106
Functions (in spreadsheets), 138, 142
Funk, Paul, 134
Future of computing, 432–43, 469–70
  MIS, 401–3
  networks, 374–75
  peripherals, 341
Fuzzy logic, 292

G

Garbage in, garbage out, 53
Gas plasma display, 327
Gates, Bill, 6, 436
Generations of computers, 454–71
Geoprocessing Information System
  (GIS), 187
GIGO, 53
Grammatik, 121
Graphic interface, 69–71
Graphics, 144–45, 212–17
Grosch's Law, 458

Groupware, 421
Guru (DBMS), 159

H

Hackers, 370
HAL, 432
Handshaking, 355
Hard copy, 86, 326
Hard disks, 67–68, 336–38
Hardware, 15–17, 36–42, 276–345; *see also* Peripherals
    future of, 439–40
    in MIS, 398–401
    processing, 278–313
Hayes, Dennis, 349
Help (in software), 101
Hewlett-Packard, 464
Hexadecimal number system, 449–50
HGC, 326
Hidden file, 81–82
Hierarchical DBMS's, 164, 166
High-level languages, 255–63
Highlighting, 107
High-resolution displays, 326
High-resolution graphics, 212
HIPO charts, 238–39
History of computing
    generations, 455–67
    origins, 12, 29, 46, 279
    spreadsheets, 127–28, 154
    word processing, 117–18, 414
Hoff, Marcian E. "Ted," 279, 465
Hollerith, Herman, 12, 315, 458
Hopper, Grace M., 257, 259
Huang, Alan, 440
Human-computer interface, 69
HyperCard, 224, 225
Hypertext, 437–38

I

IBM, 29, 305, 397
    early history, 14, 315, 458
    EBCDIC, 450
    introduces System/360, 15, 303, 462
    major hardware products, 414, 457–58, 460, 461
    major software products, 164, 185, 204, 424, 463
IBM MT/ST, 414, 415
IBM PC and compatibles, 63, 64, 193, 286–88, 394
    operating systems, 201–2
IBM PS/2, 63, 65, 288–89, 327
Icons, 70
IDMS, 164
IMS, 164
Index generator (in word processing), 115
Indianapolis 500, 159
Information, 53–54
Information Age, 10
Information anxiety, 442
Information center, 394
Information services, 365–66
Information utilities, 367–68
Inkjet printers, 330, 331

Input devices, 38, 318–25; *see also particular devices, e.g.,* Keyboards
Input/output control (by operating system), 198
Input/output devices, 458, 463, 466, 469; *see also* Input devices *and* Output devices
Insert mode, 101
Instruction, 13
Integrated CASE, 270
Integrated circuits (IC's), 51, 279, 456–57, 462; *see also* Silicon chips
Integrated desktop, 422–23
Integrated office systems, 426
Integrated software, 208–11
Integration (of circuitry), 456–57
Intel, 279, 287, 465
Interactive services, 367–68
Interfaces, 69–71, 316–18
International Business Machines; *see* IBM
Interpreters, 247
Intruders, 370–72, 374–75
ISDN, 365
Iverson, Kenneth, 414

J

Jacopini, Giuseppe, 237
Jacquard, Joseph-Marie, 12, 233
Jacquard loom, 233
Jobs, Steven, 289, 298
Josephson Junction, 306
Joystick, 320, *320*

K

Kahn, Philippe, 221
Kapor, Mitchell D., 129, 209, 376; *see also* Lotus 1-2-3
Keyboards, 17, 319, 343
    layout, 96, 97, 100, 106, 107
Keyword, 181
Kilby, Jack, 279, 457
Kilobyte, 66
Knowledge workers, 410
Kurzweil, Raymond, 332, 434

L

Labels (in spreadsheets), 132
LANs, 360–63
Laptop personal computers, 291–95
Large system integration, 424–25
Laser printers, 328–30, 331
Laventhol & Horwath, 125
Lecht, Charles P., 426–27
Ledger sheet, 126
Leibniz, Gottfried Wilhelm von, 12
Letter-quality printers, 328
Light pen, 320
Liquid crystal display, 327
Local area networks, 360–63
Logical data representation (in DBMS), 166
Logical operations, 11

Lotus Notes, 421
Lotus 1-2-3, 128, 129, 209, 210, 275; *see also* Kapor, Mitchell D.
    mainframe version, 153
    newsletter, 155
Low-resolution displays, 326
Luddites, 20

M

MacDraw, 213
Machine language, 247, 254
Macintosh, 63–64, 65
    applications, 153, 213, 229
    hardware, 289–90, 326
    operating system, 84, 202–3
Macros (in spreadsheets), 144
Magnetic core, 459
Magnetic drum, 459
Magnetic ink character recognition (MICR), 323
Magnetic tape, 339–40, 460–61
Mail/merge (in word processing), 116
Mailing list program, 116
Main memory; *see* Storage
Mainframe computers, 15, 16, 302–4, 464
Maintenance of software, 249
Management information systems; *see* MIS
Management of MIS, 392
MANs, 363
Mark I, 457
Mark IV, 459
Martin, James, 267
Massachusetts Institute of Technology, 204
Masuda, Yoneji, 10
Mathematical operations, 11
McGrath, Jack, 155
McLuhan, Marshall, 374
Mean time between failures (MTBF), 460
Media, 34–35; *see also* Storage
Megabyte, 66
Memory; *see* Storage
Menu line (in spreadsheets), 132
Menu-driven interface, 69
Metropolitan area networks, 363
MICR (magnetic ink character recognition), 323
MicroAmerica, 25
Microcomputers; *see* Personal computers
Micro-floppy, 34, 35
Micrographics, 331–32, 417, 419
Microsoft, 6, 61
Microsoft Windows, 467
Microsoft Works, 422, 423
Millions of instructions per second, 51
Minicomputers, 16, 17, 300–301, 464–65
Mini-floppy, 34
MIPS, 51
MIS, 380–407
    executives, 393, 402–3
    future of, 401–3
    hardware, 398–401
    overview, 381, 383–91

MIS—*Cont.*
software, 395–97
staffing, 391–94
Modems, 349, 351–54
Module, 238
Monitor, 17
Motherboard, 37
Mouse, 42, 43, 319, 321, 466
Mrs. Fields Cookies, 387–88
Multifinder, 202–3
Multimedia, 225
Multimedia home PC, 439
Multiprogramming, 199
Multitasking, 200, 201, 296
MVS, 204
Myers, Therese, 193

N

Napier, John, 12
NASA, 298, 396
Natural language, 266
NAVSTAR, 308–9
Navy MIS, 388–90
Near-letter-quality printers, 328
Nelson, Theodor, 437–38
Network and communication management systems, 420
Network DBMS's, 164, 165, 166
Network manager, 402–3
Networks, 24, 348–79
components, 350–56
future of, 374–75
security, 370–74
services, 365–70
tips for using, 364
types of, 358–65
work session, 356–57
Neural computing, 438, 468
News services, 365–66
Newsletters, Etc., 229
NeXT Computer System, 298–99
Node, 350
Nolan, Richard, 381
NOMAD (DBMS), 184, 266
Nonprocedural languages, 266
Nonvolatile memory, 39; *see also* Storage
Number, 445
Number systems, 444–52
Numeral, 445

O

Object code, 246
Object-oriented programming, 267, 467
OCR (optical character recognition), 322
Octal number system, 449
Office automation, 408–31
Office of the future, 426–27
OfficeVision, 424–25
Olsen, Kenneth, 16, 300
OLTP, 50
On-line researcher, 377
On-line transaction processing (OLTP), 50
Open architecture, 286

Open Desktop, 420
Open system, 205
Operating systems, 195–206; *see also* DOS *and* Software
commands, 196–98, 204
evolution of, 459, 463, 467
Operation, 306
Operation Sun Devil, 375
Operations technicians, 394
Optical character recognition (OCR), 322
Optical computer, 440, 468
Optical disc storage, 338–39
OS/2, 201–2
OS/360, 463
Osborne-1, 291, 310
Outliner (in word processing), 114
Output devices, 38, 326–32; *see also particular devices, e.g.,* Printers
Ownership of software, 271

P

Packet-switching networks, 358–60
PageMaker, 229
Palm Top (computer), 292
Parallel processing, 307, 468
Pascal (language), 263
Pascal, Blaise, 12
Pascaline, 12, 20
Paterson, Tim, 61
PC: *see* Personal computers *and* IBM PC
PC-compatibles, 63
PC manager, 394, 404
People: role in computing systems, 30–33, 53–54
Peripheral devices, 38, 39, 40
Peripherals, 38, 39, 40, 314–45
external storage, 333–40
future of, 341
input devices, 318–25
output devices, 326–32
Perot, H. Ross, 399
Personal computers, 62, 465; *see also* DOS *and* IBM PC
care of, 66
desktop, 285–90
hardware, 17, 62–68, 284–99
interfaces, 69–71
laptop, 291–95
operating systems, 63
origins, 16–17
Personal information managers, 181–82
Physical data representation, 166
Piracy of software, 87, 227–28
Pixels, 212
PL/1, 262–63
Plagiarism, 118–19
Plotters, 42, 330, 331
Plug-compatible machines (PCM), 463
Pointing devices, 319
Portability (of software), 203, 256–57
Powers, 446
Presentation graphics, 212–13
Presentation Manager, 424, 425, 467
Prime Computer, 187, 300, 464
Printed circuit board, 35

Printers, 17, 42, 328–31, 466; *see also particular types, e.g.,* Laser printers
Privacy of personal data, 186–87
Private networks, 360–64
Processing; *see* Data processing
Productivity in the office, 409
Program, 13
Programmers, 13, 56, 255, 392–94
Programming, 244–49, 469
Programming languages, 254–67; *see also particular languages, e.g.,* BASIC
evolution of, 461, 463, 466–67
high-level, 255–63
chart, 263
translators, 246–47, 254, 256
Project MAC, 204
Prompt, 74
Proprietary, 205
Protocols, 355
PS/2, 63, 65, 288–89, 327
Pseudocode, 242, 243
Public networks, 358–60
Punched cards, 12, 233, 234, 315, 458
Punched-card tabulating machine, *12*

Q

Quality control, 18
Quarterdeck Office Systems, 193
Query languages, 185, 266; *see also* SQL
Quick-reference guides, 253

R

RAM; *see* Storage
RAMAC, 333, 461
Random access memory; *see* Storage
Ratliff, Wayne, 168
Read only memory (ROM); *see* Storage
Recalculate (spreadsheet command), 143–44
Record (in DBMS), 167
Reduced-instruction-set computing (RISC), 299, 468
Reference documentation, 252
Relational DBMS's, 164–65, 166
Remington Rand, 29
RENAME (DOS command), 83
Replace (word processing command), 109–10
Report writer, 180
RISC, 299, 468
ROM; *see* Storage
Rows (in spreadsheets), 131
RPG, 263

S

Sabotage, 308–9
SABRE, 360
Saving files, 110
Scanners, 322
Scheduling (by operating system), 198–99

SCISOR, 418–19
Scrolling, 100–101, 133
Scrooge, 126
Scully, John, 440–41
Search (word processing command), 109–10
Sectors, 335
Security, 370–74, 397, 403
Semiconductor, 456
Sensor Frame, 440
Sequential access storage devices, 339–40
Shannon, Claude, 448
Shugart, Alan, 333
Sidekick, 221–22
Sideways, 134
Silicon chips, 34–35, 36, 51–52
    history, 279, 456–57, 465
        table, 280
    manufacturing, 281
Silver, Jackie, 229
Snyder, Tom, 434–35
Soft copy, 326
Software, 13, 33–35, 192–275
    application, 33, 206–25, 467
    evolution of, 459, 461, 463–64, 467
    future of, 436–39, 469
    graphics, 212–17
    in MIS, 395–97
    operating systems, 33, 195–206
    telecommunications, 354–56
    tips for buying, 226
    utilities, 221–25
Software development, 232–75
Software documentation, 251–52
Software maintenance, 395
Solomon, Robert, 343
Sort key (in DBMS), 177
Source code, 244
Source data input, 323–24
Spelling checker (in word processing), 112–13
Spreadsheet, 13, 124–57
    add-ons, 134
    advanced features, 141–45
    applications and examples, 145–52
    basic features, 130–33
    graphics, 144–45
    tips for using, 153
    work session, 134–41
SQL, 185, 266

Staffing of MIS, 392–94
Stand-alone programs, 208
Standards, 461
Statement, 256
Status line (in spreadsheets), 132
Stibitz, George, 12
Storage, 38–40, 333; *see also particular media, e.g.,* Floppy disks
    auxiliary (nonvolatile), 38, 68, 333–40
    disks, 338–39, 340
    evolution of, 463–466, 469
    RAM (random access memory), 37, 38, 66–67, 68

Storage—*Cont.*
    ROM (read only memory), 38
    tape and tape cartridges, 339–40, 460–61
Storage allocation (in operating system), 199–200
Storage device, 316
Structure charts, 238
Structured analysis, 237
Structured programming, 244–45
    control structures, 245
Structured Query Language (SQL), 185, 266
Structured techniques, 237–43
Subdirectories, 73
Supercomputers, 15, 305–7
Superminicomputers, 301
Switchboard, 343
Symphony, 209
System development life cycle, 234
System software; *see* Software
System unit, 17
System/360, 15, 303, 462
Systems analysis and design, 235–43, 272
Systems analyst, 235, 272
Systems integration, 398–400
Systems programmers, 393

T

Table of contents generator (in word processing), 115
Tabulating, 459
Tabulating Machines Company, 315
Tandem, 300, 464
Tape and tape cartridges, 339–40, 460–61
Templates (in spreadsheets), 144
Terminals, 328
Terminate and stay resident programs, 222
Text editors, 244
Text management systems, 413–15
Thermal printers, 331
Thesaurus (in word processing), 113–14
Time-sharing, 204, 464
Toggle key, 99
Topology, 360
Trackball, 319, 320
Tracks (on disks), 335
Transistors, 456, 459–60
Translators (for programming languages), 246–47
Triode, 456
TSR programs, 222
Turing, Alan, 227
Tutorials, 252
TX-0, 459–60
Typeover mode, 101
Typewriter, 414

U

Unbundling, 463
UNIVAC, 54–55, 303, 457
UNIX, 203, 205
Uploading, 354
User documentation, 252
Utility software, 221–25

V

Vacuum tubes, 455–56, 458
Values (in spreadsheets), 128
Vatican Library, 419
VAX computers, 203, 300, 465
Vector graphics, 212
VGA, 326
Video monitors, 326–28
Viruses, 372–73
VisiCalc, 125, 127–28, 155
VMS (operating system), 203, 205
    commands, 204
Voice input, 323
Voice output, 332
Volatile memory, 38; *see also* Storage
Von Neumann, John, 46

W

Waks, David J., 439
Wallach, Steve, 310
Wang, An, 459
Wang Freestyle, 423
Wang Laboratories, 300, 414, 464
Wang WPS, 414, 415
WANs, 363
Watson, Thomas J., Jr., 15, 303
Watson, Thomas J., Sr., 14, 303
Weiner, Norbert, 21
What-if analysis, 128
Whittaker, James B., 388–90
Wide area networks, 363
Wildcard, 82–83
WingZ (spreadsheet), 153
Wohl, Amy, 429
Word processing, 13, 94–123
    advanced features, 112–15
    applications, 115–17
    editing features, 99–102, 107–10
    in office automation, 413–15
    tips for using, 111
    work session, 103–11
Word wrap, 100
WordPerfect, 120–21
WordPerfect Executive, 209
WordPerfect Office, 422, 424
Words and word length, 52–53
Work group computing, 421
Workstations, 16, 295–99
Write-protect, 81
Writing, 103
Wurman, Richard Saul, 442
WYSIWYG (in word processing), 118